# Competing Economic Paradigms in China

T0331342

When the Chinese economic reforms began in 1978, Marxist economics infused all the institutions of economic theory in China, from academic departments and economics journals to government departments and economic think tanks. By the year 2000, neoclassical economics dominated these institutions and organized most economic discussion. This book explains how and why neoclassical economic theory replaced Marxist economic theory as the dominant economics paradigm in China. It rejects the idea that the rise of neoclassical theory was a triumph of reason over ideology, and instead, using a sociology of knowledge approach, links the rise of neoclassical economics to broad ideological currents and to the political-economic projects that key social groups inside and outside China wanted to enable. The book concludes with a discussion of the nature of economic theory and economics education in China today.

**Steven Mark Cohn** is a Professor in the Department of Economics at Knox College, Galesburg, Illinois, USA.

# Routledge Contemporary China Series

For our full list of available titles:
www.routledge.com/Routledge-Contemporary-China-Series/book-series/
SE0768

# Competing Economic Paradigms in China

The Co-Evolution of Economic Events, Economic Theory and Economics Education, 1976–2016

**Steven Mark Cohn**

Routledge
Taylor & Francis Group

LONDON AND NEW YORK

First published 2017
by Routledge

2 Park Square, Milton Park, Abingdon, Oxfordshire OX14 4RN
52 Vanderbilt Avenue, New York, NY 10017

*Routledge is an imprint of the Taylor & Francis Group, an informa business*

First issued in paperback 2019

*British Library Cataloguing in Publication Data*
A catalogue record for this book is available from the British Library

*Library of Congress Cataloging in Publication Data*
A catalog record for this book has been requested

ISBN: 978-1-138-67815-6 (hbk)
ISBN: 978-0-367-87802-3 (pbk)

Typeset in Bembo
by Wearset Ltd, Boldon, Tyne and Wear

For Nancy and Maury and all people trying to build a better world

# Contents

# Preface

I am a heterodox economist. I find the methodology and basic assumptions of neoclassical economics (such as the assumption of hyper rational human behavior) helpful for thinking about some partial equilibrium, microeconomic issues, but ultimately inadequate for understanding many important economic problems, including the origins of unemployment and macroeconomic crises, the causes of economic inequality, and the economic roots of potential environmental crises. I believe that Chinese policy makers will need a richer framework than that provided by neoclassical theory to best guide their economy. I explained many of my reservations about neoclassical theory in my book *Reintroducing Macroeconomics: A Critical Approach* (Sharpe 2007). Some of these topics are briefly discussed in Chapter 1 of this book. Readers interested in more detailed explanations of the methodological differences between neoclassical, Marxist, and heterodox economics may want to consult this book.

I believe that the study of economics cannot be separated from a larger analysis of the socio-political dynamics that economic practices create. In the case of China, this means studying the logic of State Socialism and State Capitalism as reproducing social systems. Neoclassical economics endorses the separation of economic analysis from analysis of larger social dynamics. This separation denies economists the ability to fully explore important economic topics, such as the origins of tastes and preferences, the socially constructed reactions of economic agents to uncertainty, the full range of factors shaping the evolution of economic institutions, the two way causal relationship between the economy and the state, and the relationship of the economy to human well-being. All of these topics are critically important to understanding the evolution of the Chinese economy and the current policy choices confronting Chinese leaders and their advisors.

I came to economics through a circuitous route. I went to college during a very idealistic time in America and majored in American Studies at Amherst College. It was my hope to contribute to the elimination of poverty in the United States. I initially went to graduate school in public policy at Princeton University and focused on anti-poverty policy. While at Princeton I realized that neoclassical economists dominated policy discussions. I was dissatisfied, however, with the unrealistic assumptions of neoclassical economic models. I felt they biased analyses toward recommending free market oriented (though not entirely laissez-faire) outcomes, without much reflection about the limitations of these models. Therefore, after graduating from Princeton with an MPA in public policy, I decided to pursue a PhD in economics at the University of Massachusetts in Amherst, which had the leading heterodox economics program in the United States. I studied with brilliant people at U. Mass-Amherst, including Sam Bowles and Herb Gintis, Rick Wolff and Steve Resnick, and Jim Crotty. I owe my ability to think about economic issues in multiple paradigms to these teachers.

I studied economics because I thought it could be useful in figuring out how to build a world in which everyone's basic needs were met; a world where people had meaningful work, self-respect, and economic security; a world were inequality was modest and democracy present in the workplace as well as the town hall. I was interested in the long term possibility of democratic socialism and the short term project of social reform in the United States. Somewhat later, I became interested in sustainability.

While some of the concepts of neoclassical economics can be used to pursue most of the above goals, I believe the paradigm ultimately truncates many of these projects. The assumptions of classical liberalism which underlie neoclassical economics promote a policy framework that varies between laissez-fair-strong and laissez-faire lite, thereby limiting social reform. This has been the case in the United States and I will argue it is also the case in China. As we shall see in the chapters that follow, Chinese neoclassical economists usually told stories about the economy that fit events into neoclassical theory's master narrative about the merits and inevitable triumph of private enterprise and laissez-faire oriented government policies.

This may seem strange to some readers, as the "Beijing Consensus" has often been portrayed as an alternative to the neoliberal oriented "Washington Consensus." I will try to demonstrate, however, that the difference between Chinese neoclassical economists' long run goals and the Washington Consensus is relatively modest. Aspects of the Beijing Consensus, such as restrictions on the privatization of land, for example, probably have been opposed by most neoclassical economists. Many other "activist" government policies of the Beijing Consensus were endorsed by neoclassical theorists as temporary measures. These policies were tolerated in recognition of domestic political constraints or accepted as transitional policies that avoided the disruptive effects of a "shock therapy" transition to a free-market lite economy. The long run aims of Chinese neoclassical economists have consistently been to "extend the reform process," which usually means moving Beijing closer to Washington.

One of the goals of this book is to demonstrate the presence of a "homing instinct" in neoclassical theory which tends to conform economic analyses to findings consistent with the world view of classical liberalism. While it is easy to show this with reference to writings on China by economists like Milton

Friedman and Steven Cheung, I will try to show that this is also the case with respect other important American neoclassical economists writing about China (such as Gregory Chow, Dwight Perkins, and Nicholas Lardy) and other important Chinese neoclassical economists (such as Lin Yifu, Li Yining, and Wu Jinglian). There are obviously exceptions to this claim, but I think it true for the paradigm as a whole.

One particularly vexing issue is how to draw the boundaries distinguishing debates within neoclassical economics from debates between neoclassical economics and other paradigms, such as Marxist economics and heterodox economics. I have relied on two related criteria: (1) the methodology used to construct economic arguments and (2) the assumption or rejection of the basic neoclassical narrative about Chinese economic history since 1949. The neoclassical narrative paints the Maoist years as catastrophic and the reform years as miraculous. Reflecting the assumptions of classical liberalism, the narrative attributes the success of economic reform to the expansion of markets and material incentives, privatization, and the greater openness of the economy to global markets. It ties the failures of the Mao years to the inevitable result of dulling material incentives, the inherent inefficiencies of economic planning, and the costs of withdrawing from the global division of labor. The neoclassical narrative foresees only one viable future path for China involving laissez-faire lite and strong options. It is a TINA [There Is No Alternative] vision. Marxist and heterodox histories of the Chinese economy construct different narratives and imply different potential futures.

Many chapters in this book will demonstrate how the logic of neoclassical economics has influenced the framing of Chinese economic analysis. I will also demonstrate the plausibility of alternative Marxist and heterodox economic framings and, by extension, the possibility of alternative futures for the Chinese economy to the neoclassical vision. My hope is that by demonstrating the paradigmatic nature of Chinese economic discourse, the book will encourage the evolution of a more pluralistic Chinese economics profession.

In writing this book, I have come to have more respect for the neoclassical position, both in terms of acknowledging the shortcomings of the Maoist period and recognizing some of the economic achievements of the reform period. I still find the neoclassical narrative seriously flawed and overdrawn, but consider it a much more serious and honest attempt to explain Chinese economic history than when I started this project. I also still find the paradigm unlikely to generate a research agenda that would help combat the consolidation of a highly unequal and unsustainable socio-economic system in China.

I suspect that revelations about the violent excesses of the Cultural Revolution caused many left leaning economists originally sympathetic to aspects of Mao's policies, to have second thoughts about their critiques of the neoclassical narrative in the 1980s and 1990s. While such rethinking is healthy, I do not think that excessive enthusiasm for Maoism should deter thoughtful critiques of contemporary Chinese economic policies or neoclassical framings of Chinese economic issues. The Cultural Revolution was a great tragedy and it would be ironic if its last harm to the Chinese people was to inhibit thoughtful criticism of China's drift toward free market capitalism.

## Audiences and reader resources

The book has three different intended audiences: American and Chinese economists, American and Chinese historians and other social scientists, and the educated lay public. The different expertise of these different audiences presents problems with respect to the appropriate level of background information for many discussions. I have tried to provide the minimal level of background necessary for all groups to follow the analysis. There is a list of abbreviations following this preface.

## A note on the treatment of Chinese names

Most Chinese names have been ordered with family name followed by first name, as is the custom in China. This convention has not been followed for Western economists of Chinese descent who use traditional Western naming conventions putting family name last.

Galesburg, IL. May 1, 2017

# Acknowledgments

I begin this project with a sense of modesty. I am not a lifelong China scholar. For 35 years I have focused my research on thinking about the logic of paradigms in economic thought and economic policymaking. For the last five years I have studied the Chinese economy and Chinese economic thought. Given this background, the contribution I could potentially make to understanding the evolution of Chinese economic theory and the Chinese economy is to unpack the impact of paradigms on both, and this is what I have tried to do in this book.

I have benefitted from the help of many friends, China scholars, and participants in China's political-economic life who have shared their experiences and thoughts with me. The list below is necessarily incomplete, as one incurs intellectual debts that elude specific recognition, but shape one's thinking none the less. Thus, thanks to these unnamed teachers as well, if only anonymously.

I would like to acknowledge financial support for this research from the Knox College faculty research fund, Knox College conference travel fund, and Knox College Mellon grant fund. I would also like to thank the China Studies Institute in Beijing for inviting me to teach in their program winter term 2014. I would also like to thank the Knox library and computer staffs for their assistance.

It is a pleasure to thank the many people who have helped me with this research. I benefitted from hearing views from very different perspectives. Nothing in this acknowledgment should be mistaken for an endorsement of the positions expressed in the book by any of the people thanked. I alone am responsible for any errors. Among the people who have helped me are: Bai Runtian; Chen Long; Cheng Enfu; Gerry Epstein; Fang Min; James Galbraith; David Goodman; Gu Limei; Guo Fei; Guo Yuhua; He Yin; Stan Helm; David Kotz; Mehrene Larudee; Fred Lee; Li An; Li Bingyan; Li Minqi; Liu Zhen; Daniel Lund; Ryan Lynch; Keith Maskus; Michael Pettis; Thomas Rawski; Mike Schneider; Shuyan Shipplett; Barbara Schulze; Song Jianmin; Sun Youli; Wang Fang; Wang Yanjun; Wang Yougui; James Watson; Ruby Watson; Wen Jiaoxiu; Xia Lu; Xie Fusheng; Xiang Tang; Xiong Wanting; Yang Yuan; Yao Jie; Yao Xianguo; Yin Xing; Yuan Jian; Zhao Zhun; and Zhu Andong. I would also like to thank Lucy McClune of Routledge Press, Ashleigh Phillips, Amit Prasad, Richard Skipper, and Maria Whelan for their help in preparing the book for publication. Special thanks to Routledge editor Peter Sowden.

Special thanks also to: Marc Blecher; Victor Lippit; Malcolm Warner; Norton Wheeler; Zhou Yi; and my partner in everything, Nancy Eberhardt. Acknowledgement and gratitude are also extended to the following publishers and authors for permission to quote from their works:

Excerpt from "The challenge China's economy poses for Chinese economists" by Dwight Perkins, published in the *China Economic Review* 13(4) 2002. Permission granted by the publisher.

Excerpt from "China's Neglected Informal Economy: Reality and Theory," by Philip C.C. Huang, published in *Modern China* 35(4) 2009. Permission granted by the publisher.

Excerpts from "Western Neoclassical vs Marxist Economics in the PRC after Mao," by Steve Cohn. Contained in *The Diffusion of Western Economic Ideas in East Asia*, (2017) edited by Malcolm Warner. Permission granted by the publisher.

Excerpts from "The Evolution of Chinese Entrepreneurial Firms: Township-Village Enterprises Revisited" by Chenggang Xu and Xiaobo Zhang, IFPRI Discussion Paper 00854, (2009), used with permission of the publisher, International Food Policy Research Institute.

Excerpts from "The Chinese Road to Capitalism," by Richard Smith, published in the *New Left Review* I/199, (1993). Permission granted by the publisher."

# Abbreviations

| | |
|---|---|
| AEA | American Economic Association |
| CASS | Chinese Academy of Social Sciences |
| CCER | China Center for Economic Research |
| CEERC | Committee on Economics Education and Research in China |
| CES | Chinese Economist Society |
| CIPE | Center for International Private Enterprise |
| CPC | Chinese Communist Party (Sometimes also rendered as CCP) |
| CR | Cultural Revolution |
| CRS | Contract Responsibility System |
| CSCPRC | Committee on Scholarly Communication with the People's Republic of China |
| FDI | Foreign Direct Investment |
| FIE | Foreign Invested Enterprise |
| FSU | Former Soviet Union |
| FTCs | Foreign Trading Companies |
| GATT | General Agreement on Tariffs and Trade |
| GLF | Great Leap Forward |
| H (HS) | Holism (Holist-structuralism) |
| HRS | Household Responsibility System |
| IoE | Institute of Economics |
| IMF | International Monetary Fund |
| INGO | International Non-Governmental Organization |
| KMT | Kuomintang |
| LTV | Labor Theory of Value |
| MI | Methodological Individualism |
| MoE | Ministry of Education |
| NIE | New Institutionalist Economics |
| NRRM | New Rural Reconstruction Movement |
| NSC | New Socialist Countryside |
| PRC | People's Republic of China |
| SASS | Shanghai Academy of Social Sciences |
| SEZ | Special Economic Zone |
| SHC | Shareholding Cooperative |

| | |
|---|---|
| SOE | State-Owned Enterprise |
| SSA | Social Structure of Accumulation |
| TFP | Total Factor Productivity |
| TINA | There Is No Alternative |
| TVEs | Township Village Enterprises |
| UNDP | United National Development Programme |
| WTO | World Trade Organization |

# 1 Introduction and overview

## 1.1 Main themes

This book is about one of the great ideological revolutions shaping the modern world, the triumph of classical liberalism over Marxist theory in China. The replacement of Marxist economics by neoclassical economics was neither a triumph of reason over ideology, as often portrayed by neoclassical economists, or simply a self-serving embrace of a legitimizing ideology by a rising class of property owners, employers, and their representatives, as suggested by some Marxist theorists. The triumph of neoclassical economics reflected a complex social process and feedback loop: mixing intended and unintended consequences; bouncing across numerous dimensions of Chinese society; and running along globalizing filaments, such as the World Bank and even the Social Science Citation Index. The decline of Marxist economics in China redefined the questions asked (and unasked) in economics, and the basic assumptions adopted about human nature and historical change.

In the chapters that follow we will look closely at how the revolution took place in economic theory and in economics education. While the battles were fought on an academic terrain, the revolution had enormous implications for daily life in China. The triumph of neoclassical economics has legitimized and empowered a "laissez-faire lite" economic agenda. This, in turn, has created a domestic Chinese capitalist class, accelerated economic growth, increased social inequality, and expanded environmental destruction. It has also tended to restrict economic debate over future policies to those ideas congenial with the assumptions of neoclassical economics—putting the "free market cart," so to speak, before the horse of economic analysis. From the perspective of Marxist and heterodox economists, the current dominance of neoclassical economics severely limits the ability of Chinese economic thought and policy to address problems of inequality, macroeconomic instability, and sustainability. How did such a radical change in thinking occur among Chinese economists?

Applying ideas from Kuhn's theory of paradigmatic discourse, this book analyzes the process by which a new "scientific community" of neoclassical economists was created and eventually came to replace the older "scientific community" of Marxist economists as the recognized experts within China on economic topics. The book stresses that the transition involved new ways of both "seeing" and "not seeing," in a framing sense. Rather than simply learning how to use a set of tools (which is a common neoclassical economics metaphor for the study of economics), Chinese economists and their students were putting on different pairs of theoretical spectacles. The new lenses conditioned what economists saw, even before they reflected upon it. Using the new glasses presupposed fundamental changes in some basic assumptions underlying economic inquiry and a revised agenda for economic research.

But what do these changes in academic approach have to do with actual changes in the Chinese economy? There is a complex two way relationship between economic theory and economic events. This book tries to illuminate that relationship. It discusses how economic theory influenced economic policy and how economic outcomes influenced the evolution of economic theory. As we will see, both neoclassical and Marxist economists attempted to understand and fit events into their different pre-existing master narratives. These narratives, in turn, evolved within themselves and influenced how decision makers managed the Chinese economy.

To a surprising extent, economics is a kind of storytelling. Economists supplement raw economic data (often after crafting the categories that define or constitute data) with narratives that attempt to fill in the gaps and explain very complicated events with manageable theories. This book details how Chinese economists over the last 25 years gradually began to fill in the gaps with a different set of narratives and thereby learned to tell neoclassical rather than Marxist stories about economic development.

The book concludes with an analysis of the current state of Chinese economic theory, emphasizing its paradigmatic character, its accompanying tendency to narrow economic education to neoclassical training, and emerging efforts to transcend that narrowness.

## 1.2  Overview

The book has 10 chapters. In the remainder of this chapter I introduce the argument and discusses the basic differences between neoclassical, Marxist, and heterodox economic paradigms. Chapter 1 lays the groundwork for understanding why members of these different paradigms "saw" different things in Chinese economic history and recommended different policy responses.

Chapter 2 identifies the domestic and foreign influences that have pressed for the expansion of neoclassical economic theory and economics education in China since 1976.

Chapter 3 describes the political-economic history and immediate economic context that stimulated economic restructuring. It analyzes the distinct outlooks and policy initiatives of different groups of reformers. It highlights generational differences among Chinese economists, noting how different formative events (such as the Long March and the Cultural Revolution) helped shape the political-economic outlook of different cohorts of Chinese economists. It provides a description of the economic environment within which different economic species (i.e., different economic paradigms) co-evolved, gradually changing their economic environment and themselves.

Chapters 4, 5, and 6 illustrate this process in more detail by analyzing the co-evolution of economic theory and economic events in three different sectors of the Chinese economy over three different time periods. The three sectors are: the rural sector (Chapter 4), the international sector (Chapter 5), and the urban, state-owned enterprise sector (Chapter 6). The time periods are: 1978–1989, the first era of restructuring; 1989–1991, the Tiananmen Square interregnum; and 1992–2001, the second era of restructuring. The goal of the chapters is to illustrate how and why neoclassical, heterodox, and Marxist theorists thought differently about the periods' economic events, fitting them into different pre-existing, but somewhat flexible, master narratives. (For much of this discussion we lump together Marxist and heterodox economists.)

Chapter 7 offers some conclusions about the patterns observed across sectors and time periods.

Chapters 8 and 9 examine the evolution of Chinese economics education, from 1978 to 2000 and from 2000 to the present. These chapters analyze the internal and external forces that led China to replace Marxist with neoclassical economic theories in its university curriculum, its journal editorial policies, and its research support.

Chapter 10 sums up the book's findings and situates the development of Chinese economics with respect to global patterns of change in the economics profession as a whole. The analysis finds that the Chinese economics profession has accepted much of the spirit of classical liberalism and largely abandoned the goal of constructing socialism, replacing it with the task of maximizing economic growth. The Chinese economics profession has also elevated the role of mathematics and reduced the role of historical analysis in economic practice and education. When doing economic history Chinese economists have tended to replace historical materialism with new institutionalist theory. The Chinese economics profession has also tended to endow market outcomes with a privileged status (if not exactly a presumed optimality) that recommends guarding against "excessive" government "intervention" in the economy.

The book concludes with a discussion of the likely future of Chinese economics education and some suggestions for creating a pluralist economics profession in China.

## 1.3 A note on sources

The analysis in this book is based on two main sources of information. The first are written sources and conference presentations, which are endnoted in the usual fashion. The second are a series of formal interviews I conducted in the spring and summer of 2011 and winter/spring of 2014 in the US, Beijing, Shanghai, and Hangzhou, supplemented by many informal discussions with Chinese and American academics. Many aspects of these discussions were off the record and, in these cases, names are not cited.

## 1.4 A topology of economic schools

The history of the changing terms used to refer to neoclassical economics in China is revealing of the paradigm's changing status. Before 1978 neoclassical economics would have generally been referred to as "bourgeois economics," or "vulgar economics." After the initial reform period, the descriptive term was "Western economics." Around 1983 the term "modern economics" replaced "western economics" (Chow 2000, p. 52, Fang 2013, 304). While common usage is moving toward conflating neoclassical economics (or what is called mainstream economics today in the US) with economics, the transition is not complete.[1]

It would be helpful to define more precisely what is meant by terms like "Western/neoclassical economics" and "Marxist economics" in China. Unfortunately this is not as straightforward a task as it might seem. By "Western economics," do we mean the economics of Milton Friedman and Friedrich Hayek, two very popular Western economists in China, or the economics of John Maynard Keynes and Joseph Stiglitz, also popular in China? By "Marxist economics," do we mean the economics of *Das Kapital* and the USSR's five-year plans, the economics of Mao's mass mobilizations, or perhaps Jiang Yiwei's ideas of enterprise democracy? Are there any fundamental characteristics that we can use to distinguish all neoclassical economists and neoclassical economics from Marxian economists and Marxian economics?

In exploring these questions, I think it is helpful to use a modified version of distinctions introduced by Lin (1981) and elaborated by Robert Hsu (1991).[2] The authors divide Marxian economics in China into two "branches," diagnostic and functional economics. They define diagnostic economics as an ideological exercise demonstrating how a particular argument relates to the fundamental ideas of Marxian theory and the goal of socialist construction. They define functional economics as a practical exercise addressing public policy questions, often related to economic planning. Diagnostic economics is characterized by highly abstract and often philosophical argument. Functional economics uses more quantitative techniques, such as econometrics and input-output analysis, to analyze empirical data and offer practical advice.

Using a somewhat similar distinction as Hsu and Lin, but built around the difference between *texts* and *subtexts* (rather than "functional" and "diagnostic"), I want to distinguish the narrowly technical dimensions of *both* Western and Marxian economics from their broader philosophical dimensions.[3] The *texts* of each school of economics are the school's, or paradigm's, formal theories about how an economy works. For Western economics (neoclassical economics) this would include abstract theories, such as general equilibrium theory, and empirical analyses, such as studies of the price elasticity of demand for housing. Similarly, for Marxian economics, *texts* would include abstract theories, such as the labor theory of value, and quantitative planning models, such as input-output tables.

Explaining what I mean by *subtexts* will require a bit more elaboration.[4] To some extent, *subtexts* involve the philosophical orientations suggested by Lin and Hsu's term "diagnostic economics," but they are broader in scope. A paradigm's *subtexts* bookend its formal texts. They define starting points (unprovable basic assumptions) and anticipate ending points (what the theory will be used for). They infuse *texts*. *Subtexts* are what animate economics books and economic theories, transforming the lifeless logic of cause and effect into a kind of practical and moral calculus for human action.

*Subtexts* are built upon unprovable, and often tacit, assumptions about how the world works, such as assumptions about human nature. *Subtexts* reflect beliefs about the kinds of questions and projects that are important for economists to work on. *Subtexts* influence what topics are covered in introductory economics textbooks or in graduate curriculum. They influence how complex ideas are simplified to make them accessible to beginning students. Many simplifying (but unrealistic) assumptions are tolerated in introductory textbooks (or scholarly articles, for that matter) as long as the analysis gets the "fundamental" story "correct." What counts as "fundamental" and "correct," of course, is a paradigmatic judgment and usually echoes a paradigm's subtexts.

*Subtexts* are partially explicit and partially implicit. One often has to tease them out of a scholarly discussion. They are more visible in popular oriented writings, but even here much is left implicit. The basic *subtexts* of Western economics (neoclassical economics) and Marxian economics relevant to our discussion of Chinese political economy are listed below. We begin with Western-neoclassical economics. As we will see, its main subtexts tend to legitimize capitalist organization of economic activities.

## 1.5 Neoclassical economics

The following seven claims are the major subtexts of neoclassical economics:

### 1.5.1 On epistemology (the nature of economic knowledge)

Neoclassical economics is a scientific theory with claims on belief similar to modern physics. Mathematics is the bedrock language of science and thus should also serve as the bedrock language of economics.

### 1.5.2  On ontology (the nature of being)

There is no independent entity called Society. There are only individuals. Economics needs to study how individuals make choices and how various institutions, such as markets, aggregate them. This is known as the theory of methodological individualism (MI). It leads neoclassical economists to demand that all theories have micro foundations. It also requires treating people's tastes and preferences as exogenous independent variables.

### 1.5.3  On human nature

Neoclassical economics assumes "*homo economicus*," that is, that people are naturally rational and self-interested. Most people are assumed to have insatiable consumer appetites. As noted above, neoclassical economics does not concern itself with the origins of people's tastes and preferences (although insatiability tends to be implicitly treated as reflecting human nature). Competitive markets permit the harnessing of self-interest and human nature in the service of the common good. According to this logic, capitalism has been successful, in part, because it organizes the economy in accord with human nature.[5]

### 1.5.4  On the contribution of economic theory to human well-being

The task of economic theory is to understand and promote economic efficiency and economic growth, as both provide a basis for human happiness and the solution for many of our social problems. Many troubling aspects of market outcomes, such as inequality or concentrated economic power, are tolerable because of their contribution to economic growth.

### 1.5.5  On markets

Market outcomes reflect free choice and produce results that make all parties in an exchange better off. Markets are generally self-regulating. They usually automatically find the price that equates supply and demand, spur institutional innovation, and generally facilitate economic growth.

### 1.5.6  On the role of government

The basic role of the government is to secure the playing field for competitive markets (e.g., define private property rights) and fill in where competitive markets cannot operate. Even when there are clear "market failures," such as monopolies, recognition of the potential for "government failures" should temper government "intervention in the economy." A third potential role involves addressing equity issues, but this is limited by the need for incentives to promote economic efficiency and economic growth.

### 1.5.7 On socioeconomic choices

Neoclassical economics assumes the "TINA" (There Is No Alternative) perspective. The fall of the former Soviet Union and the travails of China before Deng's reforms are taken to prove that socialism and other attempts at more egalitarian and planned economies cannot work. The "take-away" message of the twentieth century is said to be "let capitalist markets work." Therefore, the burden is always on the government to justify an "intervention" in the market.

For neoclassical economists, the answer, regardless of the question, is usually economic growth, and the facilitators of this growth are "free markets."

Illustrative neoclassical texts influential in China include *Capitalism and Freedom* and *Free to Choose* by Milton Friedman (the latter with Rose Friedman) and the textbook *Economics* by Paul Samuelson. Currently popular neoclassical textbook authors include Gregory Mankiw and Paul Krugman.

## 1.6 Marxian economics

The subtexts of Marxian economics overlap neoclassical/Western economics in some cases, but diverge significantly in others. They are listed below.

### 1.6.1 On epistemology

Marxian economics is a scientific theory with claims on belief similar to modern physics. There is no special status for mathematics. There is a frequent use of historical analysis.

### 1.6.2 On ontology

Economics cannot be limited to studying individual behavior because there are logics to individual behavior that are generated at the societal level. Economic analysis needs to be part of a broader analysis of the reproducing logic of a social system.[6] This is known as holism (H). Historical materialism is the preferred holist methodology for studying modern social systems.[7] This approach points to macro foundations for micro behaviors.

### 1.6.3 On human nature

Economic activities involve less "natural" individual behavior and more socially constructed behavior than is generally suggested by neoclassical economics.

### 1.6.4 On the contribution of economics to human well-being

As in neoclassical economics, a high priority is assigned to understanding and promoting economic growth. This is treated, however, as an intermediate rather than a final goal. The ultimate goal of economic understanding is enabling the transition to socialism and increasing human well-being.

### 1.6.5  On markets

The study of markets must be situated within an analysis of the social system deploying them. While potentially very useful social institutions, markets have dysfunctional (e.g., Great Depression and Great Recession) interludes as well as self-regulating moments. Wage labor and labor markets within capitalism are exploitive and alienating. Markets have strong feedback effects on culture and the structure of the rest of society. A good society needs to reflect carefully on the proper role for markets.

### 1.6.6  On the role of government

The government and community decision-making institutions need to play a large role in the economy, at least during the transition to socialism.

### 1.6.7  On socioeconomic choices

The future will be a choice between socialism and barbarism. Capitalism is like a bicycle; it is only stable when in motion. Its great triumph has been enabling and imposing relentless capital accumulation and economic expansion. But this process contains within itself no limiting principle and will eventually explode the environmental envelope surrounding the economy. In the short run, capitalist economies need to be embedded in a system of social governance to prevent huge inequalities, protect workers' dignity, and ensure sustainability. In the long run, capitalism needs to be superseded for human life to endure. Thus, one of the major tasks of economics is to help construct socialism.

Illustrative Marxist texts popular in China include the *Communist Manifesto* by Marx and Engels, and Engels's *The Condition of the British Working Class*. Many articles form the journal *World Review of Political Economy* are illustrative of more current Marxist scholarship in China.

This book focuses on how the subtexts infusing Chinese economic theory and Chinese economics instruction shifted from Marxian to neoclassical themes. We will look at evidence of the shift and how it took place. We will also link these shifting approaches to economic analysis to shifting recommendations for public policies, with particular attention to the logic of neoliberalism.

## 1.7  Heterodox economics

In order to complete the topology of Chinese economic thought, I need to introduce a third position, in some ways located between the Marxian and neoclassical schools and in other ways, located alongside them. It is called heterodox economics in the West. It is illustrated by schools of Western economic thought known as institutionalist economics (of the "old" variety), Post Keynesian economics, radical economics, feminist economics, ecological economics, and social economics. Along with these paradigms, heterodox economic thinking in China would include writings from the Chinese New Left and New Rural Reconstruction movement. They all share a common ground in rejecting the adequacy of neoclassical theory's world of *homo economicus* and general equilibrium, but they do so in different ways. Illustrative heterodox subtexts are:

### 1.7.1 On epistemology

Economic analysis is paradigmatic. It is always constructed by looking through a lens. It thereby contains more "subjective" or stylized content than acknowledged in either Marxist or neoclassical analysis. Recognition of this recommends intellectual modesty and openness to alternative ideas. Economics should employ a variety of methods, ranging from mathematical models to anthropological-style fieldwork and behavioral experiments. Most heterodox economists believe that the pendulum has swung too far toward mathematical formalism and over-simplified assumptions in the name of parsimony.

### 1.7.2 On ontology

Economics needs to study the logic of individual behavior within a system of social reproduction. Economics needs to study institutions as well as individuals.

### 1.7.3 On human nature

*Homo economicus* is much too narrow a psychological foundation for economic analysis. In order to understand economic behavior, much more attention should be given to the impact of culture, custom, habit, tendencies for reciprocity, panic, imitation, and so forth.

### 1.7.4 On the contribution of economics to human well-being

The link between economic growth and human well-being is much more complicated than is often implied in neoclassical and Marxist analyses, and this link has weakened considerably in the advanced economies. Equity and environmental concerns, as well as the nature of the nonmarket economy (for example the household economy), deserve increased attention in economic analysis and are often mistakenly devalued in relationship to market efficiency and growth concerns in both neoclassical and Marxist analyses.

### 1.7.5 On markets

The study of markets must be situated within an analysis of the social system deploying them. All markets are not the same and must be studied in their concrete particularity. While extremely useful social institutions for making many kinds of decisions, markets are not appropriate institutions for organizing all kinds of social interaction.

### 1.7.6 On the role of government

Market economies need strong forms of social governance to best meet human needs.

### 1.7.7 On socioeconomic choices

Heterodoxy has no immediate allegiance to capitalism or socialism, with a tendency for eclecticism and experimentation. It prioritizes "quality of life" (defined ambiguously and independently from GDP/capita), sustainability, and equity, alongside material advance.

Heterodox economics tends to be a more diverse school of thought than either neoclassical or Marxist economics. While there are very significant variations within neoclassical economics (from libertarians like Milton Friedman to Neo-Keynesians like Paul Krugman) and within Marxist economics (from orthodox Marxists like Ernest Mandel to Post Modern Marxists like Richard Wolff), the range is even broader in heterodox economics. As a result, the examples of heterodox economic theories noted below tend to be illustrative of an approach rather than shared belief.

John Kenneth Galbraith's analysis of the modern economy in terms of the special characteristics of the large corporation illustrates the importance of institutionalist analysis to heterodoxy. Hyman Minsky's analysis of the effects of herd behavior on financial markets illustrates the importance of emotional responses to uncertainty within heterodoxy. Both authors are relatively well known in China.

## 1.8 What's at stake: the significance of competing paradigms and subtexts

The debate among economics paradigms is a debate about how to frame economic discussion. It is a debate over the basic assumptions used to build economic models, over the most important goals for the economy, and over which questions the discipline of economics needs to answer. It is a debate that determines which metaphors will be used to represent economic processes, and which simplifications and anomalies in the models can be tolerated. It is a debate that *precedes* analysis. Where do these contrasting visions of the economy take us?

### 1.8.1 Impact of neoclassical thought

The models built within the neoclassical paradigm reflect the heritage of classical liberalism. They start with the assumption of *homo economicus* (rational economic man) and end with the goal of maximizing GDP as a proxy for human welfare. Even when leavened with thoughtful concerns about market imperfections and equity issues, the models necessarily tend to generate laissez-faire lite policy conclusions. There is minimal discussion of "capitalism" or "socialism" as social systems in neoclassical writings.[8]

The great exception to this is, of course, Milton Friedman and the Austrian economics tradition. Friedman's formal economic theory is built on methodological individualism, but his political economic writings are full of holist claims about the impact of economic policies on culture and political life. Like Margaret Thatcher, Friedman asserts "there is no such thing as society" (i.e., only individuals exist). Nevertheless, he simultaneously argues that an economy built around property rights, the legal fiction of corporations as citizens, and institutions that promote markets can create a harmonious society with democracy and civil liberties along with a culture that supports these practices. Thus, Friedman, the Austrians and many neoclassical economists in China appeal to an implicit holist theory of their own. They argue that capitalism produces an attractive society and way of life. There is nothing wrong with their attempts to make such arguments, but they should be acknowledged as holist claims and open to challenge and debate.

Serious discussion of the basic assumptions underlying economic models is adamantly rejected by Milton Friedman and most neoclassical economists.[9] They argue that only a model's predictions matter, not its assumptions—a strange position for a paradigm that usually wants to make use of all available information in making decisions. It is also a strange position in a field with very poor predictive success on major issues and a notoriously difficult time of interpreting the implications of failed predictions due to an inability to carry out controlled experiments.

Taken together, the logical structure, social networks, and de facto social theory of neoclassical economics in China have tended together to relentlessly (and somewhat unreflectively) push Chinese economic policy and economic restructuring in a laissez-faire direction.[10]

### 1.8.2 Impact of Marxist thought

Traditional Marxist economic theorizing in China asked how to simultaneously increase economic growth and create a path to an egalitarian socialist society. The relative weight accorded to these two goals (socialism and growth) fluctuated. During orthodox Marxist periods (such as the first five-year plan in the mid-1950s), attention focused on promoting economic growth. During Maoist periods, attention focused more on promoting socialist consciousness.

The different ultimate goals of Marxist and neoclassical theory (socialism vs. economic growth) and the different assumptions made about human behavior led theorists in each paradigm to concentrate on different problems. While neoclassical oriented economists studied the perceived inefficiencies of state-owned enterprises, characterizing socialism as a "shortage economy" in the goods market, Marxist oriented economists studied the hardships of the "Reserve Army of the Unemployed," characterizing capitalism as a "labor surplus economy."

It appears that Chinese Marxism has tended to emphasize philosophical and qualitative analysis over empirical and quantitative analysis. This characterization (and potential criticism) can, however, be taken too far. Chinese Marxists may have not done the same kind of market studies as neoclassical economists, but this does not mean that they did not do empirical work. Chinese Marxist economists built input-output models of the Chinese economy and Marxian growth models for economic planning purposes and prepared detailed institutional analyses of different sectors of the economy.[11] They also prepared detailed critiques of the inefficiencies of Chinese firms and failures of economic coordination between firms, that resulted in excess capacity in some areas and shortages in others. Nevertheless, the multiple goals of Marxist economic analysis (studying economic outcomes and their larger feedback on social development) probably resulted in less attention to the cost minimizing choices faced by enterprise managers than that given by neoclassical economists.

A more serious problem for Chinese Marxism was its manipulation for short run political purposes. Because Marxist economics was (and is) part of the official discourse used to justify Chinese government policies, it was subject to opportunist interpretations by political figures. While there was (and is) more genuine debate over theoretical principles among Chinese Marxist economists than is sometimes portrayed in Western accounts, the boundaries of debate and intellectual conclusions were (and are) sometimes constrained by political conditions. The potential for intellectual argument to degenerate into apologetics is one of the hazards incurred by a social theory (or religion) when it becomes a state ideology.

Despite its challenges, Marxist economics in China kept the goal of socialist construction in sight and situated economic discussion within a larger social context than neoclassical economics.

## Notes

1 Reflecting the growing hegemony of neoclassical economics in China, Fang reports, "Others propose to change the term 'Western economics' into 'modern economics' [arguing] ... the term 'Western economics' was redundant" (Fang 2013, 304). Universities are also dropping prefaces and simply labeling courses as micro or macroeconomics (Ibid., 302).

2 Chen (1995) takes a fairly similar approach, distinguishing between what he calls "fundamental principles" and "instrumental principles" (Chen 1995, Introduction).

3 Hsu acknowledges that it would also be theoretically possible to characterize Western economics in terms of its ideological and functional aspects, and notes that Chinese scholars have actually done this. He reports that at a conference on economic reform in 1987, Chinese economists endorsed efforts to

> absorb the 'scientific components' of Western economic theories ... the "essence-oriented theories" (*benzhi lun*) of Western economics should be rejected, but its "operation-oriented theories" (*yunxing lun*) ... should be studied ... and its "method-oriented-theories" (*fangfalun*), such as input-output analysis, should be learned.
>
> (Hsu 1991, 8)

This is in keeping with a long rhetorical history of pledges by Chinese leaders to maintain a Chinese essence (*ti*) while deploying Western techniques (*yong*). In 1978, Hu Qiaomu, the president of the Chinese Academy of Social Sciences, called for China to adopt the functional aspects of Western management theory, while rejecting the ideologically driven practices in the service of capitalist relations of production (Hu 1978, 7–11). In the early 1980s, when Western economics was being re-examined in China, Chen Daisun and others urged efforts to distinguish the "vulgar" aspects of neoclassical economics (apologetics for capitalism) from its useful operational aspects (Fang 2013, 297–300).

4 Much of this discussion of texts and subtexts is taken from and elaborated in Cohn 2007, especially Chapter 2. See also Chapters 1 and 3.

5 The centrality of this assumption to neoclassical economics and its Chinese derivative is nicely illustrated by Lin Justin Yifu in his 2012 book *Benti and Changwu: Dialogues on Methodology in Economics*. Lin writes,

> The common element in all economic theories is rationality. ... This premise ... distinguishes economics from other social sciences. ... In economics, rationality is the *Dao* [emphasis in the original]. ... [T]he economist's job is to ... explain the rationality behind the phenomenon.
>
> (Lin 2012c, xix)

6 Thus the interest in historical analysis.

7 Historical materialism embodies Marx's theory of history. It calls for, among other things: dialectical analyses of social wholes; the theoretical construction of social wholes with reference to class structures; and definitions of classes with respect to the relations of different groups to the means of production and control of the social surplus.

8 As Robert Heilbroner once remarked, "The best kept secret in [neoclassical] economics is that economics is about the study of capitalism" (Palley 1998, 15).

9 For an excellent discussion of this issue, see Hodgson 1986.

10 In discussing shifting ideas about the merits of privatization and joint ventures in China, Edward Gu reaches a similar conclusion, writing, "Advances in social science knowledge, as Alexander Gerschenkron has argued, have contributed more to institutional change by reinforcing ideology than by advancing analytical capacity" (Gu 1997, 61).

11 Liu Guoguang, for example, indicates that as early as 1959 the Institute of Economics of the Chinese Academy of Sciences set up the Research Group for Quantitative Economics (Liu Guoguang interview, 9).

# References

Chen, Feng. 1995. *Economic Transition and Political Legitimacy in Post-Mao China: Ideology and Reform*. Albany, NY: State University Press of New York.

Chow, Gregory. 2000. "The Teaching of Modern Economics in China." *Comparative Economic Studies* 42 (2): 51–60. doi:10.1057/ces.2000.8.

Cohn, Stephen M. 2007. *Reintroducing Macroeconomics: A Critical Approach.* Armonk, NY: M. E. Sharpe.

Fang, Fuqian. 2013. "The Changing Status of Western Economics in China." In *Thoughts on Economic Development in China*, edited by Ying Ma and Hans-Michael Trautwein, 295–305. New York: Routledge.

Gu, Edward X. 1997. "Foreign Direct Investment and the Restructuring of Chinese State-Owned Enterprises (1992–1995): A New Institutionalist Perspective." *China Information* 12 (3): 46–71. doi:10.1177/0920203X9701200303.

Hodgson, Geoff. 1986. "Behind Methodological Individualism." *Cambridge Journal of Economics* 10 (3): 211–224.

Hsu, Robert C. 1991. *Economic Theories in China 1979–1988.* New York: Cambridge University Press.

Hu, Qiaomu. 1978. "Observe Economic Laws, Speed Up the Four Modernizations." *Peking Review* 21 (45): 7–12.

Lin, Cyril Chihren. 1981. "The Reinstatement of Economics in China Today." *The China Quarterly* (85): 1–48. doi:10.1017/S0305741000028010.

Lin, Justin Yifu. 2012c. *Benti and Changwu: Dialogues on Methodology in Economics.* Beijing: Peking University Press.

Liu, Guoguang. "Interview with Dr. Heng Lin." Chinese Academy of Social Sciences website: experts, 1st group CASS members, Liu Guoguang, http://casseng.cssn.cn/experts/experts_1st_group_cass_members/201402/t20140221_969619.html.

Palley, Thomas. 1998. *Plenty of Nothing: The Downsizing of the American Dream and the Case for Structural Keynesiansim.* Princeton, NJ: Princeton University Press.

# 2 Factors shaping Chinese economic theory and education

## 2.1 Introduction

The spread of neoclassical economics in China can be analogized in some respects to the spread of Christianity during the initial period of Western colonialism. Like the early missionaries, the economists from the American Economic Association (AEA) passionately believed that they were sharing ideas that would benefit both the Chinese people and Western nations. The economists enjoyed support from commercial economic interests, the US government, and Western philanthropic institutions, without being under their direct supervision. Aided by international institutions designed to facilitate the expansion of global capitalism, such as the World Bank, the IMF, and the GATT, the AEA economists actively promoted the free market friendly theories of neoclassical thinking.

It would be incorrect, however, to claim that neoclassical economic ideas were imposed on a hostile Chinese economics profession, recalcitrant Chinese state, or resistant general public. The process which revolutionized Chinese economic theory and economics education reflected the preferences of powerful interests inside as well as outside China. Norton Wheeler's memorable phrase, "invited influence," provides a good picture of the relationship between Chinese adopters and Western proselytizers of neoclassical economics (Wheeler 2012).

The dynamics spreading neoclassical economics were multi-dimensional. They reflected the unintended consequences of activities undertaken for other reasons, as well as conscious promotion. The insinuation of neoclassical motifs into Chinese institutions and habits of thinking provides a good illustration of Gramsci's concept of ideological hegemony. Neoclassical economics was not just "taught" to Chinese economists and students in lectures, conferences, and formal classes. The creation of neoclassical frames was also an experiential residue of practical interactions with Western accountants and bankers, journalists, and business partners. The growth of neoclassical economics was partially a linguistic shift reflecting the spread of a language helpful for participation in international commerce, in international credit markets, in global economic planning discussions, and in international academic conferences.

Like the reproduction of gender roles, the ideology of free market think-ing was a product of lived experience (expanded market activities) mediated through a newly available lens (neoclassical economics). The result was not the inevitable product of exposure to logical ideas or even the inevitable product of market experience. It was the result of a conjuncture of factors elaborated below. It was not accidental but it was also not inevitable.

This chapter is divided into two parts. Part 1 discusses the domestic factors inside China pressuring for the adoption of neoclassical economics by Chinese universities. Part 2 discusses foreign influences promoting neoclassical expansion.

## 2.2 Domestic reasons for the popularity of neoclassical economics after 1978

There were nine main domestic factors responsible for the growing interest in neoclassical economics in China after 1978: (1) the legacy of several chronic problems in the Chinese economy which invited new methods of analysis; (2) the expertise that Western economists were presumed to have in dealing with market economies and the desire of Chinese intellectuals to participate in international economics discourse with Western economists; (3) the eagerness of some older Chinese economists trained in the West before the 1949 revolution to reestablish ties with Western colleagues; (4) the increasing familiarity of Chinese citizens with market terms like prices and profits, which tended to make Marxist terms like surplus value and contradic-tion, seem artificial; (5) the scientific appearance of neoclassical theory's math-ematical format; (6) the desire of Chinese economics professors and students to study in the US, and/or find jobs with Western firms; (7) the use of neo-classical training as an indicator of business-friendly values by business firms within China; (8) the discrediting of Marxism by the Cultural Revolution; and (9) the appeal of neoclassical economics' reliable pro-market perspective to advocates of marketization within the Chinese Communist Party. The dis-cussion below looks in more detail at each of these phenomena.

### 2.2.1 Search for new strategies to deal with chronic problems

The problems faced by the Chinese economy during the late 1970s and early 1980s which invited increased interest in neoclassical economics are discussed in the historical narratives presented in Chapters 3–6.

### 2.2.2 Credibility of Western experts about Western economies

In the aftermath of the Communist Party's decision in December 1978 to adopt more market-oriented economic mechanisms, it seemed natural to many Chinese government leaders, local economic decision makers, and stu-dents to listen to Western economic experts and to study mainstream Western economic theory.[1] To a large extent this view has persisted. As a Marxist economic scholar told me, "Although western economists defend exploitation, our common goal is growth, so we can learn from western economies" —and presumably, Western economists.

In 1979 the Chinese Academy of Social Sciences (CASS) invited the US Committee on Scholarly Communication with the People's Republic of China (CSCPRC) to sponsor a trip to China by a prestigious group of US economists to plan future economics exchanges. The delegation's report indicates that the Chinese were very interested in obtaining access to contemporary Western economic theory.[2]

The same year a group of Chinese officials and academics visited business schools in the US and recommended that similar schools be set up in China (Warner 2014, 124). Deng was especially supportive of this initiative. The goal was to transplant Western management practices in China, with, of course, "Chinese characteristics."[3] In 1980 plans were initiated for an American oriented business school in Dalian, in partnership with State University of New York at Buffalo and with support from the US government. The Dalian MBA program was established in 1984, about the same time as other joint projects with Japanese and European institutions. By the turn of the century China had 62 MBA programs.[4] The training of public officials, at least at the highest levels, appears to have also turned to Western models. Lin Chun indicates that "Harvard's Kennedy School of Government is jokingly called China's 'second party school,' as senior officials are regularly dispatched there to be trained in proper modern thinking" (Lin Chun 2013, 69).

The Chinese leadership probably looked to Western economics to prepare managers to succeed in a market environment by limiting their gaze to "the bottom line," independent of social or political objectives. Deng's reforms had to create both a "class of residual claimants," and an ideology that legitimized pursuing these claims. Classical liberalism's view of the market's transformation of private vices into public virtues, which is echoed in neoclassical theory, filled this role.

In the late 1970s and early 1980s almost all university economists in China were Marxist economists. For the most part, only those trained before 1949 had studied Western economics in serious detail. There were a modest number of Chinese trained PhDs after 1949 who taught history of thought courses or contemporary bourgeois economic theory classes that included neoclassical micro theory and Keynesian macro theory. As the older group retired, there was a partial vacuum in terms of people who could present informed assessments of neoclassical economics. This vacuum was eventually filled by voices sympathetic to neoclassical economics.

The history of the World Bank's role in Chinese economic policy making illustrates the sustained interest of China's highest leaders after December 1978 in acquiring economic advice from Western experts. Beijing rejoined the World Bank in 1980. Bank inputs were avidly consumed by Chinese leaders during the first decade of reform, highlighted by the wide distribution given to the Bank's thousand-page assessment of the Chinese economy in 1981 and a follow-up study in 1985. Senior economists and government officials took part in several Bank organized conferences, such as the Muganshan conference in 1982 on Eastern European economic reforms and the Bashanlun conference in 1985 on macroeconomics and plan-market relationships. Two World Bank delegations sent to China in 1984 "proposed the concept of socialist joint-stock ownership, an idea that apparently inspired Chinese theorists" to support broad enterprise reform (Ma 1998, 383). The Bank contributed heavily to discussions of Chinese economics education, especially curricular changes, in 1986 and 1987. Key Chinese leaders, such as Zhao Ziyang and Zhu Rongji, seem to have been especially interested in World Bank research and recommendations.[5]

During the 1980s, fears of inflation were persistently near the top of Chinese policy makers' concerns. This priority probably reflects memory of the lethal effects of hyperinflation on the survival of the KMT government in the late 1940s. It also reflects the political sensitivity to inflation in modern China. Both during the Maoist period and the "reform" period, the pulse of the economy has been defined by a cycle of expansion, inflationary pressures (which during the Maoist period surfaced as shortages and expanded rationing, due to price controls) contractionary disinflation policies, renewed expansion, more inflationary pressures, further contraction, etc. It appears that Chinese leaders, especially Zhao Ziyang and Zhu Rongji, believed that neoclassical methodologies and econometric techniques could be practically useful in understanding and controlling inflation (Chow 1988, 9–11, Bottelier 2006, 21). The World Bank responded to these sentiments by co-sponsoring the Bashanlun conference on macroeconomic management in 1985 and conferences in Cambridge Massachusetts and Dalian China in 1993. Beijing appears to have adopted some of the advice emerging from these meetings.[6]

Aspects of neoclassical economics probably also appealed to Chinese planners faced with certain practical planning problems. For linear programmers with limited training in social theory, it was probably quite easy to shift from Marxist to neoclassical language. Advanced econometrics was probably seen as potentially useful by economists in many fields.[7]

Some of the leadership's openness to neoclassical economic ideas may also have been the result of the weakness of China's research and university infrastructure in the aftermath of the Cultural Revolution. The latter had an especially devastating effect on the economics profession.[8] As we shall see in later chapters, Western economic techniques often came combined with broader ideological overtones.

### 2.2.3 Revival of ties to Western economics by older professors originally trained in the West

After returning from China, the Committee on Scholarly Communication with the People's Republic of China (CSCPRC) delegation reported in

1980, "A number of the Chinese economists whom we met had studied in American universities during the 1940's and 1950's. They were particularly anxious to renew ties ... and to help groom a younger generation"[9] By 1984 these contacts and interests had been reestablished (Watson 1987, 85; Chow 1994, 114). Jacobson and Oksenberg indicate that this cohort of Chinese economists was active in facilitating China's membership in the World Bank.[10]

### 2.2.4 Growing use of market categories to describe market experience

Several people I talked with indicated that as the vocabulary of daily life included more and more references to market experiences, the explanatory world of Marxist economics, which deployed categories like value, surplus value, and contradiction, seemed increasingly artificial. The practical usefulness of concepts associated with Western economics, such as supply and demand, for explaining short run market phenomena reinforced this trend. These familiarities eased the way for popular acceptance of neoclassical economics for framing more complex and less immediately accessible ideas.[11]

My impressions of contemporary campus culture in China suggest that neoclassical economics is perceived as empirically grounded and practically oriented, while Marxist economics is perceived as philosophically grounded and ideologically oriented.

Chinese television has also played a role in popularizing and normalizing market thinking. Currently, China's national TV network (CCTV) has several programs that seem to resemble US financial news programs (Zhu 2012, Chapter 5). One of the programs was modeled after Donald Trump's *The Apprentice* (Zhu 2012, 110)!

In the 1990s CCTV produced several economics programs sympathetic to economic reform in the 1990s. The topics covered included: 20 episodes on village economic reform, 16 episodes on urban enterprise reform, and 12 episodes on the market and ethics. The programs championed marketization and globalization (Zhu 2012, 113–114).

Lin *et al.* report:

> in the mid-1990s, the marketized media arose as a platform to make neoliberalists' voices prominent in the Chinese intellectual community. ... The revival of liberalism has thus become an organizational construction, rather than merely the result of the action of individuals.
>
> (Lin et al. 2015, 56)

The authors highlight the role of *Southern Weekend*, a popular weekly magazine headquartered in Guangzhou.

Liu Changyuan and Wang Song's content analysis of the popular PRC magazine entitled *Chinese Youth* from 1980–2000 explores the evolution of individualism among Chinese young people. Their discussion of the Pan Xiao debate offers a fascinating glimpse into the emergence of a lay version of Adam Smith's invisible hand and Mandeville's "Fable of the Bees" in China. Searching for a meaningful life, Pan Xiao (a pseudonym) wrote a letter to the magazine which generated 20,000 responses. In the core paragraph Pan Xiao averred, "I've gradually come to an understanding: everyone, no matter what he/she is doing, is working just to make basic living … and he/she is working subjectively for himself/herself, but objectively for others…" (Liu and Wang 2009, 63).

### *2.2.5) Appeal of mathematical language*

When Chinese students went abroad to study economics their comparative advantage lay in mathematical techniques, as they had relatively weaker English language skills, so this is where many concentrated their studies. Having specialized in econometrics and mathematical modeling, they naturally taught and published in these areas, and valorized this part of economics upon returning home.

More importantly, the mathematical language of neoclassical economics gave it an a-political, scientific appearance which encouraged belief.[12] Some of the appeal of this language was in contrast to the highly politicized, anti-intellectual rhetoric of the Cultural Revolution. The privileging of mathematical language in Chinese economics has persisted. It is rewarded by referees in leading Chinese journals and in academic administration. It has been difficult, for example, to get articles published in the leading Chinese economic journal (*Economic Research*, [*Jingji Yanjiu*]) that do not rely heavily on econometric arguments.[13] At the Shanghai University of Finance and Economics (SUFE), an important university in Shanghai which I visited, the deans of both the economics and business schools had been math majors as undergraduates. At a higher level of the bureaucracy, many of China's current political leaders have been trained in engineering.[14] They probably find the surface similarities between neoclassical economics and engineering models attractive.

Song Longxiang's 1995 PhD dissertation provides a particularly clear statement of what might be called "mathematical fetishism" in Chinese economic thought.[15] He argues:

> James Buchanan, a Nobel laureate, writes that what economists can learn from one of its neighbors, mathematics, is '*a* language' (2) … the increased respect for economics as a separate scientific discipline since World War II has been largely due to the massive application of rigorous mathematical and statistical tools.
>
> (24)

Song contrasts neoclassical theory's successful embrace of mathematics with Chinese economists' lamentable "opposition to mathematics"[16] (156–157).

One of China's leading economists, Lin Justin Yifu, elevates the role of mathematics even higher. He argues that the industrial revolution occurred in England rather than China, and global economic leadership shifted to the West because of England's embrace of mathematical projects (and controlled experiments) and China's retreat from mathematical training. He writes,

> The precondition for the Industrial Revolution was the Scientific Revolution, which featured mathematics and controlled experiments. The Scientific Revolution did not take place in China because its civil service system discouraged talented persons from acquiring the capacity for mathematics and controlled experiments (Lin 2012a, 22).[17]

### 2.2.6 Interest in studying in the West (especially in the US)

Ever since the mid-1980s Chinese economics students have had a strong interest in studying in the United States for personal and professional reasons.[18] Advanced American economics degrees have been very helpful and are now almost required for obtaining teaching positions at China's elite universities. American degrees also help with employment in Western firms. Almost all of the entrance exams as well as course requirements in US economics education require neoclassical training.

Studying Western economics in the US was also attractive to some Chinese young people because it appeared likely to increase the opportunity for migrating to the US.

### 2.2.7 Job market concerns

Many people I spoke with described Chinese university students in general, and economics majors in particular, as being preoccupied with the pursuit of wealth. Careerist pressures appear to have accelerated over time. In response to changing student interests, for example, the Hopkins-Nanjing Center for Chinese and American Studies (a Sino–US joint venture on the campus of Nanjing University) replaced some history and area studies courses with more career oriented classes in the 1990s (Wheeler 2012, 23–24). The employment priorities of graduate students at CASS (one of China's elite think tanks) similarly shifted from idealist to materialist concerns.[19] Many Chinese students seem to have believed that studying neoclassical economics would enable them to get a good job with a prestigious Chinese firm[20] or international organization.[21]

### 2.2.8 Backlash against the Cultural Revolution

The Cultural Revolution left deep scars in Chinese society across many groups. Among these were loyal Communist Party members. Economists of all stripes were particularly vulnerable to attack by Red Guards. Their personal traumas served as a precondition for what might be called "conversion experiences" to alternative systems of belief. For many Chinese social groups, backlash against the Cultural Revolutions valorized previously transgressive beliefs like neoclassical economics and organized religion. For some young people, Western economics represents a break with the past. Like becoming a Christian in some traditional societies, it represents a shift in identity and signals an affiliation with "being modern." It is the "new music" of the market place, and echoes "modernity" in academia. In this vein, Wang Hui writes

> denunciation of the Cultural Revolution became the sole foundation of the moral rationale behind this rethinking … repudiating the Cultural Revolution has become the guardian of the dominant ideology … any criticism directed against the present can be cast as regression to the Cultural Revolution, and thus as being wholly irrational.
>
> (Wang 2003a, 76)

I think it is difficult to overestimate the negative impact of the Cultural Revolution on interest in Marxism and "leftist" projects in China.

### 2.2.9 Usefulness to government leaders and lower level party officials

Chinese leaders at the highest level of government were probably the most important group encouraging the expansion of neoclassical economics. The leadership was motivated in part by neoclassical theory's predictable support for marketization, which was useful in political battles over economic reform. In the 1980s they exhorted Chinese economists "to 'catch up' with the advances in reform practice, that is, to come up with theories and suggestions that would justify and perfect the reforms" (Hsu 1991, 10). The linkage between Western economics and marketization was so well understood that Chinese leaders sometimes signaled their support for accelerating "marketization" by highly publicized meetings with conservative Western neoclassical economists (see section 2.3). Most notable were two celebrated meetings of China's highest leaders, Zhao Ziyang in 1988, and Jiang Zemin in 1993, with Milton Friedman.

Deng and other supporters of marketization in the 1980s also used Western institutions, such as the World Bank, deploying the language of neoclassical economics, to push China toward marketization. This kind of leveraging was repeated in the 1990s by proponents of privatization who used "membership conditions" in the WTO to undermine the position of state-owned enterprises in China.

Neoclassical economics' predictable support for privatization probably also appealed to some middle level Communist Party members in China. David Kotz, in his study of the collapse of the former Soviet Union (FSU), argues that many middle level Communist Party officials in the FSU felt it would be easier to transfer their elevated economic and social standing inter-generationally through a system of private property than through bureaucratic privilege.[22] He credits these officials, numbering around 100,000, with spear-heading the replacement of the Soviet system of state ownership with more private ownership in the hands of former Party officials. The same process of insider privatization, led by Chinese Communist Party members, has been occurring in China.[23] Kotz's perspective challenges the conventional view of CPC officials as resistant to economic reform, due to a fear of losing special privileges.[24]

## 2.3 Foreign influences promoting neoclassical economics within China

### 2.3.1 Sources of influence

Five external groups actively promoted the expansion of neoclassical eco-nomics within China: (1) the American Economic Association (AEA); (2) several Western foundations; (3) several international organizations, such as the World Bank and IMF; (4) Western governments; and (5) foreign inves-tors. While foreign influence was motivated by foreign interests, much of this influence was welcomed by the Chinese.

### 2.3.2 Influence of American Economic Association (AEA)

The American Economic Association played a crucial role in turning Chinese economics toward neoclassical economics. It mobilized the prestige of Western academic institutions and Nobel Laureates to assume the role of expert advisor to the Chinese government. It also nurtured a Chinese eco-nomics profession in its own image.

While there were many economists involved with the AEA's initiatives, Gregory Chow of Princeton was probably the most important. Chow was born and raised in China.[25] He received his economics PhD from the Uni-versity of Chicago in 1955, where he was a student of Milton Friedman. He chaired the AEA's Committee on Exchanges in Economics with the People's Republic of China from 1981 to 1994. He also co-chaired the US Commit-tee on Economics Education and Research in China (CEERC) from 1985 to 1994. The CEERC was created by the Ford Foundation and financed key aspects of many of the AEA's China initiatives.

As noted above, significant dialogue between US and Chinese economists resumed in 1979 when the Chinese Academy of Social Science (CASS) hosted a visit to China of a distinguished delegation of US economists. The US side of the visit was coordinated by the Committee for Scholarly Com-munication with the People's Republic of China (CSCPRC). Among the topics discussed during the visit were: China's current economic challenges, the economics curriculum at the university level, economics textbooks, and the organization of Chinese economics research. Plans were laid for coordinating future visits to China and the US by economists of each country. Members of the planning group were to be appointed by the CSCPRC and the AEA (CSCPRC 1980, 3). The US delegation called specifically for AEA involvement (8).

The AEA, through formal and informal networks, helped field a series of seminars and lecture tours in China in the early 1980s.[26] Of special importance were a series of summer workshops organized by Professor Chow from 1984–1986 and co-sponsored by the Chinese Ministry of Education (Chow 1994, 40). The seminars were designed to introduce Chinese economists to a different area of neoclassical economics each year. They focused on microeconomics, macroeconomics, and econometrics. They were attended by about 50–100 Chinese economists and "the best and brightest" Chinese economics students. The latter went through an elaborate two-stage selection process for admission to the seminars. At the end of the 1984 session, Chow had a highly publicized meeting with Chinese Premier Zhao Ziyang, which he judged to have signaled that China officially endorsed modern economics.[27]

At the invitation of Zhao, Chow invited several Western economists to work with the Chinese Economic Restructuring Commission. He organized a three-day meeting in Hong Kong in January 1986 and a five-day meeting in Beijing in June 1986. Key members of the Chinese Economic Reform Commission and People's Bank met with John Fei of Yale, Anthony Koo of Michigan State, and Lawrence Lau of Stanford (and perhaps other Western economists) (Chow 1986, 9–10).

Probably the most important initiative of Professor Chow and the AEA was the establishment of a program to funnel promising Chinese graduate students into US economics PhD programs. The project ran from 1985–1998 and its graduates eventually redefined economics education in China (Chow 2002, 358–359). Chow designed a selection process that was heavily weighted toward students with backgrounds in the natural sciences, mathematics, and engineering (Chow 2000, 53). The two qualifying exams tested mathematical skills and mastery of a neoclassical economics oriented textbook on the Chinese economy that had been written by Professor Chow.[28]

In 1985 the Ford Foundation established and largely financed the US Committee on Economic Education and Research in China (CEERC) (Chow 1988, 7). The Committee was chaired by Chow and Harvard Professor Dwight Perkins. Besides helping to finance Chinese graduate students in US PhD programs, the committee supported summer workshops, yearlong graduate economics training centers in China focused on neoclassical economics, a visiting scholars program for Chinese professors, and some research projects.

I interviewed one of the participants in the year round graduate study program jointly sponsored by CEERC and the Chinese Committee on Cooperation in Economics Education and Research with the US The members of this group joined the summer workshop as their third semester of study. When I asked him if he thought ideology had been involved in the selection process for participation in the program, he gave a very interesting answer:

> I don't think there was any evidence of "ideological" criteria in the selection process. I did not find any enthusiastic Marxist thinkers selected and did not find any young economists who were critical of the reforms in any way in our class, either. Interesting combination.

He added that alongside the courses taught by Western economists, there was a course called Economic Problems of Socialism, which included lectures by some leading Marxist economists. Summing up, he concluded, "credit needs to be given to Chow *et al.* for apparently not censoring ideas in a heavy handed way."

I think the perception of inclusiveness alongside the absence of students with alternative perspectives is telling. The World Bank's seminars and advisory impact seems to have been experienced in the same way. It is always difficult to "see" absences, for example, the absence of Western heterodox economists alongside Western neoclassical economists, or the absence of attention to certain methodological issues in the syllabus. Nevertheless, I think the absence of crude censorship is both a credit to the neoclassical organizers of the seminars and a testimony to how influential and limiting underlying subtextual discourse can be.

I think an analogy can probably be drawn to the ideological cast of the Nobel Prize in economics. The Bank of Sweden prize, which is a more accurate name, has been heavily influenced by a small group of Swedish economists. The nominating committee was led for many years by Assar Lindbeck, the author of an important book criticizing the New Left in economics in 1971. From an ideological point of view, the Nobel Prize has been distinguished by the large number of winners from the University of Chicago. There has been, however, a large enough presence of non-Chicago economists to maintain the allegiance of the economics profession and appearance of broad-mindedness, despite its ideological character. In much the same way, the economists tapped by Chow and the AEA for China delegations and seminars included distinguished members who would be recognized as "left of the Chicago school," such as Joseph Stiglitz, and Roger Gordon.[29]

In May 1984 Chow met with a small group of students interested in founding a society of young Chinese economists. The meeting was held at the home of Liang Heng, the co-author of *Son of the Revolution*, a first-hand account of the suffering of the Cultural Revolution. A follow up meeting in 1985 of more than 50 Chinese students studying economics, management, and related subjects in the US established the Chinese Young Economists Society (later re-named the Chinese Economist Society) (Chow 1988, 11). By 1990 the group had 300 members, an annual conference, and a Journal

(*China Economic Review*). It became part of the ASSA, an umbrella organization created by the AEA in 1992, and organizes academic panels at the AEA meetings every year. By 1997, the CES was the largest Chinese overseas organization in the social sciences, with over 400 members. It saw itself as a medium for promoting "modern economics" (neoclassical and new institutionalist economics) in China.[30] I attended some of its sessions at the AEA meetings in Denver in January 2011 and in Beijing in June 2011. The discussions were heavily dominated by neoclassical orientations. While it is difficult to characterize the views of a large group of neoclassical economists, the CES appears to have been especially influenced by the Chicago school.

### 2.3.3 Influence of the Chinese diaspora and foreign foundations

From 1949–1979, China had very little interaction with American NGOs and private sector philanthropy. Remittances from the Chinese diaspora were also reduced, as some funds were redirected to Taiwan (Yin 2004, 71). After a century of foreign humiliation, in an assertion of Chinese sovereignty, the new government sent Western NGOs packing (Yin 2009, 521). Hostility toward Western influence was especially high during the Korean War and the early years of the Cultural Revolution.

On the flip side of the coin, the US trade embargo began in 1950, during the Korean War. It continued for about 20 years and cut off almost all American financial interactions with the PRC, including foundation work and remittances from Chinese Americans (Peterson 2014, 68).

US–China relations began to thaw in 1971, in the glow of ping pong diplomacy[31] and the end of the US trade embargo (though several other barriers to expanded trade continued). President Nixon's visit to China in 1972 continued the thaw, as did "people to people" diplomacy in the form of visits by US academics (chiefly natural scientists) to China. These visits were sponsored by the US Committee on Scholarly Communications with the People's Republic of China (an organization created by the National Academy of Sciences, the American Council of Learned Societies, and the Social Science Research Council). The beginning of the Chinese economic reforms and the resumption of normal diplomatic relations between the US and China in 1979 jumpstarted American NGOs and philanthropic interests in China.[32]

It is remarkable how quickly American foundations and NGOs created an infrastructure for nurturing the spread of neoclassical economics. The foundations and NGOs, without any master plan or apparent governing body, coordinated efforts with each other, diverse US government agencies, and private individuals. Among the projects supported were: Western (primarily American) economists' trips to China to teach neoclassical economies; Chinese professors and students trips to America to study neoclassical economics; Western neoclassical economists' research on the Chinese economy; joint research by Western and PRC economists (which served as an apprenticeship for PRC researchers in neoclassical ways of framing issues and discursive practices); joint economics conferences; book donations, and the growth of Western oriented business/management schools.[33] The seemingly natural flow of economics and management education along neoclassical and Western business models illustrates Gramsci's notion of hegemony.[34]

Of course there was more planning, screening, and self-selection of participants, and focusing of aid on some projects rather than others, than initially meets the eye. But the appearance of spontaneity was important. It is precisely the image of naturalness and the easy coalescence of diverse initiatives for collective action that defines a hegemonic discourse. There is no need for formal lines of authority when everyone in the game (or nearly everyone) is on the same page. For example, as just noted earlier, the AEA was very active in creating a Chinese economics profession in its own image. This ambition was funded by the Ford Foundation (see below) which created and financed the US Committee on Economic Education and Research in China (CEERC). The history of the 1990 Institute tells a similar story.

The 1990 Institute was founded by C. B. Sung and Hang-Sheng Cheng. Mr. Sung was the founder of Unison Corporation, which had many joint venture investments in China.[35] Dr. Cheng was a Vice-President of the San Francisco Federal Reserve Bank and director of the Center for Pacific Basin Monetary and Economic Studies. He also had worked for a decade at the IMF (Wheeler 2012, 52–53, Galenson 1993, 262). The Institute promoted joint research by US-PRC economists on China's economic reforms. Under Secretary of State Philip Habib and Senator Adlai Stevenson III served as honorary co-chairs (Wheeler 2012, 59–60, 146). They also received some help from the San Francisco Federal Reserve Bank (Wheeler 2012, 145–146).[36]

The Institute's first book analyzed China's first decade of economic reform. The research was co-sponsored by the San Francisco Federal Reserve Bank and directed by Walter Galenson, who had led a major research project on the Chinese economy for the Ford Foundation in the 1950s and 1960s. The book offered a rich collection of economic data and a skillful presentation of the neoclassical narrative on economic reform. It urged greater reliance on market mechanisms, expanded privatization, termination of permanent employment guarantees, increased wage differentials, and recognition of the contribution to economic activity made by venture capital and risk takers.[37]

Galenson was a veteran of Cold War politics in international labor research. A formerly confidential document offers a window into his thinking.[38] The excerpt below is from a memo discussing plans for an International Labor Organization meeting. It illustrates Galenson's attempt to manage discussion within what he and the US government thought were reasonable boundaries. Similar efforts would be made to frame Chinese economic issues in "reasonable ways." The memo appears to be commenting on Galenson's discussion with a Japanese policy maker.

Cornell University Professor Walter Galenson ... detailed U.S. Objections to basic conference document. ... noted some specific danger signals ... Marxist influenced draft conference paper "employment: basic needs approach," ... stresses "redistribution" of land and other productive assets as panacea for problem of poverty. ... it focuses almost exclusively on government planning as agent of redistribution while ignoring private sector. ... it sharply criticizes multinationals as "bad news" for LDCS without furnishing evidence. ... it claims that poverty does not exist in so-called socialist states and totally ignores contribution of "spirit of entrepreneurship" to economic growth and consequent creation of productive employment. ... Galenson indicated he hoping to urge Germans to make similar presentation. Galenson said that if U.S., Germany and Japan, Major Ilo budget contributors, stand together at WEC, so called Third World majority will back down.

(US Embassy, Tokyo April 12, 1976)

Under Galenson's direction, the 1990 Institute's publications appear to have carried some weight in Beijing. The Institute's first book, *China's Economic Reform* (1993), was presented to Jiang Zemin, China's second in command under Deng Xiaoping in December 1992. The event was reported on Chinese television (Wheeler 2012, 60). Zhu Rongji, China's chief economic strategist in the 1990s, credited an early Institute paper on inflation as influencing his thinking (Wheeler 2012 61; Yin 2004, 86). The Institute's 1993 book project also helped shape the evolution of Chinese economic theory by including nine scholars from the People's Republic on the research teams preparing the book's chapters. The Institute subsequently arranged for cooperative research with some leading research institutions in China to study the next round of economic reforms (Galenson 1993, viii). While some of the book's research was collaborative, it appears that editorial control of the 1993 book project was vested in American hands.[39]

US foundations frequently worked together, in concert with US government bodies and private corporations in funding projects related to economic thinking in China. This collective way of financing projects may have given Western foundations and government agencies more bargaining power with the Chinese, than if each project was funded solely by an individual sponsor. It also probably helped facilitate a group consciousness about shared projects, while permitting opportunities for experiments and widespread feedback.[40]

US support for Chinese students' study in America predates the Chinese reforms and Chinese Revolution. After the Boxer Rebellion, for example, which saddled China with indemnity payments for rebelling against its Western occupiers, the US government decided to use some of its indemnity receipts to help finance Chinese students' study in the US.

The government's motives reflected the principle of enlightened self-interest, as the President of the University of Illinois advised then president Theodore Roosevelt,

The nation which succeeds in educating the young Chinese ... will be the nation which for a given expenditure of effort will reap the largest possible returns in moral, intellectual, and commercial influence.

(Wheeler 2012, 119)

The image of an all powerful, orchestrating American academic-philanthropic-private sector-government alliance should not be pushed too far. The Chinese state strongly regulated NGO activities, especially their interactions with Chinese organizations. American foundations' financial outlays were modest, and not always easy for project managers in China to obtain. While the funding and activities of American foundations were highly leveraged during this period, allowing a little funding to go a long way toward forging an intellectual development path, the travelers on the path were interested in going where the foundations were pointing. While the Ford Foundation's statements that it "eschewed a strategy of 'coming here to change things' ... [and] 'to help people you have to let them determine the agenda'" (Wheeler 2012, 114), seem a bit disingenuous about the foundation's goals, the agendas of the Ford Foundation and many Chinese participants had large overlaps.[41] This situation is nicely captured in Norton Wheeler's phrase "invited influence."

The most important foundation facilitating the spread of Western economics in China was the Ford Foundation. The Center for International Private Enterprise (CIPE) also played an important role. A number of projects received some Rockefeller money.[42] The Mont Pelerin Society may have also contributed to the expansion of neoclassical economics in China. Working alongside these groups are many foundations that support international students' graduate study in the US and neoclassical oriented economics research around the globe. Groups like the CATO Institute,[43] the National Bureau of Economic Research (NBER), and the Rand Corporation[44] for example, have sponsored joint conferences or discussions with Chinese economists that promote neoclassical analyses of economic issues. The Asia Foundation has sponsored visiting Chinese scholars in the US and funded library acquisitions of books and professional journals.[45] The Sloan Foundation, Luce Foundation, some Christian organizations, and the US government have also supported Chinese students studying economics in the US Probably the largest source of funds came from scholarships offered by US colleges and universities.[46] The US government also funded a management training school in Dalian, a city in northeast China.

The discussion below outlines the activities of the Ford Foundation and Center for International Private Enterprise. It illustrates the role of foundations in transmitting embedded knowledge. By "embedded knowledge" I mean functional information that comes attached or embedded within broader conceptual frameworks. A classic example of embedded knowledge would be literacy skills that have been acquired from reading religious texts. In economics, an example would be the explanation of econometrics using examples that assume the texts and subtexts of neoclassical economics.

As a National Academy of Sciences (NAS) report indicated, "The Ford Foundation … has consciously sought to contribute to the development of fields in China that are central to that country's economic success and 'open' policy" (Lampton et al. 1986, 79). To this end, the Foundation worked closely with Professor Chow and other AEA economists. It was a major funder for the following programs: Professor Chow's summer neoclassical economics workshops (1984–1986), the establishment of year-long graduate study programs in neoclassical economics at Fudan and Renmin universities in the 1980s, doctoral fellowships for students to study economics in the US, and collaborative research between US and Chinese economists.[47] The Foundation also funded some research and training in agricultural economics.[48] In 1988, the Foundation was the first foreign NGO to obtain official legal status in China (Shieh and Knutson 2012). The foundation negotiated with the State Council to be "sponsored" and supervised by the Chinese Academy of Social Science (CASS) which was staffed by China's leading economic reformers.

Dwight Perkins (Co-Chair with Gregory Chow of the Ford Foundation financed US Committee on Economics Education and Research in China), has described the vision behind these educational programs. While their immediate goal was merely to give Chinese students the skills they needed to succeed in Western economics PhD programs, their long term goals were more ambitious. The programs initially enrolled 50–100 graduate students a year. It was expected that many would eventually earn American doctorates and return to teach at China's leading universities. The latter

> "would be rapidly transformed" and "in turn would train the economics teachers at the less prestigious universities." Within 20 years "the economics teaching programs of China would be dominated by this cohort of young, Western-trained economists."
>
> (Perkins 1999, 2)[49]

While it took longer than expected for this process to take off, due to an initial reluctance of Chinese PhDs to return to China, the project ultimately worked as designed. Thomas Rawski finds that the normalization of relations between the US and China permitted American researchers to "recruit Chinese students to study in their home institutions," with returning graduates assuming important positions in universities and government institutions, including the People's Bank of China, Peking University and Tsinghua University (Rawski 2013 [2009], 176, 183).

The National Academy of Sciences study of US–China educational exchanges reported similar successes, concluding:

> In part because of the increased scholarly exchange and in part because of improved access to Western publications within China, China's understanding of Western economics has grown considerably since the late

1970s. … Current issues of Chinese scholarly journals now often contain articles applying neoclassical economic theory. … Increasingly, Western economists can find Chinese counterparts whose skills and research priorities are compatible with their own.

(Lampton et al. 1986, 147)

The Center for International Private Enterprise (CIPE) partnered with AEA economists and the Ford Foundation in several "embedded" economics education projects. The Center's newsletter (*Economic Reform Today*: Number Four 1999) described how the organization had overcome some of the barriers to the expansion of private enterprise in China posed by the government's socialist orientation. The report highlighted CIPE's support (aided by the National Endowment for Democracy) for the Chinese Economist Society, which it credits with "educating thousands on market economics and influencing many high-level policymakers." The report also showcases CIPE support for the China Center for Economic Research, which included collaboration on "the development of a market-economics textbook series … [and] an electronic clearinghouse for economic reform research" (17–21).

The report lists other CIPE-supported CES activities involving sponsored books on market economics and business management and economics conferences. CIPE's most important contribution to the expansion of neoclassical economics was probably its support for CES programs aimed at repatriating American trained economics PhDs in China. As noted above, despite the success of the Chow-AEA-Ford Foundation program in attracting the "best and brightest" mathematically inclined economics students for study in the US, few graduating students were returning to China.

In 1999, CIPE asked Dwight Perkins to review the activities of the Chinese Economic Society in order to determine whether CIPE should continue funding the organization. Perkins's report highlighted the importance of CES efforts to help young Western-trained economists return to China for short economics conferences. He found these visits, and CES-inspired networking among overseas Chinese economists, critical ingredients for encouraging the subsequent return to China of Western educated economics PhDs. He finds that CIPE money would have been well spent if it encouraged the return of an additional two to three dozen sea turtles with economics PhDs (Perkins 1999, 2–4).

Perkins goes on to discuss the positive, but difficult to measure impact of CIPE-supported CES conferences on market oriented reforms in China. He also recommends funneling support for China based think tanks, such as the CCER and Unirule, that reproduce the libertarian-conservative tradition of the CATO Institute or American Enterprise Institute through CES (Perkins 1999, 12–13).[50]

Tian Guoqiang's career is illustrative of the kinds of projects and professional trajectories supported by CIPE and other Western foundations. Tian received an undergraduate and Masters degree in mathematics from

Huazhong University. He was a recipient of an Alfred P. Sloan doctoral Dissertation fellowship in 1986–1987 for his work in economics. He received a Center for International Private Enterprise Grant of $78,000 in 1992 for a project entitled "Education Program in Modern Economics in China." He has also enjoyed grants of $5,000 per year for at least a decade from the Texas A&M Private Enterprise Research Center.

Tian has had a prolific publishing career. He has also been President of Chinese Professors of Social Sciences in the United States, President of the Chinese Economist Society and is currently Dean of the School of Economics at the Shanghai University of Finance and Economics.[51] He has used his position as Dean to promote neoclassical economics within the department.

Because the indirect influence of Western foundations on the evolution of Chinese economics education and economic thought is well illustrated by the activities of CCER and Unirule, their history is briefly outlined below.

The China Center for Economic Research (CCER), like the CES, has been active in creating a scientific community of neoclassical economists in China. As elaborated below, the CCER has trained graduate students, organized important conferences, authored a series of textbooks, published an important journal, maintained electronic networks, and credentialized researchers. The CCER was established in 1994 at Peking University with seed monies and endorsement from the Ford Foundation and the World Bank (Lin 2005, 5). At least through 2000, it continued to receive significant funding from these organizations (Naughton 2002, 629). It grew from a staff of six economists in 1994 to 27 economists by 2005, and was judged the most important independent think tank in China by Barry Naughton in 2002 (Naughton 2002, 629). The Center is the brain child of Lin Justin Yifu. The CCER reflects the legacy of Lin's University of Chicago PhD "with Chinese characteristics."[52] Lin was appointed chief economist for the World Bank in 2008.[53] The Center also reflects the imprint of its other co-founder, Zhang Weiying. Zhang was deeply influenced by Austrian economics and is a well known conservative critic of Keynesian theory. He was Dean of the Peking University Guanghua School of Management until 2010.[54]

The CCER was designed as a self-consciously American beacon inside the Chinese economics profession. Twenty of its 23 economists in 2005 held American economics PhDs. The three other degrees were from the UK, Belgium, and Japan. The Center was also designed to facilitate China's market-oriented reforms and "has participated, since its founding, in almost every single policy dialogue in China …" (Lin 2005, 8–9).

In the teaching field, CCER offered minors, majors, MA and PhD degrees in economics involving over 2,500 students in 2005. Its faculty has written 14 economics and/or management textbooks (Lin 2005, 8). Its faculty is credited with redesigning the economics curriculum at Peking University "in line with the American model, particularly the 'Chicago model.'"[55]

The CCER runs advanced training programs in economics and management for faculty from other universities. In 2005 it ran the number one ranked international MBA program in China (according to *Fortune Magazine*'s ratings) and jointly oversaw a highly ranked Masters program in finance with a leading Hong Kong university (Lin 2005, 7). It also sponsors special training programs for women economists and for faculty members in China's hinterland.

The CCER has attempted to influence the public discussions of economic policy by creating special economics programs for journalists as well as government officials. As Lin explained it:

> journalists are the key players in the formation of public opinions. Since 1999, the CCER together with *Caijing* Magazine ... has jointly sponsored 10 fellowships for outstanding economics and finance journalists and editors in the Chinese media to study at CCER.

The three-month fellowships were "tailor made" for the kinds of issues the journalists would write about (Lin 2005, 11).[56]

In the research field, CCER faculty have authored over 70 books. From 1994–2004 the faculty published 49 articles in leading neoclassical journals, such as the *American Economic Review*, the AEA's flagship journal (Lin 2005, 8). The Center publishes a peer reviewed journal (*China Economic Quarterly*), the CCER Economic papers (a project of CCEER graduate students), and a public policy oriented newsletter. The CCER website was said to receive 22,000 visits a day in 2005.

The CCER has maintained active relationships with economists at other institutions. For example, the World Bank has funded a Visiting Fellows program for residence at CCER. With financial help from the Hong Kong and Shanghai Banking Corporation, the CCER sponsors an annual lecture by a Nobel Laureate at Peking University. With the US National Bureau of Economic Research (NBER), the CCER sponsors an annual conference on US-China-global economic issues (Lin 2005, 13). Since 2001 the CCER has sponsored the China Economics Annual Conference, which it claims "has become the largest gathering of economists in China" (Lin 2005, 13).

In terms of its prestige and its function as a magnet for the "best and the brightest," CCER's success suggests the emergence of neoclassical theory as a new Confucianism, at least with respect to economic thinking. As Lin reports, the CCER has grown from two small offices in a Soviet style building when it was founded into a beautiful and spacious complex on the site of an old royal garden (Lin 2005, 5).

The Unirule institute was established in 1993 by five economists (Mao Yushi, Sheng Hong, Zhang Shuguang, Fan Gang and Tang Shouning), and Beijing Universal Culture Co, Ltd (Unirule Website, July 12, 2013). Mao has been a Chinese champion of classical liberalism and received the Cato Institute's Milton Friedman Prize in 2012. His essay "Paradox of Morality" draws on Chinese metaphors reminiscent of Mandeville's *Fable of the Bees*. In 1998, Mao commissioned a Chinese translation of Hayek's *The Constitution of*

*Liberty*, and many top liberals met at the Unirule institute to discuss Hayek's ideas.[57]

Sheng Hong has also championed classical liberalism, asserting that traditional Chinese culture included many aspects of classical liberalism's view of the economy. Sheng argues that traditional Chinese thought linked market behavior to natural law, favored government protection of property rights and limited state intervention in the economy, and treated market generated economic institutions as the appropriate self-organized institutions to coordinate economic activity. Sheng also highlighted the impact of Chinese ideas on the development of classical liberalism in the West, especially through their influence on the Physiocrats (Hermann-Pillath 2011, 7–9). Sheng's papers illustrate the tendency of paradigms to read themselves back into history. Sheng also cites recent revisionist economic histories of China that find many more "green shoots" of promising market development in pre-1949 China, than previously supposed.

Unirule has been, in Naughton's words, "a consistent advocate of liberalization" (Naughton 2002, 630). It has

> cooperative relationships with many international private institutions, such as the Center for International Private Enterprises (CIPE), the Ford Foundation, Alton Jones Foundation, US-China Chamber of Commerce, and the International Institute of Economics (IIE), as well as with international public institutions, such as the World Bank, International Monetary Fund, Asian Development Bank, and African Development Bank.
>
> (Unirule website, July 10, 2016)

The Institute sponsored research on institutional change within China, presumably in the tradition of new institutionalist economics (Sheng 1996, 34–35).

Foreign support for neoliberal oriented economic think tanks appears relatively widespread. In 2009 the Hoover Institute's *China Leadership Monitor* reported that many Chinese think tanks "have received funding from American and other foreign foundations," adding, "A two-decade long effort to promote China's social science research and the diffusion of international norms now seems to have come to fruition" (Li 2009, 16–18). Supporting this finding, Li points to the influence that sea turtles have over research agendas and policy discussions "in the fields of economics, [and] management" (Li 2009, 16–18).

### 2.3.4 The World Bank and IMF[58]

As noted earlier, the World Bank's direct influence on Chinese economic thought began in 1980, after China indicated it might be interested in rejoining the IMF and World Bank.[59] The decision was part of a larger decision by the Chinese leadership to become more involved in world trade.[60]

Discussions were held at the highest levels, symbolized by World Bank President Robert McNamara's meeting with Deng Xiaoping. As a precondition for extending loans, the Bank insisted on conducting a large study of the Chinese economy in order to assess the country's development needs. The study appears to have been welcomed by Beijing and included active participation by Chinese researchers, including future Premier Zhu Rongji.[61] It eventually led to tens of billions of dollars of World Bank loans, as China became the largest recipient of Bank support.[62]

The 1,000-page study was translated into Chinese and made required reading for economics faculties (Bottelier, 2006, 7). It was also widely distributed inside China, and made available at public bookstores at a relatively low price. The ease of public access to this Western economic analysis was described as a publishing "breakthrough" by Pieter Bottelier, the Chief of Mission in China for the World Bank (1993–1997) (Bottelier 2006, 7).[63] The report created a new context for economic discussion in China. It initiated Chinese economists into a global neoclassical economics discourse.[64] A second major study in 1985 had a similar effect (Bottelier 2006, 9–10), and seems to have had significant impact on China's seventh five-year plan (Vogel 2011, 460).[65]

In 1982, the Bank put together a group of foreign economists for an influential conference in Moganshan China on the implications of recent Eastern European and Russian experiments with economic restructuring. In 1985 the Bank helped organize a conference on topics related to the transition from a planned to market economy. The two conferences were credited by the Bank's director of economic research in China with demonstrating "that the dysfunctionality of a planned economy was systemic," rather than the result of policy mistakes by Chinese leaders (Lim 2014, 49).

The 1985 conference is perhaps emblematic of the Bank's impact on Chinese economists. The week-long conference took place on a boat traveling down the Yangtze River. The Boat's name was *Ba Shan*, which became the conference's name. The Chinese contingent included almost all of China's leading economists (Lim 2014, 50). Because of the unusual venue, participants shared many hours of formal and informal dialogues, which were helpful mechanisms for recasting paradigmatic identities. The conference's report became part of the economics curriculum in Chinese universities (Lim 2005, 104).

Besides sponsoring conferences, the Bank also helped shape development discussion within China by sponsoring: (1) a China specific Economic Development Institute; (2) an influential one-year economic training program at Oxford University for senior economists;[66] (3) an active collaborative research program with Chinese economists [including support for the CCER];[67] and (4) an active Chinese language publications project. Many of the Chinese participants in these activities became influential Chinese economists.

In 1985 the Bank and the Institute of Economics of CASS, with financial help from the Ford Foundation, co-sponsored "the first comprehensive, systematic research" on China's township and village enterprises (Byrd and Lin,

1990, viii). In 1993, then Vice Premier and future Premier Zhu Rongji had an eight-page analysis of China's macroeconomic situation written by the Bank's chief economist published in the *People's Daily* (Bottelier 2006, 22–23). The Bank also contributed $20,000 to the 1990 Institute's banking reform study (Communication from Norton Wheeler).

In March of 1995 the Bank sent a research team to study Chinese state-owned enterprises (SOEs). The team recommended imposing market discipline on the SOEs by permitting foreign firms to compete with the SOEs in basic industries and infrastructure (Wang 2011, 457). The study appears to have been endorsed by important government officials, offering added ammunition to privatization advocates inside Chinese policy making circles.[68] In June 1995, the Bank co-sponsored a conference on Chinese enterprise reform with the Chinese Ministry of Finance and Chinese State Economic and Trade Commission (Broadman 1996). A key paper at the conference written by Magdi Iskander, the Bank's Director of Private Sector Development, offered a scathing criticism of state-owned enterprises.

At a 1997 seminar sponsored by the Bank, soon-to-be Premier Zhu Rongji promised to "expedite the opening up" of several infrastructure and service sector industries, including banking (Wang 2011, 459). In 1999, a leading Chinese reform economist and policy maker, Gao Shangquan, dedicated his book analyzing Chinese economic reform to the World Bank.[69]

Describing the Bank's presence, Meisner offers the impressions of a *New York Times'* Beijing correspondent, "when Chinese economists debated vigorously about the stock markets and privatization, the World Bank was there … offering strategy tips … always ready to back up the ideas with money … The Bank had a direct line to China's research organizations" (Meisner 1996, 285).

In 2012, the Bank co-authored *China 2030* with the Development Research Center, the State Council's policy think tank. The study offered the Chinese cabinet a roadmap for securing China's emergence as a fully developed capitalist economy.

*The Economist* (a leading voice for neoclassical economics in the UK), highlighted the large impact the report was likely to have due to its DRC co-authorship and support from the Finance Ministry. In addition Li Keqiang (China's then premier) apparently "played an active role in arranging this co-operation between officialdom and the bank." *The Economist* added, "it's believed, the DRC used the World Bank as cover. … ('Don't blame us for these proposals, blame the bank')."[70]

The World Bank also helped shape economics instruction at Chinese universities. A study commissioned by the Bank in the mid-1980s was critical of existing Chinese economics textbooks and university economics curricula.[71] In its aftermath, the State Education Commission mandated the addition of many neoclassically-oriented economics classes to university course offerings. A committee was also established to write economics textbooks that would be similar to those used in the US (Chow 2000, 53; Chow 1994, 50–51).

The IMF sponsored a similar injection of Western economic ideas into Chinese discourse, but at a lower level of intensity.[72] Jacobson and Oksenberg report that the Fund co-sponsored two major economic symposia in China in the 1980s,[73] oversaw publication of IMF materials in Chinese that were disseminated in China, and coordinated academic exchanges under which IMF representatives lectured in China and Chinese officials received training in Washington (Jacobson and Oksenberg 1990, 122–125). Chinese economists working on Chinese related research issues also worked at the IMF from time to time, such as Huang Fanzhang (one of the early Ford Foundation financed students) (Wheeler 2012, 117–118).

A number of observers have claimed that China maintained its intellectual independence in dealings with the World Bank. The Bank's historical accounts of the relationship that I have reviewed have been respectful of China's desire and ability to find its own economic path. The Bank has been hesitant to publicly chastise the Chinese in the fashion of the IMF's demands on other developing countries for structural adjustment.[74] The reform process has generally followed Chinese rhythms, not the drum beat of the so-called Washington Consensus.[75] On the other hand, the theoretical context underlying the World Bank's imagination and neoclassical economics more broadly, remained unchanged and have clearly infused Chinese economic thinking. In his farewell address, China's first director on the board of the IMF, Zhang Zicun (PhD Cambridge University), argued that the Fund treated market economies as the norm and offered uniform policy prescriptions. He indicated that the idea of socialist development also largely disappeared from World Bank publications (Jacobson and Oksenberg 1990, 80, 134). The story came full circle with the appointment of CCER director Lin Justin Yifu as the chief economist of the World Bank in 2008. Another American educated Chinese economist, Zhu Min, became the deputy managing director of the IMF in 2011. Wang Shuilin was serving as a senior economist at the World Bank in 2002 (Brahm 2002, ix).

### 2.3.5 The impact of foreign governments and businesses

US government policies also encouraged the expansion of neoclassical economics in China. Obvious mechanisms include financial support for educational exchanges, encouragement of World Bank efforts to promote neoclassical analyses,[76] funding for academic conferences in China, and support for Western business training, such as support for a management training school in Dalian. It would be interesting to research State Department documents to see if there were any explicit efforts to increase attention to neoclassical economic ideas in China through academic analogies to the Voice of America, which has been active in China since the 1940s.[77]

The US Federal Reserve Bank has also probably had a significant impact on Chinese monetary theory and central bank policy. It would be helpful in general to know who the People's Bank of China's major advisers have been, as the Bank has been a strong force for continued economic reform.[78] The Fed's influence has probably been exercised through indirect routes, such as graduate student fellowships, the hosting of delegations from China's banking sector, the return to China of former Fed employees, etc.[79] It would be interesting to see if the Fed has had any more formal programs aimed at a Chinese audience. The Fed oversees an enormous research and public relations program in the United States. Free Fed publications fill library shelves in economics departments across the country. Our college economics department common room, for example, showcases at least eight Federal Reserve periodicals. From what I have seen, the analysis tends to be overwhelmingly neoclassical with sometimes a tilt toward monetarist ideas, though this varies across the district banks.[80]

The impact of business initiatives on economics education in China is hard to track. Potential routes of influence include financial support for economics and business conferences, think tanks, and university departments. Exxon, for example was one of the listed contributors to the Hopkins-Nanjing Center, along with some wealthy Hong Kong businessmen (Wheeler 2012). Yin Yanheng gave $10 million to the Guanghua School of Management at Peking University, which has had a strong free market orientation. A Shanghai billionaire has supported the publication of many books promoting the opening of Chinese financial markets (Zhou 2006, 63). Along a different dimension, there were about 2,500 foreign chambers of commerce operating in China ~2009 (Yin 2009, 522). Shieh and Knutson report

> foreign chambers of commerce … have been given preferential treatment compared with other INGOs … [they] do not need to find a 'professional supervisory unit'. … [They] only need to get approval of the Ministry of Foreign Economy and Trade … which serves only as an approval agency not as a supervising agency.
>
> (Shieh and Knutson 2012, 14)

If these chambers function at all like those in the US, they cultivate free-market oriented subcultures among their members. This kind of learning by doing is akin to Pierre Bourdieu's notion of "habitas," whereby daily habits and implicit ideas sustaining these habits, create frames for organizing ideas about the world.

Many academic economists appear to have engaged in some business consultancy work and/or direct participation in start-up firms. In the immediate aftermath of reform and the inflow of foreign capital, English-speaking business-oriented partners were at a premium. Chow indicates "….good economists have also done well, by consulting…" (2000, 59).[81] My interviews suggest that some economists also became wealthy as partners in new businesses.[82] This probably created incentives for supporting privatization programs. Neoclassical economists have often spoken out against insider privatization, crony capitalism, and authoritarian rule in China, but when push comes to shove, it appears some have been willing to sacrifice due process, equity concerns, and democracy to the higher goal of privatization (Wang Chaohua 2003, 63).[83]

China's deepening relationship with neoclassical economics was also facilitated by the Chinese diaspora. As late as 1990, when Japanese investment in China took off, investment from Hong Kong and Taiwan accounted for 75 percent of all foreign investment in China. Even after the turn of the century overseas Chinese investment in the mainland totaled more than half of all foreign investment.

## 2.4 Conclusion

There were numerous factors promoting the expansion of neoclassical economics in China after 1978. Many of these factors were related to the projects the paradigm was expected to enable. In particular, the spread of neoclassical theory was expected to support: Deng's project of marketization and its goal of rapid economic growth; lower-level Party officials' interest in transforming their bureaucratic privilege into heritable property; and the academic interests of students and faculty in foreign study, employment by international organizations, and employment by multinational private firms. To a large extent, the spread of neoclassical economics in China reflected its role as the *lingua franca* for formal discussions of world markets and the global capitalist system.

Neoclassical economics was the language of the World Bank and IMF, as well as the language of the economic advisors to foundations and bankers. Even those who did not "formally" speak this language (such as most journalists) used the basic grammar and vocabulary of neoclassical economics to communicate about the economy. Phrases derived from neoclassical analyses (such as "general equilibrium," "the marginal product of capital," "Pareto optimality," "transaction costs," "rent seeking," "cost benefit ratios," and "institutional entrepreneurs") framed nearly all economic discussions. Hence, neoclassical economic discourse came to assume the appearance of a "natural language," that is, an "objective" description of the economy, unmediated by a point of view. This status illustrates and reflects its hegemonic position. This appearance of objectivity was reinforced by neoclassical economics' frequent use mathematical expressions and the declaration of conclusions in terms of "theorems" (e.g., "the Coase theorem") and "laws" ("the law of diminishing marginal utility"). While the Chinese were aware that Western economics carried its own subtexts, and vowed to make use of only its functional categories, this distinction was gradually lost over time. Nevertheless, even today, the Chinese leadership is a little more selective in its use of Western economics than is the Chinese economics profession.

The relationship between the Chinese users of neoclassical economics and foreign proselytizers for the discourse, such as the AEA or the World Bank, was very congenial. Western influence over Chinese economic thinking is best summarized by Norton Wheeler's phrase, "invited influence."

The expansion of neoclassical economics in China was also facilitated by the weakness of the available alternative economic discourses in China in the late 1970s and 1980s. The Maoist period had dismissed Western heterodox paradigms, like "old" institutionalist economics, as well as neoclassical economics, and no strong movements emerged to resuscitate these other Western discourses. The backlash against the Cultural Revolution severely limited interest in new initiatives in Marxist economics and socialist projects. In this vacuum, neoclassical economics had little effective competition. It raced ahead on rails greased by powerful global interests.

## Notes

1  Fang Fuqian, for example, reports that the practical needs of marketization encouraged Chinese economists "to study, introduce, and apply Western economics" (Fang 2013, 301). In a similar vein, Vogel emphasizes the impact on Chinese leaders of fact finding tours of capitalist economies, as well as innovative Eastern European economies, during the early reform period. He highlights the impact of Deng's trips to France in 1975 (217–218), Japan in 1978, and the US in 1979; Yu Guangyuan's trip to Yugoslavia and Romania in 1978; trips by members of the State Planning Commission and Ministry of Foreign Trade to Hong Kong in 1978; and Gu Mu's trip to Western Europe in 1978. (Vogel 2011, 217–219, Chapters 10 and 11). The dominant impact of the trips, from Vogel's perspective, was to reinforce the notion that China was seriously behind the West technologically and needed to adopt some Western economic techniques and ideas to catch up.
2  The Chinese were especially interested in learning modern econometric techniques, public sector economics, microeconomics (to the extent it was relevant to promoting enterprise efficiency), and perhaps Western theories related to trade and economic planning (Report of the Committee on Scholarly Communication with the People's Republic of China (CSCPRC), Economics Delegation to the People's Republic of China, 1980, National Academy of Sciences).
3  As with other aspects of Western culture, Chinese importers of Western management education tried to distill out the functional from the ideological in Western management ideas. The effort was consistent with Chinese intellectuals' "*ti-yong*" (Chinese values [essences]-Western tools) strategy for modernization. From a Marxist perspective they did not succeed, in that they ended up facilitating, consciously or unconsciously, the spread of classical liberalism, even if with Confucian tones.
4  The number grew to more than 130 by 2010. In 2013 there were more than 35,000 Chinese students enrolled in MBA programs. Warner reports "Today … adopting Western ways of doing things is very much done in a matter of fact way. … Chinese business schools now teach management theory and practice … derived from North American sources, as a mainstream activity" (Warner 2014, 111).
5  See for example, Bottelier 2006, Jacobson and Oksenberg 1990. While Zhao Ziyang and Zhu Rongji were especially sympathetic to neoclassical economics, the paradigm had broad appeal as a modernist theory. In September 1982, for example, Hu Yaobang, the head of the Communist Party, told the Party's 12th National Congress, "We must improve our study and application of economics and scientific business management …" Chow finds, "A manifestation of this policy is the series of short courses on project evaluation sponsored by the World Bank" (Chow 1994, 45–46).

6 Wu Jinglian reports that James Tobin discredited the claim that inflation was good for economic growth at the Bashanlun conference (Wu 2005, 365). The 1993 meetings led to Chinese policies designed to constrain the creation of credit on the local level during times of national inflationary pressures (Bottelier 2006, 17–25). Painting a somewhat different picture, Coase and Wang report that the economists at the Bashanlun conference warned that the economy was overheating and on the verge of hyperinflation, but claim their advice was ignored by the Chinese government (Coase and Wang 2013, 108).

7 The background of Zhou Xiaochuan, the long time head of China's central bank, suggests this dynamic. Zhou was an engineer by training, earning his undergraduate degree from the Beijing Institute of Chemical Technology and his doctorate in economic system engineering from Tsinghua University. His intellect and sympathetic computer modeling of the impact of lifting price controls apparently caught the eye of economic reformers. Zhou was assigned several important posts in organizations designing market reforms in the 1980s. He is apparently well known for the motto "if the market can solve the problem, let the market do it. I am just a referee." He seems to have favored staff members trained overseas (the so-called sea turtles).

8 The US delegation of economists visiting China in 1980 reported there was "unanimous agreement among our counterparts that university education had been essentially destroyed during the Cultural Revolution" (Committee on Scholarly Communication with the People's Republic of China (CSCPRC) 2010 [1980], 21). The World Bank's 1981 study found that Chinese materials balance planning models were surprisingly weak. Forecasts of expected net exports of oil were wildly optimistic. The latter error would subsequently de-rail Chinese plans to import large amounts of Western technology with oil export revenues. Gregory Chow complained that macro statistics were insufficient for accurate macro forecasting. His criticism led Zhao Ziyang to create a new macroeconomic data center at the People's University (Renmin University) (Chow 1994, 65). Fred Herschede (1985) paints a similar picture, noting for example the lack of formal training of the economics faculty in the NanDa economics department (311).

Thomas Rawski's review of Chinese political-economy textbooks in 1986 found them highly polemical, weak in empirical analysis, and largely limited to writings by Marx, Engels, Lenin, Stalin, and Mao (Rawski 1986, 19–21).

It is hard to judge whether the critical assessments of Western observers is fully balanced. There is some evidence to suggest that Marxist scholarship prior to the import of Western inputs was not as thin as portrayed. Liu Guoguang, Sun Yefang and others for example, appear to have done thoughtful work on growth theory and macro imbalances in the Chinese countryside in the early 1960s. Still, there seems to have been large gaps in Chinese economic education, data collection, and analytical capabilities. To fill some of these gaps, the Chinese Academy of Social Sciences set up three new economic institutes in 1978. There was also an explosion of new economics journals (Chow 1994, 44; Hu 1988).

9 Committee on Scholarly Communication with the People's Republic of China 2010 [1980], 3–4.

10 Jacobson and Oksenberg (1990) write, "Chinese economists, mostly over sixty years of age in the early 1980s, guided China's approach to the KIEOs [Keystone International Economic Organizations]" (19). Elsewhere they add "Leading Chinese economists—many of whom had been trained in Western universities in the late 1940s … guided the policymakers when the appropriate opportunity arose" (60).

11 Interview.

12 Relatedly, Warner reports that one of the appeals of Taylorism in China was its appearance as modern and "scientific" (Warner 2014, 17), citing a popular slogan

in the 1950s: "Let's be Soviet, Let's be Modern" (Ibid., 76). Li and White (1991) emphasize that technocratic and engineering-like mindsets increasingly dominated the thinking of Chinese intellectual elites in the 1980s. This esthetic likely benefitted neoclassical theory, which presented itself as a kind of eco-physics for maximizing social utility.

13 Discussions with Chinese economists, summer of 2011.

14 In 1986, 45 percent of all government ministers had engineering degrees (Naughton 1995, 132). At the highest levels of government in the 1990s and 2000, Jiang Zemin, Li Peng, Zhu Rongji, Hu Jintao and Wen Jiabao were trained as engineers. In 1986 around two-thirds of Chinese mayors held engineering degrees (Li 2001, 74).

15 Song 1995.

16 Song (1995) estimates that from 1978 to 1987 only 15 of the more than 1,000 papers published in *Economic Research* were on mathematical economics (154).

17 Lin's brief discussion of the role of mathematics in England's industrial revolution tends to be reductionist. Situating his discussion of mathematics in a richer institutional-ideological and cultural analysis could provide interesting insights.

   Part of the issue here probably involves the role of Confucianism in Chinese political-economic development and the basis for that role. To draw an analogy, economists sometimes argue that China's retreat from long distance maritime trade (rather than retreat from mathematics) helps explain its subsequent defeat by the British navy. The analysis stops where it should begin, by not asking why the British turned toward trade and the Chinese away. Similarly, why did the Protestant Ethic arise in Europe and not in China, and so on. Lin's basically methodologically individualistic outlook precludes him from pursuing these ideas very far. Marxism's holist methodology asks these questions, but sometimes has responded with rather mechanical answers, especially after Marxism became the language of state justification rather than a social science.

   In the English version of *Benti and Changwu: Dialogues on Methodology in Economics* (2012c), Lin offers a surprisingly weak explanation for the misuse (overuse) of mathematics in neoclassical economics. He argues that traditional economic theory has explained the world so well, that there is little to do for modern economists. As a result, they can only distinguish themselves by showing off their mathematical skills. He writes,

   > the giants of Western economics, like Adam Smith and John Maynard Keynes, have explained the main Western economic phenomenon very clearly, leaving little for others to discuss. ... Since there are fewer new phenomena to study, the level of mathematical sophistication has become the criteria for publication ...
   >
   > (Lin 2012c, 7)

18 See for example Kwong 1994.

19 Sleeboom-Faulkner reports a shift in attitudes in the 1990s away from the idealism of earlier periods. She indicates that graduate students at CASS, "wanted to earn money most of all." Their top four employment goals were: (1) going abroad; (2) working for foreign companies; (3) working for the Party (presumably for its economic benefits); and (4) staying on at CASS (Sleeboom-Faulkner 2007, 166, 171). Lin et al. report that many surveys in the 1990s found a similar prioritizing of money-making in student job searches (Lin et al. 2015, 58).

   To balance this impression, I tried to look for counter signs of idealism alongside the pursuit of material self-interest on the part of Chinese students. I asked one professor in Beijing, for example, if the popularity of Michael Sandel's campus lectures on ethical issues in China (Friedman 2011) indicated there were reservoirs of idealism. He thought there were, but that these beliefs faded once graduates joined the workforce. This decline was partially due to enormous pressures to amass enough money to buy a house, which is still an important prerequisite for marriage. Rosen (2009) cites numerous surveys, especially one conducted among history majors by CASS in 2007, implying similar conclusions. There is felt to be a yearning "to believe in something" (Rosen 2009, 361), but past disillusionments have left only nationalism and the pursuit of self-interest as energizers. (For an interesting discussion of the evolution of philosophical and existential debates among China's youth 1980–2000, see Liu and Wang 2009.) There is a "New Left" in China, but few of the economists I spoke with thought it had had much impact on economics departments and economics students. Only 8% of the students surveyed in a recent campus opinion study self-identified as either nationalist or leftist, with most of them, I suspect, linked to nationalism (Lin et al. 2015, 64).

20 While this may be true, the linkage may not be as straightforward as most students believe. One professor I spoke with felt that students rarely applied classroom economics (Marxist or Western economics) in their business jobs. Rather than valuing economics degrees as evidence of skill sets, he felt employers used mastery of neoclassical economics as a screening device, testifying to the applicant's general ability to learn and congeniality with business values. The firms were confident they could teach students what they needed to know about their particular business on the job.

21 There seems to be some validity to this expectation. For example, Steven Lewis indicates that Chinese economists with advanced training in Western economics have been able to find jobs with foreign governments, international organizations, and global financial firms (Lewis 2005, 231–232).

22 Kotz 2000 (online version, November 1999, 10–12). See also Kotz and Weir 1997. Kotz notes that while only 17 percent of those polled in the FSU favored "a free market form of capitalism such as found in the U.S." in 1991, 76 percent of a "focus group study of the Moscow elite" in the same year "had an ideological position of support for capitalism" (Kotz 2000, online version 1999, 10).

The economic reforms have turned out well for CPC members. Li Minqi reports that a document reputedly based on an internal report to the Chinese Politburo estimated that ~2 million current and retired government officials now own 70 percent of the total private wealth in China (Li Minqi 2008, 106).

23 Kelliher writes, for example,

> By the mid-1980s, rural cadres learned that the entrepreneurial thrust of reform made their skills lucrative. Networks of connections, lines of market information, access to telephones, and inside knowledge of rural industry gave cadres an unbeatable edge in new commercial competition … astute cadres realized what a gold mine reform could be for them …
>
> (Kelliher 1992, 81)

He adds, "the entrepreneurial local cadres emerged as a key transitional group for the transfer of political power from a collective administration to a commercial elite" (Kelliher 1992, 39). See also Arrighi (2008, 368–369). Riskin, quoting Parish, notes that during the Cultural Revolution "'the fit between parental-status and children's status was reduced to near zero or to only a fraction of the former levels'" (Riskin 1987, 253). Bramall writes "The privatizations of the late 1990s were driven not by concerns about efficiency but by a desire on the part of local cadres to raise money very rapidly and enrich themselves in the process" (Bramall 2009a, 275).

24  Heilmann and Shi provide an interesting variation on this theme, suggesting the potential self-interest of high ranking government officials in promoting Japanese style industrial policy which maintains a close working relationship between very large private firms and related government bureaucracies. They report that government "sponsored organizations facilitated a 'second career' … for retired senior government officials in … business associations … an entire cohort of industrial administrators became nominal heads of industrial associations" (Heilmann and Shi 2013, 8).

Liberal economists like Wu Jinglian have argued a similar point more generally. They find that many in the Party now support "crony capitalism," or "state capitalism," rather than socialism or competitive capitalism, because of the opportunity it affords Party members to capture insider rents.

Lin Chun highlights a reverse causality, whereby capitalists join the Party (rather than Party members becoming capitalists). She finds that the class basis of the Party has changed since 2002, when private entrepreneurs were first invited to join. She notes, for example, that one-third of China's "quasi-capitalists" are Party members, as are more than one half of all Chinese with assets greater than 100 million yuan (~$16 million) (Lin Chun 2013, 68). Michael Forsythe reports that the richest 70 members of China's National People's Congress have a combined net worth of a staggering $90 billion (Forsythe March 1, 2012).

25  The Chinese were especially open to receiving advice from the Chinese Diaspora. Joyce Kallgren indicates:

> connections with the Chinese Academy were facilitated through close personal relationships enjoyed by certain Chinese American scientists with the Chinese political and educational leadership. … American scientists of Chinese descent play an exceedingly important role in facilitating programs and progress in exchanges at all levels.
>
> (Kallgren 1987, 72)

The flow of funds and ideas from Hong Kong, Singapore, and Taiwan seems to have been especially important in economic matters.

26  The first major event appears to have been a seminar organized by Nobel Laureate Lawrence Klein in the summer of 1980, which included lectures on econometrics by Professor Chow. The CSCPRC delegation of economists that visited China in 1979 had recommended greater involvement by the AEA in future exchanges (CSCPRC 1980, 12). Chow helped organize a workshop with leading Western economists on economic development in 1981 (Chow 1994, 42) and lectured at six Chinese universities in 1982 (Chow 1994, 40–44). In 1983 Chow authored a textbook which applied neoclassical economic techniques to analyzing the Chinese economy.

27  Official approval in China sometimes seems to be conveyed through television coverage. In a 1988 article, Chow indicated that his meeting with Premier Zhao was reported on Chinese television that evening and covered on the front page of the *People's Daily*, "showing a picture of the two of us," the next day (Chow 1988, 4). Chow interpreted this as an official endorsement of neoclassical economics. In a similar vein, a TV clip broadcasting the presentation of a study of Chinese economic reform to Jiang Zemin by the 1990 Institute, a US think tank, seems to have signaled to China's economists that collaboration with the Institute was permitted or even encouraged (Wheeler, 2012, 60).

28  In 1988 the GRE test replaced the exam based on Chow's text.

29  For the identities of many of the economists involved with Professor Chow's projects and early Chinese interactions with American economists see Chow (1994, 39–71).

30  In their book dedicated to the CES, Wen and Xu depict the organization's sense of its self "as an irreplaceable bridge between the modern economic academia and

China" (Wen and Xu 1997, ix). They link this sense of mission to a series of international conferences on economic reform in China sponsored by the CES in the mid-1990s, for example: Shanghai 1995: on reforming SOEs; Hangzhou 1994: on the TVEs; and Hainan 1993: on Market-Oriented reforms.

31 Ping pong diplomacy refers to an inspiring moment of people to people diplomacy initiated by spontaneous acts of good will among championship ping pong players. For a brief account of these events see the Wikipedia entry on ping pong diplomacy. While the events were spontaneous, there was, of course, a larger context ready to welcome them.

32 Hsia and White indicate that Chinese leaders' increasing openness to NGO activities in China reflected the government's desire to use international aid organizations, initially largely UN organizations, but soon private sector groups as well, to address the needs of groups harmed by the reform process. While there were few international NGOs in China in 1978, by the early 1980s there were more than 200 UN programs operating in China, spearheaded initially by the UNDP program (Hsia and White 2002, 333). Wang Ming, head of a Chinese research center on NGOs, estimates that by ~2012 there were 6,000 foreign NGOs in China including 2,000 foundations (Yin 2009, 522). The Chinese acceptance of foreign NGOs was tempered by a constant fear that the aid groups' activities would spill over into political arenas. The attempt to mobilize the services of foreign NGOs without the independent civil society overtones that accompany these organizations in the West represented another example of the Chinese *ti-yong* strategy for appropriating Western techniques without Western culture.

33 An especially unusual example of multi-sector cooperation to promote American ideas of economic development in China took place right at the beginning of reform. Jacobson and Oksenberg indicate that in early 1979, 21 World Bank officials, led by the Bank's director of International Development and Finance, traveled to China as private citizens, paying their own way. A group of Chinese-Americans in California helped arrange their tour to prepare the staff for negotiations about China's renewal of Bank membership (Jacobson and Oksenberg 1990, 71–72).

34 Henry Paulson, former head of Goldman Sachs and Treasury Secretary under George W. Bush, illustrates how this process worked. He describes how he and fellow executives at Goldman Sachs, plus a group of professors from leading US business schools, reorganized Tsinghua University's School of Economics and Management. (Tsinghua occupies a position in China analogous to MIT or Yale in the United States.) Paulson was in China overseeing Goldman Sachs's efforts to capture a share of the Chinese financial market.

Paulson was invited to redesign Tsinghuas's economics and management program by Chinese premier (and Tsinghua alum), Zhu Rongji. Zhu, an engineer by training, seems to have conceived of management as a kind of social technology, and wanted Paulson to re-engineer Tsinghua's program. He told Paulson, "'For many years I have wanted to establish a world-class management school to complement China's reform … We need to rely on you for this'" (Paulson 2015, 109). Paulson and his colleagues averred, "China needed corporate leaders, not Marxist theoreticians" (106), and proceeded to replace Tsinghua's old curriculum with courses emphasizing Harvard University's famous case study method of business education. The visiting sages were to be successful business executives, with their triumphs the new myths of success (Paulson 2015, 104–114). Fred Hu, of Goldman Sachs's Hong Kong office, was the co-director of Tsinghua's Center for Economic research (Paulson 2015, 107).

35 As early as 1979–1980, Sung began arranging for American economic experts to visit and lecture in China. In the summer of 1979–1980 he arranged for two weeks of lectures by Harvard Business School professors. In 1984 he helped

organize a similar three-year program of month-long lecture tours. In 1984, Sung also funded a three-year program on US–China economic relations that included dialogues with Chinese officials, such as Zhu Rongji (Wheeler 2012, 52).

36 The Institute's linkages to high level US officials, like Under Secretary of State Habib (even if only symbolically), and its leadership by Chinese Americans (often an important feature for PRC officials) helped strengthen the institute's influence in China.

37 Galenson wrote the book's introduction and Yeh Kung-Chia (a 30-year veteran at the Rand corporation) wrote the overview chapter. Both analyses anchored the discussion within a neoclassical narrative. There was almost no exploration of the implications of economic events and reform strategies for the achievement of socialism. To the extent socialism was discussed, it was generally as a superseded goal whose legacy impeded current reform efforts. Assessments of the Chinese economy before 1978 offered an incomplete account of China's successes. For example, there was little mention of the improved status of women, the large increases in life expectancy, or the redistribution of land. There was a heavy emphasis on the economic inefficiencies caused by "command" oriented institutions and a persistent call for expanded privatization and market incentives. The book's subtext invited continued movement of the Chinese economy toward capitalism, without explicitly referring to capitalism.

Yeh's overview chapter, for example, complained that the leadership's thinking: gave insufficient attention to protecting property rights; arbitrarily mandated that public ownership be predominant; and ignored "the importance of returns to venture capital and rewards for risk taking, the very basis for innovation in a market economy" (Galenson 1993, 17). Yeh also discredited opposition to reform, tying it to unreflective habits, ignorance, and petty self-interest, writing, "middle-level cadres … see their positions threatened by the new system that calls for economic decisions to be made … by the market…" (Galenson 1993, 28–29). There is no discussion of the support for the reforms by party cadres interested in transforming their bureaucratic privilege into private property, which seems easier to transmit across generations.

38 The memo was originally released by WikiLeaks (April 7, 2013). Knox College librarian Ryan Lynch tracked down the original document in the State Department's archives. (See US Embassy, Tokyo in References.) The memo was declassified and released in 2006. Accessed June 15, 2016.

For additional insight into Galenson's perspective on political-economic issues see Morris Weisz's March 15, 1992 interview with Galenson. (www.adst.org/ OH%20TOCs/Galenson,%20Walter.toc.pdf, accessed September 9, 2015).

39 The 1990 Institute seems to have been especially successful in contributing to Chinese tax reform. The diverse strands of American influence re-illustrate the way that US economic thinking diffused into Chinese discussions. In 1991, Hu Angang, a research economist from CASS, left to do postdoc work at Yale. He teamed with a political science professor from the PRC at Yale to write an article on tax reform. The paper was distributed at CASS as an "internal research report," under the title "Report on State Capacity." Excerpts from the report were then recirculated to wider audiences, including higher officials, under the title "Two PhDs Who Have Studied in America Propose: Strengthen the Leading Role of the Central Government in the Transition to a Market Economy" (Wheeler 2012, 82–84). A key official at the Ministry of Finance endorsed the report, commenting, "'As people say, monks from another country can recite the sutras best'<th" (Wheeler 2012, 84).

The key official in charge of Chinese tax reform was Xu Shanda, who held an MA in public finance from the University of Bath in England. In 1992 and 1995 he attended two conferences sponsored by the 1990 Institute and was also friends with Roy Bahl, who was asked by the Institute to write a paper on Chinese tax reform. Xu indicates that Bahl's thinking was influential in Chinese discussions of tax reform (Wheeler 2012, 82–87). Xu eventually wrote an introduction to Bahl's book on Chinese tax reform, organized a team of translators to prepare a Chinese version, and had the book distributed to more than 1,000 branches of China's tax authority (Wheeler 2012, 82–87).

40 Diverse financing was the case, for example, for the Hopkins-Nanjing Center which oversaw graduate study programs for American and Chinese students at Nanjing University in China. The US government, largely through AID, covered 20–30 percent of the Center's budget (1987–2005). Donations from private corporations and individuals covered another 50 percent, while foundation grants covered the remaining 25 percent (Wheeler 2012, 18–21). The Center's foundation list included the: Asia Foundation, Henry Luce Foundation, Ford Foundation, Freeman Foundation, Star Foundation, Asia Society, and the Hong Kong Fei Yi Ming journalism Foundation (Wheeler 2012, 18–19). In 1997, 47 percent of World Bank projects in China involved collaboration with NGOs (Hsia and White 2002, 329).

41 The Ford Foundation quote is from Andrew Watson, the Foundation's China representative at the turn of the twenty-first century (Wheeler 2012, 114). In a curious way, Watson's remarks resemble Mao Zedong's "from the masses to the masses" definition of the "mass line." The latter portrayed the Party cadres as akin to community organizers, helping villages to figure out what they wanted and then organizing them to achieve their goals. Like the Ford Foundation, Mao was interested in helping certain goals to float to the surface more than others. But for both Mao and the Ford Foundation there was a degree of openness to independent initiatives by "the people."

42 The Rockefeller Foundation is reported to have actively promoted liberal and anti-communist ideas in China in the first half of the twentieth century (Busse et al. 2016).

43 The Cato Institute promoted the ideas of classical liberalism. A 1988 conference, for example, focused on economic reform and highlighted lectures by Milton Friedman, Steven Cheung, and George Gilder. It captured a front page story in the *China Daily* (Cato Institute 2001, 48). During the conference Friedman received an honorary doctorate from Fudan University, which co-sponsored the conference. The Cato website seems to have made a deep impression on Liu Junning, a leading voice for classical liberalism in China and one of the founders of the journal *Gonggonluncong (Res Publica)*. The journal was the first Chinese journal to focus on classical liberalism. For a time Liu was a fellow at the Institute of Political Science at CASS (Liu 2000; Wang Chaohua 2003, 27, 29). Liu has received financial support from the Cato and the Atlas Foundations (Zhou 2006, 59).

   The Atlas Foundation's 2014 year in review indicated it had partnerships with 9 institutes in China promoting free market economics and other classical liberal ideas: the Ronald Coase Center for the Study of the Economy at Zhejiang University, the Cathay Institute for Public Affairs in Beijing, the Babel Institute in Shanghai, the Impact Law firm in Beijing, the I, Pencil Economic Research Institute, the Shanghai Institute of Finance and Law, the Lion Rock Institute in Hong Kong, the Unirule Institute of Economics, and the Transition Institute. (www. atlasnetwork.org/assets/uploads/annual-reports/Atlas_Network_YIR_2014.pdf, accessed August 22, 2016).

44 Beginning in 1998 and continuing until at least 2003, the Rand Corporation and the Chinese Reform Forum held joint annual conferences on economics and security issues, alternating host countries (Wheeler 2012, 118).

45 A National Academy of Sciences report prepared for the Committee on Scholarly Communication with the PRC indicated,

The programs of the Asia Foundation are typical of foundation efforts to develop the social sciences in China and to strengthen Chinese libraries. From 1979 through 1983 the foundation sponsored 109 Chinese in the United States and 55 Americans in China …

The foundation also sponsored training in advanced American business law for members of the Ministry of Foreign Economic Relations and Trade (Lampton et al. 1986, 78–79).

46 A 1986 report published by the National Academy of Sciences estimated that US colleges and universities absorbed about 40 percent of the costs of Chinese students and scholars in the US on J-1 visas from 1979–1983 (Lampton et al. 1986, 3).

47 The NAS report estimated Ford Foundation China-related spending at about $1.5 million per year 1979–1984. (Lampton et al. 1986, 79). The Ford Foundation's programs on economics education and research involved the AEA (whose committee on US–China Exchanges in Economics was chaired by Gregory Chow), the Ford Foundation's own initiated committee (co-chaired by Gregory Chow and Dwight Perkins), and the CSCPRC.

The Asia Foundation served, perhaps, as a model for some of these activities. Coburn reports that the Asia Foundation gave research support to American scholars specializing in Asian studies who demonstrated strong anti-communist credentials. The Foundation also financed trips to the US by promising Asian academics and funded Asian magazines and cultural organizations congenial with US interests (Coburn 1969, 80). A large chunk of the Asia Foundation's financial resources secretly came from the CIA. The Agency was forced to cut its ties with the Asia Foundation after public disclosure of these ties by *Ramparts* magazine in 1966 (Coburn 1969, 80).

48 The Foundation arranged for exchanges and collaboration with the Chinese Academy of Agricultural Sciences as well as the Chinese Academy of Social Sciences (Sutton 1987, Lampton et al. 1986). Sutton estimates that Ford was spending about one million to two million dollars a year on China related activities 1959–1979 (Sutton 1987, 101–103).

49 In a draft report for the World Bank on the status of economics education in China in December of 1986, Thomas Rawski recommended that Chinese universities await the return of foreign trained economists before expanding their graduate programs, writing,

efforts by the Chinese government to strictly limit the growth of graduate programs, especially at the PhD level, are well advised. For the most part, high-quality graduate instruction in economics–related fields must await the return of significant numbers of Chinese students from extended periods of overseas study.

(Rawski 1986, 28)

50 Perkins writes, "Political sensitivities are such that it might also make sense to funnel much of the money … for work in institutes … through CES" (Perkins 1999, 13).

51 econweb.tamu.edu/tian/vita.pdf (accessed October 29, 2011—updated June 16, 2016).

52 In 2002 Barry Naughton wrote, "[Lin] brings a consistent commitment to liberalization and free markets that reflects, among other things, his PhD training at the University of Chicago" (Naughton 2002, 629). In 2011, Lin dedicated his book *Dialogues on Methodology in Economics* to Gary Becker. He attributed to the Chicago economist (who is a strong advocate of *homo economicus* and radical methodological individualism in economics) his understanding of "the spirit of modern economic analysis" (Lin 2012c, xviii).

Although Lin's ideas have evolved, and he gives significant attention to empirical data which challenges neoclassical expectations, his thinking remains animated by the spirit of the Chicago school and the notion of benchmarking outcomes against hypothetical perfect market outcomes. His concept of deferring to "latent comparative advantage" is a novel example of this.

When describing the CCEER's research focus in 2005, Lin argued that China needed to diverge a bit from the Washington Consensus. But this independence seemed a temporary concession to the absence of certain institutions in China, rather than a rejection of the strategic goals of neoliberalism. In effect, Lin's program was "neoliberalism with Chinese characteristics" (Lin 2005, 18).

Lin's 2012b volume on "New Structural Economics" reflects both his capacity for innovation within neoclassical theory and the limits of that theory. This combination was captured very well in an extended exchange with the heterodox economist Ha-Joon Chang in Chapter II of Lin's book. Summing up their exchange, Chang indicates that he doubts neoclassical economics is flexible enough to address his concerns, and argues, "(T)he rational-choice, individualistic foundation of neoclassical economics limits its ability to analyse the uncertain and collective nature of the technological learning process, which is at the heart of economic development" (Lin 2012b, 138).

Fine and Waeyenberge come to similar assessments of Lin's framework, writing

> (Lin) is no neo-liberal and positively insists upon an interventionist role for the state. … However … Lin's commitment to a positive role for the state is as minimal or circumscribed as it is solid.
>
> (Fine and Waeyenberge 2013, 1)

In his 2012c book on methodology, Lin often attributes the shortcomings of neoclassical policy recommendations to the misapplication of the neoclassical model by first world economists insensitive to the special conditions of third world economies. He is reluctant to fault the theory itself. He seems to have little interest in analyzing the emergence of reproducing structures of inequality, the nature of the state, the nature of work life and power relations in the workplace, the origins of tastes and preferences, and the full implications of non-rational behavior and uncertainty (of the Keynesian "fundamental" rather than neoclassical "expected value" kind). (See Fine and Van Waeyenberge 2013 for some additional critiques of *New Structural Economics*.)

53 In an interesting example of reciprocity, Pieter Bottelier, former Mission Director in China for the World Bank, and Peter Geithner, former head of the Ford Foundation's projects in China, were past members of the 12-member board of directors of the Center. Currently three past or present officials of the World Bank and Ford Foundation sit on the 12-member board (http://en.ccer.edu.cn/ReadNews.asp?NewsID=6374, accessed October 31, 2011).

54 Zhang holds a doctorate in economics from Oxford. From 1984 to 1990 he was a researcher at the Economic Systems Reform Institute under the State Commission of Restructuring the Economic System (Guanghua School of Management, faculty website). He has been a major spokesperson for Austrian free market economics. In 1984 he authored a controversial article in the *China Youth Daily* entitled "A Justification for Money" which sought to legitimize profit making (*The China Story Journal*, www.thechinastory.org/intellectuals/zhang-weiying-%E5%BC%A0%E7%BB%B4%E8%BF%8E/, accessed January 17, 2013). He has championed the development of capitalism in China as the only system that can nurture the entrepreneurs who sustain economies (Ibid). In 1999 he proposed the "Theorem of the impossibility of the entrepreneur in a state-owned economy" (Ibid).

According to Bloomberg's Business Week, Zhang "has become a household name across the country…" (Bloomberg Business Week December 16, 2010, www.businessweek.com/bschools/content/dec2010/bs2010123_043231.htm, accessed October 29, 2011). Zhang has numerous academic publications and has been an active business consultant. Zhang has also been a consultant for a World Bank project on State-Owned Enterprises in China (www.whartonbeijing09. com/bio-zw.html). See also Leonard 2008a, 19–22.

Zhang would rank as a free-market champion even within the market oriented American economics profession. In 2009, for example, he blamed the financial crisis on the Federal Reserve's excessive interference with the market, rather than on excesses originating in the private sector (Freeman and Yuan 2011, 7). In 2009 Zhang called for burying Keynesianism (*The China Story Journal*, op. cit.) He was removed as Dean of the Guanghua School of Management in 2010.

55 Li Cheng August 2009, 15–16. Li also suggests that the CCER has had significant influence on government policy deliberations (Ibid.). The heavy presence of American economics PhDs in leading Chinese think tanks is common. Many think tanks have affiliated American faculty who lecture at the centers or affiliated Chinese universities for brief periods.

56 The Asia Foundation has also been active in training Chinese journalists. The Sloan Foundation may have also helped fund neoclassical courses for journalists in China as it has done in the US.

57 "Mao Yushi Wins the Cato Institute's 2012 Milton Friedman Prize for Advancing Liberty" by James A. Dorn, *Forbes* April 5, 2012. Mao's economic thinking seems to have evolved outside of formal academic channels, which prevented him from gaining a position in one of CASS's economic institutes. He was, however, given a position in CASS's institute of American Studies in 1985 and participated in the Ford Foundation/AEA econometrics workshop organized by Lawrence Klein in 1981 (*The China Story: Mao Yushi*: www.thechinastory.org/key-intellectual/mao-yushi-%E8%8C%85%E4%BA%8E%E8%BD%BC/?/, accessed May 2, 2014). He was a visiting scholar at Harvard in 1986.

58 China's involvement with other international organizations, such as the GATT, WTO and OECD also helped integrate Cheese economists into a global neoclassical economics discourse. United Nations institutions and conferences may also have helped integrate Chinese economists into a non-Marxist global economics discourse. Gao Shangquan indicates, "I attended the International Seminar on Comparison of Economic Systems, sponsored by the United Nations. … Nobody at the meeting considered that the centralized system [of planning] was any good or viable for the future" (Gao 1999, 24).

59 Much of this section's discussion relies on Jacobson and Oksenberg (1990) and articles by World Bank insiders, Pieter Bottelier (2006) and Edwin Lim (2005, 2014). Bottelier's and Lim's assessments of the World Bank's role may be colored by their positions as head of the Bank's China Mission 1993–1997 and director of the Bank's economic research in China 1980–1990. On factual details, their comments are consistent with other observers, such as Chow. Their conclusions about the extent of Bank influence may be less reliable.

60 There were also some interesting side issues related to reclaiming part of China's gold reserves deposited much earlier with the IMF (see Jacobson and Oksenberg, Chapter 3).

61 Edwin Lim indicates that Zhu worked closely with the Bank's economists (Lim 2014, 47, 49), writing a short essay on Chinese industry (Lim 2005, 105).

62 Bottelier, 2006, 3, 15. From 1980–2005, the Bank made loans of more than $40 billion to China. There usually were at least 100 World Bank staff in China, ~10,000 Chinese government workers overseeing Bank programs, and hundreds of thousands employed in Bank projects in the late 1990s (Bottelier, 2006, 15).

63 Jacobson and Oksenberg report that the Chinese initially resisted publishing the report but subsequently changed their minds (111).

64 Jacobson and Oksenberg (1990) indicate that the influence of the World Bank and IMF grew rapidly. Chinese participation in these organizations "prompted changes in policies, policy processes, and institutions in China. … Standards of evaluation derived from Western economic theory, in the minds of many, replaced concepts imported from the Soviet Union in the 1950s" (17). Edwin Lim makes similar claims (Lim 2014, 50).

   In 2011 another IMF-World Bank research team helped organize Chinese thinking about financial liberalization. As in 1980, the consultants helped frame issues for Chinese policy makers in neoclassical terms. In July 2011, the IMF's "Survey Magazine Countries and Regions" reported,

> This year … the IMF, in collaboration with the World Bank, also conducted an assessment of the health of the Chinese financial system … laying out a clear, strategic roadmap to manage the process of financial liberalization … that both reduces the risks and delivers the full benefits of a more market-based financial system …
>
> (www.imf.org/external/pubs/ft/survey/so/2011/car072011a.htm, accessed November 2, 2011)

65 Lim indicates that tens of thousands of copies of the report were sold in China at the low price of 50 cents a copy (Lim 2005, 104).
66 Vogel indicates that the program trained almost 70 Chinese economists 1985–1995. Most of these economists eventually held important economic policy positions in China (Vogel 2011, 459; Lim 2005, 104).
67 Bottelier writes, "Perhaps the greatest contribution to China's development and modernization through Bank-supported investment projects has been institution building, i.e., the development of rules, systems and organizations for managing and supervising projects in accordance with sound economic … standards" (16).
68 Sung and Chan indicate that the Bank's 1985 report was among the most important influences on the government's decision to turn the SOEs into joint-stock companies (Sung and Chan 1987, 46). Wang 2011 similarly argues that "The political ascendancy of the liberal-minded economists enabled them to socialize top leaders with neoclassical economic ideas and convinced them of the necessity of speeding up WTO accession so as to facilitate SOE reforms" (Wang 2011, 452).
69 Gao finished his book during a research fellowship at the Bank (Gao 1999, ix). In the 1980s Gao held key posts in China's economic reform think tanks, including the directorship of the State Council Office for Economic Reform (Gao 1999, 1–2). In this 1999 book, Gao indicates that China's primary stage of socialism (involving many policies also used in capitalism) would last at least 100 years (Gao 1999, 84).
70 "China and the World Bank, 2030 vision." *The Economist*, February 28, 2012, by J. M. (www.economist.com/blogs/analects/2012/02/china-and-world-bank, accessed January 15, 2014).
71 Rawski 1986; Chow 2000, 53; Perkins 1999.
72 While China only used IMF financing mechanisms once, it appears likely that it learned the language of the IMF. Bottelier indicates that IMF consultants helped China develop its "macroeconomic institutions, policies and statistics" (Bottelier 2006, 3).
73 The 1982 symposium was on the outlook for the world economy and role of the IMF. The 1986 symposium was entitled, "Macroeconomic Management, Growth, and the Role of the IMF" (Jacobson and Oksenberg 1990 122–124). A third major conference on monetary policy was scheduled for 1989, but was postponed.
74 Jacobson and Oksenberg 1990, 33, 130; Lim 2005, 104–105.
75 Ramgopal Agarwala, a senior World Bank official, for example, argues, "China …

has listened to foreign advice but has made decisions in the light of its own social, political, and economic circumstances … it was definitely not a blind adoption of the policies of the Washington [Consensus]" (Arrighi 2008, 355).

76 The Bank's president is traditionally chosen by the US.

77 Goldman reports that the Voice of America broadcast proposals for political reform offered by Peking University economist Shang Dewen in 1997 that were denied publication in China (Goldman 2005, 133). Interestingly, Shang's arguments were articulated using Marxist language.

78 The Kudlow report indicated on November 26, 2008 that supply side economic theorist and Nobel Prize winner "(Robert) Mundell travels to China about once every other month as a key advisor to the Bank of China." (https://kudlows moneypolitics.blogspot.com/2008_11_01_archive.html, accessed December 11, 2011). Derek Scissors of the Heritage Foundation finds the reform camp has been typically led by the People's Bank…" (Derek Scissors, "Chinese Economic Reform: How the U.S. Should Prepare," Heritage Foundation Report No. 3574, April 23, 2012, www.heritage.org/asia/report/chinese-economic-reform-how-the-us-should-prepare).

79 The experience of Chen Yuan, the governor of the China Development Bank for many years illustrates this kind of influence. When he was appointed to the People's Bank of China he was sent to the US to study American banking practices. He reports, "My classroom was Washington and New York. I visited the Fed, the Treasury, investment banks and commercial banks. They were my teachers" (Kuhn 2011, 262). Chen Yuan also earned a Masters degree from CASS's Institute of industrial economics during the academy's opening up to Western economics. Chen Yuan's experiences are notable, as his father, Chen Yun, was probably the most important Marxist economic thinker/policy maker of the first 30 years of the PRC.

80 For an interesting account of the Fed's impact on the economics profession see Ryan Grim's (Huffington Post) article: "Priceless: How the Federal Reserve Bought the Economics Profession" www.huffingtonpost.com/2009/09/07/priceless-how-the-federal_n_278805.html (October 23, 2009).

81 Sleeboom-Faulkner similarly reports that some CASS economists enjoyed lucrative fees in the 1980s. She also notes central government pressure on CASS to finance part of its operation from fee for service activities (Sleeboom-Faulkner 2007, 71). In 2009, Christopher Howe lamented the "marketization of academic life," asserting, "within China … it is hard to find a single economist immune to the impact of vested interests—notably property interests" (Howe 2009, 927, accessed November 25, 2015).

82 Steven W. Lewis indicates that Chinese economists with advanced degrees in neoclassical economics were especially attractive to firms and international organizations in the global financial sector (Lewis 2005, 231–232).

See also Zhao 2008, who writes,

> … *China Youth News* …publish(ed) the most poignant critique of a dominant knowledge-money-power regime in the Chinese social structure. … It cited examples of interlocking relationships between elite economists and capital … one famous economist serves as an adviser or an independent board member in nine publicly listed companies. Another economist serves as an adviser to 15 companies, enjoying an annual income ranging from 30,000 to 200,000 yuan from each company. These individuals hold important positions in government think tanks …
>
> (Zhao 2008, 298)

83 This willingness to sacrifice or defer democracy in pursuit of capitalist development has been argued to be characteristic of Hayek. More broadly, Brad Delong

[quoting Jamie K.], reports "the position of mainstream intellectuals and economists in China … [was] 'capitalism now, democracy sometime, maybe.'" DeLong
avers that China's anti subversion laws "have a Hayekian feel to them" (Brad
DeLong Blog Spot November 20, 2006).

Wang Hui similarly argues that many liberal economists represent a Chinese
Right, appealing to Hayekian notions that the market represents a spontaneous
economic order and is the only institution capable of sustaining prosperity and
democracy. While the Right's rhetoric might cite democratic goals, the real
project, Hui argues, is market building (Wang Hui 2003b, 63). He adds that a
liberal economist once told him "Attacks on corruption are an attack on the market—we have to tolerate the one to develop the other" (Wang Hui 2003b, 68).

Sleeboom-Faulkner also notes the neoauthoritarian dimension among some
market supporters, citing for example, Xiao Gongqin's view that an intellectual
elite may be necessary to provide "a guiding hand" in the transition to the "invisible hand" (Sleeboom-Faulkner 2007, 113).

Yan Sun reports,

> Neo-authoritarianism defended Zhao by arguing that economic transition
> must precede political democratization and that the separation of the economic
> and political spheres must remain the immediate goal of political reform. …
> The period of transition to the market was therefore to be marked by strong
> central power in politics but its renunciation in the economy. … This new
> authoritarianism was partly aimed at strengthening Zhao's leadership so as to
> press through with the unpopular price reform …
>
> (Sun 1995, 145–146)

"Chen Yizhi, Wang Xiaojiang, and a few other members of Zhao's brain trust
advocated 'elite democracy,' referring to the replacement of senior policymakers
with young, knowledgeable, modern-minded elites like themselves" (Sun
1995, 146).

# References

Arrighi, Giovanni. 2008. *Adam Smith in Beijing: Lineages of the Twenty-First Century.*
New York: Verso.

Bottelier, Pieter. 2006. *China and the World Bank: How a Partnership was Built.* Stanford, CA: Stanford University Press.

Brahm, Laurence J. 2002. *Zhu Rongji and the Transformation of Modern China.* Singapore: John Wiley & Sons (Asia).

Bramall, Chris. 2009a. *Chinese Economic Development.* New York: Routledge.

Broadman, Harry G. 1996. "Policy Options for Reform of Chinese State-Owned
Enterprises. Proceedings of Symposium in Beijing, June 1995. World Bank Discussion Paper no 335." Beijing, World Bank, June 1995.

Busse, Ronald, Malcolm Warner, and Shuming Zhao. 2016. "In Search of the Roots
of 'Human Resource Management' in the Chinese Workplace." *Cambridge Judge
Business School Working Papers* February 20, 2016.

Byrd, William, and Qingsong Lin, eds. 1990. *China's Rural Industry: Structure, Development, and Reform.* Washington, DC: World Bank.

Cato Institute. 2001. *25 Years at the Cato Institute: The 2001 Annual Report:* Cato Institute.

Chow, Gregory. 1986. *Development of a More Market Oriented Economy in China
(Econometric Research Program Research Memorandum no. 326).* Princeton, NJ: Princeton Econometric Research Program.

Chow, Gregory. 1988. *Teaching Economics and Studying Economic Reform in China (Econometric Research Program Research Memorandum no. 339)*. Princeton, NJ: Princeton Econometric Research Program.

Chow, Gregory. 1994. *Understanding China's Economy*. Hong Kong: World Scientific.

Chow, Gregory. 2000. "The Teaching of Modern Economics in China." *Comparative Economic Studies* 42 (2): 51–60. doi:10.1057/ces.2000.8.

Chow, Gregory. 2002. *China's Economic Transformation*. Malden, MA: Blackwell.

Coase, Ronald, and Ning Wang. 2013. *How China Became Capitalist*. New York: Palgrave Macmillan.

Coburn, Judith. 1969. "Asian Scholars and Government: The Chrysanthemum on the Sword." In *America's Asia: Dissenting Essays on Asian American Relations*, edited by Edward Friedman and Mark Selden, 67–107. New York: Vintage.

Committee on Scholarly Communication with the People's Republic of China (CSCPRC) Delegation to the People's Republic of China. 2010 [1980]. *Report of the CSCPRC Economics Delegation to the People's Republic of China*: General Books [National Academies].

Fang, Fuqian. 2013. "The Changing Status of Western Economics in China." In *Thoughts on Economic Development in China*, edited by Ying Ma and Hans-Michael Trautwein, 295–305. New York: Routledge.

Fine, Ben, and Elisa Van Waeyenberge. 2013. *A Paradigm Shift that Never Will Be?: Justin Lin's New Structural Economics*. SOAS Department of Economics Working Paper Series. Vol. 179. London: SOAS Department of Economics.

Forsythe, Michael. 2012. "The Chinese Communist Party's Capitalist Elite: Chinese Lawmakers have Amassed Huge Personal Wealth." *Bloomberg*.

Freeman, Charles W. III, and Wen Jin Yuan. 2011. *China's New Leftists and the China Model Debate After the Financial Crisis*. Washington, DC: Center For Strategic and International Studies.

Friedman, Thomas. 2011. "Justice Goes Global." *New York Times*, June 14, 2011, A27.

Galenson, Walter, ed. 1993. *China's Economic Reform*. San Francisco, CA: The 1990 Institute.

Gao, Shangquan. 1999. *Two Decades of Reform in China*. River Edge, NJ: World Scientific.

Goldman, Merle. 2005. *From Comrade to Citizen: The Struggle for Political Rights in China*. Cambridge, MA: Harvard University Press.

Heilmann, Sebastian, and Lea Shih. 2013. "The Rise of Industrial Policy in China, 1978–2012." *Harvard-Yenching Institute Working Paper Series*: July 31, 2013.

Herrmann-Pillath, Carsten. 2011. "A Third Culture in Economics? An Essay on Smith, Confucius, and the Rise of China." *Working Paper Series, Frankfurt School of Finance and Management* 159.

Herschede, Fred. 1985. "Economics as an Academic Discipline at Nanjing University." *The China Quarterly* (102): 304–316. doi:10.1017/S0305741000029969.

Howe, Christopher B. 2009. "The Chinese Economy and 'China Economists' as seen through the Pages of *the China Quarterly*." *The China Quarterly* (200): 923–927. doi:10.1017/S0305741009990981.

Hsia, Renee Yuen-Jan and Lynn T. White III. 2002. "Working Amid Corporatism and Confusion: Foreign NGOs in China." *Nonprofit and Voluntary Sector Quarterly* 31 (3): 329–351. doi:10.1177/0899764002313002.

Hsu, Robert C. 1991. *Economic Theories in China 1979–1988*. New York: Cambridge University Press.

Hu, Thewei. 1988. "Teaching about the American Economy in the People's Republic of China." *Journal of Economic Education* 19 (1): 87–96. doi:10.1080/0022 0485.1988.10845246.

Jacobson, Harold K., and Michel Oksenberg. 1990. *China's Participation in the IMF, the World Bank, and GATT: Toward a Global Economic Order.* Ann Arbor, MI: University of Michigan Press.

Kallgren, Joyce K. 1987. "Public Interest and Private Interest in Sino-American Exchanges: De Toqueville's 'Associations' in Action." In *Educational Exchanges: Essays on the Sino-American Experience*, edited by Joyce K. Kallgren and Denis Fred Simon, 58–79. Berkeley, CA: Institute of East Asian Studies.

Kelliher, Daniel. 1992. *Peasant Power in China: The Era of Rural Reform 1979–1989.* New Haven, CT: Yale University Press.

Kotz, David. 2000. "Lessons from the Demise of State Socialism in the Soviet Union and China." In *Socialism and Radical Political Economy: Essays in Honor of Howard Sherman*, edited by Robert Pollin (pre-publication online November 1999), 300–317. Northampton, MA: Edward Elgar.

Kotz, David, and Fred Weir. 1997. *Revolution from Above.* New York: Routledge.

Kuhn, Robert. 2011. *How China's Leaders Think.* Singapore: Wiley.

Kwong, Julia. 1994. "Ideological Crisis among China's Youth: Values and Official Ideology." *British Journal of Sociology* 45 (2): 247–264. https://knox.idm.oclc.org/login?url=http://search.ebscohost.com/login.aspx?direct=true&db=sih&AN=9408 050748&site=ehost-live.

Lampton, David M., Joyce Madancy, and Kristen M. Williams. 1986. *A Relationship Restored: Trends in U.S.–China Educational Exchanges, 1979–1984.* Washington, DC: National Academy Press.

Leonard, Mark. 2008a. *What does China Think?* New York: Public Affairs.

Lewis, Steven W. 2005. "Economic Thought." In *Encyclopedia of Contemporary Chinese Culture*, edited by Edward Lawrence Davis, 230–232. New York: Routledge.

Li, Cheng. 2001. *China's Leaders: The New Generation.* New York: Rowman & Littlefield.

Li, Cheng. 2009. "China's New Think Tanks: Where Officials, Entrepreneurs, and Scholars Interact." *China Leadership Monitor* 29.

Li, Cheng, and Lynn T. White III. 1991. "China's Technocratic Movement and the World Economic Herald." *Modern China* 17 (3): 342–388. doi:10.1177/0097700 49101700302.

Li, Minqi. 2008. *The Rise of China and the Demise of the Capitalist World Economy.* New York: Monthly Review.

Lim, Edwin. 2005. "Learning and Working with Giants." In *At the Frontlines of Development: Reflecions from the World Bank*, edited by Indermit Singh Gill and Todd Pugatch, 89–119. Washington, DC: World Bank.

Lim, Edwin. 2014. "The Influence of Foreign Economists in the Early Stages of China's Reforms." In *The Oxford Companion to the Economics of China*, edited by Shenggen Fan, Ravi Kanbur, Shang-Jin Wei, and Xiaobo Zhang, 47–52. New York: Oxford University Press.

Lin, Chun. 2013. *China and Global Capitalism: Reflections on Marxism, History, and Contemporary Politics.* New York: St. Martins Press.

Lin, Fen, Yanfei Sun, and Hongxing Yang. 2015. "How are Chinese Students Ideologically Divided? A Survey of Chinese College Students' Political Self-Identification." *Pacific Affairs* 88 (1): 51–74. doi:10.5509/201588151.

Lin, Justin Yifu. 2005. *Building Up a Market-Oriented Research and Education Institution in a Transitional Economy: The Experience of the China Center for Economic Research at Peking University (CCER Working Paper no. E2005003)*. Beijing: China Center for Economic Research.

Lin, Justin Yifu. 2012a. *Demystifying the Chinese Economy*. New York: Cambridge University Press.

Lin, Justin Yifu. 2012b. *New Structural Economics: A Framework for Rethinking Development and Policy*. Washington, DC: World Bank.

Lin, Justin Yifu. 2012c. *Benti and Changwu: Dialogues on Methodology in Economics*. Beijing: Peking University Press.

Liu, Changyuan and Song Wang. 2009. "Transformation of Chinese Cultural Values in the Era of Globalization: Individualism and Chinese Youth." *Intercultural Communication Studies* XVIII (2): 54–71.

Liu, Junning. 2000. "Classical Liberalism Catches on in China." *Journal of Democracy* 11 (3): 48–57.

Ma, Shu Y. 1998. "The Chinese Route to Privatization: The Evolution of the Share-holding System Option." *Asian Survey* 38 (4): 379–397. doi:10.2307/2645413.

Meisner, Maurice. 1996. *The Deng Xiaopeng Era: An Inquiry into the Fate of Chinese Socialism 1978–1994*. New York: Hill and Wang.

Naughton, Barry. 1995. *Growing Out of the Plan: Chinese Economic Reform 1978–1993*. New York: Cambridge University Press.

Naughton, Barry. 2002. "China's Economic Think Tanks: Their Changing Role in the 1990s." *The China Quarterly* (171): 625–635. doi:10.1017/S0009443902000396.

Paulson, Henry M. Jr. 2015. *Dealing with China: An Insider Unmasks the New Economic Superpower*. New York: Twelve Hachette Book Group.

Perkins, Dwight. 1999. *Report: Supporting China's Transition to a Market Economy; an Evaluation of the Chinese Economists Society (Commissioned for the Center for International Private Enterprise)*.

Peterson, Glen. 2014. *Overseas Chinese in the People's Republic of China*. New York: Routledge.

Rawski, Thomas. 1986. "Report on Economics Curriculum in Chinese Universities (Draft)." Draft report, personal copy.

Rawski, Thomas. 2013 [2009]. "Studies of China's Economy." In *A Scholarly Review of Chinese Studies in North America*, edited by Haihui Zhang, Zhaohui Xue, Shuyong Jiang, and Gary Lance Lugar, 175–192. Ann Arbor, MI: Association for Asian Studies.

Riskin, Carl. 1987. *China's Political Economy: The Quest for Development since 1949*. New York: Oxford University Press.

Rosen, Stanley. 2009. "Contemporary Chinese Youth and the State." *The Journal of Asian Studies* 68 (2): 359–369. doi:10.1017/S0021911809000631.

Sheng, Hong. 1996. "A Survey of the Research on the Transitional Process of Market-Oriented Reform in China." *Chinese Economic Studies* 29 (2): 5–38.

Shieh, Shawn and Signe Knutson. 2012. *Special Report: The Roles and Challenges of International NGOs in China's Development*: China Development Brief.

Sleeboom-Faulkner, Margaret. 2007. *The Chinese Academy of Social Sciences (CASS): Shaping the Reforms, Academia and China*. Boston, MA: Brill.

Song, Longxiang. 1995. "The Methodology of Mainstream Economics and its Implications for China's Economic Research." PhD diss., Washington University.

Sun, Yan. 1995. *The Chinese Reassessment of Socialism 1976–1992*. Princeton, NJ: Princeton University Press.

Sung, Yun-wing and Thomas M.H. Chan 1987. "China's Economic Reforms: The Debates in China." *The Australian Journal of Chinese Affairs* (17): 29–51. doi:10.2307/2158967.

Sutton, Francis X. 1987. "American Philanthropy in Educational Exchange with the People's Republic of China." In *Educational Exchanges: Essays on the Sino-American Experience*, edited by Joyce K. Kallgren and Denis Fred Simon, 96–118. Berkeley, CA: Institute of East Asian Studies.

US Embassy, Tokyo. 2006 [1976] to Department of State, Telegram 05358, April 12 1976, 1976TOKYO05358, Central Foreign Policy Files, 1973–1979/Electronic Telegrams, RG 59: General Records of the Department of State, US National Archives (https://aad.archives.gov/aad/createpdf?rid=27162&dt=2082&dl=1345, accessed July 15, 2016).

Vogel, Ezra F. 2011. *Deng Xiaoping and the Transformation of China*. Cambridge, MA: Harvard University Press.

Wang, Chaohua, ed. 2003. *One China, Many Paths*. New York: Verso.

Wang, Hui. 2003a. *China's New Order: Society, Politics, and Economy in Transition*, edited by Theodore Huters. Cambridge, MA: Harvard University Press.

Wang, Qingxin K. 2011. "The Rise of Neoclassical Economics and China's WTO Agreement with the United States in 1999." *Journal of Contemporary China* 20 (70): 449–465. doi:10.1080/10670564.2011.565177.

Warner, Malcolm. 2014. *Understanding Management in China: Past, Present, and Future*. New York: Routledge.

Watson, Andrew. 1987. "Social Science Research and Economic Policy Formulation: The Academic Side of Economic Reform." In *New Directions in the Social Sciences and Humanities in China*, edited by Michael B. Yahuda, 67–88. New York: St Martin's Press.

Wen, G. and D. Xu, eds. 1997. *The Reformability of China's State Sector*. River Edge, NJ: World Scientific.

Wheeler, Norton. 2012. *The Role of American NGOs in China's Modernization: Invited Influence*. New York: Routledge.

Wiki Leaks. 2013 [1976]. "Wiki Leaks: "ILO World Employment Conference: Galenson Discussion with Ministry of Labor, April 12, 1976." See US Embassy, Tokyo entry for document title.

Wu, Jinglian. 2005. *Understanding and Interpreting China's Economic Reform*. Singapore: Thomson/South-Western.

Yin, Deyong. 2009. "China's Attitude Toward Foreign NGO's." *Washington University Global Studies Law Review* 8 (3/4): 521–543.

Yin, Xiao-huang. 2004. "A Case Study of Transnationalism: Continuity and Changes in Chinese Americans Philanthropy in China." *American Studies* 45 (2).

Zhao, Yuezhi. 2008. *Communication in China: Political Economy, Power and Conflict*. New York: Rowman & Littlefield.

Zhou, Kate. 2006. "Chinese Intellectuals Fighting on the Idea Front in Global Context." In *The World and China at a Time of Drastic Changes—Towards the Construction of a New and Modern Sinology*, edited by Mitsuyuki Kagami, 35–70. Japan: Aichi University Press.

Zhu, Ying. 2012. *Two Billion Eyes: The Story of China Central Television*. New York: The New Press.

# 3 The historical context for the evolution of Chinese economic theory

## 3.1 Overview

Chapter 3 analyzes the larger context within which Chinese economic theory and economics education evolved ~1976–2001. Economic events helped create the agenda and the data for testing economic theory, which in turn helped shape the next round of economic events.[1] Of course, pre-existing paradigms oriented different observers to look at different things (minimizing attention, for example, to issues of worker alienation among neoclassical economists or marketing matters among Marxist economists). Alongside this interactive feedback, both economic events and discursive shifts among economists had their own internal momentum. The relationship between economic theory and economic practice in China was thus often messy. Economic events frequently outraced efforts to theorize about them, often leaving economic explanations appearing ad hoc and arbitrary.

Three different policy agendas, based on three different theoretical frameworks, eventually emerged. The first was a central planning oriented economic policy. It built on orthodox Marxist economic theory. It called for some changes in the techniques and priorities of economic planning, but still treated markets as very junior partners alongside central planners. The second was a more "radical reformist" economic strategy. It mixed extensive use of markets with continuing but reduced public ownership of key industries, and indirect planning techniques. This approach appealed to a version of Marxism that characterized China as being in the "primary stage of socialism." The third approach called for a transition to capitalism. It developed later than the first two approaches and relied on neoclassical and new institutionalist economic theory. The second and third approaches sometimes recommended similar economic policies, but there was a profound difference in the theoretical frameworks generating these recommendations.

The narrative below is not intended to be a comprehensive history of the first quarter century of Chinese economic reform. It tries instead to understand how the economy and ideas about the economy co-evolved. In this chapter we look at general debates among economists about economic restructuring. In Chapters 4, 5, and 6 we look in more detail at the linkages between the evolution of economic events and economic theory in three specific sectors of the economy: the agricultural-rural sector, the international sector, and the state-owned enterprise sector. While there is some discussion of the impact of these changes on economics education, this feedback loop is explored in more depth in Chapters 8 and 9.

The history of economic structuring can be divided into five periods: (1) Transition: 1976–1978;[2] (2) Initial Restructuring: 1978–1989; (3): Tiananmen and its Aftermath 1989–1991; (4) Renewed Restructuring 1992–2001; and (5) WTO and Beyond: 2001-present. The latter period is covered only briefly in the concluding chapters.

We begin with a discussion in section 3.2 of the state of the Chinese economy in 1976, and the perceived problems that stimulated efforts to restructure the economy. Section 3.3 explores general debates among Chinese economists about how to carry out economic reform. Section 3.4 ties aspects of these debates to the different formative experiences of different generations of Chinese economists. Section 3.5 explores the policies offered by proponents of economic restructuring to reassure skeptics that marketization would not undermine socialist goals. Section 3.6 looks at the political-economic factors that resolved these early debates.

## 3.2 Stimuli for restructuring 1976–1978

The political-economic context that gave rise to new economic thinking and economic restructuring in China was shaped by the need to recover from the decade long disruptions of the Cultural Revolution[3] and the accumulation of several nagging economic problems, such as lagging agricultural output, the perceived economic inefficiencies of large state-owned industrial enterprises, disguised unemployment, and technological deficits.

The most intense period of the Cultural Revolution was brought to a close in the late 1960s by the army's intervention to restore order. Mao's death in 1976 and the arrest of the "Gang of Four" shortly thereafter set the stage for new economic and academic initiatives. Mao's immediate successor, Hua Guofeng, planned to re-energize the Chinese economy through the aggressive importation of foreign technology. These plans crumbled when the oil earnings anticipated to pay for the imported goods failed to materialize. Deng Xiaoping would do the repair work.[4]

The Chinese economy's performance before the economic reforms was much more successful than is suggested by the "night and day" metaphors often used to depict the impact of marketization. There were both big successes and big failures during the Maoist period of 1949–1978. Among the major achievements of the Maoist years were: an 11.3 percent annual growth rate in industrial output (1952–1977),[5] mastery of various modern military technologies (jet planes, atomic bombs, ballistic missiles, orbiting satellites), a breakthrough in the treatment of malaria,[6] a successful land reform, independent development of green revolution agricultural technologies, a major

expansion in economic infrastructure, a highly egalitarian income distribution,[7] a near doubling in life expectancy, tremendous advances in literacy,[8]
large improvements in the status of women, lifetime job security, and the
construction of a rudimentary social safety net with respect to basic health-
care, education, and retirement security.

The period also had some major economic failings. Over the course of the
30 years, the social surplus was often used inefficiently to industrialize China.
Many of the well-known inefficiencies of central planning in the former
Soviet Union appear to have been prevalent in China, from building factories
ahead of available power and input supplies to wasteful hoarding of inputs by
firms out of fear they would not be able to purchase them in the future.[9]
Many studies have found minimal growth in total factor productivity, with
increases in output coming largely from capital accumulation.[10] These sur-
pluses were re-invested to continue capital accumulation. As a result, the per
capita private spending of farmers and workers grew minimally.[11] Agricultural
output lagged behind industrial output, slightly exceeding population growth
(2.3 percent versus 2 percent from 1952–~1978).[12] Agricultural bottlenecks
often constrained national economic growth. There was significant under-
employment (disguised unemployment),[13] petty corruption, technological
sluggishness in some sectors,[14] and periodic moments of economic disarray.
Economic mismanagement is held accountable by most observers for tens of
millions of excess deaths during the Great Leap Forward.[15] Chinese economic
data collection and macroeconomic statistics were relatively weak, leaving
policy makers acting in the dark at times.[16] There was also a top down rather
than bottom up flow of power, in the workplace as well as in the state. All of
these shortcomings were exacerbated by the terror and wastefulness of the
Cultural Revolution.

Given this context, the goals of early reform were: (1) cementing an end
of the Cultural Revolution and regaining popular support for the government; (2) recreating and improving the capacity for economic planning; (3)
increasing agricultural output; (4) increasing the economic efficiency of large
state-owned enterprises; (5) accelerating technological advance, and (6)
increasing employment.

## 3.3 General debates among Chinese economists: late 1970s–late 1980s

### 3.3.1 Debates among Marxist reformers

In the late 1970s many ideas for achieving these goals circulated among
Chinese economists. Virtually all participants in these discussions remained
Marxist economists, dedicated to achieving socialism in China.[17] Most had
been trained in Marxist theory, were animated by Marxist subtexts, and were
probably comfortable with the labor theory of value. A number had studied
at Russian universities and institutes.[18] Early discussions were informed by

past debates over Chinese economic policy[19] and discussions among Eastern European and Russian economists about reform policies within their economies. The goal of these discussions was how to revitalize socialism, not how to create capitalism.[20]

The Chinese economists' tacit assumptions about human nature, human well-being, the character and ethics of capitalism, and the logic of historical causality during this period differed markedly from the assumptions of classical liberalism animating neoclassical economics. There was a commitment to socialism, a sense of mission about improving the life of the least well off, a commitment to upholding the dignity of work, and the use of a holist methodology that invited thought about social systems. Many leading economists, like Chen Yun, Ma Hong, and Xue Muqiao[21] had developed their economic outlooks as practical responses to challenges associated with central planning. Some had also conducted field work in China's villages investigating rural poverty or labor organizing in the cities. Like businessmen in a capitalist society, their thinking was "practice-led" rather than "theory-led," though their practices (experiences) differed from the commercial experiences of businessmen and were interpreted through a different conceptual framework.

When thinking about the impact of Marxism on Chinese economists it is important to remember that most of Marx's analysis was about capitalism rather than socialism. There are suggestions and hints about what a socialist mode of production might look like in Marx's writings. They are necessarily limited, however, as Marx thought that the dialectical feedback between theory and practice would be necessary to create a new way of life. Thus, what most distinguished early reform thinking in China from neoclassical analyses was the backdrop of Marx's understanding of capitalism, the goal of constructing socialism, and the use of Marxist methodology. There were also of course, the examples of Russian and Eastern European Marxist policies.

In late 1977 the social science section of the Chinese Academy of Sciences was expanded to form an independent Chinese Academy of the Social Sciences (CASS). The new academy escaped supervision by the Ministry of Education, which apparently relaxed constraints on its theorizing (Vogel 2011, 209).[22] CASS quickly became a key center for reformist economic thought.[23] Hu Qiaomu, an historian, was chosen as its first director. In a key article published in the *Peking Review* in 1978, Hu lamented the micro inefficiencies of the Chinese economy and called for new economic policies to increase efficiency.[24] Many important reform-oriented Chinese economists from the 1950s and 1960s, such as Sun Yefang, Liu Guoguang,[25] Yu Guangyan, and Ma Hong were given important posts in CASS and its six economic research institutes.[26] Ma was appointed head of research in 1977 (Brahm 2002, xxviii) and president of the Academy in 1982, at the urging of Premier Zhao Ziyang (Sleeboom-Faulkner 2007, 73). Ma brought with him a key assistant from his days organizing central planning in Dongbei in northeast China and his work on the State Planning Commission in Beijing (Brahm 2002, xxv). His assistant, Zhu Rongzhi, would eventually oversee the

Chinese economy from ~1991–2003, and serve as the fifth Chinese premier from 1998–2003. Ma also elevated Wu Jinglian, a free market oriented economist, to key posts.

New economic research institutes were also established or expanded in many government offices, such as the State Planning Commission, the People's Bank of China, and each of the economic ministries. The Planning Commission's Economic Research Institute was headed by Xue Muqiao. Du Rusheng, a key proponent of early agricultural reforms, directed the Rural Development Research Center for the State Council. Wu Jinglian was appointed to key posts in the State Council's Development Research Center and became its most influential theorist (Naughton 2013, 166). Zhao Ziyang supported many new think tanks, treating them as an institutional resource for escaping habits of thought ensconced in government ministries.[27] By 1982 there were more than 200 economic research and study associations in China and more than 60 major conferences engaging these associations (Watson 1987, 76–77).[28] Throughout the 1980s there was also an expanding flow of foreign economists visiting, consulting, and lecturing in China and hundreds of newly established cooperative programs in economics and business between Chinese and Western universities (Lichtenstein 1992, 174). Taken together, these initiatives created a critical mass of reform-oriented economists (Hsu 1991, 18–19).[29] It appears that the research institutes at CASS and those directly under the State Council had the greatest impact on Chinese government policy.

The journal *Economic Research* (*Jingji Yanjiu*) resumed publication in January 1978 after being shut down 12 years earlier during the Cultural Revolution. It was and is probably China's most important economics journal. The first five new issues of the journal focused on: whether distribution according to labor (rather than according to needs) was a slippery slope toward restoring capitalism and to what extent socialist principles might be sacrificed to develop the forces of production (Wang 1979). Sprouting themes that would echo in later debates, [and often citing Marx's remarks in his "Critique of the Gotha Program"] the reformers found distribution according to labor to be an acceptable transitional policy. They also stressed the importance of policies that would develop the forces of production.

### 3.3.2 Adjusters vs. marketeers

In the early 1980s a rough consensus emerged among many Marxist-oriented reform economists in China about the character of Chinese economic history since 1949. These economists celebrated the achievements of the 1949–1952 period, the first five-year plan (1953–1957), and the policies of the 1961–1965 period. They were highly critical, however, of the policies during the Great Leap Forward (GLF) (1958–~1961) and the Cultural Revolution (CR) ~1966–~1976. The economists fell into two camps. The first group found fault with the techniques and priorities of economic planning during the GLF and CR years. Although sympathetic to a modest expansion of markets, their main focus was on reforming planning. The second group was more interested in expanding the use of market mechanisms than in reforming planning. They criticized the ideology of the GLF-CR periods for treating China's economy as a "natural economy," rather than a "planned commodity" economy.

Both groups' criticism of economic planning faulted the GLF-CR periods for excessive rates of accumulation; excessive investment in heavy industry at the expense of light industry and agriculture; excessive investment in new construction, rather than technological upgrading within existing facilities; excessive concentration on grain and steel production;[30] adherence to local self-reliance at the expense of pursuing regional and national comparative advantage; and the setting of relative prices according to political metrics rather than the costs of production as dictated by the "law of value."

The second group also faulted the GLF and CR for the devaluation of material incentives and the stifling of markets and market competition, linking these factors to: (1) weak incentives for worker and enterprise effort; (2) inadequate information flows about supply and demand conditions; (3) insufficient attention to the immediate needs of peasants and workers in determining final demand; and as noted above (4) relative price determination by political rather than economic logic. The turn toward a greater use of material incentives and markets was a major rebuke to Maoist attempts at a rapid transition to a new communist society, but it did not necessarily imply a loss of that goal or a commitment to capitalism.

The relative weight each group placed on reforming existing planning strategies versus expanding market mechanisms would eventually define two different approaches to economic reform. The "adjustment" strategy called for maintaining central planning as the main organizing mechanism of the economy, but recommended shifting the focus of China's five-year plans and adding a modest market sector. The "marketization" strategy called for sharply reducing the role of planning and expanding the use of material incentives and market competition across the economy. There presumably was also a third strategy that favored renewing Maoist economic policies, with a preference for moral rather than material incentives, mass mobilizations, self-reliance (both regionally and internationally), and a focus on building socialist consciousness and habits of behavior rather than maximizing economic growth. After the arrest of the "Gang of Four," however, public advocacy of this perspective was probably self-censored (White 1989, 156; Watson 1987, 70–71).[31]

The plan adjusters believed that reliance on economic planning rather than market allocation was a defining part of socialism. They were led by Chen Yun, a major architect of China's first five-year plan.[32] Chen's approach was backed by most of the economists at the State Planning Commission and Renmin University (Bramall 2000, 13).[33] Other noted advocates of elements of this strategy included: Hu Qiaomu, Deng Liqun, Yao Yilin, Peng Zhen, Xu Yi, You Lin, Gu Shutang, Tao Dayong,[34] and Wu Shuqing.

Chen favored retaining public ownership and economic planning for core industries while permitting an expanded market sector comprised of small firms (often household based) in retail trade, petty production, and services. Heavy industry, transportation, and energy production were to remain within the planned economy. Chen also favored reducing the percentage of GDP allocated to new investment (as opposed to current consumption) as well as shifting some resources from investment in heavy industry to investment in agriculture and light consumer goods. He felt that China's farmers needed access to more consumer goods if motivation were to remain high (Lardy and Lieberthal 1983).

Chen used the memorable image of a bird in a cage to describe his view of the need to keep market forces in check. He also called for continued ideological struggle to maintain socialist perspectives on the economy (Shirk 1993, 295; Harding 1987, 81–82). Advocates of this approach were often referred to as "conservatives" in the Western press. Meisner and Sun's term, "adjusters," or Bramall's term "readjusters," seem more suitable.[35]

In contrast to this approach, the "marketeers" vision went well beyond Chen's tolerance of petty producer markets in the interstices of the rural economy. The marketeers called for markets in labor, capital goods, and enterprise-management, for markets in urban as well as rural areas, and for markets in economic sectors with big as well as small firms. The marketeers were not initially clandestine supporters of a transition to capitalism. Key theorists such as Liu Guoguang, Sun Yefang, and Xue Muqiao had spent their lives attempting to construct socialism. Like Keynes' self-conscious efforts to save capitalism from itself during the Great Depression, the reformers thought of themselves as doctors, not undertakers, for the socialist body politic. But, over time the imaginations of some marketeers would change.

The main theoretical justification for the marketeers' program was the theory of "the primary stage of socialism."[36] This theory implied that China's under-developed "forces of production" (or in non-Marxist terminology, the level of technology, but also inclusive of labor skills and social infrastructures) required China to utilize some techniques found in capitalism (such as competitive markets and material incentives) in order to accelerate economic growth. Only a developed economy with advanced forces of production could fully institutionalize communist relations of production and lifestyles.[37] Prioritizing the development of the forces of production (rather than "taking class struggle as the key link," as in Maoism) also invited greater openness to the world economy in order to acquire modern technology and advanced training for China's young people and workforce. Aspects of this reform strategy had been experimented with in Russia as early as Lenin's New Economic Policy in the 1920s, and more recently debated in Hungary, Czechoslovakia, and Poland. The marketeers linked their strategy to Zhou Enlai's call in 1975 for the four modernizations (in agriculture, industry, science and technology, and defense).

Many of the key "marketeer" economists, such as Liu Guoguang, Sun Yefang, Dong Fureng, Yu Guangyuan, and Sun Shangqing, were associated with CASS. During the next decade they struggled over how to conceptualize the role of markets in Chinese life. The Chinese economy went from being characterized as a "commodity economy" in 1979–1980, to a "planned commodity economy"[38] and/or "socialist commodity economy" in 1982–1984, to a "socialist market economy" in 1992. The initial tilt toward a market economy began in the late 1970s with statements by Deng Xiaoping, Hu Qiaomu, Xue Muqiao, and others, endorsing the idea that a socialist economy was a "commodity economy."[39] This characterization rejected the Cultural Revolution's extreme hostility toward markets and market related pricing. It implied:

1   that a significant number of goods in the Chinese economy were produced for exchange (the definition of a commodity)
2   that the value of a good in exchange was determined by the "law of value," which is to say that the value of a good equaled its "embodied socially necessary average labor time" [ESNALTS] (i.e., the average direct labor time it took to produce the good and the indirect labor time transferred to the product by the depreciation of the capital equipment used up in its production)
3   that the determination of the "average socially necessary labor time" required for different goods production might involve feedback from some market mechanisms[40]
4   that there could be variations in household income based on variations in labor hours worked.

The law of value was a Marxist concept derived from the labor theory of value. While very different from the marginalist theories of value and price determination in neoclassical theory, aspects of the concept invited theoretical and practical discussions about how to integrate the logic of supply and demand and market price adjustments into Marxist theories of resource allocation. Most importantly, the law of value appeared to rely partially on market outcomes to discover the average labor time it took to produce different goods. The law of value also suggested that overproduction of a commodity devalued the ESNALTS embodied in the commodity, permitting market demand to indirectly influence value.

Numerous conferences and seminars were held across China from July 1978 to spring 1979, including a national conference in April 1979, on the implications of "adhering to the law of value."[41] Many reform economists understood the law to imply that the prices of commodities in a socialist economy should reflect their costs of production (measured in labor hours). Thus, calls for adherence to the law of value were partially calls for economic and market related price determination as opposed to planner-political price determination. These calls were usually linked to complementary arguments about the need for more autonomous firms to operationalize the law of value through socialist competition. This conversation was heavily influenced by earlier work by Sun Yefang.

Attempts to maintain the labor theory of value as a frame for economic thinking and the law of value as a tool for economic planning ran into practical problems and pedagogical disadvantages in competition with neoclassical price theory. Over time, the language for discussing a commodity economy became increasingly friendly to neoclassical economic metaphors.

In 2005, Wu Jinglian, perhaps the most famous reform economist turned neoclassical economist, summed up his view of the evolving nomenclature for the Chinese economy, declaring, a "'Commodity economy' is in fact another name for market economy" (Wu 2005, 62). Wu seems to have held this definition (and economic goal) since at least 1984. In the first 15 years of reform, the marketeers frequently distinguished their vision of socialist markets from capitalist markets by citing (1) the central role of public ownership in a socialist market economy; (2) the principle of distribution based on labor, which excludes property income; (3) the absence of labor as a commodity; (4) and the control of the state by the Communist Party (Liu 2003/1992, 105–106; Hinton 1990, 28). As the reforms unfolded, however, the first three distinctions blurred. In 1997, Wu characterized socialism as "social fairness plus the market economy" (Chen 1999, 463). When asked the difference between a socialist market economy and capitalism, Li Yining, another famous reform economist, turned neoclassical economist, answered, "In my personal opinion, there is no real difference" (Kuhn 2011, 98). Through the 1980s at least, most Marxist marketeers disagreed and struggled to define and defend a difference.

Hsu (1991) was impatient with the immense efforts by Chinese economists to reconcile proposed policies with Marx's writings or classical understandings of socialism, writing,

> the recurrent Chinese debate on … whether labor power is a commodity under socialism would seem metaphysical … and meaninglessness. However. … It is only when this commodity hurdle has been cleared … that the use of the market mechanism can be legitimized.
>
> (Hsu 1991, 32)[42]

A slightly different interpretation of these debates might note their focus was on the dynamic implications of the reforms for the long run project of building socialism and communism in China. Because the latter project is not part of the research agenda of neoclassical economists, questions raised by it, such as the merits and demerits of a generalized system of wage labor (which is another way of asking whether labor is a commodity) can appear as distractions or as ideological exercises.[43] As the subtexts organizing Chinese economic thought shifted toward classical liberal frames, increasing numbers of Chinese economists came to share Hsu's impatience with Marxist inquiries.

The marketeers can be divided into three different groups based on different strategies for revitalizing markets. The first two groups focused their reform strategy on granting greater "autonomy" to enterprises and markets to coordinate their decisions. Sun Yefang and Hu Qiaomu, two classically trained Marxist theorists at CASS, were among the advocates of this strategy.[44] By enterprise autonomy was meant increased decision-making authority over economic variables, such as firms' input choices, as well as greater retention of profits and greater responsibilities for losses. The aim was to encourage more innovative activities and attention to economic efficiency at the micro level.[45] This goal animated many of the reforms. The Household Responsibility System in rural areas and the "Contract Responsibility System" in urban areas were two important manifestations of this impulse. Aspects of this microeconomic strategy were embodied in the dual-track pricing system, where above-plan-output could be sold at higher-than-plan prices (often approaching market pricing) and the proceeds retained by the producers.

The first group of "enterprise autonomy" reformers, for example Jiang Yiwei,[46] Ma Hong, and Dong Fureng of CASS, stressed the benefits of worker self-management and industrial democracy. All three theorists had deep engagements with Marxist theory. Their reform strategy was a variant of "market socialism."[47] As early as 1980, Jiang warned that more independent enterprises might lead to a new class of privileged workers or emergent capitalists. To avert this outcome, he called for vesting managerial authority in democratically elected committees of workers (Selden and Lippit 1982, 316). In the mid-1980s Jiang opposed the dominant position among Chinese economists that called for replacing the system of permanent employment in SOEs with contract employment. Speaking against the managerial responsibility system, Jiang asserted that, "(t)he 'master' of an enterprise should be the majority of workers and employees who enjoyed permanent status in the enterprise" (Sung and Chan 1987, 49).[48]

The second group of reformers favoring increased enterprise autonomy emphasized the efficiency gains accruing from firms maximizing profit, regardless of who initially captured the efficiency gains (workers, managers, or shareholders). Li Yining, known as "Mr. Stock Market" or "Shareholding Li"[49] in China, is representative of this perspective.[50] A third group of marketeers favored a package of coordinated market reforms, often giving a higher priority (at least in terms of sequencing) to decontrolling prices than the first two perspectives. Wu Jinglian (known as Market Wu or Mr. Market)[51] was an important figure in this group (Hsu 1991, 19–20, 156–161; Wu 2005, 79–82), as was Li Tieying, the director of the Economic Reform Commission (Cheng 1995, 191–193). Many of China's Western economic advisers shared this view, stressing the need for prices to be market-based— and therefore "rational"– if economic efficiency were to arise from the independent pursuit of self-interest by economic agents. Both the second and third groups drew on reform literatures from Eastern European countries, highlighting the work of economists such as Brus, Sik, Lange, and, especially, Kornai.

Chen Yun's planning group began the reform era as the dominant faction, due in part to Chen's enormous prestige within the Party as an economic thinker.[52] Chen had an intuitive and practical grasp of the interconnectedness of macroeconomic dynamics. This perspective left him a brave and some-times lonely opponent of mass mobilization economics, which he criticized for underestimating the dangers of unbalanced growth, the inflationary risks of uncoordinated credit expansion, and the bite of foreign exchange con-straints. While Chen's adjuster faction dominated reform discussions initially, it gradually ceded more and more economic territory to the marketeers. By 1984, the marketers began to dominate restructuring discussions. Chen Yun's vision had originally limited the market to a "secondary," "supplementary" role, or, as colloquially phrased, "the big plan and the small market" (Hsu 1991, 34–35). Over time the plan and market assumed more equal status. Eventually, "mandatory" economic planning, with state allocations and output targets, nearly disappeared. It was replaced by "guidance planning"[53] that relied on indirect levers like monetary policy and taxes to influence the economy. By the late 1990s, events and economic theory were deferring to the "logic of the market." Linguistic shifts in the early 1990s signaled major policy shifts. Qian and Wu highlight the different implications of policy makers pursuing a "socialist market economy" rather than "market social-ism," writing

> In market socialism, the market … is to serve the purpose of socialism … in a socialist market economy, 'socialist' is an adjective and the goal is 'market economy.'
>
> (Qian and Wu 2000, 5–6)

We will spend a lot of time in this book trying to figure out why Chinese economists reoriented their thinking about reform from redirecting plan-ning to creating market mechanisms. One relatively neglected factor seems to have been the "messiness" of strategies that would combine planning and market mechanisms and combine non-material and material incentives. Neoclassical proponents of capitalism imply that this "messiness" is due to the intrinsically impossible goal of combining inconsistent economic mech-anisms. Marxist supporters of socialism find the messiness due to the newness and complexities of the tasks as well as accumulated historical burdens (such as the aftereffects of the Cultural Revolution). They point out that Rome was not built in a day.

Regardless of the reasons, the messiness accompanying hybrid systems had a tough time competing with the self-confident, internationally endorsed, rel-atively simple, integrated view offered by newly trained neoclassical econo-mists like Wu Jinglian. Many Chinese economists were led to adopt Barry Naughton's perspective that in the early 1990s, Wu Jinglian's team had the only coherent approach to economic reform (Naughton 2013, 160).

The trends of the early 1990s continued during the rest of the decade. The guarantee of lifetime employment at state-owned firms was revoked for new hires in the mid-1980s and for existing workers in the mid-1990s. Massive layoffs followed due to competitive market pressures. The debate between proponents of worker self-management and the manager or director responsibility system was won by the managers. By 2001 China had joined the World Trade Organization and was mimicking in more and more ways capitalist management and institutional practices.

This brief history of Chinese economic reform raises at least three major questions: (1) Does introducing significant market elements into parts of an economy inevitably lead to the spread of market relations to other areas of the economy? (2) Does the expansion of market relations inevitably lead to the adoption of neoclassical economic concepts for understanding markets and economics? and (3) Does the expansion of market relations inevitably lead to a capitalist economy dominated by private enterprises and wage labor? We will return to these questions time and again in this book. Their answers remain contested.

## 3.4 Generational differences among Chinese economists

The reactions of different economists to this "march of markets" and the accompanying reshaping of Chinese economic institutions in accord with a capitalist organization of production can be characterized in many different ways. I would like to talk initially about the responses in terms of overlapping generations of economists by age. This allows the responses to be linked to the historical periods organizing the economists' lives. There are, of course, exceptions to the general pattern of behavior that I will describe, but the broad brush stroke approach taken below can give us some insight into the social-psychological dynamics accompanying the evolution of Chinese economic thought.

### 3.4.1 The elders: those born in or before 1908

The first group of economists were at least 70 years old at the time of the historic 3rd Plenary Session of the 11th Central Committee of the Chinese Communist Party in 1978 that set China on its reform course. Xue Muqiao (born 1904), Chen Yun (1905), and Sun Yefang (1908) are key figures in this group.[54] All were actively engaged in the events of the 1949 revolution and subsequent efforts to construct socialism. Chen and Xue's economic training was largely self-taught. Sun studied in Russia. Almost all remained socialist and Marxist thinkers throughout their lives. (Using a slightly different dating schema, Sleeboom-Faulkner (2007, 77–78) refers to those born before 1915 as the Long March-Yan'an model-founding generation.)

Another group of older economists had been trained in the West. Among this group were Ma Yinchu (1882–1982; Columbia PhD 1914) and Harvard PhDs Chen Daisun (1900–1997)[55] and Xu Dixin, (1906–1988).[56] Trescott (2007) finds this cohort to have been heavily influenced by the old institutionalist school, the

Social Gospel of Christian educational institutions, Keynesian theorists who emphasized the crisis prone potential of capitalist economies, and other strains of Western economic thought critical of laissez-faire capitalism. He suggests this tradition left Chinese economists interested in mechanisms for the social governance of markets.[57] Trescott (2007, 292) also notes that during the 1940s and immediately after the Revolution, a significant portion of Western trained economists left China (about 30 percent in his sample, more than 50 percent of those with PhDs, and presumably those least sympathetic to the Revolution).

The Western trained economists remaining in China transmitted a qualified endorsement of market activity, if accompanied by appropriate government constraints and complementary activity. Their influence increased as economic reform expanded. With government support, Chen Daisun became the head of the Association for the Study of Bourgeois Economic Theory in 1978 and prepared introductory economics courses for high level cadres including Zhao Ziyang (Sung and Chan 1987, 32). Xu Dixin led groups of Chinese economists to conferences and/or seminars in Hong Kong and the US in March and November 1980.[58]

### 3.4.2 Second generation: those born 1910–1929

The second group of reform economists by age were born between 1910 and 1929. Du Runsheng (b. 1913) Yu Guangyuan (b. 1915), Ma Hong (b. 1920), Jiang Yiwei (b. 1920), Liu Guoguang (b. 1923 or 1924), Pu Shan (b. 1923) He Jianzhang (b. 1925), Fang Sheng (b. 1925), Dong Fureng (b. 1927), and Zhou Shulian (b. 1929) are representative of this group. They had often been junior partners of members of the first group. They also were involved with revolutionary activity and addressing practical problems in constructing socialism. Both of these groups had identities tied to the dream of socialism. Their interest in economics was part of this larger intellectual project. Their background included a sense of history and, at times, field work involving direct contact with rural and/or urban poverty Although many of their papers elaborated the serious shortcomings of the Chinese economy, especially its economic waste, their reaction was to look for solutions within a socialist framework.

Many of these first two groups of economists were sharply attacked and some were even imprisoned during the Maoist periods, especially during the Cultural Revolution. Their experiences were traumatic, but seem not to have dislodged their commitment to socialism. Sun Yefang, for example, was prevented from publishing his criticisms of Chinese central planning after 1961, except for an article published under a pseudonym in 1963 (Lin 1984, 357). He was imprisoned from 1968–1975,[59] but would remark in 1981, " 'In the past I was a 'revisionist,' but now I seem 'conservative,' or even a little 'left.' But those labels don't matter: we should all read a little more of *Das Kapital*' " (Naughton 1986, 149).

Summing up his interviews with Chinese economists in 1988 and 1989, Robert Hsu reported that most economists favored the evolving pattern of reform, with its declared aim of building socialism with Chinese characteristics. He found only small minorities urging a return to traditional central planning or the adoption of Western capitalist arrangements (Hsu 1991, 17–19).[60] Fewsmith comes to somewhat similar conclusions, writing "Neither ideologically nor intellectually was China prepared to make an epistemological break with socialist economics" (Fewsmith 1994, 130).

### 3.4.3 Third generation: those born 1930–1945

The third group was born between ~1930–~1945. The youngest members were the first generation to be educated in post-revolution China. Perhaps half of the group would have been in college during the period of Russian guest professors. Among members of this cohort are Zhang Zhuoyuan (b. 1933), Zhao Renwei (b. 1933), and Zhang Wenmin (b. 1937). The oldest members include two key reformers, Wu Jinglian (b. 1930) and Li Yining (b. 1930). This generation contains members who adopted Western economic theory and flirted with supporting a transition to capitalism. Even this group, however, retained commitments to the egalitarian ideals of the socialist period. Most still also came to economics from a deep involvement with practical questions related to China's attempt to build a socialist economy. The key factor distancing this group from earlier ones is their experience with the Cultural Revolution, an event that rivaled the War of Resistance against Japan or the 1949 Revolution as a major psycho-historical backdrop shaping people's lives.

Wu Jinglian is probably the most influential Chinese economist of the reform period, so attention to his experiences has special significance.[61] The social context and psychological dynamics accompanying Wu's academic commitments are revealing of the complicated combination of cognitive and emotional phenomena involved with personal and community paradigm shifts. While some aspects of Wu's personal experience are undeniably unique, the centrality of the Cultural Revolution to his intellectual and emotional life is probably shared by many people of his and subsequent generations. For China's transitional generations (this one and the next), rethinking economics was emotionally charged. Because of Wu's importance, we will look at his experience in some detail.

Wu came from a very well-to-do, forward looking family, which included several generations of important business people and journalists.[62] He inherited a sense of social responsibility from his parents and extended family.[63] He began his intellectual life as a child of the enlightenment, assuming that "Mr. Democracy" and "Mr. Science" would set China free from Western domination and poverty. He thought little about social systems, and assumed he would continue his family's entrepreneurial traditions (Naughton 2013, 126).

The events of the late 1940s led to his disillusionment with the KMT and business as usual. He became an enthusiastic follower of Mao's New Democracy movement and a self-identified socialist (Naughton 2013, 127). He was

especially taken by the Marxist historical narrative, writing, "[I] was profoundly impressed by his [Marx's] picture of the miserable life of the working
class during the period of 'primitive accumulation' of British capitalism…"
(Naughton 2013, 127).[64] Wu joined the Communist Party in 1952. He has
maintained a strong interest in reducing inequality, though it now often
seems refracted through the lens of classical liberalism and supply-side
economics.

Naughton portrays Wu's intellectual journey as beginning and ending (at
least through age 83) with a middle class vision of a modern "democratic,
cultured, China," with a 15–20 year Marxist phase sandwiched in between
(Naughton 2013, 99). (I would substitute the word "capitalist" for "prosperous" in Naughton's description.)

Wu graduated from Fudan University with a degree in economics in 1954.
He was taught mainly by Russian professors.[65] His graduation at the top of his
class earned him a position at the Chinese Academy of Sciences' Institute of
Economics (IoE).[66] In the mid 1950s, he reports being puzzled by the economic fluctuations and apparent conflict of interests in the emerging planned
economy (Naughton 2013, 129). He writes,

> It was not that I doubted the socialist ideal. … I doubted that the Soviet-
> style economic management system would be able to realize the ideal of
> socialism.
>
> (Naughton 2013, 129)

In 1956 Wu embraced Mao's critique of Soviet planning ["On the 10 Major
Relationships"] as over-centralized and leaving too little room for local initiative (Naughton 2013, 129). About the same time he became interested in
Eastern European ideas about economic reform and Sun Yefang's ideas. Sun
favored a greater role for market processes, and rejected the hostility of the
"natural economy" perspective toward market adjustments. Sun did so within
a Marxist framework that interpreted the labor theory of value as endorsing
market discovery of socially necessary labor times. Wu would later hold on to
Sun's endorsement of market adjustments, but situate this role in a neoclassical (marginalist) rather than Marxist context.

Wu's exploration of reformist ideas was cut short by the Anti-Rightist
Campaign in the aftermath of the Hundred Flowers experiment and the
Movement to Criticize Yugoslavian Revisionism (Naughton 2013, 131). Wu
faced charges of being a right deviationist (Naughton 2013, 106–107). His
parents were harshly criticized, publicly humiliated, and punished economically for raising criticisms of government policy during the Hundred Flowers
Campaign. The attack on his parents and the milder attack on himself were
traumatic for Wu.[67] He writes,

> I held the conviction that I had to wash away the 'original sin' of being a
> 'bourgeois intellectual'. … I tried to persuade myself that ideas about

using economic mechanisms to steer the economy, or emphasizing material incentives ... were all dangerous ideas rooted in capitalism or revisionism.

(Naughton 2013, 2012, 131)[68]

Wu's articles in *Economic Research* (*Jingji Yanjiu*) in 1961–1962 tied China's economic difficulties to its failure to take Marxist attacks on market economies far enough. From 1964–1966, he was part of an Institute of Economics team sent to the countryside (in Naughton's words) "to criticize, remold, and replace rural leadership cadres" (Naughton 2013, 109), or from another perspective, to motivate and explain the government's economic policies.

In the aftermath of the failures of the Great Leap Forward, Sun Yefang's suggestions for expanding market mechanisms in China gained more policy attention. This brought attacks on Sun from Kang Sheng, one of the future leaders of the Cultural Revolution. Wu joined in these campaigns against Sun. He later cited his attacks on Sun and criticism of his parents during an anti-rightist campaign in the 1950s as the two biggest regrets of his life.[69]

The Cultural Revolution brought factional strife to CASS (1966–1969) and wholesale removal of its members to the countryside (1969) for re-education and physical labor (Naughton 2013, 110–111). At first Wu was asked to handle farming, carpentry, and electrician tasks. Subsequently he was labeled a counterrevolutionary and assigned more onerous or meaningless tasks (Naughton 2013, 138).[70] Eventually the "vast national catastrophe" (Wu's words) of the Cultural Revolution led him to question his beliefs (Naughton 2013, 132).[71]

Unexpectedly, the exile to the countryside allowed him to read widely in economics, politics, and world history. His partner in these readings was Gu Zhun, a similarly exiled, and more severely persecuted, unorthodox Marxist thinker. Gu's fresh ideas about the ability of market feedback to beneficially inform economic decisions, his translations of Western heterodox economists, such as Joan Robinson and Joseph Schumpeter, his persecution, and skepticism about the merits of revolutionary rather than gradual change, deeply affected Wu.

Wu was with Gu when he died in 1974. More than 30 years later Wu recounted, "Gu Zhun had a profound influence on me; I should say that it was under his influence that my life journey took a radical turn" (Liu Hong 2006, 12). The endnote below gives some additional background about Gu's life that is helpful in understanding his impact on Wu's thinking.[72]

Wu's emerging caution about revolutionary social change, echoing Gu's thinking (Naughton 2013, 90–91), may have contributed to his reservations about reducing the use of material incentives in the economy. This is because the absence of material incentives requires the development of alternative forms of social coordination and social regulation. I suspect Wu's sympathy for recruiting Adam Smith's selfish baker and butcher was fear of the alternative, which he perceived as "struggle sessions" and denunciations, public humiliations, social labeling, neighborhood watch groups within the *danweis*, public discussion of work points in Dazhai settings, and of course the mob-like terrors of the cultural revolution.[73]

In 1972, the CASS staff were sent back to Beijing (Naughton 2013, 141). It appears that there was at first little institutional direction. Wu, for example, simply went home (Naughton 2013, 141). In 1975 Wu was asked to be part of a book project analyzing the Dazhai economy. His research contradicted the popular image during the Maoist period of Dazhai as an agricultural success story and further disillusioned him about Chinese economic practices (Naughton 2013, 114–115).

After the beginning of economic reform, Wu was invited to renew his collaboration with older CASS reformers, such as Ma Hong, Yu Guangyuan and Xue Muqiao (Barboza 2009b, 8). He participated in a series of seminars arranged by Yu Guangyuan criticizing ultra-leftists (1977–1978) (Naughton 2013, 132). Building on Gu's ideas and work by Ota Sik of Czechoslovakia and Wlodzimierz Brus of Poland, Wu began to think about economic reform in terms of economic systems rather than discrete elements (Naughton 2013, 146, 179–185).

It was at this point that the last piece in the puzzle fell into place, the wholesale substitution of neoclassical economics for Marxist economics facilitated by a year's study in the United States. As early as 1978, Wu's daughter indicates that

> he started to learn Western economics. ... He started to study mathematics. ... He went to Beijing Normal University ... to take undergraduate courses. ... He went to Yale in 1983 ... and he enrolled in undergraduate and graduate courses.
>
> (Barboza 2009b, 9; see also Naughton 2013, 148–153)[74]

His experience at Yale completed his adoption of a new world view. As he explains,

> After studying at Yale, I have a different outlook on reform.[75] I got to have a vision of the market economy.
>
> (Barboza 2009b, 8)

Elsewhere, he adds,

> What bewilders me today is how utterly convinced of these views [Marxist socialism] I was then ... it was just a kind of faith in socialism itself ... reinforced by the economic achievements made by New China in early 1950s.
>
> (Naughton 2013, 128)

To some extent, Wu's intellectual shift can be analogized to a conversion experience, where a new world view fills the vacuum created by the disintegration of older beliefs. Part of this transformation involved the adoption of neoclassical theory's subtexts, including its definition of the field. He writes,

> My studies at Yale led me to new understandings … the subject of economics was the creation of material wealth … the ultimate criterion to measure the strength and weakness of any theory and practice of economic structural reform was to decide whether it would ensure effective allocation of resources.
>
> (Naughton 2013, 148–149)[76]

All references to economics' potential contribution to understanding the "laws of motion" of capitalist society as a whole or economics' contribution to building socialism are gone. Also downplayed in Wu's new outlook are concerns about the lived experiences of workers in the workplace. The focus is almost entirely on the "creation of material wealth."[77]

Wu also adopted the explanations of new institutionalist economists for England's surging state power and economic growth in the eighteenth and nineteenth centuries. He cites, for example, the work of Douglas North, Nathan Rosenberg, and James Buchanan. These histories stress the importance of private property rights and minimal government intervention in the economy (Naughton 2013, 86–89).

It is interesting to speculate on what might have caused the different intellectual outcomes for Sun Yefang and Wu Jinglian. Among the possibilities are Wu's younger age, his personal background, his potentially greater personal contact with the sufferings of the Cultural Revolution, his year in the United States, and his direct policy engagement with the reform process.

After Wu came back from Yale in 1984, he wrote a major paper with Ma Hong on the commodity economy under socialism. Their report helped shape government thinking at the highest levels. Thereafter Wu become an important policy adviser (Naughton 2013, 117).

The "conversion" experience of Yang Xiaokai (born 1948, and a member of the next generation) was even more encompassing than Wu's. The son of two relatively high-ranking CPC parents, Yang became a Red Guard during the Cultural Revolution. He was imprisoned for 10 years for writing a widely publicized essay criticizing the Chinese state for developing a new ruling class. During his imprisonment he learned English and calculus and developed a deep friendship with a devout Christian, leading to his eventual conversion to Christianity in 2002. To escape his past reputation, he changed his name and, with the help of a Ford Foundation fellowship, eventually earned a PhD in economics from Princeton University in 1988. He wrote innovative, neoclassically oriented analyses of the division of labor.[78]

Li Yining seems to have reacted in a somewhat similar, though less dramatic, fashion to his experience during the Cultural Revolution. "I suffered a great deal … I did forced labor … my head [was] shaved" (Kuhn 2011, 98). "During the six years I was in the countryside, my views about China's economy changed. … The whole of China's economy was almost destroyed. That was when I knew that China should not follow the Soviet path" (Kristof 1989a).

### 3.4.4 Fourth generation: those born 1945–1960

The fourth generation of Chinese economists were all schooled after the founding of the PRC. They reached college age just as the Cultural Revolution was closing China's universities for a decade. Like the previous generation, many had experienced the idealism and enthusiasm of the early years of the PRC and the chaos and anxieties of the Cultural Revolution.[79] Because of the suspension of higher education, many students in this cohort began their college and graduate school education later than other students. Important members of this group were strongly influenced by the return of Western economics to China. Beginning in the late 1970s and accelerating in the 1980s, there was a growing presence of visiting Western economists, Western economic texts, Western economic policy advisors, and academic exchange programs that sent Chinese economists to the West, especially to the United States. In 1987, the Ford Foundation's representative in China, Andrew Watson, judged that, "(i)n many ways, the impact of foreign scholarship has been greater in economics than in any other area of study" (Watson 1987, 85). Chapters 8 and 9 discuss the dynamics of how this presence interacted with political-economic events to reorganize Chinese economics education and academic research.

Describing this cohort, Fewsmith writes,

> a new generation of young economists were emerging … less attached to the institutions and ideas of the CCP … many of them had a mathematical background and all of them had, to some extent, studied Western economics. It might also be said, however, that their training was incomplete; few of them had studied overseas.
>
> (Fewsmith 1994, 136)

To nurture a community of reformist economists, the Economic Reform Institute and the Beijing Association of Young Economists were established, along with a related journal entitled the *Forum of Young Economists* (Fewsmith 1994, 136). While most of this group were completely educated in China, key members of this cohort did all of their graduate work in economics abroad. They would become neoclassical economists. Like many Marxist and socialist Chinese economists from earlier generations, they would support further marketization. They would do so, however, not to build socialism, but to reduce "deadweight losses," get closer to "Pareto optimality," and capture dynamic efficiency.[80] They would eventually staff and lead many of

China's elite economics departments, government posts, and think tanks. Representative of this generation of economists are Yang Xiaokai (b. 1948, Princeton PhD), Zhou Xiaochuan (b. 1948, Qinghua, engineering PhD), Lin Justin Yifu[81] (b. 1952, University of Chicago PhD), Zhu Min (b. 1952, Johns Hopkins PhD), Hua Sheng (b. 1953), Sheng Hong (b. 1954, CASS PhD), Fan Gang (b. 1953, CASS PhD, visiting fellow Harvard/NBER 1985–1987) Wang Dingding (b. 1953), and Zhang Weiying (b. 1959, Oxford PhD). It would not be until the fifth generation of reform economists (those born after 1960) that the full transition from Marxist to neoclassical economics would be complete and an environment established that took the neoclassical framework as natural.

By the late 1980s, China's economy and economic ideology were moving forcefully toward "capitalism with Chinese characteristics." Each step of marketization seemed to undermine the viability of residual institutions in the "planned-egalitarian-economy" and to invite further marketization. The process created powerful new groups with a self-interest in further economic reform. The increasing availability of readymade "free-market" frames, courtesy of the West, also helped organize discourses friendly to expanded economic reform. By the late 1980s, the enterprise reform group, for example, had added Chinese followers of new institutionalist economics, such as the Austrian-libertarian economist Steven Cheung (Zhang Wuchang). These economists were animated by the subtexts of classical liberalism rather than Marxist theory. Cheung had been mentored by Milton Friedman and Ronald Coase and had taught economics in the United States. In the early 1980s, he moved to Hong Kong and significantly influenced both Hong Kong and Chinese economic theory. As early as 1982, he predicted that China's reforms would lead China to capitalism, an outcome he applauded.

## 3.5 Safeguarding Chinese socialism

As marketization organized more and more aspects of the Chinese economy, two fundamental questions emerged: (1) Was it possible to mix planning and market allocation, or did you have to drive on only one side of the road, so to speak? and (2) For Marxist economists, can you capture the efficiency and choice enhancing aspects of markets and competition without creating the class structure and larger, darker, dynamics of a capitalist society? Over time many different answers and associated policy responses would be suggested to these questions. These included:

### 3.5.1 Segmentation

This involved relying on economic planning and markets for different tasks, for example, using economic planning to organize heavy industry and markets to run the service sector; or relying on economic planning for quota covered output and markets for above quota output (as in the dual-track system); or using economic planning for credit allocation and investment decisions and autonomous firms and market forces for judgments about current production.[82]

### 3.5.2 Diversification of ownership structures

This involved relying on markets to allocate all resources but retaining social decisions over ownership arrangements. Market socialism, with all firms owned by their workers, is an example of this strategy,[83] but there are other variants.[84] An early slogan called for public ownership of the "commanding heights." The broadest approach targets certain percentages of firms to be state owned, community owned, worker owned, family owned, small business owned, foreign owned, joint venture owned, etc. Socialist corporatization is a popular version of this strategy. Firms are privatized but large equity shares are held by employees and public bodies.

### 3.5.3 Reliance on ideological movements

The hope in this case is to infuse market activities with "socialist ethics" (a semi-socialist version of the corporate responsibility movement). Chen Yun's marriage of socialist education campaigns to market reforms illustrates a version of this strategy, as does Dong Fureng's defense of the Wenzhou model. Dong writes, "…enterprises hiring more than 20 … workers … operate within a socialist country, and their owners … know how to treat their hired workers, with due consideration" (Dong 1990, 91).[85]

### 3.5.4 Political safeguards

This strategy relies on legal-political regulations to limit the range of capitalist institutions. For many practically-oriented theorists, the trump card for maintaining the socialist character of the reforms was the continued monopoly on political power by the CPC, as enshrined in the Four Cardinal Principles. He and Zhang (1982), for example, indicate that some Chinese economists felt that, "there is no harm in having a smattering of capitalism. … After all … the Communist Party exercises leadership, the state economy is predominant" (He and Zhang 1982, 203).

In Chapters 4 through 7 we will see how pressures for expanding marketization relentlessly eroded these sorts of safeguards that were intended to preserve socialist practices in three specific sectors of the Chinese economy. We will also see how increasing marketization encouraged increasing attention to "Western" economics.

## 3.6 Resolving the debate: the road taken

As Nina Halpern and many others have emphasized, Chinese reforms appeared "experiment-led," rather than "theory-led" (Halpern 1985, 1003–1005).

Ultimately it was Deng Xiaoping's pragmatic thinking that defined the strategy and course taken. Deng seems to have had three main objectives: (1) to increase China's national power; (2) to maintain control of the state by the Communist Party; and (3) to increase economic growth.[86] The last objective was perceived as a prerequisite for the first two as well as an important goal in its own right. There was a sense of urgency in Deng's thinking, due in part to a fear that China was falling dangerously behind the West technologically and, by extension, militarily.[87] To this day, China's growing global prestige has been a major legitimizing force for the government and its economic policies across all classes in China.

Deng was a pragmatist more than a theorist when it came to economics. By this I mean that his instincts were to implement policies that would solve immediate problems without fully situating these policies in a comprehensive theoretical framework. He had, however, some general ideas about economics that informed his thinking:

1   He prioritized economic development, arguing that "development is the only hard truth,"[88] privileged bureaucratic-technocratic authority over participatory decision making, and actively opposed efforts to analyze the social, political, or distributional impact of growth enhancing policies.[89]
2   He assumed that strong material incentives were necessary to accelerate Chinese economic growth and opposed "big-pot" modes of distribution.[90]
3   He favored clear lines of responsibility and centralized decision making within organizations (perhaps because centralization clarified responsibility).[91]
4   He created an environment in which laissez-faire experiments and laissez-faire momentum could evolve, without intending to construct a laissez-faire economic order. Although he was used to exercising authority through military and party hierarchies, he gradually came to see market mechanisms as imposing their own kind of discipline on market participants.[92]
5   He believed China had to open its economy to the outside world in order to catch up with the West technologically.

While he claimed these views were empirically grounded and subject to review, they seem to have been taken as matters of faith by the time he consolidated power in 1978. They were present as early as 1961, finding expression in his policies on enterprise management. They infused his policy initiatives in 1975 before his second fall from power in 1976.[93] They undergirded his support in 1984 for the factory director responsibility system and his "stay the course" support for the Special Economic Zones (SEZs), despite their initially disappointing results. The latter stands in stark contrast to his swift jettisoning of rural collectives in favor of the Household Responsibility System in 1983. The latter decision was especially surprising given Chinese Marxists' traditional fear of the development of petty bourgeois attitudes among the peasantry.[94]

Deng's thinking about economics and markets was not constrained by the authority of a hegemonic economics paradigm, be it classical liberalism and the Washington Consensus that fostered shock therapy on the former Soviet Union (FSU), or traditional Marxism that was hostile to petty commodity production. Both his folksy comments to the effect "it doesn't matter if the cat is white or black if it catches mice," and his more Marxist-oriented rhetoric "practice is the sole criterion of truth" expressed this flexibility. Deng's relatively a-theoretical approach to economic decisions invited incremental experiments in economic policy, an approach the Chinese came to call "crossing the river, groping for stones." This strategy works best if there are no worrisome path dependent choices along the way that require looking ahead to figure out the long run implications of what you are doing.

Over time, Deng's experimental policies congealed into a recognizable pattern. His program called for utilizing capitalist-oriented economic policies to expand the forces of production;[95] while maintaining the Communist Party's monopoly of political power, perhaps to ensure the reforms did not undermine the long run goal of socialism. As early as 1979, the market-oriented economic reforms of 1978 were married to the politics of the Four Cardinal Principles upholding the Party State.[96] In 1997, the 15th National Congress of the Chinese Communist Party declared that this union (also referred to as the "primary stage of socialism") could last for at least 100 years (Wu 2005, 86).

Deng's commitment to marketization called for increased reliance on material incentives, expanded enterprise autonomy, increased competition, and expanded economic coordination through markets. The combination spawned dynamic feedback loops along intersecting economic, political and ideological axes. *Economically*, competitive pressures, and the crowding out of non-material incentives by material incentives, spread marketization across the economy. *Politically*, marketization created a supportive class of family farmers in the countryside and a constituency within the Communist Party, who supported privatization as a means for personal enrichment. *Ideologically*, the reforms gradually popularized in China the metaphors and reference points of a market society. For a while, widely shared increases in living standards also won broad approval.

As the reforms "opened China" to the rest of the world, feedback loops increasingly included influences from overseas Chinese commercial networks and Western economic institutions. The practical discourse of these interactions was the language of the marketplace, the theoretical discourse was neoclassical economics. The "buzzing blooming confusion" of China's economic chain reactions, to borrow William James' characterization of a world interpreted without an organizing framework, increasingly gave way to the organizing logic of neoclassical economics and new institutionalist economics. The historical discussion in Chapters 4 through 7 looks at the history of marketization in three sectors of the economy in order to illustrate how these feedback loops promoted the linked growth of neoclassical economics and capitalism in China.

# Notes

1 Robert Hsu writes,

> Chinese economics ... provides the theoretical underpinnings of the reforms ... theory and practice interact to shape the course of the economy, and the Chinese emphasis on the 'unity' of theory and practice makes it important to understand the theory.
>
> (Hsu 1988, 1211)

See also Sheng (1996, 25).

2 A good case could be made for beginning the period of transition on January 1, 1975 with Deng's first return to power. As Vogel's 2011 account makes clear, Deng initiated many important reforms with respect to: the military, railroads, coal and steel production, education, and scientific and technological policy from January to November 1975. One could even push the beginning of reform back to 1974 when Deng first regained influence in military affairs (Vogel 2011, Chapters 2–4). These initial reforms, however, were more narrowly orchestrated than the broad movements after Mao's death in 1976.

3 While the analysis below emphasizes the devastating effects of many aspects of the Cultural Revolution, these years included some positive accomplishments. For example, affirmative action admission policies gave students from disadvantaged backgrounds greater access to university education (see, for example, Han 2008); (2) agricultural research programs continued; and (3) a successful program of rural industrialization was begun (Meisner 1999, 358). There appears to be some debate over the economic impact of the Cultural Revolution. While most accounts I have read implied serious disruptions, Barry Naughton finds that the Cultural Revolution had only moderate impacts on the level of agricultural and industrial production (Naughton 2007, 74–77). The protection of the economy from massive disruption may have been due to the lessons learned from the Great Leap Forward. Henry Park (1986) claims that every sector of the Chinese economy expanded from 1967–1976, writing "National income grew an average of 4.9% annually; output grew 6.8% annually. ... Even the most tumultuous part of the Cultural Revolution from 1966–1969 saw rapid growth" (Park 1986, 228–229). Amartya Sen similarly notes,

> judged in terms of over-all growth rate the Chinese economy did rather well in the period of the Cultural Revolution ... the period of the Cultural Revolution was certainly not one of economic disaster in the way in which the Great Leap Forward was.
>
> (Sen 1984, 9–10)

4 One of the ironies in this history is that Hua Guofeng was pushed aside by Deng, in part due to the failure of Hua's "big push heavy industry" economic initiative. The strategy was based on planning documents drawn up under Deng's supervision in 1975.

5 Meisner 1999, 415.

6 China developed very potent anti-malaria drugs using artemisinin. Recently, it has apparently become the drug of choice for fighting malaria globally (Tu 2011).

7 For example, Riskin (1987) cites several studies finding a maximum ratio of 3:1 between the director's salary and the average worker's salary in most enterprises (251). China's Gini coefficient for urban household income in 1981 was an incredible .16. The overall Gini for China's income distribution was .33 in 1979 (Riskin 1987, 249). Because many necessities in China were allocated socially rather than through household spending, the Gini coefficient for basic needs consumption was probably even lower than that for household income.

8 Life expectancy increased from about 35 years in 1949 to 65 years in the mid-1970s (Meisner 1999, 419). Female illiteracy rates fell from ~40 percent in 1949 to ~15 percent in 1963, while male illiteracy fell from ~13 percent to ~5 percent over the same period (Bramall 2009a, 194, Figure 6.6). See also Perry and Wong (1985, 3); and Ma (1983, 34).

9 See, for example, Ma (1983) and many of the essays in Wei and Chao (1982).

10 There are debates over the rate of productivity growth during the Maoist period. Riskin cites work by Rawski in 1979 and Tang 1980 that found negative TFP (Riskin 1987, 294). Riskin warns, however, that there are methodological debates over the "appropriate weights for aggregating the various inputs" (Riskin 1987, 294). He also questions the reliability of some of the data used in TFP calculations, due to the underreporting of agricultural output. Bramall also questions orthodox TFP accounting and suggests it overestimates the contribution of capital accumulation and underestimates the role of technological progress, which is often embodied in new equipment (Bramall 2000, 462, 528–529). Regardless of these complexities, there seems to have been a significant increase in productivity growth after the economic reforms.

11 Naughton indicates that according to official Chinese statistics household consumption grew an average of 2.3 percent/year from 1952–1978, but this rate is thought to be overly optimistic by Western experts (Naughton 2007, 80). Urban incomes grew much faster than rural incomes, suggesting very little advance in the countryside. It should be remembered, however, that while private consumption, as measured by per capita income, grew minimally, popular access to public consumption in the form of public education, public health, etc. increased significantly. Ma Hong, for example, implies that SOE employees' compensation in the late 1970s included social benefits equal to at least 80 percent of real wages (Ma 1983, 16).

12 Meisner 1999, 416. Riskin indicates that average grain consumption in rural China was less from 1978–1980 than from 1955–1957, with about 100 million peasants in especially desperate conditions (Riskin 1987, 262). Blecher indicates that grain per capita increased modestly from 288kg in 1952 to 319 kg in 1978, while meat and fish per capita production increased even faster (54 percent for hogs, and 64 percent for fish) (Blecher 2010, 143). Since 1978, agricultural output per acre has about doubled and total grain output increased by ~75 percent (*The Crop Site*, Chinese 2011 Resolution boost Grain Production, Feb 7, 2011, www.thecropsite.com/articles/743/chinese-2011-resolution-boost-grain-production).

13 Riskin estimates that disguised unemployment in rural areas was one third to one-half of the labor force (Riskin 1987, 305). He also finds "overstaffing" and rising unemployment in urban areas, especially after the return to the cities of "rusticated youths" in the middle and late 1970s (Riskin 1987, 265–267).

14 Li Lanqing's account of the conditions preceding China's economic reforms stressed the leadership's concern about the technological gap between the West (and Japan) and China (Li 2009, 52–66). Between 1977 and 1980 China sent 360 fact-finding missions abroad to investigate, among other things, Western technology and management practices. Chinese science and educational institutions sent 472 delegations abroad. Typical findings lamented that China was 20 years behind the West in machine industry technology and far behind the West in computer applications for business (Ibid., 62). Fact-finding trips by Deng to Japan and Singapore and Vice Premier Gu Wu to Western Europe seem to have been especially influential. Li reports that in Japan, Deng learned that Nissan's "annual output averaged 94 vehicles per worker (whereas China's best auto manufacturer … averaged one vehicle per worker)," leading Deng to declare, "Now I know what modernization means …" (Ibid., 59).

15 While there is extensive debate over the magnitude of "excess deaths," 12 million–38 million seems a reasonable range (see for example Bramall (2009a

126–130)). Lin Chun is especially skeptical of common estimates of famine deaths that derive from estimates of "missing people" in the 1960s. She points to doubts about the accuracy of the 1953 census, which reported a 30 percent increase in China's population 1947–1953 (Lin Chun 2013, 218).

16  Riskin reports that during the Cultural Revolution

> ... a large part of the staff that prepared, implemented, and supported planning was attacked and purged. The work of the State Statistical Bureau (SSB) virtually ground to a halt ... for almost 3 years. ... During the 1966–1976 period statistical offices were disbanded, personnel were transferred, and 'large quantities of materials were burned.' ... Without a statistical system, planning is out of the question.
>
> (Riskin 1987, 282)

The staff of the State Statistical Bureau fell from a peak of 675 in 1957 to just 15 people in 1969 (Bramall 2009a, 290). Oksenberg reports the SSB's manpower ceiling feel from 400 on the eve of Cultural Revolution to 13–14 (Oksenberg 1982, 185). Lin (1981, 36) depicts similar conditions. Oksenberg also notes that no statisticians were trained in China's universities from 1966–1981 (Oksenberg 1982, 185).

17  See for example Hsu (1991, 172–174). Based on personal interviews as well as library research, Hsu reported in 1991,

> Chinese reform theory and practice amount to a reinterpretation of socialism but not the abandonment of it in favor of capitalism ... the *ideals* and *potentials* (emphasis in the original) of socialism are still alive and important to many Chinese economists, particularly the older ones who saw the ills of early capitalism in the pre-1949 economy.
>
> (25, 171)

See also Meisner (1996, 213).

18  Among the key reformers who had studied at Russian universities were: Sun Yefang, Dong Fureng, and Liu Guoguang. Chen Yun spent some time in Russia in the 1930s.

19  See Solinger (1981) for an interesting discussion of experiments in the mid-1950s and early 1960s with market oriented reforms. Sung and Chan (1987) find similar echoes (32). The most common reform cycles rotated planning authority between central government institutions and local government institutions.

20  The shift was from concentrating on building socialist institutions and cultural practices to more narrowly defined goals of economic growth. In Marxist language the shift was from prioritizing the restructuring of the social relations of production and the social superstructure to developing the forces of production. The change built on Zhou's call for the "Four Modernizations" in the mid-1970s. Zhou first used the phrase in 1958 (Fang 2013, 305).

21  Chen worked as an underground union organizer in the 1920s and had no formal training after elementary school (Wudunn 1995). He spent the mid-1930s in Moscow (Lardy and Lieberthal 1983), presumably absorbing Soviet economic ideas. Chen began to focus on economic issues in the 1940s. From 1949–1954 he headed a key government committee in charge of economic policy. He seems to have had an excellent grasp of macro coordination issues and practical institutional questions. In the mid-1950s, Chen's intuitive understanding of economic concepts like input-output analysis was reinforced by an evolving partnership with more formally trained reformist economists, such as Dong Fureng and Liu Guoguang, at CASS's Institute of Economic Research, (Lardy and Lieberthal 1983, xxxiii). From early on Chen favored the continuation of limited petty production markets in the countryside and the overall coordination of Chinese economic

growth, especially investment decisions, through central planning. He paid attention to empirical data.

Xue was a self-taught economist. He was a member of the CPC and active in the railways workers' union in the 1920s. This led to his arrest and three-year imprisonment during Chiang Kai-shek's anti-leftist campaign of 1927. A fellow prisoner apparently lent him a Soviet textbook on political economy, leading him to quip, "he had graduated from prison." He apparently only read Marx's Capital during the Cultural Revolution (*Times* online: www.mayacafe.com/forum/topic1sp.php3?tkey=1123762016) He subsequently did extensive field work and empirical research on the conditions of rural life, during which he was influenced by Chen Han-seng, a giant of Chinese social science. He later became director of the National Bureau of Statistics and an ally for Chen Yun's central planning oriented economic policies. He was attacked as a "capitalist roader" during the Cultural Revolution and spent 18 months in detention. Thereafter was "brought back to work in Beijing, sent down again, and brought back once more in 1975," before beginning his leading role in economic reform (Gittings 2005).

Like Xue Muqiao, Ma Hong was also largely a self-taught economist, a youthful member of the CPC and active in the railway workers' union. Aided by Chen Yun, he was accepted into the CPC's Central Party School and after graduation did empirical research on the economy of northeastern China. After the revolution he worked on policy research related to topics such as central planning and the management of manufacturing enterprises. (Sources: Ma 1983; Zhang and Alon 2009; Wikipedia).

22 Plans for an independent Academy of Social Science were actually begun in 1975, but were suspended when Deng lost power for a second time (Vogel 2011, 130). From 1977 to 1982 many new research groups on economics were established at CASS including: the Institute of Industrial Economics, the Institute of Rural Development, the Institute of Finance and Trade Economics, the Institute of World Economics and Politics, and the forerunner of the current Institute of Quantitative and Technical Economics (CASS websites). For a history of CASS, see Sleeboom-Faulkner (2007).

23 Su Shaozhi, director of CASS's Marxism-Leninism-Mao Zedong Thought Institute, indicates that CASS was established to be "a think tank for the reform leaders" (Su 1995, 114).

24 Hu Qiaomu (1978) wrote, "we have not produced enough of the things we need and … some of the things we have produced are not in demand." He laments that the supply of power and raw materials failed to keep up with the needs of production, leaving workers idle at construction and factory sites. He complains that firms paid little attention to economic concerns, adding, "All this points to our lack of ability to do things according to economic laws" (11). By the early 1980s Hu would find the reforms abandoning their socialist goals and would become a major opponent of the direction of change in China.

25 Liu Guoguang was deeply versed in Marxist theory. He was the first Chinese student sent by the PRC to do graduate work in economics in Russia in the early 1950s. His initial research involved Marxian reproduction theory (which corresponds roughly to growth modeling in neoclassical terms). He was heavily influenced by the thinking of Sun Yefang, one of China's earliest Marxist reform economists. Liu Guoguang held important posts in CASS's administrative hierarchy (e.g., one of several Vice Presidents of CASS during much of the 1980s) and was a key official in the parallel Party structure responsible for overseeing CASS in the 1980s and early 1990s. He was removed from that his Party post in 1993, but subsequently returned as an advisor (Sleeboom-Faulkner 2007, Appendix IV).

In 2005 Liu warned that Chinese economic thinking was becoming overly Westernized. Explaining his concerns in 2007, he indicated, "Western economics is necessary. However, it becomes problematic if it replaces Marxism as the mainstream economic system" (Liu Guoguang, Heng Lin interview; website of Chinese Academy of Social Sciences).

26 Among other important reform economists associated with the Chinese Academy of Social Sciences were: Xu Dixin, Hua Sheng, Zhang Zhuoyuan, Dong Fureng, Jiang Yiwei, Xiao Liang, Zhou Shulian, Wang Haibo, Zhang Yulin, Liang Wensen, Xiang Qiyuan, Zhao Renwei, Lin Wei, Zhang Wenmin, and Wang Zhenshi.

27 Oksenberg emphasizes the policy influence of market oriented economists in the early days of reform. He writes, "such people as Du Run-sheng ... or Ma Hong ... played crucial roles ... holding a variety of posts in the commissions, the State Council apparatus, and the CASS research institutes. ... (T)heir influence was very great" (Oksenberg 1982, 177). Cheng Xiaonong highlights the input of young economists "using modern theories and methods," (code words for Western trained economists) in Zhao's think tanks (Cheng Xiaonong 1995, 191).

28 See Keyser (2003, especially Chapter 3) for a detailed discussion of the numerous new research institutes, monthly discussion groups, conferences, and professional organizations that sprouted in the early years of economic reform. Keyser stresses the partnership between Zhao Ziyang and younger reform oriented economists, giving particular attention to the impact of the System Reform Institute.

29 Hsu singled out economists at CASS's Institute of Economics and Institute of Industrial Economics as being especially important to the reform movement. Among the economists he highlights are: Sun Yefang, Liu Guoguang, Jiang Yiwei, Dong Fureng, and Zhou Shulian (Hsu 1991, 18). The collaboration between the World Bank and economists at CASS was probably especially influential.

30 Wu Jiang nicely illustrates this view by satirically characterizing the popular slogan, "taking steel as the key link" as "heavy industry is for heavy industry's sake" (*Peking Review* October 13, 1980, 20).

31 Maoist critiques of Deng's "Twenty Points" agenda, circa 1975, illustrate this suppressed perspective. The critiques called for renewed commitments to self-reliance, class struggle against managerial authoritarianism in the work place, skepticism about specialization, renewed commitments to a long run vision of socialism, and resistance to increasing wage differentials (Riskin 1987, 194–200). The similar outlook of the economics textbook *Fundamentals of Political Economy* (1974) is also frequently assumed to reflect late Maoist and "Gang of Four" viewpoints.

32 For over 20 years Chen had criticized Maoist strategies of continuous mass mobilization for achieving high rates of investment to GDP (> 40 percent). Along with favoring lower rates of investment, Chen advocated a shift in the composition of investment from heavy industry to agriculture and light industry, and an increased use of material incentives (though nothing approaching a pure market system) (Meisner 1996, 209, Schurmann 1968, 196, 198, 202–204). Since the mid-1950s Chinese economists in favor of economic planning have also debated the proper balance between centralized planning at the national level (in the image of the USSR) and more decentralized planning devolving administration to lower levels of government. Mao was an early critic of the Soviet model. Naughton (1995, 64–70) emphasizes a slightly different debate within the planning camp. He contrasts Chen's prudency path with Hua Guofeng's renewed big push heavy industry strategy. He suggests the failure of the latter initiative opened the door to reforms that went beyond revising planning strategies.

33 Xue Muqiao is an exception to this, as he backed the marketization strategy associated more with CASS than the State Planning Commission (Bramall 2000, 474).

34 Fewsmith 1994, 92–96, 112–113.

35 Chen seems to have been well respected by all factions of China's political and economic elite. He seems to have often stood against the tide for ideas he believed in, unrelated to his personal benefit. He was an early critic of excessive centralization in Soviet planning models and one of the few voices brave enough to question Mao's Great Leap Forward plans prior to their failure. He was an early supporter of economic reform, but became a critic when policies seemed to threaten the logic of the kind of planned socialist economy he believed in.

Ma Hong's work was very influential and included aspects of both the adjusters' and marketeers' economic strategies. Besides serving as the director of the Industrial Economic Institute and president of the Chinese Academy of Social Sciences, Ma held key posts in China's policy making bureaucracies, such as the State Council and several commissions. He also mentored and then advised Premier Zhu Rongji. In a very interesting 1983 book entitled *New Strategy for China's Economy*, Ma lays out a critique of past practices similar in many ways to Chen Yun's criticism. He calls for major revisions in the priorities of Chinese economic planning, but not for an abandonment of planning. Specifically, he calls for:

1   lowering the share of investment and raising the share of consumption in national income
2   lowering the share of investment dedicated to heavy industry and raising the share allocated for light industry and agriculture
3   raising the share of funds for energy and transportation within heavy industry spending
4   increasing the resources dedicated to services and commerce
5   reducing commitments to regional self-reliance and encouraging greater specialization based on local economic parameters
6   reducing emphasis on grain and steel production
7   elevating the goal of increased economic efficiency (cost minimization) in economic planning
8   greater attention to environmental issues.

Besides urging the above shift in planning priorities, Ma recommends some broader institutional changes involving:

1   greater use of markets and feedback from supply and demand to coordinate resource allocation (often expressed in terms of adherence to the Law of Value)
2   greater enterprise independence
3   greater use of material incentives in the form of responsibility systems and the socialist principle of compensation according to work (sometimes expressed as substituting the image of the Chinese economy as a planned socialist commodity economy for the image of the Chinese economy as a natural economy)
4   development of a more "rational" price structure
5   greater attention to population issues.

Alongside these reform measures, Ma retained many commitments to classical Chinese socialist policies, such as

1   the centrality of public ownership
2   continued economic planning (though alongside a supplemental market sector) with planning taking the form of "guidance" as well as "mandatory" planning
3   compensation according to labor
4   a commitment (at least rhetorically) to maintaining the workers as managers of their enterprises (120)

5    a call for ideological work to counter the avarice likely to accompany the expansion of markets and material incentives (100).

What is not clear in Ma's very thoughtful book is whether the recommended reforms for increasing economic efficiency carry a dynamic inconsistent with the maintenance of the text's traditional socialist principles. I suspect that Ma's policies took reform further than Chen Yun's preferences. Zhao's comments in *Prisoner of the State* support this impression (Zhao 2009, 91–94).

36  Hsu 1991 indicates that the term "primary stage of socialism" was first used in 1981 and became part of the CCP's official ideology in 1987 (Hsu 1991, 11–12). Margaret Sleeboom-Faulkner credits Yu Guangyuan with popularizing the idea of China as being in the "first stage of socialism" (Sleeboom-Faulkner 2007, 63). The term "advanced primary" stage of socialism might actually have been more appropriate. In defending the expanded use of markets, for example, Liu Guoguang argued that central planning was effective in the early days of China's socialist development. However, "once there is a higher level of economic development ... a planned economy ... is less and less suitable, and it needs to move as soon as it can towards becoming a market economy..." (Liu 2003/1992, 104).

    Primary stage theory was used by advocates of reform in many different sectors of the economy. In 1982, for example, Fang Sheng wrote in favor of expanding self-employment and family businesses in economic sectors with relatively low levels of technological development (such as restaurants and handicrafts). He cited many passages from Marx's writing in support of maintaining the "individual economy," noting the persistence of small family businesses

> bears out the Marxist truth that a social order never perishes before all the productive forces for which it is broadly sufficient have been developed.
>
> (Fang 1982, 174)

His appeal to Marxist theory seems genuine and not an after the fact apology for capitalist production (Fang 1982). Whether he still felt the same way in 1992 is uncertain. In an interview in the *People's Daily* he "urged 'absorbing certain views, models, and methods from contemporary bourgeois economic theories'—even if it meant that 'exploitation' would exist in China for a while" (Fewsmith 2008, 65).

37  Illustratively, in 1980, Yu Guangyuan, a leading Chinese political economist and Vice-President of the Chinese Academy of Social Sciences, declared: "The basic Marxist approach to socialist ownership is: anything that can best promote the development of the productive forces..." (*Peking Review* December 8, 1980, 13).

38  Naughton provides a very interesting analysis of the political-theoretical battles involved with naming the Chinese reforms. He argues that Chinese political economic discourse has been bounded by proactive limitations on the discussion of public policies. These boundaries are marked to a degree by the adoption of approved slogans or what Naughton calls "authorized expressions." He argues that Wu was instrumental in defining Chinese economic reform in 1984 as constructing a "commodity economy with planning" (Naughton 2013, 162). The key shift was from reorienting planning (the adjusters' strategy) to creating a market economy with planning, with the degree and kind of planning conditioned by the logic of a market economy.

    In 1992 Liu Guoguang also stressed the significance of the naming shift from a "planned economy" to a "socialist market economy," and the difference between a "socialist market economy" and a "capitalist market economy." The latter difference basically boiled down to control of the state by the Communist Party and public ownership of key enterprises (Liu 2003/1992).

39  See, for example, Hsu (1991, Chapter 2); Sun (1995, Chapter 2); Misra (1998, Chapter 3); Liu (2003/1992); and Wu (2005, 61–62).

40 There was significant debate over the role of markets in operationalizing the law of value. Both Sun Yefang and Hu Qiaomu, for example, believed that planners could calculate ESNALTs without market feedback. Liu Guoguang, Zhao Renwei, and Zhang Zhuoyuan argued that market forces were necessarily involved with the functioning of the law of value (Fewsmith 1994, 62, 64–66).

41 Sung and Chan (1987, 33); Fewsmith (1994, 62); Brugger and Kelly (1990, 99).

42 Cyril Lin (1984) seems similarly impatient with Sun Yefang's efforts to relate his theory of price determination, enterprise autonomy, and profit targeting to classical Marxist texts.

43 Wu Jinglian, for example, seems impatient with efforts by Marxist policy makers to determine when the number of wage workers transforms an enterprise from a family business, or petty commodity firm into a capitalist firm, with broader implications for the direction of the economy (Wu 2005, 65, note 44).

44 Meisner 1996, 209–219. See Naughton (1986) for an interesting account of Sun's life and his ideas about how to combine market forces and economic planning. Trescott (2007, 306) indicates Sun had studied in Moscow with Leontief and was familiar with work by Lange and Liberman on socialist economic policy.

45 Wu finds Sun's reform strategy very similar to that of the Polish economist Wlodzimierz Brus (Wu 2005, 37). China's Marxist economists explored many different ownership options, from the traditional Chinese practice of large central government State-Owned Enterprises (SOEs), to more provincial and local government owned enterprises, to worker-owned enterprises, to joint stock owned enterprises, to small privately owned (chiefly self-employed) enterprises, in varying degrees and combinations. The discussions attempted to understand the dynamic implications of each change in ownership relations, that is, not only how the changes might address China's perceived economic problems but also what kind of pressures for additional changes the alternations would generate. The participants seemed to understand very well that the economy was a complicated web of relationships and that changes in one area were likely to set off pressures for change in many other areas. They therefore constantly asked what the implications were of these shifts for maintaining a path to socialism, a process which required linking the discussion to various theories about markets and socialism.

46 Jiang is credited by Selden and Lippit with coining the term of an "enterprise based economy." Jiang was deputy director of the Institute for Industrial Economics and editor of an important economics Journal (*Economic Management*) at CASS in the early 1980s ((Selden and Lippit 1982, 321).

47 The term "market socialism" can refer to two related but different kinds of economic systems. The approach cited here imagines a market economy in which wage labor is largely replaced by worker owned firms coordinating their activities through self-interested decisions in markets. The second approach imagines an economy of semi-publicly owned firms in which central planners seek to set prices equal to hypothetical competitive market prices (such that price equals marginal cost) and firms and households are free to maximize profit and utility.

48 As Hsu has suggested, some of the policy debates among PRC economists reflected a broader divide in the socialist camp between those promoting socialism as a cure for the alienation of labor in capitalist societies and those promoting socialism as a response to the "anarchy of the market," and capitalism's tendency for periodic macroeconomic crises, economic inefficiencies, and economic insecurity (Hsu 1991, 82).

49 Zhao Yuezhi (2008, 295); Wang (2003a, 196).

50 Li may have been one of the relatively few economists already sympathetic toward capitalism. He told Robert Kuhn,

My intellectual conversion occurred during the 1960s when I began wondering why we Chinese were so poor while other countries were so developed. ... I realized that our problems could only be blamed on our system. That was when I surreptitiously started to desert the planned economy and accept the market economy.

(Kuhn 2011, 97)

Like the Hungarian economist Janos Kornai, Li believed there was no middle ground between market and planned economies, asserting, "the market economy and the planned economy cannot coexist and cannot be merged ... China is not merging the two systems. ... China is deleting the planned economy and enabling the market economy" (Kuhn 2011, 98).

51 Zhao Yuezhi 2008, 295.
52 In the fall of 1980, for example, Vogel reports that Deng Liqun gave four lectures at the Central Party School, that were so celebratory about Chen's economics, that Deng was accused of promoting a cult of personality (Vogel 2011, 431).
53 "Guidance planning" (as opposed to "mandatory planning") was in many ways analogous to a combination of Keynesian macro policy and industrial policy.
54 Sung and Chan (1987) adopt a similar generational concept. They emphasize these reformers' close past connections with senior political leaders. They portray Xue et al. as "more orthodox" and "dogmatic" than "second-generation" reform economists who they imply were more open to the reformist ideas of Eastern European economists (31).
55 Chen led the Qinghua economics department from 1928–1952 and the Peking University economics department from 1953 until the 1980s (Trescott 2007, 249, 253). He taught courses on the history of economic thought which included sections on Western economics. Trescott reports that he "wrote influential articles on the advantages of market economy" (Trescott 2007, 253). In 1994 Chen warned Chinese economists against uncritically accepting Western economics (Ma and Trautwein 2013, 302).
56 Xu is credited with bringing ecological economics to China in 1980 (Wang Songpei et al. 2004, 1). He presided over several important early conferences and edited some important volumes on ecological economics. He is also the editor of an influential three volume book on Western Marxism entitled *Dictionary of Political Economy* (Brugger and Kelly 1990, 16). While the volume includes an impressive range of Western Marxists and neo-Marxists (ranging from Robert Heilbroner to Harry Braverman and Harry Magdoff), Brugger and Kelly argue the analysis is frequently crude and polemical.
57 Liu Guoguang, a key reform economist, for example, studied with Chen Daisun and Xu Yunan ((Liu-Heng Interview). Xu had been a student of Keynes and Joan Robinson at Cambridge University and translated Keynes's *General Theory* into Chinese (Trescott 2012, 347, 356). The influence of John Dewey's ideas, which received a great deal of attention in the early 1920s, seems to have contributed to the popularity of institutionalist economics in China and may have also predisposed Chinese intellectuals to a more active state role in the economy (Campagnolo 2013).
   Liu Junning, an enthusiastic Chinese Hayekian, repeats Trescott's lament about Chinese intellectuals' historical attraction to John Dewey, Harold Laski, and the French Enlightenment, rather than Karl Popper, Friedrich Hayek, and the Scottish Enlightenment (Liu Junning 2000).
58 Summing up these developments, Andrew Watson, the Ford Foundation's representative in China (circa 1999–2008) reported that these Western trained economists "have been re-appointed to prominent positions ... and are playing an important role in the examination of foreign scholarship" (1987, 85). Watson

contrasts this older group, including those scarred by past attacks on Western economics and those trained in the USSR and China during the 1950s, with China's
younger economists who had no direct contact with older debates. The younger
cohort, which emerged after a generation gap created by the lost decade of the
Cultural Revolution, seems much more comfortable with Western economic
thinking.

59  Naughton 1986, 147. The virulence of the attacks on Sun were difficult for him
to assimilate. In the mid seventies he admitted, "It never occurred to me that an
old Communist Party member like myself could be thrown into a Communist
prison!" (Naughton 1986, 124).

60  Harry Harding reaches a similar conclusion (1987, 79). Hsu also found that economists at research institutes sponsored by the Chinese Academy of Social Sciences
were among the first to utilize Western economic concepts.

61  Naughton (2013) emphasizes Wu's broad influence on post 1980s Chinese economics. He highlights three routes of influence: First, he emphasizes Wu's direct
impact through his own students (such as Guo Shuqing, who became head of
China's Securities Regulatory Commission) and those he mentored (such as Zhou
Xiaochuan, who became head of China's central bank). Other 4th generation
economists who remained close to Wu (according to Naughton) included: Lou
Jiwei, Finance Minister and key manager of China's sovereign wealth fund [major
in computer science and graduate work in econometrics]; Li Jiange, holder of
important posts in the State Council's economic reform institutes [undergrad
mathematics, graduate work at CASS]; Shi Xiaomin, and Wang Xiaoqiang
(Naughton 2013, 168).
   Second, he highlights Wu's direct influence on public policy, through direct
access to Zhao Ziyang, Zhu Rongji, and Wen Jiabao.
   Third, he stresses Wu's influence as a public intellectual, with a large presence
on the internet and in other media (Naughton 2013, ix-xv).

62  Wu's great grandfather set up the first modern factory in Sichuan. His grandfather
and great uncle were involved with major mining and other industrial enterprises.
His father led a major newspaper group. His mother was also a business professional and a social activist (Naughton 2013, 125–126).

63  His mother was active in movements for democracy, the rule of law, and women's
liberation (Naughton 2013, 99–100). His mother's prenuptial agreement (which
preserved her financial independence) was cited by Zhou Enlai as an example of
the material basis necessary for gender equality (Naughton 2013, 121). Three of
his uncles joined the communist party and went to Yan'an (Naughton 2013, 100).
His father co-founded an important independent newspaper.

64  Even after his conversion to neoclassical economics and strong disparagement of
most Marxist economic policy recommendations, Wu's analyses often included
favorable comments about numerous Marxist theories. Naughton's collection of
Wu's writing, for example, includes recent essays with favorable comments about
Marx's theory of underconsumptionism (28), the falling rate of profit (62), and
Engels's *The Condition of the Working Class in England* (93).

65  Naughton 2013, 128; Barboza 2009a.

66  Naughton indicates that among the eight new economists at the institute that year
were Zhang Zhuoyuan and Wu Jiapei, who would be friends with Wu for the
next 50 years.

67  Naughton describes an earlier, milder incident at the IoE which foreshadowed the
potential for the arbitrary exercise of power by high ranking officials. In this case
junior members of the IoE were attacked by the head of the institute for insufficient deference to the latter's agenda for the institute (Naughton 2013, 103).

68  Wu's emotional anguish about his class background seems representative of many
people's experience in these decades. Jonathan Spence describes the "criticism and

self-criticism" groups that many intellectuals participated in. During these sessions people were required to publicly reflect on how their own class backgrounds had shaped and limited their thinking. Spence writes,

> they met with small groups of other intellectuals in joint sessions for discussion and self-criticism, and prepared "autobiographies" in which they analyzed their own past failings and those of their parents. This last requirement caused profound crises for many who had been brought up believing in the strict tenets of filial piety as derived from the Confucian tradition, and in general the entire process subjected the intellectuals to severe mental stress.
>
> (Spence 1990, 564)

69 Barboza 2009b; Liu Hong 2006 11; Naughton 2013, 131–132.
70 Barboza reports Wu was also beaten (Barboza 2009b, 8).
71 Alongside his own hardships and those of his parents and his new friend in exile, Gu Zhun, seven of Wu's uncles were casualties of different political campaigns, including four deaths (Naughton 2013, 101).
72 The discussion below is based on Naughton 2013, especially pages 111–113 and 135–141. Like so many of China's important economists, Gu was an extremely interesting man. He came from a poor family, but seems to have been a child prodigy in accounting and was widely published in the field. When he first met Wu, Gu had been a committed revolutionary for decades. He joined the Party in 1935 and worked as an underground organizer in Shanghai. He later fought with the New 4th Route Army (Naughton 2013, 111–113). After the revolution, Gu was appointed head of Shanghai's Fiscal Bureau (Ibid., 112).

Gu's independence of mind repeatedly caused him problems with the Party's hierarchy. He was fired from his Shanghai post and expelled from the Party in 1952 for reasons thought to involve disagreements over business tax policy. In the mid-1950s he was assigned to the Institute of Economics, where he recommended that firms' performance be assessed using prices that "adjusted according to market forces" (Ibid., 113). While similar to Sun Yefang's thinking, Gu recommended using actual rather than planner calculated market prices (Ibid., 113, 134).

Through a complex turn of events, the anti-rightist campaign following the Hundred Flowers campaign led to his second purge. He was sent to the country-side to do hard labor and while there witnessed the Great Famine (Ibid., 135).

Gu returned to the IoE in 1962, where, among other things, he translated Schumpeter's *Capitalism, Socialism, and Democracy*. He was again designated a rightist and sent to the countryside (~1964) as part of a larger campaign against Sun Yefang (Ibid., 136). He seems to have been officially labeled a rightist for criticizing Mao's cult of personality. From 1968–1972 Wu and Gu's friendship seems to have flourished. They discussed all sorts of books together, from the Bible and Confucianism to Greek history and Western economic and intellectual history (Ibid., 135–136).

In 1972 the staff of CASS returned to Beijing and Gu and Wu discussed the Institute's Western economic journals, such as the *American Economic Review*. Gu translated the *Collected Economic Papers of Joan Robinson*, and, with his help, Wu translated Robinson's *The Crisis of Economics* (Ibid., 141),

Much as with Wu, the Cultural Revolution destroyed Gu's faith in China's revolutionary path. He searched for the origins of the tragedy in structural factors rather than idiosyncratic personalities (Ibid., 138). This lead Gu to support liberal ideas about limited government with checks and balances to prevent the abuse of power by political authorities. Gu's structural critique helped prepare the way for Wu's later break with Marxist economics. Just as some Chinese people's interest in Western religion arose as a transgressive alternative to the ideologies of the Cultural Revolution, some Chinese economists may have been drawn to explore neoclassical economics as an alternative to the political-economy of the Great Leap Forward and Cultural Revolution, which they associated with Marxism.

73 Heilbroner, in *Marxism For and Against*, raises similar concerns about the viability of economic systems that don't rely primarily on material incentives, though more sympathetically; there is a "For" as well as an "Against."

74 During 1983–1984 Wu was officially a guest professor at Yale's Socio-Political Institute (*Chinese Economic Studies* 30(1): 8).

75 In his 1980 essay, "Economic System Reform and Adjustment of the Economic Structure," Wu explores systemic reasons for China's economic problems (Naughton 2013 179–185). He seems to have adopted a classical liberal orientation, without the formal architecture of neoclassical theory. While at Yale, Wu read Samuelson's introductory text, took Michael Montias's Comparative Economic Systems course, and audited undergraduate micro and macro classes.

76 Wu's conversion to neoclassical discourse is reflected in his language, which carries all of the overtones of thinking about the world in a neoclassical fashion. For example, Wu could have used many metaphors and phrasings to describe his mother's work on women's liberation, rule by law, and newspaper publishing. He chose, however, to describe her in market terms. "I feel that my mother's distinctive characteristic was to use an entrepreneur's methods and an entrepreneur's attitude to pursue her goals" (Naughton 2013, 120). Though this description seems partly appropriate, from Wu's other descriptions of his mother, it nevertheless seems reductionist, in a fashion stemming from habits of orthodox economics.

77 Wu felt that the nature and strengths of Western economics had been withheld from him. Neoclassical economics was not, as he had been taught, simply a pure apology for capitalism. This realization left him open to bolder claims by Western economists critical of Marxism and socialism. Huang Fanzhang's account of his interest of neoclassical economics seems quite similar to Wu's experience. From 1954 to 1980 Huang worked at CASS as an economist. He was one of the first five social scientists funded by the Ford Foundation to study in the US, 1980–1982. In a 2006 interview with Norton Wheeler he reported,

> "Before I came to Harvard, I studied at Peking University. … Marxism was the only economics." Learning about market economics from scholars like Martin Feldstein, who became Chairman of President Regan's Council of Economic Advisors in 1984, gave Huang insights into how China might move toward its stated goal of a socialist market economy.
>
> (Wheeler 2012, 118)

Huang later became one of China's directors at the IMF, a vice president of the State Planning Commission's Economic Research Center, and vice chairman of the office of the China Reform Forum (CRF), a think tank associated with the Chinese Communist Party School (Wheeler 2012, 117). It is interesting to think about how intellectual trajectories are maintained. Beginning in 1998 the CRF co-sponsored an annual conference with the RAND Corporation on Chinese economic and security issues. Huang gave a paper on Chinese industrialization at the 2003 conference. He was criticized by his discussant (John Despres) for not addressing the full neoclassical agenda. In a bit of hyperbole Despres ended his remarks with the comment, "too much Karl Marx (and technological dirigisme) and not enough Adam Smith (and market mechanisms)" (www.rand.org/content/dam/rand/pubs/conf_proceedings/2005/RAND_CF195.pdf, accessed September 7, 2014).

78 Interestingly, at the end of his life, after being diagnosed with lung cancer, Yang criticized the materialism and competitive egoism of China's emerging capitalist society (Carol Lee Hamrin, "Rethinking 'Modernity' and its Hold on our Lives," *Pathways* 3–4/2009). (www.globalchinacenter.org/pathways/2009/04/rethinking-modernity-and-its-hold-on-our-lives-part-one.php, accessed July 15, 2014).

79 Besides eventually disillusioning many young people, the Cultural Revolution put millions of "sent down" youth in daily contact with rural life. Some of these rusticated youths with family ties to the Chinese leadership did empirical studies of early rural reforms that helped promote their expansion. Several authors have suggested that the youths' focus on empirical data rebuked a priori Marxist critiques of the reforms.

80 Huang Yasheng, for example, finds, "The most powerful intellectual justification for China's partial reforms is that they have produced a Pareto-optimal outcome" (Huang 2008, 237).

81 Lin's journey to a Chicago economics PhD is Odyssean and illustrates how broad currents sweep up individual participants. Lin grew up in Taiwan. His undergraduate degree is from a Taiwanese military academy. He also holds an MBA from a Taiwanese University (Chou 2008). In May 1979 he defected to the PRC by swimming across the Taiwanese strait! He was motivated by a sense of Chinese nationalism that transcended political tensions between the Taiwanese and Chinese polities. In 1982, he was studying economics at Peking University (Chou 2008) when Theodore Schultz, a University of Chicago economist and Nobel Prize winner was a guest lecturer. At least partially due to his English fluency (a byproduct of his Taiwanese education), Lin was picked to translate. Schultz subsequently helped arrange a scholarship for Lin to study economics at the University of Chicago. When Lin returned to China in 1987, he joined other newly minted US PhDs in revolutionizing China's economics departments. I suspect Lin's "University of Chicago economics with Chinese characteristics," differs from many of his cohort's economics, partially because of his early life in Taiwan (an American protectorate) and lack of direct contact with the Cultural Revolution. Lin has treated the Chicago assumption of rationality as the "Dao" (or underlying essence) of economic thinking (See Lin 2012c). Much of Lin's achievements, of course, reflect his extraordinary talents, but like anyone else, he is both empowered and limited by his background.

82 Interestingly, Keynes liked this option. He felt it a reasonable response to potential aggregate demand problems arising from weak private investment due to the large uncertainties associated with long term capital commitments. Variants of this strategy were put forward by Liu Guoguang and Zhaoi Renwei, who recommended that the plan determine investment levels and the overall level of construction investment, with the details left to autonomous enterprises (Sung and Chan 1987, 33–34; Lin 1984). Sun Yefang similarly favored allowing enterprises to control their own depreciation fund for replacement investment, but called for the state to make new investment choices (Sung and Chan 1987, 35, 39). Traditionally, China had followed Soviet policies, under which the means of production were allocated by planners, explicitly denying that means of production were commodities, thereby limiting market dynamics to a select group of consumer goods (Zhou Shulian 1982, 98–103).

In another variation on this theme Xu Dixin argued, "In the macroeconomy it is necessary to implement strict planned management. In the microeconomy … it is necessary to fully bring to bear the role of market regulation" (Fewsmith 1994, 112). In another dichotomy, market mechanisms were treated as temporary crisis recovery measures, rather than normal parts of the economy (Fewsmith 1994, 111–112).

83 In many ways, collective firms seem the enterprise form most consistent with socialism in a commodified, market economy. Marx was quite explicit in arguing that state-owned firms employing wage labor were likely to reproduce the alienated labor relationship of private capital. Securitization, regardless of the distribution of share ownership, would seem to produce similar results.

84 The simplest form of this strategy held that as long as there was significant public ownership of the means of production, the socialist character of the reforms was

assured. One strategy permitted small private firms, but reserved large scale production for public firms. Until 1988, for example, private firms were officially prohibited from employing more than seven wage laborers who were not family members (Carson 1990, 270). Riskin (citing Jiang Yiwei) highlights a view popular around 1980 that public ownership plus payment according to work were the guarantors of socialism (Selden and Lippit 1982, 316). Lin Zili defended the socialist character of the household responsibility system on the same grounds (Hua, Zhang, and Luo 1993, 54–56).

The shareholding textile firms in Gaoyang offer an interesting model. All shareholders are both workers (usually managers) and investors. In the partnership form of the Gaoyang model, there are relatively high share prices and few partners. The partners often raise capital from friends and relatives in the tradition of micro finance. In the collective form, there are low share prices and many workers-owners. "(T)his creates a work environment that resembles collectively run enterprises" (Grove 2006, 231).

It appears that most firms are fairly small and focused on a single task within textile production: fine wool spinning for knitting yarns, coarse wool spinning for carpet yarn, wool weaving for toweling, wool weaving for woolen fabrics and blankets (Grove 2006, 204–206). The social relations of production would seem to resemble family firms. Most larger firms appear to have a participatory group of owner/managers, lower level managers (who are paid relatively similarly to production workers), and hired labor. There does seem the possibility of a significant divide between investor/manager owners and migrant worker employees.

The "industrial sector" model offers the hope that these small firms can survive as largely worker (family)-owner entities due to their ability to appropriate system wide economies of scale from the clustering (co-location) of many firms. Shares cannot be sold or traded to outsiders. If shareholders wish to leave the company, their shares are bought out by residual members (Grove 2006, 229).

85  A particularly interesting variant of this strategy required owners of firms to labor in their enterprises. This requirement avoided legitimizing the idea of property income, by linking the owner's share of output to their entrepreneurial labor, rather than their property ownership (Carson 1990, 266). It also was intended to keep owners and managers in touch with the work experience of their employees, a goal that baffled some foreign observers (Carson 1990, 344). Carson reports that a West German technician found the Chinese head of a Volkswagen subsidiary sweeping the floor, and "asked, with astonishment, what the man was doing. The reply was that the party leadership required him to do manual labor regularly, so as not to lose touch with the working class" (Carson 1990, 344).

Another practice sought to cultivate quality control concerns among workers by fostering closer personal contact between workers and consumers of their product. Carson reports, for example, that quality control increased significantly at a factory making mining tools after the workers visited the mines and saw the damages caused by their carelessness (Carson 1990, 274).

86  In his famous South China speeches in 1992, for example, Deng argued that the main criterion for judging a public policy should be whether it "'promotes the growth of the productive forces ... increases the overall strength of the socialist state and raises living standards'" (Wu 2005, 88). These so called "Three Favorables" were reaffirmed in a 1997 call by Jiang Zemin to judge different ownership formats in terms of these goals rather than traditional Marxist preferences for public ownership.

87  Deng estimated Chinese science and technology were about 20 years behind the developed world (Vogel 2011, 198; Naughton 1995, 63; Park 1986, 223–224; and Vogel 2011, 122, 128–133, 137–144, 200–2010).

Vogel (2011) argues that in normalizing relations with the US, Deng was interested in expanded trade, but even more interested in educational exchanges. His plans called for sending tens of thousands of students within a few years (Vogel 2011, 321–323).

88 Naughton 2007, 99.

89 Very early in the reform period, for example, he supported the use of competitive exams, rather than workplace recommendations and affirmative action policies, to determine college admission. He also thought it wasteful to require high school graduates to engage in physical labor before going to college. Maximizing economic growth trumped almost all other goals, except for national defense and the political supremacy of the Communist Party.

Li and White (1991) find Chinese intellectuals of all stripes enthralled by the goal of technological advance in the 1980s. They link this infatuation to an elitist, technocratic view of government. They find that the *World Economic Herald*, a leading newspaper hosting debates over economic reform, gave much attention to how to accelerate technological change in China, but relatively little attention to issues involving social welfare, the environment, labor, women, and the elderly (Li and White 1991).

90 In a February 1984 meeting with Shanghai leaders Deng declared, "The 'big pot' practice never worked and never will" (Li Lanqing 2009, 175). Deng, of course, also asserted, "to get rich is glorious" and "some must get rich first."

91 Both Naughton (1993, 498) and Vogel (2011) cite Deng's policies in 1975 (e.g., toward the railroad, steel, and petroleum industries) as foreshadowing his later commitment to centralizing authority and delineating clear lines of responsibility. One of the unintended casualties of this strategy appears to have been interest in participatory management. Naughton finds, "Clearly delineated authority, reinforced by increasingly significant material incentives ... is the most characteristic 'Dengist' element of reform. Of the various 'responsibility systems,' the most important was the 'factory manager responsibility system'" (Naughton 1993, 502).

92 In this regard, Naughton concludes, "Deng displayed a personal talent for *laissez-faire*: he has mastered the ruler's art of non-acting" (Naughton 1993, 492).

93 Deng's efforts in 1975 to restructure the Chinese military, railroads, coal and steel production, education, and scientific and technological policy involved administrative type reforms. As Vogel (2011) makes clear, Deng's initiatives were practically oriented and micro focused on accountability, deploying new leadership teams, modernizing equipment, better workplace discipline, and increased strategic planning (Vogel 2011, 97–114). Deng also created a more theoretically oriented working group (the Political Research Office) to explore more systemic issues (Vogel 2011, 122).

94 During the Cultural Revolution, for example, even modest agricultural product markets were attacked as dangerous "tails of capitalism." A popular Chinese textbook for self and group study of economics in the 1970s (*Fundamentals of Political Economy*), for example, was especially harsh in condemning small peasant markets as "a hotbed of capitalism" (Wang 1977, 262). Lin Chun similarly notes the "peculiarly negative connotation associated with the traditional petty peasant aspiration ... for small holdings of the land" (Lin Chun 2006, 75). Deng's embrace of de facto family farming may have been motivated in part by a desire to create a reliable constituency for economic reform.

Deng's commitments to: (1) clearly delineated lines of responsibility accompanied by strong incentive systems; (2) economic growth as the number one economic goal; and (3) lack of an overall economic vision or theory that could offer an alternative to letting the market work are nicely laid out in Barry Naughton's 1993 article *Deng Xiaoping: The Economist*. Deng's a-theoretical approach to economic policy made it extremely difficult for him to attend to the unintended consequences of numerous short run growth enhancing economic policies.

I suspect, the safeguarding backstop for Deng was continued Communist Party control of the state. The centrality of this control allowed Deng to ignore concerns about the by-products of market-capitalist oriented economic restructuring. It also made challenges to this political monopoly extremely threatening and helps explain the Tiananmen tragedy.

95 In October 1984, the Third Plenary of the 12th CCCPC (a key governing body in China) declared, "'the fundamental task of socialism is to develop social productivity. ... Whether it promotes the growth of the productive forces ... is the most important criterion for the success of any reform'" (Wu 2005, 75).

96 In his crackdown against the Democracy Wall 1979–1981, the anti-spiritual pollution campaign in 1983, or the anti bourgeois liberalization campaign in the late 1980s, Deng repeatedly made it clear that he would not tolerate any ideological challenge to control of the state by the Chinese Communist Party. At the same time, his insulation of economic reformers from severe attacks during the anti-spiritual pollution campaign of 1983 and quick curtailment of the campaign when it appeared to interfere with economic reform, reflected his prioritizing economic restructuring (Watson 1987, 83). Deng's preference for the Hungarian managerial contract responsibility system, over the Yugoslavian, worker self-management, contract responsibility system seems to have reflected a similar preference for the maintenance of centralized authority.

# References

Barboza, David. 2009a. "China's Mr. Wu Keeps Talking." *New York Times*, September 26, 2009, BU1–7.

Barboza, David. 2009b. "Interviews with Wu Jinglian, Shelly Wu and Wu's Biographer." *New York Times*, September 26, 2009.

Blecher, Marc. 2010. *China Against the Tides: Restructuring through Revolution, Radicalism and Reform*. 3rd ed. New York: Continuum.

Brahm, Laurence J. 2002. *Zhu Rongji and the Transformation of Modern China*. Singapore: John Wiley & Sons (Asia).

Bramall, Chris. 2000. *Sources of Chinese Economic Growth 1978–1996*. New York: Oxford University Press.

Bramall, Chris. 2009a. *Chinese Economic Development*. New York: Routledge.

Brugger, Bill, and David Kelly. 1990. *Chinese Marxism in the Post-Mao Era*. Stanford, CA: Stanford University Press.

Campagnolo, Gilles. 2013. "Three Influential Western Thinkers during the 'Break-Up' Period in China: Eucken, Bergson, and Dewey." In *Thoughts on Economic Development in China*, edited by Ying Ma and Hans-Michael Trautwein, 101–121. New York: Routledge.

Carson, Richard L. 1990. *Comparative Economic Systems: Part II Socialist Alternatives*. Armonk, NY: M. E. Sharpe.

Chen, Feng. 1999. "An Unfinished Battle in China: The Leftist Criticism of the Reform and the Third Thought Emancipation." *The China Quarterly* (158): 447–467. doi:10.1017/S0305741000005853.

Cheng, Xiaonong. 1995. "Decision and Miscarriage: Radical Price Reform in the Summer of 1988." In *Decision-Making in Deng's China: Perspectives from Insiders*, edited by Carol Lee Hamrin and Suisheng Zhao, 189–204. Armonk, NY: M. E. Sharpe.

Chou, Jennifer. 2008. "World Bank's Chief Economist Swam to China?" *The Weekly Standard*, February 11, 2008.

Dong, Fureng. 1990. "The Wenzhou Model for Developing the Rural Commodity Economy." In *Market Forces in China: Competition and Small Business; the Wenzhou Debate*, edited by Peter Nolan and Fureng Dong, 77–96. Atlantic Highlands, NJ: Zed Books.

Fang, Fuqian. 2013. "The Changing Status of Western Economics in China." In *Thoughts on Economic Development in China*, edited by Ying Ma and Hans-Michael Trautwein, 295–305. New York: Routledge.

Fang, Sheng. 1982. "The Revival of Individual Economy in Urban Areas." In *China's Economic Reforms*, edited by Lin Wei and Arnold Chao, 172–185. Philadelphia, PA: University of Pennsylvania Press.

Fewsmith, Joseph. 1994. *Dilemmas of Reform in China: Political Conflict and Economic Debate*. Armonk, NY: M. E. Sharpe.

Fewsmith, Joseph. 2008. *China since Tiananmen: From Deng Xiaoping to Hu Jintao*. 2nd ed. New York: Cambridge University Press.

Gittings, John. 2005. "Xue Muqiao: The Architect of China's Market Transformation." *Guardian*, August 17, 2005, 24.

Grove, Linda. 2006. *A Chinese Economic Revolution: Rural Entrepreneurship in the Twentieth Century*. Lanham, MD: Rowman & Littlefield.

Halpern, Nina P. 1985. "China's Industrial Economic Reforms: The Question of Strategy." *Asian Survey* 25 (10): 998–1012. doi:10.2307/2644177.

Han, Dongping. 2008. *The Unknown Cultural Revolution: Life and Change in a Chinese Village*. New York: Monthly Review.

Harding, Harry. 1987. *China's Second Revolution: Reform After Mao*. Washington, DC: Brookings.

He, Jianzhang and Wenmin Zhang. 1982. "The System of Ownership: A Tendency Toward Multiplicity." In *China's Economic Reforms*, edited by Lin Wei and Arnold Chao, 186–204. Philadelphia, PA: University of Pennsylvania Press.

Hinton, William. 1990. *The Great Reversal: The Privatization of China 1978–1989*. New York: Monthly Review.

Hsu, Robert C. 1988. "Economics and Economists in Post-Mao China: Some Observations." *Asian Survey* 28 (12): 1211–1228. doi:10.2307/2644742.

Hsu, Robert C. 1991. *Economic Theories in China 1979–1988*. New York: Cambridge University Press.

Hu, Qiaomu. 1978. "Observe Economic Laws, Speed Up the Four Modernizations." *Peking Review* 21 (45): 7–12.

Hua, Sheng, Xuejun Zhang, and Xiaopeng Luo. 1993. *China: From Revolution to Reform*. Studies on the Chinese Economy, edited by Peter Nolan and Fureng Dong. London: Macmillan Press.

Huang, Yasheng. 2008. *Capitalism with Chinese Characteristics: Entrepreneurship and the State*. New York: Cambridge University Press.

Keyser, Catherine. 2003. *Professionalizing Research in Post-Mao China: The System Reform Institute and Policymaking*. Armonk, NY: M. E. Sharpe.

Kristof, Nicholas. 1989a. "'Mr. Stock Market': Li Yining; Selling China on a 'Public' Privatization." *New York Times*, January 8, 1989.

Kuhn, Robert. 2011. *How China's Leaders Think*. Singapore: Wiley.

Lardy, Nicholas, and Kenneth Lieberthal, eds. 1983. *Chen Yun's Strategy for China's Development*. Armonk, NY: M.E, Sharpe.

Li, Cheng, and Lynn T. White III. 1991. "China's Technocratic Movement and the World Economic Herald." *Modern China* 17 (3): 342–388. doi:10.1177/0097700 49101700302.

Li, Lanqing. 2009. *Breaking Through: The Birth of China's Opening-Up Policy*. New York: Oxford University Press.

Lichtenstein, Peter M. 1992. "The Political Economy of Left and Right during China's Decade of Reform." *International Journal of Social Economics* 19 (10): 164–180. doi:10.1108/EUM0000000000510.

Lin, Chun. 2006. *The Transformation of Chinese Socialism*. Durham, NC: Duke University Press.

Lin, Chun. 2013. *China and Global Capitalism: Reflections on Marxism, History, and Contemporary Politics*. New York: St. Martins Press.

Lin, Cyril Chihren. 1981. "The Reinstatement of Economics in China Today." *The China Quarterly* (85): 1–48. doi:10.1017/S0305741000028010.

Lin, Cyril Chihren. 1984. "*Review of Social Needs Versus Economic Efficiency in China. Sun Yefang's Critique of Socialist Economics* ed. by K. K. Fung." *The China Quarterly* (98): 357–361. www.jstor.org/stable/653821.

Lin, Justin Yifu. 2012c. *Benti and Changwu: Dialogues on Methodology in Economics*. Beijing: Peking University Press.

Liu, Guoguang. "Interview with Dr. Heng Lin." Chinese Academy of Social Sciences website: experts, 1st group CASS members, Liu Guoguang, http://casseng.cssn.cn/experts/experts_1st_group_cass_members/201402/t20140221_969619.html.

Liu, Guoguang. 2003 [1992]. "Some Issues Relating to the Theory of the Socialist Market Economy." In *China's Economic Reform: A Study with Documents*, edited by Christopher Howe, Y. Y. Kueh, and Robert Ash, 97–107. New York: Routledge.

Liu, Hong. 2006. "'My Life is Closely Connected with China's Reform'—A Brief Biography of Professor Wu Jinglian." *The Link*: 9–15.

Liu, Junning. 2000. "Classical Liberalism Catches on in China." *Journal of Democracy* 11 (3): 48–57.

Ma, Hong. 1983. *New Strategy for China's Economy*. Beijing: New World Press.

Ma, Ying, and Hans-Michael Trautwein, eds. 2013. *Thoughts on Economic Development in China*. New York: Routledge.

Meisner, Maurice. 1996. *The Deng Xiaopeng Era: An Inquiry into the Fate of Chinese Socialism 1978–1994*. New York: Hill and Wang.

Meisner, Maurice. 1999. *Mao's China: A History of the People's Republic*. 3rd ed. New York: Free Press.

Misra, Kalpana. 1998. *From Post Maoism to Post-Marxism: The Erosion of Official Ideology in Deng's China*. New York: Routledge.

Naughton, Barry. 1986. "Sun Yefang: Toward a Reconstruction of Socialist Economics." In *China's Establishment Intellectuals*, edited by Carol Lee Hamrin and Timothy Cheek, 124–154. Armonk, NY: M. E. Sharpe.

Naughton, Barry. 1993. "Deng Xiaoping: The Economist." *The China Quarterly* (135): 491–514. doi:10.1017/S0305741000013886.

Naughton, Barry. 1995. *Growing Out of the Plan: Chinese Economic Reform 1978–1993*. New York: Cambridge University Press.

Naughton, Barry. 2007. *The Chinese Economy: Transitions and Growth*. Cambridge, MA: MIT Press.

Naughton, Barry, ed. 2013. *Wu Jinglian: Voice of Reform in China*. New York: Cambridge University Press.

Oksenberg, Michel. 1982. "Economic Policy-Making in China: Summer 1981." *The China Quarterly* (90): 165–194. doi:10.1017/S0305741000000308.

Park, Henry. 1986. "Postrevolutionary China and the Soviet NEP." *Research in Political Economy* 9: 219–233.

Perry, Elizabeth J., and Christine Wong, eds. 1985. *The Political Economy of Reform in Post-Mao China*. Cambridge, MA: Harvard University Press.

Qian, Yingyi, and Jinglian Wu. 2000. *China's Transition to a Market Economy: How Far Across the River?* Working Paper no. 69. Stanford, CA: Center for International Development, Stanford University.

Riskin, Carl. 1987. *China's Political Economy: The Quest for Development since 1949*. New York: Oxford University Press.

Schurmann, Franz. 1968. *Ideology and Organization in Communist China*. 2nd ed. Berkeley, CA: University of California Press.

Selden, Mark and Victor Lippit, eds. 1982. *The Transition to Socialism in China*. Armonk, NY: M. E. Sharpe.

Sen, Amartya. 1984. *Resources, Values and Development*. Cambridge, MA: Harvard University Press.

Sheng, Hong. 1996. "A Survey of the Research on the Transitional Process of Market-Oriented Reform in China." *Chinese Economic Studies* 29 (2): 5–38.

Shirk, Susan. 1993. *The Political Logic of Economic Reform in China*. Los Angeles, CA: University of California Press.

Sleeboom-Faulkner, Margaret. 2007. *The Chinese Academy of Social Sciences (CASS): Shaping the Reforms, Academia and China*. Boston, MA: Brill.

Solinger, Dorothy J. 1981. "Economic Reform Via Reformulation in China: Where do Rightist Ideas Come from?" *Asian Survey* 21 (9): 947–960. doi:10.2307/2643824.

Spence, Jonathan D. 1990. *The Search for Modern China*. New York: Norton.

Su, Shaozhi. 1995. "The Structure of the Chinese Academy of Social Sciences and Two Decisions to Abolish its Marxism-Leninism-Mao Zedong Thought Institute." In *Decision-Making in Deng's China: Perspectives from Insiders*, edited by Carol Lee Hamrin and Suisheng Zhao, 111–117. Armonk, NY: M. E. Sharpe.

Sun, Yan. 1995. *The Chinese Reassessment of Socialism 1976–1992*. Princeton, NJ: Princeton University Press.

Sung, Yun-wing and Thomas M. H. Chan 1987. "China's Economic Reforms: The Debates in China." *The Australian Journal of Chinese Affairs* (17): 29–51. doi:10.2307/2158967.

Trescott, Paul B. 2007. *Jingji Xue: The History of the Introduction of Western Economic Ideas into China, 1850–1950*. Hong Kong: Chinese University Press.

Trescott, Paul B. 2012. "How Keynesian Economics Came to China." *History of Political Economy* 44 (2): 341–364. doi:10.1215/00182702-1571737. https://knox.idm.oclc.org/login?url=http://search.ebscohost.com/login.aspx?direct=true&db=bsh&AN=76282605&site=ehost-live.

Tu, Youyou. 2011. "The Discovery of Artemisinin (Qinghaosu) and Gifts from Chinese Medicine." *Nature Medicine* 17 (10): 1217–1220. doi:10.1038/nm.2471. https://knox.idm.oclc.org/login?url=http://search.ebscohost.com/login.aspx?direct=true&db=a9h&AN=66445377&site=ehost-live.

Vogel, Ezra F. 2011. *Deng Xiaoping and the Transformation of China*. Cambridge, MA: Harvard University Press.

Wang, George C. ed. 1977 [1974]. *Fundamentals of Political Economy*. The China Book Project: Translations and Commentaries. Translated by K. F. Fung. White Plains, NY: M. E. Sharpe.

Wang, George C. 1979. "Editor's Introduction." *Chinese Economic Studies* 12 (3).

Wang, Hui. 2003a. *China's New Order: Society, Politics, and Economy in Transition*, edited by Theodore Huters. Cambridge, MA: Harvard University Press.

Wang, Songpei, Maoxu Li, and Dai Wang. 2004. *The Emergence and Evolution of Ecological Economics in China Over the Past Two Decades* (Presentation given at the 8th Biennial Scientific Conference of the International Society for Ecological Economics).

Watson, Andrew. 1987. "Social Science Research and Economic Policy Formulation: The Academic Side of Economic Reform." In *New Directions in the Social Sciences and Humanities in China*, edited by Michael B. Yahuda, 67–88. New York: St Martin's Press.

Wei, Lin, and Arnold Chao, eds. 1982. *China's Economic Reforms*. Philadelphia, PA: University of Pennsylvania Press.

Wheeler, Norton. 2012. *The Role of American NGOs in China's Modernization: Invited Influence*. New York: Routledge.

White, Gordon. 1989. "Restructuring the Working Class: Labor Reform in Post Mao China." In *Marxism and the Chinese Experience*, edited by Arif Dirlik and Maurice Meisner, 152–168. Armonk, NY: M. E. Sharpe.

Wu, Jinglian. 2005. *Understanding and Interpreting China's Economic Reform*. Singapore: Thomson/South-Western.

WuDunn, Sheryl. 1995. "Chen Yun, a Chinese Communist Patriarch Who Helped Slow Reforms, is Dead at 89." *New York Times*, April 11, 1995.

Zhang, Wenxian and Ilon Alon, eds. 2009. *Biographical Dictionary of New Chinese Entrepreneurs and Business Leaders*. Northampton, MA: Edward Elgar.

Zhao, Yuezhi. 2008. *Communication in China: Political Economy, Power and Conflict*. New York: Rowman & Littlefield.

Zhao, Ziyang. 2009. *Prisoner of the State: The Secret Journal of Premier Zhao Ziyang*. Translated by Bao Pu, Renee Chiang, and Adi Ignatius. New York: Simon & Schuster.

Zhou, Shulian. 1982. "The Market Mechanism in a Planned Economy." In *China's Economic Reforms*, edited by Lin Wei and Arnold Chao, 94–113. Philadelphia, PA: University of Pennsylvania Press.

# 4 Economic restructuring in the countryside 1978–2001

## 4.1 Introduction

The next three chapters analyze how the general factors influencing Chinese economic theory discussed earlier found expression in specific analyses of the rural, international, and state-owned enterprise sectors of the Chinese economy. This chapter focuses on agricultural and rural economic issues. The reorganization of the rural economy proved to be the cornerstone for economic restructuring. The rapid increase in farm output and sideline production 1978–1984 provided the economic, ideological, and political energy for expanded economic restructuring across the Chinese economy. By the turn of the century, however, significant problems plagued the countryside.

This chapter explores the different ways neoclassical and Marxist economists, (and, at times, heterodox economists) thought about economic events and economic restructuring in the countryside. There are, of course, differences within paradigms as well as differences between paradigms. This makes it impossible to compare "the" neoclassical view with "the" Marxist, or "the" heterodox view of particular issues. It is possible, however, to identify different tendencies and different generative logics in the three paradigms, and this is what is attempted below.

We will demonstrate how Marxist and neoclassical economists fit events in the rural economy into their different conceptual frameworks and pre-existing master narratives about economic development. We will compare their different counterfactuals about what could have happened if different policies had been followed and different predictions about the future trajectories of existing policies. We will highlight occasions where the paradigms attended to different issues. The gradual substitution of neoclassical for Marxist ways of thinking tended to legitimize market related outcomes and inhibited efforts to reverse the inequalities in China's emerging new class structure. The reforms tended to outrun academic efforts to guide them, however, and it would be incorrect to blame neoclassical economics for China's extreme inequality, or credit neoclassical economics for China's rapid increases in GDP in the initial years of reform.

We begin in section 4.2 with an historical account of the major events in the rural sector from 1978 until the Tiananmen Square tragedy in 1989. Sections 4.3–4.6 explore the different ways that Marxist and neoclassical political-economists understood these events. Later sections discuss the 1989–1991and 1992–2001 periods, which had their own distinct logics.

## 4.2 Rural economic reforms 1978–1989: historical narrative

When Deng assumed power in December 1978, past state investments in seed breeding and irrigation, and recent investments in fertilizer production had set the stage for China's enjoyment of its own version of the green revolution. The after effects of the Cultural Revolution and Lin Biao affair had concurrently weakened the ability of appeals to socialist solidarity to motivate work effort. Deng's reforms helped rekindle rural energies by expanding material incentives. Deng's initiatives were supported by both Marxist and neoclassical economists, often for somewhat different reasons.

The initial reforms reoriented planning priorities toward the production of consumer goods and expanded unplanned petty commodity markets. The maximum size of permissible private household plots was increased from 5 percent to 15 percent of cultivatable land. The prices paid farmers for government-mandated agricultural output and above-quota output increased by more than 20 percent and 50 percent respectively, while the regulated prices charged farmers for agricultural inputs declined.[1] Farmers were also given greater freedom to decide what to plant and license to sell above quota output and sideline production (from animal husbandry to handicrafts) in reinvigorated rural and urban markets. Sideline production grew by more than 18 percent per year 1978–1984 (Riskin 1987, 286, 291).[2]

Deng encouraged local experiments in agricultural policy. One experiment permitted groups of households to contract with their commune for control of a portion of communal lands. In return for meeting the commune's pro-rated quota of output from the contracted land, they were allowed to use the land as they saw fit. If their output exceeded quota requirements, they enjoyed the difference. Even before the 1978 reforms, some commune team leaders had allowed smaller subgroups of production teams to disaggregate their activities, as long as the production team as a whole met its responsibilities.[3] When disaggregated to the household level, the system was called the Household Responsibility System (HRS). It reintroduced family farming in China and spread rapidly.

The reforms generated their own internal momentum. For example, the expansion of private plots and market opportunities made it more difficult for the commune to mobilize village labor and attract talented people to leadership positions. This weakened the returns to collective labor and further encouraged families to shift toward family farming. The development of sideline industries spawned the development of service markets which outraced the ability of planners to accommodate them. The expansion of sideline industries created a demand for credit that quickly outraced the ability of state-owned financial institutions and rural credit cooperatives to supply credit (Qian and Huang 2011). This led to the expansion of relatively unregulated informal credit markets.

The Chinese leadership quickly decided not only to tolerate decollectivization and family farming, but essentially to require it everywhere. By 1983 almost all communes had been dissolved and assets redistributed to participating households (excluding the formal ownership of land which remained in local government hands).[4] While this reorganization was welcomed in most areas, some well managed communes preferred to remain integrated units of production, partially to take advantage of the economies of scale accompanying the large machinery they had purchased.[5] Other communities seem to have preferred a somewhat less complete dissolution of the commune than occurred, perhaps attracted to the risk-sharing aspects of collective production, and its egalitarian ideology. Survey research by He Xuefeng suggested that "at least one third [of Chinese peasants] had considerable reservations about complete decollectivization" (Xu Zhun 2013, 20). The Chinese state overruled these reservations and disallowed hybrid options.[6]

Partially in response to the need to encourage long-term thinking by family lease holders, the length of contracted leases constantly expanded, increasing from 1–3 years in the early 1980s, to 15 years in 1984, to 45–50 years in 1993, and apparently to as many as 70 years in a village growing nut trees that I visited near Beijing in 2014.

Perhaps, even more challenging to the logic of China's Marxist countryside was the emergence of a grey market in rural land-use rights by 1982. The practice was legalized in 1983. In addition, new regulations in 1983 and 1984 permitted those with land-use rights to hire wage labor and/or rent their holdings to tenant farmers. In the late 1970s households or private firms could hire a maximum of seven employees. These limits were quickly raised or ignored and disappeared entirely in 1987.[7]

There is relatively little dispute over what happened next, but some debate over why it happened. Agricultural output increased rapidly, growing by more than 33 percent from 1978–1984 (Naughton 2007, 89). The increase in agricultural output (1978–1984) and agricultural prices had numerous positive effects. The increases dissolved the agricultural bottlenecks that had restrained overall Chinese economic growth, increasing the availability of food and agricultural feedstocks for industry, such as cotton for the textile industry. The increases raised rural incomes, probably by more than 150 percent (1978–1984) and created a new market overnight for light industry production of consumer goods and expanded housing construction.[8] This market absorbed some of the surplus labor in the countryside. The leap in agricultural output also added several billion US dollars to China's foreign exchange account, permitting larger imports of capital goods (Lardy 1990, 21).

Light industry production was overseen by the spectacular expansion of township and village enterprises (TVEs), initially under the direction of local governments.[9] The new markets for light industrial goods seem to have been relatively competitive. Some TVEs were granted a fair amount of enterprise autonomy under various kinds of managerial or collective responsibility contracts (Xu and Zhang 2009, 3). Other TVEs were administered by local government cadres as if they were part of a public conglomerate. Profits from different TVEs were pooled and reinvested in new projects promising the highest total returns (Whiting 2000, 119). Richard Smith elaborates,

> Local governments function somewhat like miniature, locally-founded versions of the Japanese state capitalist *zaibatsu*: setting up firms, restricting competition within the community by preventing duplication, pooling their enterprises' after-tax profit for investment, directing resources from "sunset" to "sunrise" industries, controlling wages, cushioning subordinate enterprises from short term market fluctuations, transferring funds from firms with surpluses to those with deficits, and so on.
>
> (Smith 1993, 88)

The cadre evaluation system gave local officials incentives to: increase social services (such as education and family planning) and maintain local employment, as well as to increase industrial output and local firms' profitability. To some extent, the TVE governance system acted like a public sector version of stakeholder capitalism, recognizing much broader claims on economic output than simply maximizing shareholder value. Whiting attributes some of China's success in achieving relatively high degrees of "service delivery in education, health services, and water and sanitation" in the 1980s and 1990s to this governance system (Whiting 2000, 115–120).[10]

The dynamics of competition (both in terms of narrow economic pressures and inducements for institutional change) created powerful forces for further changes. As we shall see repeatedly in the next three chapters, competition spread initial market reforms across the economy and eroded many would be safeguards against the slide of China's economy into capitalism. The rise of the TVEs was facilitated by the dual-track pricing and allocation system which permitted state-owned enterprises to sell unused inputs to the TVEs. Some SOEs also subcontracted aspects of production to lower cost TVEs spurring inter-firm competition (Xu and Zhang 2009, 5). In addition, the institutional decentralization of the Cultural Revolution had shifted the governance of many large SOEs from the national to regional level. Local political rivalries quickly added another dimension to the competitive pressures among Chinese firms (Xu and Zhang 2009, 2; Xu 2011, 1086).[11] Rapid local economic growth promised rapid political promotion for the regional officials overseeing local TVEs and SOEs (Xu 2011 and Whiting 2000).

The expansion of the service sector also fueled Chinese economic growth in rural and urban areas. This sector had been discouraged during the Maoist

period and offered opportunities for large increases in employment with relatively little capital investment.

From 1981–1990 TVE industrial output grew at 28 percent per year.[12]
The TVEs' share of Chinese GDP increased from 14 percent in 1980 to 24
percent in 1990, to 37.5 percent of GDP in 1995.[13] TVE employment grew
from 28 million in 1978 to 123 million in 1993, reaching a startling 135
million in 1996.[14] The firms achieved impressive increases in total factor productivity (Xu and Zhang 2009, 5) while still maintaining social ties to the
local community (Lin Chun 2006, 82).

Several factors created an undercurrent for privatization; among these were
(1) competitive ("race to the bottom") pressures that rewarded firms eschew-
ing social responsibilities; (2) private households' entrepreneurial initiatives;
and (3) Party insiders' interests in transforming their "institutional capital"
into private property rights. These pressures gradually eroded many of the
safeguards put in place by Chinese policy makers to prevent China's slide into
capitalism.

The TVEs in some areas, such as Wenzhou, appear to have been disguised
family businesses or small private firms from the start, or what came to be
called "red hat enterprises."[15] In a marriage of convenience, these firms
bought the TVE label and production licenses from local authorities, but
were run entirely as private firms. In 1985 the central government gave its
tacit approval to Wenzhou's private enterprises.[16] In 1987, the State Council
officially approved the Wenzhou experiment (Xu and Zhang 2009, 7; Huang
2008, 131). In 1987 private TVEs already produced 32 percent of TVE
output and in 1989 they accounted for 50 percent of TVE employment
(Huang 2008, 127, 134).

As the 1980s progressed, the golden age of agricultural expansion faded.
Agricultural GDP growth fell from 8.8 percent per year in 1978–1984 to 3.8
percent for 1985–1995 and 4.2 percent in 1996–2000. This compares with a
4.9 percent annual growth rate for 1970–1978 in the eight years preceding
reform (Huang et al. 2008, 479).[17] In section 4.8 we shall see how the TVEs
were eventually largely superseded by capitalist-oriented firms.

## 4.3 Differing master narratives

Many Chinese economists fit events in the 1980s into master narratives
infused with paradigmatic subtexts. Neoclassically oriented economists situated China's experience within conventional neoclassical explanations of
global economic history. They drew analogies between China's situation in
the reform period and classical liberalism's master narrative about Western
economic history. The latter harkens back to John Locke's celebration of
England's "Glorious Revolution" in 1688. The narrative treats the historical
creation of private property rights as the basis of human rights and economic
growth.[18] The heroes of the story are the emerging capitalists, be they the
rural gentry in England or the captains of industry in America. The narrative

finds characteristic expression in the work of neoclassical economic historians such as Douglas North. China's economic reform process is discussed and often benchmarked by neoclassical economists with reference to this triumphant story of the payoffs to expanding property rights in the West. Chinese neoclassical economists tend to identify with this intellectual tradition (Qian and Wu 2000, 18–19).

The Chinese mass media has adopted motifs from this narrative in a retelling of Western and Chinese history in CCTV's mini-series "The Rise of Powerful Nations." The documentary celebrated England's Glorious Revolution as a model for Chinese development.[19] CCTV2 has produced several documentaries praising market economies, including a program that challenged the claim that markets produced "spiritual pollution," and several shows celebrating consumerist lifestyles (Zhu 2012, 112–113).

Marxist economic histories (such as Perry Anderson's *Passages from Antiquity to Feudalism* and *Lineages of the Absolutist State*) tell a different story and describe the relentless destruction of traditional ways of life and the creation of class inequalities during capitalist development. The focus in this case is not on the class gaining property rights, the capital accumulators who are enclosing farmland, organizing the putting out system, innovating in production, plundering the new world, and overseeing the slave trade. The focus is on the creation of a mass of workers separated from the means of production and desperate for employment. Marxists tend to focus on the process by which wage labor becomes a necessity, an imperative, rather than an opportunity.[20] This focus conditioned how Chinese Marxists viewed decollectivization in the countryside, laissez-faire oriented special economic zones in the international sector, the elimination of guaranteed permanent employment in state-owned firms in the 1980s, and the rise of the informal sector in Chinese cities.

Marxist histories of Western economic development emphasize darker pictures than highlighted in John Locke's account of the "Glorious Revolution" and contemporary neoclassical histories of capitalism. Marxist narratives situate Chinese events in the 1980s with reference to different historical accounts, such as those found in Marx's *Capital*, Engels's *The Condition of the Working Class in England* and Karl Polyani's *The Great Transformation*.[21] In these accounts, private property rights often trump rather than sponsor human rights.[22] And while Marxists acknowledge that capitalism does accelerate economic growth, they find the sharing of the results of that growth very unequal and its cost, in terms of by-products like alienated labor, very high.

## 4.4 New versus old institutionalist economics

The standard neoclassical model reduces to the equations of static general equilibrium theory and the relatively unsatisfying assumptions about automatic dynamic adjustments that are necessary in order to guarantee equilibrium. Analysis of the rapidly changing Chinese economy during this period required a more complicated model of economic outcomes involving discussion of institutional design and institutional change. There was a venerable heterodox economics tradition of institutionalist economics practiced by Veblen, Ayers, and Galbraith, among others, that added a rich historical, cultural, and political dimension to economic analysis. This paradigm had many adherents in the US and China in the first half of the twentieth century. It recognized the achievements of competitive markets but also acknowledged path dependency, irrationality, and the exercise of power in the economy. This approach did not endow market outcomes (even "perfect markets" without the presence of market failures) with the automatic optimality implied by neoclassical theory. Its subtexts conflicted with neoclassical subtexts. When Western economics was reintroduced in China, older institutionalist traditions were relatively, but not totally, neglected.[23]

The "new" institutionalism of Coase, Williamson, and North, among others, fit more comfortably within the market-affirming subtexts of neoclassical economics. It assumes *homo economicus* and treats market institutions as the Darwinian survivors of a battle to capture economic efficiencies. The framework tends to focus analysis of institutional design on analyses of transactions costs. It emphasizes the importance of private property rights and material incentives for economic efficiency. New institutionalist economics arrived in China in the 1980s and has flourished in academic and policy circles.[24] We will see below how new institutionalist economics influenced neoclassical discussions of rural and SOE issues.

## 4.5 Neoclassical thinking: the long shadow of classical liberalism

The neoclassical story begins with the assumption of "economic man."[25] It downplays the impact of culture on human behavior. It has deep roots in the subtexts of classical liberalism. Neoclassical economists like Steven Cheung (Zhang Wuchang), one of the most famous economists in China in the 1990s, based their defense of market reforms on classical liberal assumptions. Cheung writes:

> Communist doctrine misjudges the nature of man. Dialectical materialism argues that man's behaviour can be altered. ... Economic analysis, on the other hand, rests on the assertion of 'selfishness' or self-interest ... if man is born selfish and *cannot* be changed, then reforms based on the premise of altruism will lead to disaster. Biologists are now beginning to produce evidence that selfishness, like skin pigmentation, is inherited and cannot be changed.
>
> (Cheung 1986, 61–62)[26]

Neoclassical accounts portray China's rural restructuring and the household responsibility system as a process that liberated human energy by providing an escape from irrational and inefficient constraints imposed by poorly informed economic planners and Maoist ideologues. An econometric paper by Lin Justin Yifu, the head of the China Center for Economic Research (CCER) in Beijing and a University of Chicago-trained economist, was very influential in shaping interpretations of the period's reforms. The paper attributed about 50 percent of the increase in output during 1978–1984 to the household responsibility system (Lin 1992, 46). The paper was enthusiastically embraced by neoclassical economists and was the most widely cited paper in the *China Economic Review*, the journal of the Chinese Economist Society, over the entire 1989–2010 period (Du Yuxin 2011, Table 3, p. 33). Lin notes, "My research findings on Chinese rural issues were quickly accepted by mainstream academia. But when I began to challenge the Washington Consensus … I found it hard as I was the only person clapping" (Lin 2012c, xvi).

Lin's rural story is Milton Friedman's story in *Free to Choose*, and it was repeated in his highly publicized lectures in China in 1988 (Friedman 1990a). The market in neoclassical analyses of Chinese experience is portrayed as a realm of free choice and opportunity, permitting people to escape the shackles of state assigned jobs in urban areas and commune assigned tasks in rural areas. The entrepreneur and emerging capitalist is the focus of neoclassical analyses of the Chinese countryside, shifting crops in response to market signals or setting up sideline enterprises that become privately-run TVEs. The entrepreneur replaces the communal villagers of Dazhai, selfless Lei Feng,[27] or class conscious factory workers, as cultural hero. The 10,000 yuan household is the new icon of success (McCoy 2000, 85). The rapid growth of the rural economy after the initial market reforms was, and is, portrayed as vindication of classical liberalism by many neoclassical economists in China (Coase and Wang 2013).

Drawing on North's work and interviews with cadres, Nee and Su argue that the household responsibility system (HRS) reduced the free-rider problem inherent in collectivization (Nee and Su 1990, 22). They conclude: "North and Thomas rightly insist that 'if a society does not grow it is because no incentives are provided for economic initiative'" (22).

Jean Oi and others have applied new institutionalist theory and principal agent theory to explain the explosive expansion of the TVEs in the 1980s. Oi writes,

> North and Weingast, among others, point to the importance of secure property rights for economic development. … There is, however, no inherent reason why only individuals or privately held companies, as distinct from governments, can be entrepreneurs. … Publicly owned firms may be capable of playing the same role as privately held firms.
>
> (Oi 1999, 10)

From one perspective, Oi's analysis challenges neoliberal narratives as it implies that the key preconditions for rapid economic growth are markets and material incentives. Private ownership is not required as long as the public owners (in this case township and village governments) are the residual claimants from efficient production.

From another perspective, however, this analysis can reinforce neoliberal projects. It generally organizes analysis of economic development in terms of the behavior of *homo economicus*. It largely ignores the project of constructing socialism.[28] It sets the stage for a theory of Chinese development that finds public firms better than Maoist bureaucrats, but inferior to private firms, as agents of growth.[29]

Lin Justin Yifu combined classical liberalism's assumption of *homo economicus* with game theory to explain the cause of the Great Famine in China in the late 1950s and early 1960s (Lin, Justin Yifu 1990, 1243). Using game theory, he argued that the government's 1958 decision to deny households the right to withdraw from a commune was the main cause of the famine. His argument rested on the idea that households were discouraged from shirking by the threat of productive members leaving the commune if others evaded their responsibilities. The cost of shirking was therefore the risk of losing the economies of scale made possible by the commune. The state's denial of people's option to leave the commune lowered the costs of shirking and thereby undermined the incentive structure of the commune. More than anything else, it was the collapse of incentives for hard work that caused the famine (Lin, Justin Yifu 1990, 1228).

Lin's analysis seems to assume a 100 percent selfish agent with little sense of reciprocity or social solidarity. The decision to remain or leave a collective, or the decision to work diligently or shirk is modeled entirely as a self-interested net benefit calculation (1241–1242). The framework of explanation seems quite narrow and, given the serious problems of measuring some important variables used in his analysis, his conclusion is surprisingly assertive.[30]

> From the game theory point of view … the sudden collapse of agricultural production … was mainly a result of the deprivation of the right to withdraw. … Bad weather, bad policy and management, and the size of communes definitely all contributed to the severity of the catastrophe; however, they were only secondary reasons for the crisis.
>
> (1243)

Despite its limited focus, new institutionalist economics has been able to construct some interesting analyses of many economic phenomena in the US and Europe. This is also true of its application to Chinese economic issues. Xu Chenggang (University of Hong Kong and Tsinghua University) and Zhang Xiaobo (Zhejiang University and the International Food Policy Research Institute) for example, offer a very interesting analysis of the TVEs. They acknowledge that the early success of these firms, despite the absence of well-defined property rights, appears to contradict neoclassical expectations (Xu and Zhang 2009). Their resolution of this anomaly illustrates the ability of creative thinkers to make adjustments within a paradigm that reconcile it with seemingly contradictory data without relinquishing its underlying tenants and subtexts.

Xu and Zhang explain the TVEs' success by characterizing them as the closest version of private firms in rural China, given the "ideological taboo" against formal private ownership (2009, 9). In this role they link the TVEs' success to the development of an entrepreneurial spirit among local government officials or private individuals acting under the protective cover of TVE labels. Xu and Zhang push the limits of neoclassical analysis by also appealing to a series of implicit handshakes between local governments, TVEs, and their employees. This analysis echoes aspects of neo-Marxian Social Structure of Accumulation models (see Chapter 6). Xu and Zhang assert that the glue of "local social norms, such as trust, may be an important factor behind the informal institutions of TVEs..." (8). They find the origin of these cultural norms, however, to be rooted primarily in the enlightened self-interest of individuals engaged in repeated contracting, rather than in broader cultural phenomena created by social institutions. This strategy allows them to elide the troubling Marxist concern that the growth of capitalist markets will erode social capital built up in periods of non-capitalist institutions. They write,

> most TVE employees and managers and a substantial number of township-village officials lived in the same community for generations.[31] ... Under certain conditions, close long-term interactions among community members (virtually infinitely repeated overlapping generational relationships) might foster a social norm within the community that may facilitate informal institutions such as TVEs. ... [R]egion-specific local social norms, such as trust, may be an important factor behind the informal institutions of TVEs ... and between TVE employees and between TVEs themselves. ... This explanation shares the same spirit of the evolutionary repeated game theory of social norms.
>
> (8)

The hustling and bustling household entrepreneurs of the Wenzhou TVEs are the heroic survivors of the neoclassical story, a story that resonated among many Chinese economists.

When viewed from a neoclassical perspective, the 1980s demonstrated the wisdom of classical liberalism and the vitality of neoclassical theory in conveying these lessons. As free market champion Lin Justin Yifu put it, many regulatory obstacles limiting market determination of factor prices had been weakened. "Land can be leased out for rent. Interest can be charged for credit. Labor can be hired with a limitation that is not enforced" (Lin 1988, 196). Lin lamented that residual socialist-Marxist beliefs inhibited a complete transition to a capitalist market economy in the countryside. He singled out the unwillingness of the government or public opinion to support lenders' rights to seize land-use rights put up as collateral for rural loans (Lin 1988, 173). This "timidity," he felt, raised rural borrowing costs and inhibited credit based economic expansion. Lin appeared optimistic, however, that "lenders rights" would be protected sooner than expected. He acknowledged that "the government may have to tolerate the emergence of a landless population," something it has been unwilling to accept, but he reminded readers that "rent, hired labor, and interest were all not acceptable to policy-makers a few years ago; they are all legal now" (197).

The overriding message of neoclassical and new institutionalist economic theory was and is "to let the market work" in the countryside, even the imperfect market. The theory acted as a legitimizing force for private capital accumulation and discouraged state efforts to alter China's emerging new class structure. The initial across-the-board increase in most rural people's income deflected attention from potential social problems accompanying market-led growth.

## 4.6 Marxist thinking about rural restructuring

### 4.6.1 Overview

There were four major Marxist strategies for restructuring rural policy during the 1978–1989 period:

1   Chen Yun's adjustment strategy (which reoriented central planning to allocate more resources to agriculture and accepted small rural markets on the margins of the planned economy);[32]
2   The marketeers' strategy, (which limited economic planning to the use of indirect levers, such as state control of credit and gave free rein to the expansion of family farming and household petty commodity production);
3   Market socialism strategies (which emphasized the importance of worker self-managed enterprises); and
4   the Maoists' mass mobilization, non material incentives economic strategy, (which after the arrest of the "Gang of Four" was not usually advocated publicly).[33]

The strategies all retained Marxist theory's holist methodology and thought about rural reforms in terms of their dynamic, long term, "systemic" implications. The strategies sought to avoid the re-emergence of a landlord class. They also prioritized preventing the creation of a desperate working class, housed in urban slums and employed intermittently in sweatshop conditions at subsistence wages. The rural commune (guaranteeing everyone at least basic subsistence), the state-owned enterprise (guaranteeing workers lifetime employment) and the *hukou* system (a resident permit system limiting rural migration) were part of earlier attempts to accomplish these goals. Suggestions for altering these institutions invited discussion of the impact of any changes on China's class structure.

The common ground among Marxist theorists retained the goal of social-ism and traditional Marxist concerns about alienated labor and control of the state by interests friendly to the capitalist class. All but the Maoists also retained Marx's focus on the importance of developing the forces of produc-tion for achieving socialism. Many debates among Marxist theorists would turn on the relative weight given different Marxist goals, such as ending alienated labor, reducing inequality, avoiding capitalist business cycles, or advancing the forces of production.

When the reforms began, most Marxists were open to cautious experi-ments with expanded market mechanisms and material incentives in the countryside. They rejected pressures from Maoist partisans for increasing the level of aggregation for workers' compensation from the production team (consisting of 20–30 households) to the production brigade (consisting of ~7 production teams). Brigade accounting peaked in 1978 at 9.5 percent of pro-duction brigades and had fallen to 5 percent by 1981 (Zweig 1989, 178). The reformers also supported linking individuals' compensation within the pro-duction team more closely to levels of work and output. They wanted to ensure, however, that restructuring did not lead to rural capitalism.[34] Shifting control of land and tools, and the distribution of income to the household level, was unsurprisingly more controversial.[35] As late as September 1980 two-thirds of the leaders of China's provinces opposed allowing household-based agricultural production (Fewsmith 1994, 45). Despite this resistance, Deng signaled his support for family farming by appointing Du Runsheng, a strong supporter of family farming, to high ranking positions in agricultural think tanks and policy making.

The expansion of wage labor is the signature characteristic of capitalism from a Marxist perspective. It is more causally significant than either the pres-ence of markets or self-employment with private property. The hiring of wage labor in agriculture and in small-scale petty commodity production was thus even more troubling to Marxist theorists than family farming or family sideline businesses. In deference to these concerns, reformers in favor of wage labor, called rural hired hands "asked-to-help-labor" (*qing bang gong*) rather than hired labor (*gu yong*) (Fewsmith 1994, 124). The euphemism did not reassure Chen Yun and other traditional Marxists.[36] William Hinton, a Marxist ethnographer and agricultural specialist, warned,

> At the start, of course, the contractor maintains the old relationships. … But no one has control over later developments. … What is involved in all of this is not just income differentiation but class differentiation. Those who get rich first preempt the high ground and end up exploiting those who have lagged behind.
>
> (Hinton 1990, 81)

Chinese Marxists designed many policies to discourage the emergence of capitalism from competition between petty producers. Among these safeguards were prohibitions on private ownership of land, limits on the number of wage employees farmers could hire, and channeling credit away from large privately owned enterprises. These policies conflicted with neoclassical recommendations which urged that market competition and profitability determine the character of firms and the social organization of the economy.

### 4.6.2 Feasibility of collective agricultural enterprises

Marxists tended to be more hopeful than neoclassical economists about the long run potential performance of collective enterprises. Most Marxists (and heterodox economists) acknowledged that stronger material incentives in the late 1970s and 1980s had helped spur agricultural output. They also admitted that by the late 1970s, flawed projects, such as the Great Leap, the bureaucratic nature of some communes, the Cultural Revolution, and Lin Biao affair had stifled economic initiatives and depleted rural households' responsiveness to non-material incentives.[37] They challenged, however, the inference made by many Western and Chinese neoclassical economists that these outcomes were *the inevitable* result of organizing economic activity in a non-capitalist fashion.[38] They highlighted important successes of some communes and opposition to decollectivization among some farmers.

Jonathan Unger's interviews of former villagers found that team-based agriculture might have succeeded in the countryside if not for the heavy hand of relentless Maoist political campaigns. Unger concluded,

> team-based collective agriculture ultimately failed largely due to political pressures and irrational agricultural policies imposed from above … [the interviewees] were almost all of the opinion that the system of teams had its good points. They concurred that the teams provided members with economic security, noted that members felt a loyalty to their teams, and believed that if left to their own devices the teams were capable of spurring agricultural development.
>
> (Unger 2002, 223, 224)[39]

### 4.6.3 Claims of "over-painting" HRS achievements

Many Marxist and heterodox analyses of the impact of the Household Responsibility System on agricultural output accuse its advocates of over-painting their canvasses, that is, fitting ambiguous events into a preconceived neoclassical narrative. Marc Blecher, for example, criticizes the tendency of market reformers to impose metaphors from classical liberalism about inherently unmotivated selfish workers onto retrospective accounts of collective agriculture. He writes:

the frequently heard argument that Chinese agricultural collectives did not provide labor incentives is dubious both in theory and in practice. ... During the 1970s, farmers and rural cadres did not complain primarily about indolence among their fellow villagers; on the contrary, their biggest complaint was that they worked very hard but did not seem to be reaping much in the way of rewards (author's interviews).

(Blecher 2010, 144; See also Arrighi 2008, 369–370)

Other observers have criticized mainstream accounts of the agricultural reforms for giving excessive weight to the HRS in explaining increases in farm output and insufficient weight to human capital, infrastructural, and technological investments made during the Maoist years. They emphasize that several key agricultural innovations came on line just as the reforms kicked in.[40] As noted above, the "green revolution" is built on the triad of new, specially-bred seeds, increased irrigation, and expanded use of chemical fertilizer. The revolutionary aspect of the new seeds is their increased responsiveness to fertilizer. The full benefits of the green revolution therefore could only be captured if accompanied by expanded fertilizer use. The use of chemical fertilizer more than doubled during the 1978–1984 period, as new manufacturing facilities came on line (Huang and Rozelle 1995, 855).[41]

Chris Bramall provides the most extensive challenge to neoclassical portrayals of Maoist collective agriculture as a dismal failure, characterizing neoclassical accounts as "The Fable of Decollectivization" (Bramall 2009a, 250). Although not a Marxist, Bramall does not subscribe to all of the assumptions or subtexts of the neoclassical paradigm, a stance that allows him to view the history of collective agriculture in China with a different lens. In addition to stressing the role of technological changes in increasing output after 1978, Bramall raises questions about the data underlying neoclassical claims that total factor productivity stagnated during the collective years and took off after the implementation of the HRS.[42]

Marxist critics of the HRS have also stressed the advantages collective agricultural institutions offered: (1) for supplying social goods, such as public health; (2) for utilizing surplus seasonal labor in the countryside for rural infrastructural projects,[43] such as expanded irrigation systems; and (3) for capturing potential scale economies in farming from mechanization. Writing in 1990, William Hinton, for example, lamented.

the 'responsibility system' ... fracturing the land into countless small strips ... has destroyed all economies of scale and has rendered meaningful mechanization all but impossible (63). ... New theories defining agriculture as a uniquely individualistic occupation have added ideological barriers to any future joint tillage.

(64)[44]

### 4.6.4 Viability of collective agriculture: democratic solutions

One theme that runs through many contemporary "left" discussions of the feasibility of socialism in China is the failure of Maoist and later leaders to rely on democratic and participatory institutions to mobilize support for non-capitalist institutions. The inference is that you cannot maintain an economic system that does not rely heavily on material incentives without participatory institutions that mobilize voluntary cooperation.[45]

Chinese Marxism's failure to take a more democratic form was significantly influenced by Deng's decision in late 1983 to reject Hu Yaobang's attempt to elevate the humanist tradition in Marxism. The latter is prominent in many Western Marxist traditions and often associated with Marx's *1844 Manuscripts* and *The German Ideology*. Wang Ruoshui, Su Shaozhi, Ru Xin, among others, attempted to recapture the idealism of earlier Chinese Marxism by embracing this tradition (Fewsmith 1994, 125–126; Brugger and Kelly 1990, 148–149).[46]

The *1844 Manuscripts* and many subsequent Western Marxist classics, such as Braverman's *Labor and Monopoly Capital*, and Fromm's *Marx's Concept of Man* also emphasized the problem of worker alienation in their critique of capitalism. Deng aggressively rejected this strand of Marxist theory, claiming, "people who loved to discuss the 'value of people, humanism, and so-called alienation'; such people were not interested in criticizing capitalism but in criticizing socialism" (Fewsmith 1994, 126). Deng likely took this position, at least in part, because his strategy for rapid Chinese economic growth involved high levels of worker alienation. The same calculations lay behind Stalin's adoption of Taylorism in Soviet workplaces.[47] Both decisions foreclosed more participatory forms of Marxism and were at least partially motivated by the leaders' desire to generate and capture a large economic surplus for national defense.

The merits of household farming were still in dispute among Chinese Marxists in the early 1980s. The rush of events, however, largely superseded debate. With Deng Xiaoping's strong promotional support, by 1983 94 percent of all farms were organized under the household responsibility system (Bramall 2009a, 338). The flow of early positive feedback helped establish "the "primary stage theory" of Chinese socialism as a context for economic strategy.

### 4.6.5 Marxist assessments of sideline enterprises

For quite some time all Chinese economists had agreed that it was important to develop rural industry. The debate was over how to accomplish this. Mao, had promoted commune and brigade industries, and by the mid-1970s they employed 10 percent of the rural labor force (Meisner 1999, 465).[48] The development of family farms and rural sideline businesses in the 1980s (especially along the Wenzhou model) spurred far-ranging discussions among

Chinese economists. A group of reform economists, many from CASS, over-rode traditional Maoist reservations about petty commodity production. They published very favorable reviews of Wenzhou's private household network of competitive firms in six articles in *Economic Research* in 1986. Dong Fureng's favorable description of the Wenzhou model, for example, reminds one of Adam Smith's panegyric in the *Wealth of Nations* about the gains from special-ization in pin-making.[49] Dong also expressed concerns about the widening inequalities and return of usury to the countryside, and a potential shift from largely family labor to wage labor accompanying the Wenzhou model. Nevertheless he was so impressed with the productivity of the system that he endorsed it as a vehicle for socialist modernization.

In the name of advancing the "commodity economy" and the "forces of production," and with, at times, tortuous reasoning to reconcile their conclu-sions with traditional Marxist theory, other CASS economists similarly toler-ated the creation of income differentials greater than 10:1 and as high as 3,000 to 1 (Bramall 1990, 45), the accumulation of wealth from interest on loans as high as 3 percent per month (Lin Zili 1990, 169), and the expansion of wage labor in Wenzhou.

Lin Zili grounded his acceptance of the Wenzhou model in its conformity with the goals of the "commodity economy," and acknowledged that skeptics concerns could not be assuaged by traditional socialist doctrines (Lin, Zili 1990, 165). He defended income differentials as necessary "to encourage the adoption of advanced production methods" (166). He defended the payment of interest on savings in order to mobilize funds for new investment (167). He defended capitalist profits and interest accumulation as long as the funds were reinvested, arguing, "As long as the savings enter the process of expanded reproduction, and continue circulating, their role is no different from that of public accumu-lation and has the same characteristics as socialized property" (172). He even seemed to imply that the meaning of private ownership of the means of repro-duction needed to be re-evaluated in the presence of progressive income taxes (172–173). Ultimately, Lin's endorsement of the Wenzhou model reflected his awe for its impressive results. His writing mirrored Schumpeter's imagery of the entrepreneur as hero (Lin Zili 1990, 175).[50]

Lin Zhang similarly celebrated the famous button market of Qiaotou where the price of goods and services "are not determined by … an official's subjective decision, but are regulated entirely by the market's 'invisible hand' …" (Lin Zhang 1990, 102). Echoing Lin Zili's endorsement of market behavior, he found competition to be character building (106).[51]

Li Shi reinforced these affirmations, finding economic growth in Wenzhou "astonishing" and "forming a virtuous cycle." Li concludes, "J. A. Schum-peter regarded innovative entrepreneurs as the dynamic for economic devel-opment and when we analyse the emergence and growth of household industry in rural Wenzhou, we can see their critical role" (Li Shi 1990, 112).

Dong Fureng, the team leader for the CASS study of the Wenzhou model, summarized the Faustian bargain struck by the Marxist economic reformers with petty commodity production. While acknowledging that "income differentials have widened in Wenzhou" (Dong 1990, 89), he advised, "This should be regarded as an inevitable phenomenon and a price that has to be paid" (90).

Other Marxist defenders of the reforms, such as Du Runsheng, parried increasing concerns about growing rural economic inequalities in 1985, by predicting that continued economic growth would reverse that trend (a la Kuznets curve notions of the distributional stages of economic growth) (Hsu 1991, 108–109). Similar reassuring projections have been made about China's environmental problems. While many Marxist endorsements of private enterprise oriented reforms had qualifiers after them, the tone of the essays suggests a significant shift from Marxist to neoclassical subtexts and frames of reference. Andrew Watson reaches similar conclusions about the emerging tolerance of capitalist institutions among some Marxist economists, including acceptance of the "extraction of surplus value" from workers by employers (Watson 1987, 81).

There were, however, Marxist theorists who held on to traditional Marxist reservations about deploying capitalist techniques to promote economic growth and technological advance. Marxist critics of Wenzhou's system of small scale, clustered private enterprises raised concerns about its trajectory similar to those raised about the household responsibility system. They favored the "Sunan model" of local government-owned TVEs and/or presumably independent cooperatives. At times they criticized both Wenzhou and Sunan enterprises for eliciting short-term self-interested behavior. They criticized some firms, for example, for polluting the environment and engaging in unscrupulous business behavior (Hsu 1991, 128). They also feared the eventual replacement of family firms with capitalist firms. In the absence of strong state guidelines, they expected competition to eventually create dismal work lives for most workers. Some pointed to the terrible record of local government-owned coal mining TVEs with respect to the environment, worker health and safety issues, and resource conservation, to illustrate how a competitive system embracing short-term measurements of success could produce grim outcomes whether firms are publicly or privately managed.

Many economists (Marxist, neoclassical, and heterodox) have raised concerns about the growing inequality in the countryside accompanying the demise of the communes. Marxists have distinctively expressed these concerns in terms of emerging class structures, rather than simple distributions of income. Meisner, for example, writes,

> a new rural bourgeoisie. … This class-in-the-making emerged from … a system that favored the aggressive and ambitious, the entrepreneurially inclined, the physically strong, the skilled, the clever, the families with greatest labor power, and especially individuals and families with political power or access to it. … [T]he way to prosper in the post-Mao countryside was not to till the soil but to manage the labor and the products of the labor of others
>
> (Meisner 1996, 251)

He adds,

> China ... is hardly unique in suffering the incongruous coincidence of economic progress and social deterioration. Such has been the price of capitalist development everywhere, beginning two centuries ago with the social and cultural degradation of the common people of England.
>
> (Meisner 1996, 492)

Marxist supporters of the Wenzhou system were often sensitive to these concerns. They did not yet feel comfortable appealing to the benefits of the unadorned pursuit of self-interest celebrated by classical liberalism. Instead, they appealed to many of the traditional safeguards adduced by reformers to reassure skeptics that restructuring would not lead to capitalism. Chen Ruiming's ~1985 review of labor-hiring firms in Wenzhou offers a classic example of this middle ground defense of private enterprises. He writes,

> None of these labour-hiring enterprises ... is a pure capitalist enterprise. ... they have been supervised and restricted by the socialist finance, banking and tax systems ... [the employers] have been brought up and educated by the party.
>
> (Chen Ruiming 1990, 143–144)[52]

The pure capitalist firm (hardened in the kiln of tooth and claw competition), is, of course, the haunting image feared by Marxist critics of decollectivization and rural private enterprises. The Marxist narrative anticipates the inevitable emergence of a Reserve Army of the Unemployed. These victims of "development" are the by-products of a competitive struggle for existence among independent units of capital. The competition threatens to reproduce the desperate working conditions of the industrial revolution, albeit in modern garb, and transforms previously shared under-employment in the countryside into high rates of unemployment, and even higher rates of feared unemployment. As Meisner argues,

> What is most distinctively capitalist about the reformed rural economy is not the contracting of land to households but rather the increasing prevalence of wage labor. ... [M]any rural laborers have been transformed into commodities. ... By 1989 it was estimated that there were at least 50 million *youmin*, former peasants who roamed the country seeking temporary employment in the cities.
>
> (Meisner 1996, 233)

The First Round of rural economic reforms ended with the Tiananmen Square tragedy in June 1989.

## 4.7 Reconsidering rural reforms after Tiananmen Square: 1989–1991

A number of factors came together to produce the Tiananmen Square tragedy in June 1989. Most notable were the inflationary pressures that accompanied economic restructuring. Many groups whose wages were not keeping up with prices, such as workers at state-owned enterprises, felt that implicit social contracts were being violated. Anger over the corruption accompanying marketization also fueled discontent. Efforts to curb inflation led to sharp reductions of credit and rising unemployment rates, which disproportionately affected TVEs and rural employment.

Things came to a head in June of 1989 when student protests for increased democracy were joined by workers' anger over inflation, unemployment, corruption, and increased social inequality.[53] The combination was an explosive mixture. On June 4, 1989 Chinese troops violently cleared Tiananmen Square of protesters, killing at least several hundred people, and perhaps many thousands of people.[54] The palpable threat to the state posed by the Tiananmen alliance between students and workers ended the first round of economic restructuring.

Some reform leaders were replaced and some economic restructuring policies reversed.[55] Ideologically, dampers were placed on institutions thought to have spurred challenges to the Party's authority.[56] During earlier ideological campaigns in the reform era, such as the anti-spiritual pollution campaign of 1983 and the anti-Bourgeois Liberalization campaign of 1987, economic reformers were relatively insulated from sharp attacks (Watson 1987, 83; Sleeboom-Faulkner 2007, 95). It is not clear how much of the post-Tiananmen Square crackdown extended to supporters of economic liberalization as opposed to political liberalization. At least two of the key people appointed to the Party's oversight committee for CASS in 1993 were strong supporters of economic reform.[57] While the research topics of CASS were tied more closely to projects supported by the political leadership, the research agenda managed to obtain World Bank loans of $100 million (Sleeboom-Faulkner 2007, 147), suggesting the projects were congenial with continued marketization.

As intended, the austerity anti-inflation measures dampened economic activity,[58] but they caused greater than expected employment problems. Deng expressed dissatisfaction with 6 percent growth targets. His famous 1992 "Southern Tour" set off another round of market reforms. Ma Hong's former protégée Zhu Rongji, eventually took over leadership of economic policy-making. The prioritizing of economic growth, whether by appeal to the logic of "primary stage of socialism" within a Chinese Marxist framework, Deng's goal of maximizing China's national power, or the principles of neoclassical economics, encouraged a return to the pre-Tiananmen reforms. Heterodox political-economist Marc Blecher finds that "the national narrative of modernization led to 'workers' acceptance of the core values of market and state'"

(Pringle 2013, 194).[59] Marxist economist Li Minqi links the self-interest of newly empowered capitalist elites to renewed restructuring (Li Minqi 2008, 60–65). Neoclassical theorists Naughton (1995) and Jefferson and Rawski (1995) find the transparent failures of interregnum policies responsible for renewed restructuring.

## 4.8 Round two: agricultural and rural restructuring 1992–2001

### 4.8.1 Historical narrative

The flow of migrant workers from the countryside to China's cities, increased from ~30 million in 1989 to ~80 million in 2001,[60] though *hukou* regulations limited permanent and family migration. Land ownership remained in public hands, though households retained user rights that were usually transferable across generations. Most households held on to their land as a form of subsistence insurance.[61] Local governments retained the power to reshuffle land use rights in certain circumstances, as when family size changed, opportunities arose for land consolidation, or the possibility of converting local agricultural land for industrial, commercial, or high density residential uses. The seizure and resale of rural people's land without fair compensation by corrupt officials ("land grabbing") became relatively widespread and explosive politically.[62]

The earlier spurt of government investment in rural areas years was not continued,[63] while rural taxes and fees usually increased during these years. The slowdown in rural income growth that began in the mid-1980s continued in the 1990s, falling from ~14 percent 1978–1984 (Huang 2008, 117) to about 4 percent over the entire 1985–2000 period.[64] Farming income grew more slowly than income from rural industries. Income inequality within rural areas increased as did the difference between average rural and average urban incomes. Health and educational services in rural areas also eroded as did some economic infrastructure. The great counterweight to these socially undesirable outcomes was the continued decline in extreme poverty. The number of people living below the World Bank's extreme poverty level of $1.90/day (purchasing power parity [PPP] 2011 standard) fell from 756 million in 1990 to 508 million in 1999.[65] The number of people living on less than $2/day (PPP standard) fell from 960 million to 770 million over the same period (Ibid.).

The golden age of non-private TVE expansion begun in 1978 ended ~1996. The TVE sector as a whole began losing money in the mid-1990s (Huang 2008, 125) and experienced rapid privatization. Naughton estimates that the share of collectively owned TVEs fell from ~60 percent in 1995 to ~40 percent in 2000, to less than 10 percent by 2007 (Naughton 2007, 286). In absolute numbers, township and village owned TVE employment fell from 61 million in 1995 to 29 million by 2003 (Bramall 2009a, 423).[66]

By the early 2000s it was clear to many observers and government officials that there were serious socio-economic problems in the countryside (the so called three rural questions). The Hu Jintao administration made significant efforts to address some of these questions, but did not fully "solve" them. The initial super-nova of Chinese economic reform, rural economic growth, had clearly dimmed. Whether the new rural countryside was still a bright star that exceeded other hypothetical reconfigurations, or an example of the short term successes, but long term liabilities of China's transition to capitalism, was debated amongst neoclassical and Marxist/heterodox economists.

### 4.8.2 Feedback between economic theory and economics events 1992–2001: neoclassical views

On *Agriculture and the Legacy of Decollectivization:* Neoclassical theorists and national government policy recognized the need for land consolidation and larger agricultural production units,[67] a concern that had worried Marxist critics of decollectivization 15 years earlier. Their basic response to Chinese rural problems was similar to the strategy recommended by neoclassical economists for addressing US rural populations: move people to the cities.

Neoclassical theorists urged the full privatization of land in order to encourage long term thinking and capital investments. They also recommended allowing rural households to post their land as collateral in order to increase their access to credit. They favored "protecting creditors rights" to seize assets for non-payment.

Neoclassical economists portrayed many agricultural sector problems as the result of incomplete marketization.[68] They were especially concerned about the opportunities for corruption presented by residual government "interferences" in rural land, labor, and financial markets.

On *Township and Village Enterprises*: The neoclassicals explained the decline of local government and/or collectively owned and operated TVEs as a result of market efficiency pressures. Comparisons between the vitality of Wenzhou's economy and bankruptcies of Sunan's economy were often drawn in support of these conclusions. Huang and Rawski, among others, portray some privatizations as the spontaneous initiative of TVE workers much like the action of rural households in the first days of the HRS (Huang 2008, 131).

The earlier success of government led TVEs are treated as temporary, second best solutions to ownership issues. Once the market niches initially filled by traditional TVEs were open to competition from fully private firms, including joint ventures and 100 percent foreign firms, the older TVEs naturally lost ground. Xu and Zhang portrayed the efficiency of the TVE's format in the 1980s as being in-between the ideal efficient capitalist firm and the lamentably inefficient state-owned enterprise. The TVEs flourished as one-eyed warriors in a land of blind men, and perished when all gained sight. They conclude their story in the 1990s:

The decline of the TVE sector is a happy ending. That is, it comes as a result of privatization and further development, rather than of shrinkage of the firms in the TVE sector. ... TVEs lost ground in the marketplace through competition with private firms. ... In hindsight, it seems natural that all three TVE models should converge to the model dominated by private or shareholding firms.

(Xu and Zhang 2009, 9)

Summing up the neoclassical message, Huang Yasheng concludes, "(t)he unstated takeaway ... is that the demise of the TVEs should be appropriately viewed as a sign of progress and deepening reforms" (Huang 2008, 126).

The neoclassicals also explain some of the apparent decline in TVE numbers and output as an artifact of accounting. Many "red hat" enterprises that were really private firms from the start, were finally able to acknowledge their true identity in the 1990s. Huang offers a slight variation on this theme, arguing that many rural private firms were simply ignored in the enterprise data of the 1980s and recognized in the 1990s.

Neoclassical economists have also tied some of the economic difficulties of the TVEs in the 1990s to much tougher macroeconomic conditions and market environments.[69] To some extent this was a product of economy-wide excess capacity, moments of macro policy contraction in order to reduce inflationary pressures, and government efforts to curtail shadow banking and other mechanisms of informal finance, to protect the Chinese economy from financial sector meltdowns.

Huang also cites and rejects a popular explanation within "official Chinese circles." This rationale appears to reflect classic urban biases against rural entrepreneurs, suggesting that the TVEs faltered because they lacked sophistication with respect to international markets, brand status, and modern technology or as Huang puts it, "They were ill-suited for a more modern and technologically advanced China" (Huang 2008, 126).

To summarize, the neoclassicals and Chinese officials wove rural events into their pre-existing narratives, bounding the topics discussed by the focal length of their paradigm's vision. They focused on causal explanations that derived perceived outcomes from the self-interested behavior of competitive individuals. They assessed the implications of events for market-defined efficiency. They gave relatively little attention to the implications of events for the subjective experience of work, survival of village culture, or socialist goals. Their analysis invited further steps toward capitalism.

Many neoclassical analyses of the immediate causes of economic outcomes (such as their analysis of the impact of increasing competition on market structure) are shared by Marxist and heterodox economists. When these analyses are situated in a different context, however, they can lead to different conclusions about the viability of non–capitalist rural institutions, different expectations about the trajectory of current arrangements, and different policy recommendations.

### 4.8.3 Feedback between economic theory and economic events
### 1992–2001: Marxist-heterodox views

On *Agriculture and the Legacy of Decollectivization:* Marxist and heterodox economists emphasized the barriers to efficient agricultural production in the 1990s created by the fragmentation of private rural plots. They also highlighted the decline in rural education and health care that accompanied the dissolution of collective mechanisms for funding social services.[70] These benefits were part of the "social wage" accompanying collectivized life. The commune's financing mechanisms had also supported rural infrastructural investments like irrigation systems.[71]

All of these formerly collectively financed projects eroded in the 1990s. The decline in rural education following the shift to individualized production was especially severe, with illiteracy increasing from 85 million to 115 million 2000–2005 (Huang 2008, 43, 243–248).[72] Illustrative health care problems included the return of schistosomiasis, a parasite borne disease, and China's fall from a country with relatively equal access to health care to one of the most unequal health care systems in the world, as ranked by the World Health Organization (Huang 2008, 251).

While some neoclassical economists (such as Huang Yasheng) also noted and even emphasized the deleterious effect of decollectivization on rural social services, there tended to be a fatalist undercurrent in most neoclassical accounts that accepted these outcomes as acceptable collateral damage in a transition to capitalism. Their burden was softened in many neoclassical accounts by the assumption of long run Kuznets curves and supply side economics claims that all boats will rise when the tide comes in. Marxist and heterodox economists anticipated more enduring health and educational inequalities.

Marxists have drawn analogies between the seizure of communal lands in this period, at a fraction of their resale value, and the British enclosures. Some have termed the practice "Primitive Accumulation with Chinese Characteristics." Tens of millions of villagers may have been dispossessed in this privatization process (Pils 2006, 1216; Harvey 2005, 146; Andreas 2012). Along with asset stripping and insider privatization of public firms, the corrupt seizure and resale of village land helped endow an emerging Chinese capitalist class with the financial resources necessary to stand on the employer side of the labor market (Harvey 2005, 145–146). The flip side of this relationship was the creation of a labor force, lacking attractive alternatives to wage labor (such as successful rural collectives or employment guarantees in well functioning SOEs or urban collectives). From a Marxist perspective, these outcomes were contingent events, reflecting historical circumstances and balances of power, rather than technical rationality and the competitive discovery of optimal institutional formats. Reflecting on the evolution of Chinese labor markets, Meisner writes,

> the communes had provided at least minimal security for most of the
> rural population, but the abolition of the commune system … revealed

that nearly half of the rural labor force of 400 million was redundant. Of the 200 million ... half eventually found employment as wage laborers. ... The remainder, about 100 million people ... were thrust into the ranks of a new rural *lumpenproletariat* ... forming the "floating population" (*youmin*) of migrant workers. ... Living in shantytowns and working for pitiful wages, they supply much of the labor for the construction boom that has made Chinese cities appear modern and seemingly prosperous.

(Meisner 1999, 468)

Drawing on seven years of research, Anita Chan describes the working conditions faced by rural migrant workers in China in the 1990s,

Migrant workers numbered about 80 million in 1999. ... They constitute a cheap and flexible source of labor in the new free labor market ... the legal minimum-wage standards set by labor intensive, export-oriented Asian countries such as China ... are the lowest possible price at which a government can sell their workers' labor in the international labor market while maintaining their workers' physical survival.

(Chan 2001, 12)

Li Cheng's account of work life in Wenzhou's factories in 1995 illustrates Chan's claim and provides a nice counter weight to earlier heroic images of Wenzhou enterprises. Based on a site visit and interviews, Li indicates "[P] rivate entrepreneurs ... seem to be only interested in making their fortunes. No one is really concerned about the socioeconomic well-being of the community" (Li Cheng 1997, 71). Li goes on to describe factories with dim lighting, claustrophobic working conditions, hazardous environments, and extremely long hours, all made possible by the existence of Marx's Reserve Army of the Unemployed. He continues,

"We want to know whether your workers have any concerns". ... I said to her straightforwardly. "If they have any problems, they can quit their jobs here any time," the woman replied. "My workers should be grateful to be able to work here. Go see the jobless people in the 'labor markets'". ... In virtually every large and medium sized city that I visited, there were places in which hundreds of young adults, both men and women ... waited for hours and days, hoping to be picked up by anyone who could offer them jobs, including temporary or hourly work.

(Li, Cheng 1997, 73)[73]

By the early 2000s, 120 million rural migrants worked in the shadows of the informal economy. They worked an average of 11 hours a day without job security. Few had medical insurance or retirement benefits. They were paid about 60 percent of the average wage of workers within urban *hukous*. They constituted the bulk of the 700,000 workers crippled on the job each year (Huang 2009b, 407–408). Along with their siblings who remained under-employed in the countryside, they fulfilled the role of Marx's Reserve Army of the Unemployed.[74]

Huang highlights the relative invisibility of these workers in conventional accounts of the Chinese reforms. He writes,

> The one-sided acceptance of neoclassical economics and of the American model by mainstream economists in China today has in fact greatly influenced not just the presentation of statistical data but also the kinds of data gathered and not gathered. To a great extent, the indecent treatment of laborers of the informal economy is simply assumed away.
>
> (Huang 2009a, 423–424)[75]

He adds,

> The difference between the ideological neoclassical point of view and the more empirical informal-economy point of view is that while one is preoccupied with a particular variety of economic theorizing, the other is concerned about actual economic development and also about social equity.
>
> (428)

Partially in response to the plight of migrant workers, Marxist and many heterodox economists have supported efforts to avoid the full privatization of land. The goal is to preserve a minimal fallback position for rural people (Unger 2002, 225; Amin 2013). Heterodox and Marxist economists also note that some rural households also had reservations about jettisoning the current system. Unger, for example, found

> most Chinese farmers … are worried about the prospect of private land-holdings. They *prefer* [in original] to retain the current system of use rights rather than be granted outright ownership … the farmers preferred a system that periodically reassigns fields in line with changes in the size and composition of families.
>
> (Unger 2002, 225)

On *Township and Village Enterprises*: Marxist and Heterodox economists tend to highlight different factors from neoclassical economists when assessing the relative performance and survival rates of TVEs and private firms. Marxists give greater attention to equity issues. Their focus goes beyond simply looking at income inequality. They explore the emergence of structures of inequality that help reproduce class differences. They study the linkages among evolving differences in income, education, savings, access to credit, and networking that have accompanied the shift from collective to private organization of production in the countryside.

For example, from 1980–2001, rural income inequality increased significantly. The poorest decile's income increased by 3 percent per year while the richest decile's income grew by 8 percent (Huang et al. 2008, 487). At the same time the cost of rural education rose and public funding fell. This squeezed poor families and resulted in dramatic increases in rural illiteracy 1995–2000. The combination of rising income inequality, heightened dispersion of rural educational outcomes, and return to the national exam system for university admission virtually assured an elitist university campus.[76]

Reflecting Marxism's traditional focus on labor issues and alienation, Marxist and heterodox economists also give heightened attention to the implications of different enterprise forms for the nature of work.

In explaining the successes of private firms, Marxist and heterodox economists highlight "race to the bottom" logics, the erosion of a supportive social infrastructure for collective ownership, and the self-interest of corrupt officials benefitting from insider privatization.

While not as formally structured as SOE obligations, government and collectively owned TVE's had broader purposes than pure profit maximization. Among these goals were maintaining local employment and egalitarian wage structures. Official regulations limited top management's wages to 5x the average worker's wagers (Vermeer 1999, 125). In a study of village enterprises in Wuxi County in 1994, James Kung found the average ratio of the enterprise managers' income to workers income was less than 3:1 (Kung 1999, 98, 104), noting,

> Seeing themselves as the nominal owners of the "collective enterprises," villagers have refused to accept large income differentials between the manager and themselves.
>
> (Kung 1999, 104)

This kind of practice appears to have disadvantaged many village firms in competition for managerial talent (Naughton 2007, 289; Qian and Wu 2000, 10). In a different cultural climate, perhaps before the disillusionment of the Great Leap Forward and Cultural Revolution, this might have been an attractive attribute. The TVEs also appear to have used some of their profits to finance local social welfare programs and the incomes of local farmers (Smith 1993, 89). As early as 1993, Richard Smith observed,

> private capitalist firms … increasingly out-compete community enterprises … because they have lower labour costs, they rely on cheaper female labour, they exploit cheaper migrant labour, they offer few or no benefits, and they can close down and layoff workers when demand falls off and resume when it is profitable, whereas collective firms are obliged to maintain full-employment. They can also more easily conceal income, evade taxation.
>
> (Smith 1993, 90)

Li Shi indicates that from the start of economic reform, private and foreign enterprises were given greater opportunity to hire migrant workers (Li Shi 2008, 9).

The TVEs had broader notions than private firms of who were the enterprises' legitimate stakeholders. Lin Chun, for example, indicates in township and village enterprises, "Responsibilities, benefits, and risks were shared among managers, local governments, surrounding communities and workers in shareholding cooperatives" (Lin Chun 2006, 31). "For quite a while they [TVEs] tended to be community-oriented in their public functions (in terms of productive or educational infrastructure and cultural entertainment) due to traditional collectivist ties, both kinship and communal" (Lin Chun 2006, 82).[77]

Official government regulations defining TVEs also tended to impose limitations on the way profits could be used that "socialized" the surplus generated by the TVEs (Vermeer 1999, 126).

In the fiercely competitive market of the 1990s, characterized by excess capacity and tight credit, it was difficult for socially minded firms to compete with their private, profit driven rivals. Whether "tooth and claw" competition, as exhibited in the razor thin profit margin environment of Wenzhou, is a humane context for organizing work is controversial. Less contestable is the finding that this environment selects for private firms.[78]

From a Marxist perspective the most enduring impact of economic restructuring in the countryside 1992–2001 was the solidifying of inequality. Key to this process, was the ongoing creation of a capitalist class of employers and owners of financial capital. Asset stripping of the TVEs and "land grabs" became part of Chinese "primitive accumulation." Workers in formerly publicly or collectively owned TVE's became more like wage laborers. Rural migrant workers already filled that role in the cities, but their complete proletarianization was restrained by their continued "ownership" or control of use rights over small rural plots.[79]

## 4.9 Rural shareholding cooperatives

In the 1990s, shareholding cooperatives (SHCs) became an important option for TVEs. Shareholding cooperatives can combine elements of worker self-management with the capital-raising ability of privately owned shareholding firms, and the community linkages of stakeholder governance.[80] The maneuvering around SHCs reflects the competing projects of the institution's conflicted supporters. Socialist-oriented supporters hoped that SHCs would gradually collectivize small private firms. A special experiment in Wenzhou was designed to channel the city's famous family firms in a collectivist direction (Vermeer 1999, 126). Local government leaders saw SHCs as mechanisms to raise capital for local companies, largely from the firms' own workers. They were especially concerned with maintaining local employment and the influence of local cadres in overseeing TVEs. Advocates of private enterprise saw the SHCs as offering a "red hat" or "red umbrella" under which small private firms could safely expand. SHC status, for example, allowed otherwise private businesses to employ more than seven wage workers or to offer stock options that allowed top managers to earn more than five times the average worker's salary. SHCs were also seen as mechanisms to raise capital in political waters usually unfriendly to private firms (Vermeer 1999, 125). SHC status also carried significant tax advantages.

The implications of shareholding cooperatives have depended very much on how they are structured. The original regulations were announced in 1990, during the "reevaluate reform years" that followed the Tiananmen Square tragedy. The rules were infused with traditional socialist principles. Over time these principles weakened. The initial regulations encouraged: voluntary participation, democratic management, distribution mainly according to work, limits on managerial salaries, and reliance on internal accumulation (Clegg 1996, 121). There were constraints on how profits could be used that were intended to preserve the firms' SHC identity. At least 60 percent of after-tax profits were earmarked for reinvestment, with distributions to shareholders or worker's bonuses each limited to less than 20 percent of profits. If the SHC were liquidated, assets had to be used to support new businesses, local agriculture, or a staff insurance fund. Assets could not be divided up among existing shareholders (Clegg 1996, 121). Other socialist oriented regulations adopted by some SHCs included:

> Obligations to be guided by the state plan (Vermeer 1999, 127).
> Voting rules based on the principle of one person one vote (rather than one share one vote).
> Limitations on the sale of state-owned SHC shares to private individuals (which was intended to preclude private sector buyouts of public sector firms).
> Regulations requiring worker-owned shares to be tradable only among workers.
> Ceilings on the percentage of shares managers could own.
> Ceilings on the degree of unequal share ownership among workers.

After the renewal of economic reform in 1992, many of the socialist-oriented 1990 regulations were ignored, although the regulations were never formally rescinded (Vermeer 1999 126, 127,130, 142–144). More free-market, private enterprise versions of SHCs included: release from guidance by the state plan and restrictions on profit distribution, voting rights based on the number of shares owned, removal of restrictions on managers' salaries, and tolerance of concentrated stock ownership by managers or other private parties.

Analytic treatment of SHC has varied by paradigm. While it is possible for neoclassical economists to embrace socialist versions of SHC strategies (and a few important neoclassical economists, such as James Meade, have done so), the thrust of most neoclassical research has been on how to solve the agency problem within capitalist firms. Milton Friedman's version of Calvin Coolidge's declaration that the "business of America is business," still rules the day.[81] Most neoclassical observers probably fell into the "convergence" camp described by Sachs and Woo (2000). These economists treated modern capitalist firms as the historical solution to the problem of business organization. They treated the TVEs as institutional concessions to political constraints and found that they inhibited economic growth. Sachs and Woo's other group of neoclassical economists, the "experimentalists," treated the TVEs more favorably. They saw the TVEs as innovative responses to the problems posed by various market failures in China's economic environment, such as imperfect information about local firms' credit worthiness (Oi and Walder 1999) or agency problems (Naughton). Even for this group, however, one gets the impression that the TVEs and socialist oriented SHCs were halfway houses on the way to the ideal private firm.

The criteria for judging enterprise forms in neoclassical accounts is almost always their ability to mobilize resources for economic growth. There is little attention to the implications of different enterprise forms for the construction of socialism, vis a vis factors like cultural feedback, the direction of technological change, political feasibility, etc. There is attention to distributional issues, but not to the implications of different policies for the kind of social structures that might underlie distributional outcomes.

Marxist and heterodox analyses of SHCs gave attention to these social structure concerns.[82] Interestingly, while some SHCs furthered some socialist goals, such as relatively egalitarian income distributions and limits on private ownership, there seems to have been relatively little movement toward worker self-management, with local cadres or the firms' managers autocratically directing SHC enterprises.

There have been both optimists and pessimists about the future of SHCs within Marxist and heterodox circles. Cautious optimists point to various aspects of Chinese culture and contemporary Chinese politics (such as the cooperative spirit of Chinese villages, and Chinese culture) to argue that SHCs have strong traditions to draw on.[83] The pessimists, like Richard Smith (1993), expect "race to the bottom" pressures to overwhelm the socialist potential of SHCs, leaving them little more than disguises for privatization.

## 4.10 An alternative heterodox view of rural issues

Some heterodox political economists have developed another set of ideas about rural economic issues that is different from both neoclassical and Marxist economics. This approach focuses on the village as a social institution and village life as a reproducing way of life. The key claim is that village life needs to be studied as a social system that creates its own kinds of satisfying human relationships, meaningful experiences, and (perhaps) sustainable practices toward the environment.

Despite its long history, Chinese village life is disappearing. This is not usually seen as a problem in Marxist theory. Marx himself characterized traditional village life as "rural idiocy." Subsequent generations of Marxist theorists have tended to have similar urban biases, to associate cities with advanced forces of production, and to fear peasant village consciousness as tending toward petty bourgeoisie or even feudal thinking.

Neoclassical economists assume that the market will register people's preferences for different styles of life. If village life is dying, it is because people prefer to live in cities, or as independent households rather than as "villagers" in the countryside. There is no reason to lament or celebrate this. The important thing is to respect people's revealed preferences as recorded in the market. As noted earlier, the solution to the "rural question" is expected to be migration to the cities.[84]

A major problem with the Marxist perspective, from a heterodox "village studies" point of view, is that it ignores the potential for village life to nurture meaningful human relationships. It similarly neglects the potential for modernization to create a satisfying and sustainable shared way of life in the countryside. The methodological problem with the neoclassical perspective is that it mistakenly assumes that aggregating people's marginal choices can accurately reflect their system preferences. No one can "buy a sense of community," or a system of social relationships. Many key outcomes determining the viability or non-viability of village life are the unintended consequences of decisions made for other reasons. In neoclassical terms, there are numerous positive and negative externalities, coordination failures, and path dependencies that make private, marginal market choices potentially misleading about people's preferences concerning the survival of rural communities.

In China these themes have been developed by the New Rural Reconstruction Movement (NRRM). The ideas are not unique to China. In Thailand, for example, they have been developed under the rubric of "village studies" and are associated with the "sufficiency economy" movement.[85] While there is some overlap with Hu Jintao's "New Socialist Countryside" project and the call for a "harmonious society," the latter is really closer to the ideas of the welfare state than the New Rural Reconstruction Movement.[86] Chinese NRR thinkers have drawn more directly on the experiences of Kerala's development model in India.

The NRR school shares many of the criticisms of capitalist development raised by Marxist theorists, but differs somewhat in their policy response. Like Marxists, they criticize capitalist development strategies for inevitably creating large and enduring inequalities and a consumer culture that threatens the environment. NRR school theorists like Wen Tiejun, the Dean of the School of Agricultural Economics at Renmin University, and He Xuefeng, the director of the Center for Rural Governance Studies at Huazhang University of Science and Technology, argue that the development path traveled by the West is not viable for highly populated latecomers like China.[87]

Wen laments that capitalist development strategies are expected to drive small farmers out of business due to their inability to capture mechanization's economies of scale. As the process pushes the losers to marginal lands, he foresees subsistence farming accelerating soil erosion. He finds capitalist agriculture and animal husbandry creating excessive use of pesticides, herbicides, heavy metals, chemical fertilizers, steroids, antibiotics, and other dangerous practices. Because of China's enormous population and low percentage of arable land, he argues the long run dangers of Western agriculture are magnified many times in China (Wen 2008).

NRR theorists add to these criticisms a defense of the human relationships and opportunities for participatory institutions made possible by the smaller scale and personalized interactions of village life. Many of their ideas resemble Schumacher's thinking in *Small is Beautiful*. NRR policy recommendations call for public support for cooperative institutions in the countryside that renew villages' social capital. Besides actively promoting rural economic cooperatives, such as producer, marketing, and credit cooperatives, NRR activists have tried to renew rural cultural life. To some extent, the goal is to make villages attractive place to live, rather than reservoirs for people waiting to move to the cities. The late Liu Xiangbo, an associate of Wen Tiejun, for example, wrote,

> In the past, ... poverty alleviation focused on physical and monetary investment. Such measures ... have ... failed ... the fundamental reason is ... (r)ural society today lacks cohesion, "like a sheet of loose sand"... individual competitiveness and interpersonal alienation has flooded the countryside.[88]

Wen Tiejun writes,

> we must rethink ... widely accepted concepts. ... I ... was also a radical advocate of the market reforms in the 1980s. ... By the 1990s, however, these problems no longer looked so simple (11) ... the question is not whether GDP can continue to double. The question is whether this is what we really want.
>
> (Wen 2007, 14)

In a similar vein He Xuefeng has called for a "low-consumption, high benefit" rural development strategy (He 2007).

NRR activists have treated cultural projects as a kind of alternative economic development strategy, linking credit cooperatives and cultural initiatives, for example, in a process of community building. Illustratively, Alexander Day describes the work of He Huili, an NRR activist and an Assistant Professor at the Agricultural University of China:

> In He Huili's experience, the cultural troupes were vital in developing cooperative relationships that formed the basis for economic cooperatives. ... In Chenzhai Village ... for example, a women's cultural troupe was established first, and its members later formed the core for the

establishment of an economic cooperative ... [W]ithout overcoming the atomization produced by the household responsibility system, rural ... development would be impossible. This conviction differentiates their analysis from mainstream economic approaches to rural problems.

(Day 2013, 177, 179)

Marxist and neoclassical economists tend to criticize NRR views for being unrealistic and utopian. They portray NRR priorities as condemning rural residents to second class economic status. Neoclassical economists warn that only profit driven, competitive, market mechanisms are capable of deploying the technologies necessary to sustain the world's 7 billion people. While not in favor of capitalist strategies for maintaining economic growth, Marxist economists frequently endorse similar growth goals.

It can be asked, however, whose models are really utopian? The current American macroeconomic model requires annual economic growth of at least of 1–2 percent per year to avoid macroeconomic crises and social disorder. China's mirroring of many aspects of the US model (from a romance with the automobile to the incitement of competitive consumption among middle and upper income groups), have put it in a position where economic growth rates below 3–5 percent might trigger social chaos.

The level of aggregate demand in the US economy necessary to maintain economic growth is buoyed by consumers' positional competition and massive advertising. Extending the American model of incited consumption and permanent exponential growth to China (not to mention the rest of the developing world), seems to threaten environmental disaster (and perhaps resource exhaustion, though this is more uncertain) to meet "incited" needs. Thus it is anything but irrational, to question conventional growth models and their implicit assumption that the answer to global economic questions lies in the institutions and economic practices of the advanced capitalist countries.

In addition, a lot of research problematizes the link between GDP and happiness, once economies pass a minimal level of GDP per capita. Richard Easterlin is probably the most respected economist working in this field. His team's review of six studies of subjective well-being found that despite China's four fold increase in per capita income from 1990–2010, self-reported happiness levels showed no significant increase. The greater sense of well-being enjoyed by those at the top of China's income distribution was offset by losses in subjective well-being by those at the bottom. The negative impact of rising inequality, increased economic insecurity, and material aspirations that outraced even China's rapid economic growth, undergirded the failure of aggregate measures of subjective well-being (SWB) to increase (Easterlin et al. 2012).[89] In a follow-up paper in 2017, Easterlin et al. found that SWB levels ended their decline around 2005, but were still at or below their 1990 level in 2015 (Easterlin et al. 2017, 3). The authors highlighted the importance of unemployment and social safety net levels to people's sense of well-being (Ibid., 4). The

Chinese data mirrors the findings of the Stiglitz-Sen-Fitoussi Commission's study of measures of nations' economic performance. Stiglitz et al. were highly critical of relying on GDP/capita statistics to judge a country's economic performance. While the measuring of well-being by self reported levels of happiness or life satisfaction seems inadequate, the questioning of simple relationships between GDP/capita and well-being seems 100 percent correct.

The neoclassical model does not permit research on where people's aspirations and/or tastes and preferences come from. The paradigm also tends to ignore the implications of "positional competition" (i.e., status competition) for assessing the implications of economic growth. The paradigm also leaves unexplored the preconditions for meaningful community lives. To some extent this is reasonable, as there is a case for an intellectual division of labor. Where the neoclassicals are open to potentially serious criticism, however, is their claim that their conclusions about the merits of different economic systems and policies are valid regardless of answers to these broader questions.

## Notes

1 Grain quota (and above quota) purchase prices were raised by 20 percent (and 50 percent) in the summer of 1979. Prices for other crops, such as cotton and seed oil, were also raised by an average of about 22 percent (Riskin 1987, 285). By 1981 procurement prices had risen 38 percent (Selden 1993, 202).

2 As early as 1956 Chen Yun had proposed allowing elements of sideline production in rural areas as well as market feedback on the perceived quality of consumer goods. Solinger (1981) notes that many of the reform proposals put forward in the early 1970s by Xue Muqiao closely mirrored Chen's 1956 ideas.

3 Lynn White III argues this claim more broadly. He asserts that China's devolution of economic decision making to the local level, especially with respect to rural industry, but also with respect to agriculture, accelerated in the mid-seventies. He portrays national leaders racing to get in front of an already powerful movement (White 1998).

4 While the Chinese experience of decollectivization is sometimes termed accumulation without dispossession (for example, Arrighi 2008, 364–365), Hinton argues that privatization of many of the communes' non-land physical assets had many of the same inequities that accompanied later urban privatization of the SOEs' assets, creating new groups of wealth holders and wealth losers in both cases (Meisner 1996, 245).

5 This was especially true in northern China where flat lands and wheat crops were much more amenable to mechanization than the wet rice agriculture of southern China.

6 Meisner 1996, 229–230; Unger 1985; Hinton 1990, Chapter 3; Chan et al. 1992, 272; Putterman 1993, 35; Blecher 2010, 179; Hartford 1985, 38–43; Kelliher 1992, 82–84, 96, 105–106.

   Based on survey data from 28 villages, Jonathan Unger paints a different picture of decollectivization to family farms from the democratic images offered in most contemporary newspaper reports. The latter portrayed the shift to be a response to overwhelming grassroots demand. Unger indicates that "Reports from interviewees suggest a rather different scenario" finding that "the decision as to precisely what type of system would be adopted was made exclusively by officials at levels far above the village" (587). While there had been no conspiratorial decision to force a uniform outcome, "due to the nature of Chinese political organization, that is precisely what occurred" (Unger 1985, 593).

Kelliher writes,

> The speed of decollectivization ... meant that opposition to family farming received virtually no hearing from the government. Women who recognized that family farming would deepen their subordination to patriarchal authority had no recourse. Poor families dependent upon collective welfare were instantly imperiled. And ... whole regions in ... the North China plain ... stood to lose their natural advantage in mechanized farming. ... The final irony of family farming is that what began as an innovation by communities seeking more self-determination ended up being forced upon a minority of communities against their will.
>
> (Kellilher 1992, 106)

The imposition rather than voluntary adoption of the HRS should not be taken to mean that decollectivization was unpopular. Unger's interviews found roughly 75 percent in favor of decollectivization and 25 percent opposed (Unger 1985, 597). Nee and Su's (1990, 7, 19) interviews found about 10 percent of the cadres and 13 percent of the households in their sample were critical of the HRS and preferred collective farming. At least one scholar claims that some villages voted to remain as collectives and were allowed to do so. Meisner blames the fears of being labeled "leftist" on the part of lower level party officials for the pressures on peasants to adopt the HRS (Meisner 1999, 462).

7  Meisner 1996, 232; Kraus 1991, 34; Lau 2001, 222; Cheung 1986, 66; Watson 1987, 80–81.

8  See Nolan (1990, 26) for some eye catching statistics on the expansion of consumer durables from 1978–1985. Bicycle ownership, for example, increased from 31 percent of all households to 81 percent of households, radio ownership from 17 percent to 54 percent, and watches from 27 per 100 households to 126.

9  Xu and Zhang (2009, 2) indicate that, spurred by the Cultural Revolution's push for institutional decentralization, there were over a million commune and brigade enterprises in 1976 which became TVE's after the dissolution of the communes. This number grew to more than 25 million TVEs by 1993 (Hart-Landsberg and Burkett 2005, 44).

10  Whiting notes that the TVE's governing arrangements created some "agency problems" vis a vis corrupt behavior by public officials, incentives for excessive credit creation, and the potential for short sighted decisions (due to the three-year term and evaluation period for public officials). Overall, however, she paints a relatively positive picture of the TVEs behavior. See also Lin Chun 2006, 82.

11  Zhao Ziyang's appointment as premier followed the perceived success of his market innovations in Sichuan province. Wan Li's appointment as executive deputy premier of the state council, followed his oversight of HRS experiments in Anhui Province, and Xi Zhongxun's rise to be vice Chairman of the National People's Congress followed his promotion of special economic zones in Guangdong province (Xu 2011, 1098). Xu concludes,

> excellent performance at the provincial level becomes necessary for anyone to be nominated and eventually promoted as a top leader ... without a single exception, from 1992 to 2008 every president, every premier, and every newly elected Politbureau Standing Committee member of the four CCP congresses during this period was promoted from a provincial position.
>
> (1094–1095)

12  Xu and Zhang 2009, 5.

13 Xu and Zhang 2009, 3 and Table 3, p. 5.
14 National Bureau of Statistics of China, *China Statistical Yearbook* 2010, 119. Also Hart-Landsberg and Burkett 2005, 44; Naughton 2007, 274.
15 Kellee Tsai reports that "[b]y 1986 it was estimated that 89 percent of all collective enterprises in Wenzhou were wearing red hats" (Tsai 2006, 3). See also Xu and Zhang 2009, 7–8; Huang 2008, 127; Li Cheng 1997, 83–84; and Whiting 2000. Lynn White III describes this phenomenon more generally. He notes private firms often registered under the auspices of a larger state or collective firm. The private firm paid a kind of rent for political cover and lower taxes and sometimes office space and access to banking services (White 1998, 446).
16 National coverage of events in Wenzhou was encouraged by visits from high ranking government leaders. Splits in the leadership were evident, however, as illustrated by Hu Qiaomu's attempts in 1986 to limit attention to Wenzhou's experiments. Hu called on Wenzhou officials to emphasize socialist education and restrict visits to the area by outside cadres (Liu, Alan 1992, 704.) The leadership in Shanghai seems to have promoted the Wenzhou model. The city's party paper, *Liberation Daily*, gave events in Wenzhou wide attention and invited the rest of China to study its success (Liu, Alan 1992, 704, and Garner, 2011).

   There were also many books published by "reformist intellectuals" about Wenzhou (White 1998, 146). The ideological impact of these discussions seems to have been to legitimize market outcomes. White reports, for example, that "[p]ublicity ... about Wenzhou ... lent some political legitimacy to collective companies that paid their executives high salaries" (White 1998, 443). Elsewhere he adds "[t]he ideological function of the Wenzhou model ... was to make operations on the larger and wealthier Shanghai delta look almost anti-reformist. By comparison, Shanghai and Sunan seemed staid, loyal, and conservative" (White 1998, 148).
17 Huang et al. 2008 cite slightly different growth rates elsewhere in the article: 7.1 percent for 1979–1984, 4.0 percent for 1985–1995, and 3.4 percent for 1996–2000 (482). Agricultural diversification, especially a continuing shift in farm output from grain production into higher value crops as well as livestock and fisheries, did help increase rural incomes, but the countryside still fell further behind urban areas.
18 Liu Junning has been one of the most outspoken advocates of this view in China, arguing "Property rights are the core of human rights..." (*New York Times* September 28, 1999, A13.)
19 According to Zhu Ying's account, the series downplayed the role of Western colonialism and imperialism in the rise of the West and highlighted the role of social stability in promoting economic growth (Zhu Ying 2012, 109). The precedent for this kind of celebration of Western institutions was *River Elegy* (1988) which coupled celebration of the West with denigration of traditional Chinese culture.
20 Du Runsheng writes, for example, "in Western countries ... peasants typically lost their land ... becoming the 'reserve army' of the proletariat. ... The Chinese government, concerned to ensure an equitable growth in peasants' incomes, chose a different path" (Du 1988, 373).
21 Arif Dirlik has stressed the centrality of historical analysis to many Chinese Marxists. Li Dazhao, one of the two founders of the Chinese Communist Party, for example, considered historical materialism the most distinctive and important dimension of Marxism (Dirlik 1978, 25). Dirlik argues that China's early intimidation by imperialism and modernity encouraged a self-consciousness about the construction of Chinese society and an impulse for historical study of the origins of China's "relative backwardness." Historical materialism came to dominate Chinese historical studies by the 1930s, in part because of its focus on revolutionary change.

To some extent, battles over China's future are reflected in recent debates over its history. Dirlik notes, "By the sixties and seventies, Chinese leaders could point with pride at the pictures of peasants discussing the Marxist interpretation of Chinese history" (266). As capitalist institutions and neoclassical analysis have gotten more rooted in China's academic and cultural life, there are growing pressures to retell China's pre-1949 history, transforming the traditional "failed experiment" picture of twentieth-century pre-revolutionary capitalist development into green shoots that would have flourished had not the revolution cut them down.

22  Discussing current economic conditions in China, for example, Lin Chun writes

> The boom of sweatshops, filled by migrants working long hours for low wages and in insecure working conditions, made a mockery of the Labor Law. ... Engels's description of the conditions of the working class in nineteenth-century England became applicable to Chinese workers...
>
> (Lin Chun 2006, 9)

Citing Marx's *Capital*, Victor Lippit also draws analogies between the sufferings of independent peasants and emerging wage laborers in England and China, though he suggests the hardships accompanying the enclosures in England were worse than those suffered thus far by rural Chinese households (Lippit 1987, 165–166). It is also worth noting that the "Glorious" Revolution denied political rights to the vast majority of English men and women and established the landed gentry as the rulers of England for 150 years.

23  See Chapter 9, sections 9.6.4 and 9.6.6.

24  For example, there is a Coase society in China, dedicated to promoting Coasean economics. His last book, co-authored with Wang Ning (*How China Became Capitalist*), is a celebration of the defeat of Chinese socialism (Chapter 4). Most of Douglas North's books have been translated into Chinese. In 1995, North gave the keynote address at the opening of an economics research center at Peking University. Today, he is one of the most well known Western economists in China (Li and Trautwein 2013, 235). His students have had a major impact on Chinese economic thought.

25  Lin Justin Yifu (University of Chicago PhD 1986), the founding director of the China Center for Economic Research [CCER] at Peking University, treats the assumption of rationality [economic man] as the "Dao" of economics. In his 2005 book dedicated to Gary Becker (*Benti and Changwu: Dialogues on Methodology in Economics*), he defines economics as the study of rational choice (Lin 2005 Chinese edition; 2012c English edition).

Sometime between 1995 and 1997 an anonymous article entitled "Reform and Economic Man," written under the pseudonym of "Xin Mao," circulated widely in China. It grounded the rationale for many of the economic reforms on the assumptions of classical liberalism's "economic man." The article is believed to have been written by members of China's New Left (Fewsmith 1999).

26  Putterman, a sympathetic skeptic about the long run efficacy of non-material incentives, offers probably the most optimistic neoclassical view, writing,

> I do not suppose that nonmaterial incentives were of no efficacy. ... The important question ... is one of the sustainability and self-sufficiency of such motivation ... history suggests that social systems based on high levels of mobilization rarely last for as long as a generation. ... Perhaps ... the social energy required to maintain mobilization eventually sags.
>
> (Putterman 1993, 24–25)

27  Lei Feng was a Chinese soldier whose life was transformed into a cultural symbol for socialist idealism. There has been debate over whether Lei Feng was a real person or a public relations creation.

28 Oi does note the Party's attempt "to restrain the private sector from becoming an independent economic class" and cadre efforts, at times, to use local industry revenues for redistributive purposes (Oi 1999, 13).

29 Oi writes,

> The point of this study is ... [c]ountries in transition to a market economy need not immediately privatize. Intermediate forms of property rights are capable of engendering economic growth. ... But ownership forms have evolved ... original forms of collective ownership have become outdated. ... Those who maintain that individual private property rights provide the best basis for growth may ultimately be proved right...
>
> (Oi 1999, 193–194)

30 Lin reaffirmed these arguments in 2005 and 2012. Bramall offers some thoughtful criticisms of Lin's paper. He points out that the ability to withdraw from agricultural collectives was more limited before 1958 than portrayed by Lin, undermining the "before and after" 1958 claim made in the article (Bramall 2009a, 128–130). Putterman cites many authors making the same point (Putterman 1993, 29). He also undermines the total factor productivity claims used in Lin's piece to measure Chinese agricultural performance. (Bramall 2009a, Chapter 7). Most importantly, Bramall and others have emphasized the impact of resource diversion on agricultural output. Xu (Yong) (2011) offers a more culturally focused analysis of the basis for trust and cooperation in China's economy than Lin. He treats peasants' traditional capacity for mutual aid and honest interaction as a form of social capital. Xu finds cooperative behavior flowing from habits of cooperation built up over thousands of years, rather than from immediate rational calculations of self-interest. He warns that market dynamics are eroding this social capital. Lin's analysis would also seem challenged by recent research involving "the ultimatum game," which finds additional bases for reciprocity other than immediate self-interest.

31 Feminist theorists point out that discussions of village life often reflect the vantage point of male experience. Before the 1990s, there was of course, large scale women's out migration from their home villages. It would be interesting to reflect upon the interaction of Chinese marriage customs, informal economic relations, and gender inequality. Attention to these kinds of linkages is part of the project of feminist economics.

32 This position mirrored Chen's past beliefs. For example, in a 1956 speech to the 8th National Congress ("New Issues Since the Basic Completion of the Socialist Transformation") Chen urged several reforms combining economic planning and market mechanisms in a way that still prioritized economic planning. Chen recommended maintaining some market feedback loops in the rural economy. He criticized monopolized, automatic state procurement for failing to signal to producers what were successful and unsuccessful products, and for dulling incentives for the introduction of new varieties of consumer goods (Chen 1982a [1956a], 12–13, 18). At the same time, he favored maintaining unified procurement for necessities and key industrial inputs.

   In a second speech at the 8th National Party Congress in 1956 ("Methods of Solving the Tensions in Supplies of Pork and Vegetables"), Chen called for improved planning techniques (e.g., better allocation of inputs to pork production), price incentives (raising pig and manure prices) and increased household pig production for family consumption or the market. Chen also called for a greater market role in the production of locally grown vegetables. He recommended that the urban vegetable market "become a free market under the leadership of the state." The latter role involved a kind of indicative planning, the use of state companies to support list prices during off-seasons, and the imposition of price ceilings during periods of shortage. He adds, the market is "free to a certain extent because the producers can make and change their plans according to the demands of the market, freely negotiate prices with consumers, and have direct transactions within the range stipulated by the state" (Chen Yun 1982b [1956b], 28).

   Chen also criticized amalgamation of producers where the necessary preconditions for collectivization, such as economies of scale from advanced technologies, were absent. He gave special attention to the handicraft industry, which he thought suffered a fall in quality in some areas due to the sharing of profit and loss under common management (Chen Yun 1982a [1956a], 11–12).

33 See for example Oksenberg 1982, 173–174.

34 He and Zhang, for example, note that some Chinese economists believed "if the country is to adhere to the socialist road, this development [individual ownership] must be limited and controlled, because individual economy … leads to capitalism" (He and Zhang 1982, 202). Chen seems to have reluctantly supported the HRS in the early 1960s as a desperate measure to address the famine conditions left by the Great Leap Forward (Fewsmith 1994, 26). In addition to likely concerns about the instabilities of the petty commodity mode of production, Chen feared that the HRS would weaken the ability of China's economic planners to manage the economy and extract the targeted social surplus from the countryside (Fewsmith 1994, 47). He was unwilling to normalize this policy for non-crisis times.

35 Flirtations with variants of the HRS had occurred in the early and mid-1950s, supported by Deng Zihui and Du Runsheng, leaders of the CPC's rural work department. The strategy resurfaced as part of the recovery package implemented after the failures of the GLF. Both initiatives were eventually reversed by Mao, and Du Runsheng was removed from agricultural policy making.

36 Another illustration of the ideological minefield surrounding wage labor is the controversy in 1983–1984 involving a reforesting project. The contractor, Liu Guosheng, temporarily employed up to 200 workers. He apparently paid generous wages for the time and did an excellent job of ecological restoration. He earned a surplus of 3,500 yuan. The *People's Daily* (*Renmin Ribao*) asked whether Liu had violated the law, precipitating major debate and intervention on Liu's behalf by Hu Yaobang (Kraus 1991, 33–34).

37 For a thoughtful analysis of the roots of peasant cynicism, see Chan et al. 1992, esp. 264–266. Noble Prize winner Amartya Sen notes,

> It is tempting to think that this question [the viability of moral incentives] has been answered firmly in the negative, since the Cultural Revolution is now regarded by the Chinese government as a total failure … and … 'eating from the same big pot' … (has) been condemned. … But it is difficult to separate out the problems created by the reliance on moral incentives from the chaos of the political movement that went with it. With screaming Red Guards taking over factories, intellectuals being banished to rural areas, etc., more was happening in China during the Cultural Revolution than just the use of a different incentive system …
>
> (Sen 1984, 9–10)

   See also Bramall 2009a, 239 and Sun Yan 1995, Chapter 8.
   Gittings concludes,

> Whether the communes, if properly managed, could have provided a smoother path, is now an unrealistic question. … Most Chinese peasants were no longer willing to be mobilized for "hard struggle" without more immediate returns, and had been alienated by dogmatic policies restricting initiative and flouting rural common sense.
>
> (Gittings 1989, 128–129)

38 Hinton cites an economic study that found 30 percent of the communes were successful (40 percent middling and 30 percent unsuccessful), as proof that collectivization can succeed (Hinton 1990, 140–14). He finds that collectivization needs the right infrastructure to work. He links poor leadership to inadequate training, over centralization, bureaucratic maladies, and "commandism."

Bramall argues that the failure to pursue earlier collectivization (1949–1955) was one of the great mistakes of the Maoist period (Bramall 2009a, 545). Emphasizing the viability of collectivization, Samir Amin writes,

> the recorded results are far from having been disastrous, as the right would have us believe. A commune in the Beijing region, which resisted the order to dissolve the system, continues to record excellent economic results linked with the persistence of high-quality political debates, which disappeared elsewhere.
>
> (Amin 2013)

Zhang Zhuoyuan also blames "adventurous" excesses rather than inherent problems with socialist planning for most of China's economic problems in the 1970s. He writes, "the present disproportions in China are an abnormal phenomenon which is not a necessary concomitant of her economic setup, and ... can be remedied even without a change in the latter" (Zhang 1982, 19–20).

For a "glass is half empty rather than half full" interpretation of the data, see Putterman 1993, esp. 348–350. Putterman grants that collective agriculture "did not perform badly, overall, compared to the agricultures of other densely populated Asian countries" in the 1960s and 1970s (348). He suggests, however, that inherent problems with; the anti-incentivist policies, authoritarian imposition, diseconomies of scale, and the state's extraction of surplus, limited the trajectory of collective projects.

39 Unger elaborates:

> the state did not leave the teams alone. ... The system of collectives was, as a result, repressive. ... [M]any were relieved to escape the heavy hand. ... They were exhausted by their experience of the 1970s, when bewildering and at times tense political campaigns had been funneled through the collectives, and they were irritated by the commandist style of so many team and village leaders, which was in keeping with ... the broader political atmosphere of Party rule.
>
> (Unger 2002, 224)

40 William Hinton, for example acknowledges that the contract system may have helped motivate farmers in Fengyang County to take advantage of new opportunities, but he attributes the increase in output largely to massive increases in the use of fertilizers, new hybrid rice varieties, expanded irrigation, and increased pest control (Hinton 1990, Chapter 2). Bruce Stone (1988, 818–821; 1990, 48) reaches similar conclusions.

Chris Bramall finds Maoist institutions for diffusing modern farm technology responsible for a lot of the increase in farm output during the transition period (251–252) He emphasizes "heavy Maoist investment in chemical fertilizer production, high-yielding crop varieties, and irrigation" (Bramall 2000, 459–460). Bramall also reiterates Carl Riskin's finding that "output in those areas which decollectivized early grew no faster than in late-comers" (Bramall 2000, 468). In 2009, Bramall reconfirms these judgments, writing,

> Contrary to the views expressed in the literature, the Chinese economy was not on the verge of collapse. ... China's long-run growth path was shifting upwards in the 1970s as a result of the application of green revolution technology in agriculture, the growing maturity of its rural industries, and producer good imports.
>
> (Bramall 2009b, 448)

Mark Selden highlights the tripling of tubewells and quadrupling of electricity consumption in the countryside, as well as the massive expansion of fertilizer plants from 1970–1980. He concludes. "The gains in rural productivity achieved in the first half of the 1980s rested in part on foundations of twenty-five years of heavy accumulation and investment in agricultural infrastructure" (Selden 1993, 34). Lynn White III also emphasizes the impact of technological change in the countryside, reporting the following leaps in mechanization from 1970 to 1978: water pumps +246 percent, rice transplanting machines +262 percent, walking tractors +631 percent, large and middle sized tractors: +355 percent, and agricultural pick up trucks +914 percent (White 1998, 85, 88).

Xu Zhun is a Marxist economist and Assistant Professor at Renmin University in Beijing. He has pulled together evidence for a counter narrative to the "miracle of markets" interpretation of agricultural expansion in the early 1980s. See: Xu Zhun 2012, 2013. See also Hart-Landsberg 2011, 56; and Meisner 1996, 235–238.

41  Huang and Rozelle report that fertilizer use increased from <1 kg/ha in 1952 to 24kg/ha in 1970, to 59 kg/ha in 1978 and 121 kg/ha in 1984. The percentage of new hybrid seeds sown also increased from <1 percent in 1976 to 25 percent in 1984. Huang and Rozelle also link maintenance problems with irrigation systems, formerly handled by the collectives, to the slow down in grain yield growth rates from 5.9 percent 1978–1984 to 1.6 percent 1984–1990. Yields grew at a 3.3 percent rate 1964–1978 (Table 1).

Many observers have also pointed out that China's agricultural output began to increase rapidly before the expansion of the HRS. Carl Riskin, for example, writes

> the beginning of the spurt in agricultural growth preceded both the price changes and the more radical decollectivization measures. Total agricultural output surged forward by 8.9% in 1978 and 8.6% in 1979. ... Yet the new prices took effect only with the summer harvest in 1979, and in early 1980 only about 1 per cent of farm households had adapted any form of HRS
>
> (Riskin 1987, 297–298. See also Unger 2002, 224)

42  Bramall argues that during the collectivist period there was significant under-reporting of rural output, due to the exclusion of private plots from rural output data and the communes' under-reporting of output in order to evade higher procurement targets. He finds that reporting biases may have been as large as 40 percent (Bramall 2009a, 228–229). Putterman (1993) also highlights the potential for uncertainties over the treatment of output from private plots to significantly reduce the estimated contribution to output increases of the HRS (225–227).

Bramall joins Hinton in suggesting that some of the reported increases in output after the reforms were the result of drawing down accumulated stocks rather than new production (Bramall 2009a, 228; Hinton 1990, 22).

Bramall links part of the slower growth in agricultural output during the collectivist years to external constraints (such as the need for grain self-sufficiency in response to threatening international situations) and poor weather conditions (immediately preceding the shift to the HRS).

Bramall criticizes conventional TFP analyses which find TFP declining by 1 percent per year from 1955–1981 and increasing by ~4 percent/ year 1981–1996 (Bramall 2009a, 235). He argues that land inputs have been poorly measured, the weights assigned to factor inputs quite arbitrary (partially due to the divergence of prices from marginal costs), and fish and livestock production exaggerated. He concludes that, if adjustments are made for the mistreatment of output from private plots and the increase in labor hours during the 1981–1985 period, "the alleged superiority of family farming is wiped out" (Bramall 2009a, 236).

In discussing Justin Lin's famous econometric analysis of the impact of the HRS, which he deems the strongest of the econometric analyses of the causes of increased output, Bramall faults Lin for inadequately dealing with the lagged effects of better irrigation and the big change in the weather between 1978–1981, and 1982–1984. He also notes measurement problems due to the level of aggregation (at the province rather than country level) and the treatment of labor and capital inputs (Bramall 2000, 333–339).

43 One study by authors sympathetic to the HRS, for example, found problems with maintaining roads and irrigation systems and other public goods after decollectivization in about half of the villages sampled (Nee and Su 1990, 19–20). The authors counter-balanced this observation, however, with the suggestion that new social mechanisms could be created to address these problems. Coase and Wang offer similarly optimistic projections (2012, 77). Huang and Rozelle (1995) highlight the negative environmental impact of deteriorating irrigation systems. They indicate that,

> the neglect of water conservancy infrastructure became so serious in the late 1980s that … [t]he use of corvee labor was in part reinstituted widely across China in the early 1990s in order to remove the accumulation of silt in major canals and reservoirs
>
> (Huang and Rozelle 1995, 856)

Putterman points out that coverage under China's rural health insurance scheme fell from 85 percent in 1979 to 5 percent in 1985 (Putterman 1993, 40). He also reports statistics on declining school enrollments, but suggests the drop in attendance was more due to heightened opportunities for youth labor in the economy than declining public funding. Stone (1988) also notes that some of the statistics on declining irrigation are misleading.

44 At a 2002 symposium in Beijing on the Chinese Model of Modern Development, Du Runsheng addressed the problems created for Chinese farmers by their small holdings. He predicted a gradual rise in farm size due to continuing urban migration, but acknowledged average land holding would still be small (~2 hectares per household). He suggested, however, that there were modern technologies available that did not require large firms, such as walking tractors and remote sensing systems that can increase the efficiency of fertilization. He noted that the family farm has survived quite well in modern capitalist countries, and in good Marxist fashion asserted, "As long as the operation of family farms still accommodates the development of production power, it will not end" (Du, 2005, 12–13).

45 Bramall 2009a, 242. Bramall cites the claim of New Left theorist Cui Zhiyuan that workplace democracy might be the answer to SOE efficiency problems (Bramall 2009a, 328). Selden stresses the importance of volunteerism to the potential success of collective enterprises (Selden 1993, 59–61, 108). Putterman 1993 notes the obstacle for group farming introduced by the top down structure of economic decisions and heavy-handed political campaigns (20, 25, 349–350). David Zweig echoes Putterman, writing, "for collectives to succeed, peasants must join them voluntarily, and internal decision making must occur within a democratic forum … had peasants been actively involved in its internal decision making, they might have developed strong attachments to the collective" (Zweig 1989, 198).

46 Su Shaozhi was attacked in 1983 and in 1987, and was eventually replaced as head of the Marxism-Leninism-Mao Zedong Institute of the Chinese Academy of Social Sciences (Su 1995, 111–117). The Institute under Su's leadership was reportedly attacked for promoting "bourgeois liberalism." Whether this meant Western liberalism or humanist Marxism was not clear in Su's account.

47 Taylorism has a relatively long history in China. It appeared first in Japanese factories in Manchuria in 1917. It expanded during the nationalist years, was renewed

in the 1950s by Soviet advisors, fell into disrepute during the Maoist period, and resurfaced under Deng (Warner 2014). See Marglin 1974 and Braverman 1974 (esp. 11–24) for excellent critiques of Taylorism from a humanist Marxist point of view.

48 Bramall indicates that from ~1963–1978, rural industrial growth averaged about 15 percent per year, "with perhaps" 40 million workers (~half the industrial labor force) involved (Bramall 2009a, 270). From 1971–1978 commune and brigade output grew at more than 23 percent per year (Bramall 2009a, 277). After 1978 this rate increased. During the Mao years, the workers in commune and brigade industries were usually paid in work points rather than money wages (Whyte 1999, 175).

49 Dong celebrates the emergence of specialized households in the making of badges and labels. Among the household specific tasks cited are: designing, engraving, molding, stamping, painting, glazing, perforating, and assembling. He lists a similar detailed division of labor in textile production from reprocessed fibers. In this case specialized households are involved in: buying materials, sorting waste materials, disassembling materials, spinning, weaving, sewing, transporting, and marketing (Dong 1990, 78–79). The number of separate households engaged in these specific tasks is staggering. For example, there were more than 6,000 different households doing spinning, and another 6,000 different households doing weaving, with nearly 3,000 additional households doing sewing and 1,200 households disassembling old fabrics, etc. (Dong 1990, 78–79).

50 Lin declared, "The expansion of market relationships … has caused people's viewpoints to change. People … dare to take risks" (Lin Zili 1990, 175).

51 Lin Zhang avers, "*Wenzhou's rural commodity markets have provided a great school for peasant education* [emphasis in original]. … The market has taught them to be courageous and to take risks. … When markets are alive, the whole rural economy is alive" (Lin Zhang 1990, 106).

52 Chen demonstrates he is quite familiar with Marx's *Capital*, alluding to Marx's classic image in Volume 1 of *Capital* of the capitalist confidently striding forward and the worker hanging his head, after the "free contract" wage bargain is consummated. He cites several imaginative schemes to try to circumvent the creation of a class of owners accumulating the social surplus from industrial profits. These include a progressive income tax on profits three times greater than the return on bank deposits (his presumed opportunity costs of capital), requirements that 80 percent of profits be reinvested in the firm, limits on the ratio of employer to worker income, requirements that employers participate in labor, restrictions on the number of employees (an option he is especially skeptical of), and credit, and marketing regulations. He ends his discussion optimistically, asserting, "we shouldn't worry. … The socialist superstructure has the power … to change the nature of the feeble private enterprises" (Chen Ruiming 1990, 153).

53 Sounding very much like Karl Polyani, Wang Hui writes, "A movement for social self-protection, the 1989 social movement embodied a spontaneous resistance to inequalities springing from the growth of markets…" (Wang 2003a, 58). Some observers have suggested that the state's retreat from price reform in the face of public opposition emboldened the 1989 protesters.

54 See Maurice Meisner 1999 Chapter 24 for a chilling account of what seems like a Greek tragedy, as events filled with hope relentlessly slid to disaster. Meisner acknowledges that it is difficult to estimate the number of casualties immediately associated with the protest's suppression. The official government toll was less than 300. Meisner cites more credible estimates of 2,000–7,000 deaths and several times that wounded. Almost all of the deaths were civilians. Deng offered public condolences to the families of several dozen soldiers said to have died in the battles.

55 Zhao Ziyang, who had championed market based reform and policies such as the household responsibility system, was removed from power. Li Peng was given control over economic policy. Li was an engineer by training and seems to have lacked strong ideological beliefs about economic issues. He eventually sided with Yao Yilin (an ally of Chen Yun) who favored reversing parts of the last decade's restructuring. His policies focused on macroeconomic contraction (to reduce inflation and the trade deficit) and institutional changes to increase the role of economic planning and state-owned firms in the economy. The trend toward price decontrol was mildly reversed. The list of goods allocated by planners was expanded.

56 Renewed efforts were also made to put university students in contact with the difficulties of rural life. CASS, which had been a source of support for the protests, was limited in graduate student recruitment for two years. All new students had to have a 10 month field experience in Sha'anxi Province and "moral training" was to remain part of the graduate school curriculum (Sleeboom-Faulkner 2007, 126, 164). Administratively, final management authority inside the Academy was shifted from the formal hierarchy (President, Vice President, etc.) to the parallel Party Committee alongside the bureaucracy (Sleeboom-Faulkner 2007, 14, 121–122). In response to student activism at Beijing University, the president was replaced and all new students were required to undertake military service (Sleeboom-Faulkner 2007, 126). A month-long course in patriotism was set up for academics going abroad (Sleeboom-Faulkner 2007, 132). Some members of the Rural Development Research Institute, and the Institute of Economic Structural Reform were fired (Sleeboom-Faulkner 2007, 127).

57 Wang Luolin was an economist and Liu Ji a political "heavyweight" for liberal policies. Liu was reportedly hand picked by Jiang Zemin to be his personal link to CASS (Sleeboom-Faulkner 2007, 150–152, 315). Wang Luolin edited a 2015 Routledge Press volume celebrating the benefits of China's membership in the WTO, Interestingly, Wang's grandfather had translated Marx's *Capital* into Chinese (Leonard 2008b).

58 Growth slowed to 4.4 percent in 1989 and 3.9 percent in 1990, with the four quarters in the middle of the two years basically stagnant (Naughton 1995, 287).

59 Ren Xuean, the director of many influential economics documentaries for Chinese television (CCTV), reinforces this theme. He reports,

> It hurts to see my uncle, a formerly revered factory worker, now occupying the lowest rank of the society after the reform … [but] He understands that reform is good for China and his personal loss is justified by the progress China has made … collective pride trumps that of the individual.
>
> (Zhu Ying 2012, 116)

Martin Whyte's 2004 national survey of Chinese attitudes found most respondents begrudgingly accepting inequality as part of China's meritocracy (Andreas 2012, 129). The reasons given for people being rich involved superior ability, diligence, and education. Poverty was attributed to "lack of ability, insufficient effort, poor education and poor character" (Andreas 2012, 129).

60 Li Shi 2008, 4–5. Yang and Zhao report that the number of workers laboring away from their *hukou* registration for more than six months increased from 15 million in 1987, to 30 million in 1990, to 56 million in 1995, to 80 million in 2000, to 140 million in 2004 (Yang and Zhao 2009, 108).

61 The enduring allure of land holdings by people with strong rural roots is not limited to China. Daniel Kelliher (citing E. P. Thompson's classic *The Making of the English Working Class*), notes that industrial workers in England continued to hold on to the ideal of family farming long after becoming urban workers (Kelliher 1992, 97).

62 You Ji claims that as many as 40 million peasants lost their land in insider privatization deals, underpricing land by ~2 trillion yuan from 1998–2003 (Yang and Zhao 2009, 75).

63 State agricultural investment as a percentage of total investment fell from more than 9 percent in 1980 to 3–4 percent for the1986–1991 period (Oi 1999, 21–22). In 1994, government investment in agriculture was little more than half of the 1979 level (Sachs and Woo 2000, 31).

64 Yang 2006, illustration # 4.

65 World Bank Poverty and Equity data (http://povertydata.worldbank.org/poverty/country/CHN, accessed April 22, 2017).

66 As many observers have warned, these statistics probably overestimate the decline in collectively owned TVEs. Some firms formerly labeled public TVEs were really private firms, and some currently labeled private firms have high percentages of publicly owned shares.

67 Xu Zhun 2013, 25; Huang et al. 2008, 499.

68 See for example Huang et al. 2008, esp. 491.

69 Naughton 2007, Chapter 12 is a good example of this framing.

70 For example, the share of villages covered under the "cooperative medical system" fell from more than 90 percent in 1976 to 11 percent in 1983 and remained at around 20 percent in the mid-1990s (Huang 2009b, 348).

71 These declines are also highlighted in some neoclassical analyses critical of partial marketization (especially noteworthy are accounts by Huang Yasheng (2008) and He Qinglian (*The Pitfalls of Modernization* 1998).

72 Huang ties this increase to higher dropout rates due to higher household costs for education and declining government support (2008, 246). He argues that problems in primary school education 1995–2000 manifested themselves seven to nine years later in adult literacy statistics, which refer to people over 15 years of age. He estimates that as many as 30 percent of all rural primary school students in the late 1990s may have ended up illiterate at age 15. Illiteracy rates had previously declined from 180 million in 1990 to 85 million in 2000, before rising to 115 million in 2005 (Huang 2008, 243–249).

73 Li lived in China until 1985 when he left for graduate study in the US, earning a PhD in political science at Princeton. His brother was a victim of the Cultural Revolution, apparently beaten to death for listening to the Voice of America (Li Cheng 1997, xvi, 7).

74 For a similar account see Hart-Landsberg 2011, esp. 66. Li and Qi cite data finding a slightly shorter work week. They report that a survey done by China's National Bureau of Statistics found that the average work week for migrant workers in 2009 in manufacturing, construction, social services, hotel and catering services, and wholesale and retailing, was 59–61 hours or roughly 10 hours a day, 6 days per week (Li and Qi 2014, 483). Citing a key Chinese 2002 economic survey (The Chinese Household Income Project Survey [CHIPS]), Li Shi reports that over 80 percent of the migrants worked 7 days a week, with almost 25 percent working 11–12 hours and 12 percent working more than 13 hours a day (Li Shi 2008, 14).

75 Huang finds that the China Labor Statistical Yearbook over-estimates the average wage of informal workers and underestimates their work week. He writes, "by leaving out laborers of the informal economy from its data, what the Ministry of Labor and Social Security has done, whether intentionally or not, amounts to a gross distortion of empirical reality…" (Huang 2009a, 425).

76 In contrast, during the 1970s urban/rural and male/female educational divides narrowed, and as Bramall reports, "the traditional link between the level of parental education and the educational opportunities enjoyed by their children was broken …. It was this elimination of traditional class privilege that generated such bitterness…" (Bramall 2009a, 210).

77 Lin Chun argues that this more egalitarian spirit infused private TVEs, asserting "Even privately run enterprises tended to bend to the communal pressures for social obligations, such as fair distribution of employment and regular donation to local public service facilities..." (Lin Chun 2006, 31. See also Weitzman and Xu 1994). Shifting ideological and institutional contexts would soon change this.

78 Lin Chun's explanation for the triumph of privatization seems to emphasize ideology a bit more than competitive pressures, though perhaps she was referring to the ideological underpinnings of the market environment that produced the competitive pressures. She writes,

> TVEs underwent a sweeping transition from a collective "Sunan model" to a privatized "Wenzhou model" in the late 1990s ... the change was guided less by any intrinsic need of privatization than it was forced by artificial engineering under a mounting market ideology.
>
> (Lin Chun 2006, 31)

79 Bramall (2009a, 424) develops this line of argument with respect to the SOEs and raises the linked question of who currently controls the Chinese state. Socialist defenders of the economic reforms have maintained that CPC's monopoly of state power allows current policy to mobilize the engine of capitalist accumulation without creating a self-perpetuating capitalist social structure. Critics of this strategy often cite an old saying, "He who rides on the back of the tiger, often ends up inside."

80 The first modest attempt to combine shareholding rights with employee rights was undertaken during decollectivization in 1982 (Cui 2005, 161). Not much came of this initiative. In early 1987 the Central Committee of the Chinese Communist Party advocated shareholding coops, but encountered resistance from some local governments (Vermeer 1999, 125). In response, the State Council authorized three SHC experiments to run from 1987 to 1990. At the end of this period, the Ministry of Agriculture officially endorsed SHCs projects (Clegg 1996, 120). By 1991, 10 percent of TVEs were shareholder cooperative firms (Clegg 1996, 121). The number reached 12 percent in 1995 (Vermeer 1999, 123).

81 See Friedman 1970.

82 A 1994 article by New Left theorist Cui Zhiyuan advocating shareholding cooperatives may have contributed to some government leaders support for SHCs (Cui 2005, 173).

83 See for example, Clegg 1996, 124; Bowles and Dong 1994, 58; and Lin 2006, Chapter 1.

84 This view was well represented by CASS economist Luo Xiaopeng at a key conference co-sponsored by the World Bank, and CASS's Institute of Economics in 1987. Luo wrote, "urbanization is the only way to modernize," adding, "A development strategy that pushes rural industrialization as a substitute for urbanization might prove costly ... it is necessary to consider how to speed up urbanization" (Luo, 1990, 170).

85 Day finds similarities between the NRR movement and the Zapatistas in Mexico and the Landless Workers Movement in Brazil (Day 2013, 162). I suspect the similarities may be more in terms of the perceived problems than proposed solutions.

86 The phrase "New Socialist Countryside" has a long pedigree. It was embraced by the Hu Jintao Administration and its construction held to be the country's top policy goal in Chinas 11th five-year plan (2006–2010). Hu first used the phrase in 1994. His vice premier in charge of agriculture, Hui Liangyu, wrote a book entitled *Building a New Socialist Countryside with Chinese Characteristics* in 1993. The phrase was part and parcel of Mao's 12 year agricultural plan that accelerated collectivization in 1956 (Looney 2012, 221–235).

There are competing definitions for what a NSC w/Chinese characteristics means. Unsurprisingly, the debate parallels the larger debate over the direction of the Chinese economic reforms. Neoclassical oriented definitions treat the phrase as a call for modernizing China's agricultural sector. Economists like Lin Justin Yifu highlight the goals of modernizing technology, high production, and increased rural incomes, with the latter a key part of efforts to rebalance China's macro economy by replacing export demand with consumer demand. Heterodox and Marxist economists stress the goal of creating socialist institutions in the countryside. In Marxist language, the debate is between policies that prioritize expanding the forces of production and policies that prioritize building socialist relations of production and socialist consciousness. For the most part, Hu's policies concentrated on production and modernization (Looney 2012, 211). Rhetorically, Hu's administration has tried to appropriate Maoist enthusiasm without Maoist institutions.

Wen Tiejun and proponents of New Rural Reconstruction have emphasized building new social institutions—especially those able to recreate a sense of community and collective purpose in the countryside. They implicitly challenge neoclassical interpreters of the NSC to indicate what is socialist about their countryside. The tension between a rhetoric historically tied to socialist institutions and mass mobilization campaigns, and practices geared to capitalist institutions animates both the language and policies of the NSC.

Similar debates have arisen in China over the meaning of "Chinese Ecological Agriculture" [CEA] and "Chinese Sustainable Agriculture" in the mid-1980s. McCoy treats the phrases as largely symbolic myths that give the appearance of offering a new model for Chinese agriculture, but fail to diverge very much from China's current market driven logic (McCoy 2000, 138).

Interestingly, Coase and Wang find in Wen Jiabao's remarks to the National People's Congress in 2011 a "sea change" in China's leaders' goals from "socialist modernization … to a better life with happiness and dignity…" (Coase and Wang 2013, 204). Reflecting their own assumptions, Coase and Wang then argue that capitalist institutions offer a blueprint for achieving happiness and a spiritual civilization (206–207). The history of alienation and dreadful labor conditions in capitalism, among other blemishes, are unaddressed.

87 For He's views see He 2007.
88 "Choice of Path in the Reconstruction of Rural Culture" (2007), reprinted by the China Study Group (http://chinastudygroup.net/2011/04/reconstruction-of-rural-culture/, accessed March 23, 2014). See also the CSG's obituary for Liu Xiangbo at: http://chinastudygroup.net/2011/04/liu-xiangbo/. [Unfortunately, both of these sites currently appear to have been taken down—July 10, 2016].
89 Easterlin et al. concluded,

> Despite an unprecedented rate of economic growth, China's life satisfaction over the last two decades has … no change or a declining trend. … Life satisfaction has declined markedly in the lowest-income and least-educated segments of the population while rising somewhat in the upper SES stratum.
>
> (Easterlin et al. 2012)

# References

Amin, Samir. 2013. "China 2013." *Monthly Review: An Independent Socialist Magazine* 64 (10): 14. http://monthlyreview.org/2013/03/01/china-2013/.

Andreas, Joel. 2012. "Sino-Seismology." *New Left Review* 76: 128–135.

Arrighi, Giovanni. 2008. *Adam Smith in Beijing: Lineages of the Twenty-First Century*. New York: Verso.

Blecher, Marc. 2010. *China Against the Tides: Restructuring through Revolution, Radicalism and Reform.* 3rd ed. New York: Continuum.

Bowles, Paul and Xiao-yuan Dong. 1994. "Current Successes and Future Challenges in China's Economic Reforms." *New Left Review* (208): 49–76.

Bramall, Chris. 1990. "The Wenzhou 'Miracle': An Assessment." In *Market Forces in China: Competition and Small Business; the Wenzhou Debate,* edited by Peter Nolan and Fureng Dong, 43–76. Atlantic Highlands, NJ: Zed Books.

Bramall, Chris. 2000. *Sources of Chinese Economic Growth 1978–1996.* New York: Oxford University Press.

Bramall, Chris. 2009a. *Chinese Economic Development.* New York: Routledge.

Bramall, Chris. 2009b. "Out of the Darkness: Chinese Transition Paths." *Modern China* 35 (4): 439–449.

Braverman, Harry. 1974. *Labor and Monopoly Capital: The Degradation of Work in the Twentieth Century.* New York: Monthly Review Press.

Brugger, Bill, and David Kelly. 1990. *Chinese Marxism in the Post-Mao Era.* Stanford, CA: Stanford University Press.

Chan, Anita. 2001. *China's Workers Under Assault: The Exploitation of Labor in a Globalizing Economy.* Armonk, NY: M. E. Sharpe.

Chan, Anita, Richard Madsen, and Jonathan Unger. 1992. *Chen Village under Mao and Deng.* 2nd ed. Berkeley, CA: University of California Press.

Chen, Ruiming. 1990. "A Preliminary Analysis of the 'Big-Labour-Hiring Households' in Rural Wenzhou." In *Market Forces in China: Competition and Small Business; the Wenzhou Debate,* edited by Peter Nolan and Fureng Dong, 140–156. Atlantic Highlands, NJ: Zed Books.

Chen, Yun. 1982a. [1956a] "New Issues since the Basic Completion of the Socialist Transformation." *Chinese Economic Studies* 15 (3): 7–22.

Chen, Yun. 1982b. [1956b] "Methods of Solving the Tensions in Supplies of Pork and Vegetables." *Chinese Economic Studies* 15 (3): 23–29.

Cheung, Steven. 1986. *Will China Go Capitalist?* 2nd ed. London: Institute of Economic Affairs.

Clegg, Jenny. 1996. "China's Rural Shareholding Cooperatives as a Form of Multi-Stakeholder Cooperation." *Journal of Rural Cooperation* 24 (2): 119–142.

Coase, Ronald, and Ning Wang. 2013. *How China Became Capitalist.* New York: Palgrave Macmillan.

Cui, Zhiyuan. 2005. "Liberal Socialism and the Future of China: A Petty Bourgeoisie Manifesto." In *The Chinese Model of Modern Development,* edited by Tian Yu Cao, 157–174. New York: Routledge.

Day, Alexander F. 2013. *The Peasant in Post Socialist China: History, Politics, and Capitalism.* Cambridge: Cambridge University Press.

Dirlik, Arif. 1978. *Revolution and History: the Origins of Marxist Historiography in China 1919–1937.* Berkeley, CA: University of California Press.

Dong, Fureng. 1990. "The Wenzhou Model for Developing the Rural Commodity Economy." In *Market Forces in China: Competition and Small Business; the Wenzhou Debate,* edited by Peter Nolan and Fureng Dong, 77–96. Atlantic Highlands, NJ: Zed Books.

Du, Runsheng. 1988. "Rural Employment in China: The Choices." *International Labour Review* 127 (3): 371. http://heinonline.org/HOL/LandingPage?handle=hein.journals/intlr127&div=37.

Du, Runsheng. 2005. "We should Encourage Institutional Innovations." In *The*

*Chinese Model of Modern Development*, edited by Tian Yu Cao, 9–15. New York: Routledge.

Du, Yuxin. 2011. "A Bibliometrics Portrait of Chinese Research through the Lens of *China Economic Review*." Master's thesis, Universidade do Porto.

Easterlin, Richard, Fei Wang, and Shun Wang. 2017. "Growth and Happiness in China, 1990–2015." Paper accompanying poster presentation at Annual Meetings of the American Economic Association 2017. Available at: http://conference.iza. org/conference_files/ICID_Renmin_2016/wang_f8757.pdf.

Easterlin, Richard, Robson Morgan, Malgorzota Switek, and Fei Wang. 2012. "China's Life Satisfaction, 1910–2010." *Proceedings of the National Academy of Sciences* 109: 9775–9780.

Fewsmith, Joseph. 1994. *Dilemmas of Reform in China: Political Conflict and Economic Debate*. Armonk, NY: M. E. Sharpe.

Fewsmith, Joseph. 1999. "Editor's Introduction." *Chinese Economic Studies* 32 (2): 3–4.

Friedman, Milton. 1970. "The Social Responsibility of Business is to Increase Profits." *New York Times*, September 13, 1970.

Friedman, Milton. 1990a. *Friedman in China*. Hong Kong: Chinese University Press.

Fromm, Erich. 1970. *Marx's Concept of Man*. New York: Frederick Ungar Publishing Co.

Garner, Bradley. "China's Black Market City." *Reason* December 2011 (http:// reason.com/archives/2011/11/15/chinas-black-market-city/singlepage, accessed June 28, 2012).

Gittings, John. 1989. *China Changes Face: The Road from Revolution 1949–1989*. New York: Oxford University Press.

Hartford, Kathleen. 1985. "Socialist Agriculture is Dead; Long Live Socialist Agriculture: Organizational Transformation in Rural China." In *The Political Economy of Reform in Post-Mao China*, edited by Elizabeth J. Perry and Christine Wong, 31–61. Cambridge, MA: Harvard University Press.

Hart-Landsberg, Martin. 2011. "The Chinese Reform Experience: A Critical Assessment." *Review of Radical Political Economics* 43 (1): 56–76. doi:10.1177/0486613410 383954.

Hart-Landsberg, Martin, and Paul Burkett. 2005. *China and Socialism: Market Reforms and Class Struggle*. New York: Monthly Review.

Harvey, David. 2005. *A Brief History of Neoliberalism*. New York: Oxford.

He, Jianzhang and Wenmin Zhang. 1982. "The System of Ownership: A Tendency Toward Multiplicity." In *China's Economic Reforms*, edited by Lin Wei and Arnold Chao, 186–204. Philadelphia, PA: University of Pennsylvania Press.

He, Xuefeng. 2007. "New Rural Construction and the Chinese Path." *Chinese Sociology & Anthropology* 39 (4): 26–38. doi:10.2753/CSA0009-4625390402.

Hinton, William. 1990. *The Great Reversal: The Privatization of China 1978–1989*. New York: Monthly Review.

Hsu, Robert C. 1991. *Economic Theories in China 1979–1988*. New York: Cambridge University Press.

Huang, Jikun, and Scott Rozelle. 1995. "Environmental Stress and Grain Yields in China." *American Journal of Agricultural Economics* 77 (4): 853. doi:10.2307/1243808.

Huang, Jikun, Keijiro Otsuka, and Scott Rozelle. 2008. "Agriculture in China's Development: Past Disappointments, Recent Successes, and Future Challenges." In *China's Great Economic Transformation*, edited by Loren Brandt and Thomas Rawski, 467–505. New York: Cambridge University Press.

Huang, Philip C. C. 2009a. "China's Neglected Informal Economy: Reality and Theory." *Modern China* 35 (4): 405–438. doi:10.1177/0097700409333158.

Huang, Philip C. C. 2009b. "Introduction to 'Whither Chinese Reforms? Dialogues among Western and Chinese Scholars, II'." *Modern China* 35 (4): 347–351. doi: 10.1177/0097700409335385.

Huang, Yasheng. 2008. *Capitalism with Chinese Characteristics: Entrepreneurship and the State*. New York: Cambridge University Press.

Jefferson, Gary H., and Thomas Rawski. 1995. "How Industrial Reform Worked in China: The Role of Innovation, Competition, and Property Rights." World Bank, 1994.

Kelliher, Daniel. 1992. *Peasant Power in China: The Era of Rural Reform 1979–1989*. New Haven, CT: Yale University Press.

Kraus, Willy. 1991. *Private Business in China: Revival between Ideology and Pragmatic Policy*. Honolulu, HI: University of Hawaii Press.

Kung, James Kai-sing. 1999. "The Evoluton of Property Rights in Village Enterprises: the Case of Wuxi Countuy." In *Property Rights and Economic Reform in China*, edited by Jean Oi and Andrew Walder, 95–120. Stanford, CA: Stanford University Press.

Lardy, Nicholas. 1990. "Chinese Agricultural Development Under Reform and Future Prospects." In *Agricultural Reform and Development in China: Achievements, Current Status, and Future Outlook, Sixth Colloquium Proceedings*, edited by T. C. Tso, 21–35. Beltsville, MD: IDEALS Inc.

Lau, Raymond. 2001. "Economic Determination in the Last Instance: China's Political-Economic Development Under the Impact of the Asian Financial Crises." *Historical Materialism* 8 (1): 215–251. doi:10.1163/156920601100414811.

Leonard, Mark. 2008b. "China's New Intelligentsia." *Prospect Magazine*, March 2008.

Li, Cheng. 1997. *Rediscovering China: Dynamics and Dilemmas of Reform*. Lanham MD: Rowman & Littlefield.

Li, Minqi. 2008. *The Rise of China and the Demise of the Capitalist World Economy*. New York: Monthly Review.

Li, Shi. 1990. "Growth of Household Industry in Rural Wenzhou." In *Market Forces in China: Competition and Small Business; the Wenzhou Debate*, edited by Peter Nolan and Fureng Dong, 108–125. Atlantic Highlands, NJ: Zed Books.

Li, Shi. 2008. *Rural Migrant Workers in China: Scenario, Challenges and Public Policy*. ILO Working Papers. Vol. 89. Geneva: International Labour Office.

Li, Weisen, and Hans-Michael Trautwein. 2013. "Northian Perspectives on China's Economic Reform." In *Thoughts on Economc Development in China*, edited by Ying Ma and Hans-Michael Trautwein, 235–254. New York: Routledge.

Li, Zhongjin, and Hao Qi. 2014. "Labor Process and the Social Structure of Accumulation in China." *Review of Radical Political Economics* 46 (4): 481–488. doi:10.1177/0486613414537986.

Lin, Chun. 2006. *The Transformation of Chinese Socialism*. Durham, NC: Duke University Press.

Lin, Justin Yifu. 1988. "Rural Factor Markets in China After the Household Responsibility Reform." In *Chinese Economic Policy: Economic Reform at Midstream*, edited by Bruce Reynolds and Ilpyong Kim, 169–203. New York: Paragon House.

Lin, Justin Yifu. 1990. "Collectivization and China's Agricultural Crisis in 1959–1961." *Journal of Political Economy* 98 (6): 1228–1252. doi:10.1086/261732.

Lin, Justin Yifu. 1992. "Rural Reforms and Agricultural Growth in China." *The American Economic Review* 82 (1): 34–51. www.jstor.org/stable/2117601.

Lin, Justin Yifu. 2005. *Building Up a Market-Oriented Research and Education Institution in a Transitional Economy: The Experience of the China Center for Economic Research at Peking University (CCER Working Paper no. E2005003)*. Beijing: China Center for Economic Research.

Lin, Justin Yifu. 2012c. *Benti and Changwu: Dialogues on Methodology in Economics*. Beijing: Peking University Press.

Lin, Zhang. 1990. "Developing the Commodity Economy in the Rural Areas." In *Market Forces in China: Competition and Small Business; the Wenzhou Debate*, edited by Peter Nolan and Fureng Dong, 97–107. Atlantic Highlands, NJ: Zed Books.

Lin, Zili. 1990. "Privatization, Marketization, and Polarization." In *Market Forces in China: Competition and Small Business; the Wenzhou Debate*, edited by Peter Nolan and Fureng Dong, 165–175. Atlantic Highlands, NJ: Zed Books.

Lippit, Victor. 1987. *The Economic Development of China*. Armonk, NY: M. E. Sharpe.

Liu, Alan. 1992. "The 'Wenzhou Model' of Development and China's Modernization." *Asian Survey* 32 (8): 696–711. doi:10.2307/2645363.

Looney, Kristen. 2012. "The Rural Development State: Modernization Campaigns and Peasant Pollitics in China, Taiwan, and South Korea." PhD diss., Harvard University.

Luo, Xiaopeng. 1990. "Ownership and Status Stratification." In *China's Rural Industry: Structure, Development, and Reform*, edited by William Byrd and Qingsong Lin, 134–171. Washington, DC: World Bank.

Marglin, Stephen A. 1974. "What do Bosses Do?: The Origins and Functions of Hierarchy in Capitalist Production." *Review of Radical Political Economics* 6 (2): 60–112. doi:10.1177/048661347400600206.

McCoy, Michael Dalton. 2000. *Domestic Policy Narratives and International Relations Theory: Chinese Ecological Agriculture as a Case Study*. New York: University Press of America.

Meisner, Maurice. 1996. *The Deng Xiaopeng Era: An Inquiry into the Fate of Chinese Socialism 1978–1994*. New York: Hill and Wang.

Meisner, Maurice. 1999. *Mao's China: A History of the People's Republic*. 3rd ed. New York: Free Press.

National Bureau of Statistics of China. 2010. *China Statistical Yearbook 2010*. Beijing: China Statistics Press.

Naughton, Barry. 1995. *Growing Out of the Plan: Chinese Economic Reform 1978–1993*. New York: Cambridge University Press.

Naughton, Barry. 2007. *The Chinese Economy: Transitions and Growth*. Cambridge, MA: MIT Press.

Nee, Victor and Su Sijin. 1990. "Institutional Change and Economic Growth in China: The View from the Villages." *The Journal of Asian Studies* 49 (1): 3–25. doi:10.2307/2058430.

Nolan, Peter. 1990. "Petty Commodity Production in a Socialist Economy: Chinese Rural Development Post-Mao." In *Market Forces in China: Competition and Small Business; The Wenzhou Debate*, edited by Peter Nolan and Fureng Dong, 7–42. Atlantic Highlands, NJ: Zed Books.

Oi, Jean. 1999. *Rural China Takes Off: Institutional Foundations of Economic Reform*. Berkeley, CA: University of California Press.

Oi, Jean, and Andrew Walder, eds. 1999. *Property Rights and Economic Reform in China*. Stanford, CA: Stanford University Press.

Oksenberg, Michel. 1982. "Economic Policy-Making in China: Summer 1981." *The China Quarterly* (90): 165–194. doi:10.1017/S0305741000000308.

Pils, Eva. 2006. "Asking the Tiger for His Skin: Rights Activism in China." *Fordham International Law Journal* 30 (4): 1209–1287. http://ir.lawnet.fordham.edu/ilj/vol.30/iss4/6.

Pringle, Tim. 2013. "Reflections on Labor in China: From a Moment to a Movement." *South Atlantic Quarterly* 112 (1): 191–202. doi:10.1215/00382876-1891323.

Putterman, Louis. 1993. *Continuity and Change in China's Rural Development.* New York: Oxford University Press.

Qian, Meijun, and Yasheng Huang. 2011. *Financial Reversal in Rural China*: Financial Institutions Center, University of Pennsylvania.

Qian, Yingyi, and Jinglian Wu. 2000. *China's Transition to a Market Economy: How Far Across the River?* Working Paper no. 69. Stanford, CA: Center for International Development, Stanford University.

Riskin, Carl. 1987. *China's Political Economy: The Quest for Development since 1949.* New York: Oxford University Press.

Sachs, Jeffrey D. and Wing Woo. 2000. "Understanding China's Economic Performance." *Journal of Policy Reform* 4 (1): 1–50. doi:10.1080/13841280008523412.

Selden, Mark. 1993. *The Political Economy of Chinese Development.* Armonk, NY: M. E. Sharpe.

Sen, Amartya. 1984. *Resources, Values and Development.* Cambridge, MA: Harvard University Press.

Sleeboom-Faulkner, Margaret. 2007. *The Chinese Academy of Social Sciences (CASS): Shaping the Reforms, Academia and China.* Boston, MA: Brill.

Smith, Richard. 1993. "The Chinese Road to Capitalism." *New Left Review* 199: 55–99.

Solinger, Dorothy J. 1981. "Economic Reform Via Reformulation in China: Where do Rightist Ideas come from?" *Asian Survey* 21 (9): 947–960. doi:10.2307/2643824.

Stone, Bruce. 1988. "Developments in Agricultural Technology." *The China Quarterly* (116): 767–822. doi:10.1017/S0305741000037954.

Stone, Bruce. 1990. "The Next Stage of Agricultural Development: Implications for Infrastructure, Technology and Institutional Priorities." In *Agricultural Reform and Development in China: Achievements, Current Status, and Future Outlook, Sixth Colloquium Proceedings*, edited by T. C. Tso, 47–93. Beltsville, MD: IDEALS Inc.

Su, Shaozhi. 1995. "The Structure of the Chinese Academy of Social Sciences and Two Decisions to Abolish Its Marxism-Leninism-Mao Zedong Thought Institute." In *Decision-Making in Deng's China: Perspectives from Insiders*, edited by Carol Lee Hamrin and Suisheng Zhao, 111–117. Armonk, NY: M. E. Sharpe.

Sun, Yan. 1995. *The Chinese Reassessment of Socialism 1976–1992.* Princeton, NJ: Princeton University Press.

Tsai, Kellee. 2006. "Debating Decentralized Development: A Reconsideration of the Wenzhou and Kerala Models." *Indian Journal of Economics and Business*: 47–67.

Unger, Jonathan. 1985. "The Decollectivization of the Chinese Countryside: A Survey of Twenty-Eight Villages." *Pacific Affairs* 58 (4): 585–606. doi:10.2307/2758470.

Unger, Jonathan. 2002. *The Transformation of Rural China.* Armonk, NY: M. E. Sharpe.

Vermeer, Eduard B. 1999. "Shareholding Cooperatives: A Property Rights Analysis." In *Property Rights and Economic Reform in China*, edited by Jean Oi and Andrew Walder, 123–144. Stanford, CA: Stanford University Press.

Wang, Hui. 2003a. *China's New Order: Society, Politics, and Economy in Transition*, edited by Theodore Huters. Cambridge, MA: Harvard University Press.

Warner, Malcolm. 2014. *Understanding Management in China: Past, Present, and Future.* New York: Routledge.

Watson, Andrew. 1987. "Social Science Research and Economic Policy Formulation: The Academic Side of Economic Reform." In *New Directions in the Social Sciences and Humanities in China*, edited by Michael B. Yahuda, 67–88. New York: St Martin's Press.

Weitzman, Martin and Chenggang Xu. 1994. "Chinese Township-Village Enterprises as Vaguely Defined Cooperatives." *Journal of Comparative Economics* 28: 121–145.

Wen, Tiejun. 2007. "Deconstructing Modernization." *Chinese Sociology & Anthropology* 39 (4): 10–25. doi:10.2753/CSA0009-4625390401.

Wen, Tiejun and Kin Chi Lau. 2008. "Four Stories in One: Environmental Protection and Rural Reconstruction in China." *Positions: East Asia Cultures Critique* 16 (3): 491–505.

White, Lynn T. III. 1998. *Local Causes of China's Economic Reforms. Unstately Power.* Vol. I. Armonk, NY: M. E. Sharpe.

Whiting, Susan. 2000. *Power and Wealth in Rural China: The Political Economy of Institutional Change.* New York: Cambridge University Press.

Whyte, Martin King. 1999. "The Changing Role of Workers." In *The Paradox of China's Post-Mao Reforms*, edited by Merle Goldman and Roderick MacFarquhar, 173–196. Cambridge, MA: Harvard University Press.

Xu, Chenggang. 2011. "The Fundamental Institutions of China's Reforms and Development." *Journal of Economic Literature* 49 (4): 1076–1151. doi:10.1257/jel.49.4.1076.

Xu, Chenggang and Xiaobo Zhang. 2009. *The Evolution of Chinese Entrepreneurial Firms: Township-Village Enterprises Revisited.* (IFPRI Discussion Paper 00854) International Food Policy Research Institute.

Xu, Yong. 2011. "The Expansion of Peasant Rationality: An Analysis of the Creators of the 'China Miracle'—Challenging Existing Theories and Proposing New Analytical Approaches." *Social Sciences in China* 32 (1): 5–25. doi:10.1080/02529203.2011.548916.

Xu, Zhun. 2012. "The Chinese Agriculture Miracle Revisited." *Economic and Political Weekly* XLVII (14): 51–58.

Xu, Zhun. 2013. "The Political Economy of Decollectivization in China." *Monthly Review: An Independent Socialist Magazine* 65 (1): 17–36. http://monthlyreview.org/2013/05/01/the-political-economy-of-decollectivization-in-china/.

Yang, Dali L., and Litao Zhao. 2009. *China's Reforms at 30.* Singapore: World Scientific.

Yang, Weiyong. 2006. "Reforms, Structural Adjustments, and Rural Income in China." *China Perspectives* 63.

Zhang, Zhuoyuan. 1982. "Introduction: China's Economy After the 'Cultural Revolution'." In *China's Economic Reforms*, edited by Lin Wei and Arnold Chao, 1–27. Philadelphia, PA: University of Pennsylvania Press.

Zhu, Ying. 2012. *Two Billion Eyes: The Story of China Central Television.* New York: The New Press.

Zweig, David. 1989. *Agrarian Radicalism in China 1968–1981.* Cambridge, MA: Harvard University Press.

# 5 Economic restructuring in the international sector

## 5.1 Introduction

This chapter analyzes how the general factors influencing Chinese economic theory found expression in specific analyses of international trade and international finance. While restructuring in the rural-agricultural sector was the reform that jumpstarted China's reform economy and endowed Deng and other reformers with significant political capital, the rural reforms drew mainly on traditional peasant interest in family farming and household petty commodity production. Restructuring in the international sector involved much larger, non familial, private enterprises and major infusions of Western capitalist management practices. It would be the businesses in the new international trade oriented Special Economic Zones, rather than family farms, that would serve as models for future Chinese production. It was in the trade sector that China's romance with global capitalism took off.

As in the agricultural sector, China's leaders welcomed a Faustian bargain, sacrificing socialist principles to promises of accelerated economic growth and technological advance. As in the countryside, numerous safeguards (such as joint venture requirements, the isolation of the trade sector from the rest of the Chinese economy, and the insulation of key sectors from foreign competition) were designed to prevent economic restructuring from leading the economy into capitalism, and as in the countryside, these safeguards rapidly eroded. Besides being a conduit for goods and services, the international sector became a major artery for the flow of free market economic ideas and practices into China.

## 5.2 Historical narrative 1978–1989

The reformers' declared objectives in the international sector were initially similar to their objectives in the countryside. They wished to make decisions about international trade based primarily on economic principles, like that of comparative advantage, rather than based on political principles, like self-reliance. Images of openness, conveying feelings of freedom and possibility, were often invoked in support of expanding international trade and access to the Chinese economy by foreign investors. While most Chinese economists supported the expansion of trade and foreign investment, they do not seem to have been very involved with Deng's decision to open the Chinese economy (Sung and Chan 1987, 30).

As in the countryside, the reformers started first with isolated experiments, which then spread across the country. The key international sector reform during 1978–1989 was the establishment of Special Economic Zones (SEZs). These zones courted foreign investment and shifted new investments from the interior to the coasts. The four initial SEZs in 1979–1980 were designed to attract foreign investment from overseas ethnic Chinese.[1] It was anticipated that foreign direct investment (FDI) would give the Chinese access to Western management techniques, modern technology, export markets, and brand credibility.[2] In many ways the SEZs were similar to export processing zones. They offered foreign firms duty free inputs for re-export, low tax rates, subsidized infrastructural services, and relatively light regulatory environments. The SEZs initially had almost no links to the rest of the Chinese economy, limiting their potential disruption of existing economic practices (Naughton 1995, 11; Gallagher 2002). While the SEZs were set up to encourage joint ventures between foreign and domestic firms, the contracts gradually tilted toward majority and wholly foreign-owned enterprises.

The zones served as a kind of testing ground for experiments with capitalist economic mechanisms, such as market-based wages and direct foreign investment. The SEZs had a laissez-faire and anti-"independent"-union orientation.[3] SEZ workers lacked the protection of long-term contracts and guaranteed employment. Firms were given more autonomy in setting wages and fewer responsibilities for workers' social welfare than urban state-owned enterprises (SOEs). Many SEZ workers were poorly educated female migrant laborers from impoverished inland areas who lacked the "iron-rice bowl" expectations of SOE workers (Gallagher 2002, 356–358, Leung 1988). While low by global standards, wages for these unskilled workers were attractive in comparison with many options in the Chinese countryside.[4] Foreign invested enterprises (FIEs) were also able to attract higher skill workers away from SOEs and TVEs due to the foreign firms' less egalitarian wage policies, which benefitted skilled workers. Working conditions in SEZ factories exhibited the classic features of alienated labor: routinized labor, extremely hierarchical relationships with management, authoritarian dispute resolution, the absence of worker input to the design of work, the absence of any relationship between workers and the consumers of the products of their labor, and job insecurity (Leung 1988, Chapters 2, 3).

The Chinese *hukou* (household registration) system which made it difficult for migrant workers to become permanent urban residents, also contributed to the weak bargaining position of many SEZ laborers (Chan 2009, 207). Because most migrant workers thought of their jobs as temporary positions, the potential for group solidarity was diminished. Migrant workers also lacked local political connections, which might have softened employers' abuse of power. The central government's policy of granting decision-making authority about local FDI to regional governments tended to weaken China's bargaining position with foreign capital, creating what has been called "competitive liberalization."

The SEZs got off to a disappointing start. Foreign investment was slow to arrive. Infrastructural preparation proved expensive, and the zones seemed to exacerbate corruption and smuggling problems.[5] Despite these shortcomings, Deng reaffirmed support for the SEZs in 1982, added zones in 14 coastal cities in 1984, opened three major river delta areas for SEZs in 1985;[6] lowered taxes on foreign investment in 1986, designated the entire island of Hainan as an SEZ in 1988, and announced plans for the Pudong SEZ in Shanghai in 1990.[7]

Economic activity in the zones eventually took-off (Meisner 1999, 457–458). By 1990 they accounted for two-thirds of China's exports (Wu 2005, 296). While initially many enterprises were merely final assembling stations for parts produced elsewhere, it appears that the zones eventually played a role in upgrading China's technological capacity. However, the firms' most enduring legacy may have been their modeling for Chinese managers the outlook of enterprises dedicated solely to the well-being of their shareholders. Market enthusiasts refer to this as the diffusion of modern management techniques.

Spurred by the SEZs and a few other regulatory changes (such as currency devaluation and increased flexibility in foreign exchange markets), China's "degree of openness" (total imports + exports)/GDP increased from 10 percent in 1978 to 23 percent in 1985, and to 30 percent in 1990 (Lin, Cai, and Li 2003, 195). The SEZs also facilitated the increasing flow of foreign capital into China and set the stage for China's eventual turn toward export-led growth. Many market-oriented reformers lobbied hard for China's participation in the WTO (even under terms that many took to be relatively disadvantageous for China).

## 5.3 Feedback: economic theory and economic events in the international sector: neoclassical and Marxist thought

Neoclassical economists treat China's "opening up" to the world market as a rational response to potential economic gains from trade. They applaud the development of labor-intensive manufacturing facilities in the SEZs as a rational response to China's comparative advantage. They highlight the potential for increased employment and technology transfer from foreign investment. They applaud the opportunities afforded Chinese managers to learn Western management techniques from joint ventures and wholly-owned foreign subsidiaries in the SEZs. And, finally, they emphasize the ability of foreign direct investment (FDI) to put competitive pressures on domestic firms to become more economically efficient. In short, neoclassical economists see the SEZs as a medium for grafting rational Western economic practices onto Chinese stems. Wu Jinglian, for example, writes,

> ...the major contribution of FDI to the host country lies in that it not only brings in the capital, technology, and management skills necessary for the economic development of the host country, but also improves its economic efficiency and competitiveness through market competition. Another important role of FDI is to promote the economic system reform in the host country.
>
> (Wu 2005, 307)

Many different aspects of Chinese economic reform were focused on increasing competition (be it between firms, between economic regions, between potential firm managers, or between political cadres). Marxist economist Liu Guoguang's enthusiasm, for example, for creating a "buyer's market," a situation where there was mild excess supply in the economy, was designed to put competitive pressures on firms to increase their economic efficiency, quality control, and sensitivity to the market (Hsu 1991, 45–48).

While neoclassical analyses celebrated the SEZs promotion of Western management techniques and China's integration into the world market as expressions of rationality, Marxist analyses were more ambivalent. While appreciating the potential for economic gains from trade and technology transfer, Marxist analyses gave greater attention to the way in which the SEZs contributed to restructuring "the social relations of production" and the overall weakening of labor's position in the workplace. Many Marxists also challenged the characterization of Western management techniques as forms of "scientific management." While some Western management practices can be treated as practical solutions to challenges involved with coordinating labor in any context, some are specific to capitalism, and its potentially adversarial relationship between labor and management in the workplace. Some Chinese reform economists acknowledged the capitalist signature of modern Western management techniques, but appealing to Lenin's call for using capitalist techniques to develop socialist economies (a la primary stage theories of Chinese socialism) approved of the use of capitalist management techniques in the SEZs (e.g., Xu 1981).

Most Marxist-oriented analyses of the impact of SEZs on Chinese labor practices emphasized how the expansion of foreign firms created competitive dynamics that eroded labor's position in both foreign and domestic firms. Gallagher (2002), for example, notes that regional and enterprise competition for FDI, skilled labor, and market share was "a powerful force for convergence with [the] capitalist practices of foreign firms" (Gallagher 2002, 357).[8] These pressures were especially "instrumental in ending the labor protections of state socialism" (Blecher 2010, 147. See also Leung 1988, 137–138). The loss of "socialist" principles in the workplace, however, did not go unchallenged, even in the SEZs. Leung describes many battles over practices such as mandatory overtime during which workers appealed to older socialist principles (Leung 1988, 142–144). These appeals were undermined by the SEZs, which fragmented the Chinese working class, by putting some urban workers in competition with rural migrants (Gallagher 2002, 344). Ultimately, Gallagher suggests, "foreign-invested SEZs ... became laboratories of capitalism," hosting experiments with short-term labor contracting, expanded firm autonomy for wage and bonus setting, and reduced enterprise obligations for social welfare spending (355–356). Relatively quickly, the laws and regulations piloted in the SEZs for foreign-invested enterprises became the basis for national economic policy. "The market logic of FIE employment law, with its notions of contract and autonomy, trumped socialist notions of guaranteed employment and the 'working class as the master class" (358–359).

Citing the work of Muhammad Yunus, the Nobel Prize winner famous for his projects on microcredit, Philip Huang adds,

> our neoclassical construction that the entrepreneur not only is, but ought to be, bent on profit maximizing, because those impulses would somehow work through market mechanisms to result in an economic system of optimal efficiency, has actually helped to create the often rapacious behavior of capitalists, almost as a self-fulfilling prophecy.
>
> (Huang 2009a, 429)

## 5.4 The Tiananmen Square interregnum 1989–1991

China's journey toward free market capitalism seems to have been less interrupted in the international sector than in the domestic sector in the years following the Tiananmen Square tragedy. The entire reform process was renewed by Deng's famous Southern Tour in 1992 when he visited several Special Economic Zones and treated them as the future of China.

## 5.5 International sector restructuring: round two 1992–2001: historical narrative

Chinese international trade increased steadily in the 1990s and accelerated even faster after China's entrance into the WTO in 2001. Exports increased from $72 billion in 1991 to $266 billion in 2001, to more than ~$1 trillion in 2007 (National Bureau of Statistics of China 2010, 231). Imports also rose significantly, though not as fast as exports, allowing China to accumulate large foreign exchange reserves by the late 1990s. Foreign investment in China primarily took the form of direct investment. Actual FDI spending increased from $4 billion in 1991 to $47 billion in 2001 and $90 billion in 2009 (National Bureau of Statistics of China 2010, 250). In 1994, 17 percent of all fixed asset investment in China was carried out by foreign invested enterprises (Branstetter and Lardy 2008, 642).

Throughout the 1990s, a number of "commanding heights" industries (such as banking, petroleum, and petrochemicals) remained off-limits to foreign investors. Portfolio investment also remained relatively closed to foreign capital. While Chinese exporters and importers could easily convert funds in China's foreign exchange markets for trade purposes, there were tight restrictions on foreign exchange conversions for buying and selling financial assets. China limited foreign borrowing through most of the 1990s.[9] The growth in foreign loans was modest, increasing from $7 billion in 1991 to $10 billion in 2000 (National Bureau of Statistics of China 2010, 250). Foreigners could purchase only a limited number of shares in Chinese companies, listed on China's two newly created stock exchanges. These shares, known as "B" shares, were bought and sold in foreign currency (Naughton 2007, 470). Chinese citizens had limited legal means to purchase foreign financial assets.

Chinese leaders strongly supported the expansion of trade and FDI. Deng Xiaoping's lavish praise of Shenzhen and several other export-oriented cities in January 1992, helped trigger a leap in new FDI announcements from $12 billion in 1991 to $58 billion in 1992 (National Bureau of Statistics of China 2010, 250). Several additional SEZs were approved 1990–1993, including the key Pudong area in East Shanghai.[10] In 1994 China devalued the yuan from 5.8Y/$ to 8.6Y/$.[11] Exporters across China were given tax incentives and favorable financing. Many more firms were allowed to directly export or import goods (Lardy 2002, 18). The permission given to local governments to establish their own foreign trading companies (FTCs) was especially important, as it introduced another dimension to regional and firm competition. The "exchange rate regime" was partially deregulated and by 1986 the value of the yuan had fallen in real terms about 60 percent (Naughton 2007, 383). Provincial government trading companies sought out low cost producers and shifted some purchases from SOEs to TVEs. By the mid-1990s TVEs accounted for 20 percent of FTCs exports (Naughton 2007, 384).

Beginning in the early 1990s, China began to abandon its import substitution strategy in favor of a more free-trade orientation. The shift accelerated in 1996, partly in anticipation of China's plans to join the WTO. Average statutory tariffs fell from 56 percent in 1992 to 16 percent by 2000 (Lardy 2002, 34). Non-tariff barriers to imports also declined, with the percentage of goods regulated by licenses and quotas, for example, falling from ~50 percent in 1990 to ~8 percent in 2001 (Branstetter and Lardy 2008, 635).

Special efforts were made to attract FDI in exporting industries. Foreign firms were given lower tax rates, greater flexibility with respect to foreign exchange, and easier import regulations in SEZs than domestic competitors elsewhere in China. Demands that foreign investors involve Chinese partners were also relaxed, and by 2002 69 percent of FDI was in the form of wholly-owned foreign enterprises (Wu 2005, 301). The share of exports by foreign investment firms increased from ~1 percent in 1985 to about 50 percent by 2001 (Naughton 2007, 388).

After 2001 China abolished local content requirements, and seems to have abolished or reduced required technology transfer and mandatory in-country R&D initiatives (Wu 2005, 306).[12] Taking this a step further, foreign investors were given the opportunity to take partial or total control of some SOEs (Wu 2005, 302). Edward Gu argues that the first wave of privatization in China took the form of joint ventures. In these marriages, the SOEs and foreign firms created new entities from combinations of their assets, with foreign firms, like the China Strategy Company, often gaining a controlling interest. Gu notes, "What is striking … is that … through acquisition of Chinese SOEs by foreign investors, a de facto privatization is—to some extent—taking place" (Gu 1997, 47). Gu emphasizes the political sensitivity of Hong Kong investors who refused to characterize their purchases as "takeovers," "although they were in fact taking over Chinese SOEs" (Gu 1997, 61). Li Haijian describes similar dynamics, emphasizing how foreign investors gained controlling interests in joint ventures through continuous investment that "crowded out" Chinese partners (Li Haijian 2003, 388). As in the 1978–1989 period, the expansion of foreign firms in China pressured all firms to adopt a "bottom line" attitude toward economic decisions.

China began negotiations to join the GATT (precursor of the WTO) in 1986. What was expected to be a quick approval process dragged on for 15 years. In 1999, Chinese negotiators agreed to tough pre-conditions for WTO membership demanded by US negotiators. As Lardy points out, Chinese trade concessions were extensive, symbolized by the acceptance of a US demand that the developed countries have the right for as long as 12 years to curtail some Chinese imports, if they became burdensome.

When the Asian financial crisis hit in 1997–1998, China suffered a reduction in regional exports, but weathered the storm quite well, in part because of its relatively closed capital accounts. The later insulated China from the volatility of short run capital flows. China's huge exchange reserves also discouraged speculative runs on the yuan.

The debate over Chinese policy toward international trade and foreign investment 1992–2001 echoes many earlier debates of the 1978–1989 period, as well as debates over public versus private ownership of domestic firms. Free market oriented reformers were especially enthusiastic about China's potential membership in the WTO. Besides favoring expanded trade in general, key WTO supporters perceived WTO regulations as a convenient means for imposing competitive pressures and capitalist-oriented practices on state-owned enterprises as well as a means for restricting government aid to these firms.[13]

Marxist and heterodox economists also saw China's WTO membership, increased reliance on FDI, and integration into the existing global division of labor as a kind of lock-in, but the anticipated trajectory was not as rosy as the neoclassical forecast. Marxist and heterodox economists criticized China's policies for tilting bargaining power in favor of capital and extending the reach of relentless market pressures for capital accumulation into more and more areas of societal life.

## 5.6  Feedback between economic events and economic theory: neoclassical view

As Paul Krugman has noted, "If there were an Economist's [read neoclassical] Creed, it would surely contain the affirmation 'I understand the Principle of Comparative Advantage' and 'I advocate Free Trade'" (Krugman 1987, 131). In this spirit, neoclassical economists celebrated China's integration into the global, capitalist-oriented, economic order. They repeated arguments for "free trade" made during the 1978–1989 period. Their arguments were reinforced by Alan Greenspan, head of the US Federal Reserve, in a high-powered meeting with Chinese Premier Zhu Rongji in January 1999 (Brahm 2002, 262–263). Zhu subsequently used Greenspan's comments and global prestige to help win support for WTO membership among Chinese leaders (Brahm 2002, 264).

Two of the classic benefits of expanded trade for developing countries, the capture of economies of scale due to access to markets much larger than the home market, and access to capital, were diminished in China's case, due to the substantial size of its home market and China's very high domestic savings rate. Key supporters of free trade emphasized instead, that WTO membership would impose competitive discipline on the SOEs.[14]

The neoclassical take on the global division of labor, is basically "there is no alternative." Nicholas Lardy, reports, "China's top leadership in the wake of the Asian crisis saw that there was no viable alternative to the globalization of production" (Lardy 2002, 20). Wu Jinglian, perhaps China's leading neoclassical economist, adds, "The accession to the WTO is essential ... it is a necessary journey for China to increase its participation in the international division of labor" (Wu 2005, 320). China's chief trade negotiator (Long Yongtu) offered an even more expansive conclusion, arguing not only that all countries must participate in the global division of labor, but that they must adopt capitalist market practices to do so. Long argued, "'Countries with planned economies have never been a part of economic globalization. China's economy must become a market economy in order to become part of the global economic system'" (Lardy 2002, 21).

Neoclassical supporters of China's decision to join the WTO and to rely on global forces to shape its division of labor point to five key payoffs from these policies:

1  Large increases in output and employment in labor intensive export industries (with accompanying upgrading in labor skills).
2  Access to cheaper foreign sources of raw materials and land intensive products.
3  Access to more advanced technology (technology transfer from FDI).
4  Access to modern management techniques.
5  Increased economic efficiency as a result of increased competitive pressures from foreign firms (especially in sectors, like financial services, formerly closed to foreign competition).

In support of these claims free traders argue that Chinese firms have already begun moving up the "global value chain," from initially exporting primary products (like oil), to manufactured goods produced with relatively low skilled labor (like textiles, footwear and toys), to manufactured goods requiring higher skilled labor (like consumer electronics). The trade optimists expect that multinational firms producing in China will migrate more and more research and development activities to China in order to be closer to actual production lines. They also expect Chinese domestic industry to eventually acquire foreign firms' organizational capital (management techniques, training practices, market assessment, etc.). They see "learning" and human capital accumulation even at the bottom of the division of labor. They portray routinized factory labor as turning some, not all, rural migrants into market-savvy wage laborers and even entrepreneurs in their new environs or when they return to their home village. This is Milton Friedman's story in *Free to Choose*.

Most importantly, they perceive the market discipline of import competition and production from foreign-invested firms inside China, as perhaps the most important benefit of WTO membership and China's opening to the world economy. It is the imperative, rather than the opportunity, to adopt capitalist practices that ultimately insures the success of the reformers' vision of marketization. For China, the WTO accomplishes what the enclosures and putting out system accomplished in England's transition to capitalism. Both developments demanded that local producers match the ability of capitalist production to produce a re-investable surplus. For China, the reformers see this demand as delivering the final blow against the phoenix of state-owned enterprises.[15]

## 5.7 Feedback: Marxist–heterodox views

Marxist and heterodox critics of China's trade policies and neoclassical endorsements of free trade (or free-trade light) are not in favor of autarky, self-reliance, or isolation from the rest of the world. They do, however, reject the neoclassical imperative of fitting into the existing global division of labor, and favor more attention to the impact of international sector policies on the bargaining power of capital and labor in the workplace, the character of work lives, and distributional issues. They reject rather than embrace the imposition of a capitalist imperative.

### 5.7.1 *"Heterodox lite" alternatives*

Marxist and heterodox alternatives to neoclassical frames and "TINA" conclusions fall into two categories. The first perspective is marginally compatible with mainstream neoclassical theory. It argues on empirical and theoretical grounds that real world divergences from the perfect market model undermine free trade doctrines more than acknowledged in mainstream analyses of

China's international sector. Economists in this camp raise concerns about "free trade," capital account liberalization, and membership in the WTO, using ideas compatible with neoclassical economics. Neoclassical critics like Dani Rodrik, for example, emphasize how imperfect information and speculative excesses can lead to destabilizing short-term capital flows in an "overly" liberalized capital account regime. Other critics like Chris Bramall argue that developing countries need to adopt active industrial policies to protect infant industries, facilitate economy wide learning, and maintain aggregate demand to ensure full-employment. Bramall asserts

> relentless competition from Western companies will ensure that ... [China] will be locked into a development trajectory which depends on the exploitation of cheap labour. The People's Republic would therefore be well advised to leave the WTO ... and thereby regain its policy freedom.
>
> (Bramall 2009a, 531)

He adds "China's central problem is that the state is much weaker than it was a decade ago," due to China's membership in the WTO and the increased privatization of state-owned enterprises. He finds this weakness crippling China's ability to use industrial policy to catch up with the West (Bramall 2009a, 554).[16]

While Bramall emphasizes that "successful catch-up almost certainly requires that China leave the WTO" (Bramall 2009a, 395), he does not call for leaving neoclassical economics behind. He argues instead that ideologically-laden interpretations of the neoclassical model (rather than the paradigm itself) have over-estimated the contribution of export processing industries and foreign investment to China's rapid economic growth,[17] and mistakenly concluded that China must reduce its capital controls and allow competition organized by WTO regulations to determine the fate of its manufacturing sector. These analyses remind one of criticisms of neoclassical economists for "over-painting their canvas" about the need to privatize state-owned enterprises. In the final analysis, Bramall uses neoclassical language to criticize mainstream arguments for laissez-faire-oriented trade policy, arguing "The basis, then, for the heterodoxy is that market failure is pervasive in capitalist economies. There is thus a *prima facie case* for state intervention" (Bramall 2009a, 400).

### 5.7.2 More distinctive critiques: overview

The second set of Marxist and heterodox critiques of mainstream conclusions involve more fundamental methodological challenges to neoclassical theory. These analyses focus on work lives and power relations in the workplace, distributional concerns, and macroeconomic issues. They challenge China's decision to sacrifice many socialist ideals, such as the idea of workers as "the masters of their enterprises," the goal of unalienated labor, and egalitarian principles, to the goal of attracting foreign investment. Their stance reflects Marxism's treatment of labor as a defining human activity, rather than one of several inputs into production or utility functions. Attention to the character of work lives is also prevalent in the field of labor studies and these accounts are drawn on more fully in Marxist than neoclassical analyses.

Mainstream discussions tend to look at the export sector from a managerial point of view. There is much discussion of value chains, return on investment, investment environments, management skills, the transfer of technology, product branding, market access, efficiency, etc., but little discussion of worker alienation, worker participation in decision making, job security, and grievance procedures.[18] There is discussion of wages in the international sector, and some discussion of social security issues involved with pensions, medical care, unemployment insurance, but even here, the discussion seems to be in terms of what is necessary for the management project to proceed smoothly, rather than what is the best way to improve the quality of life for workers in China.[19] Heterodoxy rejects two key assumptions of classical liberalism underlying this pattern of attention: (1) that workplace issues can be ignored by assuming market forces have optimized workplace arrangements; and (2) that by increasing competition, accelerating capital accumulation, and deepening specialization in the division of labor, free trade will eventually benefit everyone.

### 5.7.3 Marxist and heterodox concerns about the impact of neoliberal "openings" on labor markets

The difficult working conditions in China's exporting industries are highlighted, rather than merely noted in Marxist, heterodox, and labor studies accounts. Greater attention is also given to the origins of power differentials in the workplace. Anita Chan's research has been particularly influential in researching and publicizing the daily life accompanying China's expansion of exports. She documents the presence of 80-hour weeks, routinized, exhausting assembly-line tasks, hazardous working conditions, and almost prison-like workplace supervision.[20] Chan also depicts some firms' dormitory housing in penal terms, noting "in some of the bigger factories that I have visited, workers are even marched to and from meals and to and from dormitories in tight military-style squads" (Chan 2003, #32). Lee Ching Kwan is another important chronicler of working environments in China. Her work describes similar conditions. Her ethnography *Gender and the South China Miracle* (Lee 1998) is especially interesting as it is based on a year's participant observation study of low wage factory work in Hong Kong and Shenzhen.[21] Drawing on her own experience and sustained interaction with migrant women workers, she finds that marketization "has led to a general deterioration of workers' livelihoods, especially in the 1990s" (Lee 2007c, 60). The literature on working conditions in China is reminiscent of Engels's *The Condition of the*

*Working Class in England*. The articles often find publication outside of economics journals.[22]

Because many workers in low wage export industries were and are migrants, the *hukou* system exacerbated their economic and social problems. Migrants often started work in debt to their employers due to the need for a large number of permits costing more than a month's wages.[23] Many employers also demanded a "deposit" from new employees of about a half a month's wages, which was forfeitable if workers left their jobs without company "approval." Many firms were also late in paying wages, adding to the sum that workers might lose if they quit their jobs. As a result, a de facto system of bonded labor emerged in the 1990s, within which it was very hard for workers to flee desperate working conditions.

These constraints and capital/labor tensions in general are highlighted more in Marxist than neoclassical accounts.[24] Greenfield and Leong, for example, note that firms in the Special Economic Zones initially hired workers from the same geographic area.

> "This formed the basis of a powerful sense of common interests ... which often challenged the power of managers and supervisors. In response, managers have implemented policies of segregation, ensuring that workers from the same province are broken up into different sections in the factory."
>
> (Greenfield and Leong, 1997, 115)

The dispersal of workers from the same geographical area to reduce labor solidarity is surprisingly similar to management strategies in the Michigan copper mines around 1900. Meyer Weinberg reports, for example, that the mining companies hoped "that language barriers would forestall the growth of unionism" and that during a strike in 1913 the companies tried to recruit workers from areas different from existing miners (Weinberg 2002, Chapter 8).

Marxists, labor studies theorists, and heterodox economists link the intense competition of global supply chains to a "race to the bottom" in the treatment of labor. The analysis is remarkably reminiscent of Marx's prediction of a subsistence wage. Along the global supply chain it appears that firms' returns increase *pari passu* with the degree of monopoly, with the lowest margins and most desperate working conditions at the bottom of the pyramid, in the most competitive markets. Tim Culpan reports, for example, that Apple's profit margin from mid 2007–2011 varied between 15–30 percent (~30 percent in January 2012), while its major Chinese supplier, Foxconn's, profit margin never exceeded 5 percent and fell to 1.5 percent in 2012.[25] Lee Ching Kwan writes,

> It seems that as the Chinese economy becomes more integrated with global capitalism, manufacturers are confronted with ever more intense competition and shrinking margins of profit ... Inside factories, these

competitive pressures turn into longer production shifts, declining real wages, neglect of production safety ... and subsequent mass layoffs."

(Lee 2007c, 163–164)

Foreign ownership of China's export factories has also sometimes contributed to the harshness of working conditions. For example, Chan writes," "physical abuse has become pervasive in some of the factories owned and managed by Taiwanese, Koreans, and Hong Kong Chinese."[26]

As we have seen in other contexts, the paradigm debate over working conditions in the export sector often boils down to a debate over trajectories (what is going to happen) and counterfactuals (what could have happened). Neoclassical defenders of China's labor practices argued that sweatshops were an inevitable stage of economic development. They stressed that rural workers actively sought out these positions. Marxist and heterodox critics acknowledged the relative attractiveness of export industry jobs. Lee, for example, found that the prospect of escaping rural patriarchal constraints was perhaps even more important than the lure of higher earnings in motivating young women to migrate.[27] Once again, however, the key issue is whether existing village opportunities or sweatshop employment were the only possible alternatives.

It is worth noting that the migrants' retention of the fallback option of returning home and claiming access to rural *hukou* land remained a constraint on factory exploitation. In an insightful comment, one worker noted,

> "if I don't want to work here, I can always go home and farm the land. ... But what can Hong Kong workers do except work for their bosses? They don't have any land to make a living. Here I can fire my boss and quit..."
>
> (Lee 1998, 77)

Over time, of course, the viability of rural homesteading was eroding.

The neoclassicals emphasize that working conditions and wages were improving and would continue to do so in export industries.[28] Marxist and other critics of China's export policies found only modest improvements in labor market conditions. The critics also found GDP growth and wage levels to be insufficient measures of the well being of Chinese workers. Most importantly, the critics saw China's export industry policies and the Washington Consensus that lay behind them, as creating a reproducing structure of inequality that would be resistant to significant improvement.

The neoclassical defenders of China's export sector portrayed the sweatshop as a ladder for individual and group upward mobility. Marxist and heterodox critics acknowledged that some workers might indeed find social mobility through these jobs, but doubted this was a common outcome. Lee reports, for example, that "a number of" her young migrant co-workers at the Shenzhen factory were taking night classes in English, typing, accounting, and computing. She also reports that some women were carefully saving parts of their modest wages to accumulate enough funds to start a small retail shop in the future. At the same time, she indicates that opportunities for promotion within the firm were very limited, and implies there were formidable obstacles to advancement outside the firm. Her study of the Hong Kong Factory staffed by older women but producing exactly the same products as the Shenzhen factory, found their wages and working conditions to be much better than those at the Shenzhen factory. At first glance this suggests the possibility of economic improvements over time. But during Lee's year-long study, the Hong Kong factory was closed, probably due to competition from low wage production at places like the Shenzhen factory. The women were laid off with severance pay with only one day's notice. Four years later, a follow-up study by Lee found unemployment rates of 27 percent among a cohort of women workers similar to those laid off from the Hong Kong factory.

Summing up her research she concludes,

> irrespective of their present employment status, women workers reported a general decline in their class and gender status in both their family and society. However much these women have contributed to the south China economic miracle, there is neither an escape from the unrelenting domination of global capitalism nor a linear path of female emancipation through wage labor.
>
> (Lee 1998, 170)

The critics highlight data about the sluggishness of changes at the bottom of the division of labor, such as: the failure of the real minimum wage to rise much in the 1990s (Chan 2003); the minimal growth in wages of the bottom 10 percent of the wage ladder 1995–2002;[29] the persistence of poverty;[30] the increase in the GINI coefficient for income inequality in China, from ~.3 in 1981 to .45–49 in 2005; and the increasing use of temporary workers (called 'dispatch labor").[31]

They also highlight the migration of alienated working conditions up the division of labor, echoing Harry Braverman's analysis of the spread of alienated labor in the West from blue collar to white collar labor. This finding is critically important, as it suggests that China's migration up the global value chain, from textiles to electronics to IT industries may do little to improve job insecurities and alienated working conditions.

Andrew Ross's analysis of China's emerging information technology (IT) industry tends to support these fears. Ross finds the physical working conditions in China's IT firms more pleasant than the assembly-line conditions of the apparel and footwear factories, and the wages somewhat higher, but the underlying character of alienated labor and economic insecurities to be roughly the same. He writes,

> As outsourcing moves up the value chain … it takes less and less time for corporate managers to submit skilled Asian workforces to the kinds of

deskilling and dehumanizing that we have seen over the course of several decades in the West.

(Ross 2007b, 189)

Ross also acknowledges that IT workers have greater freedom to quit their jobs than migrant workers on the assembly line and admits this freedom has given them some leverage in the labor market. The underlying conditions bred by cutthroat competition however, has produced a deep anxiety among most workers. Ross writes, " 'pressure' ... [was] the most common term used by my engineer interviewees to describe their economic situation" (Ross 2007a, 111). He adds,

> Both skilled and unskilled workplaces share a climate rife with distrust and disloyalty ... extreme wage pressure from the threat to move to cheaper locations, and the shedding of economic and social security in the communities where investors have set up shop. (4). ... Many of the employees I interviewed saw little reason for loyalty. ... I found [turn-over] rates of up to 40 percent. ... In their ceaseless pursuit of the cheap-est and most dispensable employees, multinational firms have made it clear they will not honor any kind of job security. ... [I]t looks as if workers in China's transitional economy might be returning the disrespect.
>
> (Ross 2007a, 16)

Social Structure of Accumulation (SSA) models, such as those developed by Li and Qi (2014) can be used to analyze the workplace patterns Ross describes. The harsh working conditions in China's export industries in the 1990s reflected what SSA theorists call low-road economic development strategies. Both firms and workers had very short relationships and minimal trust in each other. While offering firms very low wage bills, this situation increased transaction costs (due to the need for close supervision of labor and high labor turnover) and probably lowered quality control. Alternative trade-offs were possible.

While technological changes, especially in telecommunications, have made it feasible for firms to construct a global division of labor, from a Marxist and heterodox perspective, the balance of power in these electronically linked workplaces is more a product of social engineering than hardware engineer-ing. The current SSA has been enabled by capital mobility. The threat of relocation intimidates both workers and local governments. The rules of the game which empower managers in the workplace and ensure a large share of income going to capital (as opposed to labor), reflect socio-political decisions. Interestingly, the World Bank (China) Development Research Center report *China 2030* (2013), urged China to promote its own outward FDI, noting, "China's rapid increase in incomes means that firms may need to relocate to lower-wage locations" (387). The threat of such behavior influences Chinese labor markets and helps maintain capital's dominant negotiating position inside China.[32] Chinese FDI outflows increased from $1 billion in 2000 to $44 billion in 2009, though the bulk of these investments were in resource-acquiring activities, like mining, rather than manufacturing. From 2004 to 2013 there was an explosion in Chinese overseas investments, which increased from $45 billion to $613 billion.[33] Marxist analyses suggest that limits on Chinese capital mobility may be necessary to protect Chinese workers.

Those who would reform Chinese capitalism, rather than replace it with socialist institutions (such as worker-owned firms and guaranteed employment) hope that global movements for corporate responsibility will curb the worst excesses of FDI in the third world. Public pressure has caused Apple, for example, to put pressure on Foxconn to improve working conditions in its factories. Similar pressures have curbed the import of goods produced with prison labor in China. Reviews of the corporate responsibility movement seem to suggest that it has had positive impacts, but for the most part, these impacts have been modest.[34] From a Marxist and heterodox perspective, significant change requires (1) the elimination of the Reserve Army of the Unemployed composed of ~100+ million migrants[35] and tens of millions of displaced SOE workers, and (2) the reconstruction of labor market conditions to improve the bargaining position of workers. The provision of alternative employment options, limits on capital mobility, support for independent labor unions, escape from WTO limitations on industrial policy, and extensive educational assistance for low income families[36] are five possible reform policies. Worker ownership of firms, would of course be a more radical-socialist alternative.

### 5.7.4 Marxist and heterodox macroeconomic critiques of China's FDI-export-led growth strategy

Marxist macro theorists have questioned the macroeconomic sustainability of China's highly unequal income distribution. These economists foresee problems of under-consumption leading to insufficient aggregate demand and economic contraction. They argue that China was able to temporarily escape these problems by relying on investment and export led growth, but argue that neither of these strategies are viable in the long run. They foresee China's high rate of investment leading to problems of excess capacity, unless income redistribution increases domestic consumption. They also argue that a large country like China cannot continue to grow at 7–9 percent a year, while the world GDP grows at 2–3 percent, if it relies on increasing demand from the rest of the world to fuel its economy. Marxist economists also note that China's export dependence leaves it vulnerable to global business cycles and protectionist policies of leading capitalist countries interested in protecting their manufacturing base. Zhu and Kotz, for example, note that,

> Traditionally the dominant capitalist countries have exported manufactured goods, particularly the most technologically sophisticated ones. ...

China's rising exports threaten to disrupt ... part of the basis of the economically dominant position of today's leading capitalist states ... it is difficult to avoid the conclusion that China is on a path that cannot be sustained in the long-run.

(Zhu and Kotz 2011, 26)

Li Minqi concludes,

> neoliberal policies and institutions have imposed serious constraints on ... mass consumption, productive investment, and public spending. With insufficient domestic demand, many countries have attempted to pursue export-led growth by creating a low-wage, low tax, deregulated environment for foreign and domestic businesses. This has in turn led to a general 'race to the bottom' in wage rates, tax rates, and social spending ... attempts by many countries to generate [export] surpluses ... [could] lead to a general collapse of the global effective demand and send the global economy into a downward spiral. ... These dangerous tendencies have not yet materialized largely because the world's largest and hegemonic economy—the US economy—has acted as the world's 'borrower and consumer of last resort' ... providing markets for their export expansion. ... However, the large US current account deficits cannot be sustained indefinitely.

(Li 2008, 73)

While the idea that capitalist economies are inherently crisis prone and have a narrow "distributional sweet spot," (between income distributions that are "too equal" and discourage investment due to profit squeezes and income distributions that are "too unequal" and result in problems of insufficient aggregate demand) is inconsistent with the automatic full-employment implications of orthodox neoclassical theory, many neoclassical economists have also argued that China needs to "rebalance" its macro profile to include greater domestic consumption.

Many commentators, Marxist and otherwise, have also argued that ecological constraints imply that macroeconomic strategies based on national and/ or global growth rates of even 2–3 percent in perpetuity are unsustainable. This is due to resource and waste disposal constraints. Li Minqi has stressed the point, arguing that China's attempt to imitate the growth path of the US is ecologically impossible. We have not addressed environmental issues in this manuscript due to their relatively low profile in Chinese economic discussions for most of the period in question. The issues are, however, obviously of enormous importance.

## Notes

1 Shenzhen was located adjacent to Hong Kong, Zhuhai next to Macao, Xiamen across from Taiwan, and Shantou near Chaozhou (a city with ethnic ties to

Chinese living in Singapore and elsewhere in Southeast Asia). Giovanni Arrighi, among others, has stressed the role of overseas Chinese trading networks as incubators for Asian capitalism and matchmakers for the reintegration of China into global capitalist markets. As late as 1990, when Japanese investment in China took off, investment from Hong Kong and Taiwan accounted for 75 percent of all foreign investment in China. Even after turn of century, overseas Chinese investment in the mainland totaled more than half of all foreign investment (Arrighi 2008, 352). Perkins stresses the role of Hong Kong's marketing infrastructure in enabling China's emerging manufacturing capacity (Perkins 1994, 33–34).

2 Meisner 1999, 458; Naughton 2007, 408; Li Lanqing 2009, Chapter 2.

3 See for example, Meisner 1999, 457; Hart-Landsberg and Burkett 2005. Leung's account suggests that this outcome was due in part to continual pressure and complaints from foreign investors (Leung 1988, 137–140). New regulations in 1988, for example, increased the ability of foreign invested enterprises to hire and fire and recruit workers from outside their vicinity. While there were legal protections for the operation of government authorized unions, these organizations seemed to conceive of their role as accommodating workers to the needs of the firm, rather than representing the interests and dignity of the workers. In addition, even the protections of government sponsored unions (reaffirmed in 1985) were often ignored (Leung 1988, Chapter 4).

4 In 1986 in Shenzhen, for example, wages varied from \$54–\$76 per month, with social taxes raising labor costs to \$96–\$109/month (Leung 1988, 140). In 1984 the average income in Shenzhen was five times the national average for urban residents (Leung 1988, 141).

5 Naughton 2007, 406–410; Gallagher 2002, 349; Meisner 1996, 278–284; Hart-Landsberg and Burkett 2005, 49; Leung 1988, 130.

6 Naughton 2007, 409; Hart-Landsberg and Burkett 2005, 48. Li Lanqing's account of Deng's inspection visit of Shenzhen and other SEZs in early 1984 gives the impression that things were going better than Naughton's account suggests. Li's excerpt from Deng's remarks about the SEZs in February 1984 suggest he had already made up his mind about the need for new kinds of market incentives, declaring, "Our construction speed is slow … but in Shekou and Shenzhen, construction is a lot faster. … The 'big pot' practice never worked and never will" (Li Lanqing 2009, 175). As late as June 1984, however, Deng hedged his bets, declaring "Shenzhen SEZ is an experiment … a new phenomenon. … It is our wishes that it will be a success; if not, then let it be an experience" (Leung 1988, 131).

7 Wu 2005, 296, 298.

8 Gallagher notes that from 1980–1982 there were two separate sets of labor laws, one for FIEs and one for SOEs. By the mid-1980s there was some overlap among the laws, and by 1995, FIE law tended to apply everywhere (Gallagher 2002, 355–359).

9 Brahm credits Zhu Rongji with anticipating the risks of capital market liberalization that subsequently crippled many Southeast Asian economies (Brahm 2002, 31).

10 Deng discussed the idea of a Shanghai SEZ, with a focus on finance, with Zhu Rongji in February 1991 (Brahm 2002, xxi). The decision to develop Pudong was formally made in April 1990 (Wu 2005, 298).

11 The IMF estimated that the value of the yuan fell 70 percent in real terms against the dollar from 1980–1995 (Branstetter and Lardy 2008, 639). From 1995–2005 the market exchange rate stabilized at ~8.3Y/\$ (National Bureau of Statistics of China 2010, 230), as the government pegged the RMB to the dollar. From July 2005 to October 2011 "the real effective exchange rate" appreciated against the dollar, by about 30 percent, under China's managed floating exchange rate policies (World Bank 2013, 392).

12 Technology transfer requirements on foreign firms were already weakening before China joined the WTO (Nolan 2004 [1998], 222).

13 Naughton writes, "reformists … used the lure of WTO membership to help push through reforms that they favored in any case" (Naughton 2007, 388). Jacobson and Oksenberg indicate that similar reasoning contributed to China's interest in joining the GATT in the 1980s. The reformers apparently believed that China's commitments under GATT would make it nearly impossible to reverse the reform process.

14 Greenspan also averred that WTO membership would create new jobs to replace ones lost to SOE layoffs (Brahm 2002, 263).

15 See, for example, Qian and Wu 2000, 31.

16 Bramall 2009a, Chapter 11, for example has a thoughtful discussion (from a neoclassical accounting point of view) of the benefits and costs of expanding trade and FDI to China's economy. On the benefit side, he examines claims about technology transfer, human capital accumulation, remittances from areas with expanding export industries to more isolated regions, and access to cheaper imported raw materials than available at home. On the cost side, he looks at the damage to some farmers and domestic industries by foreign competition, and the loss of political autonomy. He concludes that the major drivers for Chinese economic growth 1976–1996 were agriculture and rural industry, treating foreign trade and capital flows as secondary factors (Bramall 2009a, 390–391).

17 For example, Bramall challenges the claim that Chinese concessions to foreign investors and WTO negotiators have resulted in major transfers of technology to China. He argues that while China now exports electronic goods in addition to textiles and footwear, their role in high-tech manufacturing is still primarily in assembly rather than more upscale tasks.

18 Xue and Chan's 2013 study of the global value chain literature, for example, concludes "these chain governance studies … fail to focus on working conditions and labor relationships" (Xue and Chan 2013, 58). Chan has also noted that the industrial relations literature and American human rights discourse give relatively little attention to labor rights (Chan 1998). Lee Ching Kwan similarly faults "transition studies for often "presenting too laudatory a narrative of China's 'successful' turn to capitalism, missing the seamy side of reform that blights many ordinary people's lives" (Lee 2007c, xi).

19 Ross (2007a, Chapter 3, especially 82) makes a somewhat similar point about "free market fundamentalism" dulling ethical senses of responsibility among members of Shanghai's American Chamber of Commerce.

20 The fire at the Zhili toy factory in Shenzhen in 1993, which killed 83 workers, is symbolic of these conditions. Barred windows and locked doors trapped workers inside the building (*China Labour Bulletin*, "Victims of the 1993 Zhili Fire." Originally published in CLB #51, Nov–Dec 1999; *New York Times,* November 20, 1993 "Fire Ravages a Doll Factory in Southern China, Killing 8").

21 Lee's 1998 ethnography describes the different working conditions and factory cultures in the Shenzhen and Hong Kong electronics assembly plants. Both facilities were owned by the same Hong Kong company. The Shenzhen factory employed young migrant women, under what seems to have been typical SEZ terms, although the facility was outside the formal SEZ. Lee's account offers a lived experience of working lives in these factories. She writes from the point of view of a worker rather than a manager, as digested by an ethnographer familiar with Marxist and feminist theory. She observes,

> These despotic rules were strikingly similar to those Karl Marx described for the prototypical factory of his time. … [The Shenzhen factory's] rule book stipulated "… going to bathroom without a 'leave seat permit,' folding up uniform sleeves, and having long nails are all fined RMB1 each. … Refusal to

do overtime shift is fined RMB2 for the first time, RMB4 for the second, RMB8 for the third, and deduction of all wages for the fourth."... On the assembly lines, it was not unusual to find workers sobbing...

(112–113)

Lee concludes,

All these hardships ... found objective inscriptions on women's bodies, according to women workers. Objective indicators of workers' suffering from despotic disciplines included weight loss, deterioration of "face color," and skin conditions, all indicators of worsening health in Chinese folk medicine.

(Lee 1998, 115)

In a later work, Lee depicts

a relentless intensification of the labor process ... running at such a nerve-racking pace that workers' physical limits and bodily strength are put to the test on a daily basis. In the early 1990s, a factory operator regularly worked a ten–twelve hour day, six days a week. During my visit in 2002–2003 ... workers ... regular work cycle consisted of a grueling fourteen—or even sixteen—hour work day ... It has become "normal" to work four hundred hours or more every month.

Lee adds that "Horror stories of management mistreatment ... are regular features of popular newspapers" (Lee 2007c, 162–163).

22 For illustrations of Lee's work see: *Gender and the South China Miracle: Two Worlds of Factory Women* (Lee 1998) *Against the Law: Labor Protests in China's Rustbelt and Sunbelt* (Lee 2007c), and two essays in *Working in China* [see below]. For further illustrations of a vast literature on China's brutal working conditions, see: "Labor in a Changing China" (*International Labor and Working-Class History* 73 (Spring 2008); *Working in China: Ethnographies of labor and workplace transformation* (Lee 2007a). For a helpful short review of recent literature see Mark Frazier's "Where to Begin: New Perspectives on Chinese Labor," July 2, 2010 The China Beat (www.thechinabeat.org/?p=2285, accessed November 25, 2013). For Marxists' use of this material, see, for example, Hart-Landsberg and Burkett 2005, Chapter 3.
23 Chan indicates migrants needed to purchase: border region passes, personal identity cards, marital status certificates, proof that their birth did not invalidate the one-child policy, temporary residence permits, and work permits (Chan 2003).
24 In a variation on this theme, this time involving CASS's Institute of Sociology, Marxist economist Li Minqi has criticized CASS's social strata research for inattention to topics like workplace conflict. Li argues that CASS's social strata research artificially classifies most Chinese workers as members of the middle class, and abandons Marxism's focus on social polarization and capital labor conflicts (Li Minqi 2008, Ch. 4).
25 Bloomberg Chart of the Day, January 4, 2012: "Apple Profit Margins Rise at Foxconn's Expense," by Tim Culpan (www.bloomberg.com/news/2012-01-04/apple-profit-margins-rise-at-foxconn-s-expense.html, accessed November 30, 2013).
26 Chan 2003, # 46, paragraph 33; see also Whyte 1999, 182.
27 Lee argues that economic analysis traditionally underestimated the importance of young women's desire to escape rural patriarchal constraints and over emphasized the lure of higher wages (at least three times the income levels attached to farming) in explaining migrant women's decision to relocate (Lee 1998, 82).
28 Neoclassical economists point to the imminent arrival of the "Lewis turning point," when the exhaustion of the non-market sector's pool of surplus labor occurs and firms have to raise wages to attract workers.

29 John Knight and Lina Song find the wages of the bottom 10 percent of the income ladder grew by only ~.5 RMB/hour from 1995–2002 (~4.5 percent/yr.) (Gustafsson et al. 2008, 226), which at the period's nominal exchange rates of ~8 RMB/$ implies about a penny an hour increase in wages per year and 3 cents/hour at PPP exchange rates, neither of which seems very promising. See also: Peter Kwong "China's Neoliberal Dynasty," in the *Nation* Oct. 2, 2006. Hong Xue and Anita Chan 2013 find that technological upgrading does not appear to soften strategies to "squeeze labor" and 'lean production' seems to increase pressures for workers to produce faster (Xue and Chan 2013, 59).

30 Azizur Rahman Kahn indicates that "after more than two decades of unprecedented growth, the proportion of the population below the World Bank's PPP $1 poverty line in China is higher … than in almost any other country with a comparative PPP$ per capita income" (Gustafsson et al. 2008, 146). Actual poverty rates may be even higher than officially reported due to neglect or under-counting of migrant poverty. On the other hand, Kahn found a large drop (150 million) in the number of rural poor in China 1995–2002 (Gustafsson et al. 2008, 152).

31 Stanley Lubman, "Working Conditions: The Persistence of Problems in China's Factories." CHINAREALTIME September 25, 2012 (accessed November 17, 2013). Lubman cites a *Business Week* report (March 8, 2012) indicating that dispatch workers may account for one-fifth of urban workers. It appears these workers lack even the modest protections of contract workers.

32 Among additional reasons offered for promoting outward Chinese FDI was offering backdoor support for efforts to secure more Chinese acceptance of foreign investment. The World Bank *China 2030* report noted,

> At first glance, it can be difficult to understand why a poor country like China should encourage its firms to invest overseas. … Achieving stronger protection for Chinese investors would require granting reciprocal concessions to foreign investors in China, implying a dismantling of most restrictions on FDI inflows and continued improvements in the autonomy of state enterprises. These policies also are in the long-term interest of China's development.
>
> (386)

33 Zhou Lihuan and Denise Leung, "China's overseas Investments, Explained in 10 Graphics," World Resources Institute January 28, 2015 (www.wri.org/blog/2015/01/china%E2%80%/99s-overseas-investments-explained-10-graphics, accessed July 23, 2015). Some of the outflow of capital from China is likely occurring under the radar, as wealth holders try to ensure themselves against shifts in political winds within China.

34 See for example Pun Ngai (2005) who concludes,

> While it is true that some improvement have been made. … The companies have demonstrated no genuine concern for labor rights, less still for workers' representation or participation. … The ethical code movement is supposed to keep a check on the dark side of global production. … In replacing the role of the Chinese state … this top-down process results in perpetuating authoritarian factory regimes in which, from a distance the transnational corporations appear to play a paternalistic role in 'protecting' workers from labor exploitation, all the while allowing exploitation to continue, in the form of illegally low wages per hour and excessive overtime work.
>
> (Pun 2005, 112–113).

35 It is hard to find reliable statistics for the number of migrant workers in China. There are different definitions of migrant workers and significant data collection problems. Some migrants appear to work under the radar in the informal sector or sleep at work sites not included in official statistics based on data collected at residential units. Chan

cites estimates of 50–80 million migrant workers in 2003 (Chan 2003, 8). Based on data from China's National Bureau of Statistics, Philip Huang calculates there were 120 million migrant workers in China's cities in 2006 (Huang 2009, 407–406). Li Shi cites estimates of 130 million in 2006 (Li Shi 2008, i). Migrant workers do not compete directly with urban dwellers for jobs in state-owned urban enterprises due to labor market segmentation. However, they affect SOE wages and working conditions indirectly, through, for example, the competitive threats private firms employing migrants pose to SOEs.

36 Gustafsson et al. conclude that "Education has emerged as … a growing source of inequality" (Gustafsson et al. 2008, 25). The return to educational elitism is part of the larger structural shift that is recreating a very hierarchical society in China.

# References

Arrighi, Giovanni. 2008. *Adam Smith in Beijing: Lineages of the Twenty-First Century*. New York: Verso.

Blecher, Marc. 2010. *China Against the Tides: Restructuring through Revolution, Radicalism and Reform*. 3rd ed. New York: Continuum.

Brahm, Laurence J. 2002. *Zhu Rongji and the Transformation of Modern China*. Singapore: John Wiley & Sons (Asia).

Bramall, Chris. 2009a. *Chinese Economic Development*. New York: Routledge.

Branstetter, Lee, and Nicholas Lardy. 2008. "China's Embrace of Globalization." In *China's Great Transformation*, edited by Loren Brandt and Thomas Rawski, 633–682. New York: Cambridge University Press.

Chan, Anita. 1998. "Labor Standards and Human Rights: The Case of Chinese Workers Under Market Socialism." *Human Rights Quarterly* 20 (4): 886–904. www.jstor.org/stable/762792.

Chan, Anita. 2003. "A Race to the Bottom: Globalisation and China's Labour Standards." *China Perspectives* 46: 41–49.

Chan, Kam Wing. 2009. "The Chinese Hukou System at 50." *Eurasian Geography and Economics* 50 (2): 197–221.

Friedman, Milton, and Rose Friedman. 1980. *Free to Choose: A Personal Statement*. New York: Houghton Mifflin Harcourt.

Gallagher, Mary E. 2002. "'Reform and Openness': Why China's Economic Reforms have Delayed Democracy." *World Politics* 54 (3): 338–372. doi:10.1353/wp.2002.0009.

Greenfield, Gerard and Apo Leong. 1997. "China's Communist Capitalism: The Real World of Market Socialism," In *Ruthless Criticism of all that Exists: Socialist Register 1997*, edited by Leo Panitch, 96–122. New York: Monthly Review.

Gu, Edward X. 1997. "Foreign Direct Investment and the Restructuring of Chinese State-Owned Enterprises (1992–1995): A New Institutionalist Perspective." *China Information* 12 (3): 46–71. doi:10.1177/0920203X9701200303.

Gustafsson, Bjorn A., Shi Li, and Terry Sicular, eds. 2008. *Inequality and Public Policy in China*. New York: Cambridge University Press.

Hart-Landsberg, Martin, and Paul Burkett. 2005. *China and Socialism: Market Reforms and Class Struggle*. New York: Monthly Review.

Hsu, Robert C. 1991. *Economic Theories in China 1979–1988*. New York: Cambridge University Press.

Huang, Philip C. C. 2009a. "China's Neglected Informal Economy: Reality and Theory." *Modern China* 35 (4): 405–438. doi:10.1177/0097700409333158.

Jacobson, Harold K., and Michel Oksenberg. 1990. *China's Participation in the IMF, the World Bank, and GATT: Toward a Global Economic Order.* Ann Arbor, MI: University of Michigan Press.

Krugman, Paul. 1987. "Is Free Trade Passé?" *Journal of Economic Perspectives* 1 (2): 131–144. doi:10.1257/jep. 1.2.131.

Lardy, Nicholas. 2002. *Integrating China into the Global Economy.* Washington, DC: Brookings Institution Press.

Lee, Ching Kwan. 1998. *Gender and the South China Miracle: Two Worlds of Factory Women.* Berkeley, CA: University of California Press.

Lee, Ching Kwan. 2007a. *Working in China: Ethnographies of Labor and Workplace Transformation.* New York: Routledge.

Lee, Ching Kwan. 2007c. *Against the Law: Labor Protests in China's Rustbelt and Sunbelt.* Berkeley, CA: University of California Press.

Leung, Win-yue. 1988. *Smashing the Iron Rice Pot: Workers & Unions in China's Market Socialism.* Hong Kong: Asia Monitor Resource Center.

Li, Haijian. 2003 [1997]. "Integrating FDI within the Domestic Economy (China Industrial Development Report)." In *China's Economic Reform: A Study with Documents,* edited by Christopher Howe, Y. Y. Kueh, and Robert Ash, 387–398. New York: Routledge.

Li, Lanqing. 2009. *Breaking through: The Birth of China's Opening-Up Policy.* New York: Oxford University Press.

Li, Minqi. "Capitalist Development and Class Struggle in China." Book manuscript. Available online at http://content.csbs.utah.edu/~mli/Capitalism%20in%20China/Index.htm (accessed April 22, 2017).

Li, Shi. 2008. *Rural Migrant Workers in China: Scenario, Challenges and Public Policy.* ILO Working Papers. Vol. 89. Geneva: International Labour Office.

Li, Zhongjin, and Hao Qi. 2014. "Labor Process and the Social Structure of Accumulation in China." *Review of Radical Political Economics* 46 (4): 481–488. doi:10.1177/0486613414537986.

Lin, Justin Yifu, Fang Cai, and Zhou Li. 2003. *The China Miracle: Development Strategy and Economic Reform.* Rev. ed. Hong Kong: Chinese University Press.

Meisner, Maurice. 1996. *The Deng Xiaopeng Era: An Inquiry into the Fate of Chinese Socialism 1978–1994.* New York: Hill and Wang.

Meisner, Maurice. 1999. *Mao's China: A History of the People's Republic.* 3rd ed. New York: Free Press.

National Bureau of Statistics of China. 2010. *China Statistical Yearbook 2010.* Beijing: China Statistics Press.

Naughton, Barry. 1995. *Growing Out of the Plan: Chinese Economic Reform 1978–1993.* New York: Cambridge University Press.

Naughton, Barry. 2007. *The Chinese Economy: Transitions and Growth.* Cambridge, MA: MIT Press.

Nolan, Peter. 2004 [1998]. *Transforming China: Globalization, Transition and Development.* New York: Anthem Press.

Perkins, Dwight. 1994. "Completing China's Move to the Market." *Journal of Economic Perspectives* 8 (2): 23–46. doi:10.1257/jep. 8.2.23.

Pun, Ngai. 2008. "'Reorganizing Moralism': The Politics of Transnational Labor Codes." In *Privatizing China: Socialism from Afar,* edited by Li Zhang and Aihwa Ong, 87–102. Ithaca, NY: Cornell University Press.

Qian, Yingyi, and Jinglian Wu. 2000. *China's Transition to a Market Economy: How Far*

*Across the River?* Working Paper no. 69. Stanford, CA: Center for International Development, Stanford University.

Ross, Andrew. 2007a. *Fast Boat to China: High-Tech Outsourcing and the Consequences for Free Trade—Lessons from Shanghai.* New York: Vintage.

Ross, Andrew. 2007b. "Outsourcing as a Way of Life? Knowledge Transfer in the Yangtze Delta." In *Working in China: Ethnographies of Labor and Workplace Transformation,* edited by Ching Kwan Lee, 188–208. New York: Routledge.

Sung, Yun-wing and Thomas M. H. Chan. 1987. "China's Economic Reforms: The Debates in China." *The Australian Journal of Chinese Affairs* (17): 29–51. doi:10.2307/2158967.

Weinberg, Meyer. 2002. *A Short History of American Capitalism.* New History Press.

Whyte, Martin King. 1999. "The Changing Role of Workers." In *The Paradox of China's Post-Mao Reforms,* edited by Merle Goldman and Roderick MacFarquhar, 173–196. Cambridge, MA: Harvard University Press.

World Bank and Development Research Center of the State Council, the People's Republic of China. 2013. *China 2030: Building a Modern, Harmonious, and Creative Society.* Washington, DC: World Bank.

Wu, Jinglian. 2005. *Understanding and Interpreting China's Economic Reform.* Singapore: Thomson/South-Western.

Xu, Dixin. 1981. "China's Special Economic Zones." *Beijing Review* 50, 14–17.

Xue, Hong and Anita Chan. 2013. "The Global Value Chain." *Critical Asian Studies* 45 (1): 55–77. doi:10.1080/14672715.2013.758821.

Zhu, Andong and David M. Kotz. 2011. "The Dependence of China's Economic Growth on Exports and Investment." *Review of Radical Political Economics* 43 (1): 9–32. doi:10.1177/0486613410383951.

# 6 Economic restructuring of state-owned enterprises

## 6.1 Introduction and historical narrative 1978–1989

Many of the debates about the reorganization of rural industry discussed in Chapter 4 were repeated with respect to the treatment of large state-owned enterprises (SOEs) in the cities. Initial reform efforts actually focused on the SOEs. The challenge was symbolically charged, as these firms were the icons of Chinese socialism and its commitment to the working class. The "iron rice bowl" guaranteed state-owned enterprise workers lifetime employment, old age pensions, subsidized housing, children's schooling, and medical care through their workplace. The firms were deeply tied to a system of economic planning in which the Communist Party assigned jobs, minimized wage differentials within firms, determined managerial promotion, controlled access to urban residences, and conformed firm output to plan requirements. The rhetoric (if not the reality) of official policy portrayed workers as the "masters of their enterprises," or at least future masters, as socialism evolved. The SOEs also focused on the heavy industry part of the Chinese economy and were thus deeply linked to national defense. Re-engineering the SOEs thus involved much more than narrow economic issues.

There are many parallels and some differences between the initiatives attempted in the SOE sector and the restructuring projects in the countryside and international sector. Re-engineering the SOEs came to be called "reform inside the system." Relying on new foreign-owned firms and joint ventures in the SEZs or building on new firms (the TVEs and household firms) in the countryside came to be known as "reform outside the system." As with the initial agricultural reforms that increased procurement prices and farmers' independence in crop choice, the initial SOE reforms gave state-owned firms more economic autonomy and increased material incentives for improved economic performance.

Alongside the carrot of expanded rewards for economic success, the stick of new competitive pressures also spurred economic changes. The SOEs faced increased competition from each other as barriers to entry into formerly locally-provisioned markets were relaxed. The SOEs also faced increasing competition from imports and foreign-invested firms. Their most serious competition, however, came from the rapidly expanding township and village enterprises.

The competitive pressures the SOEs faced from the TVEs in the 1980s were similar to the "race to the bottom" pressures the TVEs faced from private firms in the 1990s. As the World Bank observed in its 1995 study, *Bureaucrats in Business,*

> Compared to SOEs, TVEs are more free to hire and fire labor. ... Unlike state enterprises, TVEs are not obligated to provide such services as housing, health care, education, and lifetime employment and pensions to their employees and their dependents.
>
> (74)

For most of the 1980s, the SOEs soft budget constraints attenuated these pressures. Potential losses were covered by government subsidies. While losses were modest in the early 1980s they mounted significantly in the late eighties, at the very time government subsidies covering losses were being replaced by interest bearing loans.[1] The process was interrupted by the aftershocks of Tiananmen Square but renewed with added intensity in the middle 1990s.

The goal of the reforms was to encourage the SOEs to behave more like profit making firms, both in terms of external relations (seeking higher product quality, greater innovation, and increased attention to market demand, etc.) and internal relations (seeking more efficient use of inputs, such as raw materials, credit, and labor). The aim, however, was to reform state-owned enterprises, not to privatize them.

The long run challenge was to increase the firms' economic efficiency without sacrificing their socialist characteristics. Counted among the latter were egalitarian compensation policies, guaranteed employment, and the governance of SOE behavior by social norms that called on firms to serve a higher purpose than simple profit maximization. The challenge was also to avoid those kinds of reform that might work well in the short run but have destructive implications in the long run, turning healthy competition into an unhealthy race to the bottom.

While nearly everyone agreed that many SOEs needed to improve their economic performance, there were a range of different strategies recommended to accomplish this, including: (1) expanding incentives for existing SOEs to operate more efficiently; (2) transforming existing state-owned enterprises into worker owned enterprises; (3) leasing existing SOEs to their managers (4) allowing a small private sector to compete with a much large public sector; and (5) promoting a generalized system of private enterprise with wage laborers. In the 1980s very few Chinese economists favored the last category and everyone endorsed the first strategy.

Rather than transferring all of their net revenues to the state, companies were allowed to retain a share of their profits for bonuses and enterprise determined investment projects. They were permitted to experiment with new products. As in the countryside, producers were also permitted to sell above-quota output at market rather than plan prices.

Formal experiments with greater enterprise autonomy and profit retention among the SOEs began in 1978 and expanded quickly.[2] By 1980, 6,600 SOEs, accounting for ~60 percent of budgeted national industrial output and 70 percent of national industrial profits, were involved in these experiments (Wu 2005, 145; Naughton 1995, 100). As in the countryside, the co-existence of plan determined output quotas and product prices for a portion of production, alongside market determined prices and output levels for additional production, was a celebrated hallmark of China's emerging dual-track economic development plan. In September 1984, Hua Sheng and several other young reformist economists, many associated with CASS, proposed the dual-track system to Zhao Ziyang. He quickly approved it (Kuhn 2011, 132–133).[3] Four and a half years later, Hua would propose a widespread plan for SOE privatization (Kristof 1989b).[4]

Beginning in May 1984 local factory managers were given greater control over their companies' management at the expense of local party officials. Firm profitability was increasingly seen as a measure of managerial performance (Bramall 2000, 391). Beginning around 1986–1987, the reforms took the form of the "contract responsibility system" (CRS). Like the household responsibility system, the CRS allowed managers (or other representatives of the entire enterprise) to lease the firm from the state under terms that made the managers (or workers as a whole) the residual claimant for income and output beyond that owed to the state. A number of economists favored worker self-management versions of the CRS. Jiang Yiwei, for example, proposed that employees contract for an enterprise and hire managers (Shirk 1993, 324). While Zhao Ziyang appears to have "expressed sympathy" for the idea, it was not pursued (Shirk 1993, 325, Park 1986, 222). Deng's intervention in favor of the managerial contract responsibility system appears to have been decisive.[5]

The 1980s retreat from worker self-management appears to mirror an earlier shift from the East China or Shanghai system experiments with participatory management in the early 1950s to the "one-man management" system used in the USSR around 1953. Dissatisfaction with the shift was tapped during the Great Leap period (Blecher 2010, 141). The pendulum would swing back and forth between "rationalizing managerial authority" and workplace-participatory democracy before, during, and after the Cultural Revolution. Blecher writes,

> … experiments in broad democracy in workplace political communities conflicted with countertrends toward rationalization of authority. … [T]here was a contradiction between the participatory and democratic elements embodied in the Great Leap innovations … and the needs of an increasingly complex modern industry for efficiency, predictability, and standardization. … Efforts to reconcile the two were generally unsuccessful.
>
> (Blecher 2010, 142)

The dual-track and contract responsibility system were a clever response to many of the adjustment problems expected to accompany an expansion of market dynamics within a planned economy. The framework suggested possible ways for having planned and market activities coexist. But the strategy also created powerful temptations for corrupt arbitrage and relentless pressures for complete price decontrol and subordination of the plan to the market. Unless accompanied by very thoughtful social policy, these pressures threatened to create macroeconomic instabilities, large new inequalities, and social unrest.[6]

While the SOEs are often portrayed as unchangeable, inefficient dinosaurs, they seem to have made notable, although unspectacular, economic improvements over the first 10–15 years of economic restructuring. Jefferson and Rawski, for example, found the SOEs acting more like profit-seeking firms than routinized bureaucracies. They credited the publicly owned firms with: substantial increases in labor productivity; modest increases in total factor productivity; large increases in R&D spending; and more rapid product development and process innovation (Jefferson and Rawski 1995, 133). They also noted that the SOEs had expanded their manufacturing exports, which they took to imply increased attention to quality control and market feedback.[7] Xu reports that SOE output per worker rose 67 percent during the 1980s (Xu 2011, 1121). Other analysts have found smaller productivity gains.[8]

Spillover effects persistently undermined SOE restructuring efforts in the 1980s. Economic changes in one sector of the economy caused disequilibria in other sectors, often resulting in macroeconomic, public finance, and distributional difficulties. The most serious problems accompanying initial SOE reforms were probably macroeconomic problems. The increase in enterprise autonomy and decline in economic planning was accompanied by a decentralization of credit. Local governments attempted to promote the success of local enterprises by extending them cheap credit for new investments. The result was an explosion of aggregate demand and intolerable inflationary pressures. In 1984 the Chinese central bank exacerbated these underlying pressures. It let it be known that credit allocations for the country's four main banks in 1985 would be based on loans made in 1984. This spurred the banks to make additional loans (Coase and Wang 2013, 92–93).

Alongside allowing prices for above plan output to be market determined, the reformers also removed price controls from hundreds of commodities in 1982 and 1983. State-set prices for non-staple consumer goods (including meat, fish, and vegetables) were brought closer to market prices by significant increases in 1985. The burden of these price increases on urban dwellers was initially offset by government subsidies (Bramall 2009a, 350). Subsequent announcements of plans for complete price decontrol of meat, eggs, vegetables, and sugar without offsetting subsidies spurred panic buying in the late 1980s. This in turn caused shortages, bottlenecks and additional inflationary pressures, especially in late 1987 and 1988. In his memoirs, Zhao Ziyang emphasized the inflationary impact of households' attempts to convert their

~trillion yuan of savings deposits into physical commodities in 1987 in an effort to protect their wealth from inflation (Zhao 2009, 221–225).[9]

Besides generating inflationary pressures, the reforms helped cause large government deficits. Efforts to insulate urban SOE households from the full effect of rising agricultural prices by subsidizing some food products increased government spending.[10] At the same time, the state's changing treatment of SOE markets and profits reduced government revenues. Traditionally, a very high percentage of SOE profits had been turned over to the state. When the reforms opened SOE markets to increased competition, these monopoly profits fell. In addition the reforms permitted the firms to retain a greater share of their reduced profits. The result was a huge drop in government revenues.[11]

Distributionally, the reforms tended to concentrate the benefits of enterprise restructuring in the hands of insiders. In later decades, the extreme version of this eventually involved insider privatization, under which managers were able to borrow public money at extremely low interest rates, underprice their firm's assets, and acquire ownership rights. Milder versions of restructuring under the contract responsibility system ("managerial responsibility system") in the 1980s allowed the managers to rent the firm, often at artificially low prices, and pocket the profits from enterprise improvements. Popular perceptions of corruption in the restructuring process seriously undermined its effectiveness and political legitimacy.[12] The triad of macro, fiscal/budget, and distributional problems quickly caused the government to dim the reforms and reinstitute many planning mechanisms. The first period of restructuring was curtailed in 1981, after the experiments with increased enterprise autonomy in 1979 and 1980 led to a rapidly rising fiscal deficit and inflationary pressures. Subsequent efforts to renew the SOE reforms in 1983 and 1984 and the late 1980s ran into similar obstacles (Wu 2004, 8–9).

Most SOEs continued to operate, at least partially, in a planned bubble during the 1980s. They continued to receive their traditional allotments of inputs at below market prices and were guaranteed purchase of their output, independent of quality and outside competition, at plan dictated prices. They also increased their non-plan production, with the share of inputs and outputs purchased and sold through markets reaching about 60 percent in 1989 (Jefferson and Rawski 1994, 51). These conditions allowed the firms to continue to basically maintain traditional wages and benefits for long-time employees (Whyte 1999, 187). There were no SOE bankruptcies and minimal layoffs. The covering of losses was implicitly guaranteed by access to government credit.

Under this regime, the SOEs gradually improved their economic efficiency. Output grew at about an 8 percent rate per year (Jefferson and Rawski 1995, 132). From 1984–1989 they maintained, but did not increase, their access to state-assigned inputs. After 1985, new SOE workers were hired without the guarantee of permanent employment, a major policy shift that apparently won support among Chinese economists (Sung and Chan 1987,

49).[13] In 1988 the new Enterprise Law gave SOE managers the right to fire workers, but this power was not initially used to dismiss long-time employees (Li 2008, 60). By 1994, one quarter of all SOE workers lacked employment guarantees (Greenfield and Leong 1997, 99). In Barry Naughton's words, the economy eventually "grew out of the plan." Policy makers froze the size of the planned economy flowing through government firms and encouraged the SOEs and emerging private firms to organize economic growth along market channels. This is only half the story, however. In the late 1990s, the "iron rice bowl" was not simply overshadowed; it was smashed. We will pick up that part of the story in section 6.4.

## 6.2 Neoclassical vs. Marxist analyses of SOE restructuring 1978–1989

The debate over the viability of state-owned firms in Chinese industry and the merits of expanding market-oriented incentives illustrates once again the paradigmatic nature of the assessments of Chinese reforms. Undergirding the spread of neoclassical interpretations was the animating spirit of classical liberalism. The latter's assumptions about human nature, institutional evolution, and human well-being make it difficult to imagine how public ownership, egalitarian-oriented compensation policies and cooperative-oriented institutional designs could be economically viable in the long run.[14]

From a classical liberal perspective, production workers and their immediate supervisors need a strong system of rewards and punishment to ensure diligent labor. These supervisors similarly need overseers to monitor and motivate them, and so on up the hierarchy. The challenge is to "solve the agency problem," and nothing works as well as private property and the profit motive. Unless there are clear "residual claimants" (i.e., self-interested owners), economic efficiency will suffer.

As noted in section 4.4, innovative versions of these ideas migrated to China in the late 1980s in the form of New Institutionalist Economics (NIE) and Public Choice theory. The work of Coase, North, Buchanan, and Mancur Olson was especially influential (Sheng 1996, 9–10; Ma and Trautwein 2013, 259–269). The influence of the new institutionalist economists deepened in the early 1990s. It was augmented by the return to China of an increasing number of mainstream (non-Chicago) economics PhDs from America (Klaes and Zhang 2013, 268). All three groups, mainstream and Chicago neoclassicals and new institutionalist economists, urged greater privatization, though members sometimes disagreed about the optimal pace for privatization.

Marxist and heterodox economists' different assumptions about human nature, encouraged them to believe that well-designed institutions could rely on mobilizing voluntary cooperation with weaker material incentives than implied by classical liberalism. Other aspects of these paradigms' subtexts, made it difficult to imagine how the privatization of large firms could avoid creating enduring structures of economic inequality, undesirable concentrations of economic and political power, and despotic working conditions. (While not really an issue in the 1980s, recent Marxist theorists would add the inevitability of environmental crisis to the legacy of privatization.)[15]

An emerging heterodox perspective accepted the need for autonomous, incentivized firms, but was supportive of public ownership and active government industrial policy. At the margins, this perspective draws on heterodox aspects of neoclassically-oriented political-economists, such as Peter Nolan and Chris Bramall, and market-oriented Marxist economists, like Dong Fureng.[16]

Given these backdrops, Marxist and neoclassical economists have drawn different lessons for economic theory from the performance of state-owned enterprises over the 1978–1989 period. While aspects of the early debate revolved around technical questions concerning how to measure enterprises' total factor productivity,[17] the most important debates reflected different counter-factual assumptions about what would have happened with more or less privatization.

Neoclassical economic analyses portray marketization measures in the SOE sector as steps toward economic rationality. They attribute most accompanying economic problems to insufficient rather than excessive marketization. Defenders of the reforms, especially proponents of even larger tilts toward private enterprises, have argued that the program's market incentives in the 1980s were too small to significantly alter the SOEs behavior. On the upside, they claim that the share of profits retained by firms,[18] and the level of productivity-linked bonuses given workers or managers, were insufficient to motivate managers and workers to focus on firm profitability (Naughton 1995, Chapter 3). On the down side, they claim that "soft budget constraints" (i.e., expected government bailouts) reduced the consequences of poor performance and lowered incentives to improve performance. The neoclassicals have also argued that government and party officials retained too much influence over aspects of the firm's environment through levers such as personnel appointments and control over access to credit. The take-away message of these objections was that the main problem with the reforms was that they did not go far enough.

Milton Friedman's advice to the Chinese in 1988 typifies this a priori perspective. He writes:

> [A]s long as industrial enterprises are government-owned, there are severe limits to the ability of politically sensitive managers (bureaucrats) to respond effectively to market pressures (8). … Do not compromise by partial privatization (14). … [I]f the shift can be achieved, transitional costs will pale into insignificance. … All of the peoples of the world would benefit.
>
> (Friedman 1990b, 15)

The supporters of increased privatization tended to minimize the positive aspects of government-owned firms' performance and highlight the SOEs' shortcomings. Four of their main claims were:

1   The SOEs may have improved their economic performance and the Chinese economy may have experienced rapid economic growth, but both outcomes would have been much better with additional reforms. The SOEs generally had lower rates of productivity increase and lower profit rates than non-SOE firms. Bramall has characterized aspects of this view as: "China grew at close to 10 per cent per annum, but could have grown at (say) 15 per cent 'if only' the economy had been capitalist" (Bramall 2000, 4).[19]
2   The SOEs successes were unsustainable. The SOE's improved performance rested on harvesting one-time low-hanging fruit, such as the deployment of a backlog of obviously superior new technologies and recovery from the widespread irrationalities of the late Maoist years.[20] The "gradualist" position of some Western economists, such as Jefferson, Rawski, and Naughton (versus those advocating "shock therapy") offered a variant of this position. They acknowledged the SOEs successes in the 1980s and the imprudence of rapid privatization, but still called for long-run privatization (Bramall 2000, 5; Putterman 1995, 1060).
3   The SOEs tenuous viability was due to unfair government favors, such as biased regulation, low interest rate-bailout loans, and other hidden subsidies.
4   The SOE enterprises that genuinely succeeded (without subsidies and in sustainable ways) were really "red hat firms," that is, private firms in disguise (Bramall 2000, 4).

In contrast, Marxist and other theorists more sympathetic toward public ownership fit events into a different framework, equally resistant to definitive refutation by empirical evidence. Six of their main claims were:

1   The SOEs were quite capable of efficient production as evidenced by their increase in total factor productivity, technological sophistication, and product quality during the 1980s.[21]
2   The SOEs were able to rely on voluntary cooperation and weak material incentives in the 1950s and still generate solid performance and respectable economic growth. These conditions were undermined by the disillusionment accompanying the destructiveness of the Cultural Revolution and increasing cadre corruption, but they demonstrate the feasibility of organizing production in a cooperative fashion. Li Minqi, for example, reports,

I had some opportunity to talk to the workers in the state-owned enterprises. Many old workers told me that in 1950s workers were really enthusiastic. ... [T]hey did not need material incentives, nor the supervision of the superior management. ... Today's economists certainly cannot understand this. ... [T]he old workers told me ... the cadres took care of the workers, being the first to bear hardships and the last to enjoy comforts."

(Li, Minqi 1996, 22)

3    Much of the unfavorable financial comparisons between the SOEs and other firms (such as lower profit rates) reflected a non-level playing field, due to:

   a    the higher social safety net obligations carried by the SOEs for retired workers' pensions, and current employees' welfare benefits[22]

   b    the firms' responsibility to employ surplus labor

   c    higher government tax rates on SOEs than non SOEs[23]

   d    higher environmental and work place safety standards for SOEs than urban collectives or TVEs

   e    administratively suppressed prices in some SOE dominated markets[24]

   f    accounting conventions that historically underestimated depreciation on the SOEs capital stock,[25] and, perhaps

   g    financing rules that made it difficult for some SOEs to finance investments in new technologies.[26]

4    Even ignoring the higher tax and social welfare burdens borne by SOEs, the large SOEs' profitability was still slightly higher than average industrial enterprise profitability in the 1980s and slightly lower than average in the 1990s (Lo and Zhang 2011, 48).[27] The SOEs' fall in profitability during the 1978–1998 period mirrored that of other Chinese enterprises due to national problems of excess capacity and periods of macroeconomic stress (Lo and Zhang 2011, 49). In 1993, 40–50 percent of joint ventures also suffered losses (Nolan 2004 [1998], 159–160).

5    The metrics used by conventional analysis to assess firms' and countries' economic success are too narrow.

   a    Equity issues need greater attention along with other socialist goals, such as job security.

   b    Additional metrics should be used alongside GDP/capita to assess economic performance, such as the Human Development Index, the UN's projects to measure subjective well-being,[28] Amartya Sen's index of capabilities, and measures reflecting the potential for achieving socialist goals.[29]

   c    Special attention should be given to dynamic, long run issues involving learning effects and human capital accumulation. From this angle, the early failures of rural industrialization in the Great Leap were partially offset by the "learning by doing" of rural communities that flowered in the expansion of commune and brigade industries 1970–1978 and the TVEs in the 1980s. The motivational shortcomings of the period's SOEs can be treated as "socialist tuition," down payments for the arduous task of constructing new kinds of social institutions.

6    Most importantly, the weaknesses of existing SOE performance could be redressed without privatization, which threatens unacceptable concentrations of economic and political power in private hands.

The initial debate over SOE reform inside China was carried out mainly among Marxist economists in the early 1980s. This would change by the late 1980s and early 1990s, with the neoclassical perspective gaining traction. The economists debating SOE reforms in the earlier period were usually committed to the goal of building socialism and organized their thinking with reference to Marxist subtexts. Unlike neoclassical accounts, these analyses often asked the question, "what is the implication of these policies for building socialism?" The potential tension between the reformers' commitment to expanding market forces and maintaining socialist institutions animated their deliberations. They believed in an ethic of distribution based on labor. They accepted differences in income based on differences in labor supplied, but were uncomfortable with income received from interest on loans, or as residual claimant for income derived from the labor of more than seven hired workers.

The reformers expected SOE managers to have a " 'self-sacrificing spirit,' on the one hand, and enterprising and innovative abilities, on the other hand" (Hsu 1991, 91). They worried about maintaining "fraternal cooperation and socialist emulation for the purpose of pulling the backward [firms] up to the level of the advanced—the very antithesis of capitalist competition for profits by destroying one's rivals" (Hsu 1991, 39). And although they developed a vision of socialist competition that muted these concerns, they worried about the feedback created by totally self-interested business firms and managers.[30] Such worries are not starting points for neoclassical analysis. It does not look as though Zhao Ziyang shared all of these concerns.

Marxist arguments for tolerating the termination of employment guarantees for SOE workers hired after the mid-1980s and the existence of a modest private sector alongside the SOEs appealed to the logic of primary stage theories of socialism.[31] For the most part, it seems that the SOEs were initially reluctant to use their newly granted powers to alter employment relationships (Pringle 2013, 193).[32] The mass layoffs of longtime SOE employees in the mid and late 1990s would appeal more aggressively to "primary stage" arguments.

The SOE reforms raised many theoretical questions. Can you mix plan and market mechanisms for output and price determination? Can you increase market competition without a "race to the bottom" in social practices? Can you increase material incentives without undermining the efficiency of moral incentives and voluntary cooperation? Can you significantly increase economic efficiency without large increases in inequality? Can you have an efficient workplace without an authoritarian workplace? The neoclassicals deflected these questions by assuming the market would optimize any trade-offs. Deng's reformers deflected these questions by assuming that the Communist Party's control of the state would resolve any contradictions. Economists caught in between Deng and the neoclassicals found themselves in a more difficult situation.

The debate over SOE reforms would take on harsher tones in the 1990s as market reformers increasingly called for privatization of the SOEs and "smashing the iron rice bowl." Beginning in the middle 1980s classical liberal subtexts and frames began to become much more popular. The work of Austrian economist Steven Cheung, for example, received much popular attention.[33] Neoclassical economics began to influence university education (see Chapter 8) and the tenor of the debate. Hua Sheng (one of the Chinese economists credited with authoring the dual-track pricing system) foreshadowed the debate in 1989 with a widely publicized call for the government to privatize all of its holdings (Kristof 1989b). The proposal was sidetracked by the events in Tiananmen Square a few months later.

## 6.3 SOE restructuring 1989–1991

### 6.3.1 Historical narrative

As noted in earlier chapters, the Chinese leadership reacted to the Tiananmen Square crisis by slowing economic restructuring. This shift tended to expand the role of economic planning. It also increased the role of state-owned enterprises who were given preferential access to credit and raw materials. The autonomy of SOE managers was curtailed and increased attention given to reducing income inequalities within firms (Naughton 1995, Chapter 8; Zhao 2009, 231).[34] Deng reversed these trends and ignited a second round of reform in January 1992 with his famous "Southern Tour."

### 6.3.2 Neoclassical framings

As noted earlier, neoclassical accounts of the renewal of economic restructuring attribute the policy shift to the allegedly transparent failures of retrenchment. Naughton treats the roll-back of restructuring policies 1989–1991 as the "last hurrah" of opponents of marketization, dismissing their concerns.[35] He presents the renewal of restructuring as a triumph of rationality. His account treats marketization as a popular movement with strong spontaneous elements. He concludes, "Ultimately, the most important achievement of the conservative interlude was to finally demonstrate that there was no going back" (Naughton 1995, 288). Reflecting on the evolution of practical economic thinking among China's elite, neoclassical authors Jefferson and Rawski write

> Competition forced participants to compare the merits of alternative institutional arrangements. ... The rise of promarket sentiments among

the political and administrative elite represents the biggest feedback of all in China's partial reform process ... ambitious young bureaucrats began leaving the government to pursue private business careers.

(Jefferson and Rawski 1995, 150)

### 6.3.3 Marxist and heterodox framings 1989–1991

Political economists less favorably inclined toward the emerging transition to capitalism tell a somewhat different story. Their account challenges the spontaneous and technical rationality explanation for the emergence of a new round of restructuring. In 1987 Zhao indicated that the losers from price reform were too numerous and powerful to attempt price decontrol and reportedly "told his advisers that no statesman could carry it out unless he operated under martial law" (Shirk 1993, 321). This option came into being after Tiananmen Square. Both Blecher (2010) and Wang (2003a) argue that the major restructuring projects in the early and mid-1990s (price decontrol and mass layoffs from SOE and urban collectives) were imposed on the backs of the repression of Tiananmen Square. Wang Hui notes that the price reforms halted in 1988 were resumed in September 1989, arguing that "the violence of 1989 served to check the social upheaval brought about by ... the new pricing system..." (Wang 2003a, 66). Marc Blecher concludes "the 1989 crackdown inadvertently provided the key precondition for the difficult and previously impossible breakthrough to economic reform. This combination of state political violence and economic reform goes beyond market Leninism to what could be called 'market Stalinism'" (Blecher 2010, 81, see also Bramall 2009a, 331). Wang also points out that authoritarian voices in China were able to ideologically dismiss calls for checks on the growing inequality accompanying marketization by tarring egalitarian concerns with images of the Cultural Revolution.[36]

## 6.4 SOE restructuring 1992–2001: historical narrative

As in the 1980s, the SOE reforms of the early 1990s attempted to increase the economic efficiency of state-owned enterprises by sharpening material incentives, promoting increased competition, and deregulating prices. The dual-track pricing system ended in the mid-1990s and by 1995, 89 percent of retail sales and 78 percent of producer-good sales were conducted at market prices.[37] The SOEs faced increasing competition from TVEs, newly-constituted private firms, and foreign invested firms.[38] At the same time, firmer budget constraints from the state increased the penalties for poor economic performance. The changes accelerated under the leadership of Zhu Rongji, who took over management of the economy from Li Peng after Deng's "Southern Tour." Zhu had been mentored by Ma Hong and was conversant with the logic and practice of economic planning. He was also quite willing to use administrative authority to steer the market. Nevertheless, marketization and privatization significantly increased during his watch, suggesting that more profound structural forces were behind the changes than individual personalities.

The period's major policy change was the state's support of massive layoffs in the SOE sector and the privatization of small and medium sized SOEs. While a few reform economists, such as Dong Fureng[39] and Hua Sheng, had been sympathetic to privatization as early as the mid-1980s, there were no significant privatizations before the Tiananmen Square crackdown. Privatization began with small TVEs in the early 1990s and spread to the SOEs after 1995.

The chief public rationale for mass layoffs and SOE privatization were claims of poor economic performance by state-owned enterprises. Critics of the SOEs highlighted several worrisome statistics about SOE performance. They noted that profits from industrial SOEs fell from 14 percent GDP in 1978 to ~1 percent GDP 1996–1998 (Naughton 2007, 305). The solid productivity growth achieved in the 1980s (especially 1984–1988) seems to have disappeared 1992–1996 (Bramall 2009a, 415–416).[40] Losses among unprofitable SOEs increased from ~3–8 billion RMB/year 1978–1988, to more than 70 billion RMB in 1996–1997 (Lardy 1998, 35). The SOE sector also suffered a decline in access to government subsidies to cover these losses. As the SOEs' shortfalls escalated, the Chinese banking sector accumulated "nonperforming" SOE loans.

As in the 1980s, it is not clear to what extent the SOEs economic problems in the 1990s were due to the firms' inefficiencies, the firms' shouldering of social responsibilities (such as maintaining employment and funding pensions for already retired workers), asset stripping by corrupt insiders, and/or other economic conditions, such as antiquated equipment or economy-wide excess capacity, that made it difficult for all kinds of Chinese firms to be profitable.[41]

Comparisons between the performance of public and privately owned firms are difficult to interpret because of claims from both sides of an unlevel playing field. Supporters of privatization, for example, claimed that SOEs had privileged access to capital, while supporters of SOEs claimed that their firms had higher tax and social welfare burdens.

In response to increasing competitive pressure and new social norms weakening government commitments to guaranteed employment, the SOEs eventually laid off ~30 million workers 1993–2003 (Naughton 2007, 183–189), with most of the layoffs coming between 1996 and 2000. If job losses in other non-private sector enterprises are included (such as job losses in urban collectives), layoffs totaled nearly 50 million workers, or ~40 percent of public-enterprise workers (Naughton 2007, 179).[42] The size and speed of these layoffs, created a surge in unemployment, which reached 8–10 percent from ~1996–2002 (Naughton 2007, 187; Lau 2001, 233, Li Shi 2008, 1). If migrant workers were included the numbers would be considerably higher.[43] This crisis was obscured in official Chinese unemployment statistics. The latter, for example, exclude laid-off workers still formally identified on SOE employee lists. The Chinese government attempted with limited success to cushion the impact of job losses.[44] Millions of laid-off workers suffered significant economic hardships.[45] The period of "reform without losers" was clearly over.

In addition to pressuring SOEs to become more "bottom-line"-oriented firms, urban restructuring privatized many firms. The new Company Law (1993–1994), the "grasp the large and release the small" campaign (beginning in 1994) and the constitutional protections given private ownership after 1999 spurred the privatization of tens of thousands of mainly small SOEs.[46] Building on earlier experience with rural shareholding cooperatives, the new Company Law of 1993 was intended to corporatize China's enterprise system. Both large and small firms were encouraged to assume a shareholding corporate form; the main difference being how shares would be held. Public bodies were to hold controlling stakes in large SOEs, while private owners could control small and medium sized firms. By 1996 the ownership of China's industrial plant had been reconfigured. When the reforms began in 1978, state-owned enterprises produced about three-quarters of national industrial output and collective enterprises about one-quarter. By 1996, the private enterprise sector (including foreign-invested firms), the state-owned sector, and the collective owned sector each produced about a third of national industrial output (Naughton 2007, 300). In addition, the momentum was with the private sector.[47]

By regulating shareholding, the reformers attempted to reassure socialist skeptics that corporatization would not lead to control of major Chinese industrial firms by domestic or foreign capital. A certain percentage of government shares in large SOEs were to be non-tradable shares.[48] Similarly, some of the shares in smaller "share-based cooperatives" were to be tradable only among the firms' employees (Hart-Landsberg and Burkett 2005, 53).

These safeguards were only partially successful in avoiding concentrated ownership of firms in the hands of an emerging capitalist class. As with unsuccessful attempts to limit wage labor to seven employees in the countryside, means to circumvent the safeguards quickly surfaced (Naughton 2007, 323–325). The former managers of small and medium sized SOEs (and TVEs), for example, often ended up controlling share-based coops (Hart-Landsberg and Burkett 2005, 53; Bramall 2009a, 421). When the owners of Chinese firms gained the power to fire workers, these managers were able to claim a larger share of profits. While the first round of SOE reforms empowered enterprise managers to make more decisions, workers' bargaining power remained significant due to the guarantee of permanent employment. Naughton reports,

> [M]anagers were still forced to form coalitions with workers, who could not be fired … the disposition of profit … had to bring benefits to the workers. Most of China's enterprise-built housing, for example, was actually built during this period in the 1980s.
>
> (Naughton 2007, 312)

Later reforms ended permanent employment guarantees, thereby weakening the bargaining power of labor and enlarging the claim on output of "residual claimants," be they managers, Chinese owners of firms, or foreign capital (Naughton 2008, 128).

By the time China joined the WTO in 2001 the government sector consisted mainly of ~200 large firms in highly concentrated industries such as energy, electricity, and telecommunications. Oligopolistic competition among separate government owned firms provided some pressures for economic efficiency, while still generating significant profits (~3 percent GDP) for these companies (Naughton 2008, 123). Pressures for insider privatization and/or the temptation to address budget shortfalls by selling the state's ownership share in large industrial firms may eventually privatize these firms (see for example, Lau 2001, 221–226, 247). Up until now, however, this has not happened. State spending in response to the global financial crisis in 2007 seems to have favored large SOEs and strengthened their economic position (Freeman and Yuan 2011, 10).

## 6.5 SOE restructuring 1992–2001: neoclassical perspective

Asking many Western-trained economists about the desirability of large State-Owned Enterprises (SOEs) often seems like waving a red flag in front of a bull. The economist gets ready to charge, marshaling theoretical arguments, classical examples of failed experiments with public ownership, and excuses for any apparent successes of SOEs. Like a vampire that rises from the dead, the continued presence of SOEs in China seems to haunt Western economists, who perpetually try to drive a stake through the SOEs' inefficient hearts.

The World Bank's 1995 report *Bureaucrats in Business* portrayed China's SOEs as dinosaurs on the brink of extinction (Nolan 2004 [1998], 132). "The 'transition orthodoxy' thought that most of the large-scale SOE sector would need to close down" (Ibid., 136). This recommendation was hard to ignore as the Bank co-organized a major conference in Beijing in 1995 with the State Economic and Trade Commission on Chinese enterprise reform. A key paper by Magdi Iskander, the director of the World Bank's department of private sector development, presented a very negative interpretation of international experiences with public ownership.[49] Wu Jinglian, probably the most influential Chinese reform economist, was the commentator on the paper, and largely endorsed its viewpoint.[50]

Updating Milton Friedman's fighting words of 1988 (Friedman 1990a, Chapter 5), *The Economist* called for all-out war against the SOEs in 1998. The British voice of neoclassical policy analysis warned that "China's state enterprises as a group are efficient destroyers of wealth. It would be cheaper to close them all down, and still keep paying the workers" (*The Economist* October 24, 1998, 18). Sixteen years later the magazine was still sounding alarm bells, warning "inefficient state companies are a dangerous extra drag ... putting SOEs right is 'the most critical reform area for China in the coming decade'" (*The Economist* August 30, 2014). In a more restrained voice, Lardy restates the orthodox neoclassical view, writing

> The problem of long-run declining efficiency in the use of resources ... was most acute in the state sector. The sources of inefficiency can be traced to factors that were deeply embedded in an economic planning system that developed in the prereform era ... reforms to date have failed in large portions of the state-owned sector ... their ultimate success will depend on the willingness of the Chinese Communist Party to embrace privatization.
>
> (Lardy 1998, 21–22)

One of the "deeply embedded" aspects of the SOEs behavior criticized by neoclassical economists was the firms "serving too many masters" (the so-called three committees and three meetings problem, or even more colloquially, the "too many mothers-in-law" problem). This resulted from the firms' pursuit of institutional goals other than profit maximization, such as employment security, local community welfare, and the well-being of the Communist Party. The neoclassicals argued that the pursuit of these goals undermined the firms' profitability and opened doors to corrupt nepotistic practices. They rejected the *danwei* model of worker/community oriented-social firms of the Maoist period. While not as provocatively expressed, they echoed Milton Friedman's call for an entirely amoral and self-interested firm.[51] Many current analyses of the Chinese economy echo these sentiments.[52]

There were also some neoclassical reviews of SOE performance that acknowledged modest SOE successes. As noted earlier in this volume, Jefferson and Rawski (1994) and Chow (2002) for example, acknowledged the responsiveness of China's SOEs to the new system of incentives created by economic restructuring in the 1980s. Xu argued in 2011 that changes in ownership structures appeared less important than increasing the competitiveness of political and economic environments when explaining improved economic performance in China. Nevertheless, the tone and focus of most neoclassical accounts have been fairly one-sided, concentrating on the alleged: inefficiencies of SOEs, economic losses incurred by SOEs, the burden on China's financial system of non-performing loans to SOEs, inflationary pressures introduced by the soft budget constraints of SOEs, the lack of motivation of SOE workers, the indifference of SOE managers, the low quality of SOE output, and so on. At best, state ownership was seen as a tolerable temporary concession to political realities or to the need for gradual change to reduce the cost of adjustment by all parties.[53]

As Qian and Wu, two of China's leading economists, noted approvingly in 2000, Chinese economists had internalized much of the neoclassical worldview by the early 1990s. They link this acceptance to academic exchanges and revised economics education (Qian and Wu 2000, 11). Sheng Hong's 1996 article on market reform illustrates the complementary impact of new institutionalist economics on Chinese economic thought and policy. Sheng spent the 1993–1994 year at the University of Chicago and was a student of Coase. He was also one of the co-founders of Unirule, an important free-market think tank described in Chapter 2. In his paper, Sheng emphasizes the work of Coase, North, and Buchanan in explaining the logic of Chinese reform policy. He also highlights the methodologically individualistic roots of "modern economics." He writes

> New Institutional Economics has become, perhaps, the most successful economic theory of the late 1980s and early 1990s [11]. ... The specific practices of reform were influenced by the theoretical and strategic research, while reform practices, in turn, inspired the researchers of theories and policies.
>
> (Sheng 1996, 25)[54]

There is a metaphorical system at work in many neoclassical analyses of SOE issues that has spread to Chinese authors, suggesting images of "normal," "healthy," private firms versus "artificial" and "diseased" public firms.[55] There are "best practices" or "international standards," usually benchmarking the practices of capitalist firms.[56] There is a discourse about healthy development and a discourse about muted or even mutated development. There are lazy workers, careless and indifferent managers, and rampant corruption in the SOEs. There are nimble private firms led by heroic entrepreneurs in the private sector. There is much more than a formal critique of the SOE's generous labor policies, there is almost a Puritanical disdain for the iron rice bowl.[57] Susan Shirk, for example, writes, "Large enterprise managers changed from lazy conservatives coddled by the state to active reformers challenging the state" (Shirk 1993, 288). Blecher notes the spread of this view to the Chinese elite, writing,

> The reform leadership was particularly concerned about low labor productivity, so they urged managers in government-owned firms to get tough with workers, whom they viewed as lazy or defiant. It is true that many workers were defiant in the Maoist period, especially during the Cultural Revolution. But there is no evidence that they were lazy.
>
> (Blecher 2010, 156–157)[58]

Putterman paints a somewhat similar picture, noting,

> at the very time that Western econometric studies were finding signs of responsiveness to reform on the part of China's SOEs, Chinese officials were bemoaning their continued poor performance ... [treating them as] a bastion of economic privilege.
>
> (Putterman 1995, 1057)

Bramall concludes

> the fact that Chinese writers have increasingly criticized the performance of SOEs in the mid-1990s has much more to do with a political agenda—justifying privatization, which started to occur on a significant scale in 1996–7 mainly for budgetary reasons—than any realistic assessment of performance.
>
> (Bramall 2000, 241)[59]

Li Minqi describes the spread of this view to students, writing

> I was a student at the Economic Management Department of Beijing University during the period 1987–90 … we were taught standard neoclassical microeconomics and macroeconomics, and what later I learned was termed "Chicago School" economics. … We were convinced that the socialist economy was unjust, oppressive, and inefficient. It rewarded a layer of privileged, lazy workers in the state sector and "punished" (or at least undercompensated) capable and smart people such as entrepreneurs and intellectuals.
>
> (Li Minqi 2008, x)

From the point of view of neoclassical economics, the "shedding" of "redundant or surplus labor" by public firms was a heroic step necessary to create the foundations for a high standard of living. Qian and Wu, for example, point to the tens of millions of workers laid off from the SOEs and urban collectives in the late 1990s. They criticize the media for portraying these layoffs and associated increases in unemployment as "problems" caused by the reforms. Instead, they argue, "they should be viewed as significant achievements" (Qian and Wu 2000, 15).

## 6.6 SOE restructuring 1992–2001: Marxist and heterodox perspectives

Marxists and heterodox perspectives on SOE restructuring reflected fundamental disagreements with the neoclassicals about how to think about the economy (its structure and purpose) and narrower technical disagreements about how to measure and explain SOE performance. Elaborating these differences, section 6.6.1 looks at challenges to neoclassical assessments of SOE performance. Section 6.6.2 looks at how different conceptions of the nature of work lead to different views of how to organize work. Section 6.6.3 looks at a Marxist alternative (Social Structure of Accumulation theory) to new institutionalist economics' approach to thinking about institutional evolution. Section 6.6.4 looks at philosophical questions about how to measure an economy's success and design institutions to achieve success.

### 6.6.1 Comparing SOE and non-SOE economic performance

Because of strongly held expectations about the relative viability of public and private enterprises, Marxist and neoclassical economists tend to "fill in the gaps" differently when assessing Chinese firms' performance. They also construct different counterfactuals about what would/could have happened under different conditions and what is likely to happen in the future.[60]

As in the 1980s, the defenders of public ownership emphasized that many of the SOEs' economic difficulties were unrelated to inherent problems with public ownership, and reflected instead: (1) increased competition and excess capacity in many industries;[61] (2) the small size of many SOEs and their isolated location as part of Mao's "third-front" national defense-development strategy;[62] (3) the burden of low regulated output prices for some industries (e.g., coal prices in the early1990s);[63] (4) higher relative tax burdens;[64] (5) tougher environmental standards; (6) greater social welfare responsibilities than their non-SOE competitors;[65] and (7) the cherry-picking of public assets by private firms.

Russell Smyth offers a concrete example of cherry-picking involving joint ventures with Hong Kong firms.

> the Harbin [Ball-Bearing] Group entered into a joint venture with a Hong Kong firm … [which] hived off the profitable assets leaving the SOE to shoulder the pensions of 9,000 retired workers and 250 million yuan in other liabilities.
>
> (Smyth 2000, 4)[66]

Li Haijian likewise reported,

> foreign firms now usually choose only high-performing SOES or just take the most promising parts thereof for acquisition and merger, leaving the Chinese enterprises to struggle with the debts, retirement benefits, and resettlement fees for redundant workers. Thus, when a new joint venture is established, this often dooms an SOE to collapse.
>
> (Li Haijian 2003 [1997], 388)[67]

X. L. Ding's study of SOE management in seven Chinese cities (1995–1997) found asset stripping so widespread that he concluded,

> The constant bleeding of the state sector is one of the main reasons for its poor performance, its mountainous debts, and its shrinking share of production.
>
> (Ding 2000, 2)[68]

In a variation on this theme, Yang Famin notes that SOEs have been required to continue to pay welfare benefits to former SOE workers who have taken jobs with non-SOE firms (such as providing subsidized medical and housing benefits). The SOEs were also required to guarantee the workers taking private sector jobs the option to return to their old job, if they wished to leave their new firm (Yang 1997, 9).

Neoclassical critics of the SOEs imply that the factors cited above to excuse or at least explain poor SOE economic performances are second order effects.[69]

From a heterodox perspective, a large part of the SOE debate is about the merits of industrial policy. Supporters of public ownership call for the Chinese state to protect and nurture large firms in order to enable them to bargain and compete with large global multinationals. As Nolan puts it, "the World Bank's perspective is a-historical, lacking real world content about the role and nature of big business in the advanced countries, and of the role of the state in supporting big business" (Nolan 2004 [1998], 133).

From a Marxist perspective, the SOE-privatization debate is about whether to create capitalist firms and a capitalist class, although the privatizers are often hesitant to use that language in deference to the CPC's public commitment to build "socialism with Chinese characteristics." The classical liberal narrative treats the establishment of a capitalist economy as a social mechanism that will eventually bring prosperity, democracy, civil liberties, environmental protection, long life spans, and greater equality. There is a "grand Kuznets curve" tracing out the future in reformers' minds that promises that the corruption, economic inequality, and environmental destruction, that have accompanied China's transition to capitalism will be reversed over time. Thus with both Marxist economists (who foresee a different future under capitalism) and neo-classical economists, counterfactuals about the past and/or expectations about the future dominate judgments about the merits of public and private enterprise.

In a Marxist narrative, corrupt privatization is typical and characteristic of "primitive accumulation" in an emerging capitalist economy. It is exemplified by the theft of public property in England during the enclosures. Tolerance of this corruption was by no means universal among Chinese liberals, deeply angering, for example, He Qinglian, the author of *Pitfalls of Modernization*. Public controversy about privatization intensified 2004–2006 after the widely publicized denunciation of insider privatization by Larry Lang, a professor at the Chinese University of Hong Kong. When push came to shove, however, there was a tendency among many free market-oriented economists to overlook corrupt privatization "because it lubricates the transition to a private property-based economy" (Naughton 2001, 4; Li He 2009, 34; Sun 1995, 80).[70]

### 6.6.2 Distinctive Marxist conceptions of labor and the workplace

From a Marxist perspective, the massive layoffs in the urban sector and the surge in migrant labor from the countryside in the 1990s redefined power relationships in the Chinese workplace. Rather than painting these events as creating a "rational, efficient, and free" labor market, as done by neoclassical theory,[71] Marxists frame the events as creating a subordinate Reserve Army of the Unemployed. For example, Xin Mao finds, "in the enterprises run by contracts [rather than permanent employment] ... workers' sense of responsibility ... and their sense of collectivity were most fundamentally undermined..." (Xin Mao 1999, 35). As in the Special Economic Zones, workers were clearly no longer the masters of their workplaces.[72] The former power of the cadres had been transferred to employers (often former cadres). Neither the permanent employment nor the contract system was particularly participatory or liberating, but the former had claims and aspirations to be participatory.[73] The latter offered no such pretensions, but promised to deliver a higher standard of living (the exchange of active voice in the workplace for higher wages and exit rights, being the classic bargain hawked by capitalism).

Many Marxists rejected this bargain, such as William Hinton, who wrote in 1990

> Reformers long to apply the "stick" of job competition and enterprise failure to these people. They want to transform the relations of production in ways that ... turn their labor power into a commodity. ... But from the workers' point of view lifelong job security and its accompanying prerogatives are among the primary accomplishments of the revolution. ... They are what gives meaning to the phrase "the workers are the masters of the factories." If bosses can hire and fire at will, if the reserve army of the unemployed waits to swallow all those rendered redundant for whatever reason. ... What is left of socialism?
>
> (Hinton 1990, 170)

Lin Chun shares Hinton's perspective, writing

> the dignity and well-being of labor, morally and institutionally built into a self-consciously socialist state, was a magnificent accomplishment ... reform ... pursued changes as though security, coupled with political-social esteem, did not and would not yield dedication, creativity, and responsible performance.
>
> (Lin Chun 2006, 86)

She adds,

> the socialist workplace [the *danwei*] was designed also to nurture collective spirit and work-related identities. To be sure, without 'wage labor' ... security-loyalty came with a 'feudal element' of immobility and hierarchical attachment-conformity. Yet precisely here, on both accounts, losing *danwei* meant more than the loss of a means of living. What could

not be compensated by any safety net or alternative sources of income was social exclusion and alienation ...

(Lin Chun 2006, 87)

In an open letter to Jiang Zemin in 1991 Ma Bin, the former General Manager of the large Anshan Iron and Steel Company, and Han Yaxi, a Chinese trade union official, lamented,

> Labor has already become a commodity. ... Workers enjoy extremely little of democratic rights in enterprises ... masses of workers have lost their jobs ... masses of young peasants flow in ... how can it be said that the status of the working class has not changed?[74]

Anita Chan's account of the brutal working conditions confronting 80 million migrant workers in the 1990s echoes this question,[75] as does Yi Duming's lament "'that many of our revolutionary comrades struggled all their lives so that the people of the whole country could each have an iron rice-bowl'" (White 1989, 157).[76]

In 1995, Wu Yifeng, a Marxist Professor of Economics at Renmin University, appealed to a classic claim of Marxist theory to challenge privatization.[77] Wu reminded readers that property rights in a market economy define social relations among groups of people (Han 2012). Private ownership of the means of production endows the owners of capital (or their delegated representatives) with control over people, as well as things, in the workplace. Thus in Marxist language, "capital is a social relation," (not simply a material possession). Constructing alternative social relations that protect the dignity and bargaining power of workers is perhaps the defining feature of socialism.

Wu elaborated his ideas about a decade later, contrasting the Marxist conception of property rights with a Coasean-new institutionalist view (Wu 2008). The latter treats systems of property rights as institutional solutions to the problem of minimizing transaction costs. Wu warned "if the reform of property rights ... were carried out under the guidance of Coase's theory of property rights we would inevitably practice privatization ... and the socialist market economy would eventually become the capitalist market economy" (Wu 2008, 14).[78]

In 1997 Xin Mao rooted the wrong turn in Chinese economic theory in its acceptance of classical liberalism's starting point of economic man, arguing, "the economic man orientation ... quickly became reflected in intellectual ... and cultural circles ... [It has] been exaggerated and even 'absolutized'. ... The result is that our labor models ... are being ridiculed" (Xin Mao 1999, 44–45).[79] Somewhat later, Cheng Enfu, the head of the Academy of Marxism at CASS, and Meng Jie, an Economics Professor at Renmin University, repeated this criticism. Meng argues that "the hypothesis of economic man in neo-classical economics often leads to reform approaches that revere ... private ownership and management buy-outs" (Meng Jie 2008, 13) Cheng

Enfu's concept of "new economic man," (Cheng 2003) adds an impulse for altruism to the pursuit of self-interest animating *homo economicus*. Meng finds that appropriate social institutions can promote collective interests and "[c]rit-icism of the hypothesis of economic man in neo-classical economics 'will help us adhere to … public ownership as the mainstay in the present stage'" (Meng Jie 2008, 13).

### 6.6.3 A digression on social structure of accumulation theory

As noted in section 5.7.3, Social Structure of Accumulation (SSA) theory is a heterodox economics theory. It combines aspects of Marxist, Institutionalist, and Post Keynesian theory. Part of its agenda is to explain business cycles, but it also tries to explain historical changes in income and wealth distribution, and the evolution of economic institutions. SSA theory can be used to analyze the Chinese economy and the changing character of Chinese business enterprises. It offers an illustrative heterodox-Marxist alternative to new insti-tutionalist economic (NIE) explanations for the expansion of private enter-prises and the decline of SOEs in China.

NIE theorists explain the structure of institutions found in market eco-nomies as the result of a competitive struggle among "institutional entrepren-eurs" to organize economic activities in an efficient fashion. The main challenge to this outcome is the existence of monopoly power, which is usually assumed to involve complicity by the state. In the absence of severe political interference, market institutions are endowed with a Darwinian opti-mality, in keeping with neoclassical subtexts.

SSA theory offers an alternative theory of institutional evolution. SSA theory argues that capitalism, as a socio-economic system, has to resolve several serious structural challenges in order to avoid macroeconomic collapse or social unrest. SSA theory assumes that the relationships between capital and labor are potentially more conflictual than posited in neoclassical eco-nomics and NIE theory. One of the challenges capitalist economies confront is containing capital-labor strife. Another challenge faced by capitalist eco-nomies is muting uncertainty and maintaining aggregate demand, which can be seriously depressed by uncertainty.

A "Social Structure of Accumulation" is the inter-related cluster of institu-tions that resolve the inherent challenges facing capitalist economies. The character of these institutions, according to SSA theory, is determined by more factors than included in the economic efficiency, cost-minimizing explanations offered by NIE theory. In particular, SSA theory emphasizes the role of power, ideology, and class interests in shaping institutional designs.

Because capitalism is a dynamic system, the cluster of inter-related institu-tions needed to keep it operating changes over time. SSA theory periodizes economic history in terms of particular temporal clusters of institutions. The logic of SSA theory has been impressively demonstrated by several studies of the US economy in the post war period. These analyses were able to explain much of US economic history since 1945 by analyzing the different social structures of accumulation organizing the US economy during the 1945–1975 period and the 1975–2007 period.[80] This section looks at the implications of SSA theory for understanding the character of Chinese business enterprises, labor practices, and to some extent, levels of aggregate demand.

SSA theory rejects marginal productivity theory as an adequate explanation for the distribution of income.[81] In addition to productivity variables, SSA theory argues that wages, profits, and the salaries of managerial labor are determined by ideology, institutional designs, and the relative bargaining power of capital and labor. The latter is influenced by many factors, including the size of the Reserve Army of the Unemployed, the strength of labor unions, and social notions of fairness. As such, "management" in private enterprises (and public firms acting like private enterprises) involves more than the technically-determined coordination of labor. It involves strategic actions taken in an often adversarial environment.

Part of the calculations for choosing production technologies, for example, involves the technologies' implications for maintaining management authority. SSA theorists find that current technologies in many manufacturing industries are attractive to management partly because they involve little accumulation of skills by existing workers. This ensures that current employees are easily replaceable by potential "reserve army" recruits, weakening workers' bargaining position.[82]

From an SSA perspective the debate about privatization was and is a debate about the merits of competing clusters of institutions. The SOEs were more than a production unit. Under the *danwei* system they were linked to particular forms of housing and neighborhood organization, childhood schooling (and at times access to higher education), health care delivery, and retirement support. Similarly, the precursors of the TVEs, the brigade and commune industries, were linked to the logic of the commune and its allocative, informational, and motivational features. Public enterprises in China were also linked to mechanisms of economic planning, credit allocation, technology diffusion, as well as broader ideological contexts important for worker motivation. This is why the disillusionment created by the Cultural Revolution was much more of a solvent of public enterprises than the campaign's direct immediate impact on output. It is also why the system of public firms began to unravel, once some of its constituent parts were dissolved.

The same system-like features and clusters of institutions accompanied the reorganization of the economy to operate with private firms. These enterprises rely on new forms of motivation, information feedback, credit allocation, accounting, legal arrangements, cooperation and competition, and so on. The new institutionalist economic theorists have been especially good at exploring the linkages that make a capitalist system work, in terms of linking secure property rights, regularized legal practices, government finance reforms, and market oriented credit institutions, with expanding output and investment. The NIE theorists have been weak in exploring the potential harshness of the system in organizing the workplace, distributing income,[83] concentrating economic power, and undermining institutions and values that encourage reciprocity and empathy. SSA theory addresses this gap.[84]

The differences between SSA and NIE theory offer another example of the implications of the contrasting subtexts animating new institutionalist and Marxist-heterodox economics. Underlying Coase's vision at the heart of new institutionalist economics, is an image of capitalist markets as realms of freedom, self-actualization, independence, innovation, and voluntary cooperation through exchange. The new institutionalist view of human nature naturalizes capitalism, although not always in as simple-minded a fashion as the assumption of *homo economicus* underlying orthodox neoclassical theory. The perspective celebrates capitalism's productivity with much less attention to its darker sides. Coase and Wang summarily write,

> China's market oriented reforms ... raised the living standards for a quarter of humanity ... (and) convinced other countries ... of the benevolence of the market and the folly of state planning. Moreover, the Chinese market transformation has opened up new horizons for global capitalism. ... A global liberal economic order will be far more resilient and sustainable if capitalism grows beyond the West and blooms in varying cultural backgrounds and political systems.
>
> (Coase and Wang 2013, 179–180)

The flip side of this portrayal of benevolent, blooming capitalist institutions, is contempt for socialist institutions, such as public ownership, economic planning, industrial policy, the cooperative organization of work, and social limitations on competition and compensation. Marxist and heterodox economic visions of capitalism include much darker images and more elevated hopes for socialist projects.

Neoclassical and new institutional economists have also tended to devalue problems of insufficient aggregate demand in comparison with SSA theorists. This difference is partly due to SSA theorists' greater attention to the implications of uncertainty. There are also linkages between SSA theory's analysis of labor markets and potential macroeconomic problems. For example, if the profit rate is too high (as sometimes the case in neoliberal periods when weak labor unions and easy capital mobility, for example, tend to weaken labor's bargaining position) the economy can suffer from insufficient demand due to under-consumptionism. This problem seems to afflict China's current economy. If the profit rate is too low (as is sometimes the case during Keynesian periods of full employment and strong labor movements), the economy can suffer from weak aggregate demand due to low investment.

Acknowledging these problems weakens some attacks on SOE's for "overstaffing." The popular expectation that free markets automatically produce full-employment rests on the "simplifying" assumption that firms and consumers have perfect information. If this implausible assumption is dropped, the problem of periodic (and even chronic) involuntary unemployment arises. In the face of these problems, the SOEs emerge as a potential stabilizing mechanism for responding to unemployment and maintaining aggregate demand during downturns (Bramall 2009a, 396–540).

Acknowledging the prevalence of imperfect information also creates a potential role for public firms as part of a nation's industrial policy. Joseph Stiglitz, for example, has explored how developing economies like China "learn." He emphasizes the enormity of market failures in the information area. He portrays the output of firms as a joint product of output and information. If production is viewed in this way, what is (and was) economically efficient can change. Like government funded R&D spending, public firms' investment in key sectors may facilitate the capture of sectoral economies. What appears inefficient on the micro (firm) level may be efficient at the macro (economy) level.[85]

Marxist and neoclassical economists also tend to disagree on the political implications of privatization. Neoclassicals expect privatization to strengthen civil society and in so doing promote pluralist centers of power and the preconditions for a healthy democracy. This is the basic conclusion reached by Janos Kornai, a thoughtful Hungarian reform economist, who had significant influence on Chinese intellectuals in the first two decades of reform (Kornai 1998, 34).

Marxist critics of privatization fear the growth of a plutocracy, with the slow accumulation of political power by an emerging capitalist class. In 1995 the first of four "10,000 word" critiques of recent market reforms circulated informally in Beijing (Chen 1999, 450). Three of the four critiques were anonymous, reflecting the impact of government pressures not to challenge market reforms. The author of the initial manuscript warns that privatization is leading to the accumulation of political power by an ever more active capitalist class, pointing to participation in local government bodies by the owners of private enterprises and the formation of voluntary associations to promote their viewpoints (Chen 1999, 450–451). In 2013 the *Washington Post* reported that there were 83 $billionaires in the Chinese People's Congress and Chinese People's Political Consultative Conference.[86] The second 10,000 word manuscript warned of the danger of foreign control of economic sectors and foreign influence on Chinese politics through the purchase of equity shares in SOEs.

### 6.6.4 Broader philosophical debates

E. F. Schumacher's writings offer an even deeper critique of NIE and neoclassical calls for privatization than Marxist-SSA theory. Schumacher acknowledges that capitalist firms are usually more profitable and able to increase GDP more rapidly than public-spirited, worker-owned, or government-owned firms. But, he asks, what are we trying to produce in an economy? His work suggests we conceive of some choices in terms of their "meta-externalities," that is their implications for what kind of society we wish to live in. His vision is very different from that of the "optimal" social structure posited by classical liberalism which underlies much of neo-classical economics and new institutionalist economics.

Schumacher's heterodox ideas did not resonate with much of Chinese Marxism in the 1990s. This is partly due to the justification of many economic reforms by their ability to accelerate the development of the "forces of production." More recently, Hu Jintao's call for a "harmonious society," and Wen Tiejun's New Rural Reconstruction movement may have opened the door to Schumacher like-concerns. Some heterodox economists in China, such as Zhou Yi of Fudan University, have also called for the SOEs to serve broader public purposes than simple profit maximization.[87] Writing almost 50 years ago, Schumacher's comments on the debate over government ownership in Britain, are surprisingly relevant to the debate over SOEs in the Chinese economy. He writes,

> If the purpose of nationalization is primarily to achieve faster economic growth, ... there is bound to be disappointment ... private greed, as Marx well recognized, has shown an extraordinary power to transform the world. ... The strength of the idea of private enterprise lies in its terrifying simplicity. It suggests that the totality of life can be reduced to one aspect—profits. ... Let no one befog the issue by asking whether a particular action is conducive to the wealth and well-being of society, whether it leads to moral, aesthetic, or cultural enrichment.
>
> (Schumacher 1973, 239–240)

> There is therefore really no strong case for public ownership if the objectives to be pursued by nationalized industry are ... just as limited as those of capitalist production: profitability and nothing else. ... The campaign of the enemies of nationalization ... has not been without effect. ... The reason is ... a lack of vision on the part of the socialists themselves. ... What is at stake is not economics but culture; not the standard of living but the quality of life. Economics and the standard of living can just as well be looked after by a capitalist system, moderated by a bit of planning and redistributive taxation. But culture and, generally, the quality of life, can now only be debased by such a system. Socialists should insist on using the nationalized industries not simply to out-capitalise the capitalists—an attempt in which they may or may not succeed—but to evolve a more democratic and dignified system of industrial administration, a more humane employment of machinery, and a more intelligent utilization of the fruits of human ingenuity and effort.
>
> (Schumacher 1973, 244–245)

In the *1844 Manuscripts* Marx reaches similar conclusions in his critique of socialist strategies that retain the competitive market structure of capitalism but include significant state ownership of equity shares in corporations. He writes,

> An enforced *increase in wages* ... would be nothing more than a *better remuneration of slaves*, and would not restore, either to the worker or to the work, their human significance and worth. Even the *equality of incomes* which Proudhon demands would only change the relation of the present day worker to his work into a relation of all men to work. Society would then be conceived as an abstract capitalist (emphases in the original).
>
> (Fromm 1970, 107)

Richard Easterlin's recent research on happiness in China (Easterlin et al. 2012; Easterlin et al. 2017) offers a different route to similar conclusions. Easterlin and his colleagues find that self-reported levels of life satisfaction in China appear to depend more on relative income and economic security than absolute income, once a basic income level is reached. These findings match earlier findings reported for the American, European, and Japanese economies, as well as other developing countries like China.

Easterlin cites survey data for the period 1990 to 2010. During these years per capita income in China increased four fold. Economic inequality and job insecurity also increased significantly. Despite the increase in almost everyone's real income, the average level of self-reported life satisfaction in China was unchanged. The percentage of people in the top third of the Chinese income distribution indicating they were very satisfied with their life increased from 68 percent to 71 percent.[88] But the number of people in the bottom third of the Chinese income distribution reporting they were very satisfied fell from 65 percent to 42 percent.

While findings like Easterlin's often draw serious attention among heterodox economists, they are usually "noted but ignored" by neoclassical policy makers. The direct or indirect correlation between income and well-being is part of the subtext of neoclassical theory and taken for granted.

## Notes

1 Jefferson and Rawski 1995, esp. 134–135, 142–151.
2 Formal experiments began in 1978 with 6 firms in Sichuan Province under Zhao Ziyang's leadership. He had begun encouraging more autonomous enterprise management and market incentives in 1976 (Spence 1990, 678). In 1979, the State Council asked all local governments to experiment with expanding enterprise autonomy.
3 Zhang Weiying is often cited as the originator of the dual-track idea. It seems likely that the idea was a product of much shared discussion (see for example Fewsmith 1994, 137).
4 Robert Kuhn indicates that Hua's well-to-do family background caused him problems during the Cultural Revolution. His association with Zhao Ziyang in the 1980s apparently also impeded his reintegration into CASS in the early 1990s.

Kuhn claims that "Hua had no option but to struggle to start his own business. In 2009, Hua had a group of successful companies, including a private university of which he was president" (Kuhn 2011, 133).

5 For example, while there appears to have been initial interest in the Yugoslavian model of worker self-management in 1979 and 1980 on the part of economists such as Jiang Yiwei and Dong Fureng (Wu 2005, 58–59; Hsu 1991, Chapter 3) and even the State Council, this option was not actively pursued (Meisner 1996, 208). Especially influential seems to have been Deng's preference for the clear lines of responsibility delineated in the managerial responsibility system (Naughton 1995, 108; Naughton 1993, 498; Vogel 2011).

6 Hua Sheng offered an especially clever suggestion for curbing insider capture of economic rents under the contract responsibility system. One of the challenges that bedeviled reformers was how to price the option to be the residual claimant for the firm. The "particularist" way contracts were written allowed local officials to play favorites and invited corrupt side payments. Even without corruption, the strategy left the overseers of the SOEs with the daunting task of assessing how much the firm's net revenue was likely to be. Hua suggested leaving the judgment to the market by having managers bid for the contract. While popular with many Chinese economists, the suggestion was not widely accepted, perhaps because of the attractive patronage and side payment options accompanying negotiated contracts (Shirk 1993, 321).

7 Jefferson and Rawski 1995, 133; Nolan 2004 [1998], 160. See also Naughton 1995, 233; Naughton 1993, 511; and Bramall 2000, 468.

8 The 1995 World Bank study *Bureaucrats in Business* found improvements in SOEs TFP after the institution of contract responsibility terms, but emphasized it was difficult to assign causality to the contracts, increasing competition or other factors. After acknowledging numerous uncertainties, the Bank affirmed its master narrative, concluding, "performance contracts are a less effective incentive to improved performance than clarifying and strengthening property rights" (131).

9 Zhao makes the interesting claim that serious inflationary pressures could have been avoided had the government moved more quickly to guarantee the real value of household savings and raised the interest rate on savings (Zhao 2009, 222). He indicates that Li Peng and Yao Yilin hesitated to do this, at least in part because they feared that the banks would be squeezed by having to pay higher interest rates on their deposits than existing borrowers were paying on their outstanding loans (Zhao 2009, 222).

10 State price controls also kept oil and coal prices low, basically eliminating profits in these sectors (Naughton 1995, 238).

11 Naughton indicates that from 1978–1989 the SOEs' profit remittance to the federal government fell from 15.4 percent GNP to 1.7 percent GNP. The SOEs' indirect business tax remittances fell by only .3 percent, for a total decline in SOE contributions to central government revenues of a staggering 14 percent GNP. Naughton finds that 4–5 percent of the 14 percent decline in SOE remittances was due to the firms' higher rates of profit retention (Naughton 1992, 21–22. See also Naughton 1995, 234–241; and Lau 2001).

12 The redistribution of agricultural land in the countryside after the dissolution of the communes seems to have been much more egalitarian than the reorganization of urban assets (Wang 2003a, 48). Subsequent requisition and reallocation of rural land for non-agricultural purposes has suffered from greater corruption and insider capture of rents than the beginning rounds of the household responsibility system.

13 Hart-Landsberg and Burkett 2005, 47. Sung and Chan indicate that most economists thought that the SOEs' permanent employment guarantees amounted to "eating from the big pot" and therefore "violated the principle of distribution according to work." They favored replacing "the permanent employment system by a contract system" (Sung and Chan 1987, 48–49).

14 Chris Bramall characterizes the neoclassical frame in a similar fashion, writing,

> This master discourse, [is] built ... on the foundation of neoclassical theory ... modified and informed by the work of the Austrian school ... public choice theorists such as Buchanan and Tullock (the state is malevolent), economists trained in Eastern Europe such as Kornai (there is no resting place between the free market and state socialism), and new institutional economists like North (the state must secure private property rights). ... The upshot is the doctrine espoused by international agencies such as the IMF and the World Bank ... (t)he Washington Consensus.
>
> (Bramall 2000, 285–286)

The tenor of the World Bank's privatization project is messianic. Box 1.2 in its 1995 *Bureaucrats in Business* study (p. 39), for example, tells readers "that in eleven of the twelve cases divestiture made the world a better place (emphasis added) by fostering more efficient operation and new investment" (39). The commentary adds, "the potential benefits from successful privatization are not confined to the measured gains" (38) and speculates that in indirect ways, privatization protects the environment (39–41).

15 See, for example, Fred Magdoff and John Bellamy Foster, "What Every Environmentalist Needs to Know About Capitalism," *Monthly Review* 61(10), March 2010, and *The Ecological Rift: Capitalism's War on the Earth*, by John Bellamy Foster, Brett Clark, and Richard York, *Monthly Review Press*, 2010. For a discussion of ecological Marxism in China see: "Ecological Marxism in China" by Zhihe Wang *Monthly Review* 63(9) February 2012.

16 Interestingly, Wang Gungwu notes the similarities between the Chinese state's attempt "to have high-minded officials supervise the entrepreneurial merchants" during the self-strengthening movement in the nineteenth century and Deng et al.'s efforts at the end of the twentieth century (Wang Gungwu 2014 [1992], 58).

17 Measuring the magnitude and causes of changes in total factor productivity is fraught with methodological and data problems, which makes assessing the relative performance SOEs and private firms in China difficult. Bramall, for example, cites problems with: unreliable capital stock data; over reporting of physical output; the use of flawed price deflators; and mismeasurement of intermediate inputs. He also highlights the lack of adjustment for differences in product markets, noting that many SOEs were involved in extractive industries where the expected rate of improvement in TFP would be relatively low (Bramall 2000, 234). He concludes, "Trends in total factor productivity are impossible to measure with any degree of precision" (Bramall 2000, 251). Lardy writes, "Despite the increasing methodological sophistication, no consensus has emerged on whether the numerous reform initiatives ... have led to increases in total factor productivity in the state-owned sector" (Lardy 1998, 32). See also Lo 1997, 5, 93–96, for an interesting discussion of TFP issues.

My sense of the evidence is that the SOEs did improve their performance, though probably less than some other enterprise forms (such as TVEs and private firms). Both market oriented incentives (such as increased competition and technology transfer from foreign firms) and non-market factors (such as government policies to accelerate technological change and more attention to efficiency concerns by SOE management) improved economic performance.

18 Carson estimates that in the first round of reform, firms profit retention rates peaked at 25 percent of profits in 1986, falling in 1987–1988 (Carson 1990, 348).

19 The World Bank's 1995 *Bureaucrats in Business* study, for example, noted that the 7.8 percent annual increase in the SOE's real industrial output was impressive but still less than "any other form of ownership in China." Similarly, the SOEs estimated TFP growth of 2.4 percent to 4 percent a year (which is high by international

standards), was noted to be less than the productivity growth of other forms of ownership in China (65–66).

As early as 1982, Riskin warned that internal opponents of China's planned economy and egalitarian policies seemed to be over painting their canvasses. He notes that the case against China's planned economy "is now made with tedious regularity in journal articles." While acknowledging the problems cited in these articles, he points out that many Western economists have found that "such indefinables as organizational élan and ideological commitment … were sufficient to neutralize such problems" … despite the devastating self-criticisms coming out of China (Riskin 1982, 32).

20 Bramall 2000, 4–6; Lo and Zhang 2011, 37 citing, for example, 1994 work by Sachs and Woo; Putterman 1995, 1059. Bramall indicates that even the gradualists, who acknowledged improved SOE performance, did not think the gains were sustainable. He writes, "the orthodox approach likens [the SOE's temporary success to] a restoration (*chongxin*): a period in which the old regime enjoys an Indian summer as a prelude to its final collapse" (Bramall 2000, 5–6).

21 Nolan points to the rapid technological upgrading of China's two main power equipment companies, the Harbin Power Equipment Company and the Shanghai Electrical Company, under guidance by the State Council (Nolan 2004 [1998], 153–154). More generally, Bramall asserts, "the bulk of the statistical evidence, and economic theory both point overwhelmingly in the direction of a significant increase in state-sector TFP after 1978" (Bramall 2000, 241).

22 Lo (1999) notes, for example, that social expenditures for SOEs in this period could reach 52 percent labor costs (21 percent for subsidized housing, 21 percent for pensions, 9 percent for health benefits, and 1 percent for education). The SOEs' private sector competitors entered the market without legacy pension burdens and with lower social welfare requirements for current employees (Lo 1999, 706).

Lardy (1998) also cites the heavy burden on SOEs of social welfare expenditures, but rather than linking this to improved assessments of SOE performance, sees the burdens as evidence of institutional failure.

Linda Grove's discussion of competition between state-owned and private firms in Gaoyang County in the textile industry similarly illustrates the extra burdens borne by state firms. She reports that the SOEs were responsible for funding pensions for retired workers, higher levels of employee benefits (e.g., employee housing) and the absorption of surplus labor. Furthermore, the firms lacked a fund to finance pensions, as past profits had been turned over to the state (Grove 2006, 201, 222).

The case of competition between TVEs and SOEs in the coal industry provides a particularly compelling example of the extra burdens sometimes borne by the SOEs.

23 See, for example, Lo 1999, 695, 706; Yang Famin 1997, 8–9.

24 Bramall (2000) and Lo (1999) both note that comparisons between SOEs and private firms need to be corrected for the different markets the firms inhabited. Lo argues, for example, that low regulated prices for coal, oil, and electricity that were intended to benefit energy consumers, were responsible for a lot of the losses suffered by SOE firms in the energy supply industry (Lo 1999, 703–705). Ko, Lo, and Peng indicate that about 40 percent of total enterprise losses in 1989 were in the coal-petroleum-natural gas sectors (Galenson 1993, 53). The largest loss was in the coal industry. Ko et al. note that regulated increases in input costs and frozen output prices also squeezed SOE profits in some other industries (Galenson 1993, 70). See also Yang Famin 1997, 8 and Nolan 2004 [1998], 159.

25 Lo argues that Chinese accounting conventions underestimated depreciation on state assets and therefore over-estimated SOEs capital stock and under-estimated SOEs profit rates (Lo 1999, 48).

26 Lo also argues that the period's system of inadequate depreciation accounting, mandatory transfer of profits from the SOEs to the state, and interest charges for loans made it difficult for the SOEs to finance new investment. This in turn undermined their economic competitiveness (Lo 1999 708–709).

27 Lo and Zhang find similar pre-tax profit rates for the SOEs and non-state firms and suggest accounting reasons (involving excess valuations for the SOEs old capital stock) that may have imparted downward biases to SOE profit rate calculations. They acknowledge that SOE profit rates fell in the 1980s, but note that the profit rates of all firms tended to decline during this decade (49).

28 See, for example, the *World Happiness Report 2015*, edited by Helliwell, Layard, and Sachs.

29 While the HDI includes GDP/capita, it assumes a declining marginal utility of money, weighing increments to higher incomes less than increments to lower incomes. These metrics also give special weight to outcome variables like infant mortality rates, life expectancies, and literacy rates. In other words, all dollars are not equal.

30 Chinese economic reformers recognized the potential tension between market competition and socialist construction, but were hopeful that socialist values would civilize the impact of competition. Xu Dixin, for example, writes,

> Competition under socialism is not analogous to competition under capitalism. Under socialism, it is a lever that constantly spurs socialist enterprises to increase production and to improve management and yet creates no antagonism because socialist enterprises are either state owned or collectively owned.
> (Xu 1982, 52)

How state or collective ownership mitigates competitive pressures is left unspecified.

In an article entitled "Competition Under Socialism," Wang Haibo (1982) offers five reasons for why socialist competition is different from capitalist competition. He argues that socialist competition: (1) is between state-owned enterprises rather than between capitalists; (2) recognizes some shared common interest; (3) precludes unethical competition (through practices like deceptive advertising); (4) guarantees workers in bankrupt firms new jobs; and (5) does not lead to macro crises. Wang concludes "socialist competition among state enterprises is a means by which they promote one another's growth on the basis of a community of vital interests" (Wang Haibo 1982, 118).

31 Dong Fureng published an important article in *Economic Research* in 1979 in defense of more autonomous enterprises. In a 1981 essay, based on the logic of primary stage theories of socialism, Dong argued in favor of organizing China as a commodity economy, rather than a "natural economy." He urged that publicly owned firms be responsible for their own profits and losses and rejected the notion that the larger the level of administrative authority, the more socialist the enterprise. Dong also called for tolerating increased petty commodity production, greater economic coordination through market forces, and an experimental approach to constructing socialism, writing, "As a new social order, socialism must be created through practice. … China should search through practice for a socialist economic model that fits its conditions" (Dong 1982, 131).

32 Lin 1988 found similar sentiments in the countryside in the late 1980s, noting it was unlikely that the government would allow lenders to seize someone's home for non-payment of a loan, even if the house had been used as collateral for the loan (Lin 1988, 173).

33 Interview with a Chinese economist.

34 The shift in economic policy actually began prior to Deng's dismissal of Zhao Ziyang. Zhao writes, "The bank runs and hoarding of commodities [in 1987] led

to an overall panic. ... We decided to reassert order over economic affairs in 1988. We started to shift emphasis away from reform and toward 'adjustment and reorganization'" (Zhao 2009, 223). Zhao saw the adjustment period as a short pause to regroup for renewed marketization. Li Peng, Yao Yilin, and opponents of additional marketization treated the period as an opportunity to change course. Zhao writes, "They restored the old methods, making major cutbacks through administrative means. Powers that had been handed down to lower levels were reclaimed. Measures that had relied significantly on market mechanisms were abolished" (Zhao 2009, 224). It appears that Deng favored Zhao's strategy and insulated him personally from significant criticism by opponents of marketization. This protection disappeared, however, after Zhao opposed Deng's strategy for responding to the Tiananmen Square protests.

35 Naughton sometimes ridicules anti-marketization views, writing, for example, "The specific plans the conservatives put forward to guide their program were practically worthless. Within a short time, the conservatives had used up their stock of slogans, and had nothing left to contribute" (Naughton 1995, 280).

36 Wang emphasizes how Chinese reactions against the Cultural Revolution gave rise to intellectual movements critical of China's revolutionary traditions. Among these was a Chinese version of classical liberalism that tolerated authoritarianism in the name of market construction.

37 Bramall indicates that by 1995/2003 respectively: 78 percent/87 percent of the value of producer goods sales, 89 percent /96 percent of retail sales, and 79 percent /97 percent of farm commodities were transacted at market prices (Bramall 2009a, 354, 475). Sheng Hong reports that more than 95 percent of prices in product markets were set by the market in 1994 (Sheng 1996, 5).

38 Jefferson and Rawski, for example, report that SOE profit rates fell especially far in industries with strong TVEs, such as leather, textiles, and food processing (Jefferson and Rawski 1994, 143). Prohibition of foreign-owned firms in China were lifted in the early 1990s (Bramall 2009a, 411). Greater encouragement was also given to joint ventures.

39 Recall that Dong was tremendously impressed by the entrepreneurial initiatives in Wenzhou. He also seems to have worked closely with Western economists as head of the Institute of Economics at CASS (Naughton 1995, 11).

40 Jefferson and Rawski, who had found TFP gains of 3.8 percent /yr. 1984–1988, reported TFP declines of 1.1 percent per year for 1992–1996 (Bramall 2009a, 416).

41 The decline in SOE profitability, for example, paralleled that of its chief competitor, the TVEs. Lardy notes that all industrial enterprises with independent accounting suffered losses in 1997, with non-SOEs losing about 60 billion RMB. He suggests economy wide low capacity utilization rates as a key reason for the losses (Lardy 1998, 36).

42 Freeman and Yuan cite official statistics as tallying 63 million total layoffs from the SOEs and urban collectives 1993–2002 (Freeman and Yuan 2011, 4).

43 One estimate by officials at the Ministry of Labor and Social Security put the overall rate of unemployment at 28 percent (Gold et al. 2009, 6). Lardy 2014 notes that 20 million migrants were laid off in 2009 (about 6 percent of the urban workforce) when Chinese exports fell in response to the Great Recession. Despite the layoffs, China's official urban unemployment rate only increased from 4.2 percent to 4.3 percent (Lardy 2014, 7).

44 The government: (1) established re-employment centers to help workers find new jobs; (2) lobbied the owners of newly privatized firms to find employment for former employees (*China Labour Bulletin*, 3); (3) provided tax breaks for former SOE employees to start new businesses that hired laid off workers (*China Labour Bulletin*, 3); (4) required firms to maintain former employees' access to housing

and health insurance benefits associated with their former jobs; and (5) provided small unemployment insurance payments (which varied from ~6 percent to 43 percent of past wages, depending on locality) (Naughton 2007, 186–189).

These efforts left many people out in the cold (Easterlin et al. 2012). Large numbers of workers appear to have lost significant chunks of their pensions when SOEs went bankrupt. Ching Kwan Lee describes the efforts of tens of thousands of workers in an old industrial region in northeast China (Liaoyang) to get firms and the central government to meet their pension, unemployment insurance, and wage arrears obligations after key SOEs went bankrupt. In Shenyang, the provincial capital, more than one out of every four retired workers were owed pensions. Lee concludes, "With glaring holes in the new safety net, the estimated 27 million to 40 million workers eliminated from their work units in the state and collective sector since 1995 are plagued by a profound sense of insecurity" (Lee 2007b, 17).

Lee's account details efforts by aging workers to make their demands heard (by politely stopping traffic, for example) within a highly constrained political order that still tries to portray itself as representing the interests of working people. While not altering the retirees' basic situation, the protests tended to bring modest gains. In many cases, state policy appears to have been to make narrow concessions to aggrieved parties, as long as protesters from one SOE didn't attempt to link up with protesters from other SOEs, and didn't explicitly challenge the legitimacy of the Party.

45 Zhu clearly worried about the reforms causing unemployment. In 1994 he reputedly told a group of economists that the person who figured out how to promote enterprise reform without causing massive layoffs would win the Nobel Prize in Economics (Coase and Wang 2013, 133). Giles, Park, and Cai's study of labor conditions in five large Chinese cities in 2001 found that "unemployment reached double figures. … Urban residents faced modest levels of wage and pension arrears, and sharp declines in health benefits. Public assistance programmes for dislocated workers had limited coverage…" (Giles et al. 2006, 61). The *China Labour Bulletin* reports that by 2003 redeployment through official channels helped only 30 percent of those laid off. Among the problems encountered were corruption and neglect of the law by Chinese firms and regulators (*China Labour Bulletin*, 3).

46 Naughton 2007. The *China Labour Bulletin* estimated that by 2002 "86 percent of all SOEs had been restructured and about 70 percent had been partially or fully privatized" (Dec 19, 2007, 2).

47 In July 2008 a World Bank Report ("China: Improving Unemployment Insurance") by Milan Vodopivec and Minna Tong reported that employment in the SOE and collective sectors shrank from a peak of 145 million in 1995 (comprising 80 percent of urban employment) to ~75 million in 2005 (comprising ~30 percent of urban employment) (6).

48 Lee indicates that roughly two-thirds of all SOE shares were non-tradable in 1994 and 60 percent non-tradable in 2006 (Lee 2009, Table 7).

49 Among the "lessons" Iskander drew from global experience was the need for firms to focus on profitability and not social objectives; the importance of giving high powered material incentives to managers, and the benefits of markets for corporate control. There was no attention to role of public and private firms in creating the basis for socialism.

50 Wu did suggest that more attention might be given to Germany and Japan's corporate governance system (as opposed to the Anglo-American model).

51 In a well known passage from his classic text *Capitalism and Freedom*, Friedman argues

> there is one and only one social responsibility of business … to increase its profits. … Few trends could so thoroughly undermine the very foundations of

our free society as the acceptance by corporate officials of a social responsibility other than to make as much money for their stockholders as possible.

(Friedman 1982, 133)

See also Friedman 1970.

52 Typical are the claims of Seth Weissman, who writes, "China's state-owned banks are feeding wasteful investments since they are not lending to companies that make the wisest investment decisions. Instead, the investment goes to those SOEs that have nepotistic connections" (Freeman and Yuan 2011, 17).

53 Qian Yingyi (2002), for example, criticizes measures of institutional development that rely on simpleminded measures of current levels of privatization. His main complaint is that the indices "confuse the goal (i.e., where to finish up: privatization) with the process" (9). Other analyses stress the need for reforms to be "interest compatible," meaning politically feasible, and suggest that reformers have to privatize carefully to avoid backlash. The end goal of shifting assets from the public sector to the private sector is rarely at issue.

54 Sheng makes a point of distinguishing the static model of neoclassical economics from the dynamic model of institutional reform promoted by new institutionalist economics (NIE). In analyzing the dynamic path of adjustment from a planned economy to a market economy, Sheng stresses the importance of finding a way to compensate "losers," in order to minimize their resistance to reform. Many Chinese policies, from initially insulating urban consumers from the impact of higher government procurement prices for agricultural goods, to the maintenance of lifetime employment guarantees for existing SOE workers, but fixed year contracts for new hires, can be understood in this light. As reformers consolidated power, the political need to compensate losers weakened, as illustrated by the state's willingness to induce massive layoffs among the SOEs and urban collectives in the late 1990s and a decline in support for the agricultural sector. More recently, however, calls for a "harmonious society," may signal a modest return to earlier policies.

55 Fan Gang, an influential neoclassical economist in China, for example, depicts the SOEs as parasites with the potential to metastasize and destroy the market sector (1994, 111).

56 Han Zhenliang, for example, treats Western management techniques as if they were a technology, like the internet, rather than a social practice related to the nature of work in a capitalist society. Han writes, "Learning advanced Western management and control methods is a must ... only through management do science and technology play an effective role" (Han 1996, 89).

57 In a variation on this theme Martin Whyte cites literature comparing rural workers exposed to the alleged invigorating effects of market competition with urban workers "coddled" by state enterprises. Rural people are said to "have stronger feelings of personal efficacy" than urban SOE workers and "more faith in the ability of science to solve problems" (Whyte 1999, 188). One could imagine neglected alternative comparisons referring to the two groups' sense of community, habits of reciprocity, feelings of economic security, etc.

58 Earlier, Blecher makes a similar point about Chinese narratives about the countryside (Blecher 2010, 144).

59 In the mid-1990s, Xin Mao argued that cultural shifts glorifying private material success made it increasingly difficult to mobilize workers voluntary cooperation in public firms.

60 Bramall, for example, writes "there is no reason in principle why the governance of SOEs could not be made to work. ... Even in the case of Britain ... the evidence was far more equivocal ... than advocates of Thatcherism allowed" (2009a, 412). Kate Bayliss and Ben Fine (1998) similarly criticize the World Bank's *Bur-*

*eaucrats in Business* study for its assumed counterfactuals, trajectories, and selective use of data. They assert that "[t]he desirability of privatization is never in question" (846). "The [Bank's] Report ... as is habitual in its publications in general, overlooks the literature that questions this conclusion. ... The citations are selective and biased ..." (848).

61 Nolan notes, for example, that while about ~30 percent of SOEs suffered losses in 1993, 40–50 percent of joint ventures suffered losses, suggesting that the firms' difficulties may have been related to more general market conditions than patterns of ownership (2004 [1998], 159).

62 Peter Nolan, for example, highlights the big difference in profitability between small and large SOEs. He indicates that only 42 of the 500 largest SOEs suffered losses in 1992. Of these 42 firms, 34 were in fossil fuel industries that had artificially low prices set by planners to aid downstream industries.

63 Yang 1997, 8; Nolan 2004 [1998], 159.

64 See Lau 2001, 225; Hart-Landsberg and Burkett 2005, 56. Carsten Holz argues that the profitability gap between the SOEs and non-SOEs could be entirely explained by unequal tax treatment and the greater capital intensity of the SOEs (Holz 2002). Yang Famin also cites unfair tax advantages for non-SOE firms as biasing economic comparisons (Yang, 1997, 9–10). Nolan reports that in 1993 the SOEs tax burden was more than double that of joint ventures (Nolan 2004 [1998], 160).

65 Lo, for example, writes, "This paper reviews the available evidence on the performance of China's industrial SOEs and reaches the conclusion that this performance has been far better than generally perceived" (Lo 1999, 712). In defending this conclusion Lo notes, for example, that: (1) the SOEs social burdens accounted for as much as 52 percent of their labor costs and included responsibility for a disproportionate share of retired workers' support; (2) the SOEs' tax burden was higher than other enterprises; and (3) the opportunities for sector-wide learning offered by public ownership may provide a basis for a "collective learning paradigm" capable of generating economies of scale and scope (711–712). Hart-Landsberg and Burkett echo these sentiments, noting

> reviews of the theoretical and empirical literature on privatization have concluded that no such blanket endorsement of private over state enterprise is warranted ... the vaunted 'efficiency' of private over public enterprises is often due to the former's unencumbered pursuit of private profit, whereas state firms are often charged with additional economic and political goals such as employment and welfare provision ...
>
> (Hart-Landsberg and Burkett 2005, 54)

66 Econometric work by Sarah Tong involving 50,000 SOEs from 1988–2003 found "that relatively better performing SOEs, measured by per employee value-added, profitability, and export propensity, are more prone to privatization" (Tong 2009, abstract).

67 Li also claims that some Chinese managers purposefully under value their company's assets in joint venture discussions with foreign firms in order to retain their positions after foreign purchase (Li Haijian 2003, 389). He adds that MNCs often buy Chinese brands in order to retire and replace them with Western brands (Ibid., 388).

68 Ding's paper details numerous examples of accounting maneuvers, similar to transfer pricing, that diverted SOEs revenues and profits to new subsidiaries, while leaving costs and debts with the original state firm. He concludes, "the grabbing of state firms' assets and profits and their diversion into the private hands of managers and bureaucrats are important dynamics behind the rise of post-Communist capitalism" (Ding 2000, 28).

Edward Gu's 1997 paper also offers a fascinating look at how Chinese–foreign joint ventures tended to privatize the best assets of SOEs, leaving the residual in public hands. Gu's article details the acquisition strategy of the China Strategy Company, among others. See also Wu Jinglian 2005, 157.

69 The critics highlight instead the firms' managerial failures, claiming the firms gave insufficient attention to quality control, consumer preferences, market risks, or new product development, which they take to be inherent results of public ownership. Zhu Rongji seems to have held a variant of this view (Brahm 2002, 47–48).

Even very thoughtful neoclassical economists, who granted that the economic efficiency of public and privately owned firms in China may have been similar (after adjusting for complicating factors, like the SOEs higher tax burdens) still favored encouraging private over public enterprises. Rawski (1997), for example, found the most promising future trajectories likely to emerge from the "self-organizing" Coasean initiatives of private enterprises.

70 Sun indicates

> Some of Zhao's closest associates, such as Chen Yizi and Wan Runnan, were known to espouse toleration for cadre corruption, on the grounds that it was conducive to the accumulation of private wealth and thus to the emergence of private ownership.
>
> (Sun 1995, 80)

Fan Gang, a leading Chinese liberal economist argued similarly in 1994,

> Corruption is no doubt a source of economic distortion, income disparities, and social unrest. But it appears that wide-spread corruption may be unavoidable … during the transformation. … The unpleasant possibility during the historical stage of 'initial capital accumulation' is that big money may be the most "dirty" money.
>
> (Fan 1994, 111)

71 Misra describes the orthodox view as "the radical-reformist myth" and argues that

> "[t]he freedom and equality of opportunity accompanying the commodification of labor was more obvious to CASS economists and Zhao Ziyang's advisors than to workers where greater discretionary power was devolved to personnel managers to dismiss employees … and managers who focused more on workers' rights and benefits were assailed for not living up to the ideal of cost-cutting efficient entrepreneurs.
>
> (Misra 1998, 195)

Gordon White indicates that the restructuring of the labor market was strongly backed by foreign economists, and most importantly, by the World Bank in a key 1984 report (White 1989, 156–157).

72 Blecher (2002) reports that about 25 percent of workers surveyed by the All-China Federation of Trade Unions "said that their position as 'masters of the enterprise' had declined from 1992 to 1997" (284). Assessing the impact of labor market reforms in 1999, Martin Whyte concludes, "the average worker is … more insecure than in the Mao era. … Any pretense that the workers are the leading class has largely disappeared" (Whyte 1999, 193–194).

73 Mao, for example, had called for the two participations, workers participating in management and managers participating in manual labor (Meisner 1996, 260–261).

74 The July 15, 2001 letter from Ma Bin and Han Yaxi was reproduced in *Monthly Review* (May 21, 2002) (http://monthlyreview.org/commentary/letter-of-ma-bin-and-han-yaxi/, accessed September 2, 2016). The proximate cause of the

letter was Jiang Zemin's speech endorsing The Three Represents and capitalist membership in the Chinese Communist Party. Robert Kuhn claims that Ma had difficulty gaining signatures for his petition among China's scientific elite. He argues that China's technocrats felt employing some capitalist techniques offered a better chance for mobilizing modern technology than state-owned enterprises and guaranteed employment. He concludes, "China's scientific community supported Jiang's Three Represents" (Kuhn 2011, 109).

75 Anita Chan's research on migrant labor in China illustrates the kinds of outcomes Marxist economists feared. Chan writes,

> The millions of peasants roaming the country desperately looking for work to earn a hand-to-mouth living make up an almost inexhaustible pool of human machines. They can be worked to the breaking point, and when they flee these dreadful factories, they are simply replaced by fresh, vulnerable batches of workers.
>
> (Chan 2001, 10)

Chan's 2001 book: *China's Workers Under Assault* consists of case studies of labor abuses. The accounts are heart breaking.

Coase and Wang give the impression that workers freely exchanged their permanent employment guarantee for a cash payment. This seems unlikely. They wrote,

> After privatization was officially approved in 1997 … the state gave up its position as the sole owner of state enterprises and became a minority shareholder by inviting outside investors and/or employees to become the majority shareholders. Second, employees of state enterprises gave up their 'iron bowl' in exchange for a cash settlement, which was mainly determined by their years of service.
>
> (Coase and Wang 2013, 135)

76 Original Comments in the *Guangzhou Evening News* (February 23, 1986). See also Jiang Yiwei, "If All Workers are on the Contract system it will Not be Conducive to the Socialist Character of the Enterprise" [*Jingji tizhe gaige* no. 1 (1985)] (Misra 1998, 195).

77 Wu's article was published in the journal *Chinese Social Sciences*. "Marx's Theory of Property Right and Property Rights Transformation of the State Owned Enterprises" (Han 2012, 392).

78 In a similar vein, Marxist and neoclassical theorists have debated the implications of growing wage inequality in China. The widening differentials between educated and uneducated labor are seen as a sign of progress by neoclassical economists and a social failure by Marxist economists. One of the traditional goals of Chinese Marxism has been to reduce the wage differential between mental and manual labor. In contrast, Barry Naughton, a very thoughtful neoclassical economist, writes

> The socialist system did a fairly good job of providing basic education to the population. … But the socialist system did a very poor job of rewarding individuals who had attained higher levels of skill or education … researchers … found that incomes were not consistently higher among individuals with more education. … Perhaps the most fundamental requirement of a well-functioning market economy is that an individual is able to feel secure that she will be able to reap the income created by an investment. … It is impossible to envisage a healthy market transition in China without a substantial increase in the return to education …
>
> (Naughton 2007, 192–194)

Presumably, Naughton would favor social programs to improve access to education for disadvantaged groups, but even assuming efforts much more successful
than actual Chinese equal educational opportunity initiatives, the result of Naughton's recommendation would likely be increased inequality.

79 Xin Mao is a pseudonym.
80 The institutions organizing US economic activities ~1945–1975 were in turn a
direct response to the problems faced by a more laissez-faire-oriented US capitalism during the Great Depression of the 1930s. See Cohn 2007, 189–195 for an
introduction to the SSA literature.
81 Heterodox/Marxist economists Xu, Chen, and Li question the underlying logic of
neoclassical theory's concept of marginal productivity theory and the methods used
for empirically operationalizing it. Nevertheless they attempt to apply the theory,
using neoclassical tools, to the Chinese economy 2005–2010. They estimate that
"State-owned enterprises paid workers about half of their marginal product of labor.
Domestic private enterprises paid workers between one-fifth and one-third of their
marginal product. … Non-domestic enterprises paid workers between two-fifths
and three-fifths of their marginal product" (Xu, Chen, and Li 2015, 456).
82 Li and Qi, for example, argue,

> The first feature of the dominant labor process in China is simplicity and
> repetitiveness. … This feature effectively concentrates the power of control to
> the hands of management. … The constrained 'learning by doing' effect
> renders workers vulnerable … Thus, capitalists have an upper hand
> (Li and Qi 2014, 484)

Li and Qi also argue that the current structure of compensation makes significant
overtime work necessary for a living wage. This vests added power in the hands of
management who are able to reward favored workers with extra hours. The low
hourly wage rate also makes a mockery of Chinese labor laws defining normal
working time as 44 hours a week (482).
83 New Institutionalist economic theory also recognizes social tensions over
inequality and "rent seeking behavior," but seems to imply that there exists a
technologically determined cluster of institutions that essentially reflects rationality
and maximizes aggregate benefit. The "free" market is deemed the ideal instrument for discovering appropriate institutions—which turn out to involve private
property, active competition, and limited (but necessary) government correction
of market failures. Wu Yifeng, for example, notes that Coase's advice to Chinese
economists in 1997 was pretty simple (quoting Coase)

> the crux of the matter lies with privatization. … Once you establish the system
> you won't need to be anxious about privatization.
> (Wu Yifeng, 2008, 14)

SSA theorists challenge this depiction. See, for example, Li and Qi (2014).
84 There are striking parallels between the picture of US labor markets (1950–1975)
portrayed by SSA theorists using dual labor market theory and the labor market in
China's cities in the 1990s. In the US, women and minorities were disproportionately channeled into the secondary labor market, while primary sector jobs were concentrated among white males. In China, the migrants took the place of women and
minorities, and urban dwellers took the place of white males. (See for example, Zhao
2005.) I was struck by how similar the language used to describe and implicitly justify
the conditions of migrant workers was to the language used to depict secondary labor
market workers in the US. Of course in China some of the segmentation was done
by government fiat, reserving certain urban jobs for urban dwellers, rather than only
relying on racism, sexism, and other sorting mechanisms operating through market
decisions. In the US and China, the heterodox claim is that labor market outcomes

cannot be understood simply in terms of exogenously given workers' marginal products. Instead, labor markets have to be studied as reproducing social institutions that include individual characteristics but reflect larger social logics as well.

85  To their credit, new institutionalist economists have been better than neoclassical economists in highlighting the role of learning in economic development. Coase and Wang (2013), for example, offer an interesting defense of what appears to be a pattern of duplicative regional investments in China encouraged by local governments. They write,

> duplicative investments in the same industry is taken as unambiguous evidence [by orthodox neoclassical economists] of the presence of policy distortions ... [but] If we view the development of a market economy as an open learning process... some "waste" in duplicative investment on the part of firms is inevitable ... duplicative investment ... has ... helped to spread manufacturing technologies and significantly improve workers' skills all over China. The gains in human capital outweigh the losses from the underutilization of physical capital ... duplicative investment across China can be seen as an effective mechanism of social learning.
>
> (144, 145)

Chris Bramall has defended traditional Chinese development policy and the performance of SOEs by a similar appeal to social learning. Writing four years before Coase and Wang, he finds, "Chinese industrial development has actually been very successful ... (w)hen the concept is properly defined—to mean a sector capable of serving the wider needs of the Chinese economy," and "the process of learning–by–doing" (Bramall 2009a, 395).

Lo Dic reaches a similar conclusion, arguing that Chinese enterprise forms and development policy need to be situated in a larger economy wide context than individual firms' momentary factor productivity. Taking a somewhat Schumpeterian approach, Lo argues that the key question is how well Chinese institutions were able to promote rapid technological change. In this respect, he finds both China's development policies and the SOEs fairly successful in facilitating "collective learning" (Lo 1997).

86  www.washingtonpost.com/world/asia_pacific/chinese-national-peoples-congress-has-83-billionaires-report-says/2013/03/07/d8ff4a4e-8746-11e2-98a3-b3db6b9ac586_story.html.

87  Zhou Yi wrote a paper in 2009 taking this position (interview 4–26–14).

88  Easterlin et al. (2012) treated a self-reported level of 7 (out of a possible 1–10 ranking of life satisfaction) as being very satisfied.

# References

Bayliss, Kate, and Ben Fine. 1998. "Beyond Bureaucrats in Business: A Critical Review of the World Bank Approach to Privatization and Public Sector Reform." *Journal of International Development* 10 (7): 841–855.

Blecher, Marc. 2002. "Hegemony and Workers' Politics in China." *The China Quarterly* (170): 283–303. www.jstor.org/stable/4618737.

Blecher, Marc. 2010. *China Against the Tides: Restructuring through Revolution, Radicalism and Reform.* 3rd ed. New York: Continuum.

Brahm, Laurence J. 2002. *Zhu Rongji and the Transformation of Modern China.* Singapore: John Wiley & Sons (Asia).

Bramall, Chris. 2000. *Sources of Chinese Economic Growth 1978–1996.* New York: Oxford University Press.

Bramall, Chris. 2009a. *Chinese Economic Development*. New York: Routledge.

Carson, Richard L. 1990. *Comparative Economic Systems: Part II Socialist Alternatives*. Armonk, NY: M. E. Sharpe.

Chan, Anita. 2001. *China's Workers Under Assault: The Exploitation of Labor in a Globalizing Economy*. Armonk, NY: M. E. Sharpe.

Chen, Feng. 1999. "An Unfinished Battle in China: The Leftist Criticism of the Reform and the Third Thought Emancipation." *The China Quarterly* (158): 447–467. doi:10.1017/S0305741000005853.

Cheng, Enfu. 2003, "New 'Economic Man' Theory: A Basic Hypothesis of Shanghai School Economics." *Teaching and Research* (11): 22–26.

Cheng, Enfu. 2012. "Seven Currents of Social Thought and their Development in Contemporary China, with a Focus on Innovative Marxism." *The Marxist* 27 (4). Available at http://cpim.org/sites/default/files/marxist/201204-Cheng%20Enfu.pdf.

Chow, Gregory. 2002. *China's Economic Transformation*. Malden, MA: Blackwell.

Coase, Ronald, and Ning Wang. 2013. *How China Became Capitalist*. New York: Palgrave Macmillan.

Cohn, Stephen M. 2007. *Reintroducing Macroeconomics: A Critical Approach*. Armonk, NY: M. E. Sharpe.

Ding, X. L. 2000. "The Illicit Asset Stripping of Chinese State Firms." *The China Journal* (43): 1–28. doi:10.2307/2667530.

Dong, Fureng. 1982. "The Chinese Economy in the Process of Great Transformation." In *Economic Reform in the People's Republic of China: In Which China's Economists Make Known What Went Wrong, Why, and What Should Be Done About It*, edited by George C. Wang, 125–137. Boulder, CO: Westview Press.

Easterlin, Richard, Fei Wang, and Shun Wang. 2017. "Growth and Happiness in China, 1990–2015." Paper accompanying poster presentation at Annual Meetings of the American Economic Association 2017. Available at: http://conference.iza.org/conference_files/ICID_Renmin_2016/wang_f8757.pdf.

Easterlin, Richard, Robson Morgan, Malgorzota Switek, and Fei Wang. 2012. "China's Life Satisfaction, 1910–2010." *Proceedings of the National Academy of Sciences* 109: 9775–9780.

Fan, Gang. 1994. "Incremental Changes and Dual-Track Transition: Understanding the Case of China." *Economic Policy* 9 (Supplement): 99–122. doi:10.2307/1344602.

Fewsmith, Joseph. 1994. *Dilemmas of Reform in China: Political Conflict and Economic Debate*. Armonk, NY: M. E. Sharpe.

Freeman, Charles W. III, and Wen Jin Yuan. 2011. *China's New Leftists and the China Model Debate After the Financial Crisis*. Washington, DC: Center for Strategic and International Studies.

Friedman, Milton. 1970. "The Social Responsibility of Business is to Increase Profits." *New York Times*, September 13, 1970.

Friedman, Milton. 1982 [1962]. *Capitalism and Freedom*. Chicago, IL: University of Chicago Press.

Friedman, Milton. 1990a. *Friedman in China*. Hong Kong: Chinese University Press.

Friedman, Milton. 1990b. "Using the Market for Social Development." In *Economic Reform in China: Problems and Prospects*, edited by James Dorn and Wang Xi, 3–15. Chicago, IL: University of Chicago Press.

Fromm, Erich. 1970. *Marx's Concept of Man*. New York: Frederick Ungar Publishing Co.

Galenson, Walter, ed. 1993. *China's Economic Reform*. San Francisco, CA: The 1990 Institute.

Giles, John, Albert Park, and Fang Cai. 2006. "How has Economic Restructuring Affected China's Urban Workers?" *The China Quarterly* (185): 61–95. doi:10.1017/S0305741006000051.

Gold, Thomas B., William J. Hurst, Jaeyoun Won, and Qiang Li, eds. 2009. *Laid-Off Workers in a Workers' State: Unemployment with Chinese Characteristics*. New York: Palgrave Macmillan.

Greenfield, Gerard, and Apo Leong. 1997. "China's Communist Capitalism: The Real World of Market Socialism," In *Ruthless Criticism of all that Exists: Socialist Register 1997*, edited by Leo Panitch, 96–122. New York: Monthly Review.

Grove, Linda. 2006. *A Chinese Economic Revolution: Rural Entrepreneurship in the Twentieth Century*. Lanham, MD: Rowman & Littlefield.

Gu, Edward X. 1997. "Foreign Direct Investment and the Restructuring of Chinese State-Owned Enterprises (1992–1995): A New Institutionalist Perspective." *China Information* 12 (3): 46–71. doi:10.1177/0920203X9701200303.

Han, Yuling. 2012. "The Academic Career and Economic Thought of Yifeng Wu." *World Review of Political Economy* 3 (3): 389–401. doi:10.13169/worlrevipoliecon.3.3.0389.

Han, Zhenliang. 1996. "Draw the Line Beween Learning Advanced Things from the West and Worshiping Things Foreign." *Chinese Economic Studies* 29 (3): 85–92.

Hart-Landsberg, Martin, and Paul Burkett. 2005. *China and Socialism: Market Reforms and Class Struggle*. New York: Monthly Review.

Hinton, William. 1990. *The Great Reversal: The Privatization of China 1978–1989*. New York: Monthly Review.

Holz, Carsten A. 2002. "Long Live China's State-Owned Enterprises: Deflating the Myth of Poor Financial Performance." *Journal of Asian Economics* 13 (4): 493. https://knox.idm.oclc.org/login?url=http://search.ebscohost.com/login.aspx?direct=true&db=bsh&AN=8550003&site=ehost-live.

Hsu, Robert C. 1991. *Economic Theories in China 1979–1988*. New York: Cambridge University Press.

Jefferson, Gary H., and Thomas Rawski. 1994. "Enterprise Reform in Chinese Industry." *Journal of Economic Perspectives* 8 (2): 47–70. doi:10.1257/jep. 8.2.47.

Jefferson, Gary H., and Thomas Rawski. 1995. "How Industrial Reform Worked in China: The Role of Innovation, Competition, and Property Rights." World Bank, 1994.

Klaes, Matthias, and Yi Zhang. 2013. "Chinese Reform and Schools of Thought in Western Economics." In *Thoughts on Economic Development in China*, edited by Ying Ma and Hans-Michael Trautwein, 255–273. New York: Routledge.

Kornai, Janos. 1998. *From Socialism to Capitalism: What is Meant by the Change of the System?* London: The Social Market Foundation.

Kristof, Nicholas. 1989b. "In Beijing a Bold New Proposal: End State Ownership of Industry." *New York Times*: A1.

Kuhn, Robert. 2011. *How China's Leaders Think*. Singapore: Wiley.

Lardy, Nicholas. 1998. *China's Unfinished Revolution*. Washington, DC: Brookings Institution.

Lardy, Nicholas. 2014. *Markets Over Mao: The Rise of Private Business in China*. Washington, DC: Peterson Institute for International Economics.

Lau, Raymond. 2001. "Economic Determination in the Last Instance: China's Political-Economic Development Under the Impact of the Asian Financial Crises." *Historical Materialism* 8 (1): 215–251. doi:10.1163/15692060111100414811.

Lee, Ching Kwan. 2007b. "The Unmaking of the Chinese Working Class." In *Working in China: Ethnographies of Labor and Workplace Transformation*, edited by Ching Kwan Lee, 15–37. New York: Routledge.

Lee, Junyeop, and OECD Working Group on Privatisation and Corporate Governance of State Owned Assets. 2009. *State Owned Enterprises in China: Reviewing the Evidence*: OECD.

Li, Haijian. 2003 [1997]. "Integrating FDI within the Domestic Economy (China Industrial Development Report)." In *China's Economic Reform: A Study with Documents*, edited by Christopher Howe, Y. Y. Kueh, and Robert Ash, 387–398. New York: Routledge.

Li, He. 2009. "China's New Left." *East Asian Policy* 1 (1): 30–37.

Li, Minqi. "Capitalist Development and Class Struggle in China." Book manuscript. Available online at http://content.csbs.utah.edu/~mli/Capitalism%20in%20China/Index.htm (accessed April 22, 2017).

Li, Minqi. 2008. *The Rise of China and the Demise of the Capitalist World Economy*. New York: Monthly Review.

Li, Shi. 2008. *Rural Migrant Workers in China: Scenario, Challenges and Public Policy*. ILO Working Papers. Vol. 89. Geneva: International Labour Office.

Li, Zhongjin, and Hao Qi. 2014. "Labor Process and the Social Structure of Accumulation in China." *Review of Radical Political Economics* 46 (4): 481–488. doi:10.1177/0486613414537986.

Lin, Chun. 2006. *The Transformation of Chinese Socialism*. Durham, NC: Duke University Press.

Lin, Justin Yifu. 1988. "Rural Factor Markets in China After the Household Responsibility Reform." In *Chinese Economic Policy: Economic Reform at Midstream*, edited by Bruce Reynolds and Ilpyong Kim, 169–203. New York: Paragon House.

Lo, Dic. 1997. *Market and Institutional Regulation in Chinese Industrialization, 1978–1994*. New York: St. Martin's Press.

Lo, Dic. 1999. "Reappraising the Performance of China's State-Owned Industrial Enterprises 1980–96." *Cambridge Journal of Economics* 23 (6): 693–718.

Lo, Dic, and Yu Zhang. 2011. "Making Sense of China's Economic Transformation." *Review of Radical Political Economics* 43 (1): 33–55. doi:10.1177/0486613410383952.

Ma, Bin, and Yaxi Han. 2002. "Letter to Comrade Jiang Zemin and the Party's Central Committee." *Monthly Review* archives May 21, 2002. (https://monthlyreview.org/commentary/letter-of-ma-bin-and-han-yaxi/, accessed April 23, 2017).

Ma, Ying, and Hans-Michael Trautwein, eds. 2013. *Thoughts on Economic Development in China*. New York: Routledge.

Meisner, Maurice. 1996. *The Deng Xiaopeng Era: An Inquiry into the Fate of Chinese Socialism 1978–1994*. New York: Hill and Wang.

Meng, Jie. 2008. "The Hypothesis of Economic Man and Marxist Economics." *Social Sciences in China* 29 (1): 5–15. doi:10.1080/02529200801920855.

Misra, Kalpana. 1998. *From Post Maoism to Post-Marxism: The Erosion of Official Ideology in Deng's China*. New York: Routledge.

Naughton, Barry. 1992. "Implications of the State Monopoly Over Industry and its Relaxation." *Modern China* 18 (1): 14–41. www.jstor.org/stable/189138.

Naughton, Barry. 1993. "Deng Xiaoping: The Economist." *The China Quarterly* (135): 491–514. doi:10.1017/S0305741000013886.

Naughton, Barry. 1995. *Growing Out of the Plan: Chinese Economic Reform 1978–1993.* New York: Cambridge University Press.

Naughton, Barry. 2001. "Zhu Rongji: The Twilight of a Brilliant Career." *China Leadership Monitor* 1 (1): 1–10.

Naughton, Barry. 2007. *The Chinese Economy: Transitions and Growth.* Cambridge, MA: MIT Press.

Naughton, Barry. 2008. "A Political Economy of China's Economic Transition." In *China's Great Economic Transformation*, edited by Loren Brandt and Thomas Rawski, 91–135. New York: Cambridge University Press.

Nolan, Peter. 2004 [1998]. *Transforming China: Globalization, Transition and Development.* New York: Anthem Press.

Park, Henry. 1986. "Postrevolutionary China and the Soviet NEP." *Research in Political Economy* 9: 219–233.

Pringle, Tim. 2013. "Reflections on Labor in China: From a Moment to a Movement." *South Atlantic Quarterly* 112 (1): 191–202. doi:10.1215/00382876-1891323.

Putterman, Louis. 1995. "The Role of Ownership and Property Rights in China's Economic Transition." *The China Quarterly* (144): 1047–1064. doi:10.1017/S0305741000004720.

Qian, Yingyi. 2002. *How Reform Worked in China.* William Davidson Working Paper no. 473.

Qian, Yingyi, and Jinglian Wu. 2000. *China's Transition to a Market Economy: How Far Across the River?* Working Paper no. 69. Stanford, CA: Center for International Development, Stanford University.

Rawski, Thomas G. 1997. "China's State Enterprise Reform–an Overseas Perspective." *China Economic Review (1043951X)* 8 (1): 89. https://knox.idm.oclc.org/login?url=http://search.ebscohost.com/login.aspx?direct=true&db=bsh&AN=9709223159&site=ehost-live.

Riskin, Carl. 1982. "Market, Maoism, and Economic Reform in China." *Bulletin of Concerned Asian Scholars* 13 (3): 31–41.

Sachs, Jeffrey D. and Wing Woo. 2000. "Understanding China's Economic Performance." *Journal of Policy Reform* 4 (1): 1–50. doi:10.1080/13841280008523412.

Schumacher, E. F. 1973. *Small is Beautiful: Economics as if People Mattered.* New York: Harper and Row.

Sheng, Hong. 1996. "A Survey of the Research on the Transitional Process of Market-Oriented Reform in China." *Chinese Economic Studies* 29 (2): 5–38.

Shirk, Susan. 1993. *The Political Logic of Economic Reform in China.* Los Angeles, CA: University of California Press.

Smyth, Russell. 2000. "Asset Stripping in Chinese State-Owned Enterprises." *Journal of Contemporary Asia* 30 (1): 3, 3–16. doi:10.1080/00472330080000021.

Spence, Jonathan D. 1990. *The Search for Modern China.* New York: Norton.

Sun, Yan. 1995. *The Chinese Reassessment of Socialism 1976–1992.* Princeton, NJ: Princeton University Press.

Sung, Yun-wing and Thomas M. H. Chan 1987. "China's Economic Reforms: The Debates in China." *The Australian Journal of Chinese Affairs* (17): 29–51. doi:10.2307/2158967.

Tong, Sarah Y. 2009. "Why Privatize Or Why Not? Empirical Evidence from China's SOEs Reform." *China Economic Review* 20 (3): 402–413. doi:10.1016/j.chieco.2009.06.008.

Vogel, Ezra F. 2011. *Deng Xiaoping and the Transformation of China.* Cambridge, MA: Harvard University Press.

Wang, Gungwu. 2014. *Another China Cycle: Committing to Reform.* Hackensack, NJ: World Scientific.

Wang, Haibo. 1982. "Competition Under Socialism." In *China's Economic Reforms*, edited by Lin Wei and Arnold Chao, 114–122. Philadelphia, PA: University of Pennsylvania Press.

Wang, Hui. 2003a. *China's New Order: Society, Politics, and Economy in Transition*, edited by Theodore Huters. Cambridge, MA: Harvard University Press.

White, Gordon. 1989. "Restructuring the Working Class: Labor Reform in Post Mao China." In *Marxism and the Chinese Experience*, edited by Arif Dirlik and Maurice Meisner, 152–168. Armonk, NY: M. E. Sharpe.

Whyte, Martin King. 1999. "The Changing Role of Workers." In *The Paradox of China's Post-Mao Reforms*, edited by Merle Goldman and Roderick MacFarquhar, 173–196. Cambridge, MA: Harvard University Press.

World Bank. 1995. *Bureaucrats in Business: The Economics and Politics of Government Ownership.* New York: Oxford University Press.

Wu, Jinglian. 2004. "Market Socialism' and Chinese Economic Reform." Conference Paper Submitted to the IEA's Round Table on "Market and Socialism Reconsidered" (Draft).

Wu, Jinglian. 2005. *Understanding and Interpreting China's Economic Reform.* Singapore: Thomson/South-Western.

Wu, Yifeng. 2008. "Theory of Property Rights: Comparing Marx with Coase." *Social Sciences in China* 29 (2): 5–17. doi:10.1080/02529200802091201.

Xin, Mao (pseudonym). 1999. "Reform and Economic Man." *The Chinese Economy* 32 (2): 22–60.

Xu, Chenggang. 2011. "The Fundamental Institutions of China's Reforms and Development." *Journal of Economic Literature* 49 (4): 1076–1151. doi:10.1257/jel.49.4.1076.

Xu, Dixin. 1982. "China's Modernization and the Prospects for its Economy." In *Economic Reform in the PRC: In Which China's Economists Make Known What Went Wrong, Why, and What Should Be Done About It*, edited by George C. Wang, 43–52. Boulder, CO: Westview Press.

Xu, Zhun, Ying Chen, and Minqi Li. 2015. "Are Chinese Workers Paid the Correct Wages? Measuring Wage Underpayment in the Chinese Industrial Sector, 2005–2010." *Review of Radical Political Economics* 47 (3): 446–459. doi:10.1177/0486613414542780.

Yang, Famin. 1997. "The State-Owned Enterprises Pour Out their Hearts." *The Chinese Economy* 30 (4); 6–28.

Zhao, Zhong. 2005. "Migration, Labor Market Flexibility, and Wage Determination in China: A Review." *The Developing Economies* 43 (2): 285–312. doi:10.1111/j.1746-1049.2005.tb00263.x.

Zhao, Ziyang. 2009. *Prisoner of the State: The Secret Journal of Premier Zhao Ziyang.* Translated by Bao Pu, Renee Chiang, and Adi Ignatius. New York: Simon & Schuster.

# 7   Sociology of knowledge lessons

## 7.1 Some big questions and tentative answers

It seems worthwhile at this juncture to review the findings of the case studies discussed in the last three chapters for common themes and general conclusions. What can the history of competing analyses of China's rural, international, and SOE sectors tell us about Chinese economic development and economics discourse? Why did modest attempts to expand the role of markets in circumscribed areas of the economy quickly spread to other sectors and promote capitalist practices? How did different intellectual frameworks generate very divergent understandings of economic restructuring? This chapter pulls together threads found in earlier chapters to address these questions. Most of the larger context and data supporting the conclusions that follow can be found in Chapters 4, 5, and 6.

## 7.2 Why did restructuring spread rapidly and promote capitalist practices?

Three factors seem especially relevant for answering this question. First, the preconditions were in place for a period of rapid economic growth in the mid-1970s. This was due to past government investments in public education, public health, and economic infrastructure, as well as accumulating technological changes, especially the completion of China's own Green Revolution. The accompanying increase in agricultural productivity acted like a shot of adrenalin for the Chinese economy. It expanded food production, increased agricultural inputs for manufacturing, freed up rural labor for industrial employment, and made broad and rapid economic change possible.[1] The popularity of family farming and its additional contribution to rising agricultural productivity also endowed the reformers with significant political capital.

Second, the new energy flowed, at least in part, through market channels, as the Cultural Revolution had ideologically undermined Maoist-collectivist institutions. The Red Guards and other activists had also dismantled much of China's economic planning apparatus. The resulting gaps in socially engineered linkages encouraged the new economic energy to flow along market organized linkages. The decision of Chinese leaders to make rapid economic growth their number one priority amplified this outcome. Deng and other top officials seemed quite comfortable being "capitalist riders," that is, using techniques found in capitalism to promote economic growth, if not "capitalist roaders."

Third, and perhaps most importantly, the Chinese leadership encouraged economic competition on all levels. Because of the Cultural Revolution's dismantling of much of China's central planning institutions, local governments and economic units enjoyed significant autonomy. In this environment, competition proved an especially strong economic force. It also proved difficult to control.

The initial experiments with markets in the countryside and with markets for "above-quota" production in the cities, contained within themselves powerful expansionary tendencies. The Chinese state's welcoming of competition among SOEs, and the emergence of TVEs in the countryside pressured the SOEs to adopt more "bottom line" practices. Competition among the SOEs and TVEs encouraged firms to seek out new markets and sources of supply, spreading pressures for change to new sectors. The expansion of foreign firms in the SEZs eventually multiplied these pressures across the economy, as did the emergence of private domestic firms. Later developments, linking funds for new investment to retained earnings and interest bearing loans from financial institutions, rather than grants from central planners, also amplified the restructuring impact of competition.

Government policy offered only modest safeguards to prevent competition from precipitating a "race to the bottom" among firms. As a result, the TVEs and SOEs gradually shed many of their social obligations, taking on more and more characteristics of capitalist firms, modeled for them by private firms in the SEZs. The allure of potentially huge material rewards encouraged insiders to try to transform their privileged positions in the Party-state into property rights in a capitalist economy, creating powerful allies for expanded restructuring. The pattern of change in the rural, international, and SOE sectors demonstrates how market competition, abetted by a state intent on maximizing output, can create a path toward capitalism. While reluctant endorsement of this development strategy came from "primary stage" oriented Marxist theorists, the major lighting illuminating this path was provided by neoclassical and new institutionalist economic thought.

A major take-away lesson from this period for Marxist economists is that competition may be the tiger that inhabits Chen Yun's cage, rather than the bird of his original metaphor. The bird does not just fly away; the tiger eats the rider on its back.

## 7.3  Sources of paradigmatic argument: subtexts

### 7.3.1  Competing subtexts

It is admittedly difficult to characterize the position of an entire discourse or paradigm on a research topic, that is, to assert "the neoclassical treatment" of the SOEs or international trade was like this, and "the Marxist treatment," like that. There are, of course, variations among neoclassical and Marxist economists and disagreements over what characterizes each approach. Nevertheless, I think it is possible to distinguish common themes that separate the two paradigms discussion of rural, international, and SOE issues. It is in fact surprising how similar the differences are in each area.

One way to distinguish economic paradigms is by their subtexts, that is by their unprovable starting assumptions and expectations about the projects they are imagined to enable. The different subtexts of Marxist, neoclassical, and heterodox economics were very influential in leading economic analyses in different directions. Two of neoclassical theory's a priori assumptions (methodological individualism and *homo economicus*), and the paradigm's project of expanding markets and maximizing GDP, were especially important in shaping neoclassical research agendas. Two assumptions of Marxism (holism and a more complicated view of human nature than *homo economicus*), and the project of building socialism, were similarly influential in shaping Marxist research. The assumptions and projects of heterodox economics often overlapped those of Marxist theory but sometimes led in unique directions. In the discussion below we will concentrate on the differences between Marxist and neoclassical analyses, but will mention heterodox ideas from time to time.

### 7.3.2  Impact of subtexts on discussions of decollectivization, TVEs and SOEs

Neoclassical discussions of decollectivization and TVEs in the countryside and SOEs in the cities started with the assumption of economic man and the need for strong material incentives for efficient production. The increase in agricultural output after 1978 was thus intuitively tied to the closer link between effort and reward in the household responsibility system (HRS) than under collective production. Research was designed to test and hopefully confirm this hypothesis. Lin Yifu's econometric paper (Lin 1992), which concluded that over half of the increase in agricultural output 1978–1984 was due to the HRS, was the most widely cited article over the 1989–2010 period in the *China Economic Review*. The latter is a leading economics journal in China maintained largely by graduates of Western PhD programs. Besides the impressive technical expertise and new data exhibited in the article, Lin's work was widely cited because it confirmed key neoclassical assumptions and legitimated China's capitalist oriented reforms. He later noted sardonically that a subsequent paper of his, mildly critical of the Washington Consensus, received no such attention from neoclassical readers.

From their starting point, Marxist and heterodox economists have looked more actively than neoclassical economists for explanations for the increase in farm output after 1978 that do not discredit collective production. As noted in Chapter 4, Xu Zhun and others have criticized neoclassical analyses of decollectivization for, among other things, their accounting treatment of output from private plots, the measurement of technological change, the treatment of weather variables, and insufficient attention to the timing of HRS adoption. Bramall has characterized the neoclassical story as the "Fable of Decollectivization" (Bramall 2009a, 250).

Reflecting the starting point and tools of neoclassical theory, Lin has used game theory to reach the surprising conclusion that the most important factor explaining the Great Famine was not the government's diversion of inputs from agriculture to industry during the Great Leap Forward, or the diversion of food from the countryside to exports, or bad weather. Instead Lin emphasizes the government's termination of peasants' right to withdraw from rural collectives. He argues that this reduced the penalties for shirking (the risk of inducing productive members to withdraw from the collective) and thus reduced overall work effort and caused the famine.

Xu and Zhang have likewise appealed to evolutionary game theory to explain why self-interested agents in Chinese markets have prospered without a well-developed legal system and robust protections of private property. Little attention is given in game theoretic models to the independent role of culture and reproducing social systems in understanding behavior. All is reduced to rational calculations by self-interested agents. The impact on Chinese culture of economic institutions is also devalued as an economics research topic.

The above discussion has emphasized the work of Lin Yifu, a very important Chinese neoclassical economist, but similar results would have emerged from a discussion of other starting points, such as the work of Wu Jinglian, Li Yining, Tian Guoqian, Zhang Weiying (all well-known Chinese neoclassical economists), or research sponsored by the World Bank, the Chinese Academy of Social Sciences (CASS), or the Chinese Economist Society (CES).

Had we started our discussion with reference to research on state-owned enterprises rather than agriculture, the results would also have been similar. Recall, for example, the work of Steven Cheung, a very influential Hong Kong economist. His appeal to human nature to explain the problems with public ownership and socialism offers a classic statement of the neoclassical imagination. As you may recall he argued, "Economic analysis ... rests on the assertion of 'selfishness' ... if man is born selfish and *cannot* be changed, then reforms based on the premise of altruism will lead to disaster" (Cheung 1986, 61–62).

There is a strong a priori belief in neoclassical thought against the viability of publicly owned, collectively owned, or egalitarian oriented enterprises.

The key challenge posed by the paradigm for economic systems is how to solve the agency problem. Private enterprise with strong material incentives is seen as the ideal solution. Xu and Zhang, for example, concluded, the "TVEs lost ground in the marketplace through competition with private firms. ... In hindsight, it seems natural that all three TVE models should converge to the model dominated by private or shareholding firms..." (Xu and Zhang 2009, 9).

The metaphors used in academic papers to describe SOEs suggests at least some neoclassical economists harbor contempt for public firms. Fan Gang, for example, has warned that the SOEs might "prosper as a parasite ... (and) ... metastasize" (Fan 1994, 111). While private firms are often celebrated for their nimbleness and economic bravery ("jumping into the sea"), public firms are disparaged for laziness and economic obesity. Marxists, of course, often use metaphors with the opposite overtones, portraying private firms as sweat-shops, sweatshops in waiting, or prison-like facilities.

When SOEs or collectively owned TVEs appear to succeed, neoclassical critics of public ownership usually look for extenuating or unsustainable circumstances. This is not necessarily self-serving. Their paradigm offers good reasons for suspecting an unlevel playing field. Among the rationales offered for moments of SOE success have been: privileged (and "unfair") access to government controlled credit, hidden subsidies, and the temporary capture of "low-hanging fruit," (such as the deployment of new technologies after a period of Maoist economic isolation).

Marxist and heterodox defenders of public ownership tend to do the exact opposite, that is find extenuating circumstances for the failings of the SOEs and TVEs. Among the factors cited for the higher debt levels of many SOEs than private firms have been: higher tax burdens, asset stripping by corrupt privatizers, and higher expenditures for social responsibilities, such as main-taining employment during economic downturns or covering retired workers' pensions (liabilities new private firms don't have).

The tendency for a priori assumptions to dominate the feedback process in setting research agendas is very strong in the social sciences. Researchers tend to accept results that confirm their paradigm's subtexts and seek explanations for why anomalies are not really anomalies. Because experiments are not really possible in the social sciences it is hard to overcome confirmatory discourse.

## 7.4 Counterfactuals

One of the key ways that paradigmatic assumptions dominate empirical data in assessments of different ownership forms is by influencing the theorist's counterfactuals, that is the assumptions made about what might have hap-pened under different policies. For example, to some extent, whether the migrants of the floating population are victims or beneficiaries of Chinese economic restructuring, depends on what you imagine their alternative present to have been. Neoclassical theorists assume that the alternative to China's adoption of capitalist practices was minimal economic growth, very low productivity, sluggish technological change, widespread poverty, and the nepotistic and corrupt use of economic power. Disappointing aspects of the reforms are frequently dismissed by the argument that more complete reform could have avoided these problems. The corruption of insider privatization, for example, is tied to insufficient liberalization, rather than an inherent characteristic of early capitalism (primitive accumulation) as argued in Marxist theory. Had China avoided halfway measures like dual-track pricing, the neoclassicals have argued, many instances of corruption could have been avoided. Similarly, the economic weaknesses of the migrants could have been reduced by ending the *hukou* system and government regulation of labor mobility.

Marxist economists have assumed their own counterfactuals, which imagined hypotheticals congenial with socialist projects. Some argued that the progress made during the first five-year plan (1953–1957) could have been repeated if Maoist policies had not derailed central planning. Others have suggested that rural collectives and SOEs would have been much more successful if they had been governed democratically through participatory management. Still other proponents of rural collectives have argued that they would have been able to stand on their own, if unrealistic policies dictated by local Party leaders or officials in Beijing had not been imposed on them.

## 7.5 Trajectories

Marxist and neoclassical theorists also differed about the trajectory of different policies. As with debates over counter-factuals, disagreements over trajectories, allows a priori assumptions to dominate empirical data in assessments of economic options. The neoclassicals imagined a grand Kuznets curve, promising a future decline in corruption, inequality, and pollution as capitalism matured. Marxists foresaw the consolidation of a class society with gaping inequalities and rapacious destruction of the environment,

The Kuznets curve is part of the subtexts of neoclassical economics. It was originally applied only to the distribution of income (implying that inequality would initially increase in industrializing capitalist economies, but then decline), but has since taken on other dimensions. The claims are often assumed implicitly without formal argument. Sometimes there are acknowledgments of the ambiguity of the evidence for the curves, but such qualifiers are usually overwhelmed by implicit assurances of sunny futures.

This combination of formal qualification alongside informal adoption is consistent with the origins of the original Kuznets curve. The optimistic implication of the curve seems from the start to have been linked with the subtext of promoting global capitalism. In his recent book on inequality, *Capital in the Twenty-First Century*, Thomas Piketty notes,

Kuznets himself was well aware that the compression of high US incomes between 1913 and 1948 was largely accidental. ... But in December 1954 ... he offered a far more optimistic interpretation ... (predicting that) inequality everywhere can be expected to ... first increase and then decrease over the course of industrialization (13). ... In order to make sure that everyone understood what was at stake, he took care to remind his listeners that the intent of his optimistic predictions was quite simply to maintain the underdeveloped countries "within the orbit of the free world." In large part, then, the theory of the Kuznets curve was a product of the Cold War.

(Pikkety 2014, 14)

## 7.6 Research priorities, questions asked, and data assembled

Differences in the questions asked are probably even more important than differences in the way common or shared questions are answered. The dominant project of neoclassical economics is how to maximize GDP. Marxist and heterodox projects are more diverse, and relatively speaking, give greater attention, to equity issues, concerns about the quality of work lives, and cultural construction. This weighting informs the questions asked and topics researched by each paradigm.

The differences between Marxist and neoclassical discussions of equity issues go beyond quantitative measures of levels of attention. Marxists have focused on the creation of reproducing structures of inequality, while neoclassicals have focused on distinctions caused by differences in individual talents and work habits. Marxists have analyzed how the economic reforms created a capitalist oriented division of labor in China, with attendant inequalities of income, wealth, and access to education. Using concepts such as the "Social Structure of Accumulation" and the "Reserve Army of the Unemployed," for example, William Hinton, Maurice Meisner, Li Minqi, and Li Zhongjin have analyzed the nature of China's new class structure. They have tied the origins of China's new working class to: decollectivization; the layoffs of 30 million SOE workers; the "smashing of the iron rice bowl's" labor protections; the imposition of employer empowering labor market regulations; and the expansion of the informal sector. They have tied the origins of China's new capitalist class (and the source of its initial capital accumulation) to: insider leasing and insider privatization of the SOEs; corrupt rural land grabs; joint ventures in the SEZs with foreign capital; and profits from petty commodity production.

The emergence of a 100 million strong migrant labor force, working 11 hours a day for subsistence wages, alongside China's new super rich (568 billionaires and 320,000 households with wealth of ~1.5 million dollars)[2] is emblematic for Marxists of China's new social order.

China's class structure is not a topic for discussion within neoclassical theory, though the impact of labor market regulations on wages, employment, and output can be, and is, discussed. The Marxist approach forces attention to larger social structures. The neoclassical approach welcomes narrower inquiries that do not invite studying capitalism as a reproducing social system. Both approaches are capable of generating recommendations for reduced economic inequality. Marxist interest in structural inequalities has also generated research on how the emerging capitalist class has accumulated political power and a legitimizing worldview alongside its financial assets.

Consistent with Marxist economists' study of class relations is an intense focus on the adversarial aspect of capitalism's organization of work and the problem of alienation. In contrast, neoclassical and new institutionalist economic theorists treat capitalist firms' labor policies as solved problems involving efficient resource use. The disappearance of the phrase "workers as the masters of their enterprises" in neoclassical discussions of labor markets is reflective of the paradigm's assumption that all market participants are by definition masters of their fate, from "free laborers," to "sovereign consumers."

The goals of worker self-management associated with the idea of workers being the "masters" of their enterprises still animates many Marxist oriented studies. This linkage is well illustrated in Chapters 4–6 by the work of Hinton (1990), Lin Chun (2006), Ma Bin and Yaxi Han (2002), Ross (2007b), and Wu (2008).

Marxist and heterodox researchers have also raised questions about how to measure success in economic reform. Neoclassical economists usually measure the impact of economic restructuring by its affect on GDP growth. Marxist and heterodox economists favor more multi-dimensional measures. The Rural Reconstruction Movement (RRM), for example, calls for looking at the impact of the reforms on villages' cultural capital and social solidarity, as well as household income. Zhou Yi, an economist at Fudan University, raises similar measurement issues with respect to assessments of the SOEs. Like E. F. Schumacher, Zhou argues that economists need broader metrics than the firms' relative profitability for assessing the merits of public and private ownership. Easterlin's work on the apparent lack of a strong relationship between self-reported levels of happiness in China and national GDP/capita statistics vibrates more strings and has more overtones, in Marxist and heterodox economics than in neoclassical economics.

## 7.7 Master narratives

As Chapters 4 to 6 recounted, Marxist and neoclassical economists fit the Chinese economic events they highlighted into different master narratives. Neoclassical theorists fit decollectivization, expanded international trade, and privatization of the SOEs and TVEs into its master narrative of how the West got rich. With echoes of John Locke's depiction of England's Glorious Revolution, Douglas North's theory of history, and Oliver Williamson and Ronald Coase's theory of institutional design, China's rapid economic growth was tied to the creation and protection of private property rights in neoclassical analyses. The heroes of the neoclassical story are entrepreneurial family farmers, rural small business owners, privatizers of public firms, and government officials, opening China to the world in order to modernize a stunted, isolated economy. The focus is on the accumulators of capital through hard work and innovation, land speculation and "*guanxi*" (connections in general). The relative success of Chinese policies is often benchmarked against US institutional and regulatory practices. These practices are treated as "best practices" or international norms, rather than capitalist practices.

Marxist analyses covering the same sectors and time periods fit events into a different master narrative. It is Marx and Polyani's narrative. Its focus is not on the entrepreneurs and the accumulators of capital, it is on the mass of people separated from the means of production and required to sell their labor power to survive. It is about the market as an imperative rather than opportunity. It is about the casualties of restructuring and the emergence of China's squeezed working class, symbolized by the ~100+ million floating population.

## 7.8 Analogies in the international sector

We close this chapter by reviewing the differences between Marxist-Heterodox and neoclassical analyses of the international sector. The re-emergence of themes found in our discussion of the rural and state-owned sectors is striking, given the very different subject matter of the international sector.

The neoclassical story is again one of the triumph of economic rationality over ideology. China's "opening up" is celebrated for increasing the country's GDP and employment. Lin Yifu is second to no one in his promotion of the principle of comparative advantage (Lin 2012b). Other neoclassical economists tout the benefits of trade with respect to technology transfer and exposure to Western management practices (which are treated a kind of technology) (Wu 2005). China's chief trade negotiator for membership in the WTO, Long Yongtu argued that the PRC had no alternative but to join the global division of labor.[3]

Marxist and heterodox attitudes toward trade and the world market were and are more complicated. The GDP and employment benefits of increased trade are usually acknowledged. Other impacts are seen more critically. Marxist and heterodox economists stress the tendency for the trade sector to increase capital's bargaining power with labor. Both the SEZs and WTO are portrayed as Trojan horses for the importation into China of employer empowering labor relations (Gallagher 2002). Initially imposed to attract foreign capital, the SEZ's regulations ultimately became national standards. Labor studies oriented theorists, such Ching Kwan Lee and Anita Chan, stress the degrading, exhausting, and dead end aspects of sweatshops in the international sector.

Both neoclassical and Marxist-heterodox economists believed that Chinese membership in the WTO would consolidate rules limiting the Chinese state's ability to intervene in the Chinese economy. The neoclassicals thought the trade sector would impose the discipline of capitalist competition on the Chinese production. They applauded the dictates of this competition. Most heterodox and Marxist economists feared a "race to the bottom," and asserted the need for social management or guidance of competition. Chris Bramall (2009a) in particular, has called for China to withdraw from the WTO in order to retain its ability to manage international trade and the structure of the Chinese economy.

As in discussing agricultural and state-owned enterprises, Marxist-heterodox and neoclassical economists assumed different counterfactuals and trajectories for the international sector, making it hard for existing empirical data to definitively adjudicate the debate between the paradigms. The neo-classicals argued the TINA principle and saw economic stagnation and mass poverty as the alternative to China's opening up policies. Marxist and hetero-dox economists assumed more diverse options, with the possibility of rural reconstruction instead of mass migration to the SEZs, tougher technology transfer requirements, and a successful industrial policy.

The neoclassicals assumed that over time Chinese firms would move up the global value chain, escaping the sweatshop conditions of most current workers in the export sector and eventually reducing economic inequality. Marxist and heterodox economists anticipated a lock-in, both in terms of China's global position and the underclass in China's labor market. They noted how numerous government regulations designed to manage the SEZs had eroded, including mandatory joint ventures, mandatory local content standards, technology transfer requirements, and limits on the presence of SEZ firms in domestic markets. They also found it unlikely that the leading capitalist countries would let China permanently dominate the manufacturing sector.

Besides being an *entrepot* for foreign goods and services, the international sector was a conduit for the flow of Western business ideas into China. These ideas were generally welcomed by key Chinese trade officials, such as WTO negotiator Long Yongtu. As detailed in Chapters 4–6, Western firms in the SEZs set examples for Chinese firms and inculcated habits found in capitalist economies in their Chinese workers and management. At a higher level of abstraction, the World Bank and other globalizing market institutions framed thinking. Chinese and Western enthusiasts for transplanting capitalist business practices often tied them to respect for due process and the protections of individual rights under the law. Critics found the rights protected to be mainly property rights. Philip Huang (2009a) suggested that the neoclassical's *positive claim* that *homo economicus is* selfish often blurs into a neoliberal *normative* claim that "he" *should* be selfish.

## 7.9  Summing up

For the neoclassicals economic restructuring in China is about the rational reorganization of the economy. Capitalism is treated as a natural social system that solves motivational and informational problems. For the Marxists, restructuring in China is about the creation of a class society. The key outcomes have been the creation of a capitalist class with command of the means of production and a disenfranchised working class forced to sell its labor power under highly unfavorable conditions.

## Notes

1 As Lynn White III noted, "The liberation of agricultural labor beginning in the early 1970s conjured reforms more surely than did 1978 pronouncements. ... Here is a case where Marx's ideas on the technological causes of political shifts apply quite well" (White 1998, 111).
2 Statistics on China's billionaires can be found in Hoogewerf 2016, 1. Statistics on China's 10 million yuan (approximately $1.5 million dollars) households are found in Giroir 2011, 454.
3 Long added that participants in the global market would have to adopt capitalist market practices to survive (Lardy 2002).

## References

Bramall, Chris. 2009a. *Chinese Economic Development.* New York: Routledge.
Cheung, Steven. 1986. *Will China Go Capitalist?* 2nd ed. London: Institute of Economic Affairs.
Fan, Gang. 1994. "Incremental Changes and Dual-Track Transition: Understanding the Case of China." *Economic Policy* 9 (Supplement): 99–122. doi:10.2307/1344602.
Gallagher, Mary E. 2002. "'Reform and Openness': Why China's Economic Reforms have Delayed Democracy." *World Politics* 54 (3): 338–372. doi:10.1353/wp. 2002.0009.
Giroir, Guillaume. 2011. "Hyper-Rich and Hyper-Luxury in China: The Case of the Most Expensive Gated Communities." *Chinese Business Review* 10 (6): 454–466.
Hinton, William. 1990. *The Great Reversal: The Privatization of China 1978–1989.* New York: Monthly Review.
Hoogewerf, Rupert. 2016. *Huran Global Rich List of 2016.* Beijing: Huran Report.
Huang, Philip C. C. 2009a. "China's Neglected Informal Economy: Reality and Theory." *Modern China* 35 (4): 405–438. doi:10.1177/0097700409333158.
Lardy, Nicholas. 2002. *Integrating China into the Global Economy.* Washington, DC: Brookings Institution Press.
Lin, Chun. 2006. *The Transformation of Chinese Socialism.* Durham, NC: Duke University Press.
Lin, Justin Yifu. 1992. "Rural Reforms and Agricultural Growth in China." *The American Economic Review* 82 (1): 34–51. www.jstor.org/stable/2117601.
Lin, Justin Yifu. 2012b. *New Structural Economics: A Framework for Rethinking Development and Policy.* Washington, DC: World Bank.
Ma, Bin, and Yaxi Han. 2002. "Letter to Comrade Jiang Zemin and the Party's Central Committee." *Monthly Review* archives May 21, 2002. (https://monthlyreview.org/commentary/letter-of-ma-bin-and-han-yaxi/, accessed April 23, 2017).

Piketty, Thomas. 2014. *Capital in the Twenty-First Century*. Cambridge, MA: Harvard University Press.

Ross, Andrew. 2007b. "Outsourcing as a Way of Life? Knowledge Transfer in the Yangtze Delta." In *Working in China: Ethnographies of Labor and Workplace Transformation*, edited by Ching Kwan Lee, 188–208. New York: Routledge.

White, Lynn T. III. 1998. *Local Causes of China's Economic Reforms. Unstately Power*. Vol. I. Armonk, NY: M. E. Sharpe.

Wu, Jinglian. 2005. *Understanding and Interpreting China's Economic Reform*. Singapore: Thomson/South-Western.

Wu, Yifeng. 2008. "Theory of Property Rights: Comparing Marx with Coase." *Social Sciences in China* 29 (2): 5–17. doi:10.1080/02529200802091201.

Xu, Chenggang and Xiaobo Zhang. 2009. *The Evolution of Chinese Entrepreneurial Firms: Township-Village Enterprises Revisited. (IFPRI Discussion Paper 00854)* International Food Policy Research Institute.

# 8 Evolution of Chinese economics education 1978–2000

## The spread of neoclassical economics

The city of Shenzhen was one of the first four Special Economic Zones (SEZs). It grew from a population of less than 400,000 in 1978 to around 11 million today. It also saw the birth of a beautiful new university, Shenzhen University. The economics department offices are on the fifth floor of an academic building. When you get off the elevator there is bust of a famous person. You might have expected it to be Karl Marx, or an ancient Chinese sage, or perhaps a contemporary Chinese economist. It is none of these; it is Adam Smith.[1]

## 8.1 Historical context

We are now ready to put the evolution of economics education in China and the triumph of neoclassical economics over Marxist economics in Chinese universities, in an historical context. We begin in section 8.1 with a brief description of the state of economics education in the late 1970s. Sections 8.2 and 8.3 discuss neoclassical interpretations of the evolution of economics education in China 1978–2000. Sections 8.4 and 8.5 offer Marxist and heterodox interpretations of these same events. Chapter 9 looks at the current state of economics education, focusing on events since 2000. Both chapters include separate discussions of the status of neoclassical, Marxist, and heterodox economics education.

During the Cultural Revolution, higher education was among the most severely affected sectors. Intellectuals were harassed, Chinese universities closed for extended periods of time, and research basically suspended in the social sciences (Meisner 1999, 368; Keyser 2003, 39). Economics was singled out for criticism. Economics education was often reduced to rote memorization of classic Marxist texts (Meisner 1999, 368). Dissenting views were harshly repressed. The Cultural Revolution also undermined the economic information and administrative system used for economic planning (Lin 1981, 36; Huang 2008, x).[1] Formal economic research seems to have been largely suspended (Halpern 1989, 33).

In the late 1970s, as the political situation stabilized, university economics programs were renewed and expanded. Renmin University, the main site for training economists and others involved in economic planning, reopened in 1978–1979 (Lin 1981, 39–40). About the same time, the economic faculties at the elite universities for training academic and theoretical economists, such as Peking and Fudan Universities, were reconstituted (Lin 1981, 40). There was also a large increase in the number and size of economic research organizations. The surge was led by the establishment of the Chinese Academy of Social Sciences (CASS) and local versions of CASS at the provincial level. The Shanghai Academy of Social Sciences (SASS) was especially important, as was its newspaper the *World Economic Herald*.[2] The newspaper became one of the leading forums in China for discussing economic and political reform. It was enthralled with technological revolutions (Li and White 1991). The Chongqing Academy of Social Sciences published a key political-economic journal called *Reform* (*Gaige*). The journal was friendly to classical liberal views and overseen by Jiang Yiwei, an economist interested in worker self-management in the 1980s (Goldman 2005, 136).

Over the next decade neoclassical economics would replace Marxist economics as the dominant economics paradigm in universities. It has maintained this position and diffused into newspapers, public policy circles, and, to an extent, popular culture.

## 8.2 Neoclassical narratives

Neoclassical histories of Chinese economic thought and education characterize the subsequent economic reforms and reorganization of university economics curriculums as a triumph of reason over ideology. Many pre-1978 Chinese economic policies are portrayed as irrational for failing to pursue economic efficiency. Post 1978 reformist policies are celebrated for their rationality, for putting "logic" rather than "politics" in command of the economy. The shift toward neoclassical economic theory in China is treated in parallel fashion as a triumph of science over ideology.

After the government's turn toward marketization, Chinese leaders appointed economists historically friendly to the expanded use of market mechanisms to leadership positions in CASS. The economics research institutes of CASS became centers of reform thinking and were sympathetic to giving increased attention to Western economics. Other government agencies and the editorial boards of academic journals also opened up economic discussion, which spread to popular media, such as newspapers and magazines (Watson 1987). Economic data and statistics also became more widely available to researchers and the public. Though discussion remained bounded, the level of censorship declined and the range of discussable ideas expanded considerably.

The language used to formally analyze China's restructuring in neoclassically oriented accounts is quite revealing. As previously noted, the changes are almost always referred to as "reforms" rather than as "changes" or "restructuring." The word "capitalism" almost never appears in analytic papers. Instead there is talk of a move toward a "commodity economy," or a "market system." There are "private enterprises," but rarely "capitalist" firms. When institutional changes are recommended, they call for imitating international "best practices." With this language, opponents are cast as defenders of inferior practices.

Illustrative of the range of pre-1978 economic policies in China that are portrayed as irrational in these economic histories are: (1) an excessive rate of investment and correspondingly insufficient allocation of resources toward current consumption; (2) excessive investment in capital intensive heavy industry (despite China's labor intensive factor endowments) and underinvestment in agriculture and light industry; (3) the promotion of national and regional self-reliance rather than national and regional comparative advantage (taken to extremes in campaigns for local self-sufficiency in grain and steel production); (4) the disparagement of specialization and technical expertise; (5) the severing of links between effort and reward; (6) the suppression of the service sector; (7) insufficient attention to market feedback, especially with respect to consumer demand; and (8) irrational prices unreflective of production costs. In neoclassical accounts, these mistakes are linked to weaknesses in Marxian economics. Popular realization of the drag on economic growth caused by Marxist economics is linked to a search for alternative economic models that ultimately leads to the adoption of neoclassical theory in Chinese universities.

These histories highlight the usefulness of the "tool kit" that neoclassical theory offers students and practitioners. Illustrative of the important payoffs to studying neoclassical economics are claimed to be: (1) the insights of supply and demand for understanding market behavior; (2) a capacity for rigorous empirical analysis through the use of econometrics; (3) the clarity of cost benefit analysis for making social choices; (4) the clarity of many microeconomic concepts (such as opportunity costs) for enabling efficient economic choices; (5) and the development of policy instruments for managing the macro economy.

## 8.3 Assessment of the neoclassical narrative

There is some merit in parts of the neoclassical story, but ultimately it is an incomplete and sometimes misleading picture. It explains the triumph of neoclassical economics primarily in terms of "objective" evidence, downplaying subjective judgments about subtexts. The first part of the neoclassical story gives an incomplete explanation for the arguably "inefficient" appearing economic choices. Rather than simply reflecting irrational Marxist prejudices, for example, the tilt toward heavy industry and even regional self-sufficiency was significantly influenced by perceived national defense needs. The neoclassical narrative also wrongly implies that reservations about pre-1978 economic policies require rejection of Marxist economics. On the contrary, almost all of the above criticisms were first raised by orthodox Marxist critics of Maoist economists.[3]

In much the same vein, one does not have to be a neoclassical economist to use econometric techniques[4] or even supply and demand analysis for understanding short-term market behavior. One probably does have to be a neoclassical economist to promote real business cycle theory, the efficient market hypothesis, and shock therapy. While there is much more to neoclassical economics than reflected in these examples of market fundamentalism, the ideological impact of neoclassical economics often spawns "lite" versions of these outlooks, very different from the ideological ripples cast by Marxist theory.

The shift from Marxist to neoclassical economics at Chinese universities was not a shift from metaphysical to empirical argument, or from qualitative to quantitative reasoning, or even a shift from prioritizing economic equality to prioritizing economic efficiency. It was a broader shift in frames and sub-texts for how to think about economic issues. The triumph of neoclassical economics in China was the triumph of neoclassical subtexts. It was about a changing agenda for research, devaluing, for example, historical materialist inquiries into the implications of economic policies for the construction of socialism. It was about: the basic assumptions adopted (especially the assumption of *homo economicus*), the study of market moments versus the study of capitalism, the assumed normalcy of optimality and equilibrium versus the inevitability of macroeconomic crisis, etc.[5] It was about whether exploitation is inherent in a wage labor system. As with all such "scientific revolutions," or changes in worldview, there were broader judgments in play than are empirically testable or even fully conceptualized at the time of change.

## 8.4 Neo-Marxist narrative

We return now to 1977 and take a look in more detail at the events that reorganized Chinese economics education; this time from a sociology of knowledge, neo-Marxist perspective, rather than the neoclassical perspective.

### 8.4.1 Top-down influences

The initial reshaping of Chinese economics education was very much a top down affair. Deng Xiaoping, Zhao Ziyang, Zhu Rongji, and Jiang Zemin all welcomed the return of Western economics to China, especially Zhao. The motivations behind this support are complicated. On one level, the leadership's support for neoclassical economics was purely opportunistic. Neoclassical economists were expected to provide reliable support for economic reform initiatives (and they did). But the ties were and are deeper.

Deng, first and foremost, but other important political leaders as well, made maximizing aggregate economic growth the government's number one priority. One of the first acts of educational reform was the reinstitution of the national university exam system in 1977.[6] This decision symbolized Deng's willingness to sacrifice some social goals in order to increase economic output. Over time, maximizing economic growth came to mean adopting more and more features of capitalist economic organization. In 2001 capitalists were finally welcomed to join the CPC, legitimized by Jiang Zemin's theory of the "Three Represents." It remains unclear whether the leadership's project was [and is] to create a capitalist society or to ride the capitalist tiger to a Chinese version of socialism. In either case, many aspects of Western economics were deemed helpful to the politics and practice of maximizing economic growth.

At times, Chinese leaders treated Western theories of economics as more akin to Western theories of engineering or natural science than Western theories of politics or history. Chinese leaders were not totally blinded to other ways of thinking, however, and occasionally cast a wider net than that offered by neoclassical luminaries in the American Economic Association.

Several of the professors I interviewed emphasized that high level government support for neoclassical economics was probably the most important reason for its rapid expansion in China. There was, of course, an earlier precedent for this. Shortly after 1949, existing professional associations of economists, such as the China Rural Economics Society, were phased out or reorganized (Keyser 2003, 37–38). At least by 1952, Chinese universities and colleges were replacing Western economics with a Russian version of Marxist economics.[7] As Cyril Lin writes,

> (t)he introduction of Soviet-type planning to China ... entailed a truly impressive effort of intellectual capital transfer ... the Stalinist planning model *necessitated the concomitant import of a peculiar paradigm of Marxist economic thought* (italics in original). ... Software came with the hardware so to speak.
>
> (Lin 1981, p. 7)

In the 1980s, the new hardware of the economic reforms involved market mechanisms and this time the accompanying software was neoclassical economics.

The Chinese educational system has traditionally been more centralized than the American system, enabling national directives to carry much more weight.[8] Sometimes policy decisions are conveyed explicitly; for example, by announcements from the Ministry of Education (MoE) of curricular changes. Sometimes decisions are conveyed more symbolically, such as endorsements of the teaching of neoclassical economics by a series of highly publicized meetings of senior government leaders with leading Western neoclassical economists. The MoE has significant influence over comprehensive Chinese universities, especially the leading universities. In addition to appointing the president of the university, the MoE allocates key funding among the universities. In the 1990s, for example, several universities were each given over $100 million, in part to attract world class professors from the West, especially Chinese nationals. Access to these funds depended on the MoE's assessment of university quality. In economics, according to several people I interviewed, quality has been partially defined in terms of numbers of Western educated PhDs on the faculty and numbers of publications in Western economics journals.

### 8.4.2 Weaknesses of Chinese Marxism in the late 1970s

Several features of Chinese Marxism and the state of global socialist theory contributed to the triumph of neoclassical economics. First, there appears to have been some disillusionment (rather than mere reassessment) with the altruist psychologies associated with "big pot"-egalitarian methods of distribution. This sentiment probably smoothed the way for the adoption of opposite assumptions (*homo economicus*), rather than more nuanced views of human behavior.

Second, there was no agreement on what the prerequisites were for a socialist economic agenda. Some theorists highlighted commitments to economic planning over market mechanisms. Some highlighted public ownership as against private ownership. Others stressed the need for workplace democracy (and by extension democratic procedures across Chinese institutions). Still others emphasized payment according to labor or perhaps egalitarian income distributions in general. Deng and the "capitalist riders" stressed maximum development of the forces of production and CPC control of the state. The lack of a clear socialist agenda weakened one of main arguments in favor of Marxist economics, which was its demand that economic theory keep the goal of socialism as part of its analysis of public policy choices.

Third, and perhaps most importantly, perpetual and inconsistent political campaigns, the disasters accompanying the Great Leap and Cultural Revolution, cadre corruption, and a top down exercise of authority (even when in service of common interests) reduced the potential for mobilizing voluntary cooperation in the countryside and urban industries. This opened the door for the household responsibility system, the growth of "red hat" sideline businesses in the countryside, and calls for increased reliance on material incentives and privatization of state-owned enterprises in the cities. The combination strengthened the hand of economic theorists asserting the universality of "economic man."

Fourth and finally, the academic and practical policy standing of Marxist economics was also complicated by debates over the status of the labor theory of value (LTV). While these debates are too technical and complex to elaborate here, the bottom line is that the specialized language and apparatus of the LTV put Marxist analysis at a significant disadvantage in paradigm competition. This was true in both discussions linked to the practical world of commerce, which is dominated by "market-speak," and the academic world, where even most serious critiques of capitalism use non-LTV language.

First, some background. Marxist enthusiasts for the LTV argue that it is central to Marxist theory and Marxist economics. They praise it for exploring the implications of turning labor into a commodity (labor power) and argue that the theory is critical for understanding Marx's theory of exploitation. In a nutshell, the latter asserts that workers perform more labor than the labor embodied in the goods their wages permit them to buy. The structure of labor markets (for example, the presence [or absence] of a Reserve Army of the Unemployed, and the presence [or absence] of limits on capital mobility) influence the degree of exploitation. A key conclusion is that the relative share of national income going to owners of property and sellers of labor reflects distributions of power as well as technical aspects of production.

Supporters of the LTV also emphasize that by distinguishing between "labor" and "labor power," the theory generates important insights into the role of management in a capitalist economy, which is, in part, to extract labor from labor power. In neoclassical language, this means that the labor contract is incomplete. How hard and fast employees work, the exact conditions of work, the quality of work, etc. are not fully specified in the labor contract, or acquired in the purchase of labor power. Marxist theory focuses on the conflictual implications of this contingency. In contrast, neoclassical theory (general equilibrium theory, for example) often treats labor as if it were akin to a lump of coal, with the labor automatically released analogously to the BTUs combusted in coal. More realistic neoclassical models that recognize contingencies still tend to avoid images of conflict, preferring metaphors like non-zero sum games, and Pareto optimal outcomes to describe workplace dynamics.

Many Western economists sympathetic to the conclusions of the LTV about the potentially adversarial nature of the workplace and "extractive" function of management in capitalism, feel these insights can be obtained without most of the formal apparatus of the LTV. This is the case for neo-Ricardian theorists, institutionalist economists, and even many Marxist economists interested linking labor market analysis to historical materialism, class analysis, and the implications of labor power as a commodity,

The formal apparatus of the LTV links labor values to market prices and includes complicated adaptations for different kinds of goods. This apparatus and its adaptations to cover commodities like natural resources and skilled intellectual labor (such as computer software design) is thought flawed by some heterodox economists and cumbersome, at best, by many sympathetic critics, as it requires the construction of a discourse built around "labor values" alongside an analysis of prices. The creation of this parallel universe requires its own language, data collection, and conceptual categories. While potentially insightful in some respects, in a world where daily life is organized around market prices, detours into value categories tend to make it hard for Marxist analyses to gain popular attention. Once neoclassical economics became a commercial and media language, as well as the language of "high theory" for most of the world, it was harder and harder to argue for Marxist economic policies using the LTV. Western economists' disdain for the LTV, rather than mere criticism of the theory, also discouraged attention to it by younger Chinese economists.[9]

From the very beginning of economic reform there have been lively debates in China about the status and implications of the labor theory of value. In the late 1970s and early 1980s, leaders of the "adjustment" faction of economic reform (such as Chen Yun and Sun Yefang) appealed to the LTV (and its "Law of Value") to argue that relative prices should reflect relative costs of production (calculated in labor values) and income received should be based on labor performed (see Chapter 3).[10] Their chief opponents (such as the Shanghai school) held more Maoist ideas and favored freeing prices and income from a technically determined anchor of embodied labor (Brugger and Kelly 1990, 95–96).

In the mid-1980s debates over the LTV arose in the context of price reform. In this case the adjusters, such as Chen Yun, were battling more market oriented reformers, who wished to replace planned prices derived primarily from labor values, with market prices without reference to labor values. In 1983–1984, articles discussing market prices appeared in *Economic Research (Jingji Yanjiu)*. By 1986 Yu Guangyuan urged economists to " 'Put prices at the forefront and value at the rear' " (Hsu 1991, 149). As price reform proceeded, the labor theory of value received less and less attention.

Chinese economists who are defenders of the LTV continue to feel that relinquishing its language and unique angle of vision would make a neoclassical frame inevitable. This appears to be the perspective of some economists at Renmin University (interviews). The Chinese Communist Party also seems to believe that its legitimacy as a ruling party is partially bound up with the LTV and its particular theory of exploitation. It has thus been resistant to formally jettison the theory (interview). The Chinese state and Chinese Communist Party remain one of the few institutions large enough to support a robust alternative discourse to neoclassical economics. To date, they have taken only minor steps to sustain Marxist economics and analyses using the labor theory of value. A modest number of Marxist and neo-Ricardian theorists also continue to do research related to the LTV outside of China. A larger number of Western Marxists use the LTV as an informal heuristic to raise certain issues (like the distinction between labor and labor power). Without much more substantial intellectual investments, it is likely to remain a marginal discourse.

### 8.4.3 Western influences on Chinese economics education

The more advanced state of Western economies endowed Western economists with a degree of credibility in the eyes of Chinese leaders (Fang 2013, 301). Despite repeated expressions of concern about the ideological dimension of Western economics by some Chinese political leaders and economic theorists, the influence of Western voices of neoclassical economics constantly expanded in China's academic and policy circles. Much of this was due to the parallel expansion of market mechanisms, private property, and material incentives in the economy. As we have emphasized, this expansion reflected competitive pressures, which encouraged all firms and other economic units (such as local governments or households) to behave like capitalist firms. The key transition in Chinese political-economic life was the emergence of market dynamics as an imperative rather than an opportunity. This imperative created an audience for the official experts, interpreters, high priests, if you will, of the "market system." These academically and organizationally credentialed experts, from Nobel Laureates like Milton Friedman to World Bank officials, received increasing attention among Chinese officials responsible for organizing economic discussions.

From the start, China's economic reforms involved a guarded openness to Western economic theories. In January 1979, the 10th edition of Samuelson's introductory economics textbook was translated and published in China. It was the first complete Western economics principles (micro and macro) textbook published in China since 1949 (Fang 2013, 296). In April 1979, with the support of Party leaders, 17 Chinese economists who had majored in Western economics (presumably in the West) established the Chinese Association for Research on Foreign Economics [CARFE][11] (Fang 2013, 296, 305). Chen Daisun (Harvard PhD 1926) became CARFE's director. The Association organized introductory courses on Western economics for high-level Party members, including Zhao Ziyang (Sung and Chan 1987, 32).[12] Lecture notes were published in 1980 and 1981 and helped popularize Western economics (Fang 2013, 296).

In October 1979 a high powered group of US economists visited China. The same year a group of Chinese officials and academics visited business schools in the US and recommended that similar schools be set up in China (Warner 2014, 124). Deng was especially supportive of this initiative.

The host institution for the US economists' visit to China was the Chinese Academy of Social Sciences (CASS) which became a sympathetic venue for exploring liberal political-economic thought. The visit marked the renewal of Chinese economists' direct ties to the West. The symbolic legitimizing of neoclassical economics received a major boost in the fall of 1980 when, at the invitation of CASS, Milton Friedman lectured in several cities in China, including Beijing and Shanghai.[13] The audience appears to have been primarily invited government and party officials, and university economists (Friedman 1998, 520–522; Kwong 2006, 2). The Friedman invitation was a green light for popular investigation of Western economics.[14] It was not, however, a full endorsement of Western economics. The early "get acquainted" courses highlighted some useful ideas from Western economics but retained key Marxist subtexts and criticized Western economics for its pro-capitalist subtexts (Fang 2013, 299).[15]

Alongside enjoying support from the highest levels of the Chinese government (expressed through the Ministry of Education, CASS, major newspapers and periodicals, and other social institutions), neoclassical economic policies found allies among mid-level Party cadres who wished to transform their political capital into economic assets more easily transferable inter-generationally.

Young people interested in studying abroad and/or gaining access to relatively high paying jobs with foreign companies, were also attracted to Western (neoclassical) economics. Li Minqi indicates that Chicago oriented neoclassical theory already dominated the business school curriculum at Peking University by the late 1980s.[16] The popular appeal of Western business lore has lasted. Ethnographer Andrew Ross found that business books, followed by self-help books, were the most popular kind of Western literature among Shanghai's youth (Ross 2007a, 107).

Despite the continued use in the 1980s of economics textbooks in Chinese high schools that reflected the official views of Chinese Marxism,[17] Chinese high school students appeared to have absorbed much of the ideological overtones of neoclassical economics. For example, in 1989 students from four high schools in and around Beijing scored slightly higher than a control group of high school students from California on questions drawn from the US Test of Economic Literacy (Shen and Shen 1994, 283). The exam is based entirely on neoclassical economic teachings. Illustratively, nearly three-quarters of the Chinese students stated that "it is the social purpose of profits" to "get business to produce what consumers demand" versus only two-thirds of the California students (Shen and Shen 1994, 284).[18]

As noted in Chapter 2 there were also powerful external forces pressuring for the expansion of neoclassical economics in China, such as the World Bank, American Economic Association, and the Ford Foundation. The World Bank was probably the most important of these. The intellectual prestige of the World Bank, its potential line of credit to the Chinese government, and predictable support for the initial market oriented reforms favored by Deng encouraged Chinese leaders to allow the World Bank to do research in China. In the early 1980s the World Bank's detailed neoclassical analysis of the current state of the Chinese economy was permitted wide distribution in China. The project helped orient future discussions of China's economy. By the mid-1980s the spread of Western economics was taken to be the natural intellectual shadow of market reforms. For the next 30 years, the World Bank played a special role in shepherding Chinese economic thinking (especially in high-powered policy circles) in a neoclassical direction. The Bank's proselytizing for neoclassical economics seems to have been quite diplomatic and effective in gradually winning the confidence of its Chinese partners; quite the opposite of the more arrogant approach of the IMF with its clients.[19] The World Bank co-sponsored international conferences in China on TVEs (1985) and SOEs (1987) that were especially effective in integrating Chinese economists into World Bank led discussions. In 2013, a World Bank blueprint for the future of the Chinese economy, *China 2030*, was coauthored with a key think tank (the Development Research Center) of China's State Council (the rough equivalent of China's cabinet).[20]

In 1985 the Chinese Ministry of Education and the Ford Foundation established the economics exchange program that funneled Chinese economics students to US universities and US economists to Chinese universities. In the mid-1980s Professor Gregory Chow's summer institutes for the study of neo-classical economics enjoyed a high public profile and personal endorsement from China's Premier, Zhao Ziyang. In July of 1984, Chow met with Zhao and discussed economics education and economic reform. Pictures of the meeting were broadcast on China's TV news and appeared on the front page of the *People's Daily*, leading Professor Chow to judge that "The publicity signaled that China officially endorsed modern economics" (Chow 1988, 4). Chow also toured China "…as a guest of the Premier," talking with local leaders about economics (Chow 1988, 5).

Official Chinese opinion was not, however, unanimous in the mid-1980s. Despite legitimation at the very highest levels of state, a surprising amount of debate continued in the mass media. In December of 1985, for example, the *Beijing Review* published an article by Song Longxiang (under the pseudonym of Ma Ding) calling for more empirical content in economic analysis and a reassessment of past dismissals of Western economic theory. The article's criticism of Marxist economics spurred a large public controversy that was ultimately pacified by the intervention on Song's behalf of both Zhao Ziyang and Hu Yaobang (Goldman 1994, 160–163; Song, 1985, Brugger and Kelly 1990, 117).[21]

In 1987 the World Bank prepared a review of Chinese economics education. The conclusions were very critical of the dominance of economics education by Marxist theory. The report played a major role in the Ministry of Education's reorganization of the economics curriculum at Chinese universities (Rawski 1986; Chow 2000, 53). Western economics was added to the required course list and a committee was established to write economics textbooks that would be similar to those used in the US (Chow 2000, 53; Chow 1994, 50–51, Fang 2013, 298).

Fang reports that classes on Western economics were still supposed to retain a critical component. Quoting from two key Chinese translators and explicators of Western economics (Chen Daisun and Gao Hongye), Fang indicates that instructors were charged with explaining the useful ideas in neoclassical theory and exposing its ideological dimensions (Fang 2013, 298–299). The dominant public stance toward Western economics was that it was a synthesis of insight and ideology, requiring users to extract the "rational kernel" from the "vulgar" wrapping.[22] I suspect most Chinese students, like most American economics students today, eschewed attention to broader issues and simply struggled to learn the formalism of neoclassical theory.

Around 1986–1987, New Institutionalist economics (NIE) and Public Choice theory came to China. The schools were deeply infused with classical liberalism and found a ready audience among those interested in re-engineering Chinese institutions to be friendlier toward private property. Chicago school neoclassical economics and Austrian-libertarian economics were given a boost in 1988 by a highly publicized meeting between Milton Friedman and Zhao Ziyang. Friedman's visit was coordinated by Steven Cheung (Zhang Wuchang) whose personal reputation in China was also enhanced by the favorable publicity surrounding Friedman's meeting with Zhao.[23] Cheung promoted Austrian economics and New Institutionalist economics. After studying with Armen Alchian, Milton Friedman, and Ronald Coase, and teaching in the US for 13 years, Cheung returned to Hong Kong in the early 1980s. He was reputedly influential in revising Hong Kong's A-level economics exam[24] and wrote a prescient book in 1982 predicting that China would develop a capitalist economy. By the late 1980s Cheung had lectured at numerous mainland universities, the Chinese Academy of Social Sciences (10 hours of lectures on the theory of property rights)[25] and even at the Communist Party school in Beijing. Like the Chinese diaspora's early investment in the free-market oriented SEZs, Hong Kong's intellectual capital helped pave the way for the conversion of China's economics profession to neoclassical economics. Gregory Chow, for example, has emphasized the role played by many other Western trained economists at Hong Kong universities in Westernizing China's economics curriculum (Chow 2000, 57).[26]

I suspect Friedrich Hayek was quite popular in Hong Kong and Cheung was probably able to mobilize local support for the promotion of Hayek's classical liberal ideas on the mainland. Wang Hui has emphasized the impact of Hayek on Chinese neoliberalism (Wang 2003a, 27).[27] Xin Mao's essay in *Economic Research* (*Jingji Yanjiu*) indicates Hayek's ideas were important in challenging the viability of state-owned firms in the mid-1990s (Xin Mao1999, 48).[28] Shue Yan University in Hong Kong University hosted the 11th annual Hayek Society meeting in 2015.

The work of Coase, North, Buchanan and Mancur Olson has been especially influential in China. "Property rights" versions of NIE were especially important in the late 1980s and "principal-agent" versions popular in the 1990s.[29] While both lines of thinking emphasized the importance of competition for fostering economic efficiency, principal-agent theorists were relatively more agnostic about the short run need for rapid and complete privatization (Klaes and Zhang 2013, 261–268).

Classical liberals were quite successful in popularizing the idea that property rights were the basis of human rights. This Hayekian connection linked the struggle for democracy, civil liberties, and rule of law in China to support for privatization of state enterprises and limited government regulation of business. The rights discourse emphasized the rights of owners of firms to be free from state interference. The rights of workers to a job, to collective bargaining, to participatory management, and other aspects of the older notion of "workers as the masters of their enterprises" were de-emphasized, if mentioned at all.

The Coasean view of property rights reinforced the Hayekian "free society" argument for sanctifying private property with efficiency claims.[30] Underlying the entire edifice of Chinese liberalism was an implicit "Grand Kuznets Curve." The metaphor promised that economic growth coupled with private property would automatically address popular concerns about inequality, environmental pollution, the vitality of civil society, and the dangers of business misbehavior. The spread of classical liberal discourse also tended to shift historical understandings of the rise of capitalism from Marxist to New Institutionalist frameworks (see Chapter 4).

Klaes and Zhang find that the influence of property rights theorists ebbed in the 1990s. It was replaced by more formalistic neoclassical economic thinking, brought back to China by students who received their PhDs in the West (especially in the US) in the late 1980s (Klaes and Zhang 2013, 268). Regardless of distinctions, all three economic approaches (principal-agent theory, property rights theory, and mainstream general equilibrium theory) were undergirded by the subtexts of classical liberalism. Their practitioners may have differed in the pace or sequencing of events in an organized transition to capitalism, but not in their goal. Their frameworks helped create an intellectual landscape that made subsequent attention to Marxist theory difficult.

In the early 1990s, Deng's Southern Tour speeches encouraged further attention to Western economics. Partially because of their congeniality with Deng's free market oriented agenda, several Chicago School oriented theories received curricular attention, including: new classical economics, and monetarism, (Fang 2013, 301–302). The turn from economic planning to indirect management of the economy also stimulated interest in Keynesian macroeconomic theory.

Friedman's third visit to China in 1993 was highlighted by a meeting with China's President, Jiang Zemin. The meeting was taken as a public avowal of the government's continuing commitment to marketization, despite the crackdown at Tiananmen Square. There is a tradition in China of learning from venerated sages, and the symbolic endorsement of conservative economic theorists, such as Nobel Laureates Milton Friedman and Robert Lucas, may have shifted some of the weight of that tradition toward classical liberalism. One of my interviewees stressed that Chinese leaders during this period did not meet with leading Western Marxist economists.

Qian Yingyi and Wu Jinglian, two leading Western oriented economists in China, argue that by the early 1990s Western economics had replaced Soviet-style economics and greased the wheels for a transition to a market economy (Qian and Wu 2000, 11).

The expansion of neoclassical and new institutionalist economics and neoliberalism did not go unchallenged. In 1994, in response to academic controversy, the Ministry of Education (and the editorial board of *Front*) held three seminars on Western economics, which warned of the dangers of uncritical acceptance of Western economics. Chen Daisun repeated the same kind of warnings he had given at the beginning of CARFE's reassessment of Western economics in the 1980s (Fang 2013, 299–300, 302,). But for the most part, these warnings fell on deaf ears. The diffusion of neoclassical economics in the curriculum had by now normalized much of its paradigmatic outlook. Course titles changed from "Western economics" to simply "microeconomics" or "macroeconomics" with little critical commentary (Fang

2013, 302). The controversy subsided, not so much because of grand theoretical triumphs, like a refutation of Marxist theory of macro crises, or a rejection of Marxist analyses of financial markets, but rather because interest in larger paradigmatic issues had simply faded. Fang writes, "fewer scholars joined this kind of debate. … More attention was paid to the direct application of the theories and methods of Western economics…" (Fang 2013, 302).

By the turn of the century Western oriented microeconomics and macroeconomics classes were spreading across Chinese universities without critical commentary (Fang 2013, 302). The term "Western economics" was increasingly replaced by the term "modern economics." English language textbooks used in the US were also used in China.[31] The most popular authors according to Fang (2013) were: Mankiw; Samuelson and Nordhaus; Stiglitz; Nicholson; Varian; Dornbusch, Fischer and Startz; Mas-Colell; Romer; Mishkin; Krugman and Obstfeld; Rosen; and Kennedy (Fang 2013, 303). In June 2004, the *People's Daily* carried a picture of Wen Jiaobao meeting with conservative neoclassical economist Robert Lucas and other participants at an economics conference.

As neoclassical language pervaded economics instruction it spilled over into newspaper columns and official publications (Fang 2013, 303). As neoclassical economics expanded in university economics departments, Marxist theory shrank. The credit hours for Marxist political economy were reduced for students in economics and finance. Some compulsory political economy requirements were eliminated (Fang 2013, 302).

As in the early 1980s and mid-1990s, warning voices were again raised by Marxist theorists, in this case by Liu Guoguang, one of the most important Chinese reform economists. In 2005 Liu lamented that rather than selecting the useful aspects of Western economics and situating them within a Marxist frame, Chinese economists had allowed neoclassical economics to become the frame itself. In an interview with Heng Lin *circa* 2007, he criticized many Chinese economists for abandoning Marxism and socialism, lamenting, "they advocate … full privatization. … It's wrong to oppose reform, but it's worse to abandon socialism" (Liu, interview).

By 2007, in addition to requiring mainstream economics courses at Chinese universities, the Ministry of Education pushed for standardized exams based largely on Western oriented textbooks (Zhao 2010, 309). Zhao Haiyun reports:

> Mainstream economics, as currently taught in China, hardly differs from that offered in the west … (the) teaching plan and course design must be approved by the education department. Professors do not have discretion to change the course content. The exam method, content and answers are standardized. … And designated textbooks are, for the most part, western texts …
>
> (309)[32]

In 2007 there were 971,000 undergraduates in China specializing in economics and 3,614,000 specializing in management (Zhao 2010, 304). The combination represented about one quarter of all Chinese undergraduates and was second in popularity only to engineering (about a third of the student body). In 2007, about 5 percent of all graduating seniors specialized in economics in China (Ibid., 304).

Eventually, the content of Peking University's entrance exam (and presumably other universities as well) for graduate study in economics also shifted toward neoclassical theory.[33] This reorientation influenced undergraduate curricula as well as graduate student profiles. In 2007 there were 17,239 students enrolled in graduate economics programs in China, with about 13 percent of these in doctoral programs (Zhao 2010, 305).

## 8.5 A stage theory of intellectual diffusion

As noted above, with the endorsement of Chinese leaders, additional Western economic courses were added to many Chinese universities' curriculum in the early 1980s. We can situate this initiative in a stage theory of intellectual diffusion offered by Thomas Rawski in his study of Chinese economics education prepared for the World Bank in December of 1986. Although Rawski accepts the neoclassical narrative that explains the triumph of neoclassical economics as a result of its truth value, his discussion can also be used to illustrate a sociology of knowledge approach to understanding the changing status of neoclassical economics in China.

Rawski divides the acceptance process for Western economics into two phases. Phase one involves different degrees of skepticism and phase two, different degrees of embrace. He divides phase one into four steps:

1   "Complete neglect of western economics" (1950-mid-1960s).
2   "Critique … of western or 'capitalist' economics" (beginning in the mid-1960s).
3   "Adoption of specific technical tools" (also begun in the mid-1960s).
4   Historical analysis and "detailed scrutiny … as a prelude to selecting segments of western economics seen as suitable for application to Chinese conditions" (Rawski 1986, 32–33).

Rawski finds China to be in step 4, circa 1986 (Rawski 1986, 35). He presciently lays out several additional steps that had yet to occur in China that were necessary for the development of neoclassical economics as a dominant paradigm. Linking these steps to a sociology of knowledge perspective (something Rawski does not do), they call for

5   Situating analyses of particular economic issues against a backdrop of an integrated system of supply and demand (general equilibrium theory in a loose rather than technical sense).

6   The co-existence of neoclassical economics as a general approach (rather than an eclectic tool kit) for analyzing economic questions, alongside alternative approaches (or paradigms), such as Marxist theory.

7   A "normalizing" of neoclassical economics and its language as the theoretical spectacles worn by Chinese economists. In the language of "texts and subtexts" (which is not Rawski's language), normalization requires that economic outcomes be automatically situated in students' minds against a backdrop of micro foundations and general equilibrium theory, and, further, that economic thinking be animated by neoclassical subtexts (such as the rationality and optimality of perfect market prices).

8   The elimination of alternative paradigms as viable options in economics discussions or economics education. The co-existence of Marxist and neoclassical economics, rather than the immediate perception of the economy in neoclassical terms, would indicate the incomplete development of neoclassical economics as a dominant paradigm.

### 8.5.1 Creating a scientific community

While domestic curricular changes were important in reshaping Chinese economics education in the 1980s, the selection of the "best and brightest" Chinese graduate students for participation in Western led neoclassical economics workshops in China and enrollment in PhD programs in the West were the most influential events of the decade. The doctoral programs "intellectually socialized" Chinese students and initiated them into the neoclassical scientific community. It is these students who eventually reorganized Chinese economics departments. While there were some "self-taught" neoclassical economists in China (Rawski 1986, 27), their ability to shift the economics imagination in China would likely have been limited in the absence of returning foreign trained PhDs. This is because one does not simply "study" neoclassical economics, one *becomes* a neoclassical economist. In some ways, it is like becoming a doctor or a lawyer. It involves a process of socialization and identity formation that entails more than purely cognitive skills. Rawski's account, I believe, implies this without explicitly stating it. In describing one of the latter stages of intellectual diffusion, he writes: "A further stage of reform comes with the introduction of western economics into the core undergraduate curriculum … the clear expectation is that students will *'internalize' western concepts as part of their own basic intellectual equipment*" [emphasis added] (1986, 34). One does not generally talk about internalizing algebra or making accounting part of one's basic intellectual equipment, but one *does* talk about internalizing world views and subtexts. Rawski adds, "students exposed to this approach will, like their counterparts in the US or Japan, *instinctively* (emphasis added) reach for such methods as cost-benefit … to assess alternative technologies" (1986, 34). The attempt to re-express all dimensions of an issue in terms of monetized values (either actual market prices or shadow prices) is one of the quintessential characteristics of neoclassical policy analysis.

Another way of describing the paradigm shift in Chinese economics is to characterize it as a linguistic shift. Deng and other economic reformers initially used Marxist terminology to express ideas about economic restructuring. Phrases like "practice is the sole criterion of truth," "the primary stage of socialism," the planned commodity economy," and "socialism with Chinese characteristics," were deployed to enable market-building projects. Overtime the language of "utility" maximization, "equilibrium prices," "Pareto Optimal outcomes," and "average rates of profit" replaced the vocabulary of "labor values," "planned proportional development," and "rates of exploitation." Eventually the project of expanding markets evolved into constructing capitalism. Overtime neoclassical language dissolved the intellectual framework that Marxism offered for understanding capitalism and thinking about socialism.

The progression reminds one of Marx's remarks in the *Eighteenth Brumaire of Louis Bonaparte*,

> a beginner who has learnt a new language always translates it back into his mother tongue, but he has assimilated the spirit of the new language and can freely express himself in it only when he finds his way in it without recalling the old and forgets his native tongue in the use of the new.
>
> (Liu 2004, 52) [34]

Contemporary economists in China have lost their Marxist tongue.

Coase and Wang write about similar phenomena in terms of people assuming new identities. They argue that a major prerequisite for economic restructuring was the casting off of a collective socialist identity and embrace of a capitalist identity. While they are asserting this principle culturally, it is especially true more narrowly for the economics profession (Coase and Wang 2013, 97). The shift can also be understood in terms of the embrace of different subtexts.

### 8.5.2 Shifting editorial policies at leading economic journals

As in the United States, control of the editorial policies of the leading journals is central to control of the economics discipline in China. My interviews suggest that there is some debate over how to rank Chinese journals. Among the top three appear to be: *Economic Research* (*Jingji Yanjiu*), *World Economy* (*Shijie Jingji*), and *Chinese Social Science* (*Zhongguo Shehui Kexue*).[35] The latter journal has a broader scope than just economics, but is an important journal for economic analysis.

Currently, a publication in a leading Western neoclassical journal, such as the *American Economic Review*, seems to be taken as equivalent, or perhaps, even superior to the tier-one Chinese journals. Much less "credit" is given for publications in Western heterodox economics journals not indexed in the

Social Science Citation Index (SSCI). The latter tends to be weighted toward neoclassical journals. Chinese critics of the current journal ranking system have described it as SSCI fetishism, coining the backronym SCI or "Stupid Chinese Index." Some observers have also claimed that Marxist oriented journals, such as *Science and Society*, which are indexed in the SSCI are given less weight in Chinese faculty assessment.[36]

*Economic Research* (*ER*) (*Jingji Yanjiu*) appears to be the leading economics journal in China. Publication in its pages is a de facto requirement for promotion to full professor. Because of its significant role in the Chinese economics profession, we will dwell a bit on its history. Before 1978, *ER* emphasized Marxist scholarship and relatively non-mathematical research. Song estimates that from 1978 to 1987, *ER* "published more than 1000 papers, but only 15 of them were on mathematical economics" (Song 1995, 154). Beginning around 1992 and accelerating in the mid-1990s, the proportion of Marxist articles declined significantly. By the early 2000s the journal accepted few Marxist papers. Several Marxist professors who had published articles in *ER* previously told me they no longer submitted their research to the journal. Since 1998, *ER* has been edited by Liu Shucheng, an econometrician. His editorial policy heavily favored econometric articles relying on neoclassical assumptions. Paraphrasing one of my interviewees, Professor Zhou Yi of Fudan University, Marxist frames no longer fit the standard "assembly line for 'manufacturing' an economics paper." The template now is: literature review; adoption of an econometric model from a Western mainstream economics source; the plugging in of Chinese data; and deployment of common econometric techniques (panel data analysis being faddish), using standard computer software. If the result is consistent with mainstream expectations, the author celebrates mainstream economic theory and analytic techniques. If the result is anomalous, the author suggests that conditions in China differ from those built into the model and notes the need for further research. Malcolm Warner has made a similar observation about Chinese academia, lamenting "[a] good deal of academic research is often replication, particularly in the social sciences" (Warner 2014, 111).

The tendency for empirical work in economics to serve a "confirmatory" function rather than test an hypothesis has been stressed by McCloskey, who writes,

> Simulation is affirmative, not falsifying, asking whether one can make a case for such-and-such, not whether one can prove it wrong. … In economics … econometrics amounts to simulation. The doubting and falsifying method, enshrined in the official version of econometric method, is largely impractical.
>
> (McCloskey 1985, 14)

In other words, the neoclassical model invites practitioners to operationalize it with Chinese data. If the results conform to the paradigm's subtexts they are accepted. If they conflict with popular subtexts, I suspect they are harshly interrogated and less energy invested in that line of inquiry. This is an hypothesis, however: I have not reviewed the literature to confirm it. The popular reception given Justin Yifu Lin's 1992 paper linking the Household Responsibility System to increases in agricultural productivity and the reluctance to give social attention to alternative interpretation of the reasons for the growth in agricultural output is consistent with this hypothesis. Xu Zhun, an Assistant Professor at Renmin University in Beijing doing research on the Household Responsibility Systems, has written interesting papers pulling together evidence for a counter narrative to the miracle of private property interpretation of the expansion of agricultural output in the early 1980s.[37]

To Marxist and some neoclassical observers, *Economic Research*'s acceptance policy also showcases advanced econometric technique over substantive discussion. The journal appears to have situated itself with reference to business research rather than social science and Marxist projects. In a study of citing frequencies, Zhou et al. indicate that the "cited environment of the *Economic Research Journal* involves journals in economics, management, finance, accounting, and statistics" (Zhou et al. 2010, 28).

*ER* is published by the Chinese Academy of Social Sciences. It is edited by the director of the Institute of Economics. When I asked Chinese economists how the editorial policy was changed and who was responsible, I got the impression that the shift reflected broad forces, rather than the decisions of a single individual. While there certainly were pressures from the very top of China's authority structure (e.g., from Zhao Ziyang and Zhu Rongji[38]), many other forces were pushing in the same direction. Among these were: recommendations from the World Bank, AEA, and other global voices of mainstream neoclassical economics; pressures from returning Chinese graduates of foreign economics programs; and lobbying by new, neoclassical oriented think tanks. The result was that, even when the editor of *ER* was personally sympathetic to Marxist economic theory (unlike the recent period), he oversaw a review process that limited Marxist publications.

The Chinese ranking system of Western journals seems to rely on rankings based on the Thompson Reuters' SSCI. For Chinese journals (I am not sure this applies to the top four journals) departments seem to rely on the Chinese Social Science Citation Index developed by Nanjing University around the year 2000.

Reinforcing the selection bias of some leading Chinese journals has been the tendency for research funding in economics departments to be tilted toward neoclassical theory.[39]

### 8.5.3 *Final steps*

In sum, many separate changes set the stage for the consolidation of neoclassical economic theory's control of economics education in China. Among these were: changes in the curriculum at the graduate and undergraduate level, changes in the entrance exams for graduate study, changes in the editorial policies of leading journals and the criteria for academic promotion, changes in research funding, and changes in job market credentialing. Shifts in all of these areas gradually promoted neoclassical economics. However, the consolidation of neoclassical theory as a hegemonic paradigm, that is, one that crowds out attention to other ways of thinking rather than merely being the dominant way of thinking among recognized competing approaches, required the return to China of enough Western-socialized (and mostly American) PhDs to create a reproducing hegemonic community.[40] This did not begin to happen until the twenty-first century. The process is not totally complete and the intellectual terrain remains partially contested.

Like Rawski's observations in the mid-1980s, Song Longxiang's assessment of Chinese economics in the mid-1990s depicted a fluid situation with competing perspectives. Song (pen name Ma Ding) was an enthusiastic advocate of Western economics and lamented that neoclassical theory was not yet hegemonic. He treats neoclassical economics as a science, Marxist economics as metaphysics, and heterodox economics as irrelevant. He writes:

> Chinese economics has not been well institutionalized ... compared with Western mainstream economics ... [where] significant consensus on the fundamental principles has already been achieved. ... Indeed no dominant paradigm in the professional community shows that Chinese economics is still at the stage of transition from ideology to science.
>
> (Song 1995, 150–151)

The fluid situation that Song lamented was to rigidify during the early years of the twenty-first century. How that change occurred is the subject of the next chapter.

## Notes

1 Lin indicates that the whole discipline of economics was attacked for economism, adding that the charges initially focused on CASS, but "[e]ventually the attack ... was widened to include the professional economists and planners..." (Lin 1981, 36).

2 The Shanghai Academy of Social Sciences was founded in 1958, earlier than most other think tanks. Many of the *World Economic Herald's* senior advisors were key economic reformers associated with CASS or other Beijing government institutions. Among these advisors were Ma Hong, Xue Muqiao, Yu Guangyuan, Qian Junrui, and Xu Dixin (Li and White 1991, 348). The newspaper seems to have been especially fascinated with the work of Alvin Toffler (Li and White 1991, 361). The staff's technocratic outlook probably meshed well with the self-presentation of most neoclassical economists.

3 Chen Yun, for example, advocated the greater use of markets in agriculture, commerce and parts of light industry for decades. He criticized Chinese development plans for excessive investment rates and over-emphasis on heavy industry investment. He supported expanded use of material incentives in agriculture and price premiums for higher quality goods and changes in production conditions. All of

these market-oriented policies, however, were situated within a Marxist framework.

Ma Hong's *New Strategy for China's Economy* (1983, especially Chapter II: "Towards a Rational Economic Structure") relies heavily on the language of "rationality," and includes most of the concerns found in the neoclassical accounts noted above, beginning with his prioritizing of economic efficiency, rather than "taking class struggle as the key link." Ma criticizes Chinese economic policy for: excessive rates of accumulation, excessive investment in heavy industry, insufficient investment in agriculture, light industry, and housing, suppression of the service sector, excessive attempts at regional self-sufficiency and national autarky, and insufficient use of market feedback for resolving potential supply and demand imbalances. He concludes, "...our present economic structure is irrational in many respects..." (34). Much the same argument is made by Zhang, Zhuoyuan (1982).

Ma also shares the neoclassical faith in the fruitfulness of economic incentives. He favors vastly increased autonomy for economic enterprises in terms of decision making and responsibility for profits and losses. He criticizes past Chinese policies for premature leaps to communist rather than socialist principles of distribution, favoring payment according to work over "the iron rice bowl" and "common pot."

Despite this overlap with many aspects of neoclassical thinking, Ma holds on to many of the goals of socialism and communism. He endorses state or worker ownership of the means of production, seems to support distribution based on labor, favors a combination of economic planning and market allocation, and expresses concern about the ideological feedback from market competition and the pursuit of self-interest. His analysis suggests serious prior engagement with Marxist writings and rejection of Western capitalism as the long run goal of Chinese policy. He writes, for example,

> Ideological work must be strengthened when the responsibility system is carried out. Only by means of vigorous ideological work which is related to the actual thinking of the workers and staff members can their socialist consciousness be continuously raised. Thus, they can struggle against such unhealthy trends as seizing every chance to seek private gain at the expense of the collective.
>
> (109)

It is hard to imagine this paragraph flowing from a neoclassical pen.

The major lacuna in *New Strategy* is the text's failure to grapple with the question of whether the package of market oriented reforms favored by Ma creates a powerful dynamic that inevitably carries the economy toward concentrated private ownership of the means of production and capitalism in other dimensions of political and social life.

4 Marxist economists Sun Yefang and Liu Guoguang, for example, set up a Research Group for Quantitative Economics ~1960, which later became the Institute of Quantitative and Technical Economics. Liu also helped organize courses on quantitative economics by Nobel Prize winner Lawrence Klein in the early 1980s (Liu Guoguang, Heng Lin interview, 9).

5 The subtexts of each paradigm determine the rhythms of debate confined within each paradigm. Neoclassical macroeconomic subtexts, for example, generate cycles of return to notions of automatic equilibrium, ranging from classical theory to Keynesian theory, and back again to new classical theory; from Ricardian equivalencies to Phillips curves and back again to rational expectations theory; from the Pigou effect (and deflation as a guarantor of full employment) to Samuelson's demand gaps, and back again to real business cycle theory.

On the micro level, neoclassical notions of rationality and optimality oscillate between laissez-faire strong and laissez-faire lite. Factors are paid their marginal product and "efficient markets" call for financial de-regulation, followed by financial collapse and re-regulation in anticipation of the next de-regulation. In transitional economies "shock therapy" gives way to "gradualism," awaiting the next visit from Chicago economists.

Alternatively, Marxist subtexts have macroeconomic cycles of return to "crisis theory;" wages are too high-leading to wage-profit squeezes, or wages are too low, leading to under-consumption problems; capitalism is prone to stagnation, or capitalism is relentless in delivering economic growth that will explode our environmental envelope.

At the micro level, on the shop floor: rising exploitation leads to labor organizing, subverted by false consciousness, broken through by vanguard parties, disarmed by hegemonic discourse, renewed by globalization. The anticipated challenge to capitalism shifts from the proletariat in the advanced countries, to the peasantry in the developing world, to the professional managerial class in the advanced countries, to the proletariat in the third world, to the inability of capitalist social relations of production in the first world to fully mobilize the forces of production in an information based economy, to the environmental challenge in the third world as capitalism spreads across the globe, etc.

6 Karrie Koesel has done interesting research on the changing focus of the questions on the national college entrance exam (the "*gaokao*"). She finds, "by the late 1980s there is a shift away from class struggle toward a wider range of topics, including economics..." (Koesel 2015, 1). Using computer assisted content analysis of the politics section of the exam, she finds that after 1999 economics questions are the second largest subject matter (Ibid., 12). Even more interesting is the dramatic increase in questions on entrepreneurship, which leap from zero before 1980 to 12–32 percent of all economics questions after 2000 (13, Table 4).

7 Herschede 1985, 304; Halpern 1989, 25. These shifts are treated somewhat differently by Western observers. When Marxist economics replaced Western economics, Western trained economists (in Nina Halpern's words) were required to undergo "a process of 'thought reform' aimed at resocializing them to accept Marxist ideas" (Halpern 1989, 25). When neoclassical economics replaced Marxist economics, there was also "the personnel problem of retraining existing economics teachers and researchers and convincing them to accept modern economics..." (Chow 2002, 360).

8 This characterization should not be taken too far. China had its own version of educational decentralization. While the Ministry of Education's oversight of the elite universities in China was greater than the Department of Education's influence over elite US universities, there were many other institutions of higher education in China that were much more independent of the MoE, such as institutions run by government ministries and local governments. Interestingly, many of these institutions were much more subordinate to the training needs of employers (often government agencies) than the MoE. Rawski argues that this tended to impart a narrow vocational emphasis to higher education and militated against large investments in neoclassical theory and abstract models.

9 Robert Hsu's remarks are typical here. He writes, "A Marxist theory that has profoundly influenced Chinese economics is the labor theory of value. This theory is considered analytically invalid and operationally meaningless in the West, but it has been the theoretical foundation of China's price theory" (Hsu 1991, 4).

10 For a long time, the language of the LTV had been integrated into the official discourse of the state. From July 1978–January 1979, for example, numerous conferences and seminars were held in different cities in China focused on the implications of the law of value. These discussions culminated in the Wuxi

conference in April 1979 which helped redefine the relationship between the plan and market in China, giving greater scope to market forces (Sung and Chan 1987, 33).

11 It appears that CARFE was initially called the Association for the Study of Bourgeois Economic Theory or at least evolved from that group ((Sung and Chan 1987, 33). CARFE was commissioned by the Leading Group of Economic Theory and Methodology of the Fiscal and Economic Commission of the State Council (Fang 2013, 296).

12 Chen Daisun depicted Western economics as having both useful aspects and ideological apologetics for capitalism (Fang 2013, 297).

13 Fang indicates that the invitation to Friedman came from Qian Junrui, a former director of one of CASS's research institutes.

14 Fang confirms Friedman's impression that his visit spurred the translation of more Western economics textbooks and monographs, as well as articles about Western economics, giving a boost to the teaching of Western economics (Fang 2013, 296–297). Friedman's ideas gained additional attention from the influential *World Economic Herald* newspaper (Li and White 1991, 353).

15 Chen Daisun, for example, warned against absorbing the "apologetic functions" of Western economics (Fang 2013, 297). Gao Hongye stressed the need to "consider the politics in Western economics" (Fang 2013, 299).

16 Li Minqi: "Tiananmen Square," (http://johnshaplin.blogspot.com/2009/05/tiananmen-square-by-minqui-li.html, accessed December 26, 2013).

17 The three texts cited in the article were: *Economic Common Sense* (*Jing Ji Chang Shi*) published by Beijing Normal University in 1987 and 1988; a second text with the same name used in Tianjin, and the 4th edition of *Political Economy* (*Zhen-zhi Jing Ji Xue*), a college text widely used in universities in Southern China that also served as a reference book for high school economics courses (Shen and Shen 1994, 275).

18 In an earlier article about the same survey, the authors report that 61 percent of the Chinese high school students queried (compared with 64 percent of US students) felt private property was either a natural right or was needed to promote economic incentives (Shen and Shen 1993, 79). Summing up the image of Chinese high school students conveyed in their interpretation of the survey responses, the authors conclude "One might even describe them as natural capitalists" (Shen and Shen 1993, 79). Reflecting the Classical Liberal tone of the article, they close by arguing, "The conclusion that economic man is universal is unavoidable" (Shen and Shen 1994, 286).

19 See for example, Joseph Stiglitz, "What I learned at the World Economic Crisis," *New Republic* April 17, 2000.

20 The *Economist* reported that China's new premier, Le Keqiang, apparently helped arrange cooperation between the Bank and the Development Research Center (*Economist* February 28, 2012, www.economist.com/blogs/analects/2012/02/china-and-world-bank, accessed December 23, 2013).

21 Interestingly Merle Goldman indicates that Song's article, published in the *Workers' Daily*, did not initially generate controversy. Only after an editorial in a New York City Chinese language paper attacked the piece, did serious criticism arise in China. Deng Liqun and Hu Qiaomu attacked the article. Chen Yun called for increased emphasis on ideological education (explaining Marxism, a sympathetic interpretation of Chen's position, increased indoctrination from Goldman's point of view). Zhao Ziyang reportedly urged "caution" "in criticizing theoretical liberalism." Allies of Hu Yaobang defended the article. Yu Guangyuan, a leading CASS political economist who had helped Deng prepare his key reform speech at the 11th National Congress in 1978, also defended the article and urged increased study of Western economics (Goldman 1994, 160–162; Vogel 2011, xv).

22 Unsurprisingly, this stance (which finds both "scientific merit" and ideological nonsense in neoclassical economics) has persisted in China. In a March 12, 2015 article in the *People's Daily*, for example, the Dean of Economics at Renmin University argued, "It's undeniable that Western economics contains scientific knowledge. … But it also contains strong ideology … (and) economic hypotheses … which clearly favour the capitalist system … (S)o how can they be expected to accurately explain China's economy." ("Why Western Economics Fails to Explain China's Economy," March 22, 2015 *Sinocism* newsletter (https://chiecon.wordpress.com/2015/03/22/why-western-economics-fails-to-explain-chinas-economy-translation-5/, accessed December 26, 2015).

23 Steven Cheung (Chinese name Zhang, Wuchang) accompanied Friedman during his meeting with Zhao Ziyang. His description of the meeting is instructive. He writes,

> The meeting between Zhao and Friedman went off remarkably well … afterwards the Secretary General walked all the way to the car, and opened the door for us. Because this was the first time Zhao had made such a gesture to outsiders, stories about the meeting spread all over Beijing…
> Cheung, First Annual Arnold C. Harberger Distinguished Lecture, UCLA Nov. 17, 1997, 4). (www.pauldeng.com/pdf/stevencheung/deng.pdf, accessed November 4, 2011)

24 Cheung taught at the University of Hong Kong for many years and was the director of the School of Economics and Finance from 1992–2000. Wikipedia credits him with shaping the A-level exam without citing a source for the claim. Tian Guoqiang, a leading contemporary Chinese economist (see section 2.3.3) reports, "For our generation, the most important thinker is Zhang Wuchang. His book influenced me greatly" (Zhou 2006, 43).

25 Friedman 1990a, 98.

26 Chow indicates that Hong Kong economists helped Chinese universities redesign their curriculum. He notes that the Hong Kong University of Science and Technology has an American curriculum and American trained faculty (Chow 2000), and implies that other Hong Kong universities have similarly contributed to the "modernization" of Chinese economics. The Hong Kong Economic Association (a consortium organized by seven Hong Kong universities) publishes the *Pacific Economic Review*. The journal's editorial board has a preponderance of US economists. The Association has also overseen a biennial economics conference since the year 2000. Many of these seven universities also sponsor regular economics conferences. The City University of Hong Kong (which portrays itself as a champion of economic reform) hosts the ACE conference (All China Economics conference) and the Chinese University of Hong Kong hosts the CCE Conference (Conference on the Chinese Economy). The Hong Kong University of Science and Technology co-sponsors the China Economic Summer Institute. The Hong Kong Institute for Monetary Research (HKIMR) organizes regular conferences on monetary and macro economic issues. (Hong Kong conference information derived from "Resources for Economists," conference listing web site as well as specific schools' websites.) In the mid-1980s many associations were set up in China to study the Hong Kong economy. John Greenwood reports, "I have met with several representatives of those associations. … [T]hese Chinese economists emphasize the desirability of importing *management* and *technology* (italics in original) from Hong Kong" (Dorn and Xi 1990, 273).

Singapore may have played a similar, though much smaller role, in organizing conferences and ferrying free market ideas into China. The National University of Singapore, for example, held an important international conference on *China: the Next Decade* in 2007 (Yang and Zhao, 2009, viii).

27 Wang Hui indicates that Hayek's ideas gained readership in the late 1980s and even wider popularity in China around 1998 (Wang 2003b, 60, 83). Li Minqi argues that from 1980–1985 dissident intellectuals organized their critiques of current Chinese policies within a Marxist framework. Activists called for more democracy without questioning the legitimacy of socialism. After 1985 there was a turn toward the free market ideology of Hayek and Friedman (Li Minqi 2008, xi). Hayek's ideas came to China through political scientists, like Liu Junning (hosted by the Cato Institute in 1999) (*Cato Policy Report* 11–12/1999, 21(6)) as well as economists like Steven Cheung.

Liu reports an increase in attention to classical liberalism beginning in 1998. This interest was reflected in the spread of campus reading groups on classical liberalism and a sellout of the first printing of Hayek's *The Constitution of Liberty* (Liu Junning 2000).

More recently, Xia Yeliang, the Peking University economics professor fired in 2013, perhaps for political activism, but officially for inadequate teaching evaluations and substandard research, listed Hayek, among "his intellectual idols" (David Feith, "Xia Yeliang, The China Americans Don't See," *Wall Street Journal* October 25, 2013). In the spring of 2014, I interviewed a professor at Tsinghua University, who was an excited member of an inter-disciplinary study group. One of the two current books they were reading was Hayek's *Road to Serfdom*. The 11th annual meeting of the Chinese Hayek society was held in 2015 in Hong Kong.

28 Interestingly, Hayek's ideas also gained attention from He Qinglian and Zhu Xueqin's attack on crony capitalism in He's 1998 book *The Pitfalls of Modernization* (Liu 2004, 72–73).

29 Klaes and Zhang 2013, 259–269; Huang 2009a, 420–423.

30 Marx's theory of property rights is very different from Coase's theory, illustrating once again the framing impact of paradigms. Marx's theory is not about the ownership of consumer goods like clothes, cars, or even private homes. It is about the ownership of enterprises. Marx's distinctive claim is that property in this context involves social relationships. Property rights confer the ability to control labor and dictate the organization of work. This is the basis for Marx's otherwise odd sounding claim that "capital" (the ownership of real and financial assets) "is a social relation" (rather than a thing or object).

Illustrating the extent to which liberal discourse has organized economic discussion in China, Wang et al. (2008) note that from January 1, 1994–August 23, 2004 "there were 15,756 articles with the key term 'property rights' published in Chinese journals." Of these, the majority discussed Coase's theory of property rights, with only 74 including the term "Marxist property rights" (Wang et al. 2008, 59).

31 Tang Shouning of the Unirule Institute reinforces these conclusions, writing, "nearly all of the economic textbooks are American or British … (making it) inevitable that Chinese economists become, in a sense, Americanized or Britonized…" (Tang 2000, 2).

32 Zhao indicates that popular economics textbooks in China include, *Western Economics* by Gao Hongye, Mankiw's *Principles of Economics* and Pindyck and Rubinfeld's *Microeconomics* (Zhao 2010, 309). The transplanting of neoclassical economics took place very quickly at some leading educational institutions. Li Minqi was a student in the Economic Management Department of Beijing University 1987–1990. He indicates that neoclassical theory already dominated the department's economics curriculum, along with the paradigm's subtext that

only a free market economy with clarified private property rights and 'small government' can solve all economic and social problems rationally and efficiently.

... Thus, for China to have any chance to catch up with the West ... it had to follow the free market capitalist model.

(Li Minqi 2008, x)

33 There are four exams for students applying to Peking University's graduate economics program. The exams cover: microeconomics, macroeconomics, econometrics, and political-economy. The latter subject matter consists largely of questions about official government economic policy (interview with Peking University professor).

The micro and macro exams are based on courses taught in Peking University's undergraduate program. They are written by the professors currently teaching these courses, but the exams have become pretty standardized and do not change much from year to year. The opportunity to write these exams is based on seniority among the current instructors of these classes.

There is a special website for preparation material for the exams. Students often buy textbooks written by the Peking University professors writing the exams, and buy lecture notes from Peking University students in these courses.

One of my interviewees thought that SUFE's graduate entrance exam did not include questions on Marxist economics.

34 The source for the Marxist quote cited by Liu Kang is: Karl Marx, 1963 [1852] *The Eighteenth Brumaire of Louis Bonaparte*, 15–16 (New York: International Publishers).

35 Assessing the influence of academic journals is somewhat subjective. Different economists and different methodologies can produce varied results. A list of elite journals based on Zhou et al.'s (2010) citation web would include *Economic Research, Management World,* and *World Economy* and would add: *Journal of Finance Research, Journal of Quantitative and Technical Economics,* and *Finance and Trade Economy,* and *China Industrial Economy.*

Another list I was given by a senior scholar at Fudan University included *Economic Research, World Economy,* and the *Journal of Chinese Social Science, Financial Research, Research in Quantitative Economy and Technical Economy* [probably an alternative translation of the *Journal of Quantitative and Technical Economics*], *China Industrial Economy, Accounting Research, Economic Science, China's Agricultural Economy, International Economic Review,* and *China Countryside Outlook.*

36 See the *Heterodox Economics Newsletter* Issue 92 (December 16, 2009) for Fred Lee's discussion of the selection bias in the SSCI. (www.heterodoxnews.com/n/htn92.htm) In the commentary, Lee describes the problems faced by heterodox economists in Spain, but the same analysis would apply to Chinese heterodox economists. He writes,

> The pressure to publish in SSCI economic journals means that Spanish heterodox economists do not have the luxury of sending their papers to non-SSCI economics journals. ... Initially any SSCI publication was fine, but [now] ... only the top 50% are counted—which means that publications in the CJE, JEI, JPKE, and the AJES ... are not really recognized as acceptable research.

37 As noted in Chapter 4, Lin's 1992 paper was the most cited reference appearing in the *China Economic Review,* the journal of the Chinese Economist Society, 1989–2010 (Du, Yuxin 2011, 33). For criticism of Lin's position see Xu 2012, 2013, and Riskin 1987, 297–298, 314.

38 One of my interviewees, for example, believed that Zhu Rongji had personally intervened in the governance of Tsinghua University and overridden resistance to the appointment of Qian Yingyi as Dean of Tsinghua's School of Economics and Management. I have no independent collaboration of this impression.

39 Interview.

40 The fascinating intellectual and professional journey of Zhang Fengbo is an exception that proves the rule. Zhang was the first Chinese national to receive a post war economics PhD from a Japanese university (~1986). His study of economics was apparently celebrated by reports in the *People's Daily* (Zhang 2008, 13). He returned to China in the latter half of the 1980s and lectured at leading universities. He also led some major economic research projects for several government bodies. He left China in 1988 after an invitation from Martin Feldstein to affiliate with the NBER and Harvard University. For reasons not fully elaborated, he remained in the United States and eventually went to work for the Takenaka Corporation, a large Japanese company interested in the US real estate market. I suspect that the Tiananmen Square violence and opportunities for moneymaking in the US influenced his decision to remain in the States.

# References

Brugger, Bill, and David Kelly. 1990. *Chinese Marxism in the Post-Mao Era*. Stanford, CA: Stanford University Press.

Chow, Gregory. 1988. *Teaching Economics and Studying Economic Reform in China (Econometric Research Program Research Memorandum no. 339)*. Princeton, NJ: Princeton Econometric Research Program.

Chow, Gregory. 1994. *Understanding China's Economy*. Hong Kong: World Scientific.

Chow, Gregory. 2000. "The Teaching of Modern Economics in China." *Comparative Economic Studies* 42 (2): 51–60. doi:10.1057/ces.2000.8.

Chow, Gregory. 2002. *China's Economic Transformation*. Malden, MA: Blackwell.

Coase, Ronald, and Ning Wang. 2013. *How China Became Capitalist*. New York: Palgrave Macmillan.

Dorn, James A., and Wang Xi, eds. 1990. *Economic Reform in China: Problems and Prospects*. Chicago, IL: University of Chicago Press.

Du, Yuxin. 2011. "A Bibliometrics Portrait of Chinese Research through the Lens of *China Economic Review*." Master's thesis, Universidade do Porto.

Fang, Fuqian. 2013. "The Changing Status of Western Economics in China." In *Thoughts on Economic Development in China*, edited by Ying Ma and Hans-Michael Trautwein, 295–305. New York: Routledge.

Friedman, Milton. 1990a. *Friedman in China*. Hong Kong: Chinese University Press.

Friedman, Milton, and Rose Friedman. 1998. *Two Lucky People: Memoirs*. Chicago, IL: University of Chicago Press.

Goldman, Merle. 1994. *Sowing the Seeds of Democracy in China: Political Reform in the Deng Xiaoping Era*. Cambridge, MA: Harvard University Press.

Goldman, Merle. 2005. *From Comrade to Citizen: The Struggle for Political Rights in China*. Cambridge, MA: Harvard University Press.

Halpern, Nina P. 1989. "Policy Communities in a Leninist State: The Case of the Chinese Economic Policy Community." *Governance: An International Journal of Policy and Administration* 2 (1): 23–41.

Herschede, Fred. 1985. "Economics as an Academic Discipline at Nanjing University." *The China Quarterly* (102): 304–316. doi:10.1017/S0305741000029969.

Hsu, Robert C. 1991. *Economic Theories in China 1979–1988*. New York: Cambridge University Press.

Huang, Philip C. C. 2009a. "China's Neglected Informal Economy: Reality and Theory." *Modern China* 35 (4): 405–438. doi:10.1177/0097700409333158.

Huang, Yasheng. 2008. *Capitalism with Chinese Characteristics: Entrepreneurship and the State*. New York: Cambridge University Press.

Keyser, Catherine. 2003. *Professionalizing Research in Post-Mao China: The System Reform Institute and Policymaking*. Armonk, NY: M. E. Sharpe.

Klaes, Matthias, and Yi Zhang. 2013. "Chinese Reform and Schools of Thought in Western Economics." In *Thoughts on Economic Develoopment in China*, edited by Ying Ma and Hans-Michael Trautwein, 255–273. New York: Routledge.

Koesel, Karrie. 2015. *Learning to be Loyal: Political Education in China*. Paper Delivered at the 2015 Meetings of the Association for Asian Studies.

Kwong, Peter. 2006. "The Chinese Face of Neoliberalism." *Counterpunch* 13 (12): 1–3.

Li, Cheng, and Lynn T. White III. 1991. "China's Technocratic Movement and the World Economic Herald." *Modern China* 17 (3): 342–388. doi:10.1177/0097700 49101700302.

Li, Minqi. "Capitalist Development and Class Struggle in China." Book manuscript. Available online at http://content.csbs.utah.edu/~mli/Capitalism%20in%20China/ Index.htm (accessed April 22, 2017).

Li, Minqi. 2008. *The Rise of China and the Demise of the Capitalist World Economy*. New York: Monthly Review.

Lin, Cyril Chihren. 1981. "The Reinstatement of Economics in China Today." *The China Quarterly* (85): 1–48. doi:10.1017/S0305741000028010.

Liu, Guoguang. "Interview with Dr. Heng Lin." Chinese Academy of Social Sciences website: experts, 1st group CASS members, Liu Guoguang, http://casseng.cssn.cn/ experts/experts_1st_group_cass_members/201402/t20140221_969619.html.

Liu, Junning. 2000. "Classical Liberalism Catches on in China." *Journal of Democracy* 11 (3): 48–57.

Liu, Kang. 2004. *Globalization and Cultural Trends in China*. Honolulu, HI: University of Hawaii Press.

Ma, Hong. 1983. *New Strategy for China's Economy*. Beijing: New World Press.

McCloskey, Donald N. 1985. *The Rhetoric of Economics*. 1st ed. Madison, WI: University of Wisconsin Press.

Meisner, Maurice. 1999. *Mao's China: A History of the People's Republic*. 3rd ed. New York: Free Press.

Qian, Yingyi and Jinglian Wu. 2000. *China's Transition to a Market Economy: How Far Across the River?* Working Paper no. 69. Stanford, CA: Center for International Development, Stanford University.

Rawski, Thomas. 1986. "Report on Economics Curriculum in Chinese Universities (Draft)." Draft report, personal copy.

Riskin, Carl. 1987. *China's Political Economy: The Quest for Development since 1949*. New York: Oxford University Press.

Ross, Andrew. 2007a. *Fast Boat to China: High-Tech Outsourcing and the Consequences for Free Trade—Lessons from Shanghai*. New York: Vintage.

Shen, Ruth and T. Y. Shen. 1993. "Economic Thinking in China: Economic Knowledge and Attitudes of High School Students." *Journal of Economic Education* 24 (1): 70–84. doi:10.1080/00220485.1993.10844781.

Shen, Ruth and T. Y. Shen. 1994. "High School Economics in the People's Republic of China." In *An International Perspective on Economic Education*, edited by William B. Walstad, 273–289. Boston: Kluwer Academic Publishers.

Song, Longxiang (pseudonym Ma Ding). 1985. "Ten Major Changes in China's Study of Economics." *Beijing Review* 28(49): 17–20.

Song, Longxiang. 1995. "The Methodology of Mainstream Economics and its Implications for China's Economic Research." PhD diss., Washington University.

Sung, Yun-wing and Thomas M. H. Chan. 1987. "China's Economic Reforms: The Debates in China." *The Australian Journal of Chinese Affairs* (17): 29–51. doi:10.2307/2158967.

Tang, Shouning. "Preface to China Economics 2000." In *China Economics 2000.* Beijing: Unirule Institute.

Vogel, Ezra F. 2011. *Deng Xiaoping and the Transformation of China.* Cambridge, MA: Harvard University Press.

Wang, Hui. 2003a. *China's New Order: Society, Politics, and Economy in Transition,* edited by Theodore Huters. Cambridge, MA: Harvard University Press.

Wang, Hui. 2003b. "The New Criticism." In *One China, Many Paths,* edited by Chaohua Wang, 55–86. New York: Verso.

Wang, Yicheng, Ning Fang, Bingquan Wang, and Ruisheng Liu. 2008. *A Study on Contemporary Chinese Intelligentsia and Media Elite—Survey II of Contemporary China's New Social Structural Changes :* Institute of Political Science, Chinese Academy of Social Sciences.

Warner, Malcolm. 2014. *Understanding Management in China: Past, Present, and Future.* New York: Routledge.

Watson, Andrew. 1987. "Social Science Research and Economic Policy Formulation: The Academic Side of Economic Reform." In *New Directions in the Social Sciences and Humanities in China,* edited by Michael B. Yahuda, 67–88. New York: St Martin's Press.

Xin, Mao (pseudonym). 1999. "Reform and Economic Man." *The Chinese Economy* 32 (2): 22–60.

Xu, Zhun. 2012. "The Chinese Agriculture Miracle Revisited." *Economic and Political Weekly* XLVII (14): 51–58.

Xu, Zhun. 2013. "The Political Economy of Decollectivization in China." *Monthly Review: An Independent Socialist Magazine* 65 (1): 17–36. http://monthlyreview.org/2013/05/01/the-political-economy-of-decollectivization-in-china/.

Yang, Dali L. and Litao Zhao. 2009. *China's Reforms at 30.* Singapore: World Scientific.

Zhang, Fengbo. 2008. *A Chinese Economist's Journey* Create Space, Independent Publishing Platform.

Zhang, Zhuoyuan. 1982. "Introduction: China's Economy After the 'Cultural Revolution'." In *China's Economic Reforms,* edited by Lin Wei and Arnold Chao, 1–27. Philadelphia: University of Pennsylvania Press.

Zhao, Haiyun. 2010. "Economics Education in China." *International Journal of Pluralism and Economics Education* 1 (4): 303–316.

Zhou, Kate. 2006. "Chinese Intellectuals Fighting on the Idea Front in Global Context." In *The World and China at a Time of Drastic Changes—Towards the Construction of a New and Modern Sinology,* edited by Mitsuyuki Kagami, 35–70. Japan: Aichi University Press.

Zhou, Ping, Xinning Su, and Loet Leydesdorff. 2010. "A Comparative Study on Communication Structures of Chinese Journals in the Social Sciences." *Journal of the American Society for Information Science and Technology* 61 (7): 1360–1376.

# 9 Chinese economic theory and economics education in the twenty-first century

## 9.1 Note on sources

My thoughts on the current state of economics in China are based primarily on: (1) interviews with about 20 Chinese political-economists during the spring and summer of 2011 and the winter and spring of June 2014; (2) attendance at two economics conferences within China during the same period and sessions with Chinese economists at academic conferences in the US 2011–2016; (3) discussions with Chinese university students and business sector professionals in China; (4) a small survey of Chinese undergraduate and graduate students, and (5) many secondary sources.

Most of my discussions were with people associated with China's leading Universities.[1] Much of my reading has also been about educational issues related to elite institutions. Hence, it may not be appropriate to generalize from these discussions to the rest of China. On the other hand, China's elite universities have historically set the tone and standards for the rest of the country. They have also educated many of China's economic and political leaders, magnifying the importance of what happens on these campuses. A more serious limitation of the discussion below is the modest sample it derives from and the impressionistic basis of some conclusions. Nevertheless, while there may be some developments not covered in the analysis, I think the chapter's depiction of the basic character of Chinese economics education and the directions of change are well grounded.

## 9.2 Return of Western educated PhDs

The most important development in the first decade of the twenty-firt century was the return of a sufficient number of Western trained economists to China to create a critical mass of neoclassically socialized (as well as educated) economists. The factors responsible for the "in and out" migration of educated labor have been widely studied. The reasons given for Chinese PhDs remaining in the West include expectations of higher salaries, better research and teaching facilities, greater political and social freedom, more educational opportunities for their children, fairer and more transparent promotion procedures, and easier participation in elite global culture. Some of these rationales have weakened as China has modernized. In 1998, China significantly increased the perks offered to returning economics PhDs, such as salaries four times the normal scale at Chinese universities (Chow 2000, 57) and approval of joint positions that permitted professors to continue to teach at Western universities for significant portions of the year. This initiative was part of a broader Chinese project to repatriate scientific and technical experts living abroad. Political and cultural changes within China and the shifting fortunes of the US and Chinese economies have also encouraged greater return migration. Traditional notions of Chinese identity and increasing hints of the potential for anti-Chinese xenophobia in the US may have also played a role in some return migration decisions.

Interestingly, Cao Cong cites one other unusual factor that had formerly discouraged the return of Western educated PhDs. This is the attenuation of social networks ("*guanxi*") after long time periods spent overseas (Cao 2008, 331, 340). *Guanxi* (a Chinese version of "who you know") has traditionally played a significant role in Chinese political, economic, and social life, casting a bigger shadow than in the West. Until many foreign educated economists returned to China, Western educated economists lacked the strong social networks necessary for professional advancement in China. The recent assemblage of a critical mass of neoclassical economists holding official positions in Chinese universities, think tanks, and government offices has enabled networks like those of the Chinese Economist Society to offer social linkages to returning students. Overall, more economics degree holders have returned to China than other advanced degree holders (Cao 2008, 341). This appears to be even more the case with respect to "seasoned entrepreneurs" (Cao 2008, 331).

## 9.3  Current profile of Chinese economic thinking

The current structure organizing Chinese economic education and research has several characteristics:

1    It is very neoclassical.
2    It has been heavily influenced by the Chicago school.
3    It favors mathematical argument in both research and economics instruction and appears at times to encourage a narrow technocratic approach to economic analysis.
4    It privileges New Institutionalist economics when addressing institutional issues and has developed some innovative lines of research in this field. It asserts its intellectual independence from the West by imagining itself as neoclassical theory "with Chinese characteristics."
5    Its subtexts strongly endorse the transition to capitalism in China.
6    It gives relatively little attention to Marxist and non-Marxist heterodox economics paradigms.[2]

7   Its major critics are likely to come from outside rather than inside the economics profession.
8   It has recently opened up a little to heterodox economic thinking.

The discussion below elaborates many of these points.

## 9.4  Current status of neoclassical economics

### 9.4.1  Dominant position of neoclassical paradigm

As described in earlier chapters, the institutional expansion of neoclassical economics is visible everywhere: from an airport billboard picture of Lin Justin Yifu advertising Peking University's economic expertise, to the study guides for admission to graduate economic study; from the editorial policies of leading Chinese economics journals to the requirements for securing a university teaching position and academic promotion. Since the turn of the century, there has been a flood of academic conferences largely elaborating neoclassical theory, both in China and among Chinese economists overseas. Illustrative of these meetings are: the annual conference of the Chinese Economist Society (CES), the annual meetings of the Chinese Economic Association of North America (CEANA),[3] the China Center for Economic Research's (CCER's) China Economics Annual Conference, the CCER's annual joint conference with the National Bureau of Economic Research (NBER), the annual meeting of the Chinese Hayek Society, the Chinese annual meeting in Finance, and the annual Chinese capital markets conference.[4] Specialized associations focusing on subfields of neoclassical economics have also flourished. The Chinese Game Theory and Experimental Economics Association was born in 2010 and the inaugural China Meeting of the Econometric Society took place in 2013. Neoclassical approaches also comprise the backdrop for many business-oriented conferences in China on topics like innovation or privatization. Hong Kong's Universities have contributed actively to the neoclassical menu.

Most Chinese economics discussions give little attention to heterodox economics. A bibliometric study of the articles published in the *China Economic Review* (CER) (the journal of the Chinese Economist Society) *1989–2010*, for example, found less than 1 percent of the papers addressed heterodox economics or methodological issues as defined by JEL subject codes (Du 2011, 24). Zhang and Xu found only 3.5 heterodox articles were published per year (1977–1990) in 11 leading Chinese journals (Zhang and Xu 2013, 311). Wang et al. found a similar slant in the discussion of property rights in Chinese economics journals (Wang et al. 2008).

The evolution of Chinese economics continues to follow the path taken by the US economics profession. Three-quarters of the top 30 researchers referenced in *CER* articles (1989–2010) were affiliated with US institutions. Only ~1/6 were affiliated with Chinese institutions, despite the focus of the journal on Chinese economic issues. A foreign PhD (usually American) is required to teach at most prestigious Chinese Universities. The Americanization of Chinese economics education has had predictable consequences.

There has been a tendency in American economics education to concentrate on training students to use relatively complicated mathematical techniques. Many key assumptions are accepted uncritically, as students struggle to master quantitative skills. This habit has tended to "crowd out" reflection on the social theory embodied in economic models and attention to concrete institutional details. As Dani Rodrik of Harvard notes, North American economics "PhD programs now train applied mathematicians and statisticians rather than real economists."[5]

This training has influenced studies of the Chinese economy. As Dwight Perkins, an influential neoclassical economist specializing in China studies, observes

> The challenge for economists interested in the Chinese economy … trained in the US … is how to translate excellent training in theory and econometrics into something that is truly useful to understanding growth and structural change in China. … The culture of graduate programs in economics in the US gives the greatest prestige to theory, and then to high-powered econometric technique. … Economics graduate students and young faculty who work on developing economies often know relatively little about the institutions that shape the economies they are studying, and if they spend too much time acquiring such knowledge, they risk being labeled as "area specialists." Thus much research work on developing economies involves finding a data set and then seeing what kinds of statistically significant relationships one can find using one's econometric skills. … One does not learn much about the problems that dominate the economies in which these studies are carried out or the solutions to those problems.
>
> (Perkins 2002, 413–414)

This habit of mind seems to have migrated to Chinese shores. Ever since the entrance exams used for admission to Gregory Chow's summer workshops in the mid-1980s, the recruitment of students from math and science backgrounds has characterized the Westernizing of economics departments. Lin Yifu, one of the founders of modern neoclassical economics in China notes,

> young economists in China generally do better in mathematics than their counterparts abroad. … So, they tend to consider mathematical models as economic theories. … They take pride in constructing complicated and sophisticated models, all the while ignoring the fact that theories exist to explain phenomena.
>
> (Lin 2012c, Kindle locator 2069)

This habit of mind seems to have spilled over into the teaching of economics (Huang Bin).[6]

Mathematical requirements seem to be taken as a proxy for rigor in assessing Chinese economics programs. Expertise in political economy (the term often used to represent Marxist orientations) is devalued. For example, at the Shanghai University of Finance and Economics (SUFE), one of the most pluralist economics programs in China, all PhD students in economics and political economy (i.e., Marxist economics) have to pass three qualifying exams: one in largely neoclassical microeconomics, one in largely neoclassical macroeconomics, and one in econometrics. When suggestions were made that students have the option of substituting an exam in political economy for one of the three qualifying exams, administrators worried about "diluting the rigor" and reputation of the SUFE program.

As discussed in Chapter 6, the leading Chinese economics journal *Economic Research (Jingji Yanjiu)* has tended to emphasize econometric oriented articles similar to those published in American neoclassical journals.

### 9.4.2 Neoclassical subtexts

In many ways, the mathematics of neoclassical economics and general equilibrium theory has served as a Trojan horse for the popularization of "free-market" subtexts in China. This outcome was more a sociological result of neoclassical training than a logical result of human reason. The implicit and explicit assumptions of neoclassical theory concerning matters such as human nature (methodological individualism and *homo economicus*), market efficiency (perfect information) and the purposes of economic activity (to maximize GDP/capita) have been internalized in contemporary Chinese economic theory. The pre-1978 focus of Chinese economics on understanding the "laws of motion" of capitalism as a social system and the implications of different public policies for building socialism in China has largely been abandoned.

Epistemologically, recent Chinese economics has tended to de-politicize China's market reforms by portraying them as a form of technical rationality. Song Longxiang's doctoral dissertation, completed in the US, provides a striking example of the internalization of this stance. Song characterizes neoclassical theory as a science that should command belief in the same fashion as modern physics. In taking this stance, Song allows the paradigm's subtexts, which infuse its models, to enjoy scientific status. He writes,

> Economics has gained the status of a science. … Mainstream economists, from George Stigler to Milton Friedman, have spoken with one voice: there is no value judgment in positive economics. … Second, since positive economics is essentially concerned with *quantifiable and measurable* relations … modern mathematical tools have been widely used. … Third, laboratory experimentation has become an increasingly important tool …

economics is widely recognized as an experimental discipline much like the physical and biological sciences. ... Fourth, *analytical training* has become increasingly important for the economists' education because economic research has been highly *professionalized and technically* oriented. ... Fifth, it has been widely acknowledged among economics professors and graduate students that a knowledge of the history of economic thought is not a necessary condition for understanding current conventional economic theory. ... Sixth ... (t)here is significant *consensus* on the fundamental principles of the discipline among mainstream economists. ... Seventh, prominent philosophers of science ... hold mainstream economics in almost as great esteem as they hold physics. ... Undoubtedly, economics in the Western World is a science ...

(Song 1995, 1–4)

Song's uncritical transformation of a paradigmatic view of economics into universal truths reflects the self-image of neoclassical economics. This self-portrait has been most eloquently challenged by the University of Chicago trained economist D. McCloskey. In many scholarly articles, and most comprehensively in *The Rhetoric of Economics*, McCloskey convincingly argues that neoclassical economics cannot be treated in positivist terms as a universal, objective, science.[7] It is best understood as a plausible set of metaphors and stories that aim to make useful inferences about topics for which it is generally impossible to do experiments. The recent blindsiding of most neoclassical economists by the financial crisis of 2007 illustrates the misreading of modern economics embodied in Song's bold claim that neoclassical conclusions be afforded the status of the predictions, laws, and other claims of modern physics.

As McCloskey notes, if you look under the hood, most "proofs" of basic economic arguments, such as the benefits of free trade, are based on arguments by analogy, introspection, and similar reasoning techniques disallowed by the positivist-modernist self-image of neoclassical economics. McCloskey's aim is not to disparage neoclassical economics. McCloskey is a proud Chicago alumnus who believes that the metaphors of neoclassical economics are useful and offer a reasonable way to understand the economy. What McCloskey objects to is the misleading use of "scientistic" rhetoric to command belief.

The rhetoric of scientific authority and discovery of unbreakable natural laws has been used in China by both Marxist and neoclassical economists. Wang Qingxin (2011) argues that neoclassical economics' consolidation of professional authority in China was one of the major forces responsible for the shape of Chinese policies toward state-owned enterprises and the WTO in the late 1990s. He argues:

China's decision to conclude the WTO agreement ... was because of the gradual emergence of neoclassical economic ideas as the mainstream economic theories. ... Bureaucratic leaders increasingly used the language of neoclassical economics ... to justify new policies of SOE reforms and WTO accession.

(Wang 2011, 464–465)

Wang Hui takes this one step further. He argues that neoclassical economics has been deployed in China in the service of a broad neoliberal agenda, promoting privatization, free trade, and increasing inequality (supply side economics), all in the name of economic growth. As noted in Chapter 8, the enlightenment struggle for human rights in China, as in the West, has frequently been deflected into a battle for private property rights, sometimes at the expense of human rights. Wang describes recent developments this way:

the dominant discipline in China is neo-classical economics. ... [A]fter 1990, Hayekian ideas gained real ascendancy ... economics is not just a technical discipline, any more than its predecessors: it too is an imperative world view.

(Wang 2003b, 77–78)

Zhao Yuezhi adds,

Attaining their dominant ideological position by ignoring marginalizing, and suppressing oppositional voices in public discourses, neoliberal economists have operated as the organic intellectuals of China's rising propertied class during the reform process—serving as their board members, lobbyists, publicists, and strategists, while enriching themselves with consultant and speech fees and stock shares.

(Zhao 2008, 294)

### 9.4.3 Challenges to neoclassical and neoliberal thought

Over the last 15 or so years, a number of social, political, and economic factors opened up discursive space for reassessing Western economic policy models including, in chronological order: the 1997 Asian financial crisis and heavy handed IMF response, the American bombing of the Chinese embassy in Belgrade in 1999,[8] American opposition, in 2000, to China's hosting of the 2008 Olympics, the collision of an American surveillance aircraft and a Chinese fighter plane near Hainan in 2001, a major critical study of neoliberalism undertaken by the Chinese Academy of Social Sciences 2003–2004, public outrage over corrupt privatizations in 2004–2005, resentment over US Congressional denunciation of Chinese efforts to purchase Unocal (a US oil company) in 2005, escalating tensions over territorial boundaries in the South China Sea, continuing US–China acrimony over exchange rates, and probably most importantly, the weakness of the US and other Western economies during the recent global financial crisis and "Great Recession." Popular concerns in China about growing income and wealth inequality, unemployment and economic insecurity, corruption, environmental problems, and the crowding out of Chinese firms by large foreign corporations and traditional Chinese culture by consumerism have also contributed to potential interest in reviewing current economic theory.[9]

The famous Lang–Gu debate of 2004–2005, in which Lang Xianping (Larry), a Hong Kong economics Professor, accused several businessmen, including Gu Chujun, of corrupt privatization, reflected broader controversies at many different levels of Chinese society about neoliberalism. Popular opinion, at least as mobilized over the internet, supported Lang's critique of the current system of management buy-outs. Most mainstream Chinese economists participating in the debate seem to have supported management buyouts.[10] Zhao Yuezhi notes how the debate quickly

> deepened: from Lang Xianping versus Gu Chujun to the property rights reform of the SOEs, to the entire topic of SOE reform, to a debate between contending economic paradigms over such fundamental issues as the respective roles of the private and state sectors and ... future directions of China's entire reform process.
>
> (Zhao 2008, 296)

Liu Guoguang, a former Vice President of the Chinese Academy of Sciences and a leading reform economist of the 1980s and 1990s, linked government support of management buyouts to the decline of Marxist economics and warned that continued expansion of neoclassical economics would lead to implementation of the full agenda of neoliberalism (Fewsmith 2008, 264–265; Zhao 2008, 321). Liu repeated this concern in 2007 and 2011 (Liu interview, 14; Liu 2011). In both cases he called for maintaining the key role of State-Owned Enterprises in the economy.[11] Liu's warning was significant, because he had been an early supporter of "primary stage" theories of socialism, of guidance rather than mandatory planning, of socialist competition, and other key building blocks of the reform process. He had been a major figure in the CASS group of economists who had created a critical mass of intellectual energy for economic reform. So the fact that he was having second thoughts about the direction of restructuring was significant.

Zhao's (2008) analysis of the Lang–Gu debate emphasizes how traditional media and the internet can circumvent the near monopoly of official expertise and public discussion of economic issues enjoyed by government officials and neoclassical economists in the 1980s and 1990s. Tens of thousands of individuals appear to have participated in internet conversations about the Lang-Gu controversy (Zhao 2008, 296). Most of these participants sided with Lang (Wang et al. 2008).[12] When a draft of a new property law was released shortly thereafter, many netizens joined in acrimonious public discussion over the relative roles of private and public property in China. Defending the role of public property was Gong Xiantian, a law Professor at Beida. Defending the elevation of private property were mainstream economists at important

Chinese institutions (Fewsmith 2008, 265–266; Li He 2009, 35). Adoption of the law was delayed, but it was eventually implemented with some concessions to the opposition (Li He 2010, 14).

Similarly, there has been a rising level of social protest and labor unrest in China. The number of officially reported "mass incidents," for example, has risen from 8,700 in 1993 to more than 90,000 in 2006, and may have exceeded 175,000 in 2010.[13] Many of these protests were about the expropriation of rural peasant land for non-agricultural use without fair compensation.[14] It is not clear what the ideological spillover of these protests will be. Some echoes have surfaced in what has become known as the Chinese New Left. A New Left website, *Utopia*, had 47 million hits between 2003 and 2008 (Li He August 2008, 2). Almost all of my interviewees, however, found that the New Left had little influence within economics departments at either the student or faculty level.[15] Attacks on neoliberal policies have also emerged from the New Rural Reconstruction Movement.

As in the West there are mildly unorthodox divergences from mainstream views within Chinese neoclassical economics, analogous, for example, to the voices of Joseph Stiglitz and Paul Krugman in the United States. These economists have often criticized the Washington Consensus and tried to extend the boundaries of neoclassical economics to explain China's reform process. The "New Structural Economics" of Justin Yifu Lin is probably the most influential of these approaches. Lin's greatest affinity with heterodox economics is his deep respect for empirical data, which has led him to challenge some neoclassical shibboleths. He has a broad ranging imagination and seems to pay attention to some heterodox ideas, such as the importance of bounded rationality and the findings of behavioral economics. At times, his analysis also seems to strain the confines of neoclassical theory. In a tilt toward industrial policy, for example, he calls for countries to follow their "latent" (rather than apparent) comparative advantage.

Ultimately, however, Lin remains within the force field of neoclassical theory economics. Though more respectful of the relevance of the assumptions of economic models than many interpretations of Milton Friedman's epistemology, he adopts neoclassical starting points. He accepts the key assumptions of methodological individualism, stable tastes and preferences, *homo economicus*, the practical measurement of macroeconomic success by GDP, and the working hypothesis of perfect information,[16] however qualified his endorsements may be. He also endorses Popper's view of knowledge rather than the paradigmatic approach of Kuhn.

While Lin asserts that Chicago economics, "could offer only pale, strained, and unconvincing explanations for the problems that cropped up during China's reforms" (Lin 2012c, xiii), he attributes these limitations to first-world economists' lack of understanding of the context of choice in developing nations, rather than limitations in Chicago economics.

Lin treats the origins of tastes and preferences as beyond economic analysis, referencing Stigler and Becker's work. He links consumer behavior to universal desires, operationalized in concrete circumstances. He seems to have little interest in how capitalism (with its massive system of advertising) or any other social system might constitute the context in which people become human and develop their tastes and preferences. He seems uninterested in exploring how capitalism in China might create political-economic and cultural dynamics that put enormous strain on the environment.[17]

I am not sure what the impact of social unrest within China and the failures of orthodox economics associated with the Great Recession has been on economic theorists within the Chinese Communist Party. In 2004, Cheng Enfu, a leading Marxist economist, challenged the Party's retreat from Marxist theory. In particular, he attacked the teaching of neoclassical economics as the core of economics by some instructors from the central university of the Communist party. These teachings were offered at an educational retreat for Ministers and "leaders of promise." Cheng's attack was apparently well received by some audiences (interview notes).

There are, of course, continuing debates among Marxists and within the Chinese Communist Party between advocates of traditional central planning, proponents of Maoist mobilizations, social democratic theorists, and "capitalist riders." The latter group still seems to hold political power. In the tradition of Deng Xiaoping, it claims to use capitalist techniques to advance the forces of production in order to permit a transition to socialism. However, it has recently been forced to address distributional issues in order to maintain the social stability (a "harmonious society") necessary to achieve its economic growth goals.

Reflecting the provisional flavor of the entire reform process ("crossing the river, groping for stones"), this group has not generated a unified system of thought to compete with neoclassical economics and neoliberalism on the right, or with traditional Marxism and the economics of central planning on the left. Critics of the Party see its lack of a coherent social vision as emblematic of its transformation from a revolutionary party into an instrument for the personal advancement of its members. The intellectual vacuum within the Party persists in China today on a more general level. It is the legacy of the New Culture movement in the early 1900s that undermined Confucianism and other traditional Chinese belief systems, of the Marxist period that rejected classical liberalism, and of the Cultural Revolution that discredited Marxism. The challenge of the twenty-first century will be to fill this intellectual vacuum and reconstruct some shared way of thinking.

## 9.5 Current status of Marxist economics

Marxist economics continues to enjoy the costs and benefits of official state support. All students in Chinese universities, regardless of their major, are still required to study some Marxist theory, which includes discussion of Marxists economics. The amount of required study has been reduced significantly since 1978, as measured in terms of required courses and/or credit hours. The amount of Marxist economics required of non-economics majors has almost disappeared, having been condensed into a short section or two of a single required course. Co-curricular Marxist oriented requirements, such as required Saturday political study groups, also seem to have been discontinued (interviews 2011, 2014).[18]

One of the factors that may have contributed to the weakening of Marxist economics for non-majors was the difficulty of covering in one or two courses both traditional Marxist economics and the ideas of theorists allied with Deng Xiaoping's marketization project. One of my interviewees implied that the authorities sometimes pushed the new ideas at the expense of traditional Marxist economic analysis, leading to a loss of depth and perhaps overall coherence in the traditional segments of the course. The redesign of the curriculum seems to have been directed by the Ministry of Education.

Another criticism some students have made about university Marxist economics courses is that they repeat material covered in high school without raising the level of difficulty or subtlety to a college level. Sometimes this criticism points to the relatively low level of math used in Marxist as compared to neoclassical university economics classes. The publication of a new textbook series in Marxist political economy including many more mathematical models has tried to respond to this criticism (Zhou Yi 2015).

The current mandatory Marxist classes seem to be treated by most students and faculty as an obsolete requirement, like attendance at required chapel services in Western universities during the final stages of their transition from religiously oriented to secularly oriented institutions.[19] It appears that some, and perhaps many, of the instructors teaching these required courses are unenthusiastic about them. Much like the students, these professors experience the class as an artificial demand imposed on them.[20] Little weight is apparently given to teaching in evaluating professors for promotion in China, so there is little material incentive for instructors to invest much time and energy in preparing for these classes.

I was struck by the near unanimous ridicule of the required Marxist course among students. Descriptions like "mind numbing and useless," abounded among both proponents and critics of orthodox neoclassical economics. By student accounts, most required Marxist theory courses concentrate on memorization of key passages of Marxist literature and identification (with dates) of important Party pronouncements. They appear to repeat material covered in high school in a similarly routinized and unappealing way. As one student put it, (they) "taught us everything we don't believe." His remark elicited confirmatory laughter among a group of fellow graduate students at a meeting I attended of students interested in alternatives to neoclassical economics.

One non-economics major I interviewed had a more nuanced view of the impact of required Marxist courses, although she confirmed the classes' concentration on memorizing passages from classical Marxist texts. I asked her what she thought were the basic ideas of Marxist theory. She hesitated to answer, but suggested if I started a Marxist quotation, she might be able to finish it. When I implied that this indicated her Marxist course had had little intellectual impact, she disagreed. She mused that if she had to confront some of the issues raised in the assigned texts, she might fall back on the memorized passages, as they might echo in her mind, serving as a kind of reservoir of potential knowledge.[21] This is an interesting possibility and suggests that thoughtful public discussion of Marxist ideas might some day find an audience.

While there appear to be many dedicated professors of Marxist economics in China (especially among the older faculty), the institutional presence of Marxist economics is both more heavy-handed and less subtle than the work of these scholars and teachers. Rather than treating Marxist economics and Marxist theory as an intellectual framework open to challenge, creative evolution, and contested applications, the theory has been treated by the state as a matter of faith. This is probably due to the theory's ongoing role in legitimizing the monopoly of political power held by the Communist Party in China. Theoretical discussions among some leading Chinese Marxist economists about the status of the labor theory of value, for example, have been heavily influenced by the politics of legitimation. Rather than debate the empirical or conceptual validity of the labor theory of value, it appears the theory's status in Chinese Marxism is a function of its perceived political usefulness.

As might be expected, the Chinese Communist Party's attempt to protect Marxist theory from criticism appears to have backfired in academia. It has rendered Marxism a dead theory among many college students, and it has undermined the ability of Marxist theory to compete with other theories. This is not surprising. Historically, whenever a particular way of thinking becomes an official state ideology, there has been a tendency for intellectual opportunism. This has been true of many organized religions, for example, and now seems true for aspects of Chinese Marxism. This is unfortunate, as there has been serious Marxist thinking occurring in China that could compete with other systems of thought and contribute more actively to popular discussions of China's future.[22]

### 9.5.1 Marxist economics at the undergraduate level

Students enrolled in economics schools (which may include academic concentrations such as accounting majors as well as pure economics majors) are required to take more Marxist economics than students in other schools. Here too, however, the presence of Marxist economics has been greatly reduced.

Administratively, some Marxist economists are housed in separate "groups" (frequently termed political-economy groups) or in separate institutes for the study of Marxism, distinct from economics groups or economics departments. The latter are heavily dominated by professors trained in neoclassical economics. There does not appear to be significant collaboration or interaction between the Marxist and neoclassical groups. Undergraduate economics majors take mainly neoclassical economics courses, with an emphasis on mathematics. There remain, however, more residual Marxist classes offered (especially as electives) and a greater presence of the history of economic thought and economic history in Chinese economics programs than in the United States.

For example, while the economics major at Peking University emphasizes neoclassical economics, the major still includes a two-year, four-course history requirement.[23] This appears to be due to tradition and the reputation of the Peking department for strength in this area. The focus exceeds the attention to historical issues in many other university curriculums.[24] Even here, however, the substantive impact of history on economics education seems to be declining (interviews). The methodology used in history classes also seems to have shifted toward neoclassical models of rational, optimizing individuals. As one professor put it, some of the history courses are actually "anti-history," taught in the methodologically individualistic tradition of the rest of neoclassical economics. Professors at other Chinese universities report pressures to replace the historical components of Chinese economics education with more technique-oriented neoclassical courses.

It is not clear whether the residual required exposure of economics majors to Marxist ideas opens or closes minds to potential debates between Marxist and neoclassical approaches to economics. The latter possibility can be analogized to inoculations. Students may receive watered down, polemical versions of Marxist economics, which cannot compete with the elaborately articulated instruction they receive in "modern" looking, mathematically challenging neoclassical theory. The unsatisfying memory students have of their classes in Marxist economics may discourage them from revisiting the paradigm in the future. On the other hand, when taught by thoughtful and motivated instructors, it appears required Marxist courses can retain student interest. This seems to be the case at Renmin University, where the President and traditional campus culture have been more supportive of Marxist economics.[25] At Peking University, one thoughtful professor of Marxist economics estimated that 10–20 percent of his students get excited by his Marxist class. Eventually, however, these students seem to conclude that studying Marxist theory will not help advance their professional careers and lose interest in the subject.

My impression is that most Chinese economics majors are studying economics because they believe it will help them find a good job. Seeking employment with foreign firms in the financial sector seems to be especially popular. These students are not likely to regard Marxist economics as something that will be helpful in achieving their career goals in the business or academic world.

### 9.5.2 Marxist economics at the graduate school and faculty level

Even more than undergraduate study, graduate programs in economics departments are dominated by neoclassical economics. Getting a teaching position at an elite university, and increasingly even at a moderately good

Chinese university, almost always requires a foreign PhD with a neoclassical stamp. Many of the best undergraduate economics majors do not enroll in China's leading universities' graduate programs; they go abroad (interviews).

If they are able to get a university teaching position after they graduate, the pressures to maintain a neoclassical research agenda continue. Chinese economics departments appear to have a relatively formal set of publishing requirements for promotion. Journals are divided into several quality levels. Candidates have to publish in a predetermined number of these journals at particular levels to be promoted to associate and full professor. The journal rankings generally privilege neoclassical economics. Professors also get significant monetary bonuses (as much as 50,000–100,000 yuan) for a publication in one of the designated elite journals.

As noted earlier, beginning around 1992 and accelerating in the mid-1990s, the proportion of Marxist articles in the leading Chinese economics journal, *Economic Research* (*Jingji Yanjiu*) declined significantly. By the early 2000s the journal accepted few Marxist papers.[26] A publication in a leading Western neoclassical journal, such as the *American Economic Review*, is treated as equivalent, or perhaps even superior, to the leading Chinese journals. It appears that much less "credit" is given for publications in Western heterodox economics journals, especially journals not indexed in the SSCI.

### 9.5.3 Self-criticism by Marxist economists

Some of the Marxist economists I interviewed criticized their Marxist colleagues for failing to innovate or update Marxist thinking. They lamented the lack of attention to mathematical techniques and the continued use of old textbooks. They implied that this gave students the impression that Marxism was dated and had been superseded by more modern theories. Perry Anderson has argued that Western Marxism after the 1920s shifted its focus from economics to politics and then to philosophy (Anderson 1976, Chapter 3). The administrative separation of Marxist economists from economics departments in China may have contributed to a similar shift of emphases in Chinese Marxism.

There also appears to be a tendency among some disingenuous or poorly trained Marxist economists to abandon the substance of the theory and to use Marxist language to convey neoclassical ideas. This charade sometimes leads to statements reminiscent of Orwellian doublespeak. David Kotz, an American Marxist economist who co-directs the political economy program at the Shanghai University of Finance and Economics, has collected some memorable quotes from a conference in Beijing on property rights in 2006. Here are two brief oxymoron-like examples:

> When an SOE is turned into a joint stock corporation with many shareholders, it represents socialization of ownership as Marx and Engels described it.
>
> (Kotz 2007, 60)

The nature of ownership of the enterprise has no bearing on whether a country is capitalist. ... Enterprises should always be privately owned and operated for a profit.[27]

### 9.5.4 Reviving Marxist economics

One promising avenue for reviving Chinese Marxism is the growing popularity of Ecological Marxism in China. Interest in Ecological Marxism has been spurred by China's serious environmental problems, the global impact of green movements, and residual elements in the Communist Party still interested in Marxist critiques of capitalism. Ecological Marxism links inherent aspects of capitalism, such as commodification, capitalist competition, and consumerism, to current global environmental crises. As noted in Chapter 1, from a Marxist perspective, capitalism's great success has been enabling and imposing pressures for capital accumulation and market expansion on host societies. This has produced impressive economic growth and enormous power for leading capitalist states. But this process contains within itself no limiting principle and left unchecked threatens to destroy the environmental support system surrounding the economy. Thus what has been a strength of capitalism has turned into a potentially serious liability.[28] Ecological Marxism explores the nature of this contradiction and the design of alternative socialist principles for regulating humanity's interaction with the environment.[29]

Prior to 1990, there had been only four articles on Ecological Marxism published in Chinese academic journals. However, by 2010, an astounding 598 articles had been published, along with nine books, 15 dissertations, and 69 Masters theses (Wang Zhihe 2012, 36–37; Wang et al. 2013). An international conference on socialism and the environment was also held in Jinan, China in 2008 (Huan 2010a, 8). Based on the pattern of citations I have seen, it appears that many important initiatives are coming from platforms outside of economics departments, such as from philosophy and sociology departments, and researchers associated with Wen Tiejun's New Rural Reconstruction Movement. Attention to environmental issues has been increasing rapidly, especially since the Party's commitment to an "ecological civilization" in 2007.[30]

There are, however, serious constraints on Ecological Marxism's expansion within China. This is partly due to the subtexts of primary stage theories of socialism that call for maximizing economic growth and the advancement of the forces of production. The Dengist, statist project of maximizing Chinese national power also undermines pursuit of ecological Marxist projects. Li Minqi is a Chinese Marxist who has escaped these constraints by living in the US.[31] His work includes a very strong environmentalist critiques of both capitalism and Dengist state socialism. It seems unlikely that mainland Marxist economists will be able to develop Ecological Marxist themes as forcefully as Li.[32]

Professor Cheng is an important scholar who has undertaken several institutional initiatives to re-energize Chinese Marxism. He is the head of the

Academy of Marxism of the Chinese Academy of Social Sciences (CASS), one of the founders of the Shanghai School of Marxism and the World Association for Political Economy (WAPE), and the chief editor of WAPE's journal, the *World Review of Political Economy*. While retaining a fairly orthodox Marxist viewpoint, Professor Cheng has tried to open Marxist discourse in China to interactions with other heterodox paradigms, such as Post Keynesianism, ecological economics, Neo-Ricardian-Sraffan economics, and to some extent feminist economics. He has also tried to welcome more mathematical analysis alongside qualitative analysis. These projects are reflected in a new three volume set of Marxist political-economy textbooks co-edited by Cheng in 2012. Their attention to mathematical models is especially distinctive (Zhou Yi 2015).

WAPE has sought to build intellectual bridges between Chinese Marxists, Marxist theorists around the globe, and other interested left-oriented economists. The *World Review of Political Economy* (established in 2010) combines a focus on traditional topics of Marxist political economy, such as value theory, crisis theory, and analysis of the labor process, with an openness to issues highlighted in other heterodox paradigms, such as environmental issues. David Kotz is one of WAPE's five Vice Chairpersons. In collaboration with Terrence McDonough (a member of WAPE's standing council), he has helped develop the theory of Social Structures of Accumulation. The latter combines ideas from Marxist theory, institutionalist theory, and Post Keynesian theory to help explain the behavior of different macroeconomic periods (See section 6.6.3). This kind of analysis illustrates the spirit of the *World Review of Political Economy*.

The *China Review of Political Economy* (CRPE) is another recently established Marxist journal that seeks to re-energize Chinese Marxist theory and link Marxism to broader intellectual currents. The journal's editorial board reflects a variety of Marxist perspectives, and includes John Roemer, Robert Brenner, Makoto Itoh, and Lo Dic.

As these brief descriptions indicate, both the CRPE and WAPE combine academic goals with the political project of rebuilding a basis for socialism within China. This subtext distinguishes Marxist analyses from many other heterodox paradigms, whose projects more often involve reform or regulation of capitalism, rather than its transcendence.

Political sensitivities make it difficult to investigate how the Chinese Communist Party thinks about economics education. Chinese universities still have a dual administrative structure. The formal academic line of authority flows from university presidents through deans to department chairs. It is shadowed by a parallel Communist Party line of authority with its own equivalent of department representatives, deans, and university leaders. It seems likely that this bureaucracy endorsed or at least tolerated the shift in economics education, but I have little direct information about this. No one I interviewed identified the Party structure as a major force shaping university economic discourse.

### 9.5.5 Future prospects of Marxist economics

While Marxist economics retains official endorsement and some financial support from the Chinese government, as well as a latent familiarity among many people (critics often refer to this as "nostalgia"), Marxist economics has suffered a loss of credibility among the general public and total rejection by Western trained economists in China. While all university students are still required to take a college course on Marxism, the class does not appear to be taken seriously by most students.[33] Marxist economic research is not valued highly by many leading Chinese economics journals and a PhD from a Western or Japanese university (usually geared toward neoclassical economics) is required for most elite teaching positions. It seems likely that attention to Marxist theory in economics will lag behind attention to Marxist ideas in other disciplines. This is significant, as many key policy issues will ultimately be dominated by the prevailing economics discourse. A marriage between Marxist economics and heterodox economics among students and faculty skeptical about neoclassical economics might increase the fertility of Marxist economic ideas in China's political-economic life.

It also remains possible that Chinese industrialization has finally produced the proletariat envisioned by Marx as the agent of historical change. The size of the industrial working class when Mao took power was very small. It has swelled since then, with migrant workers reproducing many aspects of the work lives described by Engels in his famous book *The Condition of the English Working Class*. Whether Marxism can become a political-economic perspective for this group remains to be seen. It is not the language of self-understanding for this group at the moment. Should it become so, it is likely that Marxist economics will renew itself.

## 9.6 The history and changing status of heterodox economics

If I had ended this project in 2011, the review of heterodox economics would have been as discouraging as that of Marxist economics. Recently however there are signs of change. We begin this section with a brief historical review of the status of heterodox economics in China since 1900, and then concentrate on the post 2000 period.

### 9.6.1 Historical background: 1900–1949

Heterodox economics was well represented in China during the first half of the twentieth century.[34] Many Chinese students studied economics in the West, with about three-quarters of these students coming to the United States.[35] They brought home American institutionalist economics[36] and a version of Keynesianism that could be seen as a forerunner of Post Keynesianism (PK). The institutionalist influence was reinforced by other Chinese students' exposure to the German historical school of economics. The link to

PK theory was especially strong for Chinese students at Cambridge University, where Keynes's intellectual circle attacked mainstream equilibrium economics.[37] These challenges were much more fundamental than those condensed into the Hicks-Hansen formula of contemporary neoclassical Keynesianism. After 1949, noted Cambridge economist Joan Robinson kept a modest Cambridge–China link alive.

The Social Gospel movement that was taught at American missionary colleges in China also heavily influenced Chinese economic thinking. Trescott calculates that these schools enrolled about one-quarter of all college students in China in the 1920s.[38] The percentage was even higher for 1900–1920.[39] The Social Gospel criticized selfishness and urged Christians to prioritize meeting the needs of the most disadvantaged. The Gospel's distrust of powerful businesses probably resonated with traditional Confucian values. Richard Ely's thought combined aspects of mainstream economics with the Social Gospel and strong support for government activism in the economy. Many Christian colleges used his textbook, *Outlines of Economics*, which was highly critical of laissez-faire economics.[40]

Other heterodox influences present in China during the first half of the twentieth century included: Neo-Ricardian traditions imported from England; elements of Western Marxism and neo-Marxism also imported from England (through economists such as Joan Robinson, Maurice Dobb and Michael Kalecki) (Trescott 2007, 238), and the ideas of Henry George (especially with respect to land taxation). The state led economic development policies of Germany and Japan, as well as the USSR also influenced Chinese economic thinking and education. Sun Yat-sen, for example, appears to have been heavily influenced by the heterodoxy of the German historical school, Richard Ely's Social Gospel, the land economics of Henry George, and the economic policies of Lenin (Trescott 2007, 87, 20).

Of course, Chinese students who studied in the West also brought back to China Marshallian thinking that would evolve into mainstream neoclassical theory as well as Austrian economic ideas (especially those who studied with Friedrich Hayek at the London School of Economics).

### 9.6.2 Heterodox subtexts: 1900–1949

Trescott identifies two different messages, or what I have been calling subtexts, conveyed by Western economics education in China from 1900–1950. Although cognizant of the potential for market imperfections, the first subtext echoed the classical liberalism of Adam Smith. It celebrated how the profit motive and private pursuit of self-interest can be made to serve the general interest through the discipline of competitive markets. It generally recommended laissez-faire government policies.

While recognizing the usefulness of markets in many situations, the second subtext emphasized the problems of market failure and market-based inequalities. It was skeptical about the adequacy of self-interest as a basis for social morality. It rejected laissez-faire approaches and favored the social governance of markets.

Trescott identifies with classical liberalism and laments the tendency of Western economics education in pre-revolution China to disparage laissez-faire policies. While his insinuation that American institutional economists were partially responsible for the excesses of Maoism (see footnote below) seems over the top, his attention to the subtexts of economics education in China is useful. Like the distinction between diagnostic and functional economics drawn by Lin and Hsu, the categories used in teaching economics draw attention to the framing or paradigmatic nature of economic thought. Assessing the impact of Adam Smith's writings in China, for example, Trescott writes, "The most important contribution may have been the moral legitimation of business activity rather than the analysis" (8).[41]

### 9.6.3 Status of heterodox economics: 1949–1979

The status of *all* variants of Western economics fell in China after the revolution. All heterodox and mainstream Western economics texts were lumped together under the Marxian rubric of "vulgar economics" (Zhang and Xu 2013, 315). As elaborated earlier, the universities were re-organized along Soviet lines and Russian economics textbooks replaced American textbooks. After the escalation of the Korean War, Christian universities were closed and their facilities transferred to government universities (Trescott 2007, 141). Many Western oriented economists emigrated to the US and Taiwan.[42] Some would later advise Chinese leaders during the period of market reform.

Zhang and Xu's study of Chinese economics journals indicates that *Economic Research* and *Economic Perspectives* did not publish any heterodox articles from 1949 through the late 1970s (Zhang and Xu 2013, 310). There were no original heterodox economics books and only 10 translated heterodox works published in China for almost 30 years (Zhang and Xu 2013, Table 2). Further, the books that were translated were often published with a preface explaining that the purpose of translation was to facilitate critique. This approach did not invite creative modification or application of the ideas, especially on the part of younger economists hoping to launch their careers.

### 9.6.4 Status of heterodox economics: 1979–2000

When Western economics returned to China, circa 1978, it came back chiefly in modern neoclassical form. While many of the expert groups organized by AEA economists and the World Bank contained a broad range of neoclassical opinion, ranging from followers of Milton Friedman to neo-Keynesians, the spectrum did not include many explicitly heterodox economists. There seems to have been the most openness to heterodox economics in the brief period between the initial return of Western economics to China in the late 1970s and consolidation of neoclassical influence in the mid and late 1980s (Zhang and Xu 2013, 317–318).

For the period 1977–1990, Zhang and Xu reviewed 11 important Chinese economics journals.[43] They found only 51 heterodox articles over this 23-year period (23 Post Keynesian (PK), 15 institutionalist, 10 radical, and 3 "other"). For the period 1991–2009, they identified 60 heterodox articles in the same journals (20 PK, 24 institutionalist, 6 radical and 10 "other"). Chinese textbooks also appear to have largely neglected heterodox economics during this period (Zhang and Xu, 2013).[44]

The heterodox literature that survived in China was dominated by PK and institutionalist approaches,[45] as well as the work of Joan Robinson. Robinson made eight trips to China after the revolution and authored several books on the Chinese economy and Maoist economic strategy.[46] Her neo-Marxist micro and macro models, and post Keynesian ideas combined to make her one of the most well-known heterodox economists in China. John Kenneth Galbraith also appears to have been relatively well known in China (Zhang and Xu 2013).

Of course it is impossible to know all that was going on during this period. It may well be the case that Chinese leaders sought to cast a wider net than their neoclassical advisors offered them. It is difficult to know how many heterodox economists might have been quietly advising the Chinese government or have been invited to lecture at Chinese universities independent of official visits organized by the CSCPRC, World Bank, or US government.

Norton Wheeler reports that in 1993, China's State Planning Commission on Macro Economic Reform asked the UNDP for advice in recruiting a "Chief Technical Advisor." James Galbraith (son of John Kenneth Galbraith), and a well known American heterodox economist in his own right, was recommended. He got the job, and for three years was responsible for bringing to the Commission's attention "the best available expert American advice in the form of conferences, papers, and training missions." Galbraith's definition of "best" was, of course, different from the orthodox perspective. In 1995, for example, he brought the Post Keynesian economist Robert Eisner and vocal IMF critic Joseph Stiglitz to China for a conference on international monetary policy (Wheeler 2012, 71).[47]

A number of very bright Chinese graduate students have also been exposed to heterodox ideas in American graduate economics programs, such as at the University of Massachusetts. I do not know of any studies that tracked the careers of these students or the organizations that they have joined.

As noted above in the discussion of ecological Marxism, ecological economics (with or without self-consciously Marxist characteristics) has also generated interest in China.

While the first decade of Chinese economics reform has often been referred to as "reform without losers," (an overly optimistic but somewhat accurate portrayal), subsequent years have produced additional beneficiaries but also a significant number of "losers," with respect to relative income and economic security. Dissatisfaction with, among other things, rising inequality, corrupt privatizations, and serious economic insecurities has led to renewed interest in critiques of orthodox economics at the very moment when the paradigm has been consolidating control of the economics profession in China. This simultaneity has often displaced serious economic debate to terrains outside of the academy.

### 9.6.5 Status of heterodox economics: 2000–present

Zhang and Xu report that heterodox economics has become slightly more popular in the last several years. For example, one of the leading publishers in China, the Commercial Press, has announced plans to publish a series called *The Translated Works of Western Heterodox Economics* (Zhang and Xu 2013, 316). My interviews with professors and students in 2011, and probably more so in 2014, were consistent with Zhang and Xu's claim. Interest in heterodox economic ideas seemed to be increasing mainly with respect to institutionalist and Post Keynesian thought. While a number of economists were working on gender issues, there did not seem to be much self-consciously "feminist" economics theorizing. There also seem to be some openings to heterodox thinking among economists working on environmental issues.

Because of these heterodox initiatives, there are conflicting currents in contemporary Chinese economic thought and economics education. As noted earlier, the neoclassicals have continued to consolidate their hold on many formal aspects of Chinese economic theory, such as journal editorial policies, requirements for obtaining academic positions and promotion, the subject matter of entrance exams for graduate study in economics, and curriculum design. At the same time there appears to be increasing interest in heterodox economic ideas among a modest number of Chinese economists, economics students, and the general public. This interest is reflected in attendance at heterodox economics conferences and attendance at lectures by touring Western heterodox economists, invitations to Western heterodox economists for visiting professorships, Chinese students and faculty participation in heterodox workshops and study groups, Chinese translations of heterodox books and articles, and the vitality of heterodox blogs and We-Chat groups.

Four factors seem most responsible for the recent expansion of interest in heterodox economics. All four reflect pressures that have been growing over time:

1   First and most important is the continuing reaction to the policy failures that led to the global financial crisis of 2007–2008 and the Great Recession that followed. Many Post Keynesian initiatives, for example, derive from a widespread perception that orthodox economics failed to prevent or even to anticipate the collapse, and likely contributed to it. This is especially true with respect to financial sector issues.

2    Second is the Chinese government's interest in economic theories that legitimize and enable a larger state role in the economy than frequently emerges from orthodox economic theory. This interest reflects the traditional role of the Chinese state in the Chinese economy as well as the residues, both theoretical and institutional, from the Maoist period. The interest may also reflect aspects of Chinese nationalism that invite replacing the "Washington Consensus" with a "Beijing Consensus." The leadership's professed pragmatic approach to economic theory also helps to create space for heterodox discussion.

3    Third is the accumulation of social costs from the over 30 years of the movement toward capitalism, such as exploding inequality, incomplete social safety nets, and environmental pollution.

4    The fourth and final stimulus for expanded attention to heterodox economic ideas is a perception among some students that the assumptions behind neoclassical models are old fashioned, unrealistic, and unconnected to the "real world."

Nevertheless, outright objections to the evolving transition to capitalism are not widespread in the Chinese economics profession. The New Left, a non-Marxist social movement critical of current economic policy is much stronger *outside* than inside economics departments. I did not find many Chinese economists who were familiar with New Left literature. I did not attend a single session at the CES conference in China that included an explicitly heterodox paper.[48]

### 9.6.6 Institutionalist economics

While "new institutionalist" economics dominates discussion of economic institutions in economics departments in China, there continues to be some interest in "old institutionalist" economics. In fact, the promotion of new institutionalist economics by neoclassical theorists in the 1980s seems to have piqued curiosity among some Chinese economists about "old institutionalism" (Zhang and Xu 2013, 318). When significant opposition began to emerge to the privatization projects recommended by new institutionalist economists, interest in alternative ways of thinking about institutions also increased. Works by old institutionalist economists are slated to be the first materials translated by the Commercial Press's heterodox initiative.

Many aspects of "old" institutionalist theory, such as its attention to the concrete specificities of particular economic contexts, its focus on the co-evolution of technology and institutions, and its welcoming attitude toward inter-disciplinary research, seem well suited for addressing China's current economic challenges. Key among these challenges are problems of social inequality, the waste of positional competition, and the social issues that accompany rapid urbanization.

The 5th China Evolutionary Economics annual meeting was held in Shandong University in 2012, building on a workshop on evolutionary economics held at Wuhan university in 2008.[49] (Evolutionary economics is a form of institutionalist economics.) The 12th China Institutional Economics annual meeting was also held at Shandong in 2012. The latter conference appears to have included both new and old institutionalist discussion. Geoffrey Hodgson, a major institutionalist theorist and editor of the *Journal of Institutional Economics*, held a visiting position at Shandong University from 2010–2013. There was a conference on old institutional economics at Renmin University in 2014. Jia Genliang of Renmin University and Huang Kainan of Shandong University are two leading Chinese institutionalist economists.

### 9.6.7 Post Keynesian (PK) economics

PK economics is the most active heterodox paradigm in China. This may be because it actively combines all four stimuli for interest in heterodox economics mentioned earlier. Its practitioners also include participants from disciplinary homes beside economics departments, such as physicists and system theorists Chen Ping and Wang Yougui, and management and finance professionals, such as Michael Pettis and Henry C. K. Liu. Hyman Minsky's work on the financial sector seems to be especially well-known in China. The Levy Institute held a successful two-day conference in China in 2012 on Minsky's ideas. Randy Wray and Paul Davidson, two important Post Keynesian economists, have had a number of speaking engagements in China. Michael Hudson (honorary Professor of economics at Huazhong University of Science and Technology) is also well known. Post Keynesian work by Marc Lavoie, Steven Keen, and Sheila Dow has been translated into Chinese. Economists such as David Kotz (of the Shanghai University of Finance and Economics and the University of Massachusetts), Lo Dic (of Renmin University and the University of London) and John Ross (of Jiao Tong University and Renmin University) have offered Chinese economists creative ways of combing Marxist and Post Keynesian analysis.

I suspect that the more realistic assumptions of Post Keynesian theory are especially appealing to students. In May 2014, I attended the first three meetings of the newly formed Beijing Heterodox Economics Study Group. Many of the attendees were already familiar with PK theory, though much less knowledgeable about other heterodox paradigms. In explaining their interest in heterodox economics, the students criticized neoclassical theory for elevating mathematical beauty over realism. They also faulted the neoclassical paradigm for being a-historical, methodologically narrow, disconnected from other social sciences, insufficiently attentive to dynamic (rather than static) modeling, and insufficiently attentive to disequilibrium (rather than equilibrium) moments.

On a different occasion, I spoke with a PK economist from Peking University about his students' responses to PK ideas. The professor organizes part of his macroeconomics class as a debate between Gregory Mankiw (the author of one of the best selling neoclassical macroeconomic textbooks and chair of the President's Council of Economic advisors under George W. Bush) and Paul Davidson (editor of the *Journal of Post Keynesian Economics* and one of the founders of the PK paradigm). He reported that that about 10–20 percent of his students got engaged and excited by PK ideas, and noted they were usually his best students. Interestingly, this is about the same percentage of students who were energized by the aforementioned introductory Marxist economics class.

### 9.6.8 Broad heterodox economics initiatives

There have been a number of global initiatives with respect to heterodox economics in recent years that have given institutional support to heterodox economic activities in China. Two of the most important of these are the formation of the World Economics Association (WEA) in 2011 and the Institute for New Economic Thinking (INET) in 2009. The birth of the Rethinking Economics movement in 2013 may also prove to be significant. The World Economics Association is an online association of people interested in expanding economic discussion beyond orthodox neoclassical boundaries. It already has over 12,000 members and publishes three online journals (the *World Economic Review, Economic Thought,* and the *Real World Economic Review*), a newsletter, and books. It also oversees online conferences and blogs. From May 5 to June 14, 2013, it organized an online conference about reforming the economics curriculum.

The WEA enables potentially isolated critics and skeptics about neoclassical economics to participate in international discussions of heterodox ideas. Ten Chinese economists were among the original 150 or so founding members of WEA. The 10 individuals are: Chen Ping, Peking University and Fudan University; Ding Xiaoqin, Chinese Academy of Social Science; Gu Shulin, Tsinghua University; Huang Kainan, Shandong University; Huo Yanli, Chiba Institute of Technology; Lo Dic, Renmin University of China and University of London; Henry C. K. Liu; Ma Ying, Wuhan University; Wang Yougui, Beijing Normal University; and Zuo Dapei, Institute of Economics, Chinese Academy of Social Sciences.

The website of the Institute for New Economic Thinking declares, "The havoc wrought by our recent global financial crisis has vividly demonstrated the deficiencies in our outdated current economic theories, and shown the need for new economic thinking..." INET was jumpstarted by a $50 million pledge from George Soros in the midst of the financial crisis, followed by large donations from venture capitalist William Janeway and Blackberry founder James Balsillie, and gifts from Paul Volcker, David Rockefeller, the Alfred P. Sloan Foundation, and the Carnegie Foundation, among others (INET Website). There do not appear to be any people from China among INET's senior staff and only two people from China (Yu Yongding of the

Institute of World Economy of CASS and Zhu Min of the IMF) among INET's ~31-member advisory board.

INET has awarded about $4 million dollars annually in research grants and sponsors economics conferences, campus meetings, and dedicated projects. It has established two committees, one in the UK and the other in the US, aimed at reforming the economics curriculum. While including diverse heterodox perspectives, INET's main thrust seems to be to develop a Keynesian financial architecture that can protect the world economy from financial crises, great depressions, and other serious crises, like the Great Recession. Casual feedback about INET funding and review of INET's personnel suggest it might align closer to orthodox economic approaches than the WEA.[50]

INET has been able to leverage the resources available for local heterodox initiatives in China, such as the Beijing Heterodox Economics Study Group, organized by Xiong Wanting, a graduate student in the Systems Science Department of Beijing Normal University, and Professor Wang Yougui, her intellectual mentor in that department. Both Ms. Xiong and Professor Wang had attended a 2014 INET conference in Toronto with INET financial assistance. The conference seemed to have deepened their connection to heterodox ideas. Yuan Yang, a part time INET organizer-facilitator, helped the study group make "Skype" contacts with other heterodox study groups. Yuan also helped arrange for live Skype presentations to the study group by Robert Johnson, the director of INET, and by well known Post Keynesian theorists Paul Davidson and John Smithin.

One of the most interesting aspects of INET and WEA's projects is the special attention given to younger economists. INET has a Young Scholar Initiative and WEA a Young Economist Facebook group. INET has held many conferences across the globe for "young scholars." INET has also been supportive of Yuan Yang's attempts to create Rethinking Economics groups on campuses across the globe. Midwifed into existence by a London conference in 2013 (supported by the New Economics Foundation), there are now 61 Rethinking Economics groups in more than 20 countries.

In a brief presentation about the functions of Rethinking Economics groups to a monetary theory class at Peking University in the spring of 2014, Yuan stressed the groups' "modernness," and its international membership. The Rethinking website emphasizes that most members are 18–34 years old. The message is that neoclassical theory is a leaden theory of the past, while the heterodox ideas of Rethinking Economics groups are the new ideas of the future. In May of 2015 more than 70 students from 10 different Chinese Universities met at Beijing Normal University for the 1st Forum on Rethinking Economics and New Economic Thinking in China. Among the heterodox paradigms explored were Post Keynesian economics, Austrian economics, behavioral finance, and econophysics.

The Internet has created the potential for heterodox economists and heterodox ideas to circumvent some of the gatekeepers of neoclassical economics, ensconced in editorial boards, admissions committees, and pro-motion committees. Lectures by leading heterodox theorists at INET and other economics conferences, for example, are now available to students and professors around the globe, even if they cannot attend the conferences in person.

We-Chat (Weixin)[51] and micro blogs have also emerged as another medium for shared economics discourse. We-Chat was established in 2011. Among other aps, it knits together non-anonymous groups of less than 100 people and is accessible on mobile phones. There were more than 200 million We-Chat users in China in 2013 and more than 600 million in 2016. Zhou Yi, a very thoughtful heterodox–oriented but neoclassically trained economist at Fudan University, believes that changes in the economics profession are likely to be spurred by discussions outside of economics departments, espe-cially internet based discussions. Recently the Chinese government has increased surveillance of these groups and this may inhibit their range of discussion.

### *9.6.9 Barriers impeding heterodox economics*

Zhang and Xu highlight several obstacles to a significant expansion of hetero-dox economics in China. The first is heterodoxy's lack of a unified theory with which to go head to head against neoclassical economics. Steven Keen has emphasized the same point. Institutionalist economics, Post Keynesian economics, and ecological economics, for example, all offer powerful insights within their sphere of discussion, but each lacks the comprehensiveness of orthodox theory.[52] The second obstacle is the limited exposure most Chinese students have to heterodox economics. Most students continue to encounter heterodox economics (if at all) through the lens of neoclassical theory in courses on the history of economic thought. These classes tend to celebrate the success of neoclassical economics as the triumph of rationality and dismiss alternative traditions as superseded theories. The overlap between heterodox theory and aspects of Marxist economics is also a barrier for some Chinese economics students.

Zhang and Xu call for efforts to find more clearly defined common ground among heterodox theories. They recommend that heterodox economists: (1) ally with Marxist economists in a broad community of heterodoxy; (2) hold an organizational meeting during the annual meetings of the Chinese Associ-ation for Political Economy; (3) hold a seminar during the annual meeting of the Chinese Foreign Economics Research society; (4) be active in the Chinese Forum of Evolutionary Economics; (5) push for continued trans-lations of heterodox ideas under the Commercial Press project; (6) put together textbooks on heterodox economics; and (7) increase ties with foreign heterodox economists (Zhang and Xu 2013, 322–323).

## 9.7 Conclusion

Institutionally, neoclassical economics has a strong hold on the Chinese economics profession. It dominates leading journals and departments. Its language continues to defuse into popular analyses of economics issues. It faces several challenges, however. Important elements of the Chinese state seem interested in enabling a more active state role in the economy than implied by the subtexts of neoclassical economics. The official language of legitimation for assessing public polices remains Marxist economics, even if only in vocabulary rather than substance. Residues of past Marxist ideas about workers being the masters of their enterprises remain in popular culture alongside modest recent increases in attention to heterodox economics in universities.

In this environment, it seems likely that neoclassical economics will continue to dominate formal economics training, but may not be allowed by the state to become fully hegemonic. This implies some continuing government support for Marxist economics in universities and tolerance (if not encouragement) of public discussion of some heterodox economic paradigms, such as the New Rural Reconstruction movement or ecological economics. Because of their association with Maoist periods, this tolerance is not likely to include the expansion of New Left economic ideas. It remains to be seen what kind of economic project NeoConfucianism might produce.[53]

## Notes

1 The universities represented were Peking University, Tsinghua, Renmin, Beijing Normal University, the University of International Business and Economics (UIBE), Zhejiang, Fudan, and the Shanghai University of Finance and Economics (SUFE).
2 These conclusions were echoed in a March 20, 2015 article in a leading Chinese academic journal published by the Chinese Academy of Social Sciences. The author, Qiu Haiping, is a Professor of economics at Renmin University. He notes that currently:

   1 Courses in business, finance, and economics use texts stressing Western economic ideas (including new institutionalist economics)
   2 Marxist oriented and political economy oriented courses have been marginalized in economics departments
   3 Some key economic journals credentialing Chinese professors privilege Western economic analyses over Marxist and political-economy analyses.

   Qiu confirms that many universities have spent significant sums of money recruiting PRC nationals with Western economics PhDs for their economics departments. He finds Western economics courses tend to cause "indifference or even resistance to political economics and all Marxist thought, leading ... (students) to doubt socialism ... (and have) a blind faith in the Western capitalist system..." (Qiu Haiping, "Westernized Economics Education Cannot Become Mainstream," in *Chinese Journal of Social Science (Zhong Guo She Hui Ke Xue Bao)*, March 20, 2015, posted by David Bandurski [within an essay entitled "The 'cancer' of all things Western," on the Website of the China Media Project]. Accessed April 25, 2015.
   Bandurski tends to ridicule Qiu's concerns.

3 The Chinese Economic Association of North American (CEANA) has traditionally been oriented toward students from Taiwan and the Chinese Economist
Society (CES) oriented toward students from the mainland.
4 American Economic Association website, "RFE: Resources for Economists on
the Internet."
5 Dani Rodrik's weblog May 7, 2013 (http://rodrik.typepad.com/, accessed January
8, 2016).
6 Huang Bin, "Research on Modern Teaching Modes of Western Economics Based
on Research Methods of Western Economics," (www.seiofbluemountain.com/
upload/product/200909/2008jyhy02a49.pdf, accessed October 9, 2016).
7 See especially Chapters 3 and 4 of *The Rhetoric of Economics* (McCloskey 1985).
8 The bombing amplified the ill will created by the Yin He incident. In 1993, the
US navy forced a Chinese ship (the Yin He) to divert to Saudi Arabia to be
searched for the presence of chemical weapons. No chemical weapons or chem-
icals weapons materials were found. The US did not apologize for the naval con-
frontation (*New York Times* September 6, 1993).
9 See Wang 2003a for a discussion of these issues in Chinese academic journals,
such as *Dushu* and *Tianya* (99).
10 Zhao Yuezhi 2008, 291–292; Fewsmith 2008, 262–267; Guo and Zhang 2013,
226–227.
11 Liu argued: "We shouldn't simply talk about reform, but should discuss socialist
reform … we shouldn't throw away how Marxism analyzes different social classes"
(Liu interview, 15). See also Freeman and Yuan 2011, 14.
 In 2011 Liu summed up some of his ideas upon receiving the Marxian Economics Award from the World Association for Political Economy. He wrote,

> I advocated … the development of Marxism with the aid of Western theories
> of economics, [retaining the] laborer's standpoint. … The fundamental prin-
> ciples of socialism must be held against the capitalist privatization, marketiza-
> tion, liberalization and polarization…

(Liu 2011)

12 Wang et al. (2008), for example, cite a survey finding nearly 90 percent of netizens crediting Lang with " 'hitting the nail on the head' " (32, 43).
13 http://chinadigitaltimes.net/2011/10/strikes-protests-surge-in-china. Arrighi cites
a slightly different number of "officially reported cases of 'public order disruptions'": 10,000 in 1993; 50,000 in 2002; and 87,000 in 2005 (Arrighi 2008,
377–378). Esther Pan (2005) cites estimates by China's Public Security Ministry
that 3.75 million people were involved in 74,000 protests in 2004. Lagerkvist
reports 127,000 incidents in 2007 (the last year the central government released
official "incident" statistics) and suggests current rates are as high as 180,000/year
(Lagerkvist 2015, 151, 137). Arrighi finds that protests by older laid off SOE
workers were "easily contained" by the state. Unrest among younger migrant
workers and urban workers in the service sector, however, was potentially more
explosive (2008, 377–378). While the reporting criterion is inconsistent, it seems
likely that the general picture of increasing public unrest is accurate. For recent
information on growing labor unrest see numerous materials published by the
*China Labour Bulletin*. The increase in reported incidents seems to reflect both a
rise in incidents and an increase in reporting.
14 The most famous rural protest is probably the Dongzhou protests of 2005, which
led to the deaths of 3–30 protesters (there is debate over the exact number) from
police gunfire.
15 Li He also finds minimal New Left influence in economics departments (Li He
2009, 37). Many discussions of the New Left in China cite a few key authors. The
most frequently cited individuals I have come across are: Wang Hui, Cui Zhiyuan,

Wang Shaoquang, and Gan Yang. Wang Shaoguang and Cui Zhiyuan are Professors of political science. Wang Hui is a Professor of Chinese literature and Gan Yang a political philosopher.

16 While sensitive to the existence of uncertainty and imperfect information and the reality of economic development as a learning process, Lin seems to ignore the full implications of Keynes's focus on the implications of "fundamental uncertainty [as opposed to probabilistic uncertainty]." His methodological individualism similarly discourages him from thinking about the socially created limits of bounded rationality.

17 In a friendly debate with Lin, heterodox economist Ha-Joon Chang similarly argues "the rational-choice, individualistic foundation of neoclassical economics limits its ability to analyse the uncertain and collective nature of the technological learning process, which is at the heart of economic development" (Lin and Chang 2009, 501). See Fine and Waeyenberge (2013) for a more critical assessment of Lin's retention of core neoclassical economic ideas in his conception of new structural economics.

18 As late as 1983–1984, two-hour Saturday political study groups were mandatory for economics students at Nanjing University (Herschede 1985, 309).

19 The *Far Eastern Economic Review* reported similar student reactions to "political courses" in 1986 (Scott 1986, 63).

20 At Renmin University the level of professorial enthusiasm was higher and the courses appear to have been better received by students.

21 In his article "Reflections on Chinese Marxism," Robert Ware argues this point more broadly. He finds that decades of socialist-Marxist education, revolutionary ideals, and the merging of Chinese socialism with Chinese nationalism are part of China's cultural memory, concluding "Marxism continues to be a strong force" (Ware 2013, 145).

22 There have been numerous campaigns by the Party to renew Chinese Marxism among college students, especially at elite universities. Rosen (1993) recounts some of those efforts. Demonstrating the challenge the Party has faced, he cites the responses of Beijing college students to the question: "What Ideals Do You Think University Students Should Establish?" Over the two-year period 1986–1988, the percentages identifying "Communism" or Socialism fell from (38 percent, 16 percent) to (6 percent, 5 percent) (Rosen 1993, 324). Heavy handed efforts to reverse this trend after the Tiananmen Square incident led to mandatory one year military training for all Peking University and Fudan first year students that included course work on the leadership's view of the Tiananmen Square protests. Rosen argues that this program, like others, failed to renew students' adherence to ideals sympathetic to the government (317–321, 331). He cites similar attitudes among high school students. The Party's traditional methods for imparting its vision of the world (study groups, criticism-self criticism) seem poorly suited for the current period shaped by mass media and competition from market driven sources.

23 Recent requirements of the economics major at Peking University are:

1 Four math courses (two calculus classes, linear algebra, and a statistics course). To get an edge in graduate school applications, some undergraduates take additional math classes, such as courses in mathematical analysis.
2 One year of principles of economics.
3 One year of intermediate economic theory (half year intermediate microeconomics, half year intermediate macroeconomics).
4 Three years of dedicated topics courses (each at half year: game theory, information economics, money and banking, international economics, industrial organization, and economic development).

   5  Two years of economic history classes (each at half year: history of Western economic thought, history of Chinese economic thought, world economic history, history of Chinese economy).

   6  A year of political economy (half year on principles of capitalism and half year on principles of socialism).

   7  Selected reading of Capital (half a year).

(Source: interview with department professor)

24  Discussion with economics professor in Peking University economics department.

25  Interview.

26  One of my interviewees indicated that in the last few years it has again become possible for Marxist articles to be published in *Economic Research*. Zhang and Xu (2013, 314) similarly suggest that there has been an increase in interest in heterodox economics during the last few years (12).

27  Kotz 2007, 61. Cheng Enfu's description of Wang Dongjing's lecture to provincial and ministerial leaders in 2004 depicts fertile ground for similar comments. Cheng finds Wang arguing for a Marxism embracing private property, *homo economicus*, and the idea that "man dies for money as birds die for food" (Cheng 2012). Wang was a professor at and a former director of the Economics Department of the Central Party School.

28  In 2014, perhaps as many as 5 percent of pedestrians in a neighborhood near Peking University where I lived routinely wore surgical looking breathing masks due to high levels of air pollution. These images (ironically, more than the air pollution itself) imparted a visceral sense of environmental hazards. While many people I talked with adopted a fatalistic stance toward environmental hazards (telling me: "you can't live your daily life wearing a breathing mask, even if that might be the rational thing to do"), the long term message was that current policies are unsustainable.

29  Huan (2010b) offers an interesting history of recent ecological thinking and ecological politics in China, including an empirical discussion of environmental Kuznets Curves. He notes that while soot emissions have been falling and forest coverage rising (suggesting environmental improvement), other indices of pollution, such as SO2 emissions and industrial solid waste production have been growing. He implies that the aggregate direction is toward environmental deterioration (though there is no attempt at a complete accounting).

30  Huan 2010b, 200. As Huan notes, there are different interpretations within the CPC of what an "ecological civilization with Chinese characteristics" means. Huan's socialist vision rejects the relentless pressures for growth in capitalism emanating from competitive pressures for capital accumulation. Exactly how the economy might be organized to avoid these pressures is not fully addressed.

    Wang et al. indicate that James O'Connor's work initially stimulated Chinese interest in Ecological Marxism. Since 2006, John Bellamy Foster's work seems to have received the most attention, with 175 articles referring to his work since 2010 (Wang et al. 2013).

31  Li was imprisoned for his association with the Tiananmen Square unrest and free market ideology. His exile, however, was due to his subsequent conversion to a Marxist perspective and criticism of current government policies from the left. His work has often been grouped with the Chinese New Left.

32  Zhou Yi, for example, finds three new Marxist political textbooks relatively weak in attention to environmental issues (Zhou Yi 2015, 152).

33  Huang Haifeng reports that a recent survey of Chinese university students found that only 2.2 percent rated their required political education courses very highly (Huang 2015, 437 fn 39).

34 The discussion of Western economics in China in 1900–1949 relies heavily on work done by Paul Trescott, especially Trescott 2007. I have not footnoted page numbers for each separate conclusion.

35 American influence on Chinese education was facilitated by a 1908 decision to use some of the American share of the indemnity payments imposed on China after the Boxer Rebellion to fund Chinese students studying in the US and to establish Tsinghua College to prepare students for such study (Trescott 2007, 61). Tsinghua has since become one of China's elite universities.

36 Among the schools Trescott emphasizes as responsible for promoting institutional-ist economics in China are: Columbia University, the alma mater of Ma Yinchu, President of Peking University (Trescott 2007, 69–70) and Ji Chaoding, a high ranking official in the Chinese banking system (70); the University of Wisconsin, home to American economists John R. Commons ("old" institutionalism) and Richard Ely (Social Gospel theorist) and the alma mater of Yong Wenyuan, Dean of the Shanghai College of Finance and Economics, and Chow Ling, "a high official with the People's Bank" (73).

37 Xu Yunan (Cambridge PhD 1940) was the first Chinese economist to translate Keynes's *General Theory*. He was a student of both Keynes and Joan Robinson and brought their form of heterodox economics to Peking University (Trescott 2007, 251, 253).

38 Trescott 2007, 121.

39 Ryan Dutch uses a 15 percent figure for the entire 1919–1949 period ("Reflec-tions on missionary education in modern China," a paper prepared for the confer-ence on The American Context of China's Christian Colleges, Wesleyan University, September 19–20, 2002).

40 Trescott finds that Ely favored government policies to reduce inequality, did not use marginal productivity theory to explain wage differentials, and favored gov-ernment intervention in the economy to reduce the power of big firms (Trescott 2007, 128).

41 Trescott notes that "[m]any Chinese studied Economics at Columbia and Wis-consin, schools where 'institutional economics' stressed the defects rather than the virtues of free markets…" (9). He laments that the classical liberal subtexts of con-temporary neoclassical economics (that "profit maximization would achieve social efficiency" and that income distributions "reflected the marginal productivity") were not diffused more widely in pre-revolution China, adding, "A better under-standing of these matters might have mitigated the emphasis on 'class warfare' which produced much of the cruelty of the Maoist regime" (8).

42 For example, Jiang Shuojie, a student of Hayek, taught in Taiwan and the US, and worked for the IMF (Trescott 2007, 83–84). Wu Yuanli, another Hayek student, taught in the US and did research on China for the Hoover Institution (84).

43 See Table 1 in Zhang and Xu (2013) for the journals cataloged.

44 Zhang and Xu note that Daniel Fusfeld's history of thought textbook (2003) has been translated into Chinese and seems to offer the most detailed discussion of heterodox ideas (313). A Chinese textbook by Lin Zhang (2008) was identified by Zhang and Xu as the only new text that discussed heterodox ideas at length.

It is possible that some heterodox influences have been overlooked in standard reviews of Chinese economic thought because of a tendency for insular discourse within Anglo-American neoclassical economics. Heilmann and Shih, for example, report that Yang Zhi, an expert on Japanese industrial policy and one of the archi-tects of Chinese industrial economics, has been ignored in Western studies of Chinese economics. They link this neglect to "his non-neoclassical analytical and prescriptive framework." They report that his textbook on industrial economics was widely used in the 1980s and 1990s and his work was "extremely influential among Chinese economic planners" (Heilmann and Shih 2013, 9). Japanese advisors in China seem to have been especially influential with respect to indicative planning, industrial policy along the lines of MITI, and enterprise management and quality control (Vogel 2011, 462–463).

45 Professor Jia Genliang of Renmin University has been a major spokesperson for evolutionary economics within China. Recently there has been an effort to create a network of economists interested in evolutionary economics in China. To this purpose a workshop was held at Wuhan University March 22–23, 2008.

46 Warner 2014, 99.

47 A 1987 World Bank report discusses the observations of Professor John Gurley, an American Marxist teaching in China at the time and presumably offering advice to Chinese economists, if not policy makers. Song's 1985 article published in the *Beijing Review* cited work by Keynes and the neo-Cambridge school. In *Salon* in 2004, Galbraith indicated,

> "In the mid-1990s I served as chief technical advisor to a Chinese State Planning Commission project on macroeconomic reform, a job that centered on advising them as to which Western economists to talk to, and which ones to avoid. I *loved* the second part of that job."
> (James K. Galbraith, "Debunking the Economist—again"; Salon Marcy 22, 2004, www.salon.com/2004/03/22/economist/, accessed August 11, 2014)

48 There may have been some such papers, but I could not identify them from their titles. There were some papers on gender issues, but these did not appear to take a feminist methodological approach distinct from neoclassical theory. There were, however, some very interesting neoclassical papers, for example a presentation by Nobel Prize winner Eric Maskin on why global markets have not reduced inequality; a paper on intellectual property rights issues by Keith Maskus; and a paper on climate change policy by Scott Taylor. Members of the CES were also extremely friendly and welcoming to a new participant in their discussions.

49 www.dime-eu.org/node/505; and www.dime-eu.org/files/active/2/Workshop%20on%20Evolutionary%20Economics%20and%20Evolutionary%20Economic%20Geograph1.pdf.

50 Cynics might rephrase INET's mission to be protecting the world's financiers from these crises. While this goal might be accurate, I think the inference that INET was established solely or even primarily for this purpose is probably wrong. INET funders, such as George Soros, seem to be motivated by social purposes beyond their immediate self-interest. While their vision of the architecture of a good society may have serious limitations from the perspectives of some heterodox theorists, I think it is not simply a cover for the pursuit of self-interest. Rather than question the motives of INET's sponsors, I think the key issue is how far the sponsors' concepts of rethinking extend. The potential limits of INET's vision may be symbolized by INET's "dress code" advice to young people attending a recent INET conference: "While there is no formal dress code, most attendees will be wearing business attire. It's a long conference, so also try to dress comfortably." (INET web page, Young Scholar's Initiative, accessed June 26, 2014). For a discussion of heterodox concerns about INET see Haering 2014.

51 A Weibo based campaign from 2011–2013 (PM2.5) pressured the Chinese government to make greater efforts to monitor and regulate fine particle air pollution. Some of the leaders of this campaign however, seem to have been targeted for reprisals by the state, so the legacy of the campaign for public activism is ambiguous ("Air Pollution Policy Making and Social Media in Beijing 2011–2013," by Johan van de Ven. Posted by Danwei (A service of the *Financial Times*, www.danwei.com/beijing-fog-investigating-air-pollution-policy-making-in-beijing-between-2011-and-2013/, accessed March 24, 2016).

In Feb 2015 an environmental video went viral. "Under the Dome," a documentary about air pollution, especially in Beijing, quickly garnered tens of millions of views and was eventually shut down by the censors; *China Digital Times*, March 1, 2015 (http://chinadigitaltimes.net/2015/03/minitrue-dont-hype-dome/, accessed March 30, 2015). See also http://theconversation.com/deadly-air-the-smog-shrouding-chinas-future-11617, accessed May 5, 2017.

52 The demand for abstract completeness, as opposed to realistic concreteness, may itself be a source of debate. Institutionalist economics, for example, tends to abjure grand theories about how the entire economic system works in favor of detailed analysis of particular sectors.

53 Drawing on his experiences as a visiting professor in China (2007–2011), Robert Ware alludes to the possibility of a Marxist-Confucian dialogue, akin to the Marxist Christian dialogues of the 1960s and the spirit of liberation theology (Ware 2013, 150–151). He highlights the importance of ethical critiques of capitalism to socialist movements. He suggests that the amoral appearance of "scientific socialism" weakens popular activism and seems to argue that a socialist morality is imminent in Marx's historical materialism (Ware 2013, 157–158).

# References

Anderson, Perry. 1976. *Considerations on Western Marxism*. London: Verso.

Arrighi, Giovanni. 2008. *Adam Smith in Beijing: Lineages of the Twenty-First Century*. New York: Verso.

Cao, Cong. 2008. "China's Brain Drain at the High End." *Asian Population Studies* 4 (3): 331–345. doi:10.1080/17441730802496532.

Cheng, Enfu. 2012. "Seven Currents of Social Thought and their Development in Contemporary China, with a Focus on Innovative Marxism." *The Marxist* 27 (4). Available at http://cpim.org/sites/default/files/marxist/201204-Cheng%20Enfu.pdf.

Chow, Gregory. 2000. "The Teaching of Modern Economics in China." *Comparative Economic Studies* 42 (2): 51–60. doi:10.1057/ces.2000.8.

Du, Yuxin. 2011. "A Bibliometrics Portrait of Chinese Research through the Lens of *China Economic Review*." Master's thesis, Universidade do Porto.

Fewsmith, Joseph. 2008. *China since Tiananmen: From Deng Xiaoping to Hu Jintao*. 2nd ed. New York: Cambridge University Press.

Fine, Ben, and Elisa Van Waeyenberge. 2013. *A Paradigm Shift that Never Will Be?: Justin Lin's New Structural Economics*. SOAS Department of Economics Working Paper Series. Vol. 179. London: SOAS Department of Economics.

Freeman, Charles W. III, and Wen Jin Yuan. 2011. *China's New Leftists and the China Model Debate After the Financial Crisis*. Washington, DC: Center for Strategic and International Studies.

Guo, Xibao and Ping Zhang. 2013. "Thirty Years of Disputes on China's Economic Reform." In *Thoughts on Economic Development in China*, edited by Ying Ma and Hans-Michael Trautwein, 217–234. New York: Routledge.

Haering, Norbert. 2014. "George Soros' INET: A Conspiracy Theory Assessment." *World Economic Association Newsletter* 4 (2).

Heilmann, Sebastian and Lea Shih. 2013. "The Rise of Industrial Policy in China, 1978–2012." *Harvard-Yenching Institute Working Paper Series*: July 31, 2013.

Herschede, Fred. 1985. "Economics as an Academic Discipline at Nanjing University." *The China Quarterly* (102): 304–316. doi:10.1017/S0305741000029969.

Huan, Qingzhi. 2010a. "Eco-Socialism in an Era of Capitalist Globalization: Bridging the West and the East." In *Eco-Socialism as Politics: Rebuilding the Basis of our Modern Civilisation*, edited by Qingzhi Huan, 1–14. New York: Springer.

Huan, Qingzhi. 2010b. "Growth Economy and its Ecological Impacts upon China: An Eco-Socialist Analysis." In *Eco-Socialism as Politics: Rebuilding the Basis of our Modern Civilisation*, edited by Qingzhi Huan, 191–203. New York: Springer.

Huang, Haifeng. 2015. "Propaganda as Signaling." *Comparative Politics* 47 (4): 419–444.

Kotz, David. 2007. "The State of Official Marxism in China Today." *Monthly Review* 59 (4): 58–63. http://monthlyreview.org/2007/09/01/the-state-of-official-marxism-in-china-today/.

Lagerkvist, Johan. 2015. "The Unknown Terrain of Social Protests in China: 'Exit', 'Voice', 'Loyalty', and 'Shadow'." *Journal of Civil Society* 11 (2): 137–153. doi:10.10 80/17448689.2015.1052229. https://knox.idm.oclc.org/login?url=http://search.ebscohost.com/login.aspx?direct=true&db=poh&AN=103736600&site=ehost-live.

Li, He. 8/2008. "China's New Left and its Impact on Political Liberalization." *EAI Background Brief* (401).

Li, He. 2009. "China's New Left." *East Asian Policy* 1 (1): 30–37.

Li, He. 2010. "Debating China's Economic Reform: New Leftists Vs. Liberals." *Journal of Chinese Political Science* 15 (1): 1–23. doi:10.1007/s11366-009-9092-4. https://knox.idm.oclc.org/login?url=http://search.ebscohost.com/login.aspx?direct=true&db=a9h&AN=48357181&site=ehost-live.

Lin, Justin Yifu. 2012c. *Benti and Changwu: Dialogues on Methodology in Economics*. Beijing: Peking University Press.

Lin, Justin Yifu, and Ha-Joon Chang. 2009. "Should Industrial Policy in Developing Countries Conform to Comparative Advantage or Defy it? A Debate between Justin Lin and Ha-Joon Chang." *Development Policy Review* 27 (5): 483–502. doi:10.1111/j.1467-7679.2009.00456.x.

Liu, Guoguang. "Interview with Dr. Heng Lin." Chinese Academy of Social Sciences website: experts, 1st group CASS members, Liu Guoguang, http://casseng.cssn.cn/experts/experts_1st_group_cass_members/201402/t20140221_969619.html.

Liu, Guoguang. 2011. "Speech upon Receiving the Marxian Economics Award." *World Review of Political Economy* 2 (3): 366–370. www.jstor.org/stable/41931930.

McCloskey, Donald N. 1985. *The Rhetoric of Economics*. 1st ed. Madison, WI: University of Wisconsin Press.

Pan, Esther. 2005. "China's Angry Peasants." *Council on Foreign Relations Backgrounder (Archives)* (December 15, 2005).

Perkins, Dwight H. 2002. "The Challenge China's Economy Poses for Chinese Economists." *China Economic Review* 13 (4): 412–418.

Rosen, Stanley. 1993. "The Effect of Post-4 June Re-Education Campaigns on Chinese Students." *The China Quarterly* (134): 310–334. Doi: 10.1017/S0305741000029702.

Scott, Margaret. October 23, 1986. "Tinkering with Reforms to China's Universities." *Far Eastern Economic Review*, 60–63.

Song, Longxiang. 1995. "The Methodology of Mainstream Economics and its Implications for China's Economic Research." PhD diss., Washington University.

Trescott, Paul B. 2007. *Jingji Xue: The History of the Introduction of Western Economic Ideas into China, 1850–1950*. Hong Kong: Chinese University Press.

Vogel, Ezra F. 2011. *Deng Xiaoping and the Transformation of China*. Cambridge, MA: Harvard University Press.

Wang, Hui. 2003a. *China's New Order: Society, Politics, and Economy in Transition*, edited by Theodore Huters. Cambridge, MA: Harvard University Press.

Wang, Hui. 2003b. "The New Criticism." In *One China, Many Paths*, edited by Chaohua Wang, 55–86. New York: Verso.

Wang, Qingxin K. 2011. "The Rise of Neoclassical Economics and China's WTO Agreement with the United States in 1999." *Journal of Contemporary China* 20 (70): 449–465. doi:10.1080/10670564.2011.565177.

Wang, Yicheng, Ning Fang, Bingquan Wang, and Ruisheng Liu. 2008. *A Study on Contemporary Chinese Intelligentsia and Media Elite—Survey II of Contemporary China's New Social Structural Changes*. Institute of Political Science, Chinese Academy of Social Sciences.

Wang, Zhihe. 2012. "Ecological Marxism in China." *Monthly Review* 63 (9): 36–44.

Wang, Zhihe, Meijun Fan, Hui Dong, Dezhong Sun, and Lichun Li. 2013. "What Does Ecological Marxism Mean for China? Questions and Challenges for John Bellamy Foster." *Monthly Review* 64 (9): 47–53.

Ware, Robert. 2013. "Reflections on Chinese Marxism." *Socialism & Democracy* 27 (1): 136–160. doi:10.1080/08854300.2012.754214.

Wheeler, Norton. 2012. *The Role of American NGOs in China's Modernization: Invited Influence*. New York: Routledge.

Zhang, Lin and Yingli Xu. 2013. "The Transmission of Heterodox Economics in China, 1949–2009." In *Thoughts on Economic Development in China*, edited by Ying Ma and Hans-Michael Trautwein, 306–326. New York: Routledge.

Zhao, Yuezhi. 2008. *Communication in China: Political Economy, Power and Conflict*. New York: Rowman & Littlefield.

Zhou, Yi. 2015. "Review of the New Textbook Series in Modern Political Economics." *World Review of Political Economy* 6 (1): 148–152. doi:10.13169/worlrevipoliecon.6.1.0148.

# 10 Conclusion

## Situating Chinese events in a global pattern and speculations about the future

### 10.1 Introduction

The institutionalization of neoclassical economic theory as the dominant economic paradigm in Chinese universities and its gradual diffusion into popular culture has been an important element in the evolving transition from socialism to capitalism in China. In the name of economic rationality and promoting faster economic growth, the spread of neoclassical economics has helped legitimize privatization, trade liberalization, and the "smashing of the iron rice bowl." Depending on your point of view, neoclassical economics has helped bring economic policy in China in line with the logic of objective conditions and produce an "economic miracle" (Lin et al. 2003; Brandt and Rawski 2008b), or it has encouraged Chinese leaders to sacrifice hard won social capital and socialist goals for extremely inequitably distributed increases in GDP and relentless environmental destruction (Hart-Landsberg and Burkett 2005; Li Minqi 2008).

We begin this concluding chapter with a brief review of the arguments we have made in earlier chapters about the nature of Chinese economic thought and economics education and the forces influencing their evolution. We conclude with some remarks on the future of Chinese economics and the relationship of Chinese experience to broader global patterns.

### 10.2 Review of Chapter 1: paradigm differences

In Chapter 1 we highlighted the importance of paradigmatic frames in economic thought and the role of texts and subtexts in distinguishing paradigms. While texts are explicit, subtexts are often implicit. Texts refer to a paradigm's formal theories. Subtexts refer to a paradigm's underlying methodological assumptions and the projects it is anticipated to enable.

Subtexts influence how paradigms are taught to students, in part by identifying what ideas are fundamental and what ideas are secondary to the paradigm. This distinction is helpful in determining permissible simplifications for conveying complex ideas to students or for applying paradigmatic ideas to analyze complex real world situations. Subtexts also influence how paradigms evolve, that is, how paradigms respond to anomalous information and new subject matter.

Subtexts influence the likely impact a paradigm will have in the world by orienting its practitioners in certain directions. Subtexts are contestable and can change, but as part of the subculture of a paradigmatic community they are slow and difficult to change.

In Chapter 1 we outlined the different subtexts of Marxist, neoclassical, and heterodox economics. We argued that these subtexts were responsible for the different directions that the paradigms were likely to take in analyzing economic events in China and socializing their transplanted members within China. In discussing neoclassical subtexts we emphasized that the neoclassical paradigm was built on the ideas of classical liberalism involving methodological individualism, the assumptions of *homo economicus* (rational economic man), and the project of increasing GDP/capita. The latter was treated as the particular contribution that economists could make to improving human welfare.

Methodological individualism assumes that the way to understand societal outcomes is to develop a theory that explains individual behavior (in the neoclassical case, this is "maximization subject to constraint" analysis by rational actors) and a framework for adding up these behaviors (in the neoclassical case, this is supply and demand equilibrium analysis). This approach treats individual tastes and preferences, and expectations of others' behavior, as independent (exogenous) variables. These variables are "taken as given" (presumably the reflection of human nature, but this is left unspecified). There is thus no discussion of capitalism as a reproducing social system.

The subtexts of neoclassical economics tend to treat market outcomes as practical optimums, implying that although participants' information may not be "perfect," markets make as good a use of available information as possible, leaving market outcomes the expression of rational choice. This package tends to produce public policy recommendations that range from strong to lite laissez-faire. Later chapters in the book linked neoclassical discussions of Chinese economic issues in general, and events in the rural, international, and state-owned enterprise sectors in particular, to these subtexts.

In discussing Marxist subtexts we emphasized the principle of holism (in the Marxist case, the assumption that capitalism can be studied as a reproducing social system with characteristics that are not based on inherent human nature but reflect the logic of capitalism as a particular social system), the assumption that individual agents are not hyper rational and markets not inherently stable, and a focus on the organization of labor as a "constitutive activity" that helps create human identities and social structures. As for the contribution of economics to human welfare, Marxist economics, like neoclassical economics, also gives a high priority to expanding GDP/capita. This project, however, is treated as an intermediate rather than a final goal. The ultimate goal of economic understanding for Marxist theory is enabling the transition to socialism and increasing human well-being. Marxist policy recommendations call for much greater social governance of markets than usually favored in neoclassical theory and initiatives to build socialism.

Like Marxist economics, the subtexts of heterodox economics tend to involve holist methodologies and more complicated psychologies of human behavior than *homo economicus*. Because heterodox economics is more diverse than Marxist or neoclassical economics it is difficult to generalize about other characteristics of the paradigm. The analysis tends to emphasize the specificity of different subject areas in economics and take an eclectic approach to economic analysis. Like Marxist economists, heterodox economists are more skeptical than neoclassical economists of whether maximizing GDP/capita will be correlated with maximizing human well-being, leaving it an insufficient target for designing economic policies.

Later chapters highlighted the influence of subtexts in different paradigms' analysis of economic issues, noting how these beliefs served as a kind of anchor or homing device for the development of their economic analysis.

## 10.3 Review of Chapter 2: domestic and international influences

Chapter 2 explored the forces inside and outside China promoting the replacement of Marxist economics by neoclassical economics as the dominant economic paradigm in China. The panoply of forces were multi-dimensional, synergistic, and very powerful. Some of them flowed behind the backs of participants, as the unintended consequence of actions taken for other reasons. Domestically, interest in neoclassical economics was spurred by:

1   the backlash against the Cultural Revolution, which valorized formerly transgressive ideologies like "Western Economics" (and discredited Marxist economics and socialist projects)
2   the credibility of Western economists as presumed experts on market economies and the desire of many Chinese economists to find new strategies for dealing with several chronic problems in the Chinese economy
3   the usefulness of neoclassical economics as a legitimizing ideology for Deng's marketization projects and for attempts by lower level Party officials to turn their bureaucratic privilege into monetized assets more easily transferred across generations
4   the desire of many older Chinese economists to renew ties with colleagues in the West, as well as younger economists' desire to participate in global economics discussions carried out in neoclassical language, and the growing use of market categories to describe market experience in everyday life
5   the scientific and a-political image of neoclassical theory implied by its heavy use of mathematics
6   the hope of many of the "best and brightest" Chinese students to study in the West, and

7 the association of pro-business credentials with neoclassical training and linked belief that these credentials would be useful for securing good jobs with Western firms or leading Chinese companies in the new economy.

Externally, the expansion of neoclassical economics in China was promoted by:

1 the American Economics Association, interested in promoting a Chinese economics discipline in its own image
2 many Western foundations and think tanks (with the Ford Foundation and Center for International Private Enterprise being especially notable) and their offspring in China (such as the China Center for Economic Research (CCER) and the Unirule Institute) interested in promoting free enterprise and market economies in the name of global economic growth
3 the World Bank, IMF, and other international economic institutions, similarly interested in promoting capitalist market economies in the name of economic growth, and
4 foreign governments and private businesses interested in promoting economic institutions, and economic policies in China congenial with their own political and economic interests.

Most of the foreign groups promoting the expansion of neoclassical economics believed in a "fortuitous correspondence." They felt that what was in their interests and favored by neoclassical economics (for example, freer trade and expanded foreign investment opportunities in China) was also in the interest of China.

While foreign institutions had significant influence on the development of the Chinese economics profession, it was in Norton Wheeler's memorable words, a case of "invited influence." Many domestic groups welcomed foreign partners in bringing neoclassical economics back to China. Like the expansion of Christianity centuries earlier, or development of English as the international language, the spread of neoclassical economics was the product of diverse and deeply rooted social dynamics. The sprouting of neoclassical ideas in any one place had both local (proximate) and deeper (systemic) causes.

The triumph of neoclassical economics illustrates Gramsci's concept of ideological hegemony. Neoclassical economics universalizes the perspective of employers, managers, and investors for thinking about economic events, in part because employers, investors and managers are treated as the medium through which market forces and market rationality assert themselves. On a less abstract level, Marc Blecher (2002) has analyzed how market outcomes and market institutions gained legitimating authority among Chinese workers, even those seriously harmed by the collapse of state-owned enterprises and the planned economy.[1]

## 10.4  Review of Chapter 3: historical context

In Chapter 3 we focused on two subjects: the historical context for the evolution of Chinese economic thought from 1976–2001 and the pattern of
change across five generations of Chinese economists. We demonstrated how
different historically significant public events in the lives of different generations of Chinese economists influenced their economic thinking. Older
Chinese economists (aged 50 or more when the reforms began in 1978) situated the feedback between economic events and economic theory against the
backdrop of the war of resistance against Japan and the revolutionary struggle
against the KMT, using largely Marxist language. Their theoretical innovations remained within a Marxist framework. Younger generations of economists situated their interpretation of events against the backdrop of the Great
Leap Forward and the Cultural Revolution, and increasingly used neoclassical
language to organize their thoughts. Older generations of Chinese economists
maintained Marxist subtexts, including the goal of socialism, while younger
generations shifted toward classical liberal subtexts. The change in outlook for
older economists adopting neoclassical theory was sometimes analogous to a
religious conversion experience.

The final step in the creation of a community of neoclassical economists in
China was the return of PhD economists from graduate study in the West,
especially in the United States. These scholars had absorbed the subculture of
neoclassical economists as well as formal models.

Chapter 3's brief history of Chinese economic reform revealed some
important patterns. Probably the most important trend was the tendency for
economic policies that increased the use of material incentives, market mechanisms, and competition to create pressures for additional restructuring in the
same direction. Chinese economic reform began with broad agreement
among Marxist and neoclassical economists about the policy changes needed
to renew the Chinese economy. Nearly everyone recommended shifting
resources from the investment to consumer goods sector and expanding small
scale market mechanisms. In the 1970s almost all Chinese economists were
committed to reforming socialism rather than promoting capitalism. They
believed that some market oriented reforms were appropriate for the historical conditions of the Chinese economy. They tried to build in safeguards to
prevent market oriented reforms from producing a capitalist economy. Over
time, most of these safeguards were overridden, such as efforts to limit wage
labor to a maximum of seven employees or requirements that a company's
stock be held by its workers.[2]

While initial debates between the plan adjusters (~Marxist central planners)
and the marketeers (Marxists more sympathetic to a bigger role for markets)
were won by the adjusters, the marketers gradually captured more and more
intellectual terrain. Perhaps even more importantly, the arguments used to
justify the expansion of market mechanisms shifted from arguments within a
Marxist framework to arguments from a neoclassical perspective. This shift

was not immediately apparent, as the policies remained the same, while the reasons for them gradually changed. Deng's intervention in the direction of policies that would maximize GDP growth and the power of the Chinese state were often decisive.

The events described in Chapter 3 raised three big questions for economic theory: (1) Does introducing significant market elements into parts of an economy inevitably lead to the spread of market relations to other areas of the economy; (2) Does the expansion of market relations inevitably lead to the adoption of neoclassical economic concepts for understanding markets and economics; and (3) Does the expansion of market relations inevitably lead to capitalism?

## 10.5 Review of Chapters 4–7: the co-evolution of economic events and economic theory

Chapters 4 through 7 illustrated in concrete detail the powerful framing effects of paradigms on economic analysis in the rural, international, and state-owned-enterprise sectors. Paradigmatic signatures were behind what questions were asked and what issues were attended to or ignored; what counterfactuals were assumed (i.e., what would/could have happened if things had been done differently); what futures were projected for different economic strategies; what master narrative was the backdrop for analyzing current economic events; what language and system of metaphor was adopted, and so on. The discussion also demonstrated the pervasive influence of subtexts on economic theory.

Neoclassical analyses were infused with the spirit of classical liberalism. They began with the assumption of *homo economicus* and the project of maximizing GDP. While often quite creative in applying neoclassical frames to Chinese landscapes (as with new institutionalist analyses of the early successes of TVEs), the analyses almost always ended with familiar neoclassical policy recommendations calling for laissez-faire lite or laissez-faire strong policies. The typical debates about rural decollectivization, privatization of SOEs, or opening to foreign investment, for example, were about the speed of convergence with the American model not the goal of convergence. It was ultimately a debate about shock therapy versus gradualism.

Rejecting classical liberalism, Marxist economic analyses began with the assumptions of historical materialism. A subset of Marxist theorists ("primary stage theorists") argued that China's low level of economic development required postponing most socialist practices and adopting some neoclassical ideas about economic development.

Other Chinese economists maintained more traditional Marxist beliefs. Like the neoclassicals, they prioritized increasing Chinese economic growth, but under constraints consistent with the project of building socialism in the foreseeable, rather than distant, future. Their approval of expanded markets in the countryside, for example, was contingent on businesses employing less than eight wage laborers. Their plans for revitalizing the SOEs excluded widespread privatization in key industries. When analyzing policies for the special economic zones they looked at their implications for the creation of reproducing class structures.

Heterodox economists generally held more diverse views than neoclassical or Marxist economists. While rejecting the hyper rational, well-informed, self-interested, isolated, utility maximizing individual of *homo economicus*, different heterodox schools emphasized different limitations of this starting point. Heterodox economists rejected the market-triumphant spirit of neoclassical theory's master narrative about Chinese economic evolution, but were tentative about what to replace it with. They lacked the Marxists' faith in the viability of collective institutions as well as the neoclassicals' faith in "free market outcomes."

For example, many heterodox economists rejected what Chris Bramall has called the "fable" of spontaneous decollectivization, but also recognized China's past problems with collective farming. They acknowledged problems with worker motivation in SOEs, but did not see these problems as inevitably fatal (like neoclassical economists) or inherently solvable (like Marxists). They wished to expand the projects of economic theory from the neoclassical project of maximizing GDP and the Marxist project of building socialism to include alternative development paths, such as those of the New Rural Reconstruction Movement.

### 10.5.1 *Rural sector*

Neoclassical economists were able to tell compelling stories about economic restructuring in the countryside. These stories were the springboard for the expansion of the paradigm. Neoclassical analyses linked the dramatic increase in agricultural output accompanying decollectivization and the impressive development of rural sideline occupations to heightened material incentives. They also highlighted the role of price signals in spurring a better matching of local growing conditions to consumer demand. They celebrated the rise and fall of local government owned or collectively owned township and village enterprises (TVEs) in response to market forces. They treated private firms' eventual replacement of the TVEs as a sign of economic progress and a reflection of the natural order of economic organization.

They condemned insider land grabs for urbanization, but ultimately tended to look the other way in response to corrupt privatization, viewing it as an acceptable, although regrettable, necessity on the way toward economic rationality. Neoclassical analyses of China's rural development fit comfortably within the paradigm's master narrative of "how the West got rich," and the spirit of classical liberalism.

Marxist and some heterodox analyses of the rural sector criticized neoclassical discussions for excessively devaluing the achievements of the collective era, for attributing too much of the increase in rural output to decollectivization rather than recently completed technological changes, for giving insufficient attention to the loss of economies of scale caused by decollectivization, and most importantly, for denying the possibility of reforming China's rural collective sector, rather than privatizing it. Marxist economists asked what the "end game was" for the rural sector and implied the choice was between large scale agribusiness (a la US agriculture in the 1950s relying on poorly treated migrant workers) and large scale collective production.

The continued viability of family farms has forced many rural development theorists in all paradigms to give greater attention to the long run viability of family farms. I suspect Marxist theory would have done better in paradigm competition had it maintained a socialist project that integrated the family farm into a socialist economic development strategy (as Marxist theorists attempted to do in the early 1950s with a voluntary collectivization strategy).

Marxist analyses and policy recommendations in all three subject areas were aimed at preventing the emergence of a desperate class of landless (or otherwise optionless) peasants and unemployed workers facing a class of employers and financiers governed solely by profit maximization. The neoclassicals counted on competition to create a harmonious, win–win situation out of this encounter. Marxists anticipated the grim work lives of the industrial revolution to arise from this encounter.

### 10.5.2 SOE sector

The debate over public ownership of enterprises in China echoed themes from the rural sector. When discussing Chinese SOEs the neoclassicals focused on the perceived failures, and assumed inherent shortcomings of public ownership. Even when there were productivity improvements and profitable balance sheets, the neoclassicals generally argued that these results were unsustainable, the product of unfair government favors and subsidies, or less impressive than private sector outcomes. Only modest effort was directed at figuring out how to create an environment where collective ownership or state ownership could work well. Very much effort was devoted to figuring out how to create optimal incentive structures and social institutions for private profit maximizing firms. The "gradualist," rather than "shock therapy" school of neoclassical economists supported creative transition policies, such as "dual-track" enterprise policies. These hybrid systems (dual track resource allocation and pricing, differential treatment of existing and new hires, etc.), however, were conceived as temporary policies, intended to prepare the way for the private sector's dominance of the Chinese economy. The layoffs of 50 million workers from state-owned enterprises and urban collectives in the mid to late 1990s were generally applauded by neoclassical theorists.

Marxist economists perceived the layoffs as helping to create a Reserve Army of the Unemployed. The lives of China's "floating population," pouring out of rural areas into brutal working conditions and subsistence life-styles, was analogized to the travails of the victims of the enclosures in Marxist narratives about English capitalism. Rather than a march toward technical rationality, Marxist economists saw a "race to the bottom" in the displacement of SOEs by TVEs, and TVEs by private firms, especially foreign-owned firms like Foxconn. Most importantly, Marxist economists "saw" the congealing of a new class structure which promised to reproduce steep inequalities far into the future. While one should not make too much out of an unfortunate choice of metaphors by Foxconn's chairman Terry Gou that compared its Chinese workers to animals in a zoo, the goal of Chinese workers as the "masters of their enterprise," was disappearing from the Chinese economy.

Unlike new institutionalist economists who treated China's emerging private enterprise structure as the outcome of optimizing institutional innovation, Marxist economists (using Social Structure of Accumulation models, for example) saw China's drift toward private enterprise as reflecting a complex interplay of objective conditions, ideology, and distributions of power. Both Marxist and neoclassical economists tended to make optimistic "trajectory" assumptions about the Chinese economy's ability to solve problems accompanying their current policy recommendations. Neoclassical economists countered Marxist concerns about rising inequality (for instance rapid increases in the Gini coefficients for the distribution of income and wealth) with casual appeals to optimistic Kuznets curves. Marxist economists countered neoclassical concerns about the high level of non-performing loans from SOEs with optimistic forecasts of future performance.

Some heterodox economists criticized both neoclassical and Marxist theorists for measuring the success of SOEs and private enterprises largely by the firms' level of output. Their arguments echoed concerns of the New Rural Reconstruction Movement. Professor Zhou Yi of Fudan University, for example, echoed E. F. Schumacher's belief that heterodox economics involved prioritizing different ends as well favoring different means for economic organization.

### 10.5.3 *International sector*

Debates about the international sector echoed themes addressed in the rural and SOE sectors. The special economic zones dominated by foreign capital served as a kind of laboratory for laissez-faire oriented economic strategies. Many policies initiated in the SEZs, subsequently spread to the entire economy.

The neoclassical project called for integrating China into the global division of labor in ways reflecting China's comparative advantage. The neoclassicals treated openness to foreign competition as a discipline that would force Chinese firms to produce efficiently. They treated membership in the WTO as a kind of Rubicon that once crossed would severely limit the ability of the Chinese state to intervene in the economy.

Oddly, both Marxist and neoclassical economists highlighted the use of WTO membership as a mechanism to impose more capitalist oriented practices on the Chinese economy. Neoclassical economists applauded this imposition; Marxist economists resisted it. While not in favor of autarky, Marxist and some heterodox economists argued for much more state management of China's interaction with the world economy. Marxists opposed WTO policies that would limit the state's ability to favor SOEs. They urged continued capital controls and strong industrial policies. Although not entirely ruled out, these policies were treated skeptically by most neoclassical economists. Some heterodox economists, like Chris Bramall, called for China to withdraw from the WTO to ensure it was not mired at the bottom of the global value chain. Frequently the debate between Marxist and neoclassical economists boiled down to the extent to which economic life should be determined by market competition. Because of the dominance of state policy by nationalist objectives, resistance to complete deference to the world market remained strong in China.

### 10.5.4 The future

The neoclassical agenda carried clear implications for future policies. In rural areas it called for full privatization of land. In the SOE sector it called for continued privatization of public firms. In the international sector it called for opening up new industries to foreign competition, especially in the financial sector. Marxist theory called for constructing socialism. Marxist economists struggled to develop "safeguards" that would permit the use of some market mechanisms alongside socialist practices. Competitive pressures in the marketplace, however, and feedback from market activities to ways of thinking and concentrations of political power, constantly expanded the domain of capitalist oriented practices and shrank the socialist sector.

## 10.6 Review of Chapters 8 and 9: the evolution of Chinese economics education

### 10.6.1 Chapter 8: Chinese economics education 1978–2000

Chapter 8 analyzed how and why neoclassical economics replaced Marxist economics as the dominant paradigm organizing Chinese economics education. Neoclassical economists portray the change as a triumph of reason over ideology. A "sociology of knowledge"-oriented analysis tells a different and more complex story. As detailed in Chapter 2, many domestic and foreign interests worked very hard to establish neoclassical economics in China. The paradigm shift was not a spontaneous "a ha" moment when Chinese economists realized the scientific superiority of neoclassical economics. Many historical factors, at best indirectly related to economic theory (such as the backlash against the Cultural Revolution) also facilitated the ascendancy of neoclassical economics. The fundamental change involved a shift in subtexts. Many of the ideas embodied in initial reform policies were compatible with both Marxist and neoclassical paradigms. Oddly enough, for a while there was agreement on reform policies without agreement on how to think about these policies.

What engendered the triumph of neoclassical theory was the triumph of its subtexts, and this triumph reflected broad ideological currents and political projects rather than scientific principles. While it is true that some Marxist theories seemed quite irrelevant to China's economic problems in 1978, so did many neoclassical theories. While it is true that some neoclassical constructs (like the short run price elasticity of supply) or statistical tools (like econometrics) appeared quite useful, they also could be deployed within a Marxist framework. Thus, rather than a scientific reassessment, the paradigm shift in Chinese economics was more like a change in worldview.

As outlined in Chapter 8, the shift to neoclassical economics in Chinese universities was a top down affair. Neoclassical economics was perceived as a predictable ally for the state's marketization-modernization project. It also was probably thought to be "scientific," by some Chinese leaders (though its political usefulness probably outweighed its imagined practical usefulness, as technical experts were not very influential in the early days of reform). The Ministry of Education signaled its endorsement of neoclassical economics through highly publicized meetings with famous American neoclassical economists (like Milton Friedman and Gregory Chow). It also distributed funds to elite universities' economics programs partially based on their degree of Westernization, established special professorships paying up to four times standard salaries to attract foreign trained economists, and set up committees to write economics textbooks modeled on US textbooks. While the process was top down, faculty and students were largely sympathetic to the reorientation. There was a widespread desire to share in the West's prosperity and it was thought that knowing neoclassical economics might prove a valuable credential, regardless of its actual usefulness.

The World Bank was especially influential in creating a policy discourse that assumed a neoclassical frame and a neoclassical vocabulary. While very diplomatic in its proselytizing, the World Bank's advisors, economic studies, and promise of large loans, strongly influenced Chinese leaders' orientation toward economics. The Ford Foundation was influential in gathering the "best and brightest" of Chinese graduate students for seminars on neoclassical economics in China and for doctoral study in the West (especially in the US). The final step cementing the reorganization of Chinese economics departments was the return of Chinese graduate students who had recently earned their PhDs in the United States. Economics graduate school involves more than technical training. It involves socialization into a community of scholars sharing a common framework. For graduate students, neoclassical terminology becomes the language of thinking. Like becoming a doctor or a lawyer, becoming a neoclassical economist impacts one's identity as well as skills, although much of this effect goes on behind the backs of the participants. Over time, attendance at neoclassical conferences, subscriptions to neoclassical journals, and membership in neoclassical networks (*guanxi*) consolidated neo-classical identities.

The institutional advantages of neoclassical economics gradually crowded out Marxist economics in China. Undergraduate and graduate school curric-ulums were rewritten (often with the aid of American economists, or Hong Kong economists, such as Steven Cheung, trained in the US). Entrance exams for graduate study were rewritten to prioritize neoclassical subject matter. Editorial policies at leading Chinese journals shifted away from favor-ing Marxist to neoclassical subtexts. Tenure requirements at leading Chinese universities privileged publication in elite foreign neoclassical journals.

Beginning with Professor Chow's entrance exams for access to overseas economics programs, the paradigm shift from Marxist to neoclassical eco-nomics led to the recruitment of mathematicians rather than social theorists into economics. The paradigm shift recast Chinese economics from a discip-line studying the economy as part of a reproducing social system, to a discip-line studying rational behavior by maximizing individuals. The paradigm shift redirected economic theory from the project of building socialism to the project of maximizing GDP. The paradigm shift gradually changed the schol-arly voice of leading economists from that of a practical Marxist like Chen Yun, to reform oriented Marxists like Liu Guoguang, to neoclassically ori-ented economists like Wu Jinglian, to classical liberals like Lin Justin Yifu and Zhang Weiying. The latter two economists were the well known directors of the China Center for Economic Research (CCER) at Peking University. Neoclassical think tanks like the CCER played an important role in recon-structing Chinese economics education. Like Unirule, the CCER was ani-mated by classical liberalism, and passed this on to economics students.

Ultimately both neoclassical and Marxist economics had to build formal models of the Chinese economy and to offer analyses of societal outcomes, not just individual maximizing decisions. Each innovated in its own way. For example, the neoclassical paradigm offered new institutionalist economic ana-lyses of China's enterprise structure in the 1980s and 1990s. Marxist theorists developed Social Structure of Accumulation theories of China's economic evolution. The neoclassical project gained public attention, the Marxist project remained obscure.

### 10.6.2 Chapter 9: Current state of chinese economics education

Chapter 9 summarized the state of Chinese economics today. It emphasized the dominance of formal economic analysis by neoclassical theory (leavened with new institutionalist economics) and the large shadow cast by its classical liberal subtexts. On a policy level, the Chinese state retains a bigger role in the economy than recommended by the logic and subtexts of neoclassical theory. Some observers have suggested that the "Beijing Consensus," endors-ing this role, is an intellectual challenge to the "Washington Consensus" derived from neoclassical economics. The formal structure of Chinese economic theory, however, implies that the Beijing hybrid is a temporary stop on the journey to a more laissez-faire economy. In other words, the Beijing Consensus, like earlier experiments with the dual-track economy and TVEs, will probably prove to be a transitional policy rather than an alternative policy to classical liberal projects. It is possible that China will develop a theory of state capitalism that will append a big state to neoclassical economics, but this would seem an epicycle within neoclassical economics, rather than a fundamentally different way of thinking about the economy.

As also noted in Chapter 9, however, there are some more fundamental challenges to neoclassical economics developing in China. A number of factors have created an increasing openness to new ideas among some Chinese economists. Among these factors are: concerns about the 1997 Asian financial crisis and the Great Recession of 2007–2008; concerns about rampant inequality and environmental pollution; concerns about corrupt privatizations; and nationalist perceptions of the dominance of the global market by Western capital. Institutionally, Cheng Enfu, among others, has been attempting to reinvigorate Marxist theory and has some state support for this project. There have been modest increases in Chinese interest in heterodox economic paradigms such as Post Keynesian theory, institutional economics, and ecological economics. There has been some interest among young graduate students in using web-based resources to expand economic discussions from the confines of neoclassical theory. There has also been growing labor unrest, creating the potential for more Marxist oriented policy initiatives.

### *10.6.3 A digression on economics and ethics in China*

Since the beginning of the reforms and accelerating in the late 1990s, there have been debates in China about the relationship between economic theory and ethics, (Borokh 2006, 133). The neoclassical position is built around three propositions.

1   Economics is a "positive" science concerned with matters of cause and effect, rather than a "normative" discourse concerned with ethical questions.
2   Human nature is adequately represented by *homo economicus*. People's tastes and preferences are exogenous variables. Even if tastes and preferences are acknowledged to be historically contingent, the causal logic influencing them is not a legitimate subject for economic analysis. This precludes attention to the potential "structural" creation of inequality by the cultural logic of capitalism. It also precludes attention to associated ethical questions about the legitimacy of structurally determined inequality.
3   The market and capitalism are successful because they turn private vices (selfish behavior) into public virtues due to the discipline of competition. This assumption tends to treat inequality as a necessary incentive for economic efficiency, economic growth, and societal well-being.

The neoclassical paradigm offers people concerned about inequality and fairness opportunities to approach these issues in neoclassical terms (for example in terms of equity-efficiency trade-offs, social welfare functions, and social capital).

Many well known Chinese neoclassical economists, such as Fan Gang, have fully adopted Milton Friedman's positivist stance divorcing ethical issues from economic discussion (Borokh 2006, 138–139). There have also been many appeals to classical liberalism's argument that competition turns the pursuit of self-interest to the general interest. Mao Yushi, for example, echoes Friedman's claim that the social responsibility of business is to maximize shareholder value. In his article "The Paradox of Morality" he tries to show how altruistic concerns for the other party in an exchange can lead to terrible consequences (Mao 2011).

Many classical liberal economists, such as Zhang Weiying and Zhang Wuchang, blame China's morally troubling inequality on incomplete marketization. They promise that further de-regulation and privatization will reduce inequality and lead to just (even if not equal) outcomes. At times some of these economists have appeared to condone corruption as a lubricant for increased marketization, accepting short term unfairness for promises of long term, market justified, economic distributions.

Neoclassical economists, especially new institutionalist economists, have sometimes given attention to societal morality as a productive resource that can reduce transaction costs. The issue here is not what is right or wrong in an ethical sense, but how certain kinds of behavior can cultivate trust and reduce the information gathering monitoring, and enforcement costs associated with contracts (see for example Wang Xiaoxi 2012).

Criticism of neoclassical discourse about ethics has for the most part come from outside of economics and from non-neoclassical economists. Public intellectuals like He Qinglian, for example, have attacked Chinese economists for giving insufficient attention to moral issues and excessive attention to esoteric mathematical models of economic activity (Borokh 2006, 137). The critics' claims are invigorated by the legacy of China's Confucian tradition and Maoist period. The Confucian tradition celebrated the cultivation of character over the pursuit of wealth. It implicitly questioned the adequacy of *homo economicus* as a predictor of human behavior and as a guideline for human action. Neoclassical theory's Confucian critics call for an economic theory that simultaneously analyzes cause and effect, and offers guidelines for personal behavior that would enable a market economy to produce humane people as well as high levels of output (Borokh 2006).

Marxist theory's holist methodology expands the dimensions of economic outcomes to include the creation of culture and human beings. This focus has particularly strong implications for thinking about ethical issues related to the workplace. The Maoist ideal (though not reality) of workers as the "masters of their enterprises," raises all sorts of moral questions about current labor relations in China.

In general, many concerns about neoclassical economists' inattention to ethical issues are implicitly concerns about the adequacy of neoclassical theory's metric (GDP/capita) for assessing economic outcomes and allocating professional research time and course hours. Whiles these concerns may gain popular attention, the education and socialization of current economists in China make it unlikely that they will significantly alter the focus of Chinese economists.

### 10.6.4 Strategies for challenging neoclassical economics

One promising way for both Marxist and heterodox economics to expand in China involves cross fertilization among the paradigms. While no single alternative paradigm is large enough to effectively challenge neoclassical economics, the panoply of heterodox paradigms, linked with Marxist economics, could provide a critical mass for intellectual and institutional growth. The linkage of heterodox and Marxist theory to practical projects, like economic development strategies that offer special incentives for companies with workers' self-management or new special economic zones that experiment with central planning, might also strengthen tendencies in this direction.

## 10.7 Relating Chinese experience to global patterns

The role played by neoclassical economists in integrating China into the global division of labor of modern capitalism (symbolized by China's acceptance of tough preconditions for membership in the WTO), is remarkably consistent with Marion Fourcade's analysis in a 2006 article entitled "The Construction of a Global Profession: The Transnationalization of Economics." Fourcade analyzes the influence of neoclassical economics in numerous countries around the globe, though she does not refer very much to China. Borrowing from Benedict Anderson, Fourcade's analysis begins with the insight that "nations have come to 'imagine' themselves as 'economic communities'..." (Fourcade 2006, 163). In the project of nation building, economic theory and economic education has become centrally involved in the moral education of the citizenry (explaining the basis of privilege and social status) and in the technocratic training of the nation's elite in preparation for their public and private roles as overseers of the economy (161, 166).

Fourcade demonstrates how and why neoclassical theory has come to fulfill this role around the globe. She argues that the professions accompanying corporate-led economic interconnections (chiefly the economics profession, but also other professions such as accounting,[3] banking, and law) have created a global commercial culture. She writes, "Western companies investing abroad, like governments or international financial institutions lending money, carry with them scores of lawyers and consultants, who ... impose their own definition of reality—their norms, concepts, language, tools and so on" (150). After World War II she finds American norms and definitions imposing themselves on economists across the globe,[4] reporting, "… everything is happening as if American graduate and professional schools … were functioning as elite licensing institutions for much of the rest of the world" (152).[5]

Sarah Babb (2001) reaches similar conclusions about the history of economics in Mexico using a variety of data, including the character of undergraduate economics theses. Like Fourcade she links her analysis of the Mexican economics profession to similar events around the globe, noting:

> The presence of U.S.-trained economists in the governments of developing countries today is astoundingly strong. These foreign-trained technocrats tend to share a common cognitive framework and set of guiding assumptions—in short, a common ideology—with foreign policymakers and international financiers. They also have social ties with U.S. policymakers and the officials of multilateral organizations—not only from their grad school days but also from prior appointments within international organizations (often the IMF). A growing body of evidence suggests that these technocrats have been instrumental in pushing forward liberalizing reforms…
>
> (Babb 2001, 19)

Jacobson and Oksenberg write about the same process of socialization, though more approvingly.[6]

Both Babb and Fourcade's research grounds China's experience in a wider pattern. Fourcade's research implies a number of predictions about the trajectory of Chinese economics, based on the domestic histories of other countries with transplanted neoclassical economics professions. Several of these predictions have already been confirmed, such as the rise of mathematical formalism (Fourcade 2006, 159–160), strong policy support from Chinese economists for trade liberalization, an emphasis on efficiency as opposed to equity (161), and the spread of neoclassically oriented "think tanks" as an initial strategy for challenging non-neoclassical traditions in the universities (182–183).[7] More interesting are several forward looking predictions, some of which seem well underway; others are more indeterminate at this moment. Among these predictions are:

1   The decline of economic history, the history of economic thought, and area studies in economics education (160).
2   The emergence of neoclassically oriented regional economics conferences and professional organizations (174–175).
3   The collapse of "local exceptionalism" or "specificity" oriented theories (160), implying a gradual erosion of the "with Chinese characteristics" dimension of Chinese neoclassical economics.
4   A period of tension between elite universities reorganized along neoclassical lines by American trained PhDs and other universities retaining older political economy orientations and staffed by locally trained PhDs.[8]

5   And, extending Fourcade's observation about the legitimizing role of the Nobel Prize in economics (170), anticipation of Chinese Prizes affirming the intellectual capital of neoclassical experts.

On a broader plane it seems likely that the expansion of neoclassical economics in Chinese universities, public bureaucracies, and the media, will continue to facilitate neoliberal policy environments, albeit with occasional moments of "kinder-gentler" factions and interludes. The global marriage of neoliberal policy recommendations and neoclassical economics is no accident. Although some aspects of neoclassical economics are ideologically neutral, and some economists have joined neoclassical imaginations to socialist projects (such as those building models of market socialism), the dominant subtexts of the neoclassical paradigm gravitate toward neoliberal conclusions. It is almost as if the precepts of classical liberalism animating Adam Smith and many early Western economists are in the collective unconscious of the economics profession.[9] The enormous presence of the University of Chicago in the global economics profession reflects this legacy and unsurprisingly helps animate the Chinese Economist Society.

At the same time, it is not surprising that many Chinese intellectuals see state repression under the guise of Marxist rather than neoclassical theory as the greatest threat to intellectual freedom. There is, of course, a history of such repression in China, beginning with the early "rectification" campaigns in the 1940s, attacks on government critics after the Hundred Flowers opening in the 1950s, the persecutions of the Cultural Revolution in the 1960s and 1970s, the "anti-spiritual pollution" campaign of the early 1980s, the attack on bourgeois liberalization in 1987, and the crackdown after Tiananmen Square in the late 1980s. The last 20 years have witnessed Jiang Zemin's termination of the so called 1998 "Beijing-Spring"[10] and Xi Jinping's more recent efforts to tighten restrictions on internet usage. Despite this legacy, or perhaps because of it, the strongest threat to free discussion of *economic ideas* going forward is arguably the aspiring hegemony of neoclassical economics. The latter is replacing Marxist theory as the Chinese State's ideological justification for sacrificing other social goals to maximizing economic growth. Like Marxist economics, neoclassical theory can be a "jealous" and intolerant paradigm. This is because it often conceives of itself as a science and its competitors as illegitimate non-sciences (in the tradition of astronomy's view of astrology, or biology's view of creationism.) While this view misrepresents heterodox paradigms, it can motivate neoclassical partisans to resist calls for pluralist education. When combined with state power, this technocratic ideology can foreclose discussion.

## 10.8  Counter tendencies

Where will change come from? Some of the older Marxist economists I interviewed believed that the fifth generation leadership would be more sympathetic to Marxist economics. One person pointed to a recent decision by the government to finance new translations and the publication of a large number of Marxist texts as a sign of things to come. Another person felt that Xi Jinping was relatively sympathetic to Marxist economics due to his formal training in Marxist theory.[11] Until recently, elaboration of Bo Xilai's Chongqing model seemed to offer opportunities for alternative economic theorizing.

While official government support for any economic paradigm in China remains a strong social force, I think the multi-dimensional foundation of neoclassical economics' hold on the economics profession will be harder to dislodge than these economists imagine. Neoclassical theory has set down strong roots in the elite universities, in the banking and business sectors, and in elements of popular culture. These roots are further nourished by powerful linkages to the international market place. They will not be dislodged easily.

Zhang and Xu's (2013) strategy for challenging the dominance of neoclassical economics calls for building a common ground that includes Marxist and non-Marxist heterodox economists. The recent growth of heterodox economics study groups, aided by funding and linkages through INET, seems a potentially important initiative (though not without its own potential problems). Posing the debate as one between a pluralist economics profession and a one-dimensional one leaves neoclassical theory much more on the defensive.

This big tent strategy recommends that Western heterodox economic associations reach out to Chinese economists. The International Association for Feminist Economics' decision to hold its annual conference in Hangzhou in 2011 is representative of such an initiative. Even more appropriate to this "rainbow strategy" would be for umbrella organizations such as ICAPE (the International Confederation of Associations of Federations for Pluralism in Economics) and INET (the Institute for New Economic Thinking) to hold regular heterodox economics conferences in China and to subsidize attendance by Chinese scholars and graduate students at heterodox conferences in the West. I suspect it would be especially useful to invite famous heterodox economists to headline conferences in China, as this kind of personal authority carries weight in China.

Professor Zhou Yi of Fudan University argues that significant change in the economics profession will probably come from pressures outside the profession. He is an especially interesting observer, as he was one of the first Chinese graduate students to participate in Professor Chow's summer workshops and has been a visitor at Harvard University. He believes the internet has an uncertain potential for creating an alternative scientific community, though he probably would not use those words.[12] Paul Krugman has depicted a similar expansion of economic discourse in the US due to the increasing importance of the blogosphere.[13] Efforts to build a more pluralist economics profession in China should probably give special attention to internet projects aimed at Chinese audiences.

Besides noting the internet's ability to provide opportunities for broad public discussions among large numbers of people, Zhou Yi and others highlight the implications of the recent expansion of micro blogs for pluralist economics. Created in 2011, for example, China's We-Chat option now has more than 300 million users. Zhou emphasizes that We-Chat groups, by design, are almost always smaller than one hundred people. This feature reduces their perceived threat to social stability and the likelihood of state censorship, as their discussions cannot "go viral."

## 10.9 Closing thoughts: subtexts and Chinese economic theory

### 10.9.1 *Marxist subtexts*

I would like to end this book by re-emphasizing the role of subtexts in economic theory and invite readers to reflect on which set of basic assumptions and economic projects seem most appropriate for China in the twenty-first century. The assumptions and projects of Marxist economic theory especially relevant for this closing section are: (1) Marxism's holist methodology; (2) Marxism's treatment of the organization of work as a socially constitutive activity (that is, as a practice that helps create the logic of an entire way of life), and (3) Marxism's project of building socialism. Marxism's holist methodology leads to economic research on the implications of "capitalism" as a reproducing social system. Marxism's project of building socialism leads to attention to distinctive questions about the ownership of productive assets, the governance of the work place, and the determinants of the shape of technological change. There are also important debates within Chinese Marxism, between Maoists and central planners, for example, and between Marxist humanists and Marxist theorists focused on developing the forces of production, but examining these is beyond the scope of this book.

In general, the Marxist project of building socialism is supported by modest elements within the Chinese Communist Party (CPC) (certainly not a majority), and resonates with scattered supporters in rural communities (especially among older residents) and perhaps some urban migrant and working class communities. While the CPC still gives lip service to the promise that socialist goals will be renewed once the "primary stage" of economic development is completed, the socialist project has largely been abandoned in China.

### 10.9.2 *Neoclassical subtexts*

The assumptions and projects of neoclassical economics especially relevant for this closing discussion are: (1) the paradigm's methodologically individualistic starting point, (2) its classical liberal assumptions about human nature (*homo economicus*); and (3) its project of expanding and perfecting markets and private property rights in a quest to maximize Chinese GDP. There are important debates within Chinese neoclassical theory between shock therapists and gradualists. While sometimes lively, these debates are over the pace of change rather than the ends of change.

The neoclassical project remains committed to building capitalism, with varying degrees of deference to historical contexts and "Chinese characteristics." Neoclassical projects calling for expanded privatization and marketization are heavily supported in China by the new rich. They also appear to enjoy reluctant if not enthusiastic support from many workers and rural people. The promise of economic growth, despite its unequal payoffs in the past, is still alluring for most people. These projects are also heavily supported by the international institutions of modern capitalist societies, such as the World Bank and IMF, as well as by most members of the American economics profession. The legitimacy of both neoclassical economics and the Chinese state depends on the ability of the Chinese economy to continue to grow rapidly and expand employment.

### 10.9.3 Heterodox subtexts

The assumptions and projects of heterodox economics are harder to summarize than neoclassical and Marxist economics due to the paradigm's diversity of approaches. Heterodox economists typically reject some neoclassical assumptions but are agnostic or accepting of others. Post Keynesian economists, for example, reject neoclassical theory's assumption of hyper rationality. Ecological economists object to neoclassical theory's treatment of the environment as a normal commodity. Feminist economists criticize the assumptions of economic man.

The heterodox project is to expand the social guidance of markets, frequently in the service of quality of life goals rather than GDP maximization. Chinese Post Keynesian projects are supported by economists interested in protecting global markets from destructive moments like the recent financial crisis. Key supporters include George Soros through initiatives like INET. Social regulations tailored to the specifics of different sectors of the economy are supported by Chinese institutionalist/evolutionary economists. Some Post Keynesian and institutionalist economics initiatives are also supported by parts of the Chinese government interested in maintaining a larger state role in the economy than usually emerges from neoclassical analyses. Chinese ecological economics projects are supported by aspects of the environmental movement in China.

### 10.9.4 What is at stake?

Given the paradigms' different projects, what is at stake in this competition is whether the momentum of market development will define life in China, largely bereft of societal reflection and social governance. The logic of

Marxist and heterodox paradigms challenge the unfettered authority of the marketplace, where dollar votes in commercial settings and the logic of competition among private units of capital determine societal directions. The neoclassical paradigm offers only a modest basis for social challenges to the market. It permits a moderate government role in the economy to "correct" market imperfections and address equity issues. The paradigm's subtexts, historical culture, and vision of the ideal economic outcome as the "perfect market" outcome, however, make it likely that Chinese neoclassical economists will defer to relatively naked market outcomes and the priorities of GDP growth and capital accumulation. The stakes of the paradigm competition are therefore consequential, and boil down to endorsements or challenges to neoliberalism.

### 10.9.5 The future of Chinese economics education: a supply and demand model

What does all of this mean for understanding the future of economics education in China? What paradigm is likely to dominate instruction, and why? The answers, I think, will largely depend on the projects key social groups want to enable. While the Chinese state is probably the key actor, it is not the only actor in this drama. As detailed in Chapter 2, a host of other institutions have and will continue to influence the evolution of Chinese economic thought and education.

The likelihood of a successful challenge to the current dominance of Chinese economics education and public discourse by neoclassical economics can be summarized with a simple supply and demand model. On the supply side, new technologies have made the availability of alternative ideas much "cheaper" and more widespread. The internet has made it possible for Chinese students, professors, and the general public to gain direct access to economic ideas without going through institutions dominated by Chinese neoclassical economists. YouTube and other videos of economics lectures and conferences, live Skyped meetings and conferences, micro blogs and We-Chat on mobile devices have all made non-neoclassical economics more accessible. There have also been a number of translating initiatives in recent years that have made it easier for Chinese readers to access Western Marxist and heterodox economics texts.

The demand side is more complicated and perhaps more important. As an old Buddhist proverb avers, "when the student is ready, the teacher appears." The demand for heterodox and Marxist theory can be thought of in terms of the demand for the projects that these paradigms facilitate. In the current environment, the demand for heterodox and Marxist projects is increasing, but still modest. Should economic growth stall in China, however, this could change very quickly. In combination with dissatisfactions over growing inequality, environmental pollution, and poor working conditions, interest in socialism and socially governed markets could expand rapidly.[14]

The task of Marxist and heterodox economics in the present would thus seem to be to continue to "supply" alternative ideas and to ensure they are relevant to meaningful projects. As Karl Marx argued:

"The philosophers have only interpreted the world, in various ways. The point, however, is to *change it*."

(Marx, Thesis on Feurbach)

And as John Maynard Keynes concluded:

the ideas of economists and political philosophers, both when they are right and when they are wrong, are more powerful than is commonly understood. Indeed the world is ruled by little else.

(Keynes, *General Theory of Employment, Interest and Money*)

## Notes

1  Blecher (2002), see especially pages 288, 295–297, and 302–303.
2  Among the safeguards tried were:

• limits on capitalist practices, such as limiting wage labor to a maximum of seven employees
• segmenting the economy into areas of capitalist and socialist practice, with socialist principles controlling the "commanding heights" of the economy
• maintaining public ownership of large enterprises
• maintaining active ideological campaigns to pressure managers and owners of private firms to behave in a socialist manner even if in competitive markets
• relying on the ultimate power of the Party state to prevent the emergence of capitalism.

Defending the robustness of the safeguards in 1981, the economic editor of the *Peking Review* wrote,

Will individual economy engender capitalism and the bourgeoisie? The answer is no ... public ownership of the means of production holds the dominant position ... those engaged in individual economy ... [e]ven when they do employ one or two assistants ... are not capitalists because they themselves take part in labour...

(*Peking Review* August 17, 1981, 3–4)

3  I suspect some very interesting research could probably be done (and perhaps has been done) about the conceptual categories that modern business accounting imposes on popular business culture. When I was in China, I spoke with an American teaching Western accounting at a Chinese university and got the impression that a major overhaul was required in Chinese business practices at the micro level to conform its Soviet influenced accounting habits with Western accounting principles. At the macro level, Western oriented national income accounting was started in China in 1985 (Fang 2013, 298). I suspect that various Marxist accounting practices, such as calculating labor values or productive and unproductive labor totals, were proportionally diminished.
4  The US policies promoting the global spread of neoclassical economics in the 1950s and 1960s that Fourcade describes, match strikingly well with later policies toward China. She highlights the funding of foreign post-graduate economics

programs and prolonged visits by US professors (169). She indicates that the Ford Foundation was the biggest supporter of social science research in Latin America. It was also active in Asia, especially in India, Pakistan, and Indonesia (170). The Foundation's support for neoclassical economics education in China in the mid-1980s was thus a final step in a long journey.

5  To back up her claims she depicts economic policy and educational histories in numerous countries, including Brazil, Chile, Indonesia, Taiwan, Korea, and the Philippines. She points illustratively and evocatively to the impact of University of Chicago economics professor Arnold Harberger, who proudly reports teaching at least 25 government ministers and a dozen central bankers (180). Aslanbegui and Montecinos (1998) reach similar conclusions about the influence of US doctoral programs on global economics discourse. They cite the adoption of English as the *lingua franca* in economics (175) and the need for fluency in US economic discourse to interact effectively with global capital markets and international economic organizations (175–177). They conclude, "It is well known that leading the world's wave of market reforms and its associated institutional restructuring are cohesive teams of professional economists, mostly trained in the United States..." (176).

6  They report that the "socialization" of individuals from developing countries serving in international organizations diffuses the concerns, norms, and rules of international organizations. They add, "Such information may help gradually to force an international consensus on norms and behavior" (Jacobson and Oksenberg 1990, 7).

7  Many of Fourcade's other observations about transplanted economic ideas are also applicable to China, such as the rejection of "dependency theory" as a primary cause of under-development (175).

8  Li indicates this tension broke out at Beida (Peking University) in 2003 after the university announced plans to further Americanize the institution. The battle was seen by many as a struggle between the "sea turtles" (returning PhDs) and "local toads." The administration portrayed the battle as a struggle to upgrade the quality of the university (Li 2005, 99–101).

9  The Jungian metaphor is memorable, but probably not as useful as more mundane analyses of the way classical liberal ideas are reproduced through: the persistence of neoclassical subtexts and their logical implications; the apprenticeship system of graduate education; the inheritance of traditional bibliographies; and the selection of work by economists for social attention by larger social forces.

10  For a brief account of the censoring of journals, banning of book publications, dismissal of personnel, etc., see Goldman 2005, especially 157, 183–186.

11  A few web sites credit him with a doctorate in Marxist theory and ideological education; other sites suggest somewhat less intense Marxist study alongside chemical engineering. In the spring of 2011 he gave a much publicized address at the central party school emphasizing the need to read the Marxist classics; whether this was boiler plate rhetoric or more deeply held belief is hard to discern at this point.

12  Professor Zhou Yi cites a recent example of internet politics. The government proposed increasing the threshold for income tax payments from 2000 yuan a month to 3,000 yuan and invited public comment on the web. Eighty percent of respondents wanted a higher income floor. At first the National People's Congress attempted to maintain the proposed 3,000Y floor, but eventually raised the level to 3,500 (interview). Li He 2009 also highlights' the internet's ability to popularize New Left ideas.

13  Krugman notes that in the past much economic discussion was organized through the private circulation of working papers and reports among the Fed, IMF, and some research departments at investment banks. He argues, "What the blogs have done ... is open up that process ... it's easier than it used to be for little boys to get a word in..." (Krugman 2011).

14  See Andreas 2012 for an interesting discussion of this contested potential.

# References

Andreas, Joel. 2012. "Sino-Seismology." *New Left Review* 76: 128–135.

Aslanbeigui, Nahid and Verónica Montecinos. 1998. "Foreign Students in U.S. Doctoral Programs." *Journal of Economic Perspectives* 12 (3): 171–182. www.jstor.org/stable/2647038.

Babb, Sarah. 2001. *Managing Mexico: Economists from Nationalism to Neoliberalism.* Princeton, NJ: Princeton University Press.

Blecher, Marc. 2002. "Hegemony and Workers' Politics in China." *The China Quarterly* (170): 283–303. www.jstor.org/stable/4618737.

Borokh, Olga. 2006. "New Trends in Chinese Thought: Economics and Morality." In *The Power of Ideas: Intellectural Input and Political Change in East and Southeast Asia,* edited by Claudia Derichs and Thomas Heberer, 133–149. Copenhagen: Nias Press.

Brandt, Loren, and Thomas Rawski. 2008b. "China's Great Economic Transformation." In *China's Great Economic Transformation,* edited by Loren Brandt and Thomas Rawski, 1–26. New York: Cambridge University Press.

Fang, Fuqian. 2013. "The Changing Status of Western Economics in China." In *Thoughts on Economic Development in China,* edited by Ying Ma and Hans-Michael Trautwein, 295–305. New York: Routledge.

Fourcade, Marion. 2006. "The Construction of a Global Profession: The Transnationalization of Economics." *American Journal of Sociology* 112 (1): 145–194. doi:10.1086/502693.

Goldman, Merle. 2005. *From Comrade to Citizen: The Struggle for Political Rights in China.* Cambridge, MA: Harvard University Press.

Hart-Landsberg, Martin, and Paul Burkett. 2005. *China and Socialism: Market Reforms and Class Struggle.* New York: Monthly Review.

Jacobson, Harold K., and Michel Oksenberg. 1990. *China's Participation in the IMF, the World Bank, and GATT: Toward a Global Economic Order.* Ann Arbor, MI: University of Michigan Press.

Krugman, Paul. 2011. "Our Blogs, Ourselves." *New York Times,* October 18, 2011.

Li, Cheng. 2005. "Coming Home to Teach: Status and Mobility of Returnees in China's Higher Education." In *Bridging Minds Across the Pacific: US–China Educational Exchanges 1978–2003,* edited by Cheng Li, 69–109. Lanham, MD: Lexington Books.

Li, He. 2009. "China's New Left." *East Asian Policy* 1 (1): 30–37.

Li, Minqi. 2008. *The Rise of China and the Demise of the Capitalist World Economy.* New York: Monthly Review.

Lin, Justin Yifu, Fang Cai, and Zhou Li. 2003. *The China Miracle: Development Strategy and Economic Reform.* Rev. ed. Hong Kong: Chinese University Press.

Mao, Yushi. 2011. "The Paradox of Morality." In *The Morality of Capitalism: What Your Professors Won't Tell You,* edited by Tom G. Palmer, 43–54. Ottawa, IL: Jameson Books.

Wang, Xiaoxi. 2012. "On the Economic Significance of Morality." *Social Sciences in China* 33 (3): 67–80. doi:10.1080/02529203.2012.702942.

Zhang, Lin and Yingli Xu. 2013. "The Transmission of Heterodox Economics in China, 1949–2009." In *Thoughts on Economic Development in China,* edited by Ying Ma and Hans-Michael Trautwein, 306–326. New York: Routledge.

# References

Amin, Samir. 2013. "China 2013." *Monthly Review: An Independent Socialist Magazine* 64 (10): 14. http://monthlyreview.org/2013/03/01/china-2013/.

Anderson, Perry. 1976. *Considerations on Western Marxism*. London: Verso.

Andreas, Joel. 2012. "Sino-Seismology." *New Left Review* 76: 128–135.

Arrighi, Giovanni. 2008. *Adam Smith in Beijing: Lineages of the Twenty-First Century*. New York: Verso.

Aslanbeigui, Nahid and Verónica Montecinos. 1998. "Foreign Students in U.S. Doctoral Programs." *Journal of Economic Perspectives* 12 (3): 171–182. www.jstor.org/stable/2647038.

Babb, Sarah. 2001. *Managing Mexico: Economists from Nationalism to Neoliberalism*. Princeton, NJ: Princeton University Press.

Barboza, David. 2009a. "China's Mr. Wu Keeps Talking." *New York Times*, September 26, 2009, BU1–7.

Barboza, David. 2009b. "Interviews with Wu Jinglian, Shelly Wu and Wu's Biographer." *New York Times*, September 26, 2009.

Bayliss, Kate, and Ben Fine. 1998. "Beyond Bureaucrats in Business: A Critical Review of the World Bank Approach to Privatization and Public Sector Reform." *Journal of International Development* 10 (7): 841–855.

Blecher, Marc. 2002. "Hegemony and Workers' Politics in China." *The China Quarterly* (170): 283–303. www.jstor.org/stable/4618737.

Blecher, Marc. 2010. *China Against the Tides: Restructuring through Revolution, Radicalism and Reform*. 3rd ed. New York: Continuum.

Borokh, Olga. 2006. "New Trends in Chinese Thought: Economics and Morality." In *The Power of Ideas: Intellectual Input and Political Change in East and Southeast Asia*, edited by Claudia Derichs and Thomas Heberer, 133–149. Copenhagen: Nias Press.

Bottelier, Pieter. 2006. *China and the World Bank: How a Partnership was Built*. Stanford, CA: Stanford University Press.

Bowles, Paul, and Xiao-yuan Dong. 1994. "Current Successes and Future Challenges in China's Economic Reforms." *New Left Review* (208): 49–76.

Brahm, Laurence J. 2002. *Zhu Rongji and the Transformation of Modern China*. Singapore: John Wiley & Sons (Asia).

Bramall, Chris. 1990. "The Wenzhou 'Miracle': An Assessment." In *Market Forces in China: Competition and Small Business; the Wenzhou Debate*, edited by Peter Nolan and Fureng Dong, 43–76. Atlantic Highlands, NJ: Zed Books.

Bramall, Chris. 2000. *Sources of Chinese Economic Growth 1978–1996*. New York: Oxford University Press.

Bramall, Chris. 2009a. *Chinese Economic Development.* New York: Routledge.

Bramall, Chris. 2009b. "Out of the Darkness: Chinese Transition Paths." *Modern China* 35 (4): 439–449.

Brandt, Loren, and Thomas Rawski. 2008a. *China's Great Economic Transformation.* New York: Cambridge University Press.

Brandt, Loren, and Thomas Rawski. 2008b. "China's Great Economic Transformation." In *China's Great Economic Transformation,* edited by Loren Brandt and Thomas Rawski, 1–26. New York: Cambridge University Press.

Branstetter, Lee, and Nicholas Lardy. 2008. "China's Embrace of Globalization." In *China's Great Transformation,* edited by Loren Brandt and Thomas Rawski, 633–682. New York: Cambridge University Press.

Braverman, Harry. 1974. *Labor and Monopoly Capital: The Degradation of Work in the Twentieth Century.* New York: Monthly Review Press.

Broadman, Harry G. 1996. "Policy Options for Reform of Chinese State-Owned Enterprises." Proceedings of Symposium in Beijing, June 1995. World Bank Discussion Paper no 335. Beijing, World Bank, June 1995.

Brugger, Bill, and David Kelly. 1990. *Chinese Marxism in the Post-Mao Era.* Stanford, CA: Stanford University Press.

Busse, Ronald, Malcolm Warner, and Shuming Zhao. 2016. "In Search of the Roots of 'Human Resource Management' in the Chinese Workplace." *Cambridge Judge Business School Working Papers* 02/2016.

Byrd, William, and Qingsong Lin, eds. 1990. *China's Rural Industry: Structure, Development, and Reform.* Washington, DC: World Bank.

Campagnolo, Gilles. 2013. "Three Influential Western Thinkers during the 'Break-Up' Period in China: Eucken, Bergson, and Dewey." In *Thoughts on Economic Development in China,* edited by Ying Ma and Hans-Michael Trautwein, 101–121. New York: Routledge.

Cao, Cong. 2008. "China's Brain Drain at the High End." *Asian Population Studies* 4 (3): 331–345. doi:10.1080/17441730802496532.

Cao, Tian Yu, ed. 2005. *The Chinese Model of Modern Development.* New York: Routledge.

Carson, Richard L. 1990. *Comparative Economic Systems: Part II Socialist Alternatives.* Armonk, NY: M. E. Sharpe.

Cato Institute. 2001. *25 Years at the Cato Institute: The 2001 Annual Report*: Cato Institute.

Center for Internatinal Private Enterprise. 1999. "Supporting China's Transition to a Market Economy." *Economic Reform Today* (4): 17–21.

Chan, Anita. 1998. "Labor Standards and Human Rights: The Case of Chinese Workers Under Market Socialism." *Human Rights Quarterly* 20 (4): 886–904. www.jstor.org/stable/762792.

Chan, Anita. 2001. *China's Workers Under Assault: The Exploitation of Labor in a Globalizing Economy.* Armonk, NY: M. E. Sharpe.

Chan, Anita. 2003. "A Race to the Bottom: Globalisation and China's Labour Standards." *China Perspectives* 46: 41–49.

Chan, Anita, Richard Madsen, and Jonathan Unger. 1992. *Chen Village Under Mao and Deng.* 2nd ed. Berkeley, CA: University of California Press.

Chan, Kam Wing. 2009. "The Chinese Hukou System at 50." *Eurasian Geography and Economics* 50 (2): 197–221.

Chen, Feng. 1995. *Economic Transition and Political Legitimacy in Post-Mao China: Ideology and Reform.* Albany, NY: State University Press of New York.

Chen, Feng. 1999. "An Unfinished Battle in China: The Leftist Criticism of the Reform and the Third Thought Emancipation." *The China Quarterly* (158): 447–467. doi:10.1017/S0305741000005853.

Chen, Ruiming. 1990. "A Preliminary Analysis of the 'Big-Labour-Hiring Households' in Rural Wenzhou." In *Market Forces in China: Competition and Small Business; the Wenzhou Debate*, edited by Peter Nolan and Fureng Dong, 140–156. Atlantic Highlands, NJ: Zed Books.

Chen, Yun. 1982a [1956a]. "New Issues since the Basic Completion of the Socialist Transformation." *Chinese Economic Studies* 15 (3): 7–22.

Chen, Yun. 1982b [1956b]. "Methods of Solving the Tensions in Supplies of Pork and Vegetables." *Chinese Economic Studies* 15 (3): 23–29.

Cheng, Enfu. 2003, "New 'Economic Man' Theory: A Basic Hypothesis of Shanghai School Economics." *Teaching and Research* (11): 22–26.

Cheng, Enfu. 2012. "Seven Currents of Social Thought and their Development in Contemporary China, with a Focus on Innovative Marxism." *The Marxist* 27 (4). Available at http://cpim.org/sites/default/files/marxist/201204-Cheng%20Enfu.pdf.

Cheng, Xiaonong. 1995. "Decision and Miscarriage: Radical Price Reform in the Summer of 1988." In *Decision-Making in Deng's China: Perspectives from Insiders*, edited by Carol Lee Hamrin and Suisheng Zhao, 189–204. Armonk, NY: M. E. Sharpe.

Cheung, Steven. 1986. *Will China Go Capitalist?* 2nd ed. London: Institute of Economic Affairs.

China Labour Bulletin. 2007 December 19, 2007. *Reform of State-Owned Enterprises in China.*

Chou, Jennifer. 2008. "World Bank's Chief Economist Swam to China?" *The Weekly Standard*, February 11, 2008.

Chow, Gregory. 1986. *Development of a More Market Oriented Economy in China (Econometric Research Program Research Memorandum no. 326).* Princeton, NJ: Princeton Econometric Research Program.

Chow, Gregory. 1988. *Teaching Economics and Studying Economic Reform in China (Econometric Research Program Research Memorandum no. 339).* Princeton, NJ: Princeton Econometric Research Program.

Chow, Gregory. 1994. *Understanding China's Economy.* Hong Kong: World Scientific.

Chow, Gregory. 2000. "The Teaching of Modern Economics in China." *Comparative Economic Studies* 42 (2): 51–60. doi:10.1057/ces.2000.8.

Chow, Gregory. 2002. *China's Economic Transformation.* Malden, MA: Blackwell.

Chu, Victoria. 2009. "Ma Hong." In *Biographical Dictionary of New Chinese Entrepreneurs and Business Leaders*, edited by Wenxian Zhang and Ilan Alon, 110–111. Northampton, MA: Edward Elgar.

Clegg, Jenny. 1996. "China's Rural Shareholding Cooperatives as a Form of Multi-Stakeholder Cooperation." *Journal of Rural Cooperation* 24 (2): 119–142.

Coase, Ronald, and Ning Wang. 2013. *How China Became Capitalist.* New York: Palgrave Macmillan.

Coburn, Judith. 1969. "Asian Scholars and Government: The Chrysanthemum on the Sword." In *America's Asia: Dissenting Essays on Asian American Relations*, edited by Edward Friedman and Mark Selden, 67–107. New York: Vintage.

Cohn, Stephen M. 2007. *Reintroducing Macroeconomics: A Critical Approach.* Armonk, NY: M. E. Sharpe.

Committee on Scholarly Communication with the People's Republic of China (CSCPRC) Delegation to the People's Republic of China. 2010 [1980]. *Report of the Cscprc Economics Delegation to the People's Republic of China*: General Books [National Academies].

Cui, Zhiyuan. 2005. "Liberal Socialism and the Future of China: A Petty Bourgeoisie Manifesto." In *The Chinese Model of Modern Development*, edited by Tian Yu Cao, 157–174. New York: Routledge.

Day, Alexander F. 2013. *The Peasant in Post Socialist China: History, Politics, and Capitalism*. Cambridge: Cambridge University Press.

Ding, X. L. 2000. "The Illicit Asset Stripping of Chinese State Firms." *The China Journal* (43): 1–28. doi:10.2307/2667530.

Dirlik, Arif. 1978. *Revolution and History: the Origins of Marxist Historiography in China 1919–1937*. Berkeley, CA: University of California Press.

Dirlik, Arif and Maurice Meisner, eds. 1989. *Marxism and the Chinese Experience*. Armonk, NY: M. E. Sharpe.

Dong, Fureng. 1982. "The Chinese Economy in the Process of Great Transformation." In *Economic Reform in the People's Republic of China: In Which China's Economists Make Known What Went Wrong, Why, and What Should Be Done About It*, edited by George C. Wang, 125–137. Boulder, CO: Westview Press.

Dong, Fureng. 1990. "The Wenzhou Model for Developing the Rural Commodity Economy." In *Market Forces in China: Competition and Small Business; the Wenzhou Debate*, edited by Peter Nolan and Fureng Dong, 77–96. Atlantic Highlands, NJ: Zed Books.

Dorn, James A., and Wang Xi, eds. 1990. *Economic Reform in China: Problems and Prospects*. Chicago, IL: University of Chicago Press.

Du, Runsheng. 1988. "Rural Employment in China: The Choices." *International Labour Review* 127 (3): 371. http://heinonline.org/HOL/LandingPage?handle=hein.journals/intlr127&div=37.

Du, Runsheng. 2005. "We should Encourage Institutional Innovations." In *The Chinese Model of Modern Development*, edited by Tian Yu Cao, 9–15. New York: Routledge.

Du, Runsheng. 2006. *The Course of China's Rural Reform*. Washington, DC: International Food Policy Research Institute.

Du, Yuxin. 2011. "A Bibliometrics Portrait of Chinese Research through the Lens of *China Economic Review*." Master's thesis, Universidade do Porto.

Easterlin, Richard, Fei Wang, and Shun Wang. 2017. "Growth and Happiness in China, 1990–2015." Paper accompanying poster presentation at Annual Meetings of the American Economic Association 2017. Available at: http://conference.iza.org/conference_files/ICID_Renmin_2016/wang_f8757.pdf.

Easterlin, Richard, Robson Morgan, Malgorzota Switek, and Fei Wang. 2012. "China's Life Satisfaction, 1910–2010." *Proceedings of the National Academy of Sciences* 109: 9775–9780.

Fan, Gang. 1994. "Incremental Changes and Dual-Track Transition: Understanding the Case of China." *Economic Policy* 9 (Supplement): 99–122. doi:10.2307/1344602.

Fan, Shenggen, Ravi Kanbur, Shang-Jin Wei, and Xiaobo Zhang, eds. 2014. *The Oxford Companion to the Economics of China*. New York: Oxford University Press.

Fang, Fuqian. 2013. "The Changing Status of Western Economics in China." In *Thoughts on Economic Development in China*, edited by Ying Ma and Hans-Michael Trautwein, 295–305. New York: Routledge.

Fang, Sheng. 1982. "The Revival of Individual Economy in Urban Areas." In *China's Economic Reforms*, edited by Lin Wei and Arnold Chao, 172–185. Philadelphia, PA: University of Pennsylvania Press.

Fewsmith, Joseph. 1994. *Dilemmas of Reform in China: Political Conflict and Economic Debate*. Armonk, NY: M. E. Sharpe.

Fewsmith, Joseph. 1996. "Editor's Introduction." *Chinese Economic Studies* 29 (2): 3–4.

Fewsmith, Joseph. 1999. "Editor's Introduction." *Chinese Economic Studies* 32 (2): 3–4.

Fewsmith, Joseph. 2008. *China since Tiananmen: From Deng Xiaoping to Hu Jintao*. 2nd ed. New York: Cambridge University Press.

Fine, Ben, and Elisa Van Waeyenberge. 2013. *A Paradigm Shift that Never Will Be?: Justin Lin's New Structural Economics*. SOAS Department of Economics Working Paper Series. Vol. 179. London: SOAS Department of Economics.

Forsythe, Michael. 2012. "The Chinese Communist Party's Capitalist Elite: Chinese Lawmakers have Amassed Huge Personal Wealth." *Bloomberg*.

Fourcade, Marion. 2006. "The Construction of a Global Profession: The Transnationalization of Economics." *American Journal of Sociology* 112 (1): 145–194. doi:10.1086/502693.

Freeman, Charles W. III, and Wen Jin Yuan. 2011. *China's New Leftists and the China Model Debate After the Financial Crisis*. Washington, DC: Center For Strategic and International Studies.

Friedman, Edward, and Mark Selden, eds. 1969. *America's Asia: Dissenting Essays on Asian American Relations*. New York: Vintage Books.

Friedman, Milton. 1970. "The Social Responsibility of Business is to Increase Profits." *New York Times*, September 13, 1970.

Friedman, Milton. 1982 [1962]. *Capitalism and Freedom*. Chicago, IL: University of Chicago Press.

Friedman, Milton. 1990a. *Friedman in China*. Hong Kong: Chinese University Press.

Friedman, Milton. 1990b. "Using the Market for Social Development." In *Economic Reform in China: Problems and Prospects*, edited by James Dorn and Wang Xi, 3–15. Chicago, IL: University of Chicago Press.

Friedman, Milton and Rose Friedman. 1980. *Free to Choose: A Personal Statement*. New York: Houghton Mifflin Harcourt.

Friedman, Milton and Rose Friedman. 1998. *Two Lucky People: Memoirs*. Chicago, IL: University of Chicago Press.

Friedman, Thomas. 2011. "Justice Goes Global." *New York Times*, June 14, 2011, A27.

Fromm, Erich. 1970. *Marx's Concept of Man*. New York: Frederick Ungar Publishing Co.

Galenson, Walter, ed. 1993. *China's Economic Reform*. San Francisco, CA: The 1990 Institute.

Gallagher, Mary E. 2002. " 'Reform and Openness': Why China's Economic Reforms have Delayed Democracy." *World Politics* 54 (3): 338–372. doi:10.1353/wp.2002.0009.

Gao, Shangquan. 1999. *Two Decades of Reform in China*. River Edge, NJ: World Scientific.

Garner, Bradley. "China's Black Market City." *Reason* December 2011. (http://reason.com/archives/2011/11/15/chinas-black-market-city/singlepage, accessed June 28, 2012).

Giles, John, Albert Park, and Fang Cai. 2006. "How has Economic Restructuring Affected China's Urban Workers?" *The China Quarterly* (185): 61–95. doi:10.1017/S0305741006000051.

Gill, Indermit Singh, and Todd Pugatch, eds. 2005. *At the Frontlines of Development: Reflections from the World Bank*. Washington, DC: World Bank.

Giroir, Guillaume. 2011. "Hyper-Rich and Hyper-Luxury in China: The Case of the Most Expensive Gated Communities." *Chinese Business Review* 10 (6): 454–466.

Gittings, John. 1989. *China Changes Face: The Road from Revolution 1949–1989*. New York: Oxford University Press.

Gittings, John. 2005. "Xue Muqiao: The Architect of China's Market Transformation." *Guardian*, August 17, 2005, 24.

Gold, Thomas B., William J. Hurst, Jaeyoun Won, and Qiang Li, eds. 2009. *Laid-Off Workers in a Workers' State: Unemployment with Chinese Characteristics*. New York: Palgrave Macmillan.

Goldman, Merle. 1994. *Sowing the Seeds of Democracy in China: Political Reform in the Deng Xiaoping Era*. Cambridge, MA: Harvard University Press.

Goldman, Merle. 2005. *From Comrade to Citizen: The Struggle for Political Rights in China*. Cambridge, MA: Harvard University Press.

Goldman, Merle, and Roderick MacFarquhar, eds. 1999. *The Paradox of China's Post Mao Reforms*. Cambridge, MA: Harvard University Press.

Gordon, David, Richard Edwards, and Michael Reich. 1982. *Segmented Work, Divided Workers: The Historical Transformation of Labor in the United States*. New York: Cambridge University Press.

Greenfield, Gerard and Apo Leong. 1997. "China's Communist Capitalism: The Real World of Market Socialism," In *Ruthless Criticism of all that Exists: Socialist Register 1997*, edited by Leo Panitch, 96–122. New York: Monthly Review.

Grove, Linda. 2006. *A Chinese Economic Revolution: Rural Entrepreneurship in the Twentieth Century*. Lanham, MD: Rowman & Littlefield.

Gu, Edward X. 1997. "Foreign Direct Investment and the Restructuring of Chinese State-Owned Enterprises (1992–1995): A New Institutionalist Perspective." *China Information* 12 (3): 46–71. doi:10.1177/0920203X9701200303.

Guo, Xibao and Ping Zhang. 2013. "Thirty Years of Disputes on China's Economic Reform." In *Thoughts on Economic Development in China*, edited by Ying Ma and Hans-Michael Trautwein, 217–234. New York: Routledge.

Gustafsson, Bjorn A., Shi Li, and Terry Sicular, eds. 2008. *Inequality and Public Policy in China*. New York: Cambridge University Press.

Haering, Norbert. 2014. "George Soros' INET: A Conspiracy Theory Assessment." *World Economic Association Newsletter* 4 (2).

Halpern, Nina P. 1985. "China's Industrial Economic Reforms: The Question of Strategy." *Asian Survey* 25 (10): 998–1012. doi:10.2307/2644177.

Halpern, Nina P. 1989. "Policy Communities in a Leninist State: The Case of the Chinese Economic Policy Community." *Governance: An International Journal of Policy and Administration* 2 (1): 23–41.

Hamrin, Carol Lee, and Timothy Check, eds. 1986. *China's Establishment Intellectuals*. Armonk. NY: M. E. Sharpe.

Hamrin, Carol Lee, and Suisheng Zhao, eds. 1995. *Decision-Making in Deng's China: Perspectives from Insiders*. Armonk, NY: M. E. Sharpe.

Han, Dongping. 2008. *The Unknown Cultural Revolution: Life and Change in a Chinese Village*. New York: Monthly Review.

Han, Yuling. 2012. "The Academic Career and Economic Thought of Yifeng Wu." *World Review of Political Economy* 3 (3): 389–401. doi:10.13169/worlrevipoliecon. 3.3.0389.

Han, Zhenliang. 1996. "Draw the Line Beween Learning Advanced Things from the West and Worshiping Things Foreign." *Chinese Economic Studies* 29 (3): 85–92.

Harding, Harry. 1987. *China's Second Revolution: Reform After Mao*. Washington, DC: Brookings.

Hartford, Kathleen. 1985. "Socialist Agriculture is Dead; Long Live Socialist Agriculture: Organizational Transformation in Rural China." In *The Political Economy of Reform in Post-Mao China*, edited by Elizabeth J. Perry and Christine Wong, 31–61. Cambridge, MA: Harvard University Press.

Hart-Landsberg, Martin. 2011. "The Chinese Reform Experience: A Critical Assessment." *Review of Radical Political Economics* 43 (1): 56–76. doi:10.1177/0486613 410383954.

Hart-Landsberg, Martin, and Paul Burkett. 2005. *China and Socialism: Market Reforms and Class Struggle*. New York: Monthly Review.

Harvey, David. 2005. *A Brief History of Neoliberalism*. New York: Oxford.

He, Jianzhang and Wenmin Zhang. 1982. "The System of Ownership: A Tendency Toward Multiplicity." In *China's Economic Reforms*, edited by Lin Wei and Arnold Chao, 186–204. Philadelphia, PA: University of Pennsylvania Press.

He, Xuefeng. 2007. "New Rural Construction and the Chinese Path." *Chinese Sociology & Anthropology* 39 (4): 26–38. doi:10.2753/CSA0009-4625390402.

Heilmann, Sebastian and Lea Shih. 2013. "The Rise of Industrial Policy in China, 1978–2012." *Harvard-Yenching Institute Working Paper Series*: July 31, 2013.

Herrmann-Pillath, Carsten. 2011. "A Third Culture in Economics? An Essay on Smith, Confucius, and the Rise of China." *Working Paper Series, Frankfurt School of Finance and Management* 159.

Herschede, Fred. 1985. "Economics as an Academic Discipline at Nanjing University." *The China Quarterly* (102): 304–316. doi:10.1017/S0305741000029969.

Hinton, William. 1990. *The Great Reversal: The Privatization of China 1978–1989*. New York: Monthly Review.

Hodgson, Geoff. 1986. "Behind Methodological Individualism." *Cambridge Journal of Economics* 10 (3): 211–224.

Holz, Carsten A. 2002. "Long Live China's State-Owned Enterprises: Deflating the Myth of Poor Financial Performance." *Journal of Asian Economics* 13 (4): 493. https://knox.idm.oclc.org/login?url=http://search.ebscohost.com/login.aspx?direc t=true&db=bsh&AN=8550003&site=ehost-live.

Hoogewerf, Rupert. 2016. *Huran Global Rich List of 2016*. Beijing: Huran Report.

Howe, Christopher B. 2009. "The Chinese Economy and 'China Economists' as seen through the Pages of *the China Quarterly*." *The China Quarterly* (200): 923–927. doi:10.1017/S0305741009990981.

Howe, Christopher, Y. Y. Kueh, and Robert Ash, eds. 2003. *China's Economic Reform: A Study with Documents*. New York: Routledge.

Hsia, Renee Yuen-Jan and Lynn T. White III. 2002. "Working Amid Corporatism and Confusion: Foreign NGOs in China." *Nonprofit and Voluntary Sector Quarterly* 31 (3): 329–351. doi:10.1177/0899764002313002.

Hsu, Robert C. 1988. "Economics and Economists in Post-Mao China: Some Observations." *Asian Survey* 28 (12): 1211–1228. doi:10.2307/2644742.

Hsu, Robert C. 1991. *Economic Theories in China 1979–1988*. New York: Cambridge University Press.

Hu, Qiaomu. 1978. "Observe Economic Laws, Speed Up the Four Modernizations." *Peking Review* 21 (45) 7–12.

Hu, Thewei. 1988. "Teaching about the American Economy in the People's Republic of China." *Journal of Economic Education* 19 (1): 87–96. doi:10.1080/0022 0485.1988.10845246.

Hua, Sheng, Xuejun Zhang, and Xiaopeng Luo. 1993. *China: From Revolution to Reform.* Studies on the Chinese Economy, edited by Peter Nolan and Fureng Dong. London: Macmillan Press.

Huan, Qingzhi. 2010a. "Eco-Socialism in an Era of Capitalist Globalization: Bridging the West and the East." In *Eco-Socialism as Politics: Rebuilding the Basis of our Modern Civilisation*, edited by Qingzhi Huan, 1–14. New York: Springer.

Huan, Qingzhi. 2010b. "Growth Economy and its Ecological Impacts upon China: An Eco-Socialist Analysis." In *Eco-Socialism as Politics: Rebuilding the Basis of our Modern Civilisation*, edited by Qingzhi Huan, 191–203. New York: Springer.

Huan, Qingzhi, ed. 2010c. *Eco-Socialism as Politics: Rebuilding the Basis of our Modern Civilisation.* New York: Springer.

Huang, Haifeng. 2015. "Propaganda as Signaling." *Comparative Politics* 47 (4): 419–444.

Huang, Jikun, Keijiro Otsuka, and Scott Rozelle. 2008. "Agriculture in China's Development: Past Disappointments, Recent Successes, and Future Challenges." In *China's Great Economic Transformation*, edited by Loren Brandt and Thomas Rawski, 467–505. New York: Cambridge University Press.

Huang, Jikun, and Scott Rozelle. 1995. "Environmental Stress and Grain Yields in China." *American Journal of Agricultural Economics* 77 (4): 853. doi:10.2307/1243808.

Huang, Philip C. C. 2009a. "China's Neglected Informal Economy: Reality and Theory." *Modern China* 35 (4): 405–438. doi:10.1177/0097700409333158.

Huang, Philip C. C. 2009b. "Introduction to 'Whither Chinese Reforms? Dialogues among Western and Chinese Scholars, II'." *Modern China* 35 (4): 347–351. doi: 10.1177/0097700409335385.

Huang, Yasheng. 2008. *Capitalism with Chinese Characteristics: Entrepreneurship and the State.* New York: Cambridge University Press.

Iskander, Magdi. 1996. "Improving State-Owned Enterprise Performance: Recent International Experience." In *Policy Options for Reform of Chinese State-Owned Enterprises. Proceedings from a Symposium in Beijing June 1995*, edited by Harry G. Broadman, 17–86. Washington, DC: World Bank.

Jacobson, Harold K., and Michel Oksenberg. 1990. *China's Participation in the IMF, the World Bank, and GATT: Toward a Global Economic Order.* Ann Arbor: University of Michigan Press.

Jefferson, Gary H., and Thomas Rawski. 1994. "Enterprise Reform in Chinese Industry." *Journal of Economic Perspectives* 8 (2): 47–70. doi:10.1257/jep. 8.2.47.

Jefferson, Gary H., and Thomas Rawski. 1995. "How Industrial Reform Worked in China: The Role of Innovation, Competition, and Property Rights." World Bank, 1994.

Kallgren, Joyce K. 1987. "Public Interest and Private Interest in Sino-American Exchanges: De Toqueville's 'Associations' in Action." In *Educational Exchanges: Essays on the Sino-American Experience*, edited by Joyce K. Kallgren and Denis Fred Simon, 58–79. Berkeley, CA: Institute of East Asian Studies.

Kelliher, Daniel. 1992. *Peasant Power in China: The Era of Rural Reform 1979–1989.* New Haven, CT: Yale University Press.

Keyser, Catherine. 2003. *Professionalizing Research in Post-Mao China: The System Reform Institute and Policymaking*. Armonk, NY: M. E. Sharpe.

Klaes, Matthias, and Yi Zhang. 2013. "Chinese Reform and Schools of Thought in Western Economics." In *Thoughts on Economic Deveolopment in China*, edited by Ying Ma and Hans-Michael Trautwein, 255–273. New York: Routledge,

Koesel, Karrie. 2015. *Learning to be Loyal: Political Education in China*. Paper Delivered at the 2015 Meetings of the Association for Asian Studies.

Kornai, Janos. 1998. *From Socialism to Capitalism: What is Meant by the Change of the System?* London: The Social Market Foundation.

Kotz, David. 2000. "Lessons from the Demise of State Socialism in the Soviet Union and China." In *Socialism and Radical Political Economy: Essays in Honor of Howard Sherman*, edited by Robert Pollin (pre-publication online November 1999), 300–317. Northampton, MA: Edward Elgar.

Kotz, David. 2007. "The State of Official Marxism in China Today." *Monthly Review* 59 (4): 58–63. http://monthlyreview.org/2007/09/01/the-state-of-official-marxism-in-china-today/.

Kotz, David, Terrence McDonough, and Michael Reich. 1994. *Social Structures of Accumulation: The Political Economy of Growth and Crisis*. New York: Cambridge University Press.

Kotz, David, and Fred Weir. 1997. *Revolution from Above*. New York: Routledge.

Kovacs, Janos, and Marton Tardos. 1992. *Reform and Transformation in Eastern Europe: Soviet-Type Economies on the Threshold of Change*. New York: Routledge.

Kraus, Willy. 1991. *Private Business in China: Revival between Ideology and Pragmatic Policy*. Honolulu, HI: University of Hawaii Press.

Kristof, Nicholas. 1989a. "'Mr. Stock Market': Li Yining; Selling China on a 'Public' Privatization." *New York Times*, January 8, 1989.

Krugman, Paul. 1987. "Is Free Trade Passé?" *Journal of Economic Perspectives* 1 (2): 131–144. doi:10.1257/jep. 1.2.131.

Kristof, Nicholas. 1989b. "In Beijing a Bold New Proposal: End State Ownership of Industry." *New York Times*: A1.

Krugman, Paul. 2011. "Our Blogs, Ourselves." *New York Times*, October 18, 2011.

Kuhn, Robert. 2011. *How China's Leaders Think*. Singapore: Wiley.

Kuhn, Thomas. 1970. *The Structure of Scientific Revolutions*. 2nd ed. Chicago: University of Chicago.

Kung, James Kai-sing. 1999. "The Evolution of Property Rights in Village Enterprises: the Case of Wuxi Countuy." In *Property Rights and Economic Reform in China*, edited by Jean Oi and Andrew Walder, 95–120. Stanford, CA: Stanford University Press.

Kwong, Julia. 1994. "Ideological Crisis among China's Youth: Values and Official Ideology." *British Journal of Sociology* 45 (2): 247–264. https://knox.idm.oclc.org/login?url=http://search.ebscohost.com/login.aspx?direct=true&db=sih&AN=9408050748&site=ehost-live.

Kwong, Peter. 2006. "The Chinese Face of Neoliberalism." *Counterpunch* 13 (12): 1–3.

Lagerkvist, Johan. 2015. "The Unknown Terrain of Social Protests in China: 'Exit', 'Voice', 'Loyalty', and 'Shadow'." *Journal of Civil Society* 11 (2): 137–153. doi:10.1080/17448689.2015.1052229. https://knox.idm.oclc.org/login?url=http://search.ebscohost.com/login.aspx?direct=true&db=poh&AN=103736600&site=ehost-live.

Lampton, David M., Joyce Madancy, and Kristen M. Williams. 1986. *A Relationship Restored: Trends in U.S.-China Educational Exchanges, 1979–1984*. Washington, DC: National Academy Press.

Lardy, Nicholas. 1990. "Chinese Agricultural Development Under Reform and Future Prospects." In *Agricultural Reform and Development in China: Achievements, Current Status, and Future Outlook, Sixth Colloquium Proceedings*, edited by T. C. Tso, 21–35. Beltsville, MD: IDEALS Inc.

Lardy, Nicholas. 1998. *China's Unfinished Revolution*. Washington, DC: Brookings Institution.

Lardy, Nicholas. 2002. *Integrating China into the Global Economy*. Washington, DC: Brookings Institution Press.

Lardy, Nicholas. 2014. *Markets Over Mao: The Rise of Private Business in China*. Washington, DC: Peterson Institute for International Economics.

Lardy, Nicholas, and Kenneth Lieberthal, eds. 1983. *Chen Yun's Strategy for China's Development*. Armonk, NY: M.E, Sharpe.

Lau, Raymond. 2001. "Economic Determination in the Last Instance: China's Political-Economic Development Under the Impact of the Asian Financial Crises." *Historical Materialism* 8 (1): 215–251. doi:10.1163/156920601100414811.

Lee, Ching Kwan. 1998. *Gender and the South China Miracle: Two Worlds of Factory Women*. Berkeley, CA: University of California Press.

Lee, Ching Kwan. 2007a. *Working in China: Ethnographies of Labor and Workplace Transformation*. New York: Routledge.

Lee, Ching Kwan. 2007b. "The Unmaking of the Chinese Working Class." In *Working in China: Ethnographies of Labor and Workplace Transformation*, edited by Ching Kwan Lee, 15–37. New York: Routledge.

Lee, Ching Kwan. 2007c. *Against the Law: Labor Protests in China's Rustbelt and Sunbelt*. Berkeley, CA: University of California Press.

Lee, Junyeop, and OECD Working Group on Privatisation and Corporate Governance of State Owned Assets. 2009. *State Owned Enterprises in China: Reviewing the Evidence* OECD.

Leonard, Mark. 2008a. *What does China Think?* New York: Public Affairs.

Leonard, Mark. 2008b. "China's New Intelligentsia." *Prospect Magazine*, March 2008.

Leung, Win-yue. 1988. *Smashing the Iron Rice Pot: Workers & Unions in China's Market Socialism*. Hong Kong: Asia Monitor Resource Center.

Lewis, Steven W. 2005. "Economic Thought." In *Encyclopedia of Contemporary Chinese Culture*, edited by Edward Lawrence Davis, 230–232. New York: Routledge.

Li, Cheng. 1997. *Rediscovering China: Dynamics and Dilemmas of Reform*. Lanham MD: Rowman & Littlefield.

Li, Cheng. 2001. *China's Leaders: The New Generation*. New York: Rowman & Littlefield.

Li, Cheng. 2005. "Coming Home to Teach: Status and Mobility of Returnees in China's Higher Education." In *Bridging Minds Across the Pacific: US-China Educational Exchanges 1978–2003*, edited by Cheng Li, 69–109. Lanham, MD: Lexington Books.

Li, Cheng. 2009. "China's New Think Tanks: Where Officials, Entrepreneurs, and Scholars Interact." *China Leadership Monitor* 29.

Li, Cheng, and Lynn T. White III. 1991. "China's Technocratic Movement and the World Economic Herald." *Modern China* 17 (3): 342–388. doi:10.1177/0097700 49101700302.

Li, Haijian. 2003 [1997]. "Integrating FDI within the Domestic Economy (China Industrial Development Report)." In *China's Economic Reform: A Study with Documents*, edited by Christopher Howe, Y. Y. Kueh, and Robert Ash, 387–398. New York: Routledge.

Li, He. 8/2008. "China's New Left and its Impact on Political Liberalization." *EAI Background Brief* (401).

Li, He. 2009. "China's New Left." *East Asian Policy* 1 (1): 30–37.

Li, He. 2010. "Debating China's Economic Reform: New Leftists Vs. Liberals." *Journal of Chinese Political Science* 15 (1): 1–23. doi:10.1007/s11366-009-9092-4. https://knox.idm.oclc.org/login?url=http://search.ebscohost.com/login.aspx?direc t=true&db=a9h&AN=48357181&site=ehost-live.

Li, Lanqing. 2009. *Breaking through: The Birth of China's Opening-Up Policy.* New York: Oxford University Press.

Li, Minqi. "Capitalist Development and Class Struggle in China." Book manuscript. Available online at http://content.csbs.utah.edu/~mli/Capitalism%20in%20China/ Index.htm (accessed April 22, 2017).

Li, Minqi. 2008. *The Rise of China and the Demise of the Capitalist World Economy.* New York: Monthly Review.

Li, Shi. 1990. "Growth of Household Industry in Rural Wenzhou." In *Market Forces in China: Competition and Small Business; the Wenzhou Debate*, edited by Peter Nolan and Fureng Dong, 108–125. Atlantic Highlands, NJ: Zed Books.

Li, Shi. 2008. *Rural Migrant Workers in China: Scenario, Challenges and Public Policy.* ILO Working Papers. Vol. 89. Geneva: International Labour Office.

Li, Weisen, and Hans-Michael Trautwein. 2013. "Northian Perspectives on China's Economic Reform." In *Thoughts on Economc Development in China*, edited by Ying Ma and Hans-Michael Trautwein, 235–254. New York: Routledge.

Li, Zhongjin, and Hao Qi. 2014. "Labor Process and the Social Structure of Accumulation in China." *Review of Radical Political Economics* 46 (4): 481–488. doi:10.1177/0486613414537986.

Lichtenstein, Peter M. 1992. "The Political Economy of Left and Right during China's Decade of Reform." *International Journal of Social Economics* 19 (10): 164–180. doi:10.1108/EUM0000000000510.

Lim, Edwin. 2005. "Learning and Working with Giants." In *At the Frontlines of Development: Reflections from the World Bank*, edited by Indermit Singh Gill and Todd Pugatch, 89–119. Washington, DC: World Bank.

Lim, Edwin. 2014. "The Influence of Foreign Economists in the Early Stages of China's Reforms." In *The Oxford Companion to the Economics of China*, edited by Shenggen Fan, Ravi Kanbur, Shang-Jin Wei, and Xiaobo Zhang, 47–52. New York: Oxford University Press.

Lin, Chun. 2006. *The Transformation of Chinese Socialism.* Durham, NC: Duke University Press.

Lin, Chun. 2013. *China and Global Capitalism: Reflections on Marxism, History, and Contemporary Politics.* New York: St. Martins Press.

Lin, Cyril Chihren. 1981. "The Reinstatement of Economics in China Today." *The China Quarterly* (85): 1–48. doi:10.1017/S0305741000028010.

Lin, Cyril Chihren. 1984. *"Review of Social Needs Versus Economic Efficiency in China. Sun Yefang's Critique of Socialist Economics ed. by K. K. Fung."* *The China Quarterly* (98): 357–361. www.jstor.org/stable/653821.

Lin, Fen, Yanfei Sun, and Hongxing Yang. 2015. "How are Chinese Students Ideologically Divided? A Survey of Chinese College Students' Political Self-Identification." *Pacific Affairs* 88 (1): 51–74. doi:10.5509/201588151.

Lin, Justin Yifu. 1988. "Rural Factor Markets in China After the Household Responsibility Reform." In *Chinese Economic Policy: Economic Reform at Midstream*, edited by Bruce Reynolds and Ilpyong Kim, 169–203. New York: Paragon House.

Lin, Justin Yifu. 1990. "Collectivization and China's Agricultural Crisis in 1959–1961." *Journal of Political Economy* 98 (6): 1228–1252. doi:10.1086/261732.

Lin, Justin Yifu. 1992. "Rural Reforms and Agricultural Growth in China." *The American Economic Review* 82 (1): 34–51. www.jstor.org/stable/2117601.

Lin, Justin Yifu. 2005. *Building Up a Market-Oriented Research and Education Institution in a Transitional Economy: The Experience of the China Center for Economic Research at Peking University (CCER Working Paper no. E2005003)*. Beijing: China Center for Economic Research.

Lin, Justin Yifu. 2012a. *Demystifying the Chinese Economy*. New York: Cambridge University Press.

Lin, Justin Yifu. 2012b. *New Structural Economics: A Framework for Rethinking Development and Policy*. Washington, DC: World Bank.

Lin, Justin Yifu. 2012c. *Benti and Changwu: Dialogues on Methodology in Economics*. Beijing: Peking University Press.

Lin, Justin Yifu, and Ha-Joon Chang. 2009. "Should Industrial Policy in Developing Countries Conform to Comparative Advantage or Defy it? A Debate between Justin Lin and Ha-Joon Chang." *Development Policy Review* 27 (5): 483–502. doi:10.1111/j.1467-7679.2009.00456.x.

Lin, Justin Yifu, Fang Cai, and Zhou Li. 2003. *The China Miracle: Development Strategy and Economic Reform*. Rev. ed. Hong Kong: Chinese University Press.

Lin, Zhang. 1990. "Developing the Commodity Economy in the Rural Areas." In *Market Forces in China: Competition and Small Business; the Wenzhou Debate*, edited by Peter Nolan and Fureng Dong, 97–107. Atlantic Highlands, NJ: Zed Books.

Lin, Zili. 1990. "Privatization, Marketization, and Polarization." In *Market Forces in China: Competition and Small Business; the Wenzhou Debate*, edited by Peter Nolan and Fureng Dong, 165–175. Atlantic Highlands, NJ: Zed Books.

Lippit, Victor. 1987. *The Economic Development of China*. Armonk, NY: M. E. Sharpe.

Liu, Alan. 1992. "The 'Wenzhou Model' of Development and China's Modernization." *Asian Survey* 32 (8): 696–711. doi:10.2307/2645363.

Liu, Changyuan and Song Wang. 2009. "Transformation of Chinese Cultural Values in the Era of Globalization: Individualism and Chinese Youth." *Intercultural Communication Studies* XVIII (2): 54–71.

Liu, Guoguang. "Interview with Dr. Heng Lin." Chinese Academy of Social Sciences website: experts, 1st group CASS members, Liu Guoguang, http://casseng.cssn.cn/experts/experts_1st_group_cass_members/201402/t20140221_969619.html.

Liu, Guoguang. 2003 [1983]. "The Important Issues Involved with China's Strategy for Economic Development." In *China's Economic Reform: A Study with Documents*, edited by Christopher Howe, Y. Y. Kueh, and Robert Ash, 66–79. New York: Routledge.

Liu, Guoguang. 2003 [1992]. "Some Issues Relating to the Theory of the Socialist Market Economy." In *China's Economic Reform: A Study with Documents*, edited by Christopher Howe, Y. Y. Kueh, and Robert Ash, 97–107. New York: Routledge.

Liu, Guoguang. 2011. "Speech upon Receiving the Marxian Economics Award." *World Review of Political Economy* 2 (3): 366–370. www.jstor.org/stable/41931930.

Liu, Hong. 2006. " 'My Life is Closely Connected with China's Reform'—A Brief Biography of Professor Wu Jinglian." *The Link*: 9–15.

Liu, Junning. 2000. "Classical Liberalism Catches on in China." *Journal of Democracy* 11 (3): 48–57.

Liu, Kang. 2004. *Globalization and Cultural Trends in China*. Honolulu, HI: University of Hawaii Press.

Lo, Dic. 1997. *Market and Institutional Regulation in Chinese Industrialization, 1978–1994*. New York: St. Martin's Press.

Lo, Dic. 1999. "Reappraising the Performance of China's State-Owned Industrial Enterprises 1980–96." *Cambridge Journal of Economics* 23 (6): 693–718.

Lo, Dic, and Yu Zhang. 2011. "Making Sense of China's Economic Transformation." *Review of Radical Political Economics* 43 (1): 33–55. doi:10.1177/04866134 10383952.

Looney, Kristen. 2012. "The Rural Development State: Modernization Campaigns and Peasant Pollitics in China, Taiwan, and South Korea." PhD diss., Harvard University.

Luo, Xiaopeng. 1990. "Ownership and Status Stratification." In *China's Rural Industry: Structure, Development, and Reform*, edited by William Byrd and Qingsong Lin, 134–171. Washington, DC: World Bank.

Ma, Bin, and Yaxi Han. 2002. "Letter to Comrade Jiang Zemin and the Party's Central Committee." *Monthly Review* archives May 21, 2002. (https://monthlyreview.org/commentary/letter-of-ma-bin-and-han-yaxi/, accessed April 23, 2017).

Ma, Hong. 1983. *New Strategy for China's Economy*. Beijing: New World Press.

Ma, Shu Y. 1998. "The Chinese Route to Privatization: The Evolution of the Shareholding System Option." *Asian Survey* 38 (4): 379–397. doi:10.2307/2645413.

Ma, Ying, and Hans-Michael Trautwein, eds. 2013. *Thoughts on Economic Development in China*. New York: Routledge.

Mao, Yushi. 2011. "The Paradox of Morality." In *The Morality of Capitalism: What Your Professors Won't Tell You*, edited by Tom G. Palmer, 43–54. Ottawa, IL: Jameson Books.

Marglin, Stephen A. 1974. "What do Bosses Do?: The Origins and Functions of Hierarchy in Capitalist Production." *Review of Radical Political Economics* 6 (2): 60–112. doi:10.1177/048661347400600206.

McCloskey, Donald N. 1985. *The Rhetoric of Economics*. 1st ed. Madison, WI: University of Wisconsin Press.

McCoy, Michael Dalton. 2000. *Domestic Policy Narratives and International Relations Theory: Chinese Ecological Agriculture as a Case Study*. New York: University Press of America.

Meisner, Maurice. 1996. *The Deng Xiaopeng Era: An Inquiry into the Fate of Chinese Socialism 1978–1994*. New York: Hill and Wang.

Meisner, Maurice. 1999. *Mao's China: A History of the People's Republic*. 3rd ed. New York: Free Press.

Meng, Jie. 2008. "The Hypothesis of Economic Man and Marxist Economics." *Social Sciences in China* 29 (1): 5–15. doi:10.1080/02529200801920855.

Misra, Kalpana. 1998. *From Post Maoism to Post-Marxism: The Erosion of Official Ideology in Deng's China*. New York: Routledge.

National Bureau of Statistics of China. 2010. *China Statistical Yearbook 2010*. Beijing: China Statistics Press.

Naughton, Barry. 1986. "Sun Yefang: Toward a Reconstruction of Socialist Economics." In *China's Establishment Intellectuals*, edited by Carol Lee Hamrin and Timothy Cheek, 124–154. Armonk, NY: M. E. Sharpe.

Naughton, Barry. 1992. "Implications of the State Monopoly Over Industry and its Relaxation." *Modern China* 18 (1): 14–41. www.jstor.org/stable/189138.

Naughton, Barry. 1993. "Deng Xiaoping: The Economist." *The China Quarterly* (135): 491–514. doi:10.1017/S0305741000013886.

Naughton, Barry. 1995. *Growing Out of the Plan: Chinese Economic Reform 1978–1993.* New York: Cambridge University Press.

Naughton, Barry. 2001. "Zhu Rongji: The Twilight of a Brilliant Career." *China Leadership Monitor* 1 (1): 1–10.

Naughton, Barry. 2002. "China's Economic Think Tanks: Their Changing Role in the 1990s." *The China Quarterly* (171): 625–635. doi:10.1017/S0009443902000396.

Naughton, Barry. 2007. *The Chinese Economy: Transitions and Growth.* Cambridge, MA: MIT Press.

Naughton, Barry. 2008. "A Political Economy of China's Economic Transition." In *China's Great Transformation*, edited by Loren Brandt and Thomas Rawski, 91–135. New York: Cambridge University Press.

Naughton, Barry. ed. 2013. *Wu Jinglian: Voice of Reform in China.* New York: Cambridge University Press.

Nee, Victor and Su Sijin. 1990. "Institutional Change and Economic Growth in China: The View from the Villages." *The Journal of Asian Studies* 49 (1): 3–25. doi:10.2307/2058430.

Nolan, Peter. 1990. "Petty Commodity Production in a Socialist Economy: Chinese Rural Development Post-Mao." In *Market Forces in China: Competition and Small Business; The Wenzhou Debate*, edited by Peter Nolan and Fureng Dong, 7–42. Atlantic Highlands, NJ: Zed Books.

Nolan, Peter. 2004 [1998]. *Transforming China: Globalization, Transition and Development.* New York: Anthem Press.

Nolan, Peter, and Fureng Dong, eds. 1990. *Market Forces in China: Competition and Small Business; the Wenzhou Debate.* Atlantic Highlands, NJ: Zed Books.

Oi, Jean. 1999. *Rural China Takes Off: Institutional Foundations of Economic Reform.* Berkeley, CA: University of California Press.

Oi, Jean, and Andrew Walder, eds. 1999. *Property Rights and Economic Reform in China.* Stanford, CA: Stanford University Press.

Oksenberg, Michel. 1982. "Economic Policy-Making in China: Summer 1981." *The China Quarterly* (90): 165–194. doi:10.1017/S0305741000000308.

Palley, Thomas. 1998. *Plenty of Nothing: The Downsizing of the American Dream and the Case for Structural Keynesiansim.* Princeton, NJ: Princeton University Press.

Pan, Esther. 2005. "China's Angry Peasants." *Council on Foreign Relations Backgrounder (Archives)* (December 15, 2005).

Panitch, Leo, ed. 1997. *Ruthless Criticism of all that Exists: Socialist Register 1997.* New York: Monthly Review.

Park, Henry. 1986. "Postrevolutionary China and the Soviet NEP." *Research in Political Economy* 9: 219–233.

Paulson, Henry M. Jr. 2015. *Dealing with China: An Insider Unmasks the New Economic Superpower.* New York: Twelve Hachette Book Group.

Perkins, Dwight. 1994. "Completing China's Move to the Market." *Journal of Economic Perspectives* 8 (2): 23–46. doi:10.1257/jep. 8.2.23.

Perkins, Dwight. 1999. *Report: Supporting China's Transition to a Market Economy; an Evaluation of the Chinese Economists Society (Commissioned for the Center for International Private Enterprise).*

Perkins, Dwight. 2002. "The challenge China's economy poses for Chinese economists." *China Economic Review* 13 (4): 412–418.

Perry, Elizabeth J., and Christine Wong, eds. 1985. *The Political Economy of Reform in Post-Mao China*. Cambridge, MA: Harvard University Press.

Perry, Elizabeth J., and Christine Wong. 1985. "Introduction." In *The Political Economy of Reform in Post-Mao China*, edited by Elizabeth J. Perry and Christine Wong, 1–27. Cambridge, MA: Harvard University Press.

Peterson, Glen. 2014. *Overseas Chinese in the People's Republic of China*. New York: Routledge.

Piketty, Thomas. 2014. *Capital in the Twenty-First Century*. Cambridge, MA: Harvard University Press.

Pils, Eva. 2006. "Asking the Tiger for His Skin: Rights Activism in China." *Fordham International Law Journal* 30 (4): 1209–1287. http://ir.lawnet.fordham.edu/ilj/vol. 30/iss4/6.

Pringle, Tim. 2013. "Reflections on Labor in China: From a Moment to a Movement." *South Atlantic Quarterly* 112 (1): 191–202. doi:10.1215/00382876-1891323.

Pun, Ngai. 2005. "Global Production, Company Codes of Conduct, and Labor Conditions in China: A Case Study of Two Factories." *China Journal* (54): 101–113. doi:10.2307/20066068.

Pun, Ngai. 2008. "'Reorganizing Moralism': The Politics of Transnational Labor Codes." In *Privatizing China: Socialism from Afar*, edited by Li Zhang and Aihwa Ong, 87–102. Ithaca, NY: Cornell University Press.

Putterman, Louis. 1993. *Continuity and Change in China's Rural Development*. New York: Oxford University Press.

Putterman, Louis. 1995. "The Role of Ownership and Property Rights in China's Economic Transition." *The China Quarterly* (144): 1047–1064. doi:10.1017/S0305741000004720.

Qian, Meijun, and Yasheng Huang. 2011. *Financial Reversal in Rural China*: Financial Institutions Center, University of Pennsylvania.

Qian, Yingyi. 2002. *How Reform Worked in China*. William Davidson Working Paper no. 473.

Qian, Yingyi, and Jinglian Wu. 2000. *China's Transition to a Market Economy: How Far Across the River?* Working Paper no. 69. Stanford, CA: Center for International Development, Stanford University.

Rawski, Thomas. 1986. "Report on Economics Curriculum in Chinese Universities (Draft)." personal copy.

Rawski, Thomas. 1987. *"Report on Economics Curriculum in Chinese Universities (Prepared for the World Bank)."* Personal copy.

Rawski, Thomas G. 1997. "China's State Enterprise Reform–an Overseas Perspective." *China Economic Review (1043951X)* 8 (1): 89. https://knox.idm.oclc.org/login?url=http://search.ebscohost.com/login.aspx?direct=true&db=bsh&AN=9709223159&site=ehost-live.

Rawski, Thomas. 2013 [2009]. "Studies of China's Economy." In *A Scholarly Review of Chinese Studies in North America*, edited by Haihui Zhang, Zhaohui Xue, Shuyong Jiang and Gary Lance Lugar, 175–192. Ann Arbor, MI: Association for Asian Studies.

Reynolds, Bruce and Ilpyong Kim. 1988. *Chinese Economic Policy: Economic Reform at Midstream*. New York: Paragon House.

Riskin, Carl. 1973. "Maoism and Motivation: Work Incentives in China." *Bulletin of Concerned Asian Scholars* 5 (1).

Riskin, Carl. 1982. "Market, Maoism, and Economic Reform in China." *Bulletin of Concerned Asian Scholars* 13 (3): 31–41.

Riskin, Carl. 1987. *China's Political Economy: The Quest for Development since 1949.* New York: Oxford University Press.

Rosen, Stanley. 1993. "The Effect of Post-4 June Re-Education Campaigns on Chinese Students." *The China Quarterly* (134): 310–334. doi:10.1017/S0305741 000029702.

Rosen, Stanley. 2009. "Contemporary Chinese Youth and the State." *The Journal of Asian Studies* 68 (2): 359–369. doi:10.1017/S0021911809000631.

Ross, Andrew. 2007a. *Fast Boat to China: High-Tech Outsourcing and the Consequences for Free Trade—Lessons from Shanghai.* New York: Vintage.

Ross, Andrew. 2007b. "Outsourcing as a Way of Life? Knowledge Transfer in the Yangtze Delta." In *Working in China: Ethnographies of Labor and Workplace Transformation,* edited by Ching Kwan Lee, 188–208. New York: Routledge.

Sachs, Jeffrey D. and Wing Woo. 2000. "Understanding China's Economic Performance." *Journal of Policy Reform* 4 (1): 1–50. doi:10.1080/13841280008523412.

Schumacher, E. F. 1973. *Small is Beautiful: Economics as if People Mattered.* New York: Harper and Row.

Schurmann, Franz. 1968. *Ideology and Organization in Communist China.* 2nd ed. Berkeley, CA: University of California Press.

Scott, Margaret. October 23, 1986. "Tinkering with Reforms to China's Universities." *Far Eastern Economic Review,* 60–63.

Selden, Mark and Victor Lippit, eds. 1982. *The Transition to Socialism in China.* Armonk, NY: M. E. Sharpe.

Selden, Mark. 1993. *The Political Economy of Chinese Development.* Armonk, NY: M. E. Sharpe.

Sen, Amartya. 1984. *Resources, Values and Development.* Cambridge, MA: Harvard University Press.

Shen, Ruth and T. Y. Shen. 1993. "Economic Thinking in China: Economic Knowledge and Attitudes of High School Students." *Journal of Economic Education* 24 (1): 70–84. doi:10.1080/00220485.1993.10844781.

Shen, Ruth and T. Y. Shen. 1994. "High School Economics in the People's Republic of China." In *An International Perspective on Economic Education,* edited by William B. Walstad, 273–289. Boston: Kluwer Academic Publishers.

Sheng, Hong. 1996. "A Survey of the Research on the Transitional Process of Market-Oriented Reform in China." *Chinese Economic Studies* 29 (2): 5–38.

Shieh, Shawn and Signe Knutson. 2012. *Special Report: The Roles and Challenges of International NGOs in China's Development:* China Development Brief.

Shirk, Susan. 1993. *The Political Logic of Economic Reform in China.* Los Angeles, CA: University of California Press.

Sleeboom-Faulkner, Margaret. 2007. *The Chinese Academy of Social Sciences (CASS): Shaping the Reforms, Academia and China.* Boston: Brill.

Smith, Richard. 1993. "The Chinese Road to Capitalism." *New Left Review* 199: 55–99.

Smyth, Russell. 2000. "Asset Stripping in Chinese State-Owned Enterprises." *Journal of Contemporary Asia* 30 (1): 3, 3–16. doi:10.1080/00472330080000021.

Solinger, Dorothy J. 1981. "Economic Reform Via Reformulation in China: Where do Rightist Ideas come from?" *Asian Survey* 21 (9): 947–960. doi:10.2307/2643824.

Song, Longxiang. 1995. "The Methodology of Mainstream Economics and its Implications for China's Economic Research." PhD diss., Washington University.

Song, Longxiang (pseudonym Ma Ding). 1985. "Ten Major Changes in China's Study of Economics." *Beijing Review* 28 (49): 17–20.

Spence, Jonathan D. 1990. *The Search for Modern China.* New York: Norton.

Stone, Bruce. 1988. "Developments in Agricultural Technology." *The China Quarterly* (116): 767–822. doi:10.1017/S0305741000037954.

Stone, Bruce. 1990. "The Next Stage of Agricultural Development: Implications for Infrastructure, Technology and Institutional Priorities." In *Agricultural Reform and Development in China: Achievements, Current Status, and Future Outlook, Sixth Colloquium Proceedings*, edited by T. C. Tso, 47–93. Beltsville, MD: IDEALS Inc.

Su, Shaozhi. 1995. "The Structure of the Chinese Academy of Social Sciences and Two Decisions to Abolish its Marxism-Leninism-Mao Zedong Thought Institute." In *Decision-Making in Deng's China: Perspectives from Insiders*, edited by Carol Lee Hamrin and Suisheng Zhao, 111–117. Armonk, NY: M. E. Sharpe.

Sun, Yan. 1995. *The Chinese Reassessment of Socialism 1976–1992.* Princeton, NJ: Princeton University Press.

Sung, Yun-wing and Thomas Chan M. H. 1987. "China's Economic Reforms: The Debates in China." *The Australian Journal of Chinese Affairs* (17): 29–51. doi:10.2307/2158967.

Sutton, Francis X. 1987. "American Philanthropy in Educational Exchange with the People's Republic of China." In *Educational Exchanges: Essays on the Sino-American Experience*, edited by Joyce K. Kallgren and Denis Fred Simon, 96–118. Berkeley, CA: Institute of East Asian Studies.

Tang, Shouning. "Preface to China Economics 2000." In *China Economics 2000.* Beijing: Unirule Institute.

Tong, Sarah Y. 2009. "Why Privatize Or Why Not? Empirical Evidence from China's SOEs Reform." *China Economic Review* 20 (3): 402–413. doi:10.1016/j.chieco.2009.06.008.

Trescott, Paul B. 2007. *Jingji Xue: The History of the Introduction of Western Economic Ideas into China, 1850–1950.* Hong Kong: Chinese University Press.

Trescott, Paul B. 2012. "How Keynesian Economics Came to China." *History of Political Economy* 44 (2): 341–364. doi:10.1215/00182702-1571737. https://knox.idm.oclc.org/login?url=http://search.ebscohost.com/login.aspx?direct=true&db=bsh&AN=76282605&site=ehost-live.

Tsai, Kellee. 2006. "Debating Decentralized Development: A Reconsideration of the Wenzhou and Kerala Models." *Indian Journal of Economics and Business*: 47–67.

Tso, T. C., ed. 1990. *Agricultural Reform and Development in China: Achievements, Current Status, and Future Outlook, Sixth Colloquium Proceedings.* Beltsville, MD: IDEALS Inc.

Tu, Youyou. 2011. "The Discovery of Artemisinin (Qinghaosu) and Gifts from Chinese Medicine." *Nature Medicine* 17 (10): 1217–1220. doi:10.1038/nm.2471. https://knox.idm.oclc.org/login?url=http://search.ebscohost.com/login.aspx?direct=true&db=a9h&AN=66445377&site=ehost-live.

US Embassy, Tokyo. 2006 [1976] To Department of State, Telegram 05358, April 12 1976, 1976TOKYO05358, Central Foreign Policy Files, 1973–1979/Electronic Telegrams, RG 59: General Records of the Department of State, US National Archives (https://aad.archives.gov/aad/createpdf?rid=27162&dt=2082&dl=1345, accessed July 15, 2016).

Unger, Jonathan. 1985. "The Decollectivization of the Chinese Countryside: A Survey of Twenty-Eight Villages." *Pacific Affairs* 58 (4): 585–606. doi:10.2307/2758470.

Unger, Jonathan. 2002. *The Transformation of Rural China*. Armonk, NY: M. E. Sharpe.

Vermeer, Eduard B. 1999. "Shareholding Cooperatives: A Property Rights Analysis." In *Property Rights and Economic Reform in China*, edited by Jean Oi and Andrew Walder, 123–144. Stanford, CA: Stanford University Press.

Vogel, Ezra F. 2011. *Deng Xiaoping and the Transformation of China*. Cambridge, MA: Harvard University Press.

Walstad, William B., ed. 1994. *An International Perspective on Economic Education*. Boston: Kluwer Academic Publishers.

Wang, Chaohua, ed. 2003. *One China, Many Paths*. New York: Verso.

Wang, George C., ed. 1977 [1974]. *Fundamentals of Political Economy*. The China Book Project: Translations and Commentaries. Translated by K. F. Fung. White Plains, NY: M. E. Sharpe.

Wang, George C., ed. 1979. "Editor's Introduction." *Chinese Economic Studies* 12 (3).

Wang, George C., ed. 1982. *Economic Reform in the PRC: In which China's Economists make Known What Went Wrong, Why, and What Should be Done About It*. Boulder, CO: Westview Press.

Wang, Gungwu. 2014. *Another China Cycle: Committing to Reform*. Hackensack, NJ: World Scientific.

Wang, Haibo. 1982. "Competition Under Socialism." In *China's Economic Reforms*, edited by Lin Wei and Arnold Chao, 114–122. Philadelphia, PA: University of Pennsylvania Press.

Wang, Hui. 2003a. *China's New Order: Society, Politics, and Economy in Transition*, edited by Theodore Huters. Cambridge, MA: Harvard University Press.

Wang, Hui. 2003b. "The New Criticism." In *One China, Many Paths*, edited by Chaohua Wang, 55–86. New York: Verso.

Wang, Qingxin K. 2011. "The Rise of Neoclassical Economics and China's WTO Agreement with the United States in 1999." *Journal of Contemporary China* 20 (70): 449–465. doi:10.1080/10670564.2011.565177.

Wang, Songpei, Maoxu Li, and Dai Wang. 2004. *The Emergence and Evolution of Ecological Economics in China Over the Past Two Decades (Presentation given at the 8th Biennial Scientific Conference of the International Society for Ecological Economics)*.

Wang, Xiaoxi. 2012. "On the Economic Significance of Morality." *Social Sciences in China* 33 (3): 67–80. doi:10.1080/02529203.2012.702942.

Wang, Yicheng, Ning Fang, Bingquan Wang, and Ruisheng Liu. 2008. *A Study on Contemporary Chinese Intelligentsia and Media Elite—Survey II of Contemporary China's New Social Structural Changes :* Institute of Political Science, Chinese Academy of Social Sciences.

Wang, Zhihe. 2012. "Ecological Marxism in China." *Monthly Review* 63 (9): 36–44.

Wang, Zhihe, Meijun Fan, Hui Dong, Dezhong Sun, and Lichun Li. 2013. "What does Ecological Marxism Mean for China? Questions and Challenges for John Bellamy Foster." *Monthly Review* 64 (9): 47–53.

Ware, Robert. 2013. "Reflections on Chinese Marxism." *Socialism & Democracy* 27 (1): 136–160. doi:10.1080/08854300.2012.754214.

Warner, Malcolm. 2014. *Understanding Management in China: Past, Present, and Future*. New York: Routledge.

Watson, Andrew. 1987. "Social Science Research and Economic Policy Formulation: The Academic Side of Economic Reform." In *New Directions in the Social Sciences and Humanities in China*, edited by Michael B. Yahuda, 67–88. New York: St Martin's Press.

Wei, Lin, and Arnold Chao, eds. 1982. *China's Economic Reforms*. Philadelphia, PA: University of Pennsylvania Press.

Weinberg, Meyer. 2002. *A Short History of American Capitalism*. New History Press.

Weitzman, Martin and Chenggang Xu. 1994. "Chinese Township-Village Enterprises as Vaguely Defined Cooperatives." *Journal of Comparative Economics* 28: 121–145.

Wen, G. and D. Xu, eds. 1997. *The Reformability of China's State Sector*. River Edge, NJ: World Scientific.

Wen, Tiejun. 2007. "Deconstructing Modernization." *Chinese Sociology & Anthropology* 39 (4): 10–25. doi:10.2753/CSA0009-4625390401.

Wen, Tiejun and Kin Chi Lau. 2008. "Four Stories in One: Environmental Protection and Rural Reconstruction in China." *Positions: East Asia Cultures Critique* 16 (3): 491–505.

Wheeler, Norton. 2012. *The Role of American NGOs in China's Modernization: Invited Influence*. New York: Routledge.

White, Gordon. 1989. "Restructuring the Working Class: Labor Reform in Post Mao China." In *Marxism and the Chinese Experience*, edited by Arif Dirlik and Maurice Meisner, 152–168. Armonk, NY: M. E. Sharpe.

White, Gordon. 1993. *Riding the Tiger: The Politics of Economic Reform in Post-Mao China*. Stanford, CA: Stanford University Press.

White, Lynn T. III. 1998. *Local Causes of China's Economic Reforms. Unstately Power*. Vol. I. Armonk, NY: M. E. Sharpe.

Whiting, Susan. 2000. *Power and Wealth in Rural China: The Political Economy of Institutional Change*. New York: Cambridge University Press.

Whyte, Martin King. 1999. "The Changing Role of Workers." In *The Paradox of China's Post-Mao Reforms*, edited by Merle Goldman and Roderick MacFarquhar, 173–196. Cambridge, MA: Harvard University Press.

Wiki Leaks. 2013 [1976]. "Wiki Leaks: "ILO World Employment Conference: Galenson Discussion with Ministry of Labor, April 12, 1976." See US Embassy, Tokyo entry for full document title.

World Bank. 1995. *Bureaucrats in Business: The Economics and Politics of Government Ownership*. New York: Oxford University Press.

World Bank and Development Research Center of the State Council, the People's Republic of China. 2013. *China 2030: Building a Modern, Harmonious, and Creative Society*. Washington, DC: World Bank.

Wu, Jinglian. 2004. "Market Socialism' and Chinese Economic Reform." Conference Paper Submitted to the IEA's Round Table on 'Market and Socialism Reconsidered' (Draft).

Wu, Jinglian. 2005. *Understanding and Interpreting China's Economic Reform*. Singapore: Thomson/South-Western.

Wu, Yifeng. 2008. "Theory of Property Rights: Comparing Marx with Coase." *Social Sciences in China* 29 (2): 5–17. doi:10.1080/02529200802091201.

WuDunn, Sheryl. 1995. "Chen Yun, a Chinese Communist Patriarch Who Helped Slow Reforms, is Dead at 89." *New York Times*, April 11, 1995.

Xin, Mao (pseudonym). 1999. "Reform and Economic Man." *The Chinese Economy* 32 (2): 22–60.

Xu, Chenggang. 2011. "The Fundamental Institutions of China's Reforms and Development." *Journal of Economic Literature* 49 (4): 1076–1151. doi:10.1257/jel.49.4.1076.

Xu, Chenggang and Xiaobo Zhang. 2009. *The Evolution of Chinese Entrepreneurial Firms: Township-Village Enterprises Revisited. (IFPRI Discussion Paper 00854)* International Food Policy Research Institute.

Xu, Dixin. 1981. "China's Special Economic Zones." *Beijing Review* 50, 14–17.

Xu, Dixin. 1982. "China's Modernization and the Prospects for its Economy." In *Economic Reform in the PRC: In Which China's Economists Make Known What Went Wrong, Why, and What Should Be Done About It,* edited by George C. Wang, 43–52. Boulder, CO: Westview Press.

Xu, Yong. 2011. "The Expansion of Peasant Rationality: An Analysis of the Creators of the 'China Miracle' – Challenging Existing Theories and Proposing New Analytical Approaches." *Social Sciences in China* 32 (1): 5–25. doi:10.1080/02529203.2011.548916.

Xu, Zhun. 2012. "The Chinese Agriculture Miracle Revisited." *Economic and Political Weekly* XLVII (14): 51–58.

Xu, Zhun. 2013. "The Political Economy of Decollectivization in China." *Monthly Review: An Independent Socialist Magazine* 65 (1): 17–36. http://monthlyreview.org/2013/05/01/the-political-economy-of-decollectivization-in-china/.

Xu, Zhun, Ying Chen, and Minqi Li. 2015. "Are Chinese Workers Paid the Correct Wages? Measuring Wage Underpayment in the Chinese Industrial Sector, 2005–2010." *Review of Radical Political Economics* 47 (3): 446–459. doi:10.1177/0486613414542780.

Xue, Hong and Anita Chan. 2013. "The Global Value Chain." *Critical Asian Studies* 45 (1): 55–77. doi:10.1080/14672715.2013.758821.

Yahuda, Michael B., ed. 1987. *New Directions in the Social Sciences and Humanities in China.* New York: St Martins Press.

Yang, Dali L. and Litao Zhao. 2009. *China's Reforms at 30.* Singapore: World Scientific.

Yang, Famin. 1997. "The State-Owned Enterprises Pour Out their Hearts." *The Chinese Economy* 30 (4): 6–28.

Yang, Weiyong. 2006. "Reforms, Structural Adjustments, and Rural Income in China." *China Perspectives* 63.

Yin, Deyong. 2009. "China's Attitude Toward Foreign NGO's." *Washington University Global Studies Law Review* 8 (3/4): 521–543.

Yin, Xiao-huang. 2004. "A Case Study of Transnationalism: Continuity and Changes in Chinese Americans Philanthropy in China." *American Studies* 45 (2).

Zhang, Fengbo. 2008. *A Chinese Economist's Journey* Create Space, Independent Publishing Platform.

Zhang, Haihui, Zhaohui Xue, Shuyong Jiang, and Gary Lance Lugar, eds. 2013. *A Scholarly Review of Chinese Studies in North America.* Ann Arbor, MI: Association for Asian Studies.

Zhang, Lin and Yingli Xu. 2013. "The Transmission of Heterodox Economics in China, 1949–2009." In *Thoughts on Economic Development in China,* edited by Ying Ma and Hans-Michael Trautwein, 306–326. New York: Routledge.

Zhang, Weiying. 2009. *Bury Keynesianism (Speech at the Forum for Chinese Entrepreneurs).* The Free Capitalist Network.

Zhang, Wenxian and Ilon Alon, eds. 2009. *Biographical Dictionary of New Chinese Entrepreneurs and Business Leaders.* Northampton, MA: Edward Elgar.

Zhang, Zhuoyuan. 1982. "Introduction: China's Economy After the 'Cultural Revolution'." In *China's Economic Reforms*, edited by Lin Wei and Arnold Chao, 1–27. Philadelphia: University of Pennsylvania Press.

Zhao, Haiyun. 2010. "Economics Education in China." *International Journal of Pluralism and Economics Education* 1 (4): 303–316.

Zhao, Yuezhi. 2008. *Communication in China: Political Economy, Power and Conflict*. New York: Rowman & Littlefield.

Zhao, Zhong. 2005. "Migration, Labor Market Flexibility, and Wage Determination in China: A Review." *The Developing Economies* 43 (2): 285–312. doi:10.1111/j.1746-1049.2005.tb00263.x.

Zhao, Ziyang. 2009. *Prisoner of the State: The Secret Journal of Premier Zhao Ziyang*. Translated by Bao Pu, Renee Chiang, and Adi Ignatius. New York: Simon & Schuster.

Zhou, Kate. 2006. "Chinese Intellectuals Fighting on the Idea Front in Global Context." In *The World and China at a Time of Drastic Changes—Towards the Construction of a New and Modern Sinology* edited by Mitsuyuki Kagami, 35–70. Japan: Aichi University Press.

Zhou, Ping, Xinning Su, and Loet Leydesdorff. 2010. "A Comparative Study on Communication Structures of Chinese Journals in the Social Sciences." *Journal of the American Society for Information Science and Technology* 61 (7): 1360–1376.

Zhou, Shulian. 1982. "The Market Mechanism in a Planned Economy." In *China's Economic Reforms*, edited by Lin Wei and Arnold Chao, 94–113. Philadelphia, PA: University of Pennsylvania Press.

Zhou, Yi. 2015. "Review of the New Textbook Series in Modern Political Economics." *World Review of Political Economy* 6 (1): 148–152. doi:10.13169/worlrevipoliecon.6.1.0148.

Zhu, Andong and David M. Kotz. 2011. "The Dependence of China's Economic Growth on Exports and Investment." *Review of Radical Political Economics* 43 (1): 9–32. doi:10.1177/0486613410383951.

Zhu, Ying. 2012. *Two Billion Eyes: The Story of China Central Television*. New York: The New Press.

Zweig, David. 1989. *Agrarian Radicalism in China 1968–1981*. Cambridge, MA: Harvard University Press.

# Index